Identities and Ideologies in the Medieval East Roman World

Edinburgh Byzantine Studies

Innovative approaches to the medieval Eastern Roman empire and its neighbours
Edinburgh Byzantine Studies promotes new, theory-driven approaches to
the empire commonly called Byzantium. The series looks at the literary,
historical, material and visual remains of this long-living political order
and its neighbours, often from a multi-disciplinary and/or cross-cultural
vantage point. Its innovative readings highlight the connectivity of
Byzantine culture as well as of Byzantine Studies.

Series Editors

Louise Blanke, The University of Edinburgh
Ivan Drpić, University of Pennsylvania
Niels Gaul, The University of Edinburgh
Alexander Riehle, Harvard University
Yannis Stouraitis, The University of Edinburgh
Alicia Walker, Bryn Mawr College

Books available in the series

The Monotheisation of Pontic-Caspian Eurasia: Eighth to Thirteenth Centuries
Alex M. Feldman

Identities and Ideologies in the Medieval East Roman World
Yannis Stouraitis

Imperial Visions of Late Byzantium: Manuel II Palaiologos and Rhetoric in Purple
Florin Leonte

Books forthcoming

*Saints, Relics and Identity in Medieval and Modern Caucasia: The Cult of
Saints and the Body Politic*
Nikoloz Aleksidze

Social Stratification in Late Byzantium
Christos Malatras

Visit the Edinburgh Byzantine Studies website at
edinburghuniversitypress.com/series-edinburgh-byzantine-studies.html

Identities and Ideologies in the Medieval East Roman World

Edited by Yannis Stouraitis

EDINBURGH
University Press

Edinburgh University Press is one of the leading university presses in the UK. We publish academic books and journals in our selected subject areas across the humanities and social sciences, combining cutting-edge scholarship with high editorial and production values to produce academic works of lasting importance. For more information visit our website: edinburghuniversitypress.com

Edinburgh University Press Ltd
The Tun – Holyrood Road
12(2f) Jackson's Entry
Edinburgh EH8 8PJ

Typeset in 10.5/13 Warnock Pro by
IDSUK (DataConnection) Ltd, and
printed and bound in Great Britain.

A CIP record for this book is available from the British Library

ISBN 978 1 4744 9362 8 (hardback)
ISBN 978 1 4744 9364 2 (webready PDF)
ISBN 978 1 4744 9365 9 (epub)

Contents

Illustrations

Figures

Table

Abbreviations

AAJord	Annual of the Department of Antiquities of Jordan
ActAntHung	Acta antiqua Academiae Scientiarum Hungaricae
Archeol. Pap. Am. Anthropol. Assoc.	Archeological Papers of the American Anthropological Association
Ἀρχ.Δελτ.	Ἀρχαιολογικόν Δελτίον
BalkSt	Balkan Studies
BASOR	Bulletin of the American Schools of Oriental Research
BF	Byzantinische Forschungen
BMGS	Byzantine and Modern Greek Studies
BSl	Byzantinoslavica
Byz	Byzantion
ByzSym	Byzantina Symmeikta
BZ	Byzantinische Zeitschrift
CahArch	Cahiers archéologiques
CahCM	Cahiers de civilisation médiévale, Xe–XIIe siècles
CCCM	Corpus christianorum, continuatio medievalis
CFHB	Corpus fontium historiae byzantinae
ChHist	Church History
CPG	Clavis Patrum Graecorum
CSHB	Corpus scriptorum historiae byzantinae
DOP	Dumbarton Oaks Papers
EME	Early Medieval Europe

FS	*Frühmittelalterliche Studien*
GOTR	*Greek Orthodox Theological Review*
GRBS	*Greek Roman and Byzantine Studies*
JHS	*Journal of Hellenic Studies*
JJS	*Journal of Jewish Studies*
JMEMS	*Journal of Medieval and Early Modern Studies*
JMH	*Journal of Medieval History*
JÖB	*Jahrbuch der Österreichischen Byzantinistik*
JRA	*Journal of Roman Archaeology*
JRAS	*Journal of the Royal Asiatic Society*
LSJ	*A Greek-English Lexicon. Compiled by Henry George Lidell and Robert Scott. A new edition revised and augmented throughout by Henry Stuart Jones with the assistance of Roderick Mckenzie* (Oxford: Clarendon Press, 1927 and 1929)
MGH ScriptRerGerm	*Monumenta Germaniae Historica Scriptores Rerum Germanicarum in usum scholarum*
NA	*Neues Archiv der Gesellschaft für Ältere deutsche Geschichtskunde*
ODB	A. Kahzdan (ed.), *The Oxford Dictionary of Byzantium* (New York and Oxford: Oxford University Press, 1991)
PEQ	*Palestine Exploration Quarterly*
PBW	Jeffreys et al., *Prosopography of the Byzantine World*, 2016
PG	*Patrologia Graeca*
PLP	*Prosopographisches Lexikon der Palaiologenzeit*
RE	G. Wissowa and W. Kroll (eds), *Paulys Real-Encyclop. die der classischen Altertumswissenschaft*, new revised edition (Stuttgart, 1894–1978)
REArm	*Revue des études arméniennes*
RÉB	*Revue des études byzantines*
RHE	*Revue d'Histoire Ecclésiastique*
RicSlav	*Ricerche slavistiche*
RSBN	*Rivista di studi bizantini e neoellenici*

Settimane	Settimane di studio del Centro italiano di studi sull'alto Medioevo
StMed	Studi Medievali
SVThQ	St Vladimir's Theological Quarterly
TAPA	Transactions of the American Philological Association
TM	Travaux et mémoires
ZPapEpig	Zeitschrift für Papyrologie und Epigraphik
ZRVI	Zbornik radova Vizantološkog instituta, Srpska akademija nauka

Notes on Contributors

Panagiotis Agapitos is Gutenberg Distinguished Research Fellow at the University of Mainz and Emeritus Professor of Byzantine Literature at the University of Cyprus. His research interests focus on textual and literary criticism, with an emphasis on Byzantine rhetoric and its performance, poetics, erotic fiction and the representation of death in Byzantine literature. His most recent major publication is *Livistros and Rodamne* (Liverpool, 2021).

Theodora Antonopoulou is Professor of Byzantine Literature at the National and Kapodistrian University of Athens. She specialises in highbrow medieval Greek literature, with an emphasis on homiletics, hymnography and hagiography, as well as in the manuscript tradition and editions of texts. Her more recent major publications are *Mercurii Grammatici Opera iambica* (2017) and, as co-author, the *Vitae et Miracula Sancti Christoduli Patmensis* (2021).

Francesco Borri is Associate Professor at the Ca' Foscari University of Venice. He specialises in medieval aristocracies and their identities. His most recent major publications include *Alboino: Frammenti di un racconto* (Rome, 2016) and 'A Placid Island: H. P. Lovecraft's "Ibid"', *Lovecraft Studies* 12 (2018): 105–35.

Leslie Brubaker is emerita Professor of Byzantine Art and Director of the Centre for Byzantine, Ottoman and Modern Greek Studies at the University of Birmingham. She specialises in Byzantine art, culture and gender, the cult of the Virgin and Iconoclasm, and has lately focused on urban processions and images of the poor in Byzantium. Her most recent major publication is *Processions: Urban Ritual in Byzantium and Neighboring Lands*, co-edited with Nancy Ševčenko (Washington, DC, forthcoming).

Jean-Claude Cheynet is emeritus Professor of Byzantine History at Sorbonne Université and honorary member of the Institut universitaire de France. He edited the *Revue des études byzantines* and co-edited the *Studies in Sigillography*. His main works are about Byzantine aristocracy – *Pouvoir et contestations à Byzance (963–1210)* (Paris, 1990); *The Byzantine Aristocracy and its Military Function* (Aldershot, 2006) – and the edition with a commentary of lead seals catalogues.

John Haldon is emeritus Professor of Byzantine History & Hellenic Studies at Princeton University and Director of the Princeton University Climate Change and History Research Initiative. His research focuses on the history of the Byzantine empire; on premodern state systems and the impact of environmental stress on societal resilience; and on the production, distribution and consumption of resources in the late ancient and medieval world. His most recent major publication is *The De Thematibus ('On the Themes') of Constantine VII Porphyrogenitus. Translated with Introductory Chapters and Notes* (Liverpool, 2021).

Johannes Koder is emeritus Professor at the University of Vienna and full member at the Austrian Academy of Sciences. He specialises in Byzantine history, historical geography, identity, everyday life and hymnography. His most recent major publication is *Nomos Georgikos: Das byzantinische Landwirtschaftsgesetz. Überlegungen zur inhaltlichen und zeitlichen Einordnung. Deutsche Übersetzung* (Vienna, 2020).

Fotini Kondyli is Associate Professor of Byzantine Art and Archaeology at the University of Virginia. Her research interests include Byzantine and Frankish spatial practices, community-building processes and the material culture of Byzantine non-elites. She also works on cultural, economic and political networks in the eastern Mediterranean in the late Byzantine period (thirteenth to fifteenth centuries). Her most recent major publications include *Rural Communities in Late Byzantium, Resilience and Vulnerability in the Northern Aegean* (2022) and (as co-editor) *The Byzantine Neighbourhood: Urban Space and Political Action* (2022).

Dimitri Korobeinikov is Associate Professor at the University at Albany (New York). He specialises in Byzantine–Turkish relations from the eleventh to the end of the fifteenth century, especially in the interactions between the Muslim and Christian state institutions, the Christian–Muslim polemics, the history of the Christian communities under Muslim rule and the emergence of new Turkic states on Byzantine soil. His most important recent publications include *Byzantium and the Turks in the Thirteenth Century* (Oxford, 2014).

Annick Peters-Custot is Full Professor in Medieval History at Nantes University. She specialises in Byzantine and Norman southern Italy, focusing on the religious and ideological circulations between western Christianity and the Byzantine world. Her most recent major publication is *La réception des Pères grecs et orientaux en Italie au Moyen Âge* (with Camille Rouxpetel and Bernadette Cabouret, Paris, 2020).

Daniel Reynolds is Senior Lecturer in Byzantine History at the Centre for Byzantine, Ottoman and Modern Greek Studies, University of Birmingham. He specialises in the history and archaeology of Byzantine and early Islamic Arabia-Palestine c. 330–c. 1000. His most recent major publications include 'Death of a Patriarch: The Murder of Yuhanna ibn Jami (966) and the Question of "Melkite" Identity in Early Islamic Palestine' and 'History and Exegesis in the Itinerarium of Bernard the Monk (c. 867).'

Jonathan Shepard is a former University Lecturer in Russian History at Cambridge. He specialises in Byzantine diplomacy, early Rus and western Eurasia in the central Middle Ages. His most recent major publications are *Viking-Age Trade: Silver, Slaves and Gotland* (2020); and *Political Culture in the Latin West, Byzantium and the Islamic World, c. 700–c. 1500* (2021).

Alicia Simpson teaches Late Antique and Byzantine History and Classics at the American College of Greece. Her main areas of research are in Byzantine Literature and Culture and in Classical Reception Studies. She is the author of *Niketas Choniates: A Historiographical Study* (Oxford, 2013) and the editor of the collective volume *Byzantium, 1180–1204: 'The Sad Quarter of a Century'?* (Athens, 2015).

Kostis Smyrlis is Associate Researcher at the Institute of Historical Research of the National Hellenic Research Foundation. He specialises in the economy, state finances and social relations of Byzantium and the medieval documents and history of Mount Athos. His major publications include *La fortune des grands monastères byzantins, fin du xe-milieu du xive siècle* (2006) and *Actes de Vatopédi II and III* (2006 and 2019).

Vlada Stanković is Professor of Byzantine Studies, and head of the Chair for Byzantine Studies at the University of Belgrade. His areas of specialisation include the period of the Komnenian dynasty, Church–state relations in the middle Byzantine period and the medieval Balkans. His most recent major publication is *The Balkans and the Byzantine World before and after the Captures of Constantinople, 1204 and 1453* (Lanham, Boulder, New York and London, 2016).

Dionysios Stathakopoulos is Assistant Professor of Byzantine History at the University of Cyprus. He specialises in Byzantine social history, environmental history and the history of medicine and disease. His recent major publications include *A Short History of the Byzantine Empire* (Bloomsbury, 2014).

Yannis Stouraitis is Senior Lecturer in Byzantine History at the University of Edinburgh. He specialises in Byzantine social and cultural history, focusing on the socio-ideological aspects of war, collective identifications and ideological attachments and the construction of historical memory. His most recent major publications include *A Companion to the Byzantine Culture of War, ca. 300–1204* (Leiden and Boston, 2018) and, as co-editor, *Migration Histories of the Medieval Afroeurasian Transition Zone. Aspects of Mobility between Africa, Asia and Europe, 300–1500 C.E.* (Leiden and Boston, 2020).

Introduction
The Ideology of Identities and the Identity of Ideologies

John Haldon and Yannis Stouraitis

Modern scholarship has devoted a great deal of attention to the research of collective identity and political ideology in the so-called Byzantine Empire. In the context of the revived scholarly dialogue on these topics in roughly the last two decades, a workshop that was organised at the University of Vienna in 2015 aimed to approach 'identity' and 'ideology' in the Byzantine world through a broader perspective.[1] Our intention was to redirect the focus of the discussion on various kinds of identifications, the forms they took and the means through which they were articulated, as well as on the content and social function of various sets of ideas and beliefs in the medieval East Roman geopolitical sphere between roughly the sixth and fifteenth centuries. The current volume is the product of that discussion, which was enriched with additional contributions on the way. It represents what we believe to be the first effort to address a wide range of different aspects of the ways in which various groups or individuals in the geopolitical sphere of the medieval East Roman Empire perceived themselves and one another, as well as the world they lived in.

Our main goal was to broaden our knowledge about the nature of the different types of sources that throw light on 'identities', about how these 'identities' were ascribed and attributed or adopted and about the understandings and misunderstandings that different modes of identifying oneself, one's kith and kin and those outside these circles generated, while

[1] The workshop was organised by Yannis Stouraitis with the contribution of Johannes Koder and Olof Heilo in the context of the research project 'Ideologies under Scrutiny: A Study on Differentiated Perceptions of Roman Imperial Ideals In Byzantine Society, 7th–12th Centuries' (P 24752-G19). The project was funded by the Austrian Science Fund (FWF) and hosted at the Department of Byzantine and Modern Greek Studies of the University of Vienna.

unravelling the potential interrelation between identification practices and various sets of ideas and beliefs. Moreover, we wanted to address the ways in which modern researchers have attempted to describe these phenomena and make sense of them and the dynamics of 'identity' and 'ideology' in a past culture. With respect to that, this introductory chapter will touch upon the central concepts of the discussion, namely 'identity' and 'ideology', whose content may vary according to author and whose analytical usefulness is still a focus for disagreement. By offering some insight into the definitional background and the various uses of these terms, we hope to provide readers with a conceptual framework that will allow them to better assess the individual contributions to the present volume.

Given the theme of the volume, it will be appropriate to begin with the term 'identity', a topic on which there exists a vast social science and cultural history literature. It goes without saying that we can do little more than pay lip service here, and to some extent we must necessarily simplify somewhat both conceptually and theoretically. Identity is a term which has predominated the fields of the social sciences and the humanities since the second half of the twentieth century and which has increasingly come under attack for its analytical usefulness.[2] It concerns a multidimensional phenomenon, a function of conscious thought and self-awareness, of the need to define oneself and others in contrast to those around us. Moreover, it suggests different things according to the questions asked of it. A range of social-institutional roles and self-perceptions generally overlap or even contradict one another at different levels of social experience and practice – a point which immediately raises the question of whether individuals possess an 'essential' identity, a consciousness of themselves that exists beneath all other forms of context-determined identity and praxis.[3]

Individuals in all societies belong to more than one group of mutually recognised 'identity sets', but they do not all belong to the same sets. Each 'identity' carries with it a reservoir of culturally determined and inflected ways of behaving in both public and private, determined and inflected by the specific context in which other persons of one or the other group are encountered. And a person's identity is further nuanced and their behaviour

---

[2] Brubaker and Cooper, 'Beyond Identity', 11–47; Malešević, *Identity as Ideology*, 14–36.

[3] Since the 1960s there has been a series of debates around the concept of identity as used in respect of the subject/self, focusing in particular on structuralist and post-structuralist challenges to traditional psychoanalysis, and represented especially in the work of Lacan and his later adherents. For useful surveys and discussion, see Hall, 'Theories of Language and Ideology', 157–62; idem, 'Ideology/Subject Couplet', 113–21; Ellis, 'Ideology and Subjectivity', 186–94.

modified by the fact that they may also need to fulfil key criteria of some of their other social and institutional roles, such as 'parent', 'sibling' or 'relative', 'soldier', 'priest' or 'farmer', for example.[4] Perceptions and assumptions about one's own and others' social and economic status likewise directly affect patterns of behaviour and the ways in which identity is given expression – a poor man behaves differently in the presence of a rich or powerful man than before his peers, and vice versa.[5] At the same time, social and cultural values are modified according to the context in order that the individual can give expression to his or her understanding of 'self', thus presenting the desired version felt to be most appropriate (or necessary, as appropriate to the context) to the situation.

Concomitantly, social interaction embodies sets of power relations, so that not all individuals or groups are able to present the identity they would (or think they would) prefer in every situation. For example, feelings of inferiority or superiority affect such situations very markedly. Different sets of identities, based on appropriate patterns of socially determined and culturally normative behaviour, have different values according to the context in which they function: a hierarchy of interests informs most human social interaction. Observable social praxis is often the result of clashes and contradictions generated by a specific context in which an individual or a group has to adopt a particular pattern of behaviour in order to preserve their identity for that particular context. Where the evidence is sufficient, historians can try to see how such contradictions evolve, how they present themselves and are 'understood', and how they are resolved – and this, of course, can offer some insight into the structure of causal relationships leading to historical change.

The context in which a given identity is referenced is important, since we need to understand, for example, whether particular identities are adopted in a context of instrumentality or solidarity. Does an individual adopt a particular identity in order to be classed as a member of a wider group, sharing common ritual and institutional observances, modes of dress, public behaviour and so forth, or in order to achieve a local, personal

---

[4] The best introduction to this approach to the question of social roles, identities and the institutionalisation of social practices according to context and self-image, is still, in our view – and in spite of flaws pointed out by later critics – Berger and Luckmann, *Social Construction of Reality*, and Schütz, *Der sinnhafte Aufbau*. There is a vast social-psychological and social-anthropological literature on these topics, to which we cannot begin to do justice here, although some of this material will be found in the notes to several of the volumes and articles cited.

[5] Indeed, such degrees of differentness are also embodied in law: see, for example, Patlagean, *Pauvreté économique*, 25–27.

objective associated with the immediate conditions of their own individual existence?[6] The two are not mutually exclusive. Under what conditions, for example, did a person describe themselves merely as a Christian, and under what conditions would they refer to themselves as an Orthodox Christian? When do subjects of the East Roman emperors describe themselves by their city or district of origin, rather than by other criteria? These are all questions about the conscious identities adopted, or professed, by those referred to in the sources.[7] And finally, from the point of view of the historian, it is necessary to apply or generate identities as heuristic and analytical categories in order to try to explain certain phenomena – identities which may never have been, and in some contexts could never have been, explicitly recognised by those to whom we apply them (such as 'lower classes', 'social elite', 'imperial bureaucracy' or 'medieval East Roman'), but which serve a useful purpose in helping us manage the evidence.[8]

The several major categories or types of broader identity that appear in our medieval sources include: religion; race and language; region (which usually overlaps with the previous group); sex and gender; public function (e.g. soldier, priest, etc.); and, depending on context and culture, perceived social origin and solidarities. These constitute pools of mutually intersecting or overlapping identities, and there is thus always the potential for conflict and tension among them. Where, for example, do the boundaries lie between 'us' and 'them' or 'the other', and under what circumstances are such markers of difference or boundaries invoked or evoked? We might bear in mind at this point the work of Fredrik Barth, who stressed precisely the issue of boundary-forming actions in constituting identities and solidarities,[9] and it would be a simple matter to list attributes demonstrating that every identity usually carries with it a host of other possible identities which may or may not be realised by the context in which it is employed, and which may or may not all be known or understood by the different groups hearing or using the identity term in question.[10]

---

[6] What Berger and Luckmann, *Social Construction of Reality*, 102–9, refer to as 'sub-universes of meaning'.

[7] For this problematic, see Berger and Luckmann, *Social Construction of Reality*, 149–57.

[8] On the various meanings of the term 'identity' in scholarship, see Brubaker and Cooper, 'Beyond Identity', 6–8.

[9] See the essays in Barth, *Ethnic Groups*.

[10] For work which deals with different aspects of the 'Byzantine identity', see Page, *Being Byzantine*, esp. 7–10, 11–21; and, from a very different perspective and set of research questions, the important collective volume Papaconstantinou and Talbot, *Becoming Byzantine*.

In light of this, it is also worth considering the latest arguments according to which 'identity' may, after all, be an analytically deeply problematical concept that should rather be dismissed, or at least used with great caution, both in its 'strong' and 'weak' understandings. Weak understandings of 'identity' are usually characterised by a meaningless 'clichéd constructivism' which ends up repudiating the core meaning of the term it employs. Strong understandings, on the other hand, bear reifying connotations which inevitably result in a use of the term intended to assert internal sameness, distinctiveness and bounded groupness, thus designating a condition rather than a process. However, it is identification (of oneself or of others) as a process which is intrinsic to social life.[11] To remain heuristically useful, therefore, we need to be aware that under the term 'identity' we should actually understand relational and categorical modes of identification, keeping all the above-mentioned descriptive and dynamic connotations of the term in mind.[12]

How East Roman 'identity' was articulated and what forms it took under different conditions and at different times has recently been the subject of some discussion. It seems obvious that there was a dominant discourse of identification through which the population of the medieval East Roman Empire could be represented as an 'Orthodox' and Roman community to itself and to the outsider. But since, as we have said, identification is processual, functional and performative, the East Roman discourse of identification embodied a set of operational strategies in which situation and context determined which elements were invoked in which combinations, and incorporated many subsets of 'Romanness', some reflecting regional cultural, linguistic or ethnic traditions and lifeways, some heterodox beliefs, some social status and situation, some a mix of all of these.

If the crucial point about any practice of identification is that it differentiates those who self-describe in a particular way from those who do not thus describe themselves or who can be described as 'other', as different in some fundamental way, then it is apparent that historians need to understand why the term 'Roman', for example, was invoked at a given moment or in a particular context. Like many catch-all identities, 'Roman' could embrace a whole cultural system and serve as a backdrop against and within which other more localised and personalised identities operated, identities which dominated the day-to-day lives and activities of most people.

[11] Brubaker and Cooper, 'Beyond Identity', 14–21.
[12] See in particular Pohl, 'Strategies of Identification', for a useful approach to and discussion of the hermeneutic and heuristic issues associated with the term 'identity'.

Just as the question of how eastern Romans identified themselves is a topic currently under discussion,[13] so is that of 'orthodoxy' as a key feature or characteristic of Byzantine culture, as several recent publications and the debate they have engendered in both these respects testify.[14] Thus, while the notion of 'Christian/Roman' itself was to a degree a universalising discourse, it served different socio-cultural groups in different ways and came to prominence or was invoked only under certain very specific circumstances and at particular moments. On the one hand, it represented above all the self-identity and vested interests of the social elite whose continued loyalty to the status quo was essential to the survival of the state and the whole imperial edifice.[15] On the other, it represented the difference between all those who understood themselves as members of the Christian-Roman world and those outside it. It could also represent the identity of all subjects of the Roman emperor and all inhabitants of the Roman Empire, humble or elite, when contrasted with those perceived to stand outside of the boundaries of this world.

So, while elements of this particular notion clearly penetrated to the roots of society, both in the metropolitan regions as well as in the more distant provinces (even if only in the form of coins bearing the emperor's image[16]), the notion of a Roman identity needs to be deployed with care, since it had different valences according to social and cultural circumstances and according to the demands of the moment.[17] We cannot really

[13] Kaldellis, *Hellenism in Byzantium*; idem, 'From Rome to New Rome'; idem, 'Social Scope of Roman Identity'; idem, *Romanland*; Stouraitis, 'Roman Identity in Byzantium'; idem, 'Reinventing Roman Ethnicity'; and idem, 'Byzantine Romanness', 123–39. See also Leppin, 'Roman Identity in a Border Region', 241–58, at 243 and n. 12; Rapp, 'Hellenic Identity, *Romanitas*, and Christianity'; and Greatrex, 'Roman Identity in the Sixth Century'.

[14] On questions of how to understand and how to deploy the term 'orthodoxy' in respect of Byzantine cultural identity, see Cameron, *Cost of Orthodoxy*, 2–24; and idem, 'Enforcing Orthodoxy'. For an alternative view, see Magdalino, 'Byzantine Cultural Identity'.

[15] For discussion of the structure, mores and identity of late Roman elites, both senatorial and provincial, see Beck, 'Konstantinopel'; Patlagean, *Pauvreté économique*; and on the later Byzantine elite, Haldon, 'Fate of the Late Roman Elite', esp. 183–98 (with older literature); and idem, 'Social Elites'.

[16] Although, as pointed out in Morrisson, 'Displaying the Emperor's Authority', 80, people could frequently mistake a given ruler's portrait for Constantine I or another emperor. Note also the remarks on the impact of coinage in Phillips, 'Coinage and the Early Arab State', 58–62.

[17] Stouraitis, 'Roman Identity in Byzantium'; Haldon, *Warfare*, 18–27; Chrysos, 'Roman Political Identity'.

say with any confidence whether or not and when and under what circumstances it was, or would be, invoked in ordinary communities and among ordinary people – farmers, peasants, herdsmen, artisans and craftsmen in the provinces. But as with people in all socially stratified societies throughout history, it was clearly possible – as the history of the empire clearly shows – to express dissatisfaction, hostility and opposition to the established order while also being able to identify with it, a fact that illustrates the complexity associated with the concept of 'identity'.

Just like 'identity', the word 'society' has a general common-sense value that belies its inherent potential for ambiguity and analytical confusion, although it has appeared frequently in our discussions with no real attempt to define what it intends to describe.[18] But whether we speak of 'society' or 'social system', these are loaded and potentially problematic terms because they can suggest that a particular set of social relations is bounded or distinct from the other 'societies' around it.[19] This, however, is only rarely the case, since even where religious-ideological boundaries exist, the people of different creeds on either side will inevitably have certain things in common, such as agrarian practices and domestic economic organisation, for example. Below the surface of political borders and military events, farmers and peasants on either side of such divides rarely differ in these respects.

Yet, at a different level, there were real and obvious differences – in habits of worship, in language, vocabulary and expression and perhaps dress, in the instrumental value attributed to different positions within a set of kinship relations and so forth. In other words, there are multiple, layered overlaps which cross over the political, religious or linguistic divisions which we commonly identify as marking the boundaries of a given society, and we need to bear this in mind, especially when discussing, for example, such topics as the changing impact of religion on marriage, local and customary legal practice, the seasonal patterns of social and economic life and so forth.

Such overlaps can play a role in perceptions, too – the well-known commonalities which are represented in the epic of Digenes Akrites between the Roman and Arab frontier lords, for example, in respect of notions of honour and social status, which set them apart from the more urbane and court-orientated worlds of Constantinople, Aleppo, Damascus or Baghdad.[20]

---

[18] For comments on the social history of the Byzantine world, see Haldon, 'Towards a Social History'.

[19] For an eloquent statement of why this cannot be the case, with an alternative approach, see Mann, *Sources of Social Power*, 1:1–33.

[20] See, for example, Magdalino, 'Honour among Rhomaioi'.

What we refer to as 'Byzantine society' or 'Islamic society' must necessarily be understood in the widest sense, as elements within a number of overlapping social structures and sets of relationships, not just in terms of physical space – around the edges, so to speak – but also in terms of social practice, household organisation and so forth.

Finally, another term that has appeared frequently in discussions but which requires careful definition is that of 'ideology', a term that bears many meanings for many people.[21] It needs to be defined in terms that show how the beliefs or sets of ideas it intends to describe were grounded in the socio-cultural realities and relationships through which they were given expression. In everyday speech, 'ideology' is generally used to mean a particular set of ideas representing the interests of a particular party – an interest group, a social class, a political party or a government, for example – although it can also mean simply 'what people believe' as well as sets of ideas which are, to the outside observer, demonstrably false or one-sided in their account of the world.

For the most part, scholars of the later Roman and Byzantine world use the term to refer both to the generality of what people believed about their world and to particular sets of ideas – all of which impact on social practice and which operate at different levels. But how are beliefs different from ideology, and how is the latter to be understood analytically, rather than merely as a description of some sets of ideas held by some people at certain times? How is ideology tied into its cultural conditions of existence in respect of the ways in which social, economic, cultural and political conditions generated specific sets of ideas? It would be helpful if we could agree on how exactly we want to deploy the term and within what kind of framework. To that end, we first need to understand where cognition and social praxis meet and how they are mutually constitutive and to think about the relationship between social structure, on the one hand, and human cognition, on the other.[22]

The notion of a 'symbolic universe' is helpful here, a concept referring to the totality of cultural knowledge and practice in a social formation within which and through which regular everyday life continued. While the relationship between consciousness and practice must be understood as a dialectic

---

[21] There is a vast bibliography on the topic of ideology, which would be impossible to list here. Indicatively, we would like to reference two general works which contain detailed and useful critical overviews of the main epistemological and sociological strands of thought on ideology research: Eagleton, *Ideology*; Malešević and McKenzie, *Ideology after Poststructuralism*.

[22] For a more detailed account see Haldon, 'Ideology and Social Change'.

through which individuals receive their subjective awareness of self and their personal environment, it also provides these individuals with the conceptual apparatus through which they can in turn express what they know about the world and act back upon it, yet at the same time sets limits to what they can know and how they can know it. Contingently, the symbolic universe is itself generated through social practice, through which it is continuously reproduced.

According to the socio-economic and cultural situation in which they find themselves, individuals and groups maintain particular roles and identities, drawing on different strands or narrative threads depending upon context. People can thus draw on a wide range of concepts and ideas in order to situate themselves with regard to others and the world around them; narratives or discourses that permit them to make sense of their place in society and in relation to the divinity; or bundles of ideas and beliefs about the world extrapolated from the broader symbolic universe. These sets of context-bound social practices and concepts are what generate identifications in the sense described above.

But using the notion of symbolic universe also helps us to define more precisely what we should mean by 'ideology', which, we would argue, can be used specifically to define particular programmatic sets of values and assumptions, bundles of ideas that evolved in order to legitimate and justify a particular order of things – usually a political order. In this context, ideology becomes entangled with 'identity' – that is, collective attachment to a politically organised community which is the outcome of people's adherence to a set of dominant operative ideas and values. The latter determine what the community is and who counts as a member at any given time, as well as the intensity and direction of feelings of belonging to the community, the question of homogeneity and the relationship between the members of the community and the state.[23] We should also bear in mind that the activities carried out by individuals actively engaged in socially reproducing themselves, and hence in reproducing the social relations of their particular cultural system, reproduce the structural forms within

---

[23] On the principal role of a dominant operative ideology in shaping collective attachment to the vision of a political community, see the argument about the intrinsic relationship of nationhood with nationalism in Malešević, *Identity as Ideology*, 84–153. For an effort to apply this theoretical model to the East Roman community, pointing to the operative role of imperial monocracy in holding the East Roman imperial community together up to the twelfth century and the retreat of this dominant ideology after the watershed of 1204, see Stouraitis, 'Reinventing Roman Ethnicity', 76–85.

which the same individuals are inscribed. This is a useful way of think-
ing about the ways in which beliefs, rooted in social praxis, determine the
range of socio-cultural possibilities open to individuals, because it retains
a stronger emphasis on the individual's constitutive function in a socio-
cultural context.[24]

The short theoretical overview presented here is mainly intended to
underline two points: first, that ideology (both dominant and counter-
ideologies) and 'identity' (understood as processes of identification and
attachment) are closely connected and are always complex and multidimensional, not just as articulated in social and cultural practice, but also as
objects of analysis and research; and second, that we should be careful to
define the terms of our analyses if our results are to be applicable to more
than just the research enterprise of each individual scholar.[25] Against this
theoretical background, we will conclude our introduction with a short
overview of the contents and aims of the book's chapters.

The first part of the volume consists of eight chapters which deal with
issues of ideology and identity in the Byzantine world from top-down or
bottom-up social perspectives. Yannis Stouraitis opens the discussion with a
critical reassessment of modern approaches to the Byzantine Empire's identity and political ideology. He scrutinises the interrelation between relabelling, periodisation and an Orientalist structure in Byzantium's constructed
image in modern historiography. In this context, he presents a critical analysis of three holistic historiographical approaches to the political ideology and
identity of the so-called Byzantines in twentieth-century scholarship, namely
'Hellenism', 'Byzantinism' and 'Republicanism', arguing that all three should
be viewed and deconstructed as ideological by-products of European fantasy
and Western hegemony.

Johannes Koder's is the first of three chapters which focus on ideas.
Koder offers some reflections on the issue of a potential divergence between
the dominant Constantinopolitan imperial ideals and the notions and
beliefs that shaped the views of the lower strata in Byzantine society. He
seeks to identify potential channels of ideological influence of the lower
strata and stresses the need to problematise the degree of that influence.
Kostis Smyrlis explores ideology in relation to state finances and identifies
the principal Byzantine ideas concerning taxation, confiscation and the use
of public resources in the eleventh and twelfth centuries. He shows how

---

[24] For this frame of reference see Berger and Luckmann, *Social Construction of Reality*,
esp. 110–12.
[25] See Cameron, 'Late Antiquity and Byzantium'.

the unanimously accepted principle that the *dēmosia* or *koina* were not the emperor's property determined the debate on taxation and confiscation as well as the use of public wealth. The contribution of Theodora Antonopoulou, the last of this group focusing on issues of ideology, explores a sample of homiletic texts from the middle Byzantine period with regard to the political messages they conveyed, in particular as conveyors of imperial ideology. She shows how preachers were eager to employ in their sermons messages in the service of political, specifically imperial, orthodoxy, which went far beyond the standard prayer for the well-being of the emperor.

A group of four essays follows, in which the spotlight is on practices of identification. Leslie Brubaker's chapter deals with identities of gender and status and how these intersected with ideas, in particular ideas concerning religious Orthodox practice, and specifically with non-liturgical devotional practices associated with the Virgin Mary in Byzantium. Panagiotis Agapitos examines the class ideology and social-ethnic identity of the well-known teacher of the Komnenian era John Tzetzes (c. 1110–c. 1170) and shows that Tzetzes' main concern was to bridge the gap between a good family lineage and his social status after 1131. To do so, he highlighted a 'pure Hellenic' identity, an identity mainly based on his readings, which he seems to have employed as a form of critique of the 'Roman' identity of the Constantinopolitan elite.

The last two chapters of the book's first part take us to the provincial periphery of the empire. Daniel Reynolds examines the theme of rural identity in Palaestina and Arabia prior to the seventh century. Based on the surviving evidence about rural communities in the corpus of papyri and, especially, dedicatory inscriptions of the sixth century, he explores identities that were publicly conveyed by rural people themselves in the contexts of their communities. Fotini Kondyli takes a closer look at middle Byzantine Athens in search of evidence of placemaking activities in architectural transformations and the repurposing of buildings and spaces, and in new constructions that become key loci of interaction among city-dwellers. Her focus is on the role of non-elites as city makers who in the absence of a strong imperial and provincial administration assumed the role of architects, builders and urban planners of their own cities.

The book's second part consists of eight chapters that take a closer look at issues of ideology and identity from the perspective of the relation between the imperial centre and its periphery. Jean-Claude Cheynet makes a contribution to the debate on collective identity in the Byzantine Empire, focusing on provincial revolts as indicators of loyalty or disloyalty towards the imperial centre. He opts for an approach that dismisses hard notions of collective identity as sameness and takes issue with recent views about Byzantium as a nation state, stressing that regarding the question of being defined as 'Roman', the answer was surely not unanimous among the emperor's subjects. Alicia Simpson examines identities through provincial rebellions from a different perspective, focusing on three case studies: the Vlachs in the Balkans, Isaac Komnenos in Cyprus and Theodore Mangaphas in Philadelphia during the turbulent last quarter of the twelfth century. She argues that the three cases should be considered as distinct, since the Vlach rebellion represented political separatism, Isaac Komnenos attempted usurpation and Theodore Mangaphas provincial revolt.

The contribution of Dionysios Stathakopoulos looks at identity within the empire from the viewpoint of war and violence. Through a close reading of two pivotal events, the massacre of the Latins in Constantinople in 1182 and the sack and occupation of Thessalonike by the Normans in 1185, he explores how war and violence contributed to the reassertion of ethnocultural boundaries in late twelfth-century Byzantium. He argues that the detailed recording of acts of violence, especially ritualised ones, during these two events suggests a certain shift reflected in the hardening of attitudes that followed the events, which promoted the targeting of the ethnoreligious 'other'.

Jonathan Shepard's chapter is the first of the final group of contributions which deal with issues of ideology and identity on the empire's periphery. He examines the workings of imperial image-projection towards foreign courts in the early Middle Ages and compares them with ways in which the empire's condition was presented subsequently, in the reign of Alexios I Komnenos. He shows that in the Komnenian era the doings of emperors and other events in Byzantium had become open to the scrutiny of articulate outsiders in a quite different manner from those of the ninth century.

Dimitri Korobeinikov shifts our attention to border identities in Asia Minor in the thirteenth century. He analyses the cases of Michael Palaiologos and Constantine Doukas Nestongos, who switched sides between the Empire of Nicaea and the Sultanate of Rūm, in order to exemplify the situational character of political identifications that were not informed by ethnic affiliation, as well as the malleability of ethnocultural categorisations. The latter remained particularly fluid and fused on the border zones of the Nicaean imperial state and the sultanate.

The last three chapters deal with societies outside the empire's limits of authority but within a broader Byzantine sphere of cultural and political influence. Francesco Borri focuses on the ninth-century book of Andreas Agnellus, in particular on the story of the humiliation of Ravenna at the hands of Justinian II and of the eventual victory of the Ravennates against their tormentors at the Coriander Field. He suggests that Agnellus' story was created with the intention of avenging the town's honour, which had taken a serious blow during the reign of Justinian II, as well as of explaining the consequent waning of imperial authority.

Annick Peters-Custot uses the example of the realm of Sicily under the Hauteville domination to examine issues of appropriation of political culture and *convivencia*. She argues that the Hauteville monarchy propagated an ideology that could be regarded as 'ecumenical'. Its aim was not to merge the different groups but, on the contrary, to maintain diversity and make well-directed use of it, since the royal power was the only one able to wield authority over all those communities. This ideological stance enabled the ruler to integrate his Christian and non-Christian subjects alike.

Finally, Vlada Stanković takes issue with nineteenth-century misconceptions about a continuous and unchangeable ethnic identity in the regions of medieval Serbia and Diokleia, and especially with the notion that both were constantly and undoubtedly Serbian principalities. He shows that the political turnaround in the second half of the twelfth century through the installation of Stephen Nemanja as great zhupan of Serbia by emperor Manuel I Komnenos was complemented by Nemanja's conscious efforts to change the ideological basis of his polity, embracing strongly not only the primacy of the Byzantine emperor but Constantinopolitan Orthodoxy as well. This is exemplified by the analysis of two important, highly symbolic ritual transformations that the founder of the Serbian medieval dynasty underwent in the process of becoming the emperor's favourite client: his second baptism and the question of his names, their meaning and their significance.

Bibliography

Barth, F. (ed.), *Ethnic Groups and Boundaries* (Boston, 1969).

Beck, H.-G., 'Konstantinopel. Zur Sozialgeschichte einer frühmittelalterlichen Hauptstadt', *BZ* 58 (1965): 11–45.

Berger, P., and Th. Luckmann, *The Social Construction of Reality* (Harmondsworth, 1967).

Brubaker, R., and F. Cooper, 'Beyond Identity', *Theory and Society* 29 (2000): 1–47.

Cameron, A., 'Enforcing Orthodoxy in Byzantium', in K. Cooper and J. Gregory (eds), *Discipline and Diversity: Papers Read at the 2005 Summer Meeting and the 2006 Winter Meeting of the Ecclesiastical History Society* (Woodbridge and Rochester, 2007), 1–24.

Cameron, A., *The Cost of Orthodoxy* (Leiden, 2012).

Cameron, A., 'Late Antiquity and Byzantium: An Identity Problem', *BMGS* 40/1 (2016): 27–37.

Chrysos, E., 'The Roman Political Identity in Late Antiquity and Early Byzantium', in K. Fledelius (ed.), *Byzantium: Identity, Image, Influence. XIX International Congress of Byzantine Studies, University of Copenhagen* (Copenhagen, 1996), 7–16.

Eagleton, T., *Ideology: An Introduction* (New York, 1991).

Ellis, J., 'Ideology and Subjectivity', in S. Hall, D. Hobson, A. Lowe and P. Willis (eds), *Culture, Media, Language. Working Papers in Cultural Studies, 1972–79* (Birmingham, 1980), 177–85.

Greatrex, G., 'Roman Identity in the Sixth Century', in G. Greatrex and S. Mitchell (eds), *Ethnicity and Culture in Late Antiquity* (London, 2000), 267–92.

Haldon, J. F., 'Ideology and Social Change in the Seventh Century: Military Discontent as a Barometer', *Klio* 68 (1986): 139–90.

Haldon, J. F., *Warfare, State and Society in the Byzantine World, 565–1204* (London, 1999).

Haldon, J. F., 'The Fate of the Late Roman Elite: Extinction or Assimilation?', in L. Conrad and J. F. Haldon (eds), *Elites Old and New in the Byzantine and Early Islamic Near East. Papers of the VIth Workshop on Late Antiquity and Early Islam* (Princeton, 2005), 178–232.

Haldon, J. F., 'Introduction: Towards a Social History of Byzantium', in J. F. Haldon and S. Mitchell (ed.), *The Social History of Byzantium* (Oxford, 2009), 1–30.

Haldon, J. F., 'Social Elites, Wealth and Power', in J. F. Haldon (ed.), *The Social History of Byzantium* (Oxford, 2009), 168–211.

Hall, S., 'Some Problems with the Ideology/Subject Couplet', *Ideology and Consciousness* 3 (Spring 1978): 113–21.

Hall, S., 'Recent Developments in Theories of Language and Ideology: A Critical Note', in S. Hall, D. Hobson, A. Lowe and P. Willis (eds), *Culture, Media, Language. Working Papers in Cultural Studies, 1972–79* (Birmingham, 1980), 157–62.

Kaldellis, A., *Hellenism in Byzantium: The Transformations of Greek Identity and the Reception of the Classical Tradition* (Cambridge, 2009).

Kaldellis, A., 'From Rome to New Rome, from Empire to Nation State: Reopening the Question of Byzantium's Roman Identity', in L. Grig and G. Kelly (eds), *Two Romes: Rome and Constantinople in Late Antiquity* (Oxford and New York, 2012), 387–404.

Kaldellis, A., 'The Social Scope of Roman Identity in Byzantium: An Evidence-Based Approach', *ByzSym* 27 (2017): 173–210.

Kaldellis, A., *Romanland: Ethnicity and Empire in Byzantium* (Cambridge, 2019).

Leppin, H., 'Roman Identity in a Border Region: Evagrius and the Defence of the Roman Empire', in W. Pohl, C. Gantner and R. Payne (eds), *Visions of Community in the Post-Roman World. The West, Byzantium and the Islamic World, 300–1000* (Farnham, 2012), 241–58.

Magdalino, P., 'Honour Among Romaioi: The Framework of Social Values in the World of Digenes Akrites and Kekaumenos', *BMGS* 13 (1989): 183–218.

Magdalino, P., 'Orthodoxy and Byzantine Cultural Identity', in A. Rigo and P. Ermilov (eds), *Orthodoxy and Heresy in Byzantium. The Definition and Notion of Orthodoxy and Some Other Studies on the Heresies and the Non-Christian Religions* (Rome, 2010), 21–46.

Malešević, S., *Identity as Ideology: Understanding Ethnicity and Nationalism* (New York, 2006).

Malešević, S., and I. MacKenzie (eds), *Ideology after Poststructuralism* (London, 2002).

Mann, M., *The Sources of Social Power. Vol. I: A History of Power from the Beginnings to A.D. 1760* (Cambridge, 1986).

Morrisson, C., 'Displaying the Emperor's Authority and kharaktèr on the Marketplace', in P. Armstrong (ed.), *Authority in Byzantium* (London, 2013), 65–82.

Page, G., *Being Byzantine. Greek Identity before the Ottomans* (Cambridge, 2008).

Papaconstantinou, A., and A.-M. Talbot (eds), *Becoming Byzantine: Children and Childhood in Byzantium* (Washington, DC, 2009).

Patlagean, E., *Pauvreté économique et pauvreté sociale à Byzance* (Paris, 1977).

Phillips, M., 'Coinage and the Early Arab State', in A. Oddy, I. Schulze and W. Schulze (eds), *Coinage and History in the Seventh-Century Near East, Vol. 4.* Proceedings of the 14th Seventh Century Syrian Numismatic Round Table Held at The Hive, Worcester, on 28th and 29th September 2013 (London, 2015), 53–71.

Pohl, W., 'Strategies of Identification. A Methodological Profile', in W. Pohl and G. Heydemann (eds), *Strategies of Identification. Ethnicity and Religion in Early Medieval Europe* (Turnhout, 2013), 1–64.

Rapp, C., 'Hellenic Identity, *Romanitas*, and Christianity in Byzantium', in K. Zacharia (ed.), *Hellenisms: Culture, Identity and Ethnicity from Antiquity to Modernity* (Aldershot, 2008), 127–47.

Schütz, A., *Der sinnhafte Aufbau der sozialen Welt* (Vienna, 1960).

Stouraitis, Y., 'Byzantine Romanness: From Geopolitical to Ethnic Conceptions', in W. Pohl, C. Gantner, C. Grifoni and M. Pollheimer (eds), *Transformations of Romanness in the Early Middle Ages: Early Medieval Regions and Identities* (Berlin and Boston, 2018), 123–39.

Stouraitis Y., 'Reinventing Roman Ethnicity in High and Late Medieval Byzantium', *Journal of Medieval Worlds* 5 (2017): 70–94.

Stouraitis Y., 'Roman Identity in Byzantium: A Critical Approach', BZ 107 (2014): 175–220.

Part I

Top-Down and Bottom-Up Approaches

1

Is Byzantinism an Orientalism? Reflections on Byzantium's Constructed Identities and Debated Ideologies

Yannis Stouraitis

It is well known that Byzantinists, when addressing a broader audience, often feel obliged to clarify that there never was a Byzantine Empire. Byzantium was the ancient name of the city of Constantinople before its refoundation by Constantine I, and it was only occasionally used by classicising Byzantine authors to refer to the imperial city. The terms mainly used by the people of the time to designate the medieval empire were *Rhōmaiōn archē*, *Rhōmaiōn basileia*, *Rhōmaiōn politeia*, *Rhōmania* and *Rhōmaïs*.[1] This discrepancy between modern and historical terms and labels is in itself not a unique phenomenon confined to the Byzantine Empire.[2] The problem in the Byzantine case, though, is related to the ideological connotations of relabelling and their interrelation with an established negative modern image of Byzantine culture.

Scholars have often raised this issue and sought to deconstruct Byzantium's negative image. Averil Cameron was among the first to point to Byzantium's essentialised identity and its orientalised image as in

---

[1] In a recent paper, Panagiotis Theodoropoulos has pointed to a rare instance in a document from the period of Constantine IV in which the term Byzantine seems to have been used to designate the inhabitants of the eastern Roman world in a broader cultural manner. However, we are dealing with a unicum in this case, and as the author states at the end of his paper, the modern use of the term Byzantine can hardly be seen to stem from that rare instance; see Theodoropoulos, 'Did the Byzantines Call Themselves Byzantines?'

[2] The Ottoman Empire is a similar case in which modern terminology has little to do with the various names the contemporaries used to denote their state and community; see Neumann, 'Devletin Adı Yok – Bir Amblemin Okunması [The State Has No Name – The Reading of an Emblem]'. I would like to thank Elias Kolovos (University of Crete) for this reference.

opposition to the 'West'.[3] Dimiter Angelov has provided a vigorous deconstruction of the notion of 'Byzantinism' as 'an essentialist and negative
understanding of a medieval civilisation that places it into rigorous analytical categories from a Western and modern view-point'.[4] He argued that
this essentialised, negative image of Byzantine culture needs to be deconstructed by examining its structures and usages while studying the Empire
of Constantinople in its proper historical context without idealising it.[5]
In a similar vein, Przemysław Marciniak has recently pointed out the
close relationship of 'Byzantinism' with Said's Orientalism,[6] a relationship
which Olof Heilo has addressed sceptically.[7] While accepting the orien-
talising aspects of the image of Byzantium in the works of scholars of the
Enlightenment such as Voltaire, Montesquieu and Gibbon,[8] Heilo argued
that, contrary to the term 'Oriental', the term 'Byzantine' should be seen
as having foremost a chronological instead of a spatial-cultural dimension, thus not presupposing or, for that matter, tacitly imposing a certain
historical-cultural prejudice.

In the current chapter, I shall revisit the question of kinship between the
concept of Orientalism and that of 'Byzantinism', which I define here as a
historiographical discourse of negation.[9] My focus will be on the interrelation between relabelling, periodisation and a colonising Orientalist structure. Based on that, I shall seek to problematise the constructed identity of
Byzantium – that is, its ideologised modern image – as both a historical
social formation and a field of research, and I shall address the continuous
impact of historiographical 'Byzantinism' on the research of the political ideology and the historical identity of the medieval Empire of Constantinople.

The Modern Matrix of Historiographical Byzantinism

The first question one needs to raise regarding 'Byzantinism', as the essentialised modern identity of the medieval East Roman culture, pertains to its
origins. Should it be seen as a product of the modern era, or as a phenomenon

---

[3] Cameron, 'Byzance dans le débat', esp. 242–6.
[4] Angelov, 'Byzantinism'.
[5] Ibid. 19.
[6] Marciniak, 'Oriental Like Byzantium'.
[7] Heilo, 'Beyond Orientalism'.
[8] Cf. Runciman, 'Gibbon and Byzantium', 105–7; Cameron, *Byzantine Matters*, 21.
[9] The question of positive 'Byzantinisms' is beyond the scope of the current chapter.
On cases of positive 'Byzantinisms', see Stamatopoulos, 'Vyzantism'; Bodin, 'Whose
Byzantinism'.

that predates it – one that has its beginnings already in the Middle Ages? Medieval stereotyping between Byzantines and Latins was indeed a practice of constructing otherness within a Christian ecumene whose abstract boundaries had been set up through the Christianisation of the Roman Empire in late antiquity. The negative stereotypes that emerged in the high medieval Latin world about the eastern Christians undeniably contributed to the negative historical image of the Constantinopolitan Empire that emerged in the writings of the intellectuals of the Enlightenment. Nonetheless, one needs to consider that stereotyping between medieval cultures took place in a historical context of political and cultural antagonism between the emperor of Constantinople and his western counterparts, in which an image of Europe as a distinct cultural and political entity had not yet been consolidated.

Until the late Middle Ages, the dominant notion of Europe was neither cultural nor political: it was geographical and subordinate to the political and cultural notion of a Christian ecumene.[10] This ecumene included all those parts of the traditional *orbis romanus* that remained under Christian rule, and its symbolic geography did not coincide with that of Europe. Within this Christian ecumene, Constantinople was a predominant cultural and political centre for most of the Middle Ages, and the East Roman Empire did not hold the position of a historical or cultural subaltern.[11] Consequently, the political-cultural framework of the medieval Christian ecumene seems ideally suited for applying Maria Todorova's analytical concept of Balkanism, which discerns variations of identity within a single type – contrary to Said's Orientalism, which distinguishes between two different types (west vs east).[12]

The concept of Balkanism has been employed to stress the subaltern position of the modern Balkans vis-à-vis a politically and culturally superior western Europe within a single type – that of Europe as a geopolitical and cultural entity. In the medieval context, however, when the single type was not yet Europe but the Christian ecumene, one may argue for a kind of inverted Balkanism. At least up to 1204, the notion of political and cultural superiority was rooted in the eastern parts of that entity where the *Rhōmaioi* of Constantinople asserted themselves as the bearers of civilisation – that is, as the exclusive heirs to the superior Roman political and Hellenic cultural heritage, respectively. Based on these claims, they consistently subalternised

---

[10] Delanty, *Inventing Europe*, 16–29.
[11] The politically and culturally superior position of East Rome vis-à-vis Latin Europe for a considerable part of the Middle Ages is even admitted in Huntington, *Clash of Civilizations*, 50 and 95.
[12] Todorova, *Imagining the Balkans*, 3–20.

the western Latin-speaking peoples by designating them as barbarians – or as semi-barbarians when the notion of Christian brotherhood came into play to somehow bridge the gap.[13]

The gradual emergence of the image of Europe as a distinct geopolitical and cultural entity during the transitional period from the late Middle Ages to the era of Enlightenment, when the notion of western Europe as the heir to the superior Greco-Roman ancient culture was finally consolidated, marks a major turning point in regard to our modern analytical categories of thought. A new symbolic geography came into being which contrasted with that of the medieval Christian ecumene; in this new system, the Greek East and the Latin West could no longer be viewed as parts of a single type. Based on that, Todorova's argument about the differences between the concepts of Balkanism and Orientalism may prove particularly enlightening when discussing Byzantium's orientalised image. According to Todorova, Said's notion of the Orient 'il n'y a pas de hors-text' in Derridean terms, whereas the Balkans are characterised by a historical and geographical concreteness which positions them politically and geographically in Europe.[14] If that is the case, one needs to stress that, contrary to the image of the modern Balkans, the image of the realm of the emperor of Constantinople was never distinctly or even predominantly European. For the longest part of its history, the Empire of Constantinople geographically straddled Europe and Asia, with the latter representing its territorial core.

That geographical in-between position played a central role in the relabelling of the medieval East Roman Empire in the modern period, a development which made it easier for modern historians to often deprive it of its historical and political concreteness. Replacing the label 'Roman' with the label 'Byzantine' was the first step towards attributing to an historical identity an intangible and, therefore, manipulable character. Contrary to the historical concreteness of the term Roman (*Rhōmaios*), the invented term 'Byzantine', similarly to Said's 'Orient', did not exist beyond the modern historiographical context. This made it easier to apply to the Byzantine Empire the image of an Oriental kingdom which could be primarily viewed as the predecessor of the Oriental Ottoman Empire rather than the medieval successor of or, even less so, the direct continuation of (western) Rome.[15] Relabelling thus became a means to establish the

---

[13] Lechner, *Hellenen und Barbaren*, 3–106, esp. 105–6.
[14] Todorova, *Imagining the Balkans*, 12–17.
[15] Cf. Agapitos, 'Byzantine Literature', 237–8, Cameron, 'Byzance dans le débat', 243.

exclusion of the medieval Roman Empire of Constantinople both from the symbolic geography of western Europe and from the historical canon of the 'West'.

In light of this, I argue that 'Byzantinism' – as a historiographical discourse intended to deprive the medieval East Roman culture of its actual historical name and identity – cannot be considered as an outcome of the mutual stereotyping and prejudice between the Latin- and the Greek-speaking parts of the medieval Christian ecumene. It should rather be understood as a product of the new categories of thought that were established in western Europe from the period of the Enlightenment onwards. These formed the basis of the conception of 'Modernity' as a politically and culturally superior era which made use of the image of an inferior medieval era in order to be clearly demarcated.

The formulation of Edward Gibbon's influential negative assessment of Byzantium in his monumental history could be seen as a culminating moment of this process.[16] The author's programmatic statements at the beginning of his account of the Empire of Constantinople from the seventh century onwards read as follows:

> From the time of Heraclius, the Byzantine theatre is contracted and darkened: the line of empire, which had been defined by the laws of Justinian and the arms of Belisarius, recedes on all sides from our view; the Roman name, the proper subject of our inquiries, is reduced to a narrow corner of Europe, to the lonely suburbs of Constantinople . . .
>
> In the last moments of her decay, Constantinople was doubtless more opulent and populous than Athens at her most flourishing era, when a scanty sum of six thousand talents, or twelve hundred thousand pounds sterling was possessed by twenty-one thousand male citizens of an adult age. But each of these citizens was a freeman, who dared to assert the liberty of his thoughts, words, and actions, whose person and property were guarded by equal law; and who exercised his independent vote in the government of the republic . . .
>
> The territories of Athens, Sparta, and their allies, do not exceed a moderate province of France or England; but after the trophies of Salamis and Platea, they expand in our fancy to the gigantic size of Asia, which had been trampled under the feet of the victorious Greeks. *But the subjects of the Byzantine empire, who assume and dishonour the names both of Greeks and Romans, present a dead uniformity of abject vices,* which

---

[16] Cf. Haldon, 'Byzantium after 2000', 2.

are neither softened by the weakness of humanity, nor animated by the vigour of memorable crimes . . .

The freemen of antiquity might repeat with generous enthusiasm the sentence of Homer, 'that on the first day of his servitude, the captive is deprived of one half of his manly virtue'. But the poet had only seen the effects of civil or domestic slavery, nor could he foretell that the second moiety of manhood must be annihilated by the spiritual despotism which shackles not only the actions, but even the thoughts, of the prostrate votary. By this double yoke, the Greeks were oppressed under the successors of Heraclius; the tyrant, a law of eternal justice, was degraded by the vices of his subjects; and on the throne, in the camp, in the schools, we search, perhaps with fruitless diligence, the names and characters that may deserve to be rescued from oblivion . . .

From these considerations, I should have abandoned without regret the Greek slaves and their servile historians, had I not reflected that the fate of the Byzantine monarchy is passively connected with the most splendid and important revolutions which have changed the state of the world. The space of the lost provinces was immediately replenished with new colonies and rising kingdoms: the active virtues of peace and war deserted from the vanquished to the victorious nations; and it is in their origin and conquests, in their religion and government, that we must explore the causes and effects of the decline and fall of the Eastern empire.[17]

Gibbon's discourse constructed an image of spatial-cultural 'otherness' between the true (western) Roman Empire, as one of the ancestors of western European civilisation (the other one being Ancient Greece), and a medieval empire of the Greeks whose identity could be neither truly Roman nor truly Greek in the idealised political and cultural terms of the Enlightenment. The medieval realm of Constantinople was not worthy of the Roman name, because this could not be seen as reaching beyond a declining late antique Roman world whose outmost chronological boundary could be Justinian's era, presented by Gibbon as an era of decline preceding the decadent medieval Byzantine Empire.[18] Nor could its inhabitants really claim the Hellenic name, since this was bound to the classical ideals of democracy and self-freedom, to which despotism and subservience as inherent features of medieval political culture needed to be juxtaposed.

---

[17] Gibbon, *Decline and Fall*, 14–15 (emphasis in the quote is my own).
[18] On Justinian's image in Gibbon, see Cameron, 'Gibbon and Justinian'.

Gibbon prepared, thus, the ground for Byzantinism to flourish as a historiographical discourse external to the medieval East Roman society. This was a discourse intended to deny self-representation to the historical subject constructed as Byzantine and, thus, to appropriate the history of the medieval Greek-speaking Romans in order to distort and negate it.[19] As stated by the author, his account of Byzantine history came about not due to any genuine interest in the history of the medieval Empire of Constantinople.[20] He regarded a historical treatment of the Byzantine monarchy as useful only due to its passive connection with the rise of new kingdoms in the lost territories of the West Roman Empire.

Gibbon's history was not a teleological narrative of historical progress, and his treatment of medieval western Europe also did not escape his generically negative judgement of the Middle Ages.[21] However, his image of a decadent Byzantine culture provided the ideological ground on which the generically subaltern position of Byzantium vis-à-vis the culturally and politically regenerating Latin parts of Europe could be established in nineteenth-century teleological narratives of historical progress. The best example of this is Hegel's *Philosophie der Geschichte*, in which the Germanic kingdoms of post-Roman western Europe are presented as having succeeded where the Byzantine Empire had failed, namely in becoming the bearers of historical progress after the fall of Rome. In Hegel's grand narrative of the triumph of reason and Christianity in early modern western Europe, the medieval Germanic world, having adopted the education and religion of the Romans, picked up the thread of historical progress from where the fall of the West Roman Empire had left it.[22] Bringing into existence the 'Byzantines' and a decadent 'Byzantine Empire' had provided an additional means for the self-representation of the 'West.'

By the early twentieth century, the historiographical relabelling of Constantinople's Roman Empire as Byzantine had been consolidated.[23] Even though this development is regarded primarily as a result of modern scholars'

---

[19] On the theoretical background, see Said, *Orientalism*, 20–1.
[20] On Gibbon's historical treatment of the Byzantine period, see Howard-Johnston, 'Gibbon'; Bryer, 'Gibbon and the Later Byzantine Empires'; Shepard, 'Byzantine Soldiers'.
[21] McKitterick, 'Gibbon and the Early Middle Ages', 163–9; Ghosh, 'The Conception of Gibbon's History', 313–14.
[22] Hegel, *Philosophie der Geschichte*, 413–18.
[23] For exceptions to that general attitude see, for instance, the two volumes of J. B. Bury on the history of the East Roman Empire from Arcadius up to the period of Basil I; more on that below.

need to periodise, a closer look shows that this was not its main and certainly not its sole function. This is demonstrated by the ongoing debate among historians on the beginnings of the Byzantine Empire. In the introduction to his *Short History of the Byzantine Empire*, Dionysios Stathakopoulos plausibly pointed out that when defining the chronological limits of the Byzantine Empire, it is easier to start from the end, because everyone agrees that the empire ended with the Ottoman conquest of Constantinople in the year 1453. He then states his own preference for the fourth century as the appropriate starting point for an account of Byzantine history.[24]

Many scholars would agree with the historical rationale behind this longue durée perspective. There are, of course, others who would disagree, providing arguments as to why the beginning should be set in the sixth or the seventh century.[25] In my view, such disagreement mainly demonstrates one thing: the term Byzantine Empire as a category of periodisation is, in fact, problematical. Although it is intended to help us periodise, it becomes itself a matter of dispute that reinforces a paradox. Everyone is certain as to when this empire came to an end, but no one can be sure about its beginnings. To understand the paradox, we ought to accept that a main function of the term 'Byzantine' as a modern signifier was to construct the signified primarily in terms of exclusion and otherness, of something that has very little to do with its own past.

At first sight, this seems to be less the case if one opts for a beginning of the Byzantine period in the fourth century as opposed to the seventh century, where the underlying identification with the Gibbonian spatial-cultural subaltern appears to be more explicit. Nonetheless, there is no real difference between the two options. To make this point clear, suffice it to say that even though Constantine I ruled as a sole emperor over the whole Roman Empire, no historian who is willing to acknowledge this emperor as the founder of the Byzantine Empire would ever think of categorising the inhabitants of, for instance, fourth-century Gaul as Byzantines. Even when the beginnings of the Byzantine Empire are set in the fourth century, the label is still confined to the eastern parts of the Roman Empire as a spatial-cultural mode of distinction, not simply a chronological one.

---

[24] Stathakopoulos, *Short History*, 3.

[25] For the seventh century as a chronological boundary, see Whittow, *The Making of Orthodox Byzantium*, 96–7. For the sixth century, see Shepard, 'Introduction', 22–6; Schreiner, *Byzanz*, 3–6. R.-J. Lilie, 'Peter Schreiner, Byzanz 565–1453', vigorously argued in favour of the traditional fourth-century boundary; cf. the discussion in Meier, 'Ostrom–Byzanz, Spätantike–Mittelalter', 187–200.

Contrary to the historically acknowledged right of the ancient Roman Empire to undergo deep administrative and cultural changes until the fifth or even the sixth century without being deprived of its Roman label, modern historians find it hard to speak of a medieval Roman Empire after the seventh century, despite its unbroken continuity in the eastern parts. Why is this? If it were only about chronological demarcation, would it not be enough to speak of the medieval Roman Empire? Here, it is important to stress that 'medieval' as a chronological category has its own strong subalternising connotations.[26] Considering this, the fact that this established chronological category is not enough to do the work of periodisation in the case of the Roman imperial state of Constantinople indicates that the modern invention of Byzantium pertains to the construction of a subaltern within the generic medieval subaltern.

Indeed, the consolidation of the modern label 'Byzantine' had little to do with a need to chronologically demarcate the radically contracted eastern empire after the seventh century. Its signifying function operated within the ideological straitjacket of the Enlightenment, in particular Gibbon's archetypical Byzantinism, thus implicitly dismissing or, at least, blurring the historical fact of unbroken continuity of a transformed Roman imperial order in the 'decadent' world of the Middle Ages. In so doing, the label consistently directs attention away from the malleability of the content of Romanness as a collective discourse of identification in both political and cultural terms. The notion of Byzantium and the Byzantines came into being in order to maintain an idealised and essentialised image of classical Greco-Roman culture immune to any medieval mutation. It was invented with the purpose of emphasising a historical end, that of the 'true' West Roman Empire, not a beginning. This is why historians find it so difficult to agree about the starting point of the Byzantine Empire.[27]

Gibbon's archetypical Byzantinism represented a side effect of the emergence of the historical spatial-cultural prerogative of the 'West' as a constructed ontologised category. According to that prerogative, the Roman Empire as the bearer of an essentialised classical Roman civilisation of republican ideals and law, to which the mythology of origins of modern western European civilisation makes an exclusive claim, emerged with ancient Rome in the western parts of Europe and declined with it in late antiquity. Therefore, deconstructing historiographical Byzantinism means,

---

[26] Le Goff, 'Pour un long moyen âge', 24–5; Brown, 'In the Middle', 547–51; Arnold, 'Das "finstere" Mittelalter'.
[27] Cf. the discussion in Cameron, *Byzantine Matters*, 95.

first and foremost, discussing how Gibbon's legacy and the orientalised image of the so-called Byzantine Empire in the context of the predominant historical grand narrative of a 'Western Civilisation' have created a rigid framework of exclusiveness and subalternity within which generations of Byzantinists have formulated their arguments.

Gibbon's Legacy and 'Anti-Gibbonism' as 'Neo-Gibbonism'

The impact of the Enlightenment's legacy regarding an orientalised Byzantium on the research field of Byzantine Studies can be seen primarily in the debates over the nature of Byzantine political ideology and identity. If Gibbon's Byzantinism was conditioned by his era's essentialising notions of classical Roman and Greek identities as the ideal progenitors of modern European civilisation, his statement about the medieval Empire of Constantinople as neither truly Roman nor truly Hellenic set the conceptual background against which research on Byzantium's identity would be conducted.

Greek scholars of the nineteenth century were the first to respond to Gibbon by constructing the image of a Hellenic Byzantium in the context of Romanticism's conception of modern nations as primordial.[28] The pioneer of this endeavour, Spyridon Zampelios, claimed that Greeks should not accept foreigners to shape the image of the Greek past in a way that reflected their own prejudices about Greece.[29] This programmatic statement was intended as a response to Hegel and through him to Gibbon.[30] At the same time, however, Zampelios's reaction was also directed against the predominant historical scheme of nascent Greek nationalism in the early nineteenth century, which had been shaped by Greek intellectuals inspired by western European ideals. The latter promoted the notion of a direct and unmediated link between the modern Greek nation and its glorious ancient Greek past, from which the Byzantine period was excluded.[31]

As has been recently argued, the ideal image of ancient Greek civilisation – often referred to as whitewashed Hellenism – came about in the process of the emergence of western Europe's mythology of origins and has been nurtured by the academic field of Classical Studies as a product

---

[28] Stamatopoulos, *Το Βυζάντιο μετά το έθνος*, 17.
[29] Zampelios, *Άσματα Δημοτικά*, 7.
[30] Stamatopoulos, *Το Βυζάντιο μετά το έθνος*, 59; Koubourlis, *La formation de l'histoire nationale Greque*, 151–2.
[31] Liakos, 'Hellenism', 204–6; Droulia, 'Τα σύμβολα', 335–51.

of European fantasy and Western hegemony.[32] According to this argument, this is what determines the kinship between the concept of Hellenism and the concept of Orientalism, since the former's main function has been to facilitate the appropriation, distortion or negation of modern Greek history and identity. This applies in particular to the role of the discourse of white-washed Hellenism in the early stages of the process of shaping a modern Greek nation, insofar as one of its main functions has been to negate the modern Greeks' recent past – that is, the medieval East Roman culture – and to stress the theory of a nation that was resurrected from the ashes of its idealised classical past. This negation corresponds with Gibbon's 'Byzantinism', which deprived the medieval Empire of Constantinople of both a 'true' Roman and a 'true' Hellenic identity in the essentialised and idealised terms of the Enlightenment.

In this regard, Zampelios's construct of a Hellenic Byzantium could be understood as a reaction against a western European notion of Hellenism which downplayed the modern Greeks' recent past and the latter's contribution to modern Greek cultural identity. However, to the extent to which his arguments can be seen as a sort of 'insurrection' against western European intellectual hegemony, that 'insurrection' fell rather short in conceptual terms, since Zampelios's goal was not to deconstruct the ideal image of perpetual ethnic Hellenism as a carrier of democratic ideals in order to reclaim the modern Greeks' recent Christian-Roman past. Instead, he sought to force that recent past into the straitjacket of the hegemonic western European conception of whitewashed Hellenism. If for Gibbon and Hegel Byzantium should be excluded from western Europe's symbolic geography because it had nothing to do with the idealised classical Roman and Greek past, Zampelios's response was that Orthodoxy and the Church were the main vehicles of Hellenic continuity in the Byzantine Empire. He drew a clear line between a democratic Hellenic nation, consisting of the people and the Church, and the foreign Roman imperial power;[33] the latter was assimilated by the former in a long-drawn process which culminated after 1204, the period of the birth of modern Hellenism.

Zampelios's discourse thus demonstrates the impact of Gibbon's archetypical 'Byzantinism' on the way Greek scholars would approach the medieval eastern Roman culture – that is, in terms of inclusion or exclusion from the ideals of western European civilisation, whose mythology

---

[32] On 'whitewashed Hellenism' as an Orientalism, see Carastathis, 'Is Hellenism an Orientalism?', esp. 1–9.

[33] Stamatopoulos, Το Βυζάντιο μετά το έθνος, 51–63.

of origins went back to classical Rome and classical Greece. Even though Zampelios's effort to Hellenise Byzantium departed from a distinctly anti-Western attitude that aimed to understand and present Hellenic history independently from European history, it is evident that he had fully internalised and was reproducing the Enlightenment's essentialised image of Hellenism as a carrier of democracy and personal freedom. In his effort to prove the nation's unbroken continuity in time and space, his argument remained fully subordinate to the conceptual boundaries of archetypical Byzantinism, the main target of his criticism.

Zampelios's continuity scheme of a Christianised Hellenic nation in Byzantium never became predominant; it was immediately challenged by Konstantinos Paparrigopoulos. Contrary to the former, the latter had a distinct agenda to Hellenise Byzantium with the aim of presenting it as an integral part of European history.[34] Breaking away from the Zampelian antithesis of democratic Hellenic nation vs autocratic Roman imperial power, Paparrigopoulos's goal was to include the monarchy in the scheme of Hellenisation. Within this framework, he saw in the phenomenon of heresy a link with ancient Hellenism, interpreting the former as a by-product of the persistent spirit of ancient Hellenic philosophy in Byzantium. Moreover, he presented the period of Iconoclasm as the equivalent of the Reformation in western Europe.[35] It was this image of Byzantium that he incorporated into his genealogical construct of perpetual national Hellenism, which has shaped the dominant modern Greek view of the past – an approach still influential today in Greek national historiography.[36]

Despite the efforts of late nineteenth-century Greek scholarship to establish the image of a Hellenic Byzantium which implicitly or explicitly positioned Byzantine culture in the 'West', the medieval Empire of Constantinople hardly escaped its generically subaltern position within the western European grand narrative – a position owing to the persistent shadow cast on it by whitewashed Hellenism. This is made evident by the integration of Byzantine Studies into the field of Classical Studies – in particular classical philology – at the universities of the Western world, within which Byzantine literature acquired the image of Hellenic literature of a 'lower quality'.[37]

[34] Stamatopoulos, 'The Western Byzantium of Konstantinos Paparrigopoulos', 39–42.
[35] Stamatopoulos, Το Βυζάντιο μετά το έθνος, 71–89.
[36] Zelepos, 'Phönix ohne Asche', 192–205; Liakos, 'Hellenism', 210–12.
[37] On the inferior image of Byzantine literature well into the twentieth century, see Mullett, 'Dancing with Deconstructionists', 258; Agapitos, 'Contesting Conceptual Boundaries', 63–7; Agapitos, 'Byzantine Literature', 239–41; Beck, 'Die byzantinischen Studien'; Reinsch, 'Η βυζαντινή λόγια'.

In this regard, it comes as no surprise that when the image of a Hellenic Byzantium was seriously challenged in the 1960s, this challenge came first from a Byzantinist who had been trained as a classical philologist. In a series of two lectures held at the University of Cincinnati in the early 1960s, Romilly Jenkins deconstructed the image of the medieval empire of the Hellenic nation.[38] Jenkins targeted the inherently problematic notion of Hellenic national continuity based on Greek racial continuity. Of great interest in his argument is the implicit image of the medieval East Roman Empire that emerged from his deconstruction of the model of nineteenth-century Greek national historiography.

Even though he sought to distance himself from Gibbon's prejudiced view of Byzantine culture,[39] Jenkins's central argument about 'Byzantinism', the term he used to label the exclusive identity and culture of the medieval Empire of Constantinople, was fully conditioned by Byzantium's orientalised image in western Europe from the time of Gibbon onwards. His central thesis was that Byzantium's Christian identity excluded it from the notion of progress which in Western civilisation had been incrementally linked to secularism from the period of the Renaissance onwards.[40] Taking this as a point of departure, he compared Hellenic culture in Byzantium with the ancient Hellenic culture and found the former wanting in terms of quality and progress when compared to the established image of the latter in the field of Classics.[41] For Jenkins, idealised classical Hellenism was incompatible with both the autocratic culture of imperial Romanness and the rigidity of Christian theocracy, the two determinants of the very essence of 'Byzantinism'.[42]

Cyril Mango, the successor of Jenkins to the Koraes Chair at King's College London, was the next to pick up the thread of the argument from where Jenkins had left it in order to debunk any relationship between the Byzantine culture and that of modern Greece.[43] Mango reasserted the image of Byzantium as a politically autocratic culture whose background

---

[38] Jenkins, *Byzantium and Byzantinism*.

[39] Ibid. 2.

[40] Ibid. 4–5. Georgiadis-Arnakis was present at Jenkins's lectures and wrote an immediate response, 'Byzantium and Greece', which was published at around the same time as Jenkins's paper and which aimed to rehabilitate Byzantium's position in the 'Western Civilisation'.

[41] Jenkins, *Byzantium and Byzantinism*, 12–13.

[42] Ibid. 40–1.

[43] Mango, 'Byzantinism and Romantic Hellenism'.

referred neither to ancient Rome nor to ancient Greece but through Christianity to biblical Israel.[44] This was a static and backward-looking culture by modern western European standards. The Byzantines' own interest in the past focused on the period of the Christian Empire of late antiquity, downplaying both the classical Roman and Hellenic cultures. Therefore, for Mango, 'messianic Byzantinism', as he called it, was a way of thought that remained incompatible with Hellenism up to the final days of the empire and beyond, until the nineteenth century, when modern Greece was colonised with Western ideals about classical Hellenism.[45]

Jenkins and Mango set in motion a debate that would unfold in the following decades and eventually marginalise the image of Byzantium as the medieval hub of the Hellenic nation in Western academia. That said, one cannot help noticing that their refined version of 'Byzantinism' bore all the main tenets of Gibbonian archetypical 'Byzantinism'. By using classical Hellenism as an ideal measure for deconstructing Byzantium's Hellenic identity, both scholars operated with hard concepts of essential and immutable identities. If Greek national historians had striven to construct a Hellenic Byzantium as a carrier of the idealised elements of classical Hellenism, the counterargument of Jenkins and Mango presented an essentially biblical culture of theocratic autocracy, which as such was excluded from a Western civilisation of classical Hellenic and Roman origins.

In this context, the 'Byzantinism' of the 1960s did not simply deconstruct Byzantium's Hellenic identity. It also implicitly downplayed its Roman identity. Jenkins and Mango evidently chose to distance themselves from the exceptional approach of J. B. Bury in the late nineteenth century, who in the preface of the first of his two volumes on the history of the early medieval East Roman Empire had explicitly argued against the mainstream 'Byzantinism' that was on the rise at the time.[46] They reasserted, instead, the principal function of Gibbon's 'Byzantinism' that was intended to deny the malleability of both Greek and Roman identity, and to postulate the idea of a major historical break between the Roman Empire and its medieval successor state in the east.

A reaction to the image of Byzantium as a culture that had very little to do with the classical Roman past was put forward at about the same

---

[44] Ibid. 30–1. Mango reaffirmed this argument in his 'Discontinuity', esp. 54–7.

[45] Mango, 'Byzantinism', 32–5.

[46] Bury, *A History of the Later Roman Empire from Arcadius to Irene*, v–vi; cf. Bury, *A History of the Eastern Roman Empire from the Fall of Irene to the Accession of Basil I (A.D. 802–867)*.

time, in the 1960s, by the prominent German Byzantinist Hans-Georg Beck. Beck focused on the issue of the empire's political ideology, and his argument was mainly directed against the predominant image of the empire's political system as theocratic despotism.[47] If the proponents of 'Byzantinism' highlighted the idea of a major break and discontinuity, the German scholar's general approach to Byzantine civilisation was founded on the notions of *Kontinuität* and *Permanenz*.[48] Beck claimed that his goal was not to respond to Gibbon's negative image of the Byzantine Empire and that he did not intend to counter the dominant view of Byzantium as a culture in decline.[49] However, his argument regarding Byzantine political ideology and the function of the political system was, in fact, criticising Gibbon's legacy, since he deconstructed Byzantium's dominant image in scholarship as an absolutist and authoritarian state where religious beliefs made the people fully submissive in political terms and incapable of challenging their rulers.

Beck focused his criticism on the dominant role of the *Kaiseridee* within the political system and highlighted the continuity of the ideals of the Roman *res publica* in Byzantine political thought and practice. If the classical Roman *res publica* had been marked by the polarity between senate and plebs, in the Byzantine political system this polarity concerned the imperial power and the *politeia* (the Greek translation of *res publica* according to Beck). Due to the central role of the latter as the higher institution in the political system, the emperor was not a divinely ordained autocrat but a simple administrator of the state, chosen by the people and answerable to and controllable by them.[50]

Given that the refined 'Byzantinism' of the 1960s had come about as a response to nineteenth-century 'Hellenism', Beck's 'Republicanism' acquired de facto the function of a response to the former and its emphasis on a Judeo-Christian core of Byzantine culture. In this way, Beck rehabilitated the decadent Byzantium within 'Western civilisation' from a different and more convincing angle in comparison to the nineteenth-century Greek national historians. Nonetheless, his approach also did not break away from the limits of the Orientalist structure that Gibbon's archetypical 'Byzantinism' had established. His theory was, in fact, seeking to spotlight as a determinant in the last instance those elements of the medieval

[47] Beck, *Senat und Volk*; *Res publica Romana*; *Das Byzantinische Jahrtausend*.
[48] Kazhdan, *Studies on Byzantine Literature*, 12.
[49] Beck, *Das Byzantinische Jahrtausend*, 11–13.
[50] Ibid. 33–40.

East Roman culture that linked it with the idealised classical Roman past. Therefore, as a I shall relate in more detail below, he was no less prone to essentialisation when it came to the continuity and societal function of Roman republican ideals. With Beck's theory, the efforts of Byzantinists to reconstruct Byzantium's identity by focusing on a different essential core came full circle. 'Hellenism', 'Byzantinism' and 'Republicanism' can be seen as three major approaches to Byzantine culture in the twentieth century which came into being as by-products of European phantasy and Western hegemony in order to define the essentialised identity of a subaltern Byzantium, thus positioning it either within or without the grand narrative of 'Western civilisation'.

Even though Byzantine Studies experienced a belated but considerable theoretical development from roughly the last quarter of the twentieth century onwards,[51] the impact of the Orientalist structure of archetypical Byzantinism on the research of Byzantine political ideology remained traceable first and foremost in the way ideal types such as 'autocracy' or 'theocracy' continued to be applied by modern scholars to define the medieval empire's political culture. For instance, 'theocracy' has often been used to describe the Byzantine political culture in a highly problematic manner.[52] According to Max Weber, 'hierocracy' as an ideal sociological type refers to a political culture in which a ruler is legitimated by priests (either as an incarnation or in the name of God) or in which a high priest is also king. In the second case, we are dealing with a pure type of 'theocracy'.[53] On these two ideal types, Weber juxtaposed a third ideal type, namely 'Caesaropapism', as their opposite, since it refers to a political culture in which a secular ruler exercises supreme authority in ecclesiastic matters by virtue of his autonomous legitimacy.[54]

Taking this definitional background into account, one cannot help noticing that in modern scholarship Byzantium has the awkward privilege of bearing the mark of both a theocratic and a Caesaropapist political culture, notwithstanding the fact that in conceptual terms it could only be either one or the other. This muddled use of analytical terms relates to the very fact that their application in the Byzantine case is, more often than not, conditioned by Byzantium's inherently orientalised image. Theocracy

---

[51] Haldon, 'Byzantium after 2000', 3–4.
[52] One characteristic example is Runciman, *Byzantine Theocracy*, in which the author's arguments deviate to some extent from the implications of the title.
[53] Weber, *Economy and Society*, 1159–60.
[54] Ibid. 1160–1.

is applied with the intention of reasserting the inferiority of an Oriental medieval political culture which is excluded from the symbolic geography of western Europe. Caesaropapism is used as an additional means to distinguish the Orthodox Christian 'East' from the Catholic Christian 'West'.[55]

If we consider that the Byzantine ruler was not legitimated by a priesthood and was not a high priest functioning as a king, it becomes evident that the Byzantine political system can hardly fit into the Weberian ideal type of a theocracy.[56] On the other hand, Caesaropapism is a problematical concept due to its considerable definitional vagueness. Weber has argued that a pure type of Caesaropapism cannot be found in any human society. He specifically mentioned Byzantium among those Caesaropapist societies in which the ruler's control over the Church may have been extensive in terms of appointing patriarchs and bishops but had certain clear limits, in particular when it came to the ruler's ability to impose religious beliefs and norms of his own making.[57] It is exactly that vagueness of Weber's definition that has raised reasonable criticism of the analytical usefulness of the concept.[58] For instance, historians of eastern Christianity have attacked the concept of Caesaropapism and declined its applicability to Byzantium wholesale, highlighting the evident lack of dogmatic control of the emperor over the Church.[59]

Contrary to the vagueness of the concept of Caesaropapism that renders it almost analytically toothless, autocracy is a category of analysis that does not lack clarity. It is defined as

> a system of government in which supreme political power to direct all the activities of the state is concentrated in the hands of one person, whose decisions are subject to neither external legal restraints nor regularized mechanisms of popular control, except for the implicit threat of coup d'état or mass insurrection.[60]

[55] A visualised example of the exclusion of theocratic Orthodox Byzantium from the symbolic geography of the western civilisation of Catholic Christianity can be found in the maps of S. Huntington's book, where the limits of western Europe follow the limits of Catholic Christianity vis-à-vis orthodox eastern (that is, Byzantine) Christianity; see Huntington, *Clash of Civilizations*, 30.

[56] The Byzantine emperor enjoyed certain priestly privileges which distinguished his status in the church from other laymen. However, he did not have the full rights and functions of a priest; see Geanakoplos, 'Church and State', 390–2.

[57] Weber, *Economy and Society*, 1161.

[58] For a critical take on Caesaropapism in Byzantium, see Dagron, *Emperor and Priest*, 282–312; cf. the comments in Arnason, 'Byzantium and Historical Sociology', 498–9.

[59] McGuckin, 'The Legacy of the 13th Apostle', 251–3.

[60] 'Autocracy', in *A Glossary of Political Economy Terms*.

Based on this definition, there can be little doubt that autocracy as an ideal type describes the Byzantine political system accurately in politological terms. As any student of Byzantine history knows, superior political power was concentrated in the person of the emperor and the power elite around him, consisting of his closest associates, who were persons of his own choosing. There was neither a legal constitution nor any other regularised mechanism of popular control over this small group's decisions about the governance of the state. The only means that could threaten the power of an emperor was a coup d'état or a revolt, which could contingently lead to his deposition.

However, the term autocracy has often been used interchangeably with the terms 'oriental despotism' and 'theocracy' in order to draw an image of Byzantine state culture as authoritarian. Here, one needs to draw qualitative distinctions. The fact that the decisions of the Byzantine emperor and the power elite around him were not subordinate to regular, institutionalised control by the people as a political body does not mean that various social groups (the senate, the army, the citizenry of Constantinople, the clergy) were not in a position to occasionally react and restrain imperial policies. Moreover, it does not mean that the imperial state, despite its – by the standards of the time – elaborate bureaucratic apparatus, had the infrastructural capacity to penetrate society in the way the modern infrastructural state does in order to control the lives of its subjects and impose the ruler's will in all cases.[61] This becomes obvious if one considers, for instance, that the inherent intolerance of the official state ideology of religious Orthodoxy towards heretics hardly prevented large numbers of heterodox Roman subjects to maintain their beliefs for centuries and even claim positions in the provincial administration or the army against the prescriptions of Roman law.[62]

In light of the above, one may rightfully argue that autocracy has rarely been employed as an analytical concept intended to describe the functional principles of the Byzantine political system. It has rather often functioned as a denigrating label and a marker of subalternity from the viewpoint of a Eurocentric historical taxonomy of political systems in

---

[61] On the ideal types of 'despotic' and 'infrastructural' state and their differences in the modern and premodern periods, see Mann, 'The Autonomous Power of the State', 113–16.

[62] The Miaphysite Armenians and the Paulicians are a case in point; Lilie, 'Ethnischen und religiösen Minderheiten in Byzanz', 301–8 and 312–15. On the issue of the enforcement of Orthodoxy in Byzantium, see Cameron, 'Enforcing Orthodoxy'.

which modern European liberal democracies and their classical progenitors, the Athenian democracy and the classical Roman republic, set
the ideal background against which the regression and barbarism of the
Middle Ages should be measured. In this context, the debate over Byzantine autocracy has been marked by the efforts of scholars to deconstruct an
ideologically charged modern image of Byzantium as a social order where
any criticism and political action against the imperial power was unthinkable due to the divinely ordained absolute power of the emperor. A number of older and more recent studies have shown that Byzantine political
culture was anything but a culture of political passivity and unquestioned
subordination of all social groups to the will of the ruler.[63]

In my view, these studies have succeeded in problematising our understanding of autocracy in the case of Byzantium, by showing which social
groups were politically influential, and how and to what degree they were
influential, in different periods of the empire's long history. For instance,
the scrutiny of the practice of revolt in the Byzantine Empire has revealed
a great deal about the function of the political system and how that fits into
the ideal type of autocracy. The Byzantine paradigm offers insights into
the different functions of autocratic regimes in history and shows why historical analysis of past social orders can profit a lot more when its point of
departure is not the need to reassert an essentialised moralising taxonomy
of superior vs inferior systems of government.

On the other hand, efforts to interpret the large number of rebellions
and coups d'état in the Byzantine Empire as evidence that superior political
power lay not with the emperor but with the people point to the persistent
effect of 'Byzantinism's' ideological straitjacket on the analysis of the medieval East Roman political culture.[64] The proponents of this theory attempt,
in fact, to deconstruct archetypical 'Byzantinism' by its own means, namely
by seeking to downplay or marginalise the role of religious ideas which are
regarded as the main sponsors of absolutism in the political culture of the
Byzantine Empire.

The founding father of the 'republican thesis', H.-G. Beck, even though
he accepted the important role of religion in shaping Byzantine identity

---

[63] Lilie, 'Macht und Ohnmacht'; 'Der Kaiser in der Statistik'; Gizewski, *Zur Normativität und Struktur*; Garland, 'Political Power and the Populace'; Cheynet, 'La colère du
peuple'; 'Se révolter'; see also the papers in Armstrong (ed.), *Authority in Byzantium*.

[64] Beck, *Senat und Volk*; *Res publica Romana*. Beck's theory has been recently revived
and elaborated by Anthony Kaldellis, who presents the Byzantine Empire as a republic: see Kaldellis, *Byzantine Republic*.

and culture, argued that the religiously charged, mystifying concept of the *Kaiseridee*, namely the notion that the emperor's power was divinely ordained, represented simply a rhetorical construct intended to safeguard the institution of the imperial office. It was secular republican ideas that ruled political life and guided political action, with frequent revolt being their main effect. Republican ideas shaped Byzantine political reality and made the emperor expendable and politically subordinate to the people, the *politeia*.[65]

At the heart of this argument lies an artificial distinction between secular-rational and religious-irrational ideas in Byzantine political discourse and practice. Whereas the latter are considered to have represented a normative rhetorical façade that played little role in shaping political practice, the former are regarded as those operative ideas and values that justified the illegitimate practice of rebellion – the means through which the people controlled the imperial office and asserted their political sovereignty over imperial power. If this is a thesis intended to respond to and debunk archetypical 'Byzantinism' – that is, Byzantium's image as an Oriental theocracy – it goes without saying that it has fully internalised and reproduces the Orientalist structure that it seeks to deconstruct, remaining fully trapped in its main premises. Instead of asking what the actual political role of religious ideas was in enabling the deposition of emperors, it seeks to a priori marginalise their role, by expelling them to the sphere of mystifying rhetorical normativity with little or no operative political role.

The argument that recurrent revolt against the emperor in Byzantium should be seen as a phenomenon resulting from a dominant operative ideology that cut through social strata and made the people perceive themselves and act as a sovereign political body flies in the face of a sober analysis of the source evidence.[66] Rebellions and coups d'état were contingent events with a contingent outcome. As a result, their political function could not be related to that of a plebiscite, in which the people united to exercise the political right of determining the holder of the imperial office. In fact, a closer look at the phenomenon of rebellions demonstrates that their frequent recurrence was very much related to the lack of a sovereign institution in the Byzantine political system – a lack, that is, of a political body which could elect or depose an emperor in a binding manner on behalf of the whole community.

---

[65] Beck, *Das Byzantinische Jahrtausend*, 33–86.
[66] See the relevant criticisms in Haldon, 'Res publica Byzantina?' 4–16; Stouraitis, 'Civil War', 102–5; 'Review of Kaldellis, A., *The Byzantine Republic*', 296–7.

Attempts to depose an emperor were motivated by various reasons, such as the personal ambition of the throne contender, the power interests of the elite faction that supported him (in most cases) and/or dissatisfaction by one or more social groups (e.g. an army unit, the circus factions or the city guilds).[67] Whatever the motives and the justifying arguments of actions of usurpation, however, the outcome of a rebellion or a coup d'état was ultimately determined by the equilibrium of (usually military) power between emperor and contenders. In the case of military rebellions of usurpation, this was overwhelmingly in favour of the holder of the imperial office, as demonstrated by the fact that of the numerous military rebellions against emperors over the many centuries of the empire's existence, less than one in five was successful.[68] Moreover, only two popular insurrections in Constantinople ended with an emperor's deposition. These data show that revolt had very little to do with a regularised political practice through which common people throughout the empire could determine the holder of the imperial office and, as a result of this, internalise the notion that they formed and functioned as a sovereign political body vis-à-vis the imperial power.

It was the lived experience of the great risk entailed in military rebellions which led the provincial magnate Kekaumenos to stress in his late eleventh-century treatise that his peers should remain loyal to the emperor and seek to avoid participation in a rebellion against his power.[69] This statement indicates that rebellion as a political practice came nowhere near to being conceived as an expression of popular sovereignty by the provincial populations. This comes as no surprise if one considers that in the vast majority of military rebellions and coups d'état, the leaders of the movement had little need for popular approval and support to organise and fulfil their subversive plans. Moreover, public opinion was hardly a crucial factor for the outcome of a power struggle. For instance, rebels such as General Bardanios or Thomas the so-called Slav did not manage to depose the reigning emperors, even though they enjoyed popularity, according to the sources.[70]

---

[67] On a typology of the image of the usurper in the Byzantine Empire, see Cresci, 'Appunti', 90–129; on a typology of Byzantine civil wars, see Stouraitis, 'Civil War', 108–18.

[68] Treadgold, 'Reluctant Warrior', 225; see also the list of military rebellions on pages 231–3.

[69] Kekaumenos, *Consilia et Narrationes*, 64–76, ed. and tr. Roueché.

[70] See the relevant passages in *Theophanes Continuatus (libri I–IV)*, 3.5–8, 11.14–19, ed. Featherstone and Signes Codoñer, 16, 80.

In light of the above, if we want to understand the role of rebellion in the medieval East Roman political system, we need to take certain factors into consideration. The lack of a sovereign political body alongside the lack of an established tradition of hereditary rule in Byzantine political culture deprived the holder of the imperial office of classical or traditional legitimacy in Weberian terms. This made his rule a matter of provisional acceptance from various social groups that could exercise political influence: the senate, the army, the Church, and the citizenry of Constantinople. Any one of these groups or even only a part of it (for instance, a faction of the senatorial elite or one army unit) could withdraw at any time its acceptance of the emperor and attempt to depose him through a palatine conspiracy, a popular revolt in Constantinople or a military revolt in the provinces.[71]

Even though any action to depose an emperor was illegitimate in legal-political terms and, hence, punishable by law,[72] in practice anyone could revolt at any time and seek to replace the ruler. The legitimacy or illegitimacy of the action of usurpation was ultimately determined only by its successful or unsuccessful outcome, respectively – that is, by sheer power relations. Therefore, it had little to do with any established perception of the emperor's subjects being a collective political body that exercised sovereignty. In this socio-political context, the only operative idea that could help the imperial subjects explain and rationalise both the contingent outbreak and the contingent outcome of revolts against the emperor was the notion of divine will and providence. Reference to God's will and not some tacit belief in the sovereign power of the people was the main means to rationalise the function of the political system as the only way of explaining why some attempts to dethrone an emperor failed while others succeeded.

Contrary to Beck's argument, the social role of the religiously charged *Kaiseridee* went beyond the normative, mystifying function of safeguarding the institution of the imperial office – a function that marginalised and delegitimised any thought of changing the political system (that is, abolishing the monarchy to return to the ancient system of the Roman *res publica*). Instead of making the imperial subjects politically passive and fully submissive to the will of the emperor, religious ideas and values had acquired a central role in justifying acts of usurpation, which were illegitimate in legal-political terms, by rationalising both their contingent outbreak and outcome.[73] The idea that revolting against the emperor was a means to

---

[71] Flaig, 'Konzeptionalisierung der Usurpation', 15–16; cf. Stouraitis, 'Civil War', 103–4.
[72] Bourdara, Καθοσίωσις, 142–82.
[73] Fögen, 'Das politische Denken', 52–82.

enforce the will of the people could not inhabit popular thought and, therefore, could not acquire an operative ideological function within Byzantine society, because it could not explain the frequent failure of rebellions. This task could only be fulfilled by the notion that the one who remained victorious at the end of a rebellion, whether reigning emperor or usurper, was the one that had been chosen by God to rule.

Conclusion

In this chapter, I have revisited the question of archetypical historiographical Byzantinism's kinship to Said's Orientalism. I have argued that the consolidation of the label 'Byzantium' in modern scholarship effected the distortion and negation of the historical identity of the remaining eastern parts of the Roman Empire after the end of antiquity. The scholarly debate over the political ideology of the so-called Byzantine Empire, as a debate about that social order's historical identity, provides ample proof of Byzantinism's persistent role in circumscribing the conceptual horizon of scholarly research and imposing the need to categorise Byzantine culture within an ontologised 'West' or 'East', respectively. Many scholars have tried to remove Byzantium from its subaltern historical position by seeking to respond to Gibbon's legacy of an essentialised discontinuity between the Byzantine world and what came before it. However, in this effort the pendulum has sometimes swung a bit too far in the opposite direction. The goal of deconstructing Byzantium's negative image has often led to arguments that constructed essentialised continuities between Byzantium and an idealised Hellenic or Roman classical past.

Any effort to try to make the subaltern speak through its own voice, namely through the various textual and material sources handed down to us, needs to begin by respecting its historical diversity and autonomy. In other words, it needs to avoid measuring it against, or colonising it with, the ideals of an ontologised Modernity. A conducive way to do so, is to seek to define our analytical concepts clearly and to use them free of any prejudice stemming from a generic, moralising taxonomy of the inferior Middle Ages vis-à-vis the superior eras of Antiquity and Modernity. That said, if the Middle Ages should not be constructed as the negated 'other' which is there to facilitate the depiction of Modernity's ideal 'self', this does not mean that medieval cultures were not in many respects different from cultures of the modern or the ancient world. Criticism of 'Byzantinism' remains one of current scholarship's main tasks, especially with regard to ongoing research on political ideologies and collective identifications in the Byzantine world.

However, deconstructing Gibbon's image of Byzantium is not enough if we do not break free from the Orientalist structure of his legacy, which imposes questions on historical research that dictate the answers.

Acknowledgements

I would like to thank Dimitris Stamatopoulos (University of Macedonia) and Niels Gaul (University of Edinburgh) for discussing drafts of this chapter with me and for making useful remarks. I would also like to thank the participants of the seminar 'The Long History of Ethnicity and Nationhood Reconsidered' at The Oxford Research Centre of the Humanities (TORCH), where I had the chance to present a version of this chapter and receive useful feedback in 2017.

Bibliography

Sources

Kekaumenos, *Consilia et Narrationes* . . . Ch. Roueché (ed. and tr.), 'Kekaumenos, Consilia et Narrationes (2013)'. Available at <https://ancientwisdoms.ac.uk/library/kekaumenos-consilia-et-narrationes> (last accessed 20 June 2020).

Theophanes Continuatus (libri I-IV) . . . M. Featherstone and J. Signes Codoñer (ed.), *Chronographiae quae Theophanis Continuati nomine fertur Libri I-IV* (Berlin, 2015).

Secondary Literature

A Glossary of Political Economy Terms. Available at <http://www.auburn.edu/~johnspm/gloss/autocracy> (last accessed 20 June 2020).

Agapitos, P., 'Byzantine Literature and Greek Philologists in the Nineteenth Century', *Classica et Medievalia* 43 (1992): 231–60.

Agapitos, P., 'Contesting Conceptual Boundaries: Byzantine Literature and Its History', *Interfaces: A Journal of Medieval European Literatures* (2015): 62–91.

Angelov, D., 'Byzantinism: The Imaginary and Real Heritage of Byzantium in Southeastern Europe', in D. Keridis, E. Elias-Bursać and N. Yatromanolakis (eds), *New Approaches to Balkan Studies* (Dulles, VA, 2003), 3–21.

Armstrong, P., (ed.), *Authority in Byzantium* (Farnham-London-Burlington, VT, 2013).

Arnason, J. P., 'Byzantium and Historical Sociology', in P. Stephenson (ed.), *The Byzantine World* (New York, 2010), 491–504.

Arnold, K., 'Das "finstere" Mittelalter. Zur Genese und Phänomenologie eines Fehlurteils', *Saeculum* 32 (1981): 287–300.

Beck, H.-G., 'Die byzantinischen Studien in Deutschland vor Karl Krumbacher', in H.-G. Beck (ed.), *ΧΑΛΙΚΕΣ. Festgabe für die Teilnehmer am XI. Internationalen Byzantinisten Kongreß (München 15.–20. September 1958)* (Freising, 1958), 67–118.

Beck, H.-G., *Senat und Volk von Konstantinopel. Probleme der byzantinischen Verfassungsgeschichte* (Munich, 1966).

Beck, H.-G., *Res publica Romana. Vom Staatsdenken der Byzantiner* (Munich, 1970).

Beck, H.-G., *Das Byzantinische Jahrtausend*, 2nd ed. (Munich, 1992).

Bodin, H., "Whose Byzantinism – Ours or Theirs? On the Issue of Byzantinism from a Cultural Semiotic Perspective", in P. Marciniak and D. C. Smythe, *The Reception of Byzantium in European Culture since 1500* (London and New York, 2016), 11–42.

Bourdara, K. A., *Καθοσίωσις και Τυραννίς κατά τους Μέσους Βυζαντινούς Χρόνους. Μακεδονική Δυναστεία (867–1056)* (Athens and Komotene, 1981).

Brown, C., 'In the Middle', *JMEMS* 30/3 (2000): 547–73.

Bryer, A., 'Gibbon and the Later Byzantine Empires', in R. McKitterick and R. Quinault (eds), *Edward Gibbon and Empire* (Cambridge, 1997), 101–16.

Bury, J. B., *A History of the Later Roman Empire from Arcadius to Irene*, 2 vols (London, 1889).

Bury, J. B., *A History of the Eastern Roman Empire from the Fall of Irene to the Accession of Basil I (A.D. 802–867)* (London, 1912).

Cameron, A., 'Gibbon and Justinian', in R. McKitterick and R. Quinault (eds), *Edward Gibbon and Empire* (Cambridge, 1997), 34–52.

Cameron, A., 'Byzance dans le débat sur orientalisme', in M.-F. Auzépy (ed.), *Byzance en Europe* (Paris, 2003), 235–50.

Cameron, A., 'Enforcing Orthodoxy in Byzantium', *Studies in Church History* 43 (2007): 1–24.

Cameron, A., *Byzantine Matters* (Princeton, 2014).

Carastathis, A., 'Is Hellenism an Orientalism? Reflections on the Boundaries of "Europe" in an Age of Austerity', *Critical Race and Whiteness Studies* 10/1 (2014): 1–17.

Cheynet, J.-C., 'La colère du peuple a Byzance (Xe-XIIe siècle)', *Société française d'histoire urbaine* 3 (2001): 25–38.

Cheynet, J.-C., 'Se révolter légitimement contre le "Basileus"?', in P. Depreux (ed.), *Revolte und Sozialstatus von der Spätantike bis zur Frühen Neuzeit/ Révolte et statut social de l'Antiquité tardive aux Temps modernes* (Munich, 2008), 57–73.

Cresci, L. R., 'Appunti per una tipologia del Tyrannos', *Byz* 60 (1990): 90–129.

Dagron, G., *Emperor and Priest: The Imperial Office in Byzantium* (Paris, 2003).

Delanty, G., *Inventing Europe. Idea, Identity, Reality* (Basingstoke and London, 1995).

Droulia, L., 'Τα σύμβολα του νέου ελληνικού κράτους', *Ta Istorika* 23 (1995): 335–51.

Flaig, E., 'Für eine Konzeptionalisierung der Usurpation im Spätrömischen Reich', in F. Paschoud and J. Szidat (eds), *Usurpationen in der Spätantike* (Stuttgart, 1997), 15–34.

Fögen, T. M., 'Das politische Denken der Byzantiner', in *Pipers Handbuch der politischen Ideen*, 2 vols, II: Mittelalter (Munich, 1993), 41–85.

Garland, L., 'Political Power and the Populace in Byzantium Prior to the Fourth Crusade', BSl 53/1 (1992): 17–52.

Geanakoplos, D. J., 'Church and State in the Byzantine Empire: A Reconsideration of the Problem of Caesaropapism', *ChHist* 34/4 (1965): 381–403.

Georgiadis-Arnakis, G., 'Byzantium and Greece: A Review Article à propos of Romilly Jenkins, Byzantium and Byzantinism', *BalkSt* 4 (1963): 379–400.

Ghosh, P., 'The Conception of Gibbon's History', in R. McKitterick and R. Quinault (eds), *Edward Gibbon and Empire* (Cambridge, 1997), 271–316.

Gibbon, E., *The History of the Decline and Fall of the Roman Empire*, with notes by D. Milman, M. Guizot and W. Smith, 12 vols, V (New York and London, 1899).

Gizewski, C., *Zur Normativität und Struktur der Verfassungsverhältnisse in der späteren römischen Kaiserzeit* (Munich, 1988).

Haldon, J., 'Byzantium after 2000: Post-Millennial, but not Post-Modern?' in C. Sode and S. Takács (eds), *Novum Millennium. Studies on Byzantine History and Culture Dedicated to Paul Speck* (Aldershot, 2001), 1–11.

Haldon, J., 'Res publica Byzantina? State Formation and Issues of Identity in Medieval East Rome', *BMGS* 40/1 (2016): 4–16.

Hegel, G. W. F., *Vorlesungen über die Philosophie der Geschichte, auf d. Grundlage d. Werke von 1832–1845 neu ed. Ausg.* (Frankfurt am Main, 1989).

Heilo, O., 'Beyond Orientalism: Byzantium and the Historical Contextualisation of Islam', in M. Grünbart (ed.), *Verflechtungen zwischen Byzanz und dem Orient. Beiträge aus der Sektion "Byzantinistik" im Rahmen des 32. Deutschen Orientalistentages in Münster (23.-27. September 2013)* (Berlin, 2019), 47–54.

Howard-Johnston, J., 'Gibbon and the Middle Period of the Byzantine Empire', in R. McKitterick and R. Quinault (eds), *Edward Gibbon and Empire* (Cambridge, 1997), 53–77.

Huntington, S. P., *The Clash of Civilizations and the Remaking of World Order* (New York, 1996).

Jenkins, R., *Byzantium and Byzantinism. Lectures in Memory of Louise Taft Semple* (Cincinnati, 1963).

Kaldellis, A., *The Byzantine Republic: People and Power in New Rome* (Cambridge, MA, 2015).

Kazhdan, A., *Studies on Byzantine Literature of the Eleventh and Twelfth Centuries, in collaboration with S. Franklin* (New York, 1984).

Koubourlis, I., *La formation de l'histoire nationale Greque. L'apport de Spyridon Zambélios (1815–1881)* (Athens, 2005).

Le Goff, J., 'Pour un long moyen âge', in *L'imaginaire médiévale, Essais par Jaques Le Goff*, 2nd ed. (Paris, 1991), 24–9.

Lechner K., *Hellenen und Barbaren im Weltbild der Byzantiner. Die alten Bezeichnungen als Ausdruck eines neuen Kulturbewusstseins* (Munich, 1955).

Liakos, A., 'Hellenism and the Making of Modern Greece: Time, Language, Space', in K. Zacharia (ed.), *Hellenisms. Culture, Identity and Ethnicity from Antiquity to Modernity* (Aldershot, 2008), 201–36.

Lilie, R.-J., 'Des Kaisers Macht und Ohnmacht: Zum Zerfall der Zentralgewalt in Byzanz vor dem vierten Kreuzzug', in *Poikila Byzantina 4, Varia I: Beiträge von R.-J. Lilie und P. Speck* (Bonn 1984), 9–120.

Lilie, R.-J., 'Der Kaiser in der Statistik. Subversive Gedanken zur angeblichen Allmacht der byzantinischen Kaiser', in C. Stavrakos, A.-K. Wassiliou-Seibt and M. Krikorian (eds), *Hypermachos: Studien zur Byzantinistik, Armenologie und Georgistik. Festschrift für Werner Seibt zum 65. Geburtstag* (Wiesbaden, 2008), 211–33.

Lilie, R.-J., 'Peter Schreiner, Byzanz 565–1453', *BZ* 101/2 (2009): 851–3.

Lilie, R.-J., 'Zur Stellung von ethnischen und religiösen Minderheiten in Byzanz: Armenier, Muslime und Paulikianer', in W. Pohl, C. Gantner and R. Payne (eds), *Visions of Community in the Post-Roman World: The West, Byzantium and the Islamic World, 300–1100* (Farnham, 2012), 301–16.

Mango, C., 'Byzantinism and Romantic Hellenism', *Journal of the Warburg and Courtauld Institutes* 28 (1965): 29–43.

Mango, C., 'Discontinuity with the Classical Past in Byzantium', in M. Mullett and R. Scott (eds), *Byzantium and the Classical Tradition* (Birmingham, 1981), 48–57.

Mann, M., 'The Autonomous Power of the State: Its Origins, Mechanisms and Results', *European Journal of Sociology* 25/2 (1984): 185–213.

Marciniak, P., 'Oriental Like Byzantium. Some Remarks on Similarities Between Byzantinism and Orientalism', in A. Alshanskaya, A. Gietzen and Ch. Hadjiafxenti (eds), *Imagining Byzantium: Perceptions, Patterns, Problems* (Mainz, 2018), 47–54.

McGuckin, J. A., 'The Legacy of the 13th Apostle: Origins of the East Christian Conceptions of Church and State Relation', *SVThQ* 47/3–4 (2003): 251–88.

McKitterick, R., 'Gibbon and the Early Middle Ages', in R. McKitterick and R. Quinault (eds), *Edward Gibbon and Empire* (Cambridge, 1997), 162–89.

Meier, M., 'Ostrom–Byzanz, Spätantike–Mittelalter. Überlegungen zum "Ende" der Antike im Osten des Römischen Reiches', *Millennium* 9/1 (2012): 187–254.

Mullett, M., 'Dancing with Deconstructionists in the Gardens of the Muses: New Literary History vs?' *BMGS* 14 (1990): 258–75.

Neumann, C., 'Devletin Adı Yok – Bir Amblemin Okunması [The State Has No Name – The Reading of an Emblem]', *Cogito* 19 (1999): 269–83.

Reinsch D. R., Ἡ βυζαντινὴ λόγια γραμματεία στὴν Γερμανία τὸν 19ο αἰώνα, in E. Chrysos (ed.), *Ἕνας νέος κόσμος γεννιέται: Ἡ εἰκόνα τοῦ ἑλληνικοῦ πολιτισμοῦ στὴ γερμανικὴ ἐπιστήμη κατὰ τὸν 19ο αἰώνα* (Athens, 1996), 107–28.

Runciman, S., 'Gibbon and Byzantinum', *Daedalus* 105/3 (1976): 103–10.

Runciman, S., *The Byzantine Theocracy* (Cambridge, 1977).

Said, E. W., *Orientalism* (London, 1978).

Schreiner, P., *Byzanz, 565–1453*, 4th ed. (Munich, 2011).

Shepard, J., 'Byzantine Soldiers, Missionaries and Diplomacy under Gibbon's eyes', in R. McKitterick and R. Quinault (eds), *Edward Gibbon and Empire* (Cambridge, 1997), 78–100.

Shepard, J., 'Introduction', in J. Shepard (ed.), *The Cambridge History of the Byzantine Empire c. 500–1492* (Cambridge, 2008), 2–95.

Stamatopoulos, D., *Το Βυζάντιο μετά το έθνος. Το πρόβλημα της συνέχειας στις βαλκανικές ιστοριογραφίες* (Athens 2009).

Stamatopoulos, D., 'From the Vyzantism of K. Leont'ev to the Vyzantinism of I. I. Sokolov: The Byzantine Orthodox East as a Motif of Russian Orientalism', in O. Delouis, A. Courderc and P. Guran (eds), *Héritages de Byzance en Europe du Sud-Est à l'époque moderne et contemporaine* (Athens, 2013), 321–40.

Stamatopoulos, D., 'The Western Byzantium of Konstantinos Paparrigopoulos', in A. Alshanskaya, A. Gietzen and C. Hadjiafxenti (eds), *Imagining Byzantium: Perceptions, Patterns, Problems* (Mainz, 2018), 39–46.

Stathakopoulos, D., *A Short History of the Byzantine Empire* (London, 2014).

Stouraitis, Y., 'Review of Kaldellis A., The Byzantine Republic: People and Power in New Rome, Cambridge, Mass, 2015', *JHS* 136 (2016): 296–7.

Stouraitis, Y., 'Civil War in the Christian Empire', in Y. Stouraitis (ed.), *A Companion to the Byzantine Culture of War, c. 300–1204* (Leiden, 2018), 92–123.

Theodoropoulos, P., 'Did the Byzantines Call Themselves Byzantines? Elements of Eastern Roman Identity in the Imperial Discourse of the Seventh Century', *BMGS* 45 (2021): 1–17.

Todorova, M., *Imagining the Balkans* (Oxford, 1997).

Treadgold, W., 'Byzantium, the Reluctant Warrior', in N. Christie and M. Yazigi (eds), *Noble Ideals and Bloody Realities. Warfare in the Middle Ages* (Leiden and Boston, 2006), 209–33.

Weber, M., *Economy and Society. An Outline of Interpretive Sociology*, ed. Guenther Roth and Claus Wittich (California, 1978).

Whittow, M., *The Making of Orthodox Byzantium, 600–1025* (Basingstoke, 1996).

Zampelios, S., *Ἄσματα δημοτικὰ τῆς Ἑλλάδος ἐκδοθέντα μετὰ μελέτης ἱστορικῆς περὶ μεσαιωνικοῦ ἑλληνισμοῦ* (Corfu, 1852).

Zelepos, I., '"Phönix ohne Asche". Konstantinos Paparrigopoulos und die Enstehung einer griechischen Nationalhistoriographie im 19. Jahrhundert', in M. Krzoska and H.-C. Maner (eds), *Beruf und Berufung. Geschichtswissenschaft und Nationsbuilding in Ostmittel- und Südosteuropa im 19. und 20. Jahrhundert* (Münster, 2005), 191–215.

2

Ruling Elites and the Common People: Some Considerations on Their Diverging Identities and Ideologies

Johannes Koder

In Byzantium, the political ideology of the emperor and the governing class strongly emphasised the term *Rhōmaios* as a self-designation for all imperial subjects. This ideological approach regarded the Byzantine Empire as the *Basileia tōn Rhōmaiōn* or *Rhōmania*, and Constantinople as *Nea Rhōmē*, the new ruling city of the entire ecumene.[1] This claim went along with a high level of socio-political organisation of the state by the standards of the time. However, this conception was probably very remote from the views and behavioural patterns of the majority of the population, the 'lower strata' of Byzantine society.

For example, the decision to start a war (including a civil war) was in Byzantium – as elsewhere – primarily a matter determined by the ideological and economic aims and concerns of the ruling elite. Declarations of war did not need the approval of the masses. While the Byzantine power elite's discourse emphatically celebrated the ideal of peace, in practice warfare could be deployed as a means of politics irrespective of ideological and ethical reservations. After the seventh century, unfavourable economic and military conditions in the geopolitical sphere of Byzantium meant that the emperors and the ruling 'senatorial class' (ἡ συγκλητικὴ τάξις)[2] were not keen on avoiding warfare out of conformity to pacifist convictions.[3] Instead, they waged wars either for territorial defence or for expansion whenever

---

[1] Treitinger, *Die oströmische Kaiser- und Reichsidee*, 161–88; Ahrweiler, *L'idéologie politique*; Karayannopoulos, *Η πολιτικη θεωρία των Βυζαντινών*; Magdalino, 'Ο οφθαλμός της οικουμένης'; Brown, *The World of Late Antiquity*.

[2] Michael Psellos, *Chronographia*, 1:7.40, ed. Reinsch, 226–7.

[3] Such convictions can be found in the Holy Scriptures (e.g. Joel 4.10 and Luke 14.31) and in the writings of the Church Fathers, e.g. Cyril of Alexandria, *Commentary*, 1:353–4; *Letters*, 731–2; *Homilies*, 15.1.59–81; Theodore of Mopsuestia, *Commentary*, in Joel 3.9–11.

the equilibrium of power was in the empire's favour.[4] In this context, one may question the efficiency of the imperial state's ideological mechanisms in widely propagating their differentiated conceptions of peace, upon which the justification of defensive or offensive warfare depended. My aim in the current chapter is to offer, relying on several *disiecta membra*, some thoughts regarding the potential channels through which the 'lower strata' could have been influenced ideologically, as well as regarding the need to problematise the degree of that influence.

Who are the 'lower strata'? Until now I could not find in Byzantine texts a description of them that would offer something like a definition. General terms like *dēmos, ethnos, genos, laos, ochlos, phylon, plērōma, politēs* or *taxis*, which are used in Byzantine texts, often with political connotations, are not sufficient to describe the delineated social groups of the empire's population. The terms *Christianos laos* or *Christianikon plērōma*,[5] for example, as group designations describe the adherents of the Christian (in the sense of orthodox and state-conforming) religion independently of their location within or beyond the frontiers of the empire; a similar use of *taxis* may be observed in the *Ponēmata* of Demetrios Chomatenos.[6] Some of the other terms are often carriers of a negative meaning. For instance, Ephrem the Syrian says in a sermon on the crucifixion of Jesus Christ, 'The ordinary people (*dēmos chydaios*), the mob from the market (*ochlos agoraios*) and the rude crowds (*laos agroikōdēs*) from the surrounding villages, who had gathered at a feast, shouted: crucify, crucify!'[7] The meaning of *ochlos* is always disparaging,[8] whereas the term *politēs* usually has a positive connotation.[9]

A different approach can be found in Byzantine reflections on the general systems of government or *katholikōterai politeiai*,[10] as they were

---

[4] On Byzantine attitudes towards warfare, see Haldon, *Warfare*, 13–33; Stouraitis, *Krieg und Frieden*, 190–361; 'Just War and Holy War', 235–64; and the collection of essays in Koder and Stouraitis (eds), *Byzantine War Ideology*.

[5] Genesios, *On the Reigns*, 4.19. See also Demetrios Chomatenos, *Ponēmata* 146.144: τῷ λοιπῷ ἱερατικῷ πληρώματι.

[6] Demetrios Chomatenos, *Ponēmata*, 86: εἴτε τοῦ βήματος εἰσίν, εἴτε τῆς λαϊκῆς τάξεώς τε καὶ καταστάσεως; ibid. 114: ἀπό τε τῆς συγκλήτου βουλῆς καὶ τῆς ἱεραρχικῆς τάξεως, ναὶ δὲ καὶ σύμπαντος τοῦ στρατιωτικοῦ μυριοπληθοῦς ὄντος.

[7] Ephrem the Syrian, *Works*, ed. Phrantzoles, 7:47.

[8] E.g. John Apokaukos, *Notitiae et epistulae* 4, lines 39–41, and 13, lines 45–8.

[9] E.g. John Apokaukos, *Notitiae et epistulae* 99.

[10] Cf. also Demetrios Chomatenos, *Ponēmata* 6.7 and 29.146–7, ed. Prinzing, 42 and 146: καθ' ἡμᾶς πολιτεία; ibid. 1.81 and 15.14–15, ed. Prinzing, 21 and 66: χριστιανῶν πολιτεία; and different terms for monastic *politeia*; ibid. 77, 79, 88, 119 and 188: ἀγγελική, μοναδική, μοναχική, τῶν μοναχῶν.

defined in the 'mirrors of princes' and other related texts. For example, in his 'Logos eis ton porphyrogennēton kyr Kōnstantinon', a lesson to the son of the emperor Michael VII Doukas (1071–8), Theophylact of Ohrid explains three pairs of opposites, well-known since antiquity:[11]

> There exist three more or less general forms of state. One is the *monarchia*, which may be called the lawful one (*ennomos*) and *basileia* . . . The form consisting of many ruling persons, who are also fully compliant to law, is called *aristokratia*. Finally, the congregation of all citizens in order to administrate the state, is called *dēmokratia*. To these, three other forms are opposed, which deprive them of their dignity: *tyrannis* lies in wait for the *basileia*; *oligokratia* aims at *aristokratia*, when some rich and ruthless persons hypocritically dominate the best; and *ochlokratia*, the lawless and totally disordered assembly of a confused crowd, is the antagonist of *dēmokratia*.[12]

This pedagogical effort may sound rather schematic. But Michael Psellos, a near-contemporary of Theophylact, expressed clearly his preference for monarchy in his description of Constantine Porphyrogennetos' youth:

> What happened was a rule of many (*polyarchia*), not of one (*monarchia*) nor of the best (*aristokratia*), it was something like a confused ruling without order, whereas on the other hand, the ruling of the best, if someone leads it to harmony, is lawful and brings imperial care.[13]

---

[11] Jonathan Greig kindly informed me that these three pairs of opposites were discussed *in extenso* in Aristotle, *Politics*, 4.2 (1289a-1301a).

[12] Theophylact of Ohrid, *Sermons, Treatises, Poems*, no. 4, 195.9–19, ed. Gautier, 195: Τρεῖς εἰσι πολιτειῶν καταστάσεις καθολικώτεραι, ὧν ἡ μὲν μοναρχία καὶ ἔννομος καὶ βασιλεία καλεῖται . . . · ἡ δ' ἐκ πολλῶν μὲν ἀρχόντων, ἐννομωτάτων δὲ καὶ τούτων, συντέθειται· ἀριστοκρατία ταύτῃ τὸ ὄνομα· ἡ δέ τις τοῦ δήμου παντὸς συνδρομὴ πρὸς τὴν τῶν τῆς πολιτείας διοίκησιν, ἣν δημοκρατίαν ὠνόμασαν. Ἀντικάθηνται δὲ ταύταις ἕτεραι τρεῖς τῆς ἀξίας ἐκβιαζόμεναι· καὶ τὴν μὲν βασιλείαν τυραννὶς ἐνεδρεύει· τὴν δ' ἀριστοκρατίαν ὀλιγοκρατία τοξεύει, ὅταν πλούσιοί τινες καὶ βίαιοι τοὺς ἀρίστους ὑποκρινόμενοι ἄρχωσι· δημοκρατίαν δὲ ἡ ὀχλοκρατία ὁρᾷ ἀντιπρόσωπος, συγκεχυμένου τοῦ πλήθους συνέλευσις ἄνομός τε καὶ παντάπασιν ἄτακτος. Cf. a similar example in John Stobaios, *Anthology*, 2:7.26.

[13] Michael Psellos, *Short History*, 102: Πολυαρχία γάρ, οὐ μοναρχία ἦν τὸ γινόμενον καὶ οὐδὲ ἀριστοκρατία, ἀλλ' ἀρχή τις συγκεχυμένη καὶ ἄτακτος. Τὸ γὰρ ἀριστοκρατεῖν, εἰ πρὸς ὁμόνοιάν τις ἀγάγοι, ἔννομόν ἐστιν ἄντικρυς καὶ ἐπιστασία βασιλική.

On the one hand, these authors demonstrate that the discourse about monarchy did not disappear after the sixth century,[14] although unjust *tyrannis* of the 'others' often is used in contrast to the just *basileia* of the Byzantine emperor.[15] On the other hand, they cannot be taken to reflect the attitudes of the 'lower strata'. No doubt the discourse on the systems of government had changed since Constantine the Great had converted to the Christian faith and had strengthened the relationship between monotheism and monarchy. For this reason, an open and emancipated discussion about (or against) imperial government, coming from the 'lower strata', is non-existent in Byzantine sources. I am not convinced that anti-imperial discourses played any role in the reality of political processes.[16] Any effort to explore ideology from the bottom up in terms of social stratification within Byzantine society, in particular the 'ideology' of the subaltern, will need an extensive search for hints and indirect terms in records of legal cases and in historical and hagiographical texts.

The Byzantine 'lower strata' were, of course, not a homogeneous group. They consisted of differing and often spontaneously transforming social conglomerations: the great mass of citizens, 'the farmers, the merchants and those living under the open sky'.[17] However, two major groups may be singled out according to emperor Justinian, who stated in his *Novel* 85 that 'neither the *idiōtai*, who live in cities, nor the *agrotai*, who cultivate their fields shall dare to use weapons and kill each other'.[18]

The first group, the *idiōtai*, are evidently the *politai*, the crowds in Constantinople (and in other big cities) who would easily be induced to physical or at least verbal violence. A famous example of this is the outbreak of

---

[14] Börm, 'Antimonarchic Discourse', 20: 'the demise, to a large extent, of the classically educated secular elites in this period meant that those who had transmitted the Greek and Roman (anti-)monarchic discourse over centuries disappeared'.

[15] E.g. John Apokaukos, *Notitiae et epistulae* 71.1–3: the emperor as νέος Δαυίδ against the ἰταλικὴ τυραννὶς, or Demetrios Chomatenos, *Ponēmata* 144.37–45: τῶν τὴν μεγίστην τῶν Ῥωμαίων ἀρχὴν λυμηναμένων ἐθνῶν, in contrast to the βασιλέα τὸν ἀναγεγραμμένον Δούκαν κῦρ Θεόδωρον; ibid. 146.69–71: τῆς Ῥωμαϊκῆς βασιλείας καὶ τῆς κατ' αὐτὴν ἱεραρχίας τῇ τυραννίδι τῶν ἐπεισφρησάντων τῇ Ῥωμανίᾳ ἐθνῶν σαλευθείσης.

[16] On this view, see Kaldellis, *Byzantine Republic*, in particular the chapters 'The Sovereignty of the People in Theory' (pp. 89–117) and 'The Sovereignty of the People in Practice' (pp. 118–64), where the author speaks about a republican background of popular insurrections. For criticisms of this thesis, see Haldon, 'Res publica Byzantina?'; Stouraitis, 'Review of Kaldellis, *The Byzantine Republic*'.

[17] Michael Psellos, *Chronographia*, I, 7.40.9–15, ed. Reinsch, 227.

[18] Justinian, *Novellae*, 3.85.30–3.

the Nika Riot. Another one comes from the year 1201, when the supporters of the unsuccessful usurper John Komnenos held a demonstration in the imperial city directed against all foreigners, shouting εὖ γε τῇ Ῥωμαΐδι ('Hail Rome!'), and promising that the *barbaroi* – some twelve hostile nations are mentioned – should 'lick the dust from our feet – they will all submit and become our slaves'.[19] In other sources, for example Chomatenos' *Ponēmata*, *idiōtēs* is simply the private individual, without negative connotation.[20]

Michael Psellos referred to the citizens as *to politikon*, juxtaposing them to the soldiers (*to stratiōtikon*).[21] Alternatively, the term could be employed with a negative connotation to mean Constantinople's 'chosen citizens and those belonging to the rowdies from the market and the craftsmen'.[22]

The other group mentioned by Justinian, the *agrotai*, is the great mass of the principally rural population in villages and market towns, which was remote from Constantinople in terms of mentality and, in part, geography. The meaning of terms like *agrotēs* or *ochlos agrodiaitos*, in other words the *hapas holōn tōn thematōn laos*,[23] is in principle neutral, although Constantine Porphyrogennetos once wrote in a letter in a rather denigrating manner about 'the rural populace, which does not know God' (a quote from the New Testament: John 7.49).[24] But in general, the term had positive connotations: for example when Neophytos Enkleistos says about a good priest, 'He acts similar to the farmers (*agrotai*) and the shepherds (*ktēnotrophoi*)'.[25]

A negative connotation is evident when the term *chōriatēs* is used: Digenes Akrites, for example, asks his father: 'How long should I hunt

---

[19] John Komnenos, *Palace Revolt*, 21. Cf. Koder, 'Zum Bild des "Westens"'.
[20] Demetrios Chomatenos, *Ponēmata* 65.35, ed. Prinzing, 227: οὐκ ἦν ἰδιώτης καὶ ἄγροικος; ibid. 110.99–100, ed. Prinzing, 336: The *basileus* ἰδιώτης ἀμύνεται, πάθος δηλονότι θεραπεύων ἴδιον κολάζει καὶ οὐ τῷ κοινῷ, καὶ διὰ τοῦτο παρανομεῖ, καθὰ εἴρηται. In *Ponēmata* 35 he refers to *Basilika* 46.3.1: Τὰ ἱερὰ θείου δικαίου εἰσὶ καὶ ὑπ' οὐδενὸς δεσπόζονται, ἱερὸν δὲ πρᾶγμα ἐστὶ τὸ ἀνιερωθὲν δημοσίᾳ· τὰ γὰρ ἰδιωτικὰ οὐκ εἰσὶν ἱερά, ἀλλὰ βέβηλα. Εἰ δὲ καταπέσῃ τὸ οἰκοδόμημα, μένει ὁ τόπος ἱερός, ἀδιάτμητον δέ ἐστι τὸ ἱερόν.
[21] Michael Psellos, *Chronographia*, I, 7.40.9, ed. Reinsch, 227: τὸ δημοτικὸν τοῦτο πλῆθος; cf. ibid. 7.40.1 (226): ὁ τῆς Πόλεως δῆμος ξύμπας.
[22] Michael Psellos, *Chronographia*, I, 5.16.2, ed. Reinsch, 88: τὸν δ' ἀπόλεκτον δῆμον τῆς Πόλεως καὶ ὅσοι τῆς ἀγοραίου τύρβης ἢ τῶν βαναύσων τεχνῶν ᾠκειοῦτο.
[23] *Theophanes Continuatus*, ed. Bekker, 348.
[24] Constantine VII Porphyrogennetos, *Letters*, 317–41: ἀγρότης ὄχλος καὶ τὸν Θεὸν μὴ γινώσκων.
[25] Neophytos the Recluse, *Homilies*, 7.23.

hares and partridges? It is proper to rustics (*chōriates*) to hunt partridges!'[26] In another context, he receives a letter from his mother who accuses him of bringing disgrace upon his family, because everyone derides them as rustics (*chōriates*).[27]

Normally, the *agrotai* were not interested in the strategies of imperial policies in Constantinople – most of them probably knew only the name of the ruling emperor and perhaps how many years he had been in power, but not much more. The *agrotai* are described generally as 'unarmed and non-belligerent farmers'.[28] Sometimes this 'rustic populace, those who smell of spade and two-pronged fork', may take up arms and join an expedition, most of them being 'unexperienced and gathering only in the hope of profit'.[29] There were some exceptions, of course. For example, groups of 'villagers on the frontiers of Nicaea' seem to have been well trained: 'Though being farmers and working in agriculture, they were brave bowmen, who trusted also in their impassable land'.[30]

Regardless of the positive or negative connotations of the terms in the context of each account, the latter's authors belonged to (or at least expressed the attitude of) the upper class. As elite writers, they stood remote from a proper understanding of the problems and the mentality of the *agrotai* and the common people in general. They observed and described the 'lower strata' as outsiders.[31]

Another question that one may pose is where the *agrotai* received their information from regarding the ruling classes' political decisions. A main source was travellers (merchants, pilgrims and so forth) who came from the capital and visited a village or a region more or less by chance, telling

---

[26] Digenes Akrites, 744–5, ed. Jeffreys, 294.

[27] Digenes Akrites, 230–1, ed. Jeffreys, 254.

[28] Eustathios of Thessaloniki, *Sermons*, 14.9–10, ed. Wirth, 238: ἀγρόται ἄσκευοι καὶ ἀπόλεμοι.

[29] Nikephoros Gregoras, *Roman History*, 1.256: ἀγρότην ὄχλον, καὶ ὅσοι σκαπάνης καὶ δικέλλης ἀπόζουσιν, οὐ μάλα ἄκοντας ἅπαντας. ὑπὸ γὰρ ἀπειρίας οἱ πλεῖστοι ξυνελαυνόμενοι πρὸς ἐλπίδα μόνην τοῦ κέρδους ἑώρων.

[30] George Pachymeres, *Short History*, 3.12: οἱ κατὰ τῆς Νικαίας ἄκρας χωρῖται, ἀγρόται μὲν ὄντες καὶ γεωργίᾳ προσέχοντες, θαρραλέοι δὲ ἄλλως, ἄνδρες τοξόται, ἅμα δὲ καὶ ταῖς καθ᾽ ἑαυτοὺς δυσχωρίαις τὸ πιστὸν ἔχοντες. Cf. a similar report in George Pachymeres, *Historical Relations*, 259–61.

[31] Michael Psellos, *Chronographia*, I, 6.135, ed. Reinsch, 167–8, quotes a citizen who boasted of his bad behaviour towards the emperor, and calls him κάθαρμά τι βαρβαρικόν ('barbarian scum') adding that he felt the need to strangle this barbarian with his own hands.

them true or biased and fabricated news. Another, probably not so popular, source of information were the tax collectors (*praktores*) and other officials, soldiers, *apelatai* (irregulars) or marines who traversed the provinces on their way to the frontiers of the empire, requisitioning in transit what they needed or desired.[32] The *Theophanes Continuatus* mentions how much the 'wretched and miserable poor' suffered in all provinces from the tax-collecting civilian officials, but also from military commanders and their infantry and cavalry,[33] and John Apokaukos complains about the farmers' massive losses owing to thunderstorms.[34] The *agrotai* probably gained lasting negative impressions of the tax collectors.

There are two more important groups which may have potentially served as 'opinion leaders': the great landowners and the representatives of the Church. The first group, members of the upper class, i.e. the aristocracy, had places of residence in Constantinople as well as in the countryside, and their political activities (in both places) could influence the lower social strata to adopt views in favour of or against the government. Hence, at times when their political aspirations did not conform to those of the emperor, they could become dangerous and pose a threat. A detailed analysis of the revolts and attempts at usurpation from the tenth to the beginning of the thirteenth century has demonstrated the importance of the aristocratic class.[35] The epic poem of Digenes Akrites provides an interesting insight in this regard. Digenes declined an imperial request to visit Constantinople, instead inviting the emperor to visit him at the Euphrates River with the request that he come with only a small number of armed men in his entourage. This advice evidently sheds doubt on Digenes' loyalty as a *Rhōmaios* as well as on the trust that he and his adherents put in the emperor.[36] The following advice that Kekaumenos addressed to fellow magnates residing beyond the empire's borders also leads us to question his sense of loyalty to the imperial centre:

---

[32] Kekaumenos, *Strategikon*, ed. Wassiliewsky and Jernstedt, 103.26.

[33] *Theophanes Continuatus*, 6.9, ed. Bekker, 443: τῶν ἀδικιῶν καὶ ζημιῶν ὧν ὑπέστησαν οἱ ἐλεεινοὶ καὶ ἄθλιοι πένητες παρὰ τῶν στρατηγῶν καὶ πρωτονοταρίων καὶ στρατιωτῶν καὶ ἱπποτῶν.

[34] John Apokaukos, *Notitiae et epistulae*, 11.24–5.

[35] Cheynet, *Pouvoir*; see also Hoffmann, *Rudimente*. In contrast, rebellions by persons of non-aristocratic backgrounds were rare. On the Nika Riot, see Meier, 'Die Inszenierung einer Katastrophe'; Greatrex, 'Nika Riot'; Pfeilschifter, *Der Kaiser und Konstantinopel*, 178–210; on Thomas the Slav, see Lemerle, 'Thomas le Slave' and Kaegi, *Military Unrest*, 261–2.

[36] Digenes Akrites, Z, 2311–30.

If you have castles and villages in your own land, if you are *toparchēs* and owner, be not seduced by wealth or titles or great promises on the part of the emperors, to give your land to the emperor.[37]

The second group is the clergy, whose political influence was growing in parallel with both the rising importance and power of the patriarch of Constantinople and the decline of the senate. Representatives of the Church – bishops, priests, monks and holy men – were present everywhere in the empire and, using their social prestige and moral authority, could cultivate favourable or hostile public opinions towards the emperor and the ruling class.[38] This could also happen simply by propagating their own opinions or interests through their sermons[39] or by introducing hymns with a political message into the liturgy. An example of clerical opinion making is seen in a hymn by Romanos Melodos, in which he combines praise of Justinian with a somewhat critical position towards certain of the emperor's policies against heretics, pagans and infidels. In the *kontakion* 'On the New Converts', Romanos addresses the newly baptised with a strange admonition:

In fear of the laws which are in force now,
you often came to the baptismal font, and you became what you became,
in timidity of the spirit of the age.... Advise yourself, friend, in these things!
You approached in fear, so stay in desire.
Love what you received and keep what you possess.
Do not backslide to earlier behaviour![40]

This example demonstrates that hymns, besides their religiously edifying purposes, could be used (or misused) in churches to influence the masses. To be sure, Justinian and probably other emperors as well were aware of this possibility and perhaps exploited it.

To conclude, we have seen that different ways existed to potentially influence the rural lower classes. But could imperial ideology really shape

---

[37] Kekaumenos, *Strategikon*, ed. Wassiliewsky–Jernstedt, 76.16–19: ἐὰν εἰς ἰδίαν χώραν κάστρα τυχὸν ἢ χωρία ἔχῃς, εἰ δὲ ἐν αὐτοῖς τοπάρχης καὶ ἐξουσιαστής, μή σε πλανήσῃ πλοῦτος ἢ ἀξιώματα ἢ ὑποσχέσεις μεγάλαι τῶν βασιλέων καὶ δῴης τὴν χώραν σου βασιλεῖ.

[38] In particular after 1204: see e.g. John Apokaukos, *Epistulae synodales*, and Demetrios Chomatenos, *Ponēmata*, passim.

[39] See Chapter 4 in this volume.

[40] Romanos Melodos, *Hymns*, 52.14.5–7 and 15.1–4, *dies festus* January 7. See Koder, 'Imperial Propaganda'.

the public opinion of the *agrotai, banausoi, boskoi, emporoi* and other groups in the countryside? And if so, to what degree? How strong was the lower classes' Roman identity in comparison with other competing (regional, ethnic, social, cultural, linguistic) identities?

In the context of this question, it may be useful to close by mentioning that the notions of 'identity' (*tautotēs*) and its opposite 'otherness' (*heterotēs*) were discussed by pagan philosophers from the times of Plato[41] and Aristotle[42] up to the sixth century, the last one probably being Damaskios.[43]

In this traditional philosophical sense, both terms survived in the Byzantine medieval philosophical vocabulary.[44] The term had also been adapted to Christian theology by the Church Fathers: *tautotēs* was equated with *homoiotēs*,[45] and *heterotēs* with *anomoiotēs*. This was emphasised when God's *tautotēs, haplotēs* and *homoiotēs* were explained in contrast to *heterotēs* and *anomoiotēs* and difference (*diaphora*), which are in the multitude (*en tois pollois*).[46]

It seems evident, however, that neither of these terms is used in the specific sense of modern identity research (*Identitätsforschung*). Nonetheless, the sociological and political-theoretical meaning of 'identity' was indirectly discussed within explanations of other terms. For example, Nikephoros Bryennios (thirteenth century) makes general observations on the term *genos*, reflecting upon its meanings and concluding that *genos* describes the biological origin (*tou tekontos*) and the geographical origin *tēs patridos* (namely the home town) and that the term may be applied in an individual sense to a person but also in a collective sense to a tribe or a

---

[41] Jonathan Greig kindly drew my attention to the fact that this theme specifically goes back to Plato's notion of the five 'Great Kinds' (μέγιστα γένη), comprising Being (τὸ ὄν), Sameness (ταὐτόν), Difference (τὸ ἕτερον), Motion (κίνησις) and Rest (στάσις): *Sophist*, 253a–259d.

[42] Aristotle, *Metaphysics*, 1018a and passim.

[43] Damaskios, *De Principiis*, 310: Καθολικωτέρη τίς ἐστιν καὶ θεία ἡ ταυτότης καὶ ἡ ἑτερότης.

[44] See Michael Psellos, *Philosophica minor*, 2.38: Πέντε τὰ γένη κατὰ Πλάτωνα, οὐσία, ταυτότης, ἑτερότης, κίνησις, στάσις, οὐχ ὡς τὰ παρὰ τοῖς φιλοσόφοις ὑπάλληλα, ἀλλ' ὡς πανταχοῦ διήκοντα. Cf. John Italos, *Questiones*, 72: τὸ γὰρ ὂν οὐκ ἔστιν οὐσία, καθ' ὃ τῶν ἄλλων ἔρημόν ἐστι, κινήσεως, στάσεως, ἑτερότητός τε καὶ ταυτότητος, ἡ δὲ οὐσία μετὰ τούτων, καὶ ὄν· ἔστι γὰρ ταῦτα οἱονεὶ στοιχεῖα αὐτῆς, ἢ μᾶλλον εἰπεῖν παθήματα καὶ ἐνέργειαι, διὸ καὶ ἐν αὐτῇ λέγεται εἶναι.

[45] Hesychios, *Lexicon*, omicron 780: ὁμοουσιότης· ταυτότης κατὰ τὸ ὑποκείμενον, καὶ τὸ ἀπαράλλακτον κατὰ τὴν οὐσίαν.

[46] Theodoros Dexios, *Works*, cap. 53: ταυτότης καὶ ἁπλότης ... καὶ ὁμοιότης ... ἑτερότης καὶ ἀνομοιότης καὶ διαφορά, ἅπερ ἐν τοῖς πολλοῖς.

nation.[47] Thoughts along similar lines may be found by other authors like Demetrios Chomatenos or John Apokaukos,[48] the latter of whom expresses his distinct dislike of the *Latinoi* and *Italoi*.[49]

But again, the above-mentioned Byzantine authors belong to the educated upper class. With a few exceptions, which quote quasi-verbatim the direct speech of a member of the *ochlos*,[50] or at least mention it,[51] they do not represent or reproduce the authentic voices of the 'lower strata'.

Acknowledgements

I would like to thank Yannis Stouraitis (Edinburgh) and the anonymous reader for their helpful remarks on the draft of this text, as well as Jonathan Greig (Dublin/Vienna) for valuable suggestions and improvements. For most of the Greek sources, the TLG (Thesaurus Linguae Graecae® Digital Library, ed. M. C. Pantelia, University of California, Irvine <http://www. tlg.uci.edu> [last accessed June and July 2016]) was consulted.

Bibliography

Sources

Basilika . . . H. J. Scheltema and N. van der Wal (eds), *Basilicorum libri LX, Series A 1–8* (Groningen, 1955–88).

---

[47] Nikephoros Blemmydes, *Epitome logica*, 753AB.

[48] Family and marital relations: John Apokaukos, *Notitiae et epistulae*, passim; Demetrios Chomatenos, *Ponēmata* 1, passim. *Barbaroi*: John Apokaukos, *Epistulae et acta* 23 (contrasting with *Hellēnes*), Demetrios Chomatenos, *Ponēmata* 18 and 59. *Blachoi*: John Apokaukos, *Notitiae et epistulae* 5. *Boulgaroi*: Demetrios Chomatenos, *Vita Clementis* 10 and 14, *Ponēmata* 8 (ἀλλὰ μὴν οἱ Βούλγαροι οὐχ αἱρετικοί, ἀλλ' ὀρθόδοξοι . . .), 59 and 81.

[49] John Apokaukos, *Notitiae et epistulae*, 71.7–12 and 107.55–64.

[50] E.g. John Apokaukos, *Ad Nicetam Choniatem*, 4.22–7 (Σημείωμα φόνου): Ἕτερος δέ τις τῶν ἐκ τοῦ χωρίου ἐκείνου (ὄνομα αὐτῷ . . .) παρελθὼν εἰς τὸ μέσον ἐμοὶ τῷ μηδὲν αὐτῷ φθεγγομένῳ ἐνέκειτο· ἐν δὲ τῶν ἐκείνου ῥημάτων ἦν (τῶν) ἀναισχύντων, τὸ ἰδιωτικῶς παρὰ τῶν ἀφελῶς καὶ ἀγροίκως διομιλουμένων ἀναφθεγγόμενον· τὸ δὲ ἦν, ὅτι Σὺ πολλὰ τσαμπουνίζεις καὶ πρόσεχε καλά ('You are talking much nonsense, hence take well care about yourself!'). Τσαμπουνίζω is a variant of τσαμπουνῶ; cf. the noun τσαμπούνα, from Italian *zampogna*, 'bagpipe', and cf. <https://el.wiktionary. org/wiki/%CF%84%CF%83%CE%B1%CE%BC%CF%80%CE%BF%CF%85%CE%BD%CF%8E> (last accessed 30 March 2022).

[51] E.g. John Apokaukos, *Epistulae et acta*, 6.14–16 and 15.8–10.

Constantine VII Porphyrogennetos, *Letters* . . . J. Darrouzès (ed.), *Épistoliers byzantins du Xe siècle* (Archives de l'Orient Chrétien 6) (Paris, 1960).

Cyril of Alexandria, *Commentary* . . . P. E. Pusey (ed.), *Commentarius: Sancti patris nostri Cyrilli archiepiscopi Alexandrini in xii prophetas*, 2 vols (Oxford, 1868).

Cyril of Alexandria, *Homilies* . . . W. H. Burns (ed.), *Cyrilli Alexandrini homiliae paschales*, SC 434 (Paris, 1998).

Cyril of Alexandria, *Letters* . . . *PG* 77: *Cyrilli Alexandrini epistulae paschales sive Homiliae paschales* (Washington, DC, 1987), 401–981.

Damaskios, *De Principiis*, ed. C. A. Ruelle (Paris, 1889).

Demetrios Chomatenos, *Ponēmat* . . . G. Prinzing (ed.), *Demetrii Chomateni Ponemata Diaphora* (Berlin and New York, 2002).

Demetrios Chomatenos, *Vita Clementis* . . . A. Milev (ed.), *Gruckite zitija na Kliment Ochridski* (Sofia, 1966).

Digenes Akrites . . . E. Jeffreys (ed.), *Digenis Akrites. The Grottaferrata and Escorial versions* (Cambridge, 1998).

Digenes Akrites, Z . . . E. Trapp (ed.), *Digenes Akrites. Synoptische Ausgabe der ältesten Versionen* (Vienna, 1971).

Ephrem the Syrian, *Works* . . . K. G. Phrantzoles (ed.), Ὁσίου Ἐφραίμ τοῦ Σύρου ἔργα, 7 vols (Thessaloniki, 1988–98).

Eustathios of Thessaloniki, *Sermons* . . . P. Wirth (ed.), *Eustathii Thessalonicensis opera minora (magnam partem inedita)* (Berlin, 1999).

George Pachymeres, *Historical Relations* . . . A. Failler (ed.), *Georgius Pachymeres, Relations historiques*, 5 vols (Paris, 1984–2000).

George Pachymeres, *Short History* . . . A. Failler (ed.), *Historia brevis: La version brève des relations historiques de Georges Pachymérès*, 3 vols (Paris, 2001–2).

Hesychios, *Lexicon* . . . K. Latte (ed.), *Hesychii Alexandrini lexicon*, 2 vols (Copenhagen, 1953–66).

John Apokaukos, *Ad Nicetam Choniatem* . . . A. Papadopoulos-Kerameus (ed.), Ἰωάννης Ἀπόκαυκος καὶ Νικήτας Χωνιάτης, Τεσσαρακονταετηρὶς τῆς καθηγεσίας Κ. Σ. Κόντου (Athens, 1909), 375–82.

John Apokaukos, *Epistulae et acta* . . . S. Pétridès (ed.), 'Jean Apokaukos, Lettres et autres documents inédits', *Izvestija Russkago Archeologiceskago Instituta v Konstantinopolie* 14 (1909): 72–100.

John Apokaukos, *Epistulae synodales* . . . A. Papadopoulos-Kerameus (ed.), Συνοδικὰ γράμματα Ἰωάννου τοῦ Ἀποκαύκου, μητροπολίτου Ναυπάκτου, *Byzantis* 1 (1909–10): 8–30.

John Apokaukos, *Notitiae et epistulae* ... N. A. Bees (ed.), 'Unedierte Schriftstücke aus der Kanzlei des Johannes Apokaukos des Metropoliten von Naupaktos (in Aetolien)', *BNJ* 21 (1971–4): 57–160.

John Italos, *Questions* ... P.-P. Joannou (ed.), *Joannes Italos, Quaestiones quodlibetales (Ἀπορίαι καὶ λύσεις)* (Ettal, 1956).

John Komnenos, *Palace Revolt* ... A. Heisenberg (ed.), *Die Palastrevolution des Johannes Komnenos* (Würzburg, 1907).

John Stobaios, *Anthology* ... O. Hense and C. Wachsmuth (eds), *Ioannis Stobaei anthologium*, 4 vols (Berlin, 1884–1912).

Joseph Genesios, *On the Reigns* ... A. Lesmüller-Werner and H. Thurn (eds), *Josephi Genesii regum libri quattuor* (Berlin, 1978).

Justinian, *Novellae* ... W. Kroll and R. Schöll (eds), *Corpus iuris civilis*, 3 vols (Berlin, 1895).

Kekaumenos, *Strategikon* ... V. G. Wassiliewsky and V. Jernstedt, *Cecaumeni strategicon et incerti scriptoris de officiis regiis libellus* (St Petersburg, 1896).

Michael Psellos, *Chronographia* ... D. R. Reinsch (ed.), *Michaelis Pselli Chronographia*, 2 vols (Berlin and Boston, 2014).

Michael Psellos, *Philosophica minora* ... D. J. O'Meara (ed.), *Michaelis Pselli philosophica minora*, 2 vols (Leipzig, 1989).

Michael Psellos, *Short History* ... W. J. Aerts (ed.), *Michaelis Pselli Historia Syntomos*, CFHB 30 (Berlin and New York, 1990).

Neophytos the Recluse, *Homilies* ... I. E. Stephanes (ed.), 'Δέκα λόγοι περὶ τοῦ Χριστοῦ ἐντολῶν', in I. Karabidopoulos, C. Oikonomou, D. G. Tsames and N. Zacharopoulos (eds), *Ἁγίου Νεοφύτου τοῦ Ἐγκλείστου Συγγράμματα*, vols 1–6 (Paphos, 1996).

Nikephoros Blemmydes, *Epitome logica*, PG 142:675–1004.

Nikephoros Gregoras, *Roman History* ... L. Schopen and I. Bekker (ed.), *Nicephorus Gregoras, Byzantina historia*, 3 vols (Bonn 1829–55).

Romanos Melodos, *Hymns* ... ed. J. Grosdidier de Matons, *Romanos le Mélode, Hymnes*, 5 vols (Paris 1964–81).

Theodore of Mopsuestia, *Commentary* ... ed. H. N. Sprenger, *Commentarius in xii prophetas minores* (Wiesbaden, 1977).

Theodoros Dexios, *Works* ... I. Polemis (ed.), *Theodori Dexii Opera Omnia* (Turnhout, 2003).

Theophanes Continuatus ... I. Bekker (ed.), *Theophanes Continuatus, Ioannes Cameniata, Symeon Magister, Georgius Monachus* (Bonn, 1838).

Theophylact of Ohrid, *Sermons, Treatises, Poems* ... P. Gautier (ed.), *Theophylacte d'Achrida. Discours, Traités, Poésies*, CFHB 16.1 (Thessaloniki, 1980).

Secondary Literature

Ahrweiler, H., *L'idéologie politique de l'Empire byzantin* (Paris, 1975).

Börm, H., 'Antimonarchic Discourse in Antiquity: A Very Short Introduction', in H. Börm and W. Havener (eds), *Antimonarchic Discourse in Antiquity* (Stuttgart, 2015), 9–24.

Brown, P., *The World of Late Antiquity AD 150–750* (London, 2006).

Cheynet, J.-C., *Pouvoir et contestations à Byzance (963–1210)* (Paris 1990)

Greatrex, G. B., 'The Nika Riot: A Reappraisal', *JHS* 117 (1997): 60–86.

Haldon, J., *Warfare, State and Society in the Byzantine World 565–1204* (London, 1999).

Haldon, J., 'Res publica Byzantina? State Formation and Issues of Identity in Medieval East Rome', *BMGS* 40/1 (2016): 4–16.

Hoffmann, J., *Rudimente von Territorialstaaten im byzantinischen Reich (1071–1210). Untersuchungen über Unabhängigkeitsbestrebungen und ihr Verhältnis zu Kaiser und Reich* (Munich, 1974).

Kaegi, W. E., Jr, *Byzantine Military Unrest, 471–843: An Interpretation* (Amsterdam, 1981).

Kaldellis, A., *The Byzantine Republic. People and Power in New Rome* (Cambridge, MA, 2015).

Karayannopoulos, I., *Η πολιτικη θεωρία των Βυζαντινών* (Thessaloniki, 1988).

Koder, J., 'Zum Bild des "Westens" bei den Byzantinern in der frühen Komnenenzeit', in *Deus qui mutat tempora, Menschen und Institutionen im Wandel des Mittelalters. Festschrift für Alfons Becker zu seinem 65. Geburtstag* (Sigmaringen, 1987), 191–201.

Koder, J., 'Imperial Propaganda in the Kontakia of Romanos the Melode', *DOP* 62 (2008): 275–91.

Koder, J. and Y. Stouraitis (eds), *Byzantine War Ideology Between Roman Imperial Concept and Christian Religion* (Vienna, 2012).

Lemerle, P., 'Thomas le Slave', *TM* 1 (1965): 255–97.

Magdalino, P., 'Ο οφθαλμός της οικουμένης και ο ομφαλός της γής', in E. Chrysos (ed.), *Το Βυζάντιο ως οικουμένη* (Athens, 2005), 107–23.

Meier, M., 'Die Inszenierung einer Katastrophe: Justinian und der Nika-Aufstand', *ZPapEpig* 142 (2003): 273–300.

Pfeilschifter, R., *Der Kaiser und Konstantinopel Kommunikation und Konfliktaustrag in einer spätantiken Metropole* (Berlin and Boston, 2013).

Stouraitis, Y., (2009), *Krieg und Frieden in politischer und ideologischer Wahrnehmung in Byzanz (7.–11. Jahrhundert)* (Vienna, 2009).

Stouraitis, Y., 'Just War and Holy War in the Middle Ages: Rethinking Theory through the Byzantine Case-Study', *JÖB* 62 (2012): 227–64.

Stouraitis, Y., 'Review of A. Kaldellis, *The Byzantine Republic. People and
Power in New Rome, Cambridge, Mass. 2015*', *JHS* 136 (2016): 296–7.

Treitinger, O., *Die oströmische Kaiser- und Reichsidee nach ihrer Gestal-
tung im höfischen Zeremoniell. Vom oströmischen Staats- und Reichsge-
danken* (Darmstadt, 1956).

3

The *Dēmosia*, the Emperor and the Common Good: Byzantine Ideas on Taxation and Public Wealth, Eleventh–Twelfth Century

Kostis Smyrlis

How the Byzantines conceived of taxation, confiscation and the administration of public resources reflects the way they imagined the constitution of their polity and, in particular, the positions of the emperor and the people within it. In less abstract terms, these ideas also help explain imperial choices that shaped the society and the economy. The question of the emperor's relation to public wealth has usually been treated in the context of examining the ruler's position within the polity, notably by Hans-Georg Beck, Paul Magdalino and Anthony Kaldellis.[1] This scholarship and the present chapter show that there existed among the Byzantines, including the emperor and his panegyrists, a consensus that the public resources, *ta dēmosia* or *ta koina*, while under the ruler's control, were not his property but, as their name indicated, that of all the people.[2] The emperor was expected to administrate this wealth in the interests of the commonwealth (*to koinon*). Numerous texts can be invoked in support of this schema. One of the clearest statements is provided by a definition of the term *basileia* in the tenth-century *Souda* lexicon:

---

[1] Beck, *Res Publica Romana*, esp. 13–17, 21; Magdalino, 'Aspects'; Kaldellis, *Byzantine Republic*, esp. 14–19, 32–61. The uninterrupted validity of the distinction between the fisc or *publicum* and the emperor in Byzantium has also been underlined by Patlagean, *Moyen Âge*, 212–13, 380 and passim.

[2] The expressions *ta dēmosia* and *ta koina* (sometimes with *pragmata*) often indicate the common or public affairs, especially with regard to their government. But they are also used in a more limited sense, the one I refer to here, to indicate the public wealth or money: e.g. *JGR* 4:143 (*Peira*, 36.2); John Skylitzes, *Synopsis*, ed. Thurn, 398; John Zonaras, *Epitome*, ed. Pinder, 667. *Dēmosia* could also denote specifically the fiscal dues or revenues: e.g. Michael Attaleiates, *History*, ed. Tsolakes, 48; see also the *Souda* lemma below.

The empire (*basileia*) belongs to the things held in common (*ta koina*) but the fiscal resources (*ta dēmosia*) are not the possession of the emperor (*basileia*). Therefore, the forcible and violent collection of taxes should be hated as tyrannical immorality while the reasoned and benevolent tax demands should be honoured as guardianship.[3]

Although this definition reproduces notions from earlier periods, its inclusion in the *Souda* lexicon demonstrates that an interest in these ideas existed in the Middle Ages and suggests they were widely accepted. These shared concepts authorised all people to have an opinion regarding the management of the *dēmosia* and to criticise the emperor's fiscal policies. Indeed, there are a great number of statements regarding these matters in texts from the centuries discussed here, in particular historical works, speeches for the emperor, laws and official documents, and private letters. Using this material, this chapter attempts to identify the principal Byzantine ideas concerning taxation, confiscation and the use of public resources, topics that, overall, remain little studied. This is not an exhaustive investigation of the sources, nor can this chapter study in detail the evolution of ideas over the time span of two centuries. Moreover, when it comes to the assessment of imperial policies in these texts, much depends on their genre, their historical circumstances and their authors' biases and intentions, factors that cannot be analysed fully here. In all sections of this chapter, I distinguish between private opinions and the imperial discourse and actions. I consider as private those views appearing in non-official texts which the authors claim as theirs or attribute to other private individuals. This includes ideas that originated within the palace and were reproduced by our authors without admitting or realising it. Imperial discourse is preserved in official documents or is reported by contemporary authors. It can also be reconstructed on the basis of encomia and certain other texts. Imperial actions, especially laws and directives, also conveyed messages to the public. Legislation had both rhetorical and practical value. The debate over taxation and administration of public resources was a genuine one,

---

[3]   *Souda*, 1:458: Ὅτι ἡ βασιλεία κτῆμα τῶν κοινῶν, ἀλλ' οὐ τὰ δημόσια τῆς βασιλείας κτήματα. διὸ τὰς ἐξ ἀνάγκης καὶ μεθ' ὕβρεως εἰσπράξεις ὥσπερ τυραννικὰς ἀκολασίας μισεῖν δεῖ, τὰς δὲ σὺν λόγῳ καὶ φιλανθρωπίᾳ τῶν εἰσφορῶν ἀπαιτήσεις ὥσπερ κηδεμονίαν τιμᾶν; cf. Matheou, 'City and Sovereignty', 56–7. The idea somewhat clumsily expressed in the first part of this lemma comes from the imperial period; cf. Herodianus, *Regnum post Marcum*, ed. Lucarini, 172: οὐ γὰρ ἑνὸς ἀνδρὸς ἴδιον κτῆμα ἡ ἀρχή, ἀλλὰ κοινὸν τοῦ Ῥωμαίων δήμου ἄνωθεν.

because through pronouncements and actions the emperors responded to most of the issues raised by the private commentators.

Ideas Regarding Taxation

It is no surprise that the absolute right of the emperor, as the superior of the fisc (*dēmosios*), to tax is never contested in our texts.[4] Medieval Byzantium was a world where systematic and extensive taxation had been carried out without interruption since antiquity. The emperor's right to tax was obviously recognised by the principle whereby tax payment proved property rights over land, meaning that all land except public land was burdened by tax.[5] This consensus explains why texts justifying the need for taxation are rare. The clearest statement is included in a military treatise, probably dating from the ninth century, which opens with a discussion of the different groups of people constituting the polity, listed according to their occupation and utility. Among these groups is the *chrēmatikon* – that is, the people in charge of tax assessment and collection. According to the treatise,

> the *chrēmatikon* has been instituted also for certain other matters of common profit, such as the construction of ships and walls, but above all for the expenses of the soldiers, since the greatest part of the annual public revenues is spent for this purpose.[6]

As we shall see below, the texts of our period insist on the importance of using public resources for the defence of the land. The emperor's guardianship (*kēdemonia*) mentioned in the *Souda* lemma quoted above should be understood in this light.

If the absolute right to tax was not questioned, what could be fairly demanded from the subjects was debatable. Indeed, on the basis of the

---

[4] The emperor is called the ruler (*kratōn*) of the fisc in the 996 novel of Basil II: *Les novelles des empereurs macédoniens*, ed. Svoronos, 212 (no. 14); cf. Kaldellis, *Byzantine Republic*, 45.

[5] *JGR* 4:148 (*Peira*, 37.1–2). Under Alexios I Komnenos tax was not only proof but also a condition of ownership (see below, p. 79).

[6] Syrianos, *Stratēgikon*, ed. Dennis, 12: Τὸ δὲ χρηματικὸν ἔστι μὲν ὅτε καὶ ἄλλων ἕνεκεν κοινωφελῶν πραγμάτων ἐπινενόηται, οἶον ναυπηγίας, τειχοποιίας, μάλιστα δὲ διὰ τὰ ἀναλώματα τῶν στρατιωτῶν. τῶν γὰρ κατ' ἔτος δημοσίων εἰσόδων ἐνταῦθα τὰ πλεῖστα καταναλίσκεται. On the officials constituting the *chrēmatikon*, ibid. 14, 16. On the date of the *Stratēgikon*, see Rance, 'The Date'; for an analysis of its preamble, see Kaldellis, *Byzantine Republic*, 15–17.

Souda lemma, which condemns the violent collection of (obviously excessive) taxes, one may argue that it was considered the people's right to contest unreasonable requests. Essentially the same notion is found in the admonitory work of Kekaumenos. Kekaumenos counsels future emperors not to beggar their people because 'they will hate you, or rather rise up in revolt against you; for you are not dealing with animals, but with rational men, who calculate and consider whether they are being treated well or badly'.[7]

The increased demands imposed on taxpayers are sometimes denounced by our authors without any further explanation. High, new or 'unusual' taxes were seen as simply reproachable. The Byzantine vocabulary is a good indication of popular opinion. The nouns *epēreia* (abuse) and *zēmia* (damage, fine) and the correlative verbs *epēreazō* and *zēmioō* probably first became common in the vernacular to denote additional or extraordinary fiscal demands. In spite of their negative and subversive character, these terms ended up being adopted by the official language of the medieval empire.[8] Many writers in our period condemn new and allegedly unusual taxes. Kekaumenos advises emperors to avoid frequent tax increases and strange (*xenos*) and unprecedented (*kainophanēs*) demands.[9] John, patriarch of Antioch, criticises Alexios I Komnenos (1081–1118) precisely for this in the speech he addressed to him, most likely in 1091.[10] According to Niketas Choniates, the contemporaries of Manuel I Komnenos (1143–80) accused the emperor of plundering his subjects through extraordinary (*asynētheis*) taxes and censuses.[11]

Nevertheless, our texts also evaluate taxation by referring to certain moral and practical values, in particular greed, justice, the subjects' prosperity and the empire's political and economic welfare. Several authors attribute the increased demands to the greed of emperors or their counsellors, a vice that typically also led them to commit injustice. According to John Skylitzes, it was out of greediness (*aplēstia*) that John Orphanotrophos, effective ruler under Michael IV (1034–41), commuted into cash the Bulgarians' dues, thus engen-

---

[7] Kekaumenos, *Consilia et Narrationes*, ed. Roueché, 98.
[8] On these and other negatively charged terms referring to fiscal demands, see Oikonomides, *Fiscalité*, 85.
[9] Kekaumenos, *Consilia et Narrationes*, ed. Roueché, 98. On Kekaumenos' views regarding taxation, see Lemerle, *Prolégomènes*, 90–3.
[10] John Oxite, *Diatribes*, 31: τὰ καινὰ τῶν δασμῶν τε καὶ δασμολόγων καὶ πράγματα καὶ ὀνόματα; 33: ξέναι εἰσφοραί. John Zonaras, *Epitome*, ed. Pinder, 737–8, also criticised Alexios I for his 'abominable ways of money collection', which included new types of demands.
[11] Niketas Choniates, *History*, ed. van Dieten, 203.

dering a revolt in 1040.[12] The *History* of Michael Attaleiates criticises Constantine X Doukas (1059–68) for his compulsive quest to increase public wealth through higher taxes and unfair means.[13] In 1187 Michael Choniates, metropolitan of Athens, addressed an encomium to Isaac II Angelos (1185–95) in which he praised the emperor for instituting a polity contemptuous of money (*aphilochrēmatos politeia*) and for censuring the tax officials' greed (*pleonexia*).[14] Nevertheless, Niketas Choniates, brother of Michael, condemned both Isaac II and Alexios III Angelos (1195–1203) for their obsessive love of money (*philochrēmatia*), something which led them to plunder the cities, invent new taxes and commit injustice.[15]

The value most frequently cited by our authors with regard to taxation is indeed justice, often together with the value of care for the subjects.[16] For most Byzantines, justice really meant fiscal justice.[17] Few emperors or their associates and officials escape criticism for unjust taxation. What constitutes unjust demands or exactions is not always specified. It is clear, however, that the term injustice had a broad meaning that might describe a number of undesired experiences on the part of taxpayers: demands beyond one's means as well as increased or unusual taxation; illegal and abusive exactions; and unequal treatment. There was significant overlap between these experiences, as illegal and abusive demands increased the burden on taxpayers significantly. Moreover, especially during times of financial strain, the higher or new taxes imposed by the emperors tended to combine with unfair judgements and increased administrative abuses.

Unbearable or disastrous taxation is a complaint frequently related to injustice. The 'contributions beyond the people's means' are condemned by John of Antioch in his speech denouncing Alexios I Komnenos' unjust fiscal measures.[18] Another prelate, Nicholas Mouzalon, archbishop of Cyprus at the beginning of the twelfth century, left his see in protest against the

---

[12] John Skylitzes, *Synopsis*, ed. Thurn, 411–12; on this event, see also Cheynet, *Pouvoir*, 50–1 and Oikonomides, *Fiscalité*, 143.

[13] Michael Attaleiates, *History*, ed. Tsolakes, 60–1; on this passage, cf. Krallis, *Michael Attaleiates*, 124–5.

[14] Michael Choniates, *Τὰ σωζόμενα*, ed. Lampros, 1:253–4.

[15] Niketas Choniates, *History*, ed. van Dieten, 537–8.

[16] Justice and care for the subjects had been two of the cardinal virtues of the ruler since antiquity: Kazhdan, 'The Social Views', 24–7.

[17] On the close connection between justice and taxation, see Laiou, 'Law, Justice', and Magdalino, 'Justice and Finance'.

[18] John Oxite, *Diatribes*, 33: ὑπὲρ τὴν σφετέραν δύναμιν; cf. Kekaumenos, *Consilia et Narrationes*, ed. Roueché, 98, who believed the provinces should be taxed according to their wealth: κατὰ τὴν δύναμιν αὐτῶν.

injustices committed on the island by fiscal agents and the governor. In his letter of resignation, which was composed in verse and apparently addressed to the holy synod, Nicholas mentions the suffering of the poor at the hands of greedy tax officials who demanded, in taxes and gifts, more than the people possessed, thus condemning them to starvation. According to the archbishop, the earth produced everything, but all of it and more was taken.[19] Zonaras states that emperors of his day behaved towards their subjects not like shepherds towards their sheep, taking some of the wool and milk, but like thieves, 'slaughtering the sheep and devouring their flesh, or even sucking the marrow from their bones'.[20]

The intensification of taxation was not only undesirable; it was also considered unjust. Attaleiates is especially critical of Nikephoritzes, the financial minister of Michael VII Doukas (1071–8), for his creation of an official grain market (the *phoundax*) at Raidestos, an institution aimed at the more efficient taxation of the sale of grain but which apparently caused the price of the commodity to skyrocket. Attaleiates thought that the taxation of previously untaxed exchanges was unjust and motivated by greed and envy of the abundance of grain.[21]

As one would expect, the abusive or illegal practices of the emperor or imperial officials were also deemed unjust. According to Attaleiates, the unfair means Constantine X Doukas used in order to increase public revenue included unreasonable accusations, illegal judgements and demands for money not owed to the fisc.[22] Most complaints in fact concern imperial officials – tax collectors, assessors and judges – as well as other individuals invested with power. Kekaumenos advises emperors to visit the provinces in order to correct the tax collectors' injustices.[23] The abusive or illegal actions of fiscal agents and other officials is a recurring theme in the letters of Theophylact, archbishop of Ohrid in the late eleventh and early twelfth century, and in those of Michael Choniates of Athens.[24] Both prelates

---

[19] Nikolaos Mouzalon, *Resignation*, ed. Doanidou, esp. 136–7.

[20] John Zonaras, *Epitome*, ed. Pinder, 15; on the idea of the emperor as shepherd to his people: Hunger, *Prooimion*, 100–2.

[21] Michael Attaleiates, *History*, ed. Tsolakes, 155–7.

[22] See n. 13 above. The historian accuses Nikephoritzes of similar practices: Attaleiates, *History*, ed. Tsolakes, 141. On Attaleiates' concern with legality, see n. 96 below. John of Antioch also refers to the unlawfulness (*ekthesmos, athesmos, paralogos*) of Alexios I's fiscality: John Oxite, *Diatribes*, 39, 43, 49.

[23] Kekaumenos, *Consilia et Narrationes*, ed. Roueché, 103.

[24] See e.g. Theophylact of Ohrid, *Letters*, ed. Gautier, letters 19, 45, 79; Michael Choniates, *Epistulae*, ed. Kolovou, letters 58, 60, 65; *Hypomnēstikon*, ed. Stadtmüller, 283–5. Imperial officials' abuses are also denounced by John of Antioch: John Oxite: *Diatribes*, 31.

wrote to powerful people of their time to protest the injustices committed against their churches and the city of Athens. Most commonly, officials are accused of ignoring the privileges awarded to the sees or to the city, but also of demanding undue taxes or rents. Commenting on the demand of dues from men of his Church who did not exploit any fiscal land, Theophylact exclaims 'Not even the emperor can do this!'[25] Apart from fiscal rules, the archbishop also invoked the legal framework, claiming that the tax agents conceived of the divine laws and imperial orders as spider webs that caught the flies (i.e. the poor) but were torn by the wasps (i.e. the powerful), the latter being a group from which his Church is somewhat surprisingly excluded.[26] Michael Choniates is particularly concerned with the respect of the laws in the speech he addressed in 1183 to Demetrios Drimys, the judge of Hellas, newly appointed by Andronikos I Komnenos (1183–5), an emperor praised for his emphasis on justice. The metropolitan contrasts Andronikos I's regime to the previous one, in which injustice and the greed of tax collectors and other officials were rampant. Along with the general notion of justice (*dikaiosynē*), Michael Choniates frequently invokes the law (*nomos*) as well as court decisions or courts of justice (*dikē*, *bēmata*), highlighting the legal training of Drimys, whom he likens to Tribonian. Thanks to Andronikos I and Drimys, it was expected that cities would again enjoy lawful government (*ennomos politeia*) and *eunomia*, which, in this context, may be rendered as 'the rule of law'. Michael Choniates salutes the abolition of the practice of confiscating the property of the deceased, a shift which, apart from ending an injustice towards orphans and widows, also allowed the dying to pass their property to the inheritors as provided by the laws. For the metropolitan, the prior practice was an unlawful restriction on the right of bequest.[27]

Our authors occasionally expound upon their preoccupation with justice. Both Attaleiates and John of Antioch, writing during periods of frequent military reversals, claim that tax injustices provoked the wrath of God, who then punished the empire for its impiety. While discussing the reign of Michael VII Doukas, Attaleiates pauses to consider the reasons for

[25] Theophylact of Ohrid, *Letters*, ed. Gautier, 489–91 (letter 96).

[26] Ibid. 419 (letter 79).

[27] Michael Choniates, Τὰ σωζόμενα, ed. Lampros, 1:157–79, esp. 161–3, 173–9. The *eunomia* in cities was also invoked by Isaac II (see below n. 54); cf. Laiou, 'Law, Justice', 176, on *eunomia* in Attaleiates. Niketas Choniates presents an image of Andronikos I not far removed from his brother's: the emperor is credited with selecting administrators based on merit and for curbing, through fear, the greed of tax collectors and imperial officials; see n. 48 below.

the empire's recent string of defeats, ascribing them to the emperors' impious quest for profit and unjust taxation, which infected all people, leading them to plunder their fellow citizens.[28] John of Antioch's speech to Alexios I Komnenos, which was concerned, as already noted, with injustice, questions the lack of revenue invoked by the emperor – there appeared to be no lack of funds for his relatives – challenging the notion that the empire's defeats were a matter of resources. According to John, behind the defeats was God's wrath at the emperor's unrighteous and un-Christian acts. Divine help would come if Alexios abandoned unjust taxation, appointed just governors and judges and restored illegally confiscated properties.[29] Niketas Choniates seems to adopt a more secular approach. While John of Antioch considers unfair taxation an absolute evil, Choniates notes that the intense and oppressive taxation of Manuel I and his predecessors had filled the treasury.[30] Moreover, as we shall see below, Choniates relates justice in taxation not to piety but to the subjects' prosperity.

Equality in taxation is relatively rarely mentioned by our authors.[31] What we encounter are complaints of unequal treatment in comparison to other taxpayers. Theophylact of Ohrid protests in a letter that the clerics of his Church paid much more for their mills and fishponds than laymen did. Nevertheless, Theophylact was not a proponent of equality. In another letter, he invokes the special status of clerics, requesting that they be exempted from certain dues; priests, he maintains, should not be treated like the 'common people'.[32] About a century later, Michael Choniates wrote repeatedly to complain that the *epēreiai* imposed on Athens were more numerous and onerous than those levied in neighbouring cities, which was an injustice.[33]

The most commonly invoked victims of tax injustice are the poor. Almost all of our authors mention them. According to Kekaumenos, the poor (*ptōchoi*, *penētes*) require the emperors to protect them against tax

---

[28] Michael Attaleiates, *History*, ed. Tsolakes, 149–52; cf. 163. On this passage, see Tinnefeld, *Kategorien*, 138; Magdalino, 'Aspects', 332; Kaldellis, *Byzantine Republic*, 49–50.

[29] John Oxite, *Diatribes*, 31–5, 41–3; cf. 49, 55.

[30] Niketas Choniates, *History*, ed. van Dieten, 230.

[31] Kekaumenos' advice that taxes should correspond to wealth is not a reference to equality but an appeal against oppressive taxation: see above n. 18.

[32] Theophylact of Ohrid, *Letters*, ed. Gautier, 489 (letter 96), 195 (letter 19).

[33] Michael Choniates, *Hypomnēstikon*, ed. Stadtmüller, 283; *Epistulae*, ed. Kolovou, Letter 65; cf. letter 32.

officials' injustices.[34] Attaleiates mentions the 'many injustices and the groaning of the poor' through which the powerful relatives of Michael V (1041–2) amassed great wealth, a probable reference to gains from the sale of offices and tax contracts.[35] The protection of the poor, especially the peasants, is a frequent topic in the writings of prelates: Theophylact of Ohrid, Nicholas Mouzalon and Michael Choniates. The latter protests that an exemption awarded to the Athenians had not been implemented properly and had benefited only the powerful, not those who needed the most compassion.[36] For Michael Choniates, the poor ought to be protected not only from the fisc but also from the wealthy. In 1183, he declared that the arbitrary power of the wealthy (*hē tōn ploutontōn oligarchia*) had devoured what the greedy tax collectors had not taken from the cities. In the petition he addressed to Alexios III Angelos around 1198, the metropolitan also asked the emperor to confirm earlier decrees forbidding the city's powerful (*kastrēnoi*) from taking possession of peasant lands.[37] Although the concern that the poor were oppressed by the rich is expressed in texts throughout this period, Michael Choniates appears particularly invested in the issue.[38] Other classes are also singled out but less frequently. John of Antioch is notable in that, apart from the poor, he mentions a number of other categories of people that fell victim to Alexios I Komnenos' fiscal measures. Having noted the plundering of the churches, John also states that the rich were impoverished, while the poor, manual workers, farmers, tradesmen and craftsmen were forced to pay more than they could afford. As a result, John contends, some of the unjustly taxed died prematurely from hunger, while others emigrated, with many joining the 'Christian-killing barbarians' with whom life was more bearable than with the Byzantines.[39]

As noted, the political and material interests of the empire were among the values used in assessing taxation. We have already seen that injustice as a trigger of God's wrath was connected to the well-being of the empire. Our texts also mention more tangible dangers arising from high or abusive

---

[34] Kekaumenos, *Consilia et Narrationes*, ed. Roueché, 103.

[35] Michael Attaleiates, *History*, ed. Tsolakes, 12.

[36] Michael Choniates, *Epistulae*, ed. Kolovou, letter 32.

[37] Michael Choniates, Τὰ σωζόμενα, ed. Lampros, 1:174; *Hypomnēstikon*, ed. Stadtmüller, 286.

[38] The notion that lords overburden their *paroikoi* appears in several monastic foundation charters (*typika*): Michael Attaleiates, *Diataxis*, ed. Gautier, 77; Pakourianos, *Typikon*, ed. Gautier, 35; *Kosmosoteira Typikon*, ed. Petit, 56, 58–9.

[39] John Oxite, *Diatribes*, 33.

taxation. One can distinguish two main concerns. The first is that excessive taxation may push people to revolt or alienate them from the empire; the second, that high taxes actually had a negative impact on state finances. Kekaumenos warns that new or increased taxes may lead to rebellions, in particular in provinces inhabited by non-Romans.[40] Indeed, as we saw, Skylitzes states that people joined the Bulgarian revolt of 1040 on account of undesirable taxation.[41] Similarly, Niketas Choniates attributes the late twelfth-century Vlacho-Bulgarian uprising to an extraordinary demand imposed by Isaac II Angelos.[42] Over-taxation could also push the empire's subjects into the ranks of the enemy, as John of Antioch asserted took place as a result of the exactions of Alexios I Komnenos.

The second fear put forward by our authors regarded the effect excessive taxation and abusive practices had on state finances. The claim was that the flight of overburdened taxpayers from the territory meant a loss of revenue. The notion that fiscal revenues depended on settlement had a long history. It is one of the main arguments in the novel of Romanos I Lekapenos (920–44), which prohibits the acquisition of peasant lands by the powerful.[43] One finds an allusion to the demographic aspect of over-taxation in John of Antioch's speech to Alexios I in which the subjects' early death or flight appears next to their joining Byzantium's enemies. Here, leading the people to starvation and emigration is not simply an injustice but a detriment to the empire, depriving it of manpower and taxes.[44] This idea, however, appears most clearly and forcefully in Michael and Niketas Choniates. In the petition he addressed to Alexios III Angelos, Michael Choniates repeated his frequent complaint that Athens was abandoned by its inhabitants and turned into a desert because of the heavy *epēreiai* and the abuses of imperial officials. The metropolitan then noted the effect on the fisc as the tax base was reduced by emigration. Michael Choniates raised this issue again later in the petition in requesting that peasant lands be protected from the acquisitions of the city's *kastrēnoi*. According to the metropolitan, these acquisitions led to the extinction of the tax-paying village, something detrimental to the fisc.[45] In the same petition as well as in a letter, Michael Choniates raised another issue in asking for protection from various demands, namely that the fisc

---

[40] Kekaumenos, *Consilia et Narrationes*, ed. Roueché, 98, 70.
[41] See above n. 12.
[42] Niketas Choniates, *History*, ed. van Dieten, 368.
[43] *Les novelles des empereurs macédoniens*, ed. Svoronos, 85 (no. 3, a. 934).
[44] See n. 39 above.
[45] Michael Choniates, *Hypomnēstikon*, ed. Stadtmüller, 283–6.

gained nothing from the officials' exactions.[46] That injustice threatened the tax base is noted by the metropolitan in one of his earlier letters, written in the reign of Andronikos I Komnenos. Here he contended that Constantinople, to which money and resources came from all over the empire, did not provide justice to the provinces. Michael Choniates warned that insecurity and injustice would cut the flow feeding the capital.[47]

The same concepts appear in Niketas Choniates. For Niketas, Manuel I Komnenos' greatest contribution to the common good was the fortification of Neokastra, since it boosted the region's settlement and prosperity and thus its contributions to the treasury. The historian also praises Andronikos I for curbing greedy tax collectors and officials and for ensuring that judgements were fair, measures that allowed the population of the provinces and cities to grow and led to an increase in productivity and cheaper prices.[48] Niketas Choniates describes in relative detail a case in which Turks settled Byzantine captives within their territory during the reign of Alexios III Angelos. As Turkish taxation was bearable and 'philanthropic', unlike Byzantine demands, the resettled captives chose to stay, and some of their compatriots from the empire even decided to join them.[49]

After this overview of what I would call private opinions, we turn now to the imperial side. Although not contested in principle, taxation could be opposed in practice. The rulers had access to redoubtable means of coercion, including military violence and administrative and legal measures. Kekaumenos advises emperors not to neglect their army, because 'if there is no army, not even the treasury stands firm, but absolutely anyone who wants to will oppose you'.[50] This is not the place to discuss the practical aspects of coercion in taxation. We can note, however, certain examples suggesting imperial officials frequently called upon the threat of punishment for contesting taxation, even towards exalted individuals. Opposing taxation was opposing the emperor. Theophylact of Ohrid mentions repeatedly being denounced to Alexios I by tax officials, in particular for

---

[46] Michael Choniates, *Epistulae*, ed. Kolovou, letter 65; *Hypomnēstikon*, ed. Stadtmüller, 285.

[47] Michael Choniates, *Epistulae*, ed. Kolovou, letter 50.

[48] Niketas Choniates, *History*, ed. van Dieten, 150, 325–6, 330–1.

[49] Niketas Choniates, *History*, ed. van Dieten, 494–5. The demographic concern is also pronounced in the funerary speech written for Manuel I by Eustathios of Thessaloniki; the archbishop extolls at length the settlement of foreign soldiers in the empire because it led to an increase of the cities' population: *PG* 135:984–5.

[50] Kekaumenos, *Consilia et Narrationes*, ed. Roueché, 101; translation by Roueché.

tax evasion, something which demonstrated ingratitude towards the ruler. Nicholas Mouzalon of Cyprus reports that when he took actions which threatened to reduce fiscal revenues, he was accused of disloyalty towards the emperor.[51]

Although the fear of coercion and punishment was certainly in the mind of all taxpayers, emperors also relied upon persuasion. Through a variety of means, rulers emphasised their justice, especially in fiscal matters. The general argument was that the emperors were not greedy but just and concerned with their subjects' well-being and that their taxation aimed at fairness, in spite of practical difficulties and occasional unavoidable deviations. Apart from securing the taxpayers' acquiescence to fiscal demands, this argument also sought to buttress the emperor's legitimacy as a just ruler. Echoing the view of private observers, emperors related just taxation to their subjects' prosperity and unjust demands to poverty. Attaleiates quotes the proclamations Constantine X Doukas made upon his accession. The emperor promised he would be philanthropic and take care of all his subjects, and that people would prosper under his rule, as justice would reign and no one would suffer unjust deprivations.[52] It is likely that Michael and Niketas Choniates' praise of Andronikos I Komnenos for restoring justice and prosperity in the provinces reflects the official discourse of that emperor.[53] In his encomium to Isaac II Angelos, Michael Choniates praises the emperor's efforts to put an end to the abuses of tax officials, citing certain of his pronouncements. Isaac II quoted biblical precepts condemning the love of illegally acquired money and extolling justice. He also drew on Synesios' *Peri basileias* to declare that he was not a money-loving (*erasichrēmatos*) emperor, his greatest wealth being piety, and that cities enjoyed *eunomia* and were not victims of excessive taxation.[54]

The notion of equality was part of fiscal rules as well as imperial discourse. Tax assessment was largely based on the principle of proportionality. The most important commercial tax, the *kommerkion*, was a percentage duty, whereas the amount of tax demanded on land depended on its quantity and quality; the more land one owned, and the higher the quality of this, the greater the basic tax one paid. However, the surtaxes

---

[51] Theophylact of Ohrid, *Letters*, ed. Gautier, 489 (letter 96); Nikolaos Mouzalon, *Resignation*, ed. Doanidou, 127.

[52] Michael Attaleiates, *History*, ed. Tsolakes, 56.

[53] See n. 27 above.

[54] Michael Choniates, *Tὰ σωζόμενα*, ed. Lampros, 1:254; cf. Synesios of Cyrene, *Opuscula*, ed. Terzaghi, 54–5.

(*parakolouthēmata*) increased only up to a certain point, after which taxation became regressive.[55] This was not the main reason why Byzantine taxation was far removed from equality or justice. The salaries paid to imperial officials, especially before Alexios I Komnenos, and the substantial gains obtained thanks to contracts with the fisc and the sale of offices, went untaxed. Moreover, a portion of the wealthier individuals enjoyed some sort of tax exemption. The extent is unknown, but already by the tenth century it must have been significant.[56] In spite of the great disparities in the way Byzantines were taxed, equality remained a principle invoked and applied by emperors in the twelfth century in matters that went beyond the basic assessment of tax. In 1106, Alexios I issued a directive ordering that the same coin equivalence be used for the payment of the tax by peasants (*chōritai*) and great landowners (*prosōpa*); the latter profited from the numismatic confusion of the time, paying significantly less than peasant taxpayers.[57] The concern for equal treatment, this time of Constantinopolitans and provincials, can also be detected in Manuel I's law on court procedure of 1166, which, among other things, ordered the expedited adjudication of complaints regarding taxation brought to the imperial court by provincials so as to spare them the expenses of a prolonged stay away from home.[58]

There were also measures designed to alleviate the tax burden on peasants. The fisc in this period employed the technique of *sympatheia* (compassion) to temporarily exempt communities from the obligation of collectively assuming the taxes of vanished members of the same fiscal unit, so as not to cause all peasants to flee.[59] One notes the highly rhetorical tenor of the term used for this fiscal operation. According to Skylitzes, Basil II in fact transferred to the powerful (*dynatoi*) the obligation of paying the taxes of the vanished poor (*tapeinoi*).[60] Beyond general rules, there may also have been cases of exemptions aiming at assisting the less well-off

---

[55] Morrisson, 'La logarikè', table on p. 463.
[56] This is the basic assumption of the Macedonian legislation restricting land acquisition by the powerful; see Oikonomides, 'The Social Structure', 105–8. The 996 novel of Basil II refers to numerous chrysobulls issued in the earlier part of his reign, which probably awarded privileges or donations: *Les novelles des empereurs macédoniens*, ed. Svoronos, 214 (no. 14).
[57] *JGR* 1:334–5.
[58] Manuel I Komnenos, *Four Novels*, ed. Macrides, 130.
[59] Oikonomides, 'The Role', 1004.
[60] John Skylitzes, *Synopsis*, ed. Thurn, 347; the rule was abolished by Romanos III Argyros (1028–34): ibid. 375; discussion in Lemerle, *Agrarian History*, 78–80.

taxpayers of certain cities, as seems to have been the case with the privilege awarded to the Athenians by Alexios II Komnenos (1180–2).[61]

In our period, in fact, emperor and fisc continue to play the role of protectors of the poor and regulators of social relations, as they did in the tenth century. The emperors presented themselves as lovers of the poor. As we shall see, the rulers made frequent distributions to the needy and founded charitable institutions, all highly public acts. The poor were awarded special legal and judicial protection in our period. The tenth-century legislation of the Macedonians which limited the acquisition of peasant lands, whose declared aim was to protect the poor (*penētes* or *ptōchoi*) from the powerful (*dynatoi*) as well as the interests of fisc, remained in force and was apparently applied through the end of our period. It appears, in fact, that Alexios I Komnenos, or one of his eleventh-century predecessors, issued a law that reiterated the restrictions of the Macedonians. This law no longer called peasants *penētes* and *ptōchoi* but used the equally rhetorical term *tapeinoi* (humble).[62] Alexios I stands out among the emperors in our period for his use of laws and judgements to protect the weak against the oppression of the powerful.[63] In 1095 he issued a law that, through the invocation of a rule apparently originating in the Macedonian legislation, limited the rights of slave owners (as *dynatoi*) to produce witnesses in cases initiated by slaves (called *tapeinoteroi*) reclaiming their freedom.[64] The letters of Theophylact of Ohrid reveal that the emperor personally heard the

---

[61] See n. 36 above.

[62] On the continued force of this legislation and *tapeinos*, see Magdalino, 'Deux précisions', 345–8. Michael Choniates' petition to Alexios III, which refers to decrees, probably of earlier emperors, forbidding the *kastrēnoi* of Athens from taking hold of peasant lands (n. 37 above), also suggests the restrictions were still valid; at the same time, the fact that orders had to be issued and the metropolitan felt the need to explain the significance of these acquisitions suggests that the application of the law was problematic.

[63] Cf. Magdalino, 'Justice and Finance', 109–10. Other emperors who afforded legal or judicial protection to the weak include Nikephoros III, said to have judged cases providing justice to orphans and widows (Michael Attaleiates, *History*, ed. Tsolakes, 239); Manuel I, who issued a *prostagma* in 1166 ordering the quick distribution of properties left to the poor by will (Manuel I Komnenos, *Four Novels*, ed. Macrides, 134–6); and Andronikos I, called a lover of the poor (*philopenēs*) and praised for his fair judgements of the weaker (Michael Choniates, Τὰ σωζόμενα, ed. Lampros, 1:174, 179; Niketas Choniates, *History*, ed. van Dieten, 330).

[64] *JGR* 1:344–5; cf. *Les novelles des empereurs macédoniens*, ed. Svoronos, 204, 194–5 (no. 14, a. 996), This may be the earliest dated reference to the law using the term *tapeinoi*, mentioned above (n. 62).

complaints of a Bulgarian *paroikos* against his landlord, the archbishop.[65] Alexios I also enjoined a landowner to whom he had awarded *paroikoi* to treat them well and not expel them from the estate.[66]

Emperors responded to complaints of abuse by officials by issuing orders or laws aimed at curbing these practices. At the beginning of the twelfth century, Alexios I issued an order clarifying tax collection issues in which he condemned the greed of the tax collectors and requested they surrender to the fisc what had been collected illegitimately. Referring to these abuses, a memorandum of the *genikos logothetēs* later spoke of a tax collection that had been 'detrimental to the subjects'.[67] John II Komnenos (1118–43), Manuel I Komnenos and Isaac II Angelos forbade the over-taxation or plundering of Church properties at the death of the bishop.[68] We have already seen that both Andronikos I Komnenos and Isaac II were praised for their efforts to rein in unjust officials and for appointing worthy judges and governors. According to Niketas Choniates, Andronikos I personally judged cases of abuse by officials, severely punishing transgressors.[69] Almost all the emperors in our period are said to have practised personal justice, often hearing fiscal cases. Some emperors emphasised their readiness to hear from those with complaints or requests, notably Alexios I Komnenos. Zonaras reports that in a given summer he set certain days during which he would sit in an open field receiving and answering the petitions of anyone with a request.[70] A remarkable innovation was the creation of a court, apparently in the reign of Alexios I, dealing exclusively with fiscal cases. We see it in action once, in 1196, when it actually found in favour of the monastery of Lavra, a powerful taxpayer, and against a bureau of the fisc, then headed by some of the most influential

---

[65] Theophylact of Ohrid, *Letters*, ed. Gautier, 487 (letter 96); cf. 503 (letter 98). The speech the imperial official Manuel Straboromanos addressed to Alexios I stresses particularly the emperor's judgement of cases involving orphans and widows and his care of the lepers. It also mentions a case that looks remarkably similar to that of Theophylact's *paroikos*: a poor peasant who did not speak proper Greek interrupted a meeting of the emperor obtaining from him a hearing and a favourable response: Manuel Straboromanos, *Dossier*, ed. Gautier, 183.

[66] *Actes de Lavra I*, ed. Lemerle et al., 258 (no. 48, a. 1086).

[67] *JGR* 1:336.

[68] Isaac Angelos, *Decree*.

[69] See nn. 27, 48, 54 above.

[70] John Zonaras, *Epitome*, ed. Pinder, 753. The accessibility of Alexios I is confirmed by the case of the *paroikos* of Theophylact (see n. 65 above).

individuals of the time. This was a moment of actual fiscal justice against official abuse.[71]

Unlike regular taxes, emperors were sometimes obliged to justify – and once, at the end of the twelfth century, to negotiate – significant increases or extraordinary demands. In the time of Attaleiates, a period of severe military and financial challenges, emperors apparently cited the fiscal benefit in order to explain their increased demands.[72] In order to justify his heavy taxation and confiscations, Alexios I Komnenos invoked his empty treasury and the army's pressing needs, saying that these prevented him from verifying whether the measures were just or not.[73] Facing the need to pay a substantial sum to the German ruler, Alexios III Angelos was the first emperor to convoke a council of Constantinopolitan citizens, composed of aristocrats, clergy, craftsmen and tradesmen, in order to ask them for a voluntary contribution.[74]

Ideas Regarding the Confiscation of Property

We possess a remarkable amount of argumentation put forward by the imperial side in an effort to justify confiscation. Whereas the expropriation of specific individuals or institutions, in accordance with established fiscal rules or for crimes against the emperor, was a regular practice, larger-scale confiscation remained extraordinary and contested, hence the wealth of imperial statements regarding the matter. Emperors often appealed to the common good, whose value was superior to everything else, including laws and private rights.[75] The common interest was invoked in cases where it was perceived to be imperilled by financial difficulties and military emergencies. Michael Psellos' account of the measures of Isaac I Komnenos, which included the confiscation of lay and monastic properties, is preceded by an excursus on the profligacy of the predecessors of Isaac I, who are accused of undermining state finances.[76] It is likely that Psellos is here echoing the

---

[71] *Actes de Lavra I*, ed. Lemerle et al., 349–54, 355–8 (nos 67, 68); Magdalino, 'Justice and Finance', 106–15.
[72] Michael Attaleiates, *History*, ed. Tsolakes, 151: προφάσει δημοσιακῆς ὠφελείας; cf. ibid. 211, on Michael VII mentioning financial difficulties.
[73] John Oxite, *Diatribes*, 41.
[74] Niketas Choniates, *History*, ed. van Dieten, 478; cf. Kyritses, 'Political and Constitutional Crisis', 106.
[75] Cf. Kaldellis, *Byzantine Republic*, 70–82.
[76] Michael Psellos, *Chronographia*, ed. Reinsch, 231–7.

official discourse that sought to delegitimise the policies of earlier emperors. Indeed, according to the same historian, Isaac I seized the properties his predecessors had donated to various laymen by invalidating the relevant imperial acts.[77] With regard to the seizure of monastic estates, Psellos offers the terse statement that 'to those who wanted to dispute this action, the fisc was a sufficient defence.'[78] This could mean one of two things. Either Isaac I invoked the acute needs of the fisc or he referred to a fiscal rule allowing him to expropriate – a practice, as we will see, well attested in the period. Finally, as already noted, Alexios I Komnenos also attributed his unjust taxation and confiscations to a lack of resources and a military emergency.[79]

Emperors also confiscated without reference to an emergency by appealing to the simple promotion of the common good. Several rulers, beginning with Alexios I, seized private properties in order to create or expand the quarters of westerners in Constantinople.[80] In 1082 Alexios I confiscated properties to provide a quarter to Venice. In the chrysobull he issued to this effect, he stated that no one should turn against the Venetians, who were his loyal servants and were offering valuable services to the empire.[81] Although in 1082 Byzantium was in the middle of a military crisis, Alexios I was content to invoke the Venetians' contribution to the common good. The same argument was used in 1192, when Isaac II Angelos awarded real estate to Genoa. In the chrysobull addressed to that city, the emperor confirmed its newly acquired rights over the properties by stating that he had seized them 'by virtue of the lawful power entrusted to him . . . and because he donated these to Genoa for the advantage and benefit of Romania.' The emperor claimed to have the authority to disregard private property rights in order to promote the interests of the polity. As we shall see, however, Isaac offered additional arguments in relation to the confiscations he carried out in 1192.

---

[77] According to Michael Psellos, *Chronographia*, ed. Reinsch, 236, Isaac annulled all such donations made by his predecessor, Michael VI (1056–7), as well as donations made by earlier emperors. Attaleiates, *History*, ed. Tsolakes 48–9, who also discusses Isaac I's measures, does not indicate that the properties were imperial donations, simply that they were included in chrysobulls issued to the owners.

[78] Michael Psellos, *Chronographia*, ed. Reinsch, 236: Ἀπολογία γὰρ αὐτάρκης τοῖς διαβάλλειν ἐθέλουσι τὴν πρᾶξιν, ὁ δημόσιος καθειστήκει.

[79] See n. 73 above.

[80] On these confiscations see Smyrlis, 'Private Property'.

[81] *Trattati con Bisanzio*, ed. Pozza and Ravegnani, 42–3 (no. 2), and Smyrlis, 'Private Property', 117–19. It seems that the expropriated owners were not compensated: ibid. 127.

Another common way in which emperors sought to legitimise confiscation was by presenting their measures as conforming to law or precedent.
Legal pretexts were used a few times by emperors in the late eleventh century and later in order to justify expropriations. According to Attaleiates,
Michael VII Doukas seized the wharfs (*skalai*) on the coasts of Constantinople and its suburbs, which belonged to ecclesiastical and welfare institutions and other private owners. To do this, Michael VII used what the
historian calls 'obsolete and aged pretexts', a likely reference to novels of
Justinian I regarding the seashore, which the emperor liberally interpreted
to suit his purposes.[82] Soon after Alexios I Komnenos' accession to the
throne, Church treasures in the capital were seized. Apart from invoking
the empire's pressing defence needs, the emperor's brother argued, in front
of a large assembly of ecclesiastics, that the appropriation was consistent
with canon and civil law, which permitted the alienation of Church silver
in order to ransom captives. Later, Alexios I apparently also referred to
precedents set by Pericles and King David on the use of sacred possessions.
Nevertheless, less than a year later, in August 1082, because of the fierce
reaction of the Church, Alexios I issued a law by which he asked forgive-
ness for what 'he had done against his will', promised restitution and bound
himself and all future emperors to strict respect of Church property. The
emperor acknowledged that the secularisation had angered God, in spite
of the fact that he had acted under pressure and only after the imperial
treasury had been emptied.[83] Alexios I was more confident when in 1089
and later he confiscated ecclesiastical and lay properties throughout the
empire on a scale that made previous expropriations pale in comparison.
This measure was presented as the application of a fiscal rule (the *epibolē*)
stipulating that landowners forfeit to the fisc properties exceeding the
amount of holdings implied by the tax they paid. It seems, however, that
this arguably oppressive rule was an altered version of an existing principle
that Alexios I manipulated in order to confiscate on a vast scale.[84]

The use of legal arguments continued in the twelfth century. In 1158,
Manuel I Komnenos issued a chrysobull invalidating all the acts he himself had issued which went against the law. This was clearly a means of
nullifying grants and privileges he had conceded in the earlier part of his

---

[82] Michael Attaleiates, *History*, ed. Tsolakes, 213–14. On the identification of the 'pretexts'
with Justinian's novels, see Triantaphyllopoulos, 'Novelle', 314–18.
[83] Glabinas, Ἔρις, 51–98; Alexios I's law: *JGR* 1:302–4. In spite of his promise, Alexios
I was soon forced to once again confiscate Church silver: Glabinas, Ἔρις, 133–8.
[84] Smyrlis, 'Fiscal Revolution', 594–601.

reign, especially to powerful individuals and institutions, and probably led to confiscations.[85] New elements appear in official statements regarding confiscation in the late twelfth century. The two chrysobulls of 1192, by which Isaac II Angelos awarded properties to the Pisans and the Genoese, contain a clause forbidding the dispossessed owners to turn against the Italians, asking them instead to seek compensation through a lawsuit against the fisc. In the event they are not compensated, the owners are told they have no recourse, since the emperor has 'the right by law to knowingly donate belongings of third parties'. This refers to a fifth-century law which did not, however, authorise the emperor to confiscate and donate properties or allow the fisc to refuse compensation.[86] Here the emperor abuses an existing law in order to legitimise his action. However, and this is new, the invocation of this law also officially recognised the right of all owners to compensation. This is certainly significant, especially when related to contemporary events. We have seen that Isaac II's successor, Alexios III Angelos, was the first emperor to have convoked a council of the capital's citizens in order to ask them to voluntarily offer a monetary contribution.[87] And it was in the reign of Alexios III that the attempted abusive confiscation of Kalomodios, a wealthy merchant of Constantinople, was thwarted by a revolt of the citizens.[88]

Additional arguments of a moral character were used in the case of the expropriation of monasteries and churches. The emperors presented their measures as restoring proper monastic or ecclesiastical order and as alleviating the suffering of the poor. In addition to his invocation of the fisc, Isaac I Komnenos circulated such arguments with regard to his expropriation of monasteries. Both Psellos and Attaleiates state that Isaac let the monasteries keep what was appropriate for foundations that ought not be rich, attaching the rest to the fisc. Attaleiates also mentions another idea that he attributes to those who 'judged matters carefully' as opposed to 'the more pious people', who only cursorily examined the act. While the latter considered Isaac I's confiscation of monastic lands illegal and sacrilegious, the former found it doubly useful, as it both freed the monks from improper

---

[85] Manuel I Komnenos, *Four Novels*, ed. Macrides, 168–72; Magdalino, *Empire*, 286.
[86] *Acta et diplomata*, 3:18; Sanguineti and Bertolotto (eds), *Nuova serie*, 420; discussion in Smyrlis, 'Private Property', 121–6. References to this law appear frequently in eleventh-century texts; see e.g. *JGR* 4:142–4 (*Peira*, 36.2, 4–5, 12); Michael Psellos, *Poemata*, ed. Westerink, Poem 8.221–3.
[87] See n. 74 above.
[88] Niketas Choniates, *History*, ed. van Dieten, 523–4.

concerns and brought relief to the peasant neighbours of monastic estates from whom the monks were oppressively acquiring lands. The arguments Psellos and Attaleiates mention in relation to this incident (assigning to the greedy monks what befitted their vocation and protecting the farmers) echo two prominent ideas of the Macedonian legislation. In fact, what Attaleiates says about those who carefully judged the imperial measure is notably similar to the epilogue of the novel of Nikephoros II Phokas (963–9) restricting land acquisition by the monks. This epilogue states that the sensible people who did not 'examine matters superficially' would find the novel doubly useful, both to the monks and to the commonwealth.[89] It is possible that the statements regarding Isaac I's monastic expropriations reported by Attaleiates reflect his or his contemporaries' opinions, which were in turn closely based on the Macedonian legislation. It seems more likely, however, that Attaleiates is reproducing – and espousing – Isaac I's discourse, not only because the historian himself attributes one of these notions to the emperor but also because these arguments were so in line with imperial purposes. The argument that confiscation was actually good for the ecclesiastics continued being used after Isaac I. It may have circulated in relation to the expropriations carried out according to the *epibolē* principle under Alexios I Komnenos.[90] Moreover, a *prostagma* Manuel I Komnenos issued soon before 1163, which ordered that bishoprics ought to keep only those properties they rightfully held while losing the rest to the fisc, claimed that the measure aimed at providing 'assistance and complete freedom to their bishops.'[91]

We also have at our disposal a significant number of reactions to the imperial measures. The individuals deprived of their properties by Isaac I Komnenos are said to have hated the emperor.[92] In the case of the attempted

---

[89] On the need to protect the properties of the poor (peasants) from the powerful and greedy, see, in particular, *Les novelles des empereurs macédoniens*, ed. Svoronos, 82–92 (no. 3, a. 934). The novel of Nikephoros II aimed at healing the monks from the disease of greed: ibid. 157–61 (no. 8, a. 963/4), esp. 157 and 161 (epilogue). It is usually assumed that these ideas came from Attaleiates; see e.g. Laiou, 'Law, Justice', 177–8; Krallis, *Michael Attaleiates*, 104–5, 120–6.

[90] In a document of 1228 referring to these confiscations, it is stated that, during the reign of Alexios I, the metropolitan of Naupaktos chose to abandon many of his Church's properties so as to enjoy the few remaining ones in peace, free from the trouble caused by fiscal demands: *Noctes Petropolitanae*, ed. Papadopoulos-Kerameus, 251.

[91] Mentioned in a document issued to the bishopric of Stagoi: *Acta Stagorum*, 21.17–22 (no. 1): χειραγωγίαν καὶ καθόλου ἐλευθερίαν.

[92] Michael Psellos, *Chronographia*, ed. Reinsch, 236.

expropriation of Kalomodios, the people rose in revolt to protect a third person. Our authors often speak of injustice or, in the case of ecclesiastical property, of impiety and sacrilege. Attaleiates criticises Michael VII Doukas for confiscating the treasures of certain rich churches in Constantinople in his effort to counter simultaneous rebellions. This is deemed a great impiety, especially since, according to the historian, there was still cash in the imperial treasury.[93] Leo, metropolitan of Chalcedon, led the opposition to Alexios I Komnenos' seizing of Church treasures in the 1080s, which he condemned as sacrilege and even iconoclasm, invoking civil and canon law, biblical precedents, the Church Fathers and tradition.[94] As we already saw, John of Antioch censured Alexios I's taxation and confiscation as unjust and provocative of God's wrath. The people of Constantinople are said to have refuted as sacrilegious Alexios III Angelos' suggestion to melt down precious objects dedicated to churches. The same emperor's robbing of imperial tombs is considered a profanity by Niketas Choniates. The historian especially regrets the plundering of the churches in 1203. For Choniates, this was a flagrantly unlawful act that caused the empire's fall and made the Byzantines responsible for the great evils they suffered, since no one, not even he himself, had objected to this impiety.[95]

Attaleiates stands out among our authors in that he also condemns confiscation on the basis of legal arguments. He censures Michael VII's seizing of the wharfs on the capital's shores as a shameless deprivation of the proprietors from their rights upon the *skalai*, which were based upon 'ancestral customs and the imperial constitutions'. As we saw, the emperor's invocation of the law was deemed abusive.[96] Nevertheless, in contrast to John of Antioch, for whom nothing could justify unjust expropriation, Attaleiates is not absolutely opposed to confiscation. For Attaleiates, Michael VII Doukas' seizing of Church treasures was an impiety because there was still cash in the imperial treasury, implying that such expropriations could be legitimate in a true emergency. The historian is no doubt more representative of general views than is the prelate. The reactions to Alexios I Komnenos' secularisation of Church silver came essentially from the clergy, while in 1203 there was apparently no reaction.

---

[93] Michael Attaleiates, *History*, ed. Tsolakes, 199–200. It seems that Michael VII had invoked lack of funds (πρόσχημα τῆς ἀπορίας).

[94] Glabinas, Ἔρις, 65–71, 80–132, 161–93.

[95] Niketas Choniates, *History*, ed. van Dieten, 478–9, 551–2.

[96] See n. 82 above. On Attaleiates' emphasis on property rights and legality, see Tinnefeld, *Kategorien*, 136–7; Kazhdan, 'The Social Views', 41; Laiou, 'Law, Justice', 176–81, 183–4.

The neutral or approving accounts Psellos and Attaleiates give of Isaac I Komnenos' confiscation of lay and monastic properties is certainly related to their overall positive assessment of the emperor. Attaleiates, so fiercely opposed to the measures of Michael VII Doukas, does not seem particularly troubled by Isaac I's disregard of individual rights. The relative lack of sympathy for the laymen may also be attributed to the fact that they were likely a limited group of highly favoured individuals. With regard to the monasteries, another factor was present, namely, that general opinion was critical of the monks' wealth. Both authors more or less openly approved of the curtailing of monastic wealth by endorsing the claim that it freed the monks from improper concerns while, for Attaleiates, also benefiting the farmers. The condemnation of monastic greed continued to have currency in the twelfth century and beyond.[97]

Ideas on the Use of Public Wealth

There is no shortage of views, imperial or private, on how public resources should be used. Although the greatest part of the official discourse at our disposal concerns imperial liberality, at times emperors also advocated austerity. This was certainly the case with Isaac I Komnenos. As noted, Psellos' and Attaleiates' accounts of this emperor's reforms, which apart from increasing public resources also involved spending cuts, seem to reflect the official discourse to a significant extent. Much later, in 1197, Alexios III Angelos explained his invalidation of all tax exemptions of boats by contending that the excessive concessions were damaging the fisc.[98] Savings were useful even in the absence of financial difficulties. While also counselling generosity, the poem Alexios I Komnenos addressed to his son John stresses especially the importance of maintaining a great treasure in case of a military emergency.[99]

Generosity was an imperial virtue underlining the majesty of the ruler as well as his care for his subjects through redistribution. Alexios I advises his son to give in abundance and receive in return an 'abundant flow' of gold.[100] Indeed, the movement of money entering and coming out of the

---

[97] See most notably Eustathios of Thessaloniki, *De emendanda vita monachica*, ed. Metzler. On Attaleiates' lack of concern about the laymen's rights in this case, see Laiou, 'Law, Justice', 177–8, *contra* Kazhdan, 'The Social Views', 33, 41, 43.

[98] *Βυζαντινὰ ἔγγραφα τῆς μονῆς Πάτμου. Α´*, ed. Branouse, 105 (no. 11).

[99] Alexios I Komnenos, *Muses*, 357–8.

[100] Ibid. 357.

treasury is likened to the flow of a river of gold in a variety of texts reflecting imperial rhetoric. The treasury itself is sometimes called a sea of gold fed by rivers from all over and from which other rivers run in order to water the subjects.[101] This image is related to the idea that as much as emperors might empty the treasury, it would always be filled up again.[102] The public spending of the emperors often served the purpose of underlining their piety and their concern for the people, especially the needy. The encomium of Michael Choniates for Isaac II Angelos emphasises the emperor's piety as a principle guiding his spending. The emperor emptied the treasury because he trusted in God, not in money or armies.[103] Many rulers founded or restored monasteries and churches or gave them donations. Probably all the bishoprics and important monasteries in the empire enjoyed some sort of tax exemption, and many were also awarded annual subsidies. The concessions to such institutions were often explained with reference to their needs, the emperor's love of the clergy or the monks and his duty or debt towards the divine, notions stressing the emperor's piety.[104] Charitable institutions were also founded and endowed in the capital. Two noteworthy cases are the Orphanotropheion, created by Alexios I Komnenos to provide shelter for the elderly and education for orphans or sons of indigents, and the hospital attached to the monastery of the Pantokrator, founded by John II Komnenos. Both foundations were very large and endowed with vast properties.[105] Emperors also made cash distributions to the needy, endowed poor virgins and offered compensation to fire victims.[106] Andronikos I Komnenos is

---

[101] Michael Psellos, *Chronographia*, ed. Reinsch, 108, 179, 189; Manuel Straboromanos, *Dossier*, ed. Gautier, 187; Eustathios of Thessaloniki, *Opera minora*, ed. Wirth, 147; Michael Choniates, *Epistulae*, ed. Kolovou, letter 50; Τὰ σωζόμενα, ed. Lampros, 1:23.

[102] Michael Attaleiates, *History*, ed. Tsolakes, 200–1; cf. Michael Psellos, *Orationes Forenses et Acta*, ed. Dennis, 156.2–6, 158.63–4.

[103] The encomium here probably reproduces Isaac II's discourse. It is interesting to note that Michael's brother, Niketas, states that Isaac II was firmly convinced that he enjoyed God's favour and that he did not, therefore, need to take the care of government very seriously: Niketas Choniates, *History*, ed. van Dieten, 423. The notion that divine help was more important than armies was not new in imperial discourse; see e.g. *Actes de Lavra I*, ed. Lemerle et al., 112–13 (no. 7, a. 978). This concept is also the main argument of John of Antioch's speech to Alexios I; see n. 29 above.

[104] E.g. Βυζαντινὰ ἔγγραφα τῆς μονῆς Πάτμου. Α´, ed. Branouse, 33–4, 44–7 (nos 4, 5, a. 1087).

[105] On the Orphanotropheion, see Magdalino, 'Innovations', 156–64; on the Pantokrator, see Smyrlis, *La fortune*, 70–2. Isaac II is also said to have created several public welfare establishments: Niketas Choniates, *History*, ed. van Dieten, 445.

[106] E.g. Niketas Choniates, *History*, ed. van Dieten, 324 (on Andronikos I), 445 (on Isaac II).

credited with a work of public utility, the restoration of an aqueduct provisioning the capital.[107] The practice of awarding tax privileges to entire cities is attested in the eleventh and twelfth centuries. We have no direct evidence of the arguments used to justify such grants, but they likely included the poverty of the citizens, as noted in the case of Athens, and the abuses of officials.[108]

Apart from the care for the needy and religious institutions, imperial rhetoric also commented on the attribution of public resources to reward loyalty and services to the empire. These concessions included the conferral of dignities to individuals and monetary donations, grants of land, revenues or privileges awarded to individuals, institutions or communities. Providing rewards for services to the empire was an ancient practice that continued in medieval Byzantium. How the imperial state understood this function is explained in a concession document of 1045 issued to Judge Byzantios of Bari. For the assistance Byzantios provided to Constantinople during the revolt of George Maniakes and a Norman attack, he was rewarded with a village and a tax exemption. The preamble of this document states that

> It is fair that those who have a praiseworthy disposition, who display their loyalty and gratitude in a time of need, and who have shown right and sincere faith to the emperors should enjoy the appropriate favour and, in addition, receive great honours and benefactions.[109]

There are several other examples of such grants, where loyalty or outstanding services to the empire are mentioned by the emperor in order to justify the concessions. One of these grants, awarded in 1086 by chrysobull to Leo Kephalas, defender of Larissa against the Normans, is notable for the fact that the preamble specifies that the concession was not a gift but repayment for his efforts and victories.[110] Exemplary civil service was

---

[107] Niketas Choniates, *History*, ed. van Dieten, 329.
[108] On the concession of tax privileges to cities, see Smyrlis, 'Wooing the Petty Elite', 658. Michael Choniates also refers to the concession of subsidies (*dēmosia sitēresia*) to cities by Andronikos I: Michael Choniates, Τὰ σωζόμενα, ed. Lampros, 1:178. On the poor benefiting from exemptions to cities, see n. 36 above. Towards 1198, the Athenians requested that the emperor award them a privilege protecting them from extraordinary demands and the abuses of officials: Michael Choniates, *Hypomnēstikon*, ed. Stadtmüller, 285–6.
[109] Eustathios Palatinos, *Sigillion*, ed. Lefort and Martin, 528.
[110] *Actes de Lavra I*, ed. Lemerle et al., 258 (no. 48).

also deemed worthy of reward. In 1075 and 1079, Michael Attaleiates was awarded a tax privilege in recognition of the loyalty and erudition that he had put to the service of the emperor in his capacity as judge.[111]

The justification of grants in the case of churches and monasteries sometimes bore remarkable similarities to that found in concessions to imperial servants. As already noted, in their grants to ecclesiastics, the emperors invoked their piety and the institutions' insufficient means. Along with these considerations, however, official documents also mention the monks' or the clergy's services to the empire, notably their praying for the emperor, the army and the Christian subjects, and their taking care of the spiritual needs of the people.[112] The services to the empire could also concern the material world, as in the case of the bishopric of Vodena, which Basil II deemed worthy of a special tax privilege for the support it had offered him during the war with Bulgaria.[113] In the case of the cities, too, it is likely that loyalty or services to the empire were on certain occasions mentioned in the imperial charters.[114]

There is a common higher justification in all types of imperial concessions, whether they emphasised the emperor's love of the divine or his concern for the empire's defence and his subjects' well-being: they were done for the common good. The emperor's piety and justice guaranteed proper order and prosperity while ensuring God's favour for the empire. The ruler's care for the military and civil apparatuses promoted security and good government. The fact that emperors often provide justification for their grants and that the reasons are always related to the common good implied that the ruler could not use the public wealth for anything else.

Private commentators are unanimous that public wealth was not the emperor's private property. As Paul Magdalino has observed, while historians of the eleventh century criticise emperors for misusing public wealth, in particular for personal purposes, there is a remarkable change of tone and a new emphasis on the distinction between public and private in the writings of authors who were active after the establishment of a family system of government by Alexios I Komnenos.[115] John of Antioch attacked Alexios

---

[111] Michael Attaleiates, *Diataxis*, ed. Gautier, 101–23.
[112] E.g. *Actes de Lavra I*, ed. Lemerle et al., 194 (no. 32, a. 1057); *JGR* 1:376 (a. 1148); cf. Alexios I Komnenos, *Muses*, 361–2.
[113] Basil II, *Decree*, 548; cf. Oikonomides, 'Tax Exemptions', 319.
[114] Cf. nn. 144, 145 below.
[115] Magdalino, 'Aspects'.

I for liberally conceding resources to his relatives.[116] Writing about half a century later, Zonaras provides a more developed condemnation of Alexios I. The founder of the Komnenian dynasty is accused of treating the empire and its wealth as his private property and of lavishing great wealth upon his relatives and associates. Alexios is censured for not deeming the rest of the aristocracy worthy of counsel or honour and for humiliating them. More importantly, in Zonaras the criticism regarding the use of public wealth becomes the basis of a more sweeping condemnation of the imperial system of his day as tyrannical. It was a tyranny because the rulers considered the common property as their own (*idia ta koina*), using it for their own enjoyment and granting public resources (*ta dēmosia*) to whomever they pleased, while imposing upon their subjects predatory taxation.[117] At the end of our period, Niketas Choniates wrote with unmistakeable bitterness that emperors destroyed their prominent subjects, treating them as slaves so as to 'squander away in peace and have the public finances (*ta dēmosia*) all to themselves as a paternal inheritance to do with as they please'. For Choniates, emperors were not satisfied 'simply to rule, and wear gold, and treat common property (*ta koina*) as their own and free men as slaves', but also wanted to appear exceedingly wise, handsome and strong.[118]

Our authors frequently condemn imperial prodigality or misuse of public wealth, especially when they speak about the past with the benefit of hindsight. With the exceptions of Isaac I Komnenos and John II Komnenos, all emperors, from Constantine VIII to Alexios III, are accused of squandering public resources or spending them improperly. Psellos offers one of the most damning images of imperial prodigality, attributing the empire's decline to the wasteful policy of those who reigned between 1025 and 1057.[119] Niketas Choniates reserves an equally severe judgement for the two Angelos emperors, who are accused of extravagance and insouciance, attitudes that led to the capture of Constantinople by the crusaders in 1204.[120] There is an obvious parallel between Psellos and Niketas Choniates. Both highlighted the emperors' misuse of resources in their attempt to explain the collapse of imperial power that each of them experienced in their own time. The corrupt

---

[116] John Oxite, *Diatribes*, 41.
[117] John Zonaras, *Epitome*, ed. Pinder, 766 and 15; see Magdalino, 'Aspects', 330–1; Kaldellis, *Byzantine Republic*, 47.
[118] Niketas Choniates, *History*, ed. van Dieten, 143, 209; translation by Magdalino, 'Aspects', 327.
[119] Psellos, *Chronographia*, ed. Reinsch, 108–10, 231–5.
[120] See most recently Smyrlis, 'Sybaris', 159.

and purloining high-ranking officials and people close to the emperor are also castigated by our authors. Attaleiates details the ways by which Nikephoritzes enriched himself by appropriating public wealth, selling offices and obtaining a lucrative tax farm contract.[121] Niketas Choniates often presents imperial relatives and associates using their authority and influence for private gain, usually at the detriment of the fisc.[122] Besides condemnations in texts written at a certain remove from the events, we also have the benefit of more immediate reactions. In all cases, these came from people who were in the main protesting against increased fiscal demands and who perhaps also felt they did not benefit sufficiently from imperial generosity. As we saw, the speech of John of Antioch to Alexios I Komnenos criticised, among other failings, the great concessions the emperor made to his relatives. A similar complaint was apparently heard in 1197. According to Niketas Choniates, some of the citizens of Constantinople, from whom Alexios III Angelos had requested contributions, refused, telling the emperor that 'he squanders the public resources (*ta koina*) and that he has distributed the provinces to his useless relatives'. Niketas Choniates also reports that the subjects of Manuel I Komnenos criticised him for his taxation and for his spending to buy support in Italy, which they thought useless and motivated by vanity.[123]

One also finds in our texts a considerable amount of praise of imperial liberality, which may not always be explained away as hypocritical and calculated, aiming at securing the emperor's favour or as a means to safely criticise his policies.[124] Our authors might also reflect the genuine satisfaction people felt as recipients of imperial benefactions. Psellos states that Constantine IX Monomachos (1042–55), who by the later eleventh century was considered a great squanderer, was in his own time called by most people Constantine Euergetes – that is, 'the Benefactor'. In his encomium for Isaac II Angelos, Michael Choniates similarly states that the emperor ought to be called Isaac Euergetes for the benefactions he had made to all the people.[125] Attaleiates also profusely praises Nikephoros III Botaneiates (1078–81) for his lavish concessions, in the final encomiastic part of his history.[126] Michael

---

[121] Michael Attaleiates, *History*, ed. Tsolakes, 154–7.

[122] Magdalino, 'Money'; Smyrlis, 'Sybaris', 162–3, 165–7.

[123] Niketas Choniates, *History*, ed. van Dieten, 478, 199–203.

[124] The latter idea has been suggested with regard to Attaleiates' praise of Botaneiates' excessive liberality: Krallis, *Michael Attaleiates*, ch. 4, esp. 116–20, 155–6.

[125] Michael Psellos, *Chronographia*, ed. Reinsch, 233; Michael Choniates, Τὰ σωζόμενα, ed. Lampros, 1:251–2.

[126] On this praise see Kazhdan, 'The Social Views', 29–30; Kazhdan considers Attaleiates' enthusiasm genuine: ibid. 24, 30.

Choniates and Attaleiates admire what seems like reckless spending, in spite of both possessing a keen understanding of the empire's larger interests. It is no coincidence, however, that both texts date from the beginnings of the reigns of the two emperors. Obviously, all those who received benefactions were made happy. As emperors showed themselves ready to give to all, positive feelings pervaded the society, including our authors, and numbed criticism of the government. This could work for a time, but eventually the widely distributed dignities lost their value and, as state resources decreased through squandering, strict and unpopular measures became necessary to avert financial and military collapse.[127]

The necessity of spending on defence and diplomacy was accepted by all, at least in principle. Kekaumenos stresses the importance of maintaining a strong army and navy and that servicemen should be paid well and on time.[128] We already saw that for Niketas Choniates, Manuel I's greatest contribution to the common good was the fortification of Neokastra. Moreover, the historian disagreed with the critics of Manuel I's Italian spending, countering that the events that followed the emperor's death and the abandonment of his western policies proved he had been right all along.[129] The concern with defence spending, however, is mostly seen in texts criticising emperors for not directing enough resources to the army. Sometimes this is attributed to the rulers' or their counsellors' stinginess and greed. For Attaleiates, it was out of greed (*pleonexia*) that Constantine IX Monomachos withheld the fiscal revenues that had been awarded to the army of Iberia, thereby turning them into allies of the Turks. Similarly, Attaleiates maintains that Constantine X Doukas neglected the empire's defence out of stinginess (*to pheidōlon*).[130] Niketas Choniates disapproves of the reform of navy finances under John II Komnenos, which aimed at economies but instead led to the spread of piracy. The historian blames Isaac II and Alexios III Angelos for disregarding, out of greed, the tax privileges awarded to the Italians and the agreements concluded with them, thereby turning them against Byzantium.

---

[127] See the perceptive remarks of Michael Psellos, *Chronographia*, ed. Reinsch, 120, 109.
[128] Kekaumenos, *Consilia et Narrationes*, ed. Roueché, 94, 101–3.
[129] See above n. 48 and Niketas Choniates, *History*, ed. van Dieten, 203–4.
[130] Michael Attaleiates, *History*, ed. Tsolakes, 35–6 and 62–3, 64; cf. 61. The Iberian incident is also mentioned by Kekaumenos, *Consilia et Narrationes*, ed. Roueché, 18, and alluded to by Zonaras, *Epitome*, ed. Pinder, 647; both refer to an imprudent imposition of taxes on previously exempt people. On this measure, see Lemerle, *Cinq études*, 268–9.

Niketas Choniates also censures Alexios III for not providing money to an envoy he sent to Sicily.[131]

In addition to defence and diplomacy, our authors also found other causes for complaint. Attaleiates accuses Michael VII Doukas of stinginess for not making distributions to the poor in Constantinople at a time of need.[132] As noted, Michael Choniates expected the tax-collecting capital, in its role as furnisher of justice, to send judges to the provinces. This was not the typical demand for fairness but a concrete request for the manning of an administrative position.[133]

The very term Attaleiates uses to denote stinginess, *pheidōlia*, acquires a positive meaning when he speaks of the austerity measures of Isaac I Komnenos. As we saw, both Attaleiates and Psellos approved of these.[134] Niketas Choniates commends John II Komnenos for his prudent spending and also praises his finance minister, John of Poutza. Although depicted as a merciless collector of taxes and the initiator of the ill-conceived navy reform, John of Poutza is also called a fisc-loving (*philodēmosios*) auditor and a skilful and thrifty (*pheidōlos*) manager.[135]

There are a great many private comments regarding imperial concessions of dignities and privileges and the grants of lands and revenues. All commentators agree that, provided they were done properly, these concessions were a good thing. Psellos best captures this idea: 'Two things preserve the hegemony of the Romans, the dignities (*axiōmata*) and the money, and a third, the wise supervision of these two and judgement (*logismos*) in how these are distributed.'[136] Kekaumenos says much the same, recommending that benefactions should be carefully considered (*lelogismenai*) and given to those who deserve them, a statement he backs with arguments and examples.[137] Our authors usually identify imperial servants, especially the soldiers who performed well, as worthy of reward.[138] At times those who were deemed unworthy of rewards or ineligible to receive them are singled out. Psellos mentions the donations of Zoe to her flatterers and the imperial guards; according to the historian, in the case of Constantine IX

---

[131] Niketas Choniates, *History*, ed. van Dieten, 55, 537–8, 478.
[132] Michael Attaleiates, *History*, ed. Tsolakes, 163.
[133] Michael Choniates, *Epistulae*, ed. Kolovou, letter 50.
[134] See nn. 76 and 77 above.
[135] Niketas Choniates, *History*, ed. van Dieten, 59–60, 54–6.
[136] Michael Psellos, *Chronographia*, ed. Reinsch, 119; cf. 109.
[137] Kekaumenos, *Consilia et Narrationes*, ed. Roueché, 94–7.
[138] Ibid. 94; Nikephoros Bryennios, *History*, ed. Gautier, 257; cf. Michael Psellos, *Chronographia*, ed. Reinsch, 110; Niketas Choniates, *History*, ed. van Dieten, 208.

Monomachos, it was those who were most insistent in their requests and those who said something that made the emperor laugh. For Kekaumenos, dignities ought not to be awarded to mimes or to those who were called *politikoi*; higher functions ought not to be entrusted to foreigners of non-royal blood. Niketas Choniates criticises Manuel I Komnenos' giving 'with both hands' to low-born individuals, servants and Latins.[139] As we have seen, the concessions to imperial relatives are targeted by several authors, in particular because they deprived the fisc of precious resources.[140] Our authors indicate certain additional dangers of unwise concessions. Imperial servants could become lax in their duties;[141] concessions to foreigners risked alienating the indigenous subjects.[142] Niketas Choniates is unique in connecting imperial awards to a matter not directly related to the empire's interests but rather of a social nature. He states that the widespread concession of *pronoiai* by Manuel I led to the oppression of the hitherto free peasants by their new masters.[143]

The logic of the grants made to reward services is straightforward. The promotion of the talented and hardworking improved the performance of the army and the administration, while the recognition of achievements fostered excellence among the imperial servants. The question of loyalty is more complex. Allegiance to the emperor, personifying the empire, against internal or external threats contributed to political stability and territorial integrity, that is, to the common good, and was therefore worth rewarding. This notion also, however, allowed emperors to use public resources to secure loyalty to their regime. Buying the support of cities and provinces and of high-ranking people apparently seemed natural to the Byzantines. Kekaumenos mentions that during a revolt in Hellas it was suggested to emperor Constantine X Doukas that he concede a tax exemption to the people so as to bring an end to the uprising.[144] Attaleiates offered similar counsel to the regime of Michael VII Doukas on another occasion. The historian claims that in 1077, during the rebellion of Nikephoros Bryennios, he proposed that a chrysobull be issued to the inhabitants of Raidestos and other cities in the

---

[139] Michael Psellos, *Chronographia*, ed. Reinsch, 110, 119; Kekaumenos, *Consilia et Narrationes*, ed. Roueché, 94–7; Niketas Choniates, *History*, ed. van Dieten, 204.

[140] E.g. John Oxite, *Diatribes*, 41–3; Niketas Choniates, *History*, ed. van Dieten, 204.

[141] Niketas Choniates, *History*, ed. van Dieten, 208–9.

[142] Kekaumenos, *Consilia et Narrationes*, ed. Roueché, 95; cf. Niketas Choniates, *History*, ed. van Dieten, 205.

[143] Niketas Choniates, *History*, ed. van Dieten, 208–9.

[144] Kekaumenos, *Consilia et Narrationes*, ed. Roueché, 70; on the historical circumstances, see Lemerle, *Prolégomènes*, 47, and Cheynet, *Pouvoir*, 72.

vicinity so as to ensure they did not join the rebellion.[145] High-ranking imperial servants expected they would enrich themselves as a function of their proximity to the emperor. In a petition addressed to Alexios I Komnenos, Manuel Straboromanos highlights the great hopes he had when he joined imperial service and his subsequent disappointment. He says he felt as if he were in front of a river of gold which brought gold to everyone else but only pebbles and stones to himself.[146] Anna Komnene is quite eloquent regarding this matter when she pauses her narrative to express her bewilderment at the numerous rebellions against her father, Alexios I, which erupted in spite of the fact that 'he never ceased honouring [those liable to rebel] with dignities and enriching them with great donations'.[147]

Conclusion

The debate on taxation and confiscation and the use of public wealth rested upon the unanimously accepted principle that the *dēmosia* or *koina* were not the emperor's property. These resources and the mechanism of the fisc, charged with replenishing and preserving them, ought to be administrated by the ruler in order to guarantee the common good – that is, the subjects' spiritual and physical well-being. The existence of this principle authorised the participation of every Byzantine in the debate regarding fiscal policy and criticism of the emperors' actions in this domain. Although rulers might sometimes be openly challenged, criticism was usually indirect. Complaints about imperial policies appeared in letters sent to officials and individuals close to the emperor. By censuring earlier emperors, historians could safely criticise contemporary policies. Encomiastic texts might also include admonitions and indirect criticism. The emperors responded to public opinion and pressure. They explained their grants by referring to the common good, thus conceding they were restricted by a value superior to them. Imperial discourse sought to justify increased taxation and confiscations. The rulers also responded to criticism through concrete measures. They issued laws and directives aimed at satisfying the people's demands for justice. They personally heard tax-related complaints and created a fiscal court. The debate regarding fiscal matters may be interpreted as a negotiation in which rulers listened to their subjects and worked to secure acceptance of their policies through arguments and concessions. These

---

[145] Michael Attaleiates, *History*, ed. Tsolakes, 188–9; cf. Cheynet, *Pouvoir*, 83–4.
[146] Manuel Straboromanos, *Dossier*, ed. Gautier, 187.
[147] Anna Komnene, *Alexias*, 12.5, 371.

concessions were not only directed at powerful individuals or groups of people but were also general, concerning the entire population.

The participants in this debate invoked a number of ideas, all of which were ultimately connected to the common good. Emperors and private commentators referred to moral values inherited from the Christian and the Greek and Roman traditions, notably piety, justice, generosity and care for the poor, who were suffering on account of the fisc or the powerful. The notion of the poor needing protection from the greedy and oppressive rich requires special note. Although this concept had risen to prominence in the early centuries of the Christian Empire thanks to the bishops, by the Middle Ages it appears to have been attached to the state rather than the Church.[148] To some extent this was to be expected, given that resources were now concentrated in the hands of the fisc. But it was also a result of deliberate imperial policy. Of course, private commentators criticised the emperors for not fulfilling their duty towards the weaker, a criticism that could not be taken lightly. However, it seems it was principally the rulers and the fisc who promoted the concept of the poor against the rich and sought to make the most from this division. The poor were essential to the medieval emperors. On the one hand, the rhetoric presenting the ruler as the friend of the poor was a means of silencing the clergy and other potential critics; on the other, this association facilitated the application of oppressive fiscal measures directed against wealthy laymen and ecclesiastical institutions.

Besides abstract values, the debate also referred to the laws or rules inherited from antiquity or the earlier Middle Ages. The use of the laws by the emperors was sometimes selective or abusive and aimed at forestalling reactions to unpopular measures, such as expropriation or the rescinding of privileges. Even this use, however, underlined the continued importance of the law, which could also be turned against the emperors. Indeed, their critics, from Attaleiates and Theophylact to Michael Choniates, invoked the legal framework to question the fiscal practices. Emperors and private commentators also referred to the material strength of the empire, which, along with its orthodoxy, was one of the two pillars supporting the common good. The requirements of these pillars were at times in conflict. The imperial side often presented the empire's material needs as taking

---

[148] Cf. the remarks of Brown, *Poverty and Leadership*, on how the bishops of the early Christian Empire used the concept of care for the poor; see also Saradi, 'On the "Archontike"', 349, on the medieval state substituting for the Church in caring for the poor and social injustice.

precedence over other values. The emperor, it was argued, could impose unjust demands; he could ignore the right of ownership; he could even seize the sacred properties. The secular opinion, as represented by Psellos, Attaleiates and Niketas Choniates, would in many cases accept these arguments. Nevertheless, even if this approach was likely the majority view, the events of the late eleventh century demonstrated that no emperor could ignore the clerical insistence on strict adherence to Christian values and rules. Overall, in spite of the emperor's power and the numerous ways by which reality could be distorted and laws circumnavigated, the existence of Byzantium's traditional conceptual and legal framework had a significant limiting effect upon imperial freedom.

A final note concerns the private commentators' stance on privilege. None of our authors contests exceptions to the rule. In fact, all agree that, along with the other imperial grants, if done properly, the concession of privileges was beneficial to the empire. Emperors are censured for misusing rewards within the conventional framework of the debate on the use of the public wealth. It was difficult to conceive of this issue differently in a world where exception had always been common. Contrary to what is sometimes assumed in modern scholarship, privileges were widespread in Byzantium before our period, especially in the case of ecclesiastical institutions and high-ranking individuals. Although the concession of privileges expanded in the eleventh century and after, there was hardly any revolution. For our authors, exception to the rule could coexist harmoniously not only with justice but with the notion of empire itself. Even if taxation was not uniform and was apparently becoming less so, this did not necessarily put into question the ruler's sovereignty over people and territory or the power and integrity of the empire.

Bibliography

Sources

Acta et diplomata ... F. Miklosich and I. Müller (eds), *Acta et diplomata graeca medii aevi*, 6 vols (Vienna, 1860–90).

Acta Stagorum ... D. Sophianos (ed.), 'Acta Stagorum. Τὰ ὑπὲρ τῆς θεσσαλικῆς ἐπισκοπῆς Σταγῶν παλαιὰ βυζαντινὰ ἔγγραφα (τῶν ἐτῶν 1163, 1336 καὶ 1393). Συμβολὴ στὴν ἱστορία τῆς ἐπισκοπῆς, *Trikalina* 13 (1993): 7–67.

Actes de Lavra I ... P. Lemerle, A. Guillou, N. Svoronos and D. Papachrys-santhou (eds), *Actes de Lavra I, des origines à 1204* (Paris, 1970).

Alexios I Komnenos, *Muses* ... P. Maas (ed.), 'Die Musen des Kaisers Alexios I', *BZ* 22 (1913): 348–69.

Anna Komnene, *Alexias* ... D. R. Reinsch and A. Kambylis (eds), *Annae Comnenae Alexias*, 2 vols (Berlin and New York, 2001).

Basil II, *Decree* ... H. Gelzer (ed.), 'Ungedruckte und wenig bekannte Bistümerverzeichnisse der orientalischen Kirche', *BZ* 2 (1893): 22–72.

Eustathios of Thessaloniki, *De emendanda vita monachica*, ed. K. Metzler (Berlin, 2006).

Eustathios of Thessaloniki, *Opera minora*, ed. P. Wirth (Berlin and New York, 2000).

Eustathios Palatinos, *Sigillion* ... J. Lefort and J. M. Martin (eds), 'Le sigillion du catépan d'Italie Eustathe Palatinos pour le juge Byzantios (décembre 1045)', *Mélanges de l'Ecole française de Rome* 98 (1986): 525–42.

Herodianus, *Regnum post Marcum*, ed. C. Lucarini (Munich and Leipzig, 2005).

Isaac Angelos, *Decree* ... J. Darrouzès (ed.), 'Un décret d'Isaac II Angélos', *REB* 40 (1982): 135–55.

JGR ... I. Zepos and P. Zepos (eds), *Jus Graecoromanum*, 8 vols (Athens, 1931).

John Oxite, *Diatribes* ... P. Gautier (ed.), 'Diatribes de Jean l'Oxite contre Alexis Ier Comnène', *REB* 28 (1970): 5–55.

John Skylitzes, *Synopsis* ... H. Thurn (ed.), *Ioannis Scylitzae synopsis historiarum*, CFHB 5 (Berlin, 1973).

John Zonaras, *Epitome* ... M. Pinder (ed.) *Ioannis Zonarae epitome historiarum* (Bonn, 1897).

Kekaumenos, *Consilia et Narrationes*, Greek text, English translation and commentary by C. Roueché (London, 2013).

Kosmosoteira Typikon ... L. Petit (ed.), 'Typikon du monastère de la Kosmosotira près d'Aenos (1152)', *IRAIK* 13 (1908): 17–77.

Manuel I Komnenos, *Four Novels* ... R. Macrides (ed.), 'Justice under Manuel I Komnenos: Four Novels on Court Business and Murder', *Fontes Minores* 6 (1984): 99–204.

Manuel Straboromanos, *Dossier* ... P. Gautier (ed.), 'Le dossier d'un haut fonctionnaire byzantin d'Alexis Ier Comnène, Manuel Straboromanos', *REB* 23 (1965): 168–204.

Michael Attaleiates, *Diataxis* ... P. Gautier (ed.), 'La diataxis de Michel Attaliate', *REB* 39 81981): 5–143.

Michael Attaleiates, *History* ... E. Tsolakes (ed.), *Michaelis Attaliatae Historia* CFHB 50 (Athens, 2011).

Michael Choniates, *Epistulae*, ed. F. Kolovou (Berlin and New York, 2001).

Michael Choniates, *Hypomnēstikon* . . . G. Stadtmüller (ed.), *Michael Choniates Metropolit von Athen: ca. 1138–ca. 1222* (Rome, 1934), 283–86.

Michael Choniates, *Τὰ σωζόμενα* . . . S. Lampros (ed.), *Μιχαὴλ Ἀκομινάτου τοῦ Χωνιάτου τὰ σωζόμενα*, 2 vols (Athens, 1879–80).

Michael Psellos, *Chronographia*, ed. D. Reinsch (Berlin and Boston, 2014).

Michael Psellos, *Orationes Forenses et Acta*, ed. G. Dennis (Stuttgart and Leipzig, 1994).

Michael Psellos, *Poemata*, ed. L. G. Westerink (Stuttgart and Leipzig, 1992).

Nikephoros Bryennios, *History* . . . P. Gautier (ed.), *Nicephori Bryennii Historiarum libri quattuor* (Brussels, 1975).

Niketas Choniates, *History* . . . J. L. van Dieten (ed.), *Nicetae Choniatae Historia*, 2 vols (Berlin and New York, 1975).

Nikolaos Mouzalon, *Resignation* . . . S. Doanidou (ed.), Ἡ παραίτησις Νικολάου τοῦ Μουζαλῶνος ἀπὸ τῆς ἀρχιεπισκοπῆς Κύπρου', *Hellenika* 7 (1934): 109–50.

Noctes Petropolitanae, ed. A. Papadopoulos-Kerameus (St Petersburg, 1913; repr. Leipzig, 1976).

Les novelles des empereurs macédoniens, concernant la terre et les stratiotes, ed. N. Svoronos (Athens, 1994).

Pakourianos, *Typikon* . . . P. Gautier (ed.), 'Le typikon du sébaste Grégoire Pakourianos', *REB* 42 (1984): 5–145.

Sanguineti A. and G. Bertolotto (eds), "Nuova serie sulle relazioni di Genova coll'Impero bizantino," *Atti della Società ligure di storia patria* 28 (1896–1898): 337–573.

Souda . . . A. Adler (ed.), *Suidae Lexicon*, 5 vols (Leipzig, 1928–1938).

Synesios of Cyrene, *Opuscula*, ed. N. Terzaghi (Rome, 1944).

Syrianos, *Stratēgikon* . . . G. Dennis (ed.), *Three Byzantine Military Treatises* (Washington, DC, 1985), 1–136.

Theophylact of Ohrid, *Lettres*, ed. P. Gautier (Thessaloniki, 1986).

Trattati con Bisanzio . . . M. Pozza and G. Ravegnani (eds), *I trattati con Bisanzio, 992–1198* (Venice, 1993).

Βυζαντινὰ ἔγγραφα τῆς μονῆς Πάτμου. Α΄, Αὐτοκρατορικά, ed. E. Branouse (Athens, 1980).

Secondary Literature

Beck, H. G., *Res Publica Romana: Vom Staatsdenken der Byzantiner* (Munich, 1970); repr. in Herbert Hunger (ed.), *Das Byzantinische Herrscherbild* (Darmstadt, 1975), 379–414.

Brown, P., *Poverty and Leadership in the Later Roman Empire* (Hanover, NH, 2002).

Cheynet, J. C., *Pouvoir et contestations à Byzance (963–1210)* (Paris, 1990).

Glabinas, A., Ἡ ἐπὶ Ἀλεξίου Κομνηνοῦ (1081–1118) περὶ ἱερῶν σκευῶν, κειμηλίων καὶ ἁγίων εἰκόνων ἔρις (1081–1095) (Thessaloniki, 1972).

Hunger, H., *Prooimion. Elemente der byzantinischen Kaiseridee in den Arengen der Urkunden* (Vienna, 1964).

Kaldellis, A., *The Byzantine Republic: People and Power in New Rome* (Cambridge and London, 2015).

Kazhdan, A., 'The Social Views of Michael Attaleiates', in A. Kazhdan and S. Franklin (eds), *Studies on Byzantine Literature of the Eleventh and Twelfth Centuries* (Cambridge and Paris, 1984), 23–86.

Krallis, D., *Michael Attaleiates and the Politics of Imperial Decline in Eleventh-Century Byzantium* (Tempe, 2012).

Kyritses, D., 'Political and Constitutional Crisis at the End of the Twelfth Century', in A. Simpson (ed.), *Byzantium, 1180–1204: 'The Sad Quarter of a Century'?* (Athens, 2015), 97–111.

Laiou, A., 'Law, Justice, and the Byzantine Historians: Ninth to Twelfth Centuries', in A. Laiou and D. Simon (eds), *Law and Society in Byzantium, Ninth–Twelfth Centuries* (Washington, DC, 1994), 151–85.

Lemerle, P., *The Agrarian History of Byzantium from the Origins to the Twelfth Century* (Galway, 1979).

Lemerle, P., *Cinq études sur le XIᵉ siècle byzantin* (Paris, 1977).

Lemerle, L., *Prolégomènes à une édition critique et commentée des "Conseils et Récits" de Kékauménos* (Brussels, 1960).

Magdalino, P., 'Aspects of Twelfth-Century Byzantine *Kaiserkritik*', *Speculum* 58 (1983): 326–46.

Magdalino, P., 'Deux précisions sur la terminologie juridique relative aux "pauvres" au Xᵉ–XIIᵉ siècle', in B. Caseau, V. Prigent and A. Sopracasa (eds), Οὗ δῶρόν εἰμι τὰς γραφὰς βλέπων νόει: *mélanges Jean-Claude Cheynet, TM* 21/1 (2017), 343–8.

Magdalino, P., *The Empire of Manuel I Komnenos, 1143–1180* (Cambridge, 1993).

Magdalino, P., 'Innovations in Government', in M. Mullett and D. Smythe (eds), *Alexios I Komnenos* (Belfast, 1996), 146–66.

Magdalino, P., 'Justice and Finance in the Byzantine State, Ninth to Twelfth Centuries', in A. Laiou and D. Simon (eds), *Law and Society in Byzantium, Ninth–Twelfth Centuries* (Washington, DC, 1994), 93–115.

Magdalino, P., 'Money and the Aristocracy, 1180–1204', in A. Simpson (ed.), *Byzantium, 1180–1204: 'The Sad Quarter of a Century'?* (Athens, 2015), 195–204.

Matheou, N. S. M., 'City and Sovereignty in East Roman Thought, c.1000–1200. Ioannes Zonaras' Historical Vision of the Roman State', in N. S. M. Matheou, T. Kampianaki and L. M. Bondioli (eds), *From Constantinople to the Frontier: The City and the Cities* (Leiden and Boston, 2016), 41–63.

Morrisson, C., 'La logarikè: réforme monétaire et réforme fiscale sous Alexis Ier Comnène', *TM* 7 (1979): 419–64.

Oikonomides, N., *Fiscalité et exemption fiscale à Byzance (ixᵉ–xiᵉ s.)* (Athens, 1996).

Oikonomides, N., 'The Role of the Byzantine State in the Economy', in A. Laiou (ed), *The Economic History of Byzantium, From the Seventh through the Fifteenth Century*, 3 vols (Washington, DC, 2002), 973–1058.

Oikonomides, N., 'The Social Structure of the Byzantine Countryside in the First Half of the Tenth Century', *Symmeikta* 10 (1996): 103–24.

Oikonomides, N., 'Tax Exemptions for the Secular Clergy under Basil II', in J. Chrysostomides (ed.), *Kathegetria: Essays Presented to Joan Hussey on Her 80th Birthday* (London, 1988), 317–26.

Patlagean, É., *Un Moyen Âge grec. Byzance, ixᵉ–xvᵉ siècle* (Paris, 2007).

Rance, P., 'The Date of the Military Compendium of Syrianus Magister (formerly the Sixth-Century Anonymus Byzantinus)', *BZ* 100 (2007): 701–37.

Saradi, H., 'On the "Archontike" and "Ekklesiastike Dynasteia" and "Prostasia" in Byzantium with Particular Attention to the Legal Sources: A Study in Social History of Byzantium', *Byz* 64 (1994): 69–117.

Smyrlis, K., 'The Fiscal Revolution of Alexios I Komnenos: Timing, Scope, and Motives', in J. C. Cheynet and B. Flusin (eds), *Autour du* Premier humanisme byzantin *et des* Cinq études sur le xiᵉ siècle, *quarante ans après Paul Lemerle*, *TM* 21/2 (2017): 593–610.

Smyrlis, K., *La fortune des grands monastères byzantins, fin du xe–milieu du xive siècle* (Paris, 2006).

Smyrlis, K., 'Private Property and State Finances: The Emperor's Right to Donate his Subjects' Land in the Comnenian Period', *BMGS* 33/2 (2009): 115–32.

Smyrlis, K., 'Sybaris on the Bosporos: Luxury, Corruption and the Byzantine State under the Angeloi (1185–1203)', in A. Simpson (ed.), *Byzantium, 1180–1204: 'The Sad Quarter of a Century'?* (Athens, 2015), 159–78.

Smyrlis, K., 'Wooing the Petty Elite: Privilege and Imperial Authority in Byzantium, Thirteenth-mid Fourteenth Century', in O. Delouis,

S. Métivier and P. Pagès (eds), *Le saint, le moine et le paysan. Mélanges d'histoire byzantine offerts à Michel Kaplan* (Paris, 2016), 657–82.

Tinnefeld, F. H., *Kategorien der Kaiserkritik in der byzantinischen Historiographie von Prokop bis Niketas Choniates* (Munich, 1971).

Triantaphyllopoulos, K., 'Die Novelle 56 Leos des Weisen und ein Streit über das Meeresufer im 11. Jahrhundert', in *Festschrift Paul Koschaker* (Weimar, 1939; repr. Leipzig, 1977), 309–32.

4

Beyond Religion: Homilies as Conveyors of Political Ideology in Middle Byzantium

Theodora Antonopoulou

Political ideology in its various manifestations in the East Roman or Byzantine Empire has been the focus of excellent studies by eminent Byzantinists such as H. Hunger, H.-G. Beck, H. Ahrweiler and G. Dagron, to name but a few.[1] In this study, I will focus on a specific group of literary works, namely homilies, which have largely remained outside or in the margins of relevant investigations, since the existence of a political message in these religious texts *par excellence* is not self-evident. In particular, I will deal with middle Byzantine homilies, here defined as those produced between shortly before Iconoclasm began and the year 1204, in order to investigate to what extent, in what ways and for which purposes they transmitted elements of political ideology. I am not, however, going to present an exhaustive study of the chosen topic, or even a detailed list of passages related to ideology, since this is a vast subject indeed. Necessarily, the current presentation will be restricted to a few cases, such as Germanos I, Photios, Leo VI, Constantine VII Porphyrogennetos, Philagathos Kerameus and Theodosios Goudeles, that underline the significance of this genre for ideological issues on the basis of the information provided therein.

Contrary to research on the early Byzantine period, where political views in patristic homilies have been explored in more detail,[2] so far the literature concerning the middle period has been limited. For example, in my book on the homilies of Emperor Leo VI, published in 1997, I included a chapter on the political ideology expressed in those texts. In an article that

---

[1] See, in particular, Hunger, *Prooimion*; Ahrweiler, *Idéologie politique*; Beck, *Das byzantinische Jahrtausend*, 78–108; Dagron, *Empereur et prêtre*; also, see the studies gathered by Hunger (ed.), *Das byzantinische Herrscherbild*.

[2] See especially Dvornik, *Political Philosophy*, 2:683–99 (part of ch. 11: 'Political Speculation from Constantine to Justinian') on Gregory of Nazianzos, Gregory of Nyssa, Basil of Caesarea and John Chrysostom.

appeared in the same year, Antonio Garzya examined a homily by Philagathos Kerameus in relation to terms denoting political ideology.[3] There
are also scattered notes concerning individual works, but no systematic
study of the topic has appeared. Nevertheless, a number of studies on the
ideology of other religious texts have seen the light of day, with ideological
issues in hagiography – a genre closely related to homiletics – being more
familiar in scholarly literature, as in the cases of the *Synaxarion of Constantinople* and certain Lives of saints.[4] It is noteworthy that the importance
of homiletics as a source of ideology has become apparent in studies of
western medieval Europe, for example in relation to the promotion of the
Crusades.[5]

At this point comes a *caveat*: I will not argue that, generally speaking,
Byzantine homilies tell us something about the essence of the political ideology of the empire that we do not already know from elsewhere; nevertheless,
by providing some examples under a joint heading, I intend to underline that
these texts can be important for the study of ideology. In this framework, a
number of issues could be worth investigating in detail, but can only cursorily, if at all, be touched upon here. These issues could include, for example:
the extent to which the final prayer for the reigning emperor and the imperial
family was a commonplace; whether ideologies as well as identities in the
homilies were differentiated according to the author, or contained a consistent message, even with superficial variations; whether the texts conveyed
regional identity or a sense of local pride; and how these views relate to the
ideal portrait of the emperor which emerged from the Mirrors of Princes and
the *prooimia* and entered into the documents, as well as how they insist on
the qualities prescribed or mentioned in them.[6]

As I have noted in the past, homilies were a very effective and far-reach-
ing means of spreading political propaganda,[7] whether in the form of official imperial propaganda or simply propagation of the imperial idea. Due to
their wide audience, ranging from the common people to the upper strata

---

[3] Antonopoulou, *Homilies of Leo VI*, 72–80 (ch. I.5); Garzya, 'Cultura politica'.
[4] For the former, see Luzzi, 'L'ideologia costantiniana', esp. 199, arguing that the
Synaxarion 'even had the function of spreading imperial ideology'; Odorico,
'Idéologie politique'. For the latter, see, e.g., Odorico, 'Ideologia religiosa' on the
Life of St Eupraxia; Bourdara, 'Modèle', on the Life of St Euphrosyne.
[5] See Maier, *Preaching the Crusades*; *Crusade Propaganda*.
[6] On the ideal emperor according to the Byzantine Mirrors of Princes, see the useful
overviews by Paidas, Θεματική; Ἰκάτοπτρα ἡγεμόνος'. For the *prooimia*, see Hunger,
Prooimion.
[7] See Antonopoulou, *Homilies of Leo VI*, 44.

of society to the emperor himself, and including both laymen and ecclesiastics, the ideology contained in them assumes a special role in the political-
ideological formation of the audience. However, within the homiletic genre
some differentiations should be made, which may affect this investigation.
Catecheses addressed to monks will not be examined, since by their very
nature and audience they do not offer material useful for our purposes (an
exception being those of Theodore of Stoudios, which concern the iconoclastic controversy and which are a case in themselves). The same holds true
for the main body of hagiographical encomia, especially those on martyrs,
in which we encounter ample discourse between the martyr and the per-
secuting emperor, who is depicted in the darkest of colours. This negative
paradigm is explicated not only with regard to Roman times, but also in the
image of the iconoclast emperors in the encomia of iconophile saints. The
emperor is depicted as impious, arrogant and an ally of the Muslims, an
approach also known from hagiographical Lives and chronography. On the
contrary, it will be more instructive for the kind of evidence we are looking
for if we survey especially, though not exclusively, the homilies of historical interest, namely those displaying a connection with specific historical
events, circumstantial discourses and panegyrics of special feasts. Other
kinds of sermons also supplement the picture, particularly insofar as they
contain references to the reigning emperor.

Criticism of the Emperor

I will start with a perhaps unexpected issue. Despite the famous precedent of John Chrysostom, who criticised Empress Eudoxia in his sermons,
one does not usually encounter criticism of or opposition to the reigning
emperor in the homilies of the period under consideration. Of course, it is
possible – although we are not in a position to know – that a homily was
ridden of such elements following its initial public delivery with a view to
posterity, or that open criticism has been preserved in the surviving versions of homilies in cases where opponents of specific imperial policies
eventually prevailed, most notably following Iconoclasm. However, it is,
in general, surprising to find relevant evidence, whether explicit or tacit.

The latter appears to be the case regarding a homily in honour of the
Theotokos, attributed, probably correctly, to Patriarch Germanos I, a
'laudatory and thanksgiving discourse' (λόγος ἐγκωμιαστικὸς ἅμα καὶ
εὐχαριστήριος), according to the title, for the deliverance of Constantinople from the Arab siege of 717–18. The end of the siege coincided with
the feast of the Dormition of the Theotokos, while the enemy fleet was

destroyed in a sudden violent tempest. These facts, the orator says, are proof of the miraculous intervention of the Virgin Mary, to whose protection alone he attributes the salvation of the city. The editor of the sermon, V. Grumel, noted the absence of the emperor from this discourse and the absolute silence concerning his part in the deliverance of the city from the enemies. He attributed this silence to the patriarch's dispute with Emperor Leo III over the issue of icons and suggested a plausible dating to the tenth anniversary of the siege, in 728.[8] Subsequently, P. Speck expressed doubts over the authenticity of the sermon, at least in part, and dated it to the end of the ninth century, mainly for stylistic reasons.[9] J. Darrouzès, while accepting that 'nothing in the content obliges us' to accept Germanos as the author, avoided taking a position on the 'exact origin of the homily', suggesting, on the contrary, that the attribution to Germanos was based on the existence of an authentic narration on the siege.[10] Later on, D. R. Reinsch proposed that the sermon could well be authentic or, at least, was composed by an anonymous contemporary preacher and later attributed to Germanos on account of his authority.[11] Regardless of who the author was,

---

[8] Germanos I, *Homily on the Akathist* (*CPG* 8014), ed. and tr. Grumel. See Kazhdan, *History*, 59–64; Stavrianos, Γερμανός Α΄, 101–2, offers no new insights. Germanos speaks of the annual feast of the deliverance of the city, on which the oration was pronounced; see par. 17, ed. Grumel, 195: ἧς (sc. σωτηρίας) ὑπόμνημα τὴν παροῦσαν αὐτῆς ἐτησίως ἱερὰν πανήγυριν, καὶ πρὸς Θεὸν ὑμνῳδίαν πάννυχον ἄγωμεν. Grumel, 'Homélie', 186, 190, argued that the homily was preached on the feast of the Dormition of the Virgin (15 August), the actual day of the deliverance of the city from its enemies, as stated in the majority of manuscripts; that the oration was later destined for the feast of the Akathist, on Saturday of the fifth week of Lent, when all three failed sieges of Constantinople were celebrated, and that it contains no trace of the *Akathist Hymn*. In my view, however, the last assertion is erroneous, since the very beginning of this homily (par. 1, ed. Grumel, 191: Πᾶσα μὲν ἀνθρώπων γλῶσσά τε καὶ διάνοια ἡττᾶται τῶν ἐγκωμίων τῆς ἀληθῶς ὑπερενδόξου καὶ προσκυνητῆς θεομήτορος) recalls the *Akathist*, in particular Letter Υ, vv. 1–2, ed. Trypanis, 38: Ὕμνος ἅπας ἡττᾶται συνεκτείνεσθαι σπεύδων | τῷ πλήθει τῶν πολλῶν οἰκτιρμῶν σου. On the Akathist feast, see Hurbanic, 'The So-Called Feast of Akathistos'.

[9] Namely, in the words of Darrouzès, 'Deux textes', 7, because of the 'atticistic prose of the text', which 'does not accord with that' of Germanos. Speck, 'Klassizismus', had argued that no classicism existed in the eighth century. However, see below, n. 11.

[10] Darrouzès, 'Deux textes', 7–8. In fact, he published an extract from what appears to have been an authentic sermon of the patriarch on the subject (fragment from *Sermon on the Siege*, *CPG* 8017, ed. Darrouzès, 11–13).

[11] Reinsch, 'Literarische Bildung', 43–5, convincingly rejecting Speck's arguments and offering evidence for the high rhetorical formation of preachers in the late seventh and early eighth centuries.

whether the homily was genuinely by Germanos or contains an authentic kernel or was due to an unknown contemporary, the author's political stance can be described as the *damnatio memoriae* of the iconoclast emperor. Of course, the gravity of this stance differed somewhat according to whether the person responsible for the *damnatio* was the famous patriarch of the time or a lesser preacher. However, from the point of view of later audiences, who heard the homily in a church or monastery under Germanos' name, the impious emperor was effaced. And this fact was the real victory of the patriarch.

In a contrasting case, after a major catastrophe such as the sack of a city following the apparent failure of governmental apparatus to protect the citizens,[12] the reaction of the preacher could be completely detached from any political message, with the disaster being attributed to divine retribution for human sin. This was the case for Patriarch Nicholas I Mystikos' homily in the aftermath of the sack of Thessaloniki by the Arabs in 904, which makes no mention of the emperor whatsoever. This attitude only confirms that homilies were not a medium to exercise open criticism of an orthodox emperor, whose image should remain intact.

This was not always the case, however. The little-known homilies of the anonymous author of the *Theognosia*, who is now identified as none other than Metrophanes of Smyrna, a fierce opponent of Photios, crossed the accepted borderline.[13] Two of these works (nos 5 and 7) reveal that the preacher was a partisan of Nicholas I Mystikos in the Tetragamy of Emperor Leo VI, a defender of the canons and of morality, and that he joined those bishops who opposed the acceptance of the emperor's fourth marriage. At one point in Homily 7, he even attacked the emperor, speaking of the tyranny which urged people to commit illegal actions. Perhaps his views were the reason for the elimination of the prolific author's name from the homilies.[14]

It was even possible for internal enemies of the emperor to be referred to negatively in a sermon. In this respect, special mention should be made of Emperor Leo VI's Homily 29, delivered at the beginning of Lent 904 in front of a restricted audience at the Magnaura. Towards the end of his

[12] Cf. Tsiaples, 'Πολιορκίες και αλώσεις'.

[13] Metrophanes of Smyrna, *Homilies*, ed. Hansmann; on the author and his work, see Van Deun, 'La chasse aux trésors'; also Antonopoulou, 'Survey', 10–11.

[14] On these matters, see Antonopoulou, 'Homiletic Activity', 336–9. For the attack on the emperor, see *Homilies*, no. 7, ed. Hansmann, 244.12–27; 259.35–260.15; 273.5–274.15; 275.5–277.2.

speech, the emperor calls for a traitor, who had attempted to assassinate him in the Church of St Mokios on the day of his feast on 11 May 903, to be brought in before him. In a strange performance, which reminds one of a trial, the emperor plays the role of the judge, counteracting the political act with political, moral and religious arguments, not only accusing the culprit of 'a tyrannical and unjust hand' but also lamenting 'human inclination towards the worst', and being confident that his instigators will be revealed and punished in this life and the afterworld.[15]

Disseminating Imperial Ideology

I now come to the second issue of this chapter, the positive expression of political, more specifically imperial, ideology in homilies. A few significant examples from the capital at the highest levels of Church and state will illustrate the case.

Patriarch Photios

Photios' nineteen surviving homilies, which all date from his first period in office and thus from the reign of the Amorian Michael III, are a rich source of imperial ideology, namely of the various elements of the imperial idea. In them we encounter the quintessential features of the emperor as God's representative on earth, which reflect the long traditions of the Greek Mirrors of Princes and imperial oratory. Photios' views are particularly important, given that, on the one hand, he promoted the distinction between the spiritual power of the patriarch and the secular one of the emperor in the first titles of Basil I's legal book of the *Eisagōgē*,[16] and, on the other, that he exercised a great deal of influence over the emperors of the time (Michael III, Basil I and Leo VI). Notably, Photios was probably the author of a Mirror of Princes addressed by Basil I to his son Leo VI,[17] while he also composed a famous letter to the newly baptised Boris-Michael of Bulgaria, the second part of which is paraenetic in character and concerns the qualities he should possess as a Christian ruler.[18]

---

[15] On this homily, see Antonopoulou, *Homilies of Leo VI*, 64–5.

[16] See e.g. the relevant comments by Dagron, *Empereur et prêtre*, 236–42. On the *Eisagōgē*, see Signes Codoñer and Andrés Santos, *Introducción al derecho*, 53–274; Troianos, Πηγές, 240–6; *Quellen*, 191–6.

[17] On the problem of the attribution of the *Paraenetic Chapters (I)*, see Markopoulos, 'Autour des *Chapitres*', 472–4; and again Paidas, Δύο παραινετικά κείμενα, 79–89.

[18] See *Letters*, no. 1 (around 865), ed. Laourdas and Westerink, 1:2–39, esp. 19.560 to the end, with Westerink's introduction, ibid. 1:1.

Here, suffice it to present briefly a characteristic and well-known example: the case of Photios' Homily 10 on the inauguration of a palatine church
(that of the Theotokos of the Pharos). The oration was pronounced in 864
in the presence of Michael III and Bardas. It contains an extensive description of the church accompanied by encomia of the emperor and the *kaisar*,
which is a rare combination in a sermon.[19] At the beginning of the oration,
the emperor's wisdom is stressed before a large audience that has gathered
for the inauguration, including the senate and bishops (par. 8): Michael is
called the 'instigator' and 'wise architect' of the celebration; he had 'preconceived in his soul the forms of these things' (namely the church: a Platonic
reference, appropriate for a wise king)[20] and then 'in his great wisdom' created them (par. 1). Photios addresses him as 'most Christ-loving and pious
of emperors', surpassing all his predecessors. Then he refers to the emper-
or's military and foreign-policy accomplishments, his building activity and
his concern for the prosperity of his people. Michael, says the preacher, is
'the all-embracing eye of the universe' (par. 2). At the end of the oration
(par. 8), the emperor is addressed again as 'among emperors most blessed
and beloved of God', and mention is made once again of his wisdom, but
also of the expectation that he rule with 'truth, meekness and righteous-
ness' (a reference to Ps. 44:5). Photios stresses that the emperor was destined from the cradle to rule over God's people under God's guidance.[21]
He goes on to praise the *kaisar*, who was second in rank to the emperor,
for his 'wisdom and intelligence', which surpass those of his predecessors;
he 'received this high office by divine ordinance', while the emperor took
him 'as partner and sharer of the imperial dignity for the salvation of the
subjects'. It is through both of them that the Holy Trinity extends 'to all Her
providence, steers wisely and governs Her subjects'.

On the whole, the divine provenance of imperial power, the qualities of
rulership of a Christian emperor (especially justice and the concern for his
people, his building activity and his triumphs over the enemies, his piety
and role in the salvation of God's people), the participation of the emperor
in the world of ideas, the belief in God's wisdom and architecture of the
universe, and the very idea of the *oikoumenē* are essential constituents of
the imperial idea. But these are not all. In another homily, another element of imperial encomia, the emperor's role in the battle against heresies,

---

[19] *Homilies*, no. 10, ed. Laourdas, 99–104 (for the *ekphrasis*, see pars 3–7, ibid. 100–3);
tr. Mango, 184–90.
[20] As rightly observed by Laourdas, Φωτίου Ὁμιλίαι, 61*.
[21] *Homilies*, no. 10, tr. Mango, 189.

is underlined (Homily 18, par. 2 on the synod of 867). In addition, in the prayer for the emperor, which concludes some of his other homilies, Photios seizes the opportunity to return to the concept of the ideal emperor and pray for him to be victorious against his enemies and merciful towards his subjects, or the 'Roman race', as the preacher calls the people.[22] In short, in his homilies Photios took every opportunity to promote the notion of the ideal Christian emperor among his audience and before the emperor and the highest authorities of the state. The 'theory of the two powers' put forward in the *Eisagōgē* does not make its appearance in these earlier texts.

Leo VI the Wise

My second example is Leo VI, whose impressive surviving corpus of forty-two sermons poses the question of whether homilies were political texts. Given that the preacher was a political figure, in this case at the very top of the state, it would be a great surprise if politics and ideology were left out of the religious framework completely. An analysis of the content of the homilies reveals that these primarily religious works are, indeed, on a secondary level, political works, insofar as they intentionally transmit multifarious elements of the imperial ideology. As I have dealt with the issue in detail in my study of the homilies,[23] I will mention only some indicative points here.

In the tradition of his teacher Photios' homilies, which Leo imitated in various aspects of his own sermons, the majority of these texts were preached in the Constantinopolitan churches and communicated traditional official ideology to the masses that frequented them. The people heard the emperor as he concluded his sermons by speaking of the duties

---

[22] As in *Homilies*, no. 11, par. 9 on Holy Saturday, tr. Mango, 212: 'Let Christ our God . . . adorn all the more with piety and the other virtues him to whom He has granted to reign on earth in His stead, and show him worthy of the heavenly kingdom'; or in *Homilies*, no. 2, par. 15, tr. Mango, 73: 'let Him also, who has brought to light our Christ-loving and pious emperor to be provident for the Roman race, and anointed him with the imperial unction, adorn him all the more with virtues, and make him walk unswervingly and unhesitatingly in the way of truth, showing him invincible to all the enemies, merciful to subjects, and worthy of his empire'. See also *Homilies*, no. 5, par. 8; no. 6, par. 10; no. 7, par. 8; no. 12, par. 10 (see Laourdas, Φωτίου Ὁμιλίαι, 61* n. 7). On the issue of *romanitas* in Byzantium, see Stouraitis, 'Roman Identity'; and on a political-ideological level, Kaldellis, *Byzantine Republic*.

[23] Antonopoulou, *Homilies of Leo VI*, 72–80. For a critical edition, see Leo VI, *Homilies*, ed. Antonopoulou.

derived from his office, which God Himself had granted him in order to take care of His rational flock and lead it to safety on earth and salvation in the afterlife. The emperor is not only a shepherd but also the governor of the ship of the state and a father to the people. In return, he asks for the people's affection and adherence to his advice. Occasionally, Leo recognises the limitations of his power and shows some humility. Justice and philanthropy are further imperial attributes. The emperor compares himself explicitly with David and Solomon, and implicitly with Constantine the Great.

Other orations were performed in the palace and various religious locations on special occasions with a religious aspect. For example, two orations on the inauguration of churches (Homilies 31 and 37) have come down to us, which include famous descriptions of buildings no longer extant, exactly as was the case with Photios' Homily 10. These *ekphrases* are connected in the same sermons with *ekphrases* of spring, which, in turn, are most probably connected with the theme of imperial renovation. This theme was, in P. Magdalino's words, 'heavily exploited in the dynastic propaganda of the Macedonian emperors'.[24]

Since Leo is the emperor himself, his homilies are a unique case of a group of texts that allows a direct appreciation of an emperor's ideas about the relationship of the imperial office with the religious sphere. As I have noted in the past,

> the phrasing of the titles of the Homilies (ἐν Χριστῷ βασιλεῖ βασιλεύς) proclaimed the imperial power as the mirror of divine power. Leo wanted to implant this idea into the people's conscience. Through the Homilies he could reach out to a wide public and gain acknowledgment of his Orthodoxy and his ability in theological discussions, and, above all, emphasise his being the 'chosen one' for the throne.[25]

Moreover, it is probably no coincidence that no texts by Leo's brother, Patriarch Stephen I, or by his predecessor, Antony II Kauleas, survive. Not much is known about the former's education, but it seems that Photios was also his tutor. It would not be implausible to suggest that in a way Leo usurped the patriarch's role as the sole spiritual guide of the 'chosen people'.

---

[24] Magdalino, 'Bath of Leo the Wise', 105; see also ibid. 112–13; further on the theme of renovation, see Antonopoulou, *Homilies of Leo VI*, 79–80; and, especially, Antonopoulou, 'Leo VI and the "First Byzantine Humanism"'; on *ekphrases* of spring in general, see Loukaki, *Ekphrasis earos*.

[25] Antonopoulou, *Homilies of Leo VI*, 76–7; see also, Flusin, 'L'empereur hagiographe', 30–41, 52–4; and, recently, Riedel, *Leo VI*, for an overview of the religious dimension of Leo's imperial authority on the basis of his works.

Constantine VII Porphyrogennetos

Leo's son, Emperor Constantine VII, followed in his father's footsteps in his own homiletic oeuvre. Four sermons are related in some way to his name, although he may have had ghost-writers or helping hands in this endeavour; three homilies are attributed to him in (part of) the manuscript tradition and a fourth through persuasive recent arguments. In my view, his familiarity with homiletic rhetoric certainly influenced the overtly religious tone of his two military harangues (especially Harangue 2), which exceeds the relevant prescriptions for the genre as set out by Syrianos, Constantine's direct rhetorical model.[26] From his homilies, all of which have a political and ideological dimension, it emerges that Constantine and those in his environment shared in Leo's belief in the political function of homilies.

The two orations on the translations of the relics of St Gregory of Nazianzos and St John Chrysostom, respectively, which he delivered personally,

> were aimed at the celebration of the emperor's seizure of power from the relatives of his wife. The end of the struggle on 27 January 945 coincided with the relevant feasts in the same month, so that Constantine could consider his favourite saints as his patrons.[27]

Both sermons must have been delivered in the Church of the Holy Apostles, but the audience is not specified. Towards the end of the sermon on Gregory, in words that remind one of Leo, Constantine attributes to Gregory his own reign over Christ's beloved inheritance.[28] Gregory is the defender of the empire; he nourished the emperor with his words, and with his prayers protected him and seated him on the imperial throne of his father. In turn, the emperor prays to the saint for the longevity of his reign and dynasty (τοῦ γένους καὶ τοῦ κράτους).

Regarding the other two sermons (the so-called 'narration' on the translation of Christ's image not-made-by-human-hands from Edessa to

---

[26] On the importance placed by Syrianos on the religious sentiment of the army and Constantine's treatment of and insistence on the issue, see Markopoulos, 'Ideology of War', 52–4; also McGeer, 'Two Military Orations', 123, suggesting that Constantine even applied the structure of a homily to his Harangue 2.

[27] On Constantine's homilies, see Flusin, 'Panégyrique', 11–12; Flusin, 'L'empereur hagiographe', 50–4; Antonopoulou, 'Survey', 18–21, esp. 19, for the quotation cited here.

[28] Sermon on the Translation of Gregory the Theologian, par. 44–5, ed. Flusin, 77–9: ὁ διὰ σοῦ βασιλεύων ἐγὼ τῆς ἠγαπημένης Χριστοῦ κληρονομίας.

Constantinople in 944, and the homily on St Peter's chains), which could at least have been composed under Constantine's guidance or patronage, they both contain prayers for the emperor. The former sermon commemorated an event which occurred under Romanos I Lekapenos, but it was delivered on the feast day of 16 August, perhaps in 945, after Constantine had become sole emperor. It connects in eternity the translation of the relic with Constantine, 'the pious and mild emperor' according to the final prayer, who is celebrating the event and whom the holy relic by its presence elevated to the throne of his grandfather and father.[29] The preacher also prays that the emperor's son may succeed his father, as well as for peace in the state and for the safety of the reigning city. The significance of peace is also underlined in an earlier lengthy passage, where the preacher expresses his belief in the ecumenicity and autocracy of the old Roman Empire, thanks to which peace reigned when Jesus came to earth.[30] As for the latter of these two sermons, the feast of St Peter's chains was celebrated on 16 January, another January feast, close to the dates of Constantine's sermons on the two translations. The historical framework of all four sermons could have been the same.[31] In the epilogue, which may have been the product of some reworking, a political message similar to that in the previous sermons is conveyed, with the preacher praying to St Peter for 'our most pious emperor' to be victorious against the enemies and beloved by the people so that they may live in peace under his rule.[32]

On another ideological and political level, there is in the same sermon a telling comparison between Old and New Rome which places them on a par with each other. According to the preacher, St Peter literally 'distributed himself' evenly between the two cities, since he left his relics in Old Rome, while the chains (the symbols of his martyrdom) and his knife were left to the reigning city, Constantinople.[33] It should be noted that, as made clear in the sermon,[34] the relics in question lay in the palace oratory dedicated to St Peter; significantly, this was built by the founder of the dynasty,

---

[29] *Narration on the Image of Edessa*, par. 65, ed. Illert, 308–10: ὦ θεῖον ὁμοίωμα . . . σῷζε καὶ φρούρει ἀεὶ τὸν εὐσεβῶς καὶ πράως ἡμῶν βασιλεύοντα καὶ τὴν τῆς σῆς ἐπιδημίας ἀνάμνησιν λαμπρῶς ἑορτάζοντα, ὃν τῇ παρουσίᾳ σου ἐπὶ τὸν παππῷον καὶ πατρῷον θρόνον ἀνύψωσας.

[30] Ibid. par. 4, 262–4.

[31] Antonopoulou, 'Survey', 20–1.

[32] *Sermon on the Chains of St Peter*, par. 54, ed. Batareikh, 1005.20–5.

[33] Ibid. par. 40, 997.21–4: ἑαυτὸν . . . διανεῖμαι καὶ συμμετρήσασθαι, καὶ Ῥώμῃ μὲν τῇ παλαιᾷ . . . τῇ δὲ βασιλευούσῃ καὶ νέᾳ; see also par. 52, 1003.30–1004.1.

[34] Ibid. par. 49, 1002.5–14.

Basil I, and was the place where the homily was delivered. The collection of relics in the capital and in the palace (from the outset and, in particular, under the Macedonians) and their ideological significance have been analysed repeatedly in scholarly literature.[35]

Imperial Ideology Beyond the Empire: Philagathos Kerameus

Nowhere is the role of homilies as a medium of political-ideological correctness made clearer than in those homilies of the Byzantine tradition that were preached outside the empire; in this respect, too, these bear comparison to the orations analysed so far. This is the case with the monk Philagathos Kerameus (d. 1154 or later), who lived in the Norman kingdom of Sicily in the last quarter of the eleventh century.[36] He preached in Calabria, especially in the Archbishopric of Rossano, and in various places in Sicily, including Panormos (Palermo). His reputation as an orator led him to preach in the presence of King Roger II (1130–54), as testified by his Homily 50 on Palm Sunday, delivered in the old cathedral of Panormos 'before the *rex*'.[37] Moreover, Homily 27, delivered in the Palatine Chapel, which had been consecrated recently, on 28 April (probably 1140), includes a famous early description of it and praises the king in exalted terms.[38]

---

[35] See e.g. Kalavrezou, 'Helping Hands', 67–79; Flusin, 'Construire'; Mergiali-Sahas, 'Byzantine Emperors'; Klein, 'Sacred Relics', 91–3.

[36] The scholarly literature on Philagathos is extensive, underlining his excellent knowledge of the Scriptures and the Church Fathers; however, it often expresses opposing views as to his profane literary culture and consequently its testimony to Greek culture in Calabria and Sicily in his time. On the one hand, a case has been made in favour of extensive profane readings of his, whereas, on the other, arguments have been put forward against an extensive, direct use of non-Christian sources, especially taking into account the book culture of his environment. For a bibliography on both approaches, see Antonopoulou, 'Philagathos Kerameus', esp. 125–7 with nn. 29–30, where I incline towards the latter view in anticipation of a critical edition of all of Philagathos' homilies combined with a thorough search of their sources. On the present publication status of Philagathos' homilies, see Bianchi, 'Prospetto'; see also n. 38 below for another publication of part of Homily 27.

[37] *Homilies*, no. 50, *PG* 132:541–9 (no. 26), esp. 541b title: ἐλέχθη δὲ ἐνώπιον τοῦ ῥηγὸς Ῥόγου.

[38] *Homilies*, no. 27, ed. Rossi Taibbi, 174–82; *ekphrasis*: pars 1–3, ibid. 174–5; also published in Johns, 'Date', 13–14, with an excellent English translation. For the use of the description in art-historical examinations of the Chapel, see, apart from the article just cited, Tronzo, *Cultures*, passim (see index); Brenk (ed.), *Cappella Palatina*, vol. I: *Saggi*, passim and, in particular, Crostini, 'Iscrizione', 194–6.

Another homily (no. 52) contains in the epilogue a prayer for his successor, King William I (1154–66).[39]

These texts are an unequivocal testimony to the fact, also known from other sources, that the Byzantine tradition of imperial ideology was to some extent continued in the empire's former Italian territories, where the Byzantine emperors had been substituted by the Norman kings.[40] It has repeatedly been noticed that Philagathos applied the terms *basileus* and *basileia* to the Norman kings and their regime, though they themselves used the term *rex* in their documents. Antonio Garzya justified this title by reference to Philagathos' writing from the viewpoint of the periphery and because *rex* was a Latin term unsuitable for high rhetoric in Greek.[41] This is certainly true, yet the connection to the original application of the term to the Byzantine emperor cannot be underestimated, while Philagathos was not alone in this usage in the Norman kingdom.[42]

[39] *Homilies*, no. 52, ed. Caruso, 123.71–3; cf. Rossi Taibbi, *Filagato da Cerami*, p. LV. See Gigante, 'Problema Filagato', 637, for a general reference to the pagan rhetorical tradition behind this epilogue.

[40] On some elements of imperial ideology in Philagathos' works, see Pertusi, 'Aspetti letterari', 82–4; Garzya, 'Cultura politica', on Homily 27; Houben, 'Predicazione', 267–8, and Laitsos, '"Imitatio Basilei"?', 7, 22–4, on Homilies 27 and 50. For further, brief references to Philagathos in secondary literature mostly concerned with Norman political culture and/or its Byzantine tradition, see the bibliography cited below, n. 42.

[41] Garzya, 'Cultura politica', 243. For the latter point, see also von Falkenhausen, 'Κόμης', 90–1, with reference to Philagathos' homilies, among other literary texts from Norman times.

[42] On the political importance of a pre-Norman quasi-parallel, the use of the term *basileus* by St Nilos of Rossano for Otto III, see Peters-Custot, *Grecs de l'Italie*, 144. On Roger II's exclusive use of the title *rex* and the simultaneous occurrence of the words βασιλικός, βασιλεύειν and βασιλεία mainly in Greek private documents, see von Falkenhausen, 'Κόμης', 88–91; also, von Falkenhausen, 'Graeco-Byzantine Heritage', 71–2: 'For his Greek subjects, the Norman king had the function of a *basileus*', with reference, among other texts, to Philagathos' homilies. For relevant studies, which often include brief mentions of Philagathos, see also Pertusi, 'Aspetti letterari', 98–101; Brown, 'Political Use', 205–6; Houben, *Roger II*, 107–8, 134, 182; Britt, 'Roger II', esp. 31–2; Enzensberger, 'Tecniche di governo' (e.g. 18–19 on coins in Byzantine style); Rognoni, 'Donazioni', esp. 21; Puccia, 'Anonimo *Carme*', 240–1, 244, 254–5; Burkhardt, 'Sicily's Imperial Heritage', esp. 155; Acconcia Longo, 'Letteratura italo-greca', 120 n. 65. On ideology in Norman royal documents and its connection with the Byzantine tradition, see e.g. Garzya, 'Cultura politica', passim; Laitsos, '"Imitatio Basilei"?' 7–18; von Falkenhausen, 'Diploma greco'. On Roger's political ideology in general, see Tocco, *Ruggero II*, 99–107.

In Philagathos' own words in Homily 27, pronounced on the feast of saints Peter and Paul (par. 1, 175), the causes of the *panēgyris* celebrated in the Palatine Chapel are firstly God, the fountain of all goodness, then the emperor, who is pious, a saviour and benevolent towards his subjects, saving his wrath for his opponents. He is the provider of magnificence (to the people), defeating with his piety and magnanimity all present and previous rulers, like a sun defeats the shining stars. Surpassing these achievements, he has added one more feature to his imperial and great soul: the building of the most pleasant temple of the Disciples. In the epilogue (par. 26, p. 182), Philagathos addresses his dear audience (ἀγαπητοί), whom he asks to pray that the power of their pious emperor be preserved for many years to come because he steers the wheel of the state with piety, adorns the crown with his words and is adorned with the kindness of his manners, so that his virtue justly gains him praise. Garzya correctly observed the affinity of the characteristics applied to Roger with those of the Byzantine emperor in accordance with the imperial idea, as testified by the writings of Synesios and Themistios down to the documents issued by the emperors of the east: providence, piety, salvation of the people, benevolence, victories against the enemies, benefactions, munificence, magnanimity, serenity, peace, his comparison to the sun and the comparison of the state to a ship.[43] These qualities are also encountered in the homilies of Photios and Leo VI, as mentioned above. In addition, I have argued elsewhere that the *ekphrasis* of the palatine church contained in this sermon was inspired by the church *ekphrases* embedded in the homilies of Leo VI, Homily 37 in particular. In this way,

> the distinctive setting of the delivery of the suggested model furnishes a further new ideological dimension to the speech of Philagathos, to whom it would have seemed suitable to transfer the Constantinopolitan literary and imperial framework of the church *ekphrasis* to the court at Panormos.[44]

Furthermore, in Homily 50 (*PG* 132:541C), delivered on Palm Sunday 1131 in the presence of Roger II and his sons, Philagathos mentions the participation of bishops, clerics and crowds of common people in the celebrations (τῇ παμπληθεῖ δημαγωγίᾳ). In the opening part of the sermon, Philagathos praises the pious emperor, whose virtues and God-sanctioned victories and trophies have been and will be dealt with in other writings.

---

[43] Garzya, 'Cultura politica', 243–7.
[44] Antonopoulou, 'Philagathos Kerameus', esp. 125 for the quotation.

In the epilogue (549b), he prays for the God-guarded power of the pious emperor to remain unshaken for his sons, to prosper under God, who 'adorned' the emperor with wisdom and fortitude and the imperial sceptre, and to grant him a very long reign.

Such is the picture emerging from Philagathos' sermons that were delivered in an imperial establishment or in the presence of the king in Panormos. Whether and to what extent Roger, the majority of whose documents were composed in Greek by his chancery, actually understood the discourse is unknown; however, his comprehension of Greek should not be ruled out, given that he was born and grew up in environments where Greek culture was predominant.[45] As for the other members of the audience, only some of them, namely those who were native speakers of Greek and/or were educated in Greek, would have been in a position to appreciate Philagathos' rhetoric.

Similar references by Philagathos are also found in other sermons of his which had no regal connections and addressed the people alone. In one of his homilies on Palm Sunday, the above-mentioned Homily 52, which he delivered in Messene (Messina), Philagathos asks his audience to pray that the reign of their 'pious *basileus*, the most powerful *rex* William (I),'[46] be preserved for many years to come, and that his enemies might be humiliated under his feet. The presence of both terms, *basileus* and *rex*, side by side is striking, since the former is used as part of the traditional formula of prayer for the Byzantine emperor, while the second is William's title proper. In another homily on Palm Sunday (Homily 53), delivered in the cathedral of Rhegion (Reggio-Calabria), Philagathos asks his audience of men, women and children to pray for their pious emperor (he does not name him this time, but it must be the same William) so that God may preserve his glory, prudence and bravery, safeguard his power by crushing the Hagarenes under his feet like dust and keep his dominion in stability,

---

[45] See Houben, *Mezzogiorno normanno-svevo*, 222, on Roger being born in Calabria; Houben, *Roger II*, 30; see also ibid. 27, 29 on the apparently 'great impact' of Byzantine Greek culture and religiosity on his mother Adelheid, who was residing with her son in the mainly Greek city of Messina. On the language of Roger's documents as well as for his Greek signature, which was the work of his officials, see ibid. 114, with bibliography. On Roger's acquaintance with Greek, see ibid. 106. See also Metcalfe, *Muslims and Christians*, 103–4 with 249; von Falkenhausen, 'Graeco-Byzantine Heritage', 63–4, 71.

[46] See *Homilies*, no. 52, ed. Caruso, 123.71–4: διὰ παντὸς ὑπερευξώμεθα ὑπὲρ τοῦ εὐσεβοῦς ἡμῶν βασιλέως, τοῦ κραταιοτάτου ῥηγὸς Γουλιέλμου. On the imperial title *basileus*, see Rösch, *ΟΝΟΜΑ ΒΑΣΙΛΕΙΑΣ*, 37–9; and Zuckermann, 'Titles and Office'.

peace and calmness. The term used this time is *autokratōr*, which stresses the imperial status of the Norman ruler.[47]

It transpires that, in principle, these texts could have been preached anywhere in the Byzantine Empire, since they present the same imperial ideology as Byzantine homilies in general. If the author was unknown, and we left aside specific historical references, we would not be able to guess that he was writing outside the empire. The same Byzantine mentality makes its appearance throughout Philagathos' homilies. For example, in the homily at the beginning of the new indiction year (Homily 1), he explains to his audience the meaning of the term 'indiction' and its Roman origins; he does the same for the month of September, which is called *Gorpiaios* by the Greeks (with reference to the Macedonian calendar), *Thoth* by the Egyptians, *Eual* by the Hebrews and 'September by us, in the Roman tongue' (a reference to the Latin origin of the name).[48] The same attitude is true concerning the external enemies of the state. When praising the Holy Cross (Homily 4), he addresses it with a long series of attributes: among other things, the Cross is the heavenly sceptre, the invincible weapon of the emperors, the power of the Christians to which the preacher prays to 'empower our faithful emperors' so that they can defeat 'the godless Ismaelites who defy your cult'.[49] It becomes obvious that the preacher conveys to his Italo-Greek audience a sense of continuity with their Byzantine past. To achieve this, he makes no reference to either the change of rulers in Sicily and southern Italy or the religious schism (if indeed he was aware of it). For him the rulers are Christians and the sole enemies are the Muslims.

Ideological Opposition to the Enemies of the Empire: Theodosios Goudeles

Setting Philagathos' homilies aside, the employment of elements of the Byzantine imperial idea in the Norman kingdom is also indicated, indirectly, by a homily which has gone unnoticed in this respect. The final

---

[47] See *Homilies*, no. 53, ed. Caruso, 124.5, on the audience; and ibid. 126–7.88–93 for the epilogue, esp. l. 89: ὑπὲρ τοῦ εὐσεβοῦς ἡμῶν αὐτοκράτορος. On *autokratōr/ imperator*, see Rösch, *ONOMA ΒΑΣΙΛΕΙΑΣ*, 35–6; Zuckermann, 'Titles and Office'.

[48] *Homilies*, no. 1, pars 2 and 4, ed. Rossi Taibbi, 3–4: ὁ κατὰ μὲν Ἕλληνας Γορπιαῖος . . . καθ᾽ ἡμᾶς δὲ Ῥωμαϊκῇ γλώττῃ Σεπτέμβριος. On some other issues raised by this homily as well as an English translation of it, see Gaşpar, 'Praising the Stylite'.

[49] *Homilies*, no. 4, par. 23, ed. Rossi Taibbi, 31. On this homily, see Caruso, 'Note', 201–4; on the issue of Philagathos' attitude towards the Muslims, see ibid. as well as the justified criticism by Duluş, 'Philagathos of Cerami', 58 n. 36 (alongside other pertinent remarks on Philagathos' homilies).

issue in the present investigation concerns this homily, namely the encomium of St Christodoulos of Patmos (d. 1093) by Theodosios Goudeles
of Byzantium, which bridges the two worlds, Byzantine and Norman, in
another way, in that it presents the Normans and their political ideology from the point of view of a Byzantine preacher.[50] Theodosios also
comments on recent Byzantine history from a political and ideological
perspective.

The author, a Patmian monk, was the disciple and hagiographer of
Patriarch Leontios of Jerusalem. He was a very learned man, who composed the encomium of Christodoulos sometime after 1195 and before
1204 and delivered it at the Monastery of Patmos on a feast of the saint.
Theodosios was an eyewitness to the Norman raid on the island in October
1186, which forms the core of the encomium (chs 39–119).[51]

According to the encomium, the Normans arrive at Patmos with the
initially hidden purpose of acquiring, or rather snatching, the body of the
founder of the Monastery, St Christodoulos, and carrying it to Sicily. Before
placing their demand on the monks, who will vehemently refuse to surrender the precious relic, a dialogue takes place between the Normans and the
monks. The Norman fleet was led by Megarites or Margarites (Margaritus of
Brindisi), an apparently Italiote Greek, who was bilingual in Greek and Latin
and was appointed admiral by the Norman king William II (1166–89).[52] At
his own request, the admiral was accompanied by an unnamed *dux*, who
must have been Tancred of Lecce. Both deliver speeches to the monks,
which Goudeles reports and which attribute to the Norman king the royal
qualities expected of the Byzantine emperor. By way of passing comments,
Goudeles reacts to these speeches by stressing the legitimacy of the Roman
emperor and the tyranny of the Norman king. Incidentally, he also takes the

[50] On Byzantine views of the Normans and their territories on the basis of other
Byzantine texts, see Gallina, 'Mezzogiorno', with bibliography; also, Koutrakou,
'Eye of Constantinople', 47, where the present text, referred to as a *Life*, is briefly
mentioned as a testimony to the perception of Sicily as a naval power; and Gentile
Messina, 'Rapporti'.

[51] *Encomium of St Christodoulos of Patmos*, ed. Polemis and Antonopoulou; on the
work and related issues, see ibid. 45–53, 63–9, 102–22, as well as the older work of
Vranoussi, Ἁγιολογικὰ κείμενα, 67–80, 140–67. On the events in question, in correlation with the narration of Niketas Choniates, see also Lavagnini, 'Normanni', 324–34.

[52] On Margarites, see Vranoussi, Ἁγιολογικὰ κείμενα, esp. 148 (n. 2)–9, 160–1; on him
and his obscure origins, see further Ménager, *AMIRATUS*, 96–103, who, however,
was not aware of the *Encomium*; also, Polemis and Antonopoulou, *Vitae et Miracula*,
46–7, n. 101; and below, p. 118, with n. 60.

opportunity to speak of recent Roman (Byzantine) history and of tyranny within Byzantium.

According to Goudeles, Megarites was the 'archpirate of the tyrant of Sicily' (ch. 40.1–2: ὁ τοῦ τυράννου Σικελίας ἀρχιπειρατής). The designation of William II as a tyrant is noteworthy, since Roger II, William's grandfather, had already been referred to as a *tyrannus*, with the meaning of a usurper and illegitimate ruler, in some western medieval sources of that time.[53] This sense of 'oppressor of the people' appeared in connection with both Roger and his son and successor, William I.[54] The sources in question mention that the ambassadors of Emperor John II Komnenos referred to Roger as a tyrant,[55] and the same term is used for Roger in Byzantine sources such as John Kinnamos and Niketas Choniates.[56] Choniates also calls William II a tyrant.[57] Thus, Goudeles used a current political term that obviously did not refer to the circumstances of William II's ascent to the throne – which was legitimate by all means – but could be justified by association, due to his being a Norman ruler and a successor of Roger. A reference to the ancient Greek tyrants of Sicily must also have been at play here.[58] More probably, however, the designation of tyranny, with a strong implication of injustice and oppression, must have been linked to the events described in the homily regarding the illegal occupation of Byzantine lands by the Normans, who were imposing and collecting taxes from the islands of the Aegean (ch. 39.4: 'all the Roman islands').[59] The sentiment of enmity caused by these and subsequent events, as narrated by Goudeles, must have been exacerbated by

---

[53] See Wieruszowski, 'Roger II of Sicily', 54–64; also Tounta, 'Perception of Difference', 120–1, 140.

[54] See Wieruszowski, 'Roger II of Sicily', 57, n. 47; also Tounta, 'Perception of Difference', 120.

[55] See Wieruszowski, 'Roger II of Sicily', 60 with n. 62, 63 with nn. 71–2.

[56] John Kinnamos, *Epitomē*, ed. Meineke, 37.15: ὁ τῷ τηνικάδε Σικελίας τυραννῶν Ῥογέριος; ibid. 67.15: τοῦ Σικελίας τυράννου, and passim; Niketas Choniates, *Historia*, ed. van Dieten, 62.90: ὁ ἐκ Σικελίας τύραννος. See Pertusi, 'Aspetti letterari', 96; Schmitt, 'Normannenbild', 173; Koutrakou, 'Eye of Constantinople', 41–3; Gentile Messina, 'Rapporti', 53. See also Tounta, 'Perception of Difference', 127 with n. 50 on Robert Guiscard as a tyrant in Byzantine sources.

[57] See Niketas Choniates, *Historia*, ed. van Dieten, 296.75: εἰς Σικελίαν . . . καὶ τῷ ταύτης τυραννεύοντι Γιλιέλμῳ; ibid. 296.87: τὸν τῶν Σικελῶν τύραννον; ibid. 370.93–4. See also the references in Schmitt, 'Normannenbild', 162 n. 19, 167.

[58] Cf. the discussion in Wieruszowski, 'Roger II of Sicily', 52, n. 29, with reference to the Latin sources; also Tounta, 'Perception of Difference', 140–1.

[59] On these events, see Vranoussi, *Ἁγιολογικὰ κείμενα*, 140–8, 154–9.

the fact that only a year earlier Thessaloniki had been sacked by William's Normans in a brutal attack, an event which, however, is neither mentioned nor implied.

The text relates that the Norman admiral drew his origin from Megara of Attica and that because of his ancestors he was called Megarites, but 'common people who did not know correct Greek privately called him Margarites'.[60] He sailed with his fleet to Cyprus, where 'new Roman misfortunes had sprung up' (chs 40.3–41.3). Goudeles goes out of his way to compose a lengthy passage, where he explains to his audience the political situation in Cyprus at the time. The Roman emperor Isaac II Angelos (1185–95), who was descended from the Angeloi, but was a great-grandson, in the female line, of Alexios I Komnenos, destroyed the tyranny that had befallen the Romans before him because of a relative (namely Andronikos I Komnenos, 1183–5, an uncle of Isaac); in place of the tyrant, he was proclaimed the legitimate king and emperor of the Romans first by the people of Byzantium, then by the Roman army, by all the authorities and by the cities of the empire (ch. 41.3–13). It is obvious that a tyrant was a person who did not ascend legitimately to the throne, a notion used this time to denounce Andronikos, with the accompanying connotations of an unjust and cruel ruler, which also applied to that emperor. Incidentally, Goudeles describes the proclamation of Isaac II, offering information not found in other sources.[61]

The emperor sent a fleet to Cyprus to end the local tyranny of the homonymous apostate, whose genealogy is also provided. Among his distant ancestors, Emperors John II and Manuel I Komnenoi are positively mentioned, the former as the best emperor of the Romans, the latter as being of great repute (ch. 41.13–22). However, the expedition was ill-fated because of the sudden appearance of the Normans (chs 43 and 44). This time, Goudeles calls their king 'the archpirate' (ch. 45.7). On their return from Cyprus, the Norman ships stop at Patmos with the intention of taking with them the relic of Christodoulos. The negative image of the Normans, both their leaders and the soldiers, emerges with remarkable clarity and enmity: their cunning minds, which were set on deceiving the monks, their heavy weaponry, which they carried all the way up the hill to the monastery in order to scare the monks, and their hypocrisy in appearing to revere the

---

[60] Niketas Choniates, *Historia*, ed. van Dieten, 370.88–94, also calls him Μεγαρείτης.

[61] As noted by Vranoussi, Ἁγιολογικὰ κείμενα, 153. On the issue of the proclamation of Byzantine emperors, see Christophilopoulou, Ἐκλογή, esp. 163–6 on Isaac II. On the notion of *tyrannis* in Byzantium, see Bourdara, Καθοσίωσις (867–1056), esp. 131–76; Καθοσίωσις 1056–1081.

monks (chs 46–51). During vespers, Megarites and the *dux* address the monks. Megarites praises his king, the *'rex* of Sicily', in typical Byzantine terms for his ability to choose the right people to serve him, a truly regal virtue. He is wise, clever and a true king, able to judge a person's character by his very appearance, while not wasting words or time, and knows how to reward his able servants (ch. 52.1–8). But according to Goudeles, the two admirals are nothing but 'barbarians'[62] whose barbaric anger scared the monks into praising their words against their will (ch. 58.1–4); the arrogance of the *dux* was only to be expected of a barbarian (ch. 60.3–4). In his second address to the monks, Megarites introduces the demand of the *rex*, speaking 'as the tongue' of the king's 'divine words' (ch. 61.4–5). After the monks have refused to surrender the relic (chs 67 and 68), the leaders of the Normans send their priests together with servants to break up the marble sarcophagus containing the casket of the relic, which they do by applying the utmost violence (chs 69 and 70). Thus, the presentation of the barbarian enemy, whose priests commit sacrilege, culminates.

Whether the Norman speeches are reported with precision by the hagiographer is doubtful, since there is no indication that they were taken down at the moment of delivery. It seems probable that the homilist reworked them from memory. He was careful to draw clear lines between the tyranny and the legitimacy of the Roman emperors, between Romans and barbarians, between those who, like the author, spoke 'this Greek language' (ch. 38.7) and those who did not (ch. 38.9–12: all the others, including the 'barbarians'). He also draws a vivid negative picture of the enemy of the empire, who helped the tyrant of Cyprus against the legitimate emperor and committed sacrilege, for which his fleet would be duly punished by the saint. The speeches also testify to the qualities expected of a ruler, whether Roman or Norman. Goudeles probably anticipated that his audience would be shocked and appalled by the arrogance of the Normans, who even dared apply to their king the qualities of the emperor, repeatedly calling their *rex* 'the most royal/imperial' one (βασιλικώτατος). Such explicit statements on multiple ideological levels are rather unusual for homilies. The fact that the text survives in a unique Byzantine manuscript, in the library of the Monastery of Patmos, testifies to its restricted readership inside the monastery,[63] in whose circles it was produced and whose needs it covered for

---

[62] On the Byzantine notion of barbarians, see Lechner, *Hellenen und Barbaren*, 73–128.

[63] On the manuscript tradition of the text, see Polemis and Antonopoulou, *Vitae et Miracula*, 72–7. Another codex of the eighteenth century is an apograph, while other codices contain vernacular Greek paraphrases.

the purpose of recording the monastery's recent historical past and the miraculous interventions of its founder. Had the homily circulated outside the monastery and entered the liturgical collections, edges might have been smoothed.

Conclusion

From the preceding investigation of a sample of homiletic texts from the middle Byzantine period, it has become clear that it was possible for homilies to reflect political, more specifically imperial, ideology. It may well be argued that in this way the existence of a political message, which was inherent in a large part of ancient oratory, found an appropriate outlet in the ecclesiastical rhetoric of medieval times. Admittedly, such a function was present only to a limited extent and, what is more, had nothing to do, both in principle and originally, with the Christian religion which these texts served. However, at least some of the preachers were eager to employ in their sermons messages in the service of political, specifically imperial, orthodoxy which even went far beyond the standard prayer for the well-being of the emperor. Such an approach was apparently accepted, and certainly tolerated, since it was usually veiled in a religious attire of some sort. The homilies presented in this chapter reveal an array of relevant themes and targets expressed, first and foremost, by preaching emperors or by preachers with close relations to the palace, usually with the purpose of eulogising the emperor; in particular, it is noteworthy that homilies in the Byzantine tradition served the same purpose outside the empire. Furthermore, it emerged that it was possible for homilies to exercise criticism of or opposition to the emperor, whether open or veiled, as well as to express political and ideological views when referring to recent history.

The fact that homilies were a means to convey political ideology in Byzantium ensued precisely because they were an effective means to approach the broader public, both in the contemporary framework and, potentially, in eternity. They constituted a most convenient vehicle for the dominant political ideology to be transferred to the masses and reasserted for the elites, which also formed part of the audience. The solemn religious environment in which homilies were preached assured that their messages were imprinted on the minds of the listeners. In medieval homilies we do not hear the voice of the masses in matters of politics, since these were not the producers but the major recipients of this literature. Significantly, however, we witness a way in which their ideology was formulated by those responsible for their spiritual guidance. Therefore, homilies emerge as one of the few medieval literary genres that bring us directly towards the world of the people at large.

Bibliography

Sources

Akathist Hymn . . . C. A. Trypanis (ed.), *Fourteen Early Byzantine Cantica* (Vienna, 1968), 29–39.

Constantine VII, *Narration on the Image of Edessa* . . . M. Illert (ed.), *Doctrina Addai de imagine edessena. Die Abgarlegende. Das Christusbild von Edessa* (Turnhout, 2007), 260–310.

Constantine VII, *Sermon on the Chains of St Peter* . . . E. Batareikh (ed.), 'Discours inédit sur les Chaînes de S. Pierre attribué à S. Jean Chrysostome', in *Χρυσοστομικά. Studi e ricerche intorno a S. Giovanni Crisostomo a cura del comitato per il XVo centenario della sua morte 407–1907* (Rome, 1908), 973–1005.

Constantine VII, *Sermon on the Translation of Gregory the Theologian* . . . B. Flusin (ed.), 'Le Panégyrique de Constantin VII Porphyrogénète pour la translation des reliques de Grégoire le Théologien (BHG 728)', *RÉB* 57 (1999): 41–81.

Germanos I, *Homily on the Akathist* . . . V. Grumel (ed.), 'Homélie de saint Germain sur la délivrance de Constantinople', *RÉB* 16 (1958): 191–9.

Germanos I, *Sermon on the Siege of Constantinople by Souleiman* . . . J. Darrouzès (ed.), 'Deux textes inédits du patriarche Germain', *RÉB* 45 (1987): 11–13.

John Kinnamos, *Epitomē* . . . A. Meineke (ed.), *Ioannis Cinnami Epitome rerum ab Ioanne et Alexio Comnenis gestarum* (Bonn, 1836).

Leo VI, *Homilies* . . . T. Antonopoulou (ed.), *Leonis VI Sapientis Imperatoris Byzantini Homiliae* (Turnhout, 2008).

Metrophanes of Smyrna, *Homilies* . . . K. Hansmann (ed.), *Ein neuentdeckter Kommentar zum Johannes-evangelium* (Paderborn, 1930).

Niketas Choniates, *Historia* . . . I. A. van Dieten (ed.), *Nicetae Choniatae Historia* (Berlin and New York, 1975).

Philagathos Kerameus, *Homilies* . . . nos 1–35: G. Rossi Taibbi (ed.), *Filagato da Cerami: Omelie per i vangeli domenicali e le feste di tutto l'anno, I. Omelie per le feste fisse* (Palermo, 1969); no. 50: *PG* 132:541–9 (no. 26); nos 51–3: S. Caruso (ed.), 'Le tre omilie inedite "Per la domenica delle palme" di Filagato da Cerami (LI, LII, LIII Rossi Taibbi)', *EEBS* 41 (1974): 109–27.

Photios, *Homilies* . . . B. Laourdas (ed.), *Φωτίου Ὁμιλίαι. Ἔκδοσις κειμένου, εἰσαγωγὴ καὶ σχόλια* (Thessaloniki, 1959); Engl. tr. C. Mango, *The Homilies of Photius, Patriarch of Constantinople. English Translation, Introduction and Commentary* (Cambridge, 1958).

Photios, *Letters* . . . B. Laourdas and L. G. Westerink (eds), *Photii patriarchae Constantinopolitani Epistulae et Amphilochia*, 3 vols (Leipzig, 1983–5).

Theodosios Goudeles, *Encomium of St Christodoulos of Patmos* . . . I. Polemis and T. Antonopoulou (eds), *Vitae et Miracula Sancti Christoduli Patmensis* (Vienna, 2021), 169–213.

Secondary Literature

Acconcia Longo, A., 'La letteratura italogreca nell'XI e XII secolo', in R. Lavagnini and C. Rognoni (eds), *Byzantino-Sicula VI. La Sicilia e Bisanzio nei secoli XI e XII. Atti delle X Giornate di Studio della Associazione Italiana di Studi Bizantini (Palermo, 27–28 maggio 2011)* (Palermo, 2014), 107–30.

Ahrweiler, H., *L'idéologie politique de l'empire byzantin* (Paris, 1975).

Antonopoulou, T., *The Homilies of the Emperor Leo VI* (Leiden, New York and Cologne, 1997).

Antonopoulou, T., 'Homiletic Activity in Constantinople around 900', in M. Cunningham and P. Allen (eds), *Preacher and Audience. Studies in Early Christian and Byzantine Homiletics* (Leiden, Boston and Cologne, 1998), 317–48.

Antonopoulou, T., 'A Survey of Tenth-Century Homiletic Literature', *Parekbolai* 1 (2011): 7–36.

Antonopoulou, T., 'Philagathos Kerameus and Emperor Leo VI: On a Model of the *Ecphrasis* of the Cappella Palatina in Palermo', *Nea Rhome* 12 (2015): 115–27.

Antonopoulou, T., 'Emperor Leo VI the Wise and "The First Byzantine Humanism": On the Quest for Renovation and Cultural Synthesis', in B. Flusin and J.-C. Cheynet (eds), *Autour du Premier humanisme byzantin & des Cinq études sur le XIe siècle, quarante ans après Paul Lemerle = TM* 21/2 (2017): 187–233.

Beck, H.-G., *Das byzantinische Jahrtausend* (Munich, 1978).

Bianchi, N., 'Prospetto e sinossi delle edizioni delle Omelie di Filagato da Cerami', in N. Bianchi with the collaboration of C. Schiano (eds), *La tradizione dei testi greci in Italia meridionale. Filagato da Cerami philosophos e didaskalos. Copisti, lettori, eruditi in Puglia tra XII e XVI secolo* (Bari, 2011), 145–8.

Bourdara, C. A., *Καθοσίωσις καὶ τυραννὶς κατὰ τοὺς μέσους βυζαντινοὺς χρόνους. Μακεδονικὴ δυναστεία (867–1056)* (Athens and Komotini, 1981).

Bourdara, C. A., *Καθοσίωσις καὶ τυραννὶς κατὰ τοὺς μέσους βυζαντινοὺς χρόνους 1056–1081* (Athens, 1984).

Bourdara, C. A., 'Le modèle du bon souverain à l'époque de Léon VI le Sage et la Vie de Sainte Euphrosynè', in M. Balard (ed.), *ΕΥΨΥΧΙΑ: mélanges offerts à Hélène Ahrweiler*, 2 vols (Paris, 1998), 1:109–17.

Brenk, B. (ed.), *La Cappella Palatina a Palermo*, 4 vols (Modena, 2010).

Britt, K. C., 'Roger II of Sicily: Rex, Basileus, and Khalif? Identity, Politics, and Propaganda in the Cappella Palatina', *Mediterranean Studies* 16 (2007): 21–45.

Brown, T. S., 'The Political Use of the Past in Norman Sicily', in P. Magdalino (ed.), *The Perception of the Past in Twelfth-Century Europe* (London and Rio Grande, 1992), 191–210.

Burkhardt, S., 'Sicily's Imperial Heritage', in S. Burkhardt and T. Foerster (eds), *Norman Tradition and Transcultural Heritage: Exchange of Cultures in the 'Norman' Peripheries of Medieval Europe* (Farnham and Burlington, 2013), 149–60.

Caruso, S., 'Note di cronologia filagatea (omilie IV, VI e LII Rossi-Taibbi)', *SicGymn* n.s. 31 (1978): 200–12.

Christophilopoulou, A., *Ἐκλογή, ἀναγόρευσις καὶ στέψις τοῦ βυζαντινοῦ αὐτοκράτορος* (Athens, 1956).

Crostini, B., 'L'iscrizione greca nella cupola della Cappella Palatina: edizione e commento', in B. Brenk (ed.), *La Cappella Palatina a Palermo*, 4 vols (Modena, 2010), 1:187–202.

Dagron, G., *Empereur et prêtre. Étude sur le 'césaropapisme' byzantin* (Paris, 1996).

Darrouzès, J., 'Deux textes inédits du patriarche Germain', *RÉB* 45 (1987): 5–13.

Duluş, M., 'Philagathos of Cerami and the Monastic Renewal in the Twelfth-Century Norman Kingdom: Preaching and Persuasion', in N. Bianchi with the collaboration of C. Schiano (eds), *La tradizione dei testi greci in Italia meridionale. Filagato da Cerami philosophos e didaskalos. Copisti, lettori, eruditi in Puglia tra XII e XVI secolo* (Bari, 2011), 53–62.

Dvornik, F., *Early Christian and Byzantine Political Philosophy. Origins and Background*, 2 vols (Washington, DC, 1966; repr. 2020).

Enzensberger, H., 'Tecniche di governo in un paese multietnico. Alcune considerazioni', in M. Re and C. Rognoni (eds), *Byzantino-Sicula V.*

Giorgio di Antiochia: l'arte della politica in Sicilia nel XII secolo tra Bisanzio e l'Islam. Atti del convegno internazionale (Palermo, 19–20 aprile 2007) (Palermo, 2009), 3–46.

Flusin, B., 'Le Panégyrique de Constantin VII Porphyrogénète pour la translation des reliques de Grégoire le Théologien (BHG 728)', *RÉB* 57 (1999): 5–97.

Flusin, B., 'Construire une nouvelle Jérusalem: Constantinople et les reliques', in M. Amir Moezzi and J. Scheid (eds), *L'Orient dans l'histoire religieuse de l'Europe. L'invention des origines* (Turnhout, 2000), 51–70.

Flusin, B., 'L'empereur hagiographe. Remarques sur le rôle des premiers empereurs macédoniens dans le culte des saints', in P. Guran with the collaboration of B. Flusin (eds), *L'empereur hagiographe. Culte des saints et monarchie byzantine et post-byzantine* (Bucharest, 2001), 29–54.

Gallina, M., 'Il Mezzogiorno normanno-svevo visto da Bisanzio', in G. Musca (ed.), *Il Mezzogiorno normanno-svevo visto dall'Europa e dal mondo mediterraneo. Atti delle tredicesime giornate normanno-sveve. Bari, 21–24 ottobre 1997* (Bari, 1999), 197–223.

Garzya, A., 'Per la cultura politica nella Sicilia greconormanna', in A. Garzya, *Percorsi e tramiti di cultura: saggi sulla civiltà letteraria tardoantica e bizantina con una giunta sulla tradizione degli studi classici* (Naples, 1997), 241–7 = *Alpheiòs* (Catania, 1998), 105–12.

Gaşpar, C. N., 'Praising the Stylite in Southern Italy: Philagathos of Cerami on St Symeon the Stylite (BHG 822)', *Annuario dell'Istituto Romeno di cultura e ricerca umanistica a Venezia* 4 (2002): 93–109.

Gentile Messina, R., 'I rapporti tra Sicilia e Bisanzio (sec. XII) nelle fonti bizantine e occidentali', in R. Lavagnini and C. Rognoni (eds), *Byzantino-Sicula VI. La Sicilia e Bisanzio nei secoli XI e XII. Atti delle X Giornate di Studio della Associazione Italiana di Studi Bizantini (Palermo, 27–28 maggio 2011)* (Palermo, 2014), 51–61.

Gigante, M., 'Il problema Filagato', in P. L. Leone (ed.), *Studi bizantini e neogreci. Atti del IV Congresso nazionale di studi bizantini, Lecce, 21–23 aprile 1980–Calimera, 24 aprile 1980* (Galatina, 1983), 633–9.

Grumel, V., 'Homélie de S. Germain sur la délivrance de Constantinople', *RÉB* 16 (1958): 183–205.

Houben, H., 'La predicazione', in G. Musca and V. Sivo (eds), *Strumenti, tempi e luoghi di comunicazione nel Mezzogiorno normanno-svevo. Atti delle undecime giornate normanno-sveve. Bari, 26–29 ottobre 1993* (Bari, 1995), 253–73.

Houben, H., *Mezzogiorno normanno-svevo. Monasteri e castelli, ebrei e musulmani* (Naples, 1996).

Houben, H., *Roger II. von Sizilien. Herrscher zwischen Orient und Okzident* (Darmstadt, 1997).

Hunger, H., *Prooimion: Elemente der byzantinischen Kaiseridee in den Arengen der Urkunden* (Vienna and Graz, 1964).

Hunger, H. (ed.), *Das byzantinische Herrscherbild* (Darmstadt, 1975).

Hurbanic, M., 'The So-Called Feast of Akathistos and the Tradition of the Avar Siege of Constantinople in 626' (in Slovak with English summary), in M. Kulhánková and K. Loudová (eds), *EΠEA ΠΤΕΡΟΕΝΤΑ. Růženě Dostálové k narozeninám* (Brno, 2009), 129–41.

Johns, J., 'The Date of the Ceiling of the Cappella Palatina in Palermo', in E. J. Grube and J. Johns, *The Painted Ceilings of the Cappella Palatina* (Genova and New York, 2005), 1–14.

Kalavrezou, I., 'Helping Hands for the Empire: Imperial Ceremonies and the Cult of Relics at the Byzantine Court', in H. Maguire (ed.), *Byzantine Court Culture from 829 to 1204* (Washington, DC, 1997), 53–79.

Kaldellis, A., *The Byzantine Republic: People and Power in New Rome* (Cambridge, MA, 2015).

Kazhdan, A. in collaboration with L. F. Sherry and C. Angelidi, *A History of Byzantine Literature (650–850)* (Athens, 1999).

Klein, H. A., 'Sacred Relics and Imperial Ceremonies at the Great Palace of Constantinople', in F. A. Bauer (ed.), *Visualisierungen von Herrschaft. Frühmittelalterliche Residenzen. Gestalt und Zeremoniell. Internationales Kolloquium, 3.–4. Juni 2004 in Istanbul = BYZAS* 5 (2006): 79–99.

Koutrakou, N., 'The Eye of Constantinople: Continuity and Change in the 11th–12th Century Byzantine Perception of Sicily', in R. Lavagnini and C. Rognoni (eds), *Byzantino-Sicula VI. La Sicilia e Bisanzio nei secoli XI e XII. Atti delle X Giornate di Studio della Associazione Italiana di Studi Bizantini (Palermo, 27–28 maggio 2011)* (Palermo, 2014), 21–49.

Laitsos, S., '"Imitatio Basilei"? The Ideological and Political Construction of the Norman Kingdom of Sicily in the 12th Century', in S. Flogaitis and A. Pantelis (eds), *The Eastern Roman Empire and the Birth of the Idea of State in Europe* (London, 2005), 227–47.

Laourdas, B., *Φωτίου Ὁμιλίαι. Ἔκδοσις κειμένου, εἰσαγωγὴ καὶ σχόλια* (Thessaloniki, 1959).

Lavagnini, B., 'I Normanni di Sicilia a Cipro e a Patmo (1186)', in *Byzantino-Sicula II. Miscellanea di scritti in memoria de Giuseppe Rossi Taibbi* (Palermo, 1975), 321–34.

Lechner, K., *Hellenen und Barbaren im Weltbild der Byzantiner. Die alten Bezeichnungen als Ausdruck eines neuen Kulturbewusstseins* (Munich, 1955).

Loukaki, M., *Ekphrasis earos. Le topos de la venue du printemps chez des auteurs byzantins, Parekbolai* 3 (2013): 77–106.

Luzzi, A., 'L'ideologia costantiniana nella liturgia dell'età di Costantino VII Porfirogenito', *RSBN* n.s. 28 (1991): 113–24.

Magdalino, P., 'The Bath of Leo the Wise and the "Macedonian Renaissance" Revisited: Topography, Iconography, Ceremonial, Ideology', *DOP* 42 (1988): 97–118.

Maier, C. T., *Preaching the Crusades. Mendicant Friars and the Cross in the Thirteenth Century* (Cambridge, 1998).

Maier, C. T., *Crusade Propaganda and Ideology. Model Sermons for the Preaching of the Cross* (Cambridge, 2006).

Markopoulos, A., 'Autour des *Chapitres parénétiques* de Basile Ier', in M. Balard (ed.), *EYΨYXIA: mélanges offerts à Hélène Ahrweiler*, 2 vols (Paris, 1998), 2: 469–79.

Markopoulos, A., 'The Ideology of War in the Military Harangues of Constantine VII Porphyrogennetos', in J. Koder and Y. Stouraitis (eds), *Byzantine War Ideology Between Roman Imperial Concept and Christian Religion. Akten des Internationalen Symposiums (Wien, 19.–21. Mai 2011)* (Vienna, 2012), 47–56.

McGeer, E., 'Two Military Orations of Constantine VII', in J. W. Nesbitt (ed.), *Byzantine Authors: Literary Activities and Preoccupations. Texts and Translations dedicated to the Memory of Nicolas Oikonomides* (Leiden and Boston, 2003), 111–35.

Ménager, L. R., *AMIRATUS – Ἀμηρᾶς. L'Émirat et les origines de l'Amirauté (XIe – XIIIe siècles)* (Paris, 1960).

Mergiali-Sahas, S., 'Byzantine Emperors and Holy Relics: Use, and Misuse, of Sanctity and Authority', *JÖB* 51 (2001): 41–60.

Metcalfe, A., *Muslims and Christians in Norman Sicily. Arabic Speakers and the End of Islam* (London and New York, 2003).

Odorico, P., 'Ideologia religiosa e contestazione politica in una opera agiografica tarco antica', *Ricerche di Storia Sociale e Religiosa di Vicenza* 15–16 (1979): 59–75.

Odorico, P., 'Idéologie politique, production littéraire et patronage au Xe siècle: L'empereur Constantin VII et le synaxariste Évariste', *Medioevo Greco* 1 (2001): 199–219.

Paidas, K. D. S., *Η θεματική των βυζαντινών 'Κατόπτρων ηγεμόνος' της πρώιμης και μέσης περιόδου (398–1085). Συμβολή στην πολιτική θεωρία των Βυζαντινών* (Athens, 2005).

Paidas, K. D. S., *Τα βυζαντινά 'Κάτοπτρα ηγεμόνος' της ύστερης περιόδου (1254–1403). Εκφράσεις του βυζαντινού βασιλικού ιδεώδους* (Athens, 2006).

Paidas, K. D. S., *[Βασίλειος Α´ Μακεδών.] Δύο παραινετικά κείμενα προς τον αυτοκράτορα Λέοντα ϛ´ τον Σοφό. Εισαγωγή – Μετάφραση – Σχόλια* (Athens, 2009).

Pertusi, A., 'Aspetti letterari: continuità e sviluppi della tradizione letteraria greca', in C. D. Fonseca (ed.), *Il passaggio dal dominio bizantino allo stato normanno nell'Italia meridionale. Atti del secondo Convegno internazionale di studi sulla civiltà rupestre (Taranto–Mottola, 31 ottobre–4 novembre 1973)* (Taranto, 1977), 63–101.

Peters-Custot, A., *Les Grecs de l'Italie méridionale post-byzantine (IXe–XIVe siècle): une acculturation en douceur* (Rome, 2009).

Polemis, I. and T. Antonopoulou, *Vitae et Miracula Sancti Christoduli Patmensis* (Vienna, 2021).

Puccia, M., 'L'anonimo *Carme di supplica a Giorgio di Antiochia* e l'elaborazione dell'idea imperiale alla corte di Ruggero II', in M. Re and C. Rognoni (eds), *Byzantino-Sicula V. Giorgio di Antiochia: l'arte della politica in Sicilia nel XII secolo tra Bisanzio e l'Islam. Atti del convegno internazionale (Palermo, 19–20 aprile 2007)* (Palermo, 2009), 231–62.

Reinsch, D. R., 'Literarische Bildung in Konstantinopel im 7. und 8. Jahrhundert. Das Zeugnis der Homiletik', in G. Prato (ed.), *I manoscritti greci tra riflessione e dibattito. Atti del V Colloquio Internazionale di Paleografia Greca (Cremona, 4–10 ottobre 1998)*, 3 vols (Florence, 2000).

Riedel, M. L. D., *Leo VI and the Transformation of Byzantine Christian Identity: Writings of an Unexpected Emperor* (Cambridge, 2018).

Rösch, G., *ΟΝΟΜΑ ΒΑΣΙΛΕΙΑΣ. Studien zum offiziellen Gebrauch der Kaisertitel in spätantiker und frühbyzantinischer Zeit* (Vienna, 1978).

Rognoni, C., 'Donazioni e ricompense: La retorica bizantina al servizio del potere normanno', in M. Re and C. Rognoni (eds), *Byzantino-Sicula V. Giorgio di Antiochia: l'arte della politica in Sicilia nel XII secolo tra Bisanzio e l'Islam. Atti del convegno internazionale (Palermo, 19–20 aprile 2007)* (Palermo, 2009), 203–17.

Rossi Taibbi, G., *Filagato da Cerami: Omelie per i vangeli domenicali e le feste di tutto l'anno, I. Omelie per le feste fisse* (Palermo, 1969).

Schmitt, O. J., 'Das Normannenbild im Geschichtswerk des Niketas Choniates', *JÖB* 47 (1997): 155–77.

Signes Codoñer, J. and F. J. Andrés Santos, *La introducción al derecho (Eisagoge) del Patriarca Focio* (Madrid, 2007).

Speck, P., 'Klassizismus im achten Jahrhundert? Die Homilie des Patriachen Germanos über die Rettung Konstantinopels', *RÉB* 44 (1986): 209–27 = 'Classicism in the Eighth Century? The Homily of Patriarch Germanos on the Deliverance of Constantinople', in P. Speck, *Understanding Byzantium: Studies in Byzantine Historical Sources*, ed. S. Takács (Aldershot and Burlington, 2003), 123–42 (no. 11).

Stavrianos, K. S., *Ὁ ἅγιος Γερμανός Α΄ ὁ Ὁμολογητής, Πατριάρχης Κωνσταντινουπόλεως. Συμβολή στήν περίοδο τῆς Εἰκονομαχίας* (Athens, 2003).

Stouraitis, Y., 'Roman Identity in Byzantium: A Critical Approach', *BZ* 107 (2014): 175–220.

Tocco, F. P., *Ruggero II. Il Drago d'Occidente* (Palermo, 2011).

Tounta, E., 'The Perception of Difference and the Differences of Perception: The Image of the Norman Invaders of Southern Italy in Contemporary Western Medieval and Byzantine Sources', *ByzSym* 20 (2010): 111–42.

Troianos, S. N., *Οι Πηγές του Βυζαντινού Δικαίου*, 3rd ed. (Athens, 2011); German tr. *Die Quellen des byzantinischen Rechts* (Berlin and Boston, 2017).

Tronzo, W., *The Cultures of His Kingdom. Roger II and the Cappella Palatina in Palermo* (Princeton, 1997).

Tsiaples, G. B., *Πολιορκίες και αλώσεις στα βυζαντινά ρητορικά και αγιολογικά κείμενα*, PhD thesis, Aristotle University of Thessaloniki, 2014.

Van Deun, P., 'La chasse aux trésors: La découverte de plusieurs œuvres inconnues de Métrophane de Smyrne (IXe – Xe siècle)', *Byz* 78 (2008): 346–67.

von Falkenhausen, V., *Κόμης, δούξ, πρίγκηψ, ῥήξ, βασιλεύς. Zu den griechischen Titeln der normannischen Herrscher in Süditalien und Sizilien'*, in P. Schreiner and O. Strakhov (eds), *Χρυσαῖ Πύλαι – Zlataia Brata. Essays Presented to Ihor Ševčenko on his Eightieth Birthday by his Colleagues and Students = Palaeoslavica* 10/1 (2002): 79–93.

von Falkenhausen, V., 'Un diploma greco di Guglielmo II (marzo 1168)', in P. Fioretti (ed.), *Storie di cultura scritta. Studi per Francesco Magistrale*, 2 vols (Spoleto, 2012), 1: 377–89 with plate I.

von Falkenhausen, V., 'The Graeco-Byzantine Heritage in the Norman Kingdom of Sicily', in S. Burkhardt and T. Foerster (eds), *Norman Tradition and Transcultural Heritage: Exchange of Cultures in the 'Norman' Peripheries of Medieval Europe* (Farnham and Burlington, 2013), 57–77.

Vranoussi, E., *Τὰ ἁγιολογικὰ κείμενα τοῦ ὁσίου Χριστοδούλου, ἱδρυτοῦ τῆς ἐν Πάτμῳ Μονῆς. Φιλολογικὴ παράδοσις καὶ ἱστορικαὶ μαρτυρίαι* (Athens, 1966).

Wieruszowski, H., 'Roger II of Sicily, Rex-Tyrannus, in Twelfth Century Political Thought', *Speculum* 38 (1963): 46–78.

Zuckermann, C., 'On the Titles and Office of the Byzantine ΒΑΣΙΛΕΥΣ', in *Mélanges Cécile Morrisson = TM* 16 (2010): 865–90.

5

Performing Byzantine Identity: Gender, Status and the Cult of the Virgin

Leslie Brubaker

The four markers of identity most often noted in Byzantine primary sources, both written and visual, are gender, status, stage in the life course and ethnicity. Whether someone is a woman, man or eunuch is virtually always indicated: verbally, in the written sources; visually, in imagery. Status, too, is almost always described or portrayed, either in terms of wealth ('a poor man', 'a wealthy woman'), rank ('the *patrikia*'[usually named] and 'her [usually unnamed] servant'), or vocation ('a monk', 'an innkeeper', 'a prostitute'); and because this is not always crystal clear in a picture, the designation is usually also spelled out in an accompanying inscription. Position in the life course is indicated for those not in the normative mature adult stage, both in texts (a 'wise old man', 'a maiden') and images: an excellent example is provided by a miniature in a ninth-century copy of the Homilies of Gregory of Nazianzos, where an old man, a mature adult male and a beardless youth (representing the three ages of man) lower Gregory into his sarcophagus (Fig. 5.1).[1] Ethnicity is less commonly noted, though it appears in both texts (as in the sometimes despised Paphlagonians, whom Paul Magdalino has written about,[2] or in simple notations that so-and-so is Armenian, or Vlach, or some other designation) and imagery, as in the near-ubiquitous Persian Magi and the Black Ethiopians who appear in some images of the Mission of the Apostles, being baptised by Matthew.[3] The two markers I am interested in here are gender and status, which – in the textual sources – inflect each other: in Byzantine society, where masculinity was the normative gender, a high-status female could nonetheless rank above a medium-status male

---

[1] Parisinus graecus 510, fol. 452r: Brubaker, *Vision and Meaning*, 134–7, Fig. 46.
[2] Magdalino, 'Paphlagonians', 141–50.
[3] E.g. Paris. gr. 510, fol. 426v: Brubaker, *Vision and Meaning*, 243–5, Fig. 42.

Figure 5.1 Burial of Gregory of Nazianzos. By permission of the Bibliothèque nationale de France.

in the social hierarchy; but, at the same time, even a female of the highest status possible (such as an empress) never lost her female attributes, and her strengths, when recognised, were often identified as masculine traits. A classic example of this is provided by Prokopios, who described one of the few powerful women he admired – Amalasuntha, Theodoric's daughter, who was regent for her young son after 526 – as 'displaying to a great extent the masculine temper'(*Wars* V, ii.3, 21).[4] Here, I am particularly concerned with how gender and status intersect with ideology (in this case, Orthodox practice) and, specifically, with the non-liturgical devotional practices associated with the Virgin Mary, arguably the most important figure involved in such practices, in both texts and images. That the intersection between gender, status and non-liturgical devotional practices was an important issue for the Byzantines is strongly suggested by our source base: the texts, images and inscriptions that record non-liturgical devotional practices virtually always identify the practitioners specifically in terms of their gender and their status.

A good textual example is the well-known charter of the Confraternity of St Mary of Naupaktos in Thebes (Greece), preserved in a twelfth-century copy of a document originally dated to 1048.[5] The charter outlines the duties of the confraternity, which were, essentially, to take turns looking after an icon of the Virgin and to carry it from one church to another on the first day of each month.[6] The Naupaktos charter lists forty-nine members of the confraternity: eighteen are identified as priests or monks;[7] two are identified as readers;[8]

---

[4] For earlier, non-imperial, examples, see Cloke, *Female Man*.

[5] Nesbitt and Wiita, 'Confraternity', 360–84. See also Menna, 'La miniature', 1:546–7; Cutler and North, 'Gift of Service', 206–19.

[6] On the roles and goals of Byzantine confraternities, see Baun, *Tales from Another Byzantium*, 371–85, and Horden, 'Confraternities', esp. 38–9, both with earlier bibliography.

[7] In order of appearance, and with status as designated: Dionysios, monk and priest of the Monastery of Daphni; John, humble monk and priest of (the Monastery of) Hagia Photeine; Kalos Kalopragmon, priest; Soterichos, priest (in the district) of Kopais; Theophylaktos Kaletes, priest; Gregory Sakas, humble priest; Gregory Kalandos, priest; Constantine Manes, priest; Thomas Kalopteres, priest; Michael Blatas, priest; Michael Sakas, priest; Georgy Maloseiros, priest; Christodoulos Blatas, priest; Meletios, sinner, monk; Eknatiros, monk; Nicholas Koustounanos, priest; Manuel Kortos, humble priest; John Maloseiros, priest. Nesbitt and Wiita, 'Confraternity', provide prosopographical notes.

[8] Nicholas Peletakas, reader; John Blatas, reader. Nesbitt and Wiita, 'Confraternity', provide prosopographical notes.

twenty-six are laymen;[9] three are laywomen.[10] Both men and women are, then, involved in the confraternity and are clearly distinguished: gender is a recognised identifier. The other key status indicators are professional affiliation (priests, monks, readers) and geographical origin (e.g. Theodore *of Karystos*, a port in southeast Euboea; or Stephen *of Corinth*): town of origin or residence is indicated for at least twelve lay members of the confraternity and three of the priests.[11] There are also status indicators based on kinship – Maria, *wife of* Theodore Kamateros, and Nicholas, *son of* Gido – and on profession, though we cannot know from the evidence that we have whether or not the professional titles embedded in the charter's surnames remained relevant when it was signed. If so, however, the Blatas boys (Michael, Christodoulos, Andrew and John) presumably had some connection with silk, and probably specifically purple silk, the dye for which was manufactured nearby;[12] Leo Chalkeus was presumably a smith (or came from a family of smiths); and Constantine Sapoleros was, again presumably, a soap-maker, or came from a soap-making background. Finally, Maloseiros may derive from the Slavic for 'little cheese', and so Damianos and John Maloseiros may have been from cheese-making

[9] Christopher Kopsenos; George Nanaina; Theodore of Karystos; John Manes; Damianos Maloseiros; Leo Chalkeus; Leo of Preventza; Andrew Blatas; Constantine Sapoleros; Theodore (of Kourtroulion?); Gregory Cholix; Martinos (of Deka?); Stephen of Corinth; George of Sagmata; Nicholas (of Deka?); Manachos (of Phigalia?); Leo Anem(os/as?); Anchilos of Euripos; Nicholas, son of Gido; Niketas of Adrianople; Michael Kianidos; Nicholas Koukamaras; Niketas Rotrios; Constantine of Anatolikon; Eusebios (Kappadox/Kappadokes/Kappadokeios?); Nicholas Mauretanos. Nesbitt and Wiita, 'Confraternity', provide prosopographical and geographical notes.

[10] Maria, wife of Theodore Kamateros; Irene (of Skardos?); Maria. The three women appear about two-thirds of the way through the list, as signatories 30, 32 and 33. Nesbitt and Wiita, 'Confraternity', provide prosopographical notes. Neville, *Authority*, 72–3, suggests that all signatories represented their households and that Maria, Irene and Maria were thus either widows or signing because their husbands were otherwise absent.

[11] See the listings in the previous notes. As noted by Nesbitt and Wiita, 'Confraternity', 373 nn. 25–6, Niketas of Adrianople was probably not from the Thracian city of that name, but from the Adrianople that was a suffragan bishopric of Naupaktos; and Constantine of Anatolikon was from the town of that name west of Naupaktos, rather than from the theme.

[12] On silk production in Thebes, see Jacoby, 'Silk in Western Byzantium', 452–500, though his scepticism about women weavers at p. 462 is misplaced and unreferenced. For greater precision, see now Louvi-Kizi, 'Thebes', 631–8; Dunn, 'Rise and Fall', 38–71; and especially Galliker, 'Middle Byzantine Silk', 15–16, 19, 42–3, 53, 76–7, 115, 121–3, 131–3, 138.

stock.[13] Be that as it may, it is clear that both gender and status are well demarcated in the charter of the Naupaktos confraternity. What we learn here is:

1. Gender differentiation is a given, but wives and husbands are not necessarily always linked: women can appear independently (Maria appears, but not her husband Theodore Kamateros, though he is named).
2. The role of the priest was extremely important in local communities, at least as regards devotional activity.
3. It was, however, apparently not vital to group the signatories into any sort of formal hierarchies. Although the opening three signatures are of priests, and the priestly and monastic signatures cluster towards the head of the list, there is no evidence of enforced grouping by status, rank or gender. In fact, the most elaborate signature – that of Nicholas Peletakas, which is so ornate that it is almost illegible – comes late in the document (he is the twenty-ninth signatory).

An emphasis on gender and status is also found in devotional dedicatory inscriptions, whether from early Byzantine Palestine or late Byzantine Greece, as the inscriptions collected by Daniel Reynolds and Sophia Kalopissi-Verti, respectively, conclusively demonstrate.[14] For example, the eighth-century dedication inscription from Kastron Mefa'a originally portrayed the donors, clearly identified both by name and with attributes indicating their status (Fig. 5.2), while the fourteenth-century dedication images from the Church of the Archangel Michael on Crete identify the donors both by name and by distinctive costume (Fig. 5.3).[15] That the Byzantines were acutely attuned to the link between appearance, identity, gender and status – and in the context of private devotional practice – is underscored by two miniatures that portray the same woman at different stages of her life. A private prayer scroll produced in Constantinople for Eudokia Doukaina, who died after 1345, presents her as an aristocratic princess reciting her private prayers in the (anachronistic) company of John Chrysostom, one of whose prayers is included on the scroll (Fig. 5.4); after her marriage to Theodore Komnenos Doukas Palaiologos Synadenos, Eudokia was also portrayed – now as a matron, with her husband – in one

---

[13] These last speculations are from Nesbitt and Wiita, 'Confraternity', 377–8.
[14] Reynolds, 'Monasticism and Christian Pilgrimage', esp. 351–68; Kalopissi-Verti, *Dedicatory Inscriptions*.
[15] See Lymberopoulou, *Church of the Archangel*.

Figure 5.2 Kastron Mefa'a, Church of St Stephen, floor mosaic (detail): donors.
Photo courtesy © Daniel Reynolds, 2012.

of the eight non-monastic family portraits now found in the Lincoln College Typikon, under the benefaction of the Virgin Mary (Fig. 5.5).

Eudokia's status has changed from unmarried youth to married woman,
and her portrayal is accordingly modified: her unbound hair with its net
of pearls is, in the later image, swept back and restrained, and her slight
form has matured. In addition, the aristocratic status of the Typikon portrait is thrown into sharp relief by the images of monastics that precede
and follow the sequence: the status of both monastic and lay participants
is emphasised by the contrast between the two.[16] Two further examples,
the well-known miniature in the Hamilton Psalter (c. 1300) and a Russian
textile (c. 1500), confirm that gender and status remained important indicators in visual representations of non-liturgical devotional practice: the
miniature shows an older couple and six younger people, probably, as
Nancy Ševčenko has suggested, boys on the left and girls on the right,
all in special costumes that seem likely to indicate their membership in
a group dedicated to the care of the icon of the Virgin that is the central

---

[16] On the Typikon and its images, see Hutter, 'Geschichte', 79–114; Brubaker, 'Pictures';
Gaul, 'Writing'. The prayer scroll (Birmingham, private collection) is unpublished.

Figure 5.3 Kavalariana, Church of St Michael, fresco (detail): donors. By permission of the Ephorate of Chania, photograph by Angeliki Lymberopoulou, 2006.

Figure 5.4 Eudokia Doukaina and John Chrysostom: Prayer scroll (detail). Private collection, photo courtesy of owner.

Figure 5.5 Eudokia Doukaina and Theodore Komnenos Doukas Palaiologos Synadenos: Oxford, Bodleian Library, © Lincoln College, gr. 35, fol. 8r. By permission of the Rector and Fellows of Lincoln College, Oxford.

Figure 5.6 Veneration of the Virgin: Berlin, Staatliche Museen, Kupferstichkabinett 78 A 9, fol. 39v. Photo courtesy © Kupferstichkabinett. Staatliche Museen zu Berlin.

focus of the image (Fig. 5.6).[17] The textile shows the Hodegetria procession in Moscow, copied from the famous procession in Constantinople, and incorporates men and women, their differentiated statuses clearly distinguished by costume (Fig. 5.7).[18] Both the miniature and the textile provide visual parallels to the confraternity charter from Thebes discussed earlier and allow us to imagine how the activities described sketchily in the document worked in practice: how, in other words, identity was performed on the streets as part of devotional activity honouring the Virgin.

The examples we have just looked at demonstrate, in a variety of media across a broad span of time and geography, the importance that the Byzantines ascribed to recording gender and status in the practice of non-liturgical devotional activity (and I suspect that we would find this to be true across a whole range of other activities as well). The core importance of gender and status is not in itself startling (even if it has seldom been stressed), though the degree to which the Byzantines insisted

---

[17]   See N. P. Ševčenko in Vassilaki (ed.), *Mother of God*, 388–9; Parani, 'Joy'.
[18]   See A. Lidov in Vassilaki (ed.), *Mother of God*, 52–3; Parani, 'Joy'.

Figure 5.7 Procession of the Hodegetria icon in Moscow: Moscow, State Historical Museum, textile. Photo courtesy © State Historical Museum, Moscow.

on recording gender and some indication of status deserves remark. But what is more important is to recognise that descriptions and visualisations of non-liturgical devotional practice are an ideal guide – precisely because they are so mundane, so extra-liturgical, so removed from official proscriptions – to tell us which status indicators matter *most* to people when set in a public or quasi-public context. Beyond gender, the identity indicators that mattered most were: occupation or kinship, most often; place of origin, frequently; and ethnicity – which so often exercises modern scholars – very rarely.[19] This evidence tells us about ideology in practice rather than in theory – the ideological stances that filtered into (or from) the practices of daily life, that self-evident 'natural' ordering that Bourdieu calls *doxa*:[20] and this, it seems to me, is important for any understanding of the 'realities' of Byzantine daily life.

[19] In addition to the material just considered, further evidence to substantiate this claim appears in the corpus of inscriptions assembled by Reynolds, 'Monasticism and Christian Pilgrimage', and Kalopissi-Verti, *Dedicatory Inscriptions*.

[20] Bourdieu, *Outline*, esp. 164–6.

What, though, does this tell us about how Byzantine identity and ideology worked within the context of non-liturgical devotional practice? To answer that question, I would like to briefly sketch a comparative study examining responses to the Virgin Mary around the year 700 in three places: Byzantine (Orthodox) Constantinople, papal (Catholic) Rome and Umayyad (Islamic) Jerusalem.

We will start with Rome. According to the *Liber pontificalis*, around the year 700, Pope Sergius (687–701) instituted processions from Sant'Adriano to Sta Maria Maggiore, staging these on major Marian feast days. We know from later entries in the *Liber pontificalis* that these continued, and these later entries – one in 752 and one in 847 – add the detail that the pope carried the image of Christ not-made-by-human-hands with him, and that he walked at the head of a crowd formed of the populace of the city. These later two entries are incorporated into the *Liber pontificalis* because in both cases the circumstances were exceptional: faced with a threat from the Lombard king Aistulf in 752, Pope Stephen II walked barefoot at the head of the procession, and in 847 Pope Leo IV joined the procession for the feast of the Dormition with prayers to protect the inhabitants of Rome from a savage basilisk.[21] At around this same time, private devotion to the Virgin is documented through numerous commissions of Pope John VII (705–7) and several *ex voto* images, including a large and recently discovered votive image in Sta Sabina commissioned by the priests Theodore and George during the papacy of Constantine (708–15).[22]

For Jerusalem, we have two pieces of evidence for attention to the Virgin Mary around the year 700 in or near Jerusalem. The first is from the Kathisma Church just outside the city, which, as Rina Avner has shown, was the site of both Christian and Muslim veneration across the seventh and eighth centuries and, in fact, was enlarged shortly after the year 700 by Umayyad Islamic patrons.[23] The second is the Dome of the Rock, commissioned by the caliph Abd al-Malik and completed in 691/2. The inscriptions inside the building are extensive and well known, and the polemic inscription on the inner face of the arcade contains several extracts from Sura 19 of the Qur'an, which is

[21] *Liber pontificalis*, ed. Duchesne, 1:376, 443; 2:110, 158–9; for further discussion (albeit about a later period, but with useful maps), see Wickham, *Medieval Rome*, 324–8.

[22] On John VII and the Virgin, see Deshman, 'Servants of the Mother of God'; and Van Dijk, 'Domus sanctae', the latter with an extensive bibliography. For Sta Sabina, see Tempesta, *Icona murale*; Osborne, 'Rome and Constantinople'; and Gianandrea, 'Politica delle immagini'.

[23] See Avner, 'Kathisma'.

devoted to Mary. Mary (Miryam in Arabic) is, in fact, the most frequently mentioned woman in the Qur'an, and the inscription in the Dome of the Rock refers to her by name four times.[24]

And, finally, Constantinople. A well-attested procession, first recorded during the patriarchate of Timothy I (511–18) and known from other sources, ran every Friday night between the two major sites dedicated to the Virgin, the Soros Chapel at Blachernai (which housed the Virgin's robe) and the Chalkoprateia Church (which housed her belt).[25] The procession was normally headed by the patriarch, accompanied – at least by the tenth century – by the great icon of the Virgin, the monks of the city and anyone else who wished to participate in attendance. There are no early representations of the procession, but there are several later ones, including the tapestry of the Russian version enacted in Moscow, mentioned previously (Fig. 5.7). There are also a number of probably Constantinopolitan images of the Virgin from around the year 700, some of which have been well studied (and of course she appeared on the early imperial seals of Leo III around 720).[26] In an article devoted specifically to domestic use of Marian imagery in Byzantium – so certainly non-liturgical devotional imagery – Henry Maguire has demonstrated that images of the Virgin are rare before the second half of the sixth century, and only become relatively commonplace in the seventh; even then, however, she appears far less often than other saints or apotropaic images. Maguire concludes that it was only after Iconoclasm that domestic Marian imagery became a commonplace. He does, however, note that when inscriptions are engraved on wearing apparel such as armbands or rings, before Iconoclasm those with Marian imagery more frequently named women than men (after Iconoclasm, this is reversed, with more men named than women).[27]

What can we conclude from this comparison?

First, across the entire Mediterranean world – not just in the East Roman Empire – private devotional practice focused on the Virgin seems to have been a thriving activity around the year 700. It can be tracked in papal Rome, Umayyad Jerusalem and – though a bit less conclusively – in

---

[24] For the full text, with photographs and transcription, see Kessler, 'Abd al-Malik's Inscription'; for an English translation, with indications and identification of citations from the Qur'an, see Hoyland, *Seeing Islam*, 696–9.

[25] See the excellent discussion in Ševčenko, 'Icons'.

[26] E.g. a group of pectoral crosses made c. 700: see Pitarakis, 'Groupe de croix-reliquaires'. For the seals of Leo III, see Nesbitt, *Catalogue*, 57–8.

[27] Maguire, 'Byzantine Domestic Art'.

Constantinople. In all three locations, too, there was considerable input from local authority figures: the pope in Rome, the caliph in Jerusalem, the patriarch (and sometimes the emperor) in Constantinople. In short, officially sanctioned veneration of the Virgin cannot be seen as exclusive to Byzantine identity or ideology.

Second, although the Christian procession originated in Jerusalem and processions to sites associated with Mary continued into the Umayyad period, there is no evidence for procession to (or from) the Dome of the Rock.[28] (In general, across the Islamic world, processions are associated primarily with Fatimid Cairo and Ottoman Syria – both much later than the period we are considering here.[29]) In contrast, both Christian centres – Rome and Constantinople – were regularly traversed by processions honouring the Virgin that involved anyone who chose to participate, and the rare texts we have from the early periods suggest that many people did. The procession – and particularly the Marian procession – can be seen, then, as something more or less specific to Christian identity and ideology. There is, however, one important difference between the processional patterns of Rome and Constantinople: the Marian processions of Rome occurred four times a year; those in Constantinople occurred weekly. This is not a coincidence. At the height of processional ritual in Rome (generally agreed to be the twelfth century), it has been estimated that there was a procession approximately once every ten days; for Constantinople, if we believe the Typikon of Hagia Sophia and the *Book of Ceremonies*, there were processions about twice a week. So the importance of processions to Byzantine identity and ideology should not be underestimated. This is underscored by simple calculations of time and money: the sheer number of processions means that much time was expended on them by the patriarch and emperor, who surely had other things to do. As is clear from the tenth-century *Book of Ceremonies*, they also represent a huge fiscal outlay, both in terms of street decoration – which was floral and textile – and in terms of distributions from the emperor or patriarch to the people of Constantinople.[30] Neither the emperor nor the patriarch would – or could – have given up one or two days a week and allocated the sums to processions that they did, if these were not important to them. The processions, and perhaps

---

[28] Garitte, *Calendrier*, 301, 303; discussion in Avner, 'Initial Tradition'.

[29] See Sanders, *Ritual*; Grehan, 'Legend of the Samarmar'.

[30] See Constantine Porphyrogennetos, *De Cerimoniis*, ed. and tr. Dagron et al., 1:19, 31, 32 (on crosses being distributed), 70 (on vegetables and cake being given), 78 (on grapes at the vintage festival); cf. Brubaker, 'Bridging the Gap'.

especially the weekly Marian procession from Blachernai to Chalkoprateia, were evidently seen as a key factor in promoting urban identity and unity, and support for the ruling elite. The processions of Constantinople demonstrated Byzantine identity and put imperial ideology into practice. Two things corroborate this point.

First, when, in the twelfth century, John II Komnenos wanted to ensure perpetual prayers for his family, he diverted the Friday icon procession across Constantinople so that it now incorporated a stop at his new monastic complex, the Pantokrator (and he arranged to pay the participants and facilitators of that section of the procession, which presumably ensured a good turnout and proper ritual).[31] For John, buying into the great Marian procession was clearly the best way to ensure that the memory of the Komnenians remained central to Constantinopolitan identity.

Second, and even more conclusively, after the fall of Constantinople, Moscow would never have so precisely copied – and visualised – the great Friday Marian procession (Fig. 5.7) if the significance of that procession for the core identity of Byzantine Orthodoxy had not been recognised: in at least this sense, the Marian processions defined what it meant to be Orthodox.[32] The Marian procession had become a performance of Orthodox urban identity.

Bibliography

Sources

Constantine Porphyrogennetos, *De Cerimoniis* ... G. Dagron et al. (ed. and tr.), *Constantin VII Porphyrogénète. Le livre des cérémonies*, 6 vols (Paris, 2020).

Liber pontificalis ... L. Duchesne (ed.), *Le Liber pontificalis: texte, introduction et commentaire*, 2 vols (Paris, 1955).

Typikon of the Pantokrator Monastery ... P. Gautier (ed. and tr.), 'Le typikon du Christ Sauveur Pantocrator', *REB* 32 (1974): 1–145; Engl. tr. R. Jordan

---

[31] *Typikon of the Pantokrator Monastery*, ed. Gautier, 81.883–83.903, tr. Jordan, 756–7; see Ševčenko, 'Icons'.

[32] Whether or not the Moscow procession was also part of a conscious emulation of Constantinople, in an attempt to legitimise Moscow as the heart of Orthodoxy after the fall of Constantinople to the Ottomans, is uncertain. The Third Rome ideology is apparently a later invention: for a cogent discussion of this issue in English, see Bushkovitch, 'Review of Sinitsyna, *Tretii Rim*'. I thank Roman Shliakhtin for discussion and for this reference.

in J. Thomas and A. C. Hero (eds), *Byzantine Monastic Foundation Documents*, 5 vols (Washington, DC, 2000), 2: 725–81.

Secondary Literature

Avner, R., 'The Initial Tradition of the Theotokos at the Kathisma: Earliest Celebrations and the Calendar', in L. Brubaker and M. Cunningham (eds), *The Cult of the Mother of God in Byzantium, Texts and Images* (Farnham, 2011), 9–29.

Avner, R., 'The kathisma: a Christian and Muslim Pilgrimage Site', *Aram* 18–19 (2006–7): 541–57.

Baun, J., *Tales from Another Byzantium. Celestial Journey and Local Community in the Medieval Greek Apocrypha* (Cambridge, 2007), 371–85.

Bourdieu, P., *An Outline of a Theory of Practice* (Cambridge, 1977).

Brubaker, L., 'Bridging the Gap: Processions in Early Medieval Constantinople', in L. Brubaker and N. Ševčenko (eds), *Processions: Urban Ritual in Byzantium and Neighboring Lands* (Washington, DC, forthcoming).

Brubaker, L., 'Pictures Are Good to Think With: Looking at Byzantium', in P. Odorico, P. Agapitos and M. Hinterberger (eds), *L'écriture de la mémoire. La littérarité de l'historiographie* (Paris, 2006), 221–40.

Brubaker, L., *Vision and Meaning in Ninth-Century Byzantium: Image as Exegesis in the Homilies of Gregory of Nazianzus in Paris* (Cambridge, 1999).

Bushkovitch, P., 'Review of N. Sinitsyna, *Tretii Rim: Istoki I evoliutsuua russkoi srednevkovoi kontseptsii (XV–XVI vv.)* (Moscow 1998)', in *Kritika: Explorations in Russian and Eurasian History* 1 (2000): 391–9.

Cloke, G., *This Female Man of God. Women and Spiritual Power in the Patristic Age, AD 350–450* (London, 1995).

Cutler, A., and W. North, 'The Gift of Service: The Charter of the Confraternity of the Virgin of Naupaktos', in J.-M. Spieser and É. Yota (eds), *Donations et donateurs dans la société et l'art byzantins* (Paris, 2012), 206–19.

Deshman, R., 'Servants of the Mother of God in Byzantine and Medieval Art', *Word & Image* 5/1 (1989): 33–70.

Dunn, A., 'The Rise and Fall of Towns, Loci of Maritime Traffic, and Silk Production: The Problem of Thisvi-Kastorion', in E. Jeffreys (ed.), *Byzantine Style, Religion and Civilisation: In Honour of Sir Steven Runciman* (Cambridge, 2006), 38–71.

Galliker, J., 'Middle Byzantine Silk in Context: Integrating the Textual and Material Evidence', PhD thesis, University of Birmingham, 2014.

Garitte, G., *Le calendrier palestino-géorgien du Sinaiticus 34 (Xe siècle), édité, traduit et commenté* (Brussels, 1958).

Gaul, N., 'Writing "with joyful and leaping soul": sacralization, scribal hands, and ceremonial in the Lincoln College Typikon', *Dumbarton Oaks Papers* 69 (2015): 24–71.

Gianandrea, M., 'Politica delle immagini al tempo di papa Costantino (708–715): Roma *versus* Bisanzio?' in G. Bordi et al. (eds), *L'officina dello sguardo. Scritti in onore di Maria Andaloro* 1, *I luoghi dell'arte imagine, memoria, material* (Rome, 2014), 335–42.

Grehan, J., 'The Legend of the Samarmar: Parades and Communal Identity in Syrian Towns c. 1500–1800', *Past & Present* 204 (2009): 89–125.

Horden, P., 'The Confraternities of Byzantium', *Studies in Church History* 23 (1986): 25–45.

Hoyland, R., *Seeing Islam as Others Saw It: A Survey and Evaluation of Christian, Jewish and Zoroastrian Writings on Early Islam* (Princeton, NJ, 1997).

Hutter, I., 'Die Geschichte des Lincoln College Typikons', *JÖB* 45 (1995): 79–114.

Jacoby, D., 'Silk in Western Byzantium before the Fourth Crusade', *BZ* 84/5 (1991/2): 452–500.

Kalopissi-Verti, S., *Dedicatory Inscriptions and Donor Portraits in Thirteenth-Century Churches of Greece* (Vienna, 1992).

Kessler, C., 'Abd al-Malik's Inscription in the Dome of the Rock: A Reconsideration', *JRAS* 1 (1970): 2–14.

Louvi-Kizi, A., 'Thebes', in A. Laiou (ed.), *The Economic History of Byzantium From the Seventh Through the Fifteenth Century* (Washington, DC, 2002).

Lymberopoulou, A., *The Church of the Archangel Michael at Kavalariana* (London, 2006).

Magdalino, P., 'Paphlagonians in Byzantine High Society', in S. Lampakes (ed.), *Byzantine Asia Minor (6th–12th Cent.)* (Athens, 1998), 141–50.

Maguire, H., 'Byzantine Domestic Art as Evidence for the Early Cult of the Virgin', in M. Vassilaki, (ed.), *Images of the Mother of God. Perceptions of the Theotokos in Byzantium* (Aldershot, 2005), 183–93.

Menna, M., 'La miniature con la Vergine Haghiosoritissa nella pergamena della confraternità di S Maria la Naupattitissa', in M. Andaloro, (ed.), *Nobiles officinae: perle, filigrane e trame di seta dal Palazzo Reale di Palermo*, 2 vols (Palermo, 2006), 1: 546–7.

Nesbitt, J., *Catalogue of Byzantine seals at Dumbarton Oaks and in the Fogg Museum of Art* 6: *emperors, patriarchs of Constantinople, addenda* (Washington DC, 2009).

Nesbitt, J., and J. Wiita, 'A Confraternity of the Comnenian Era', *BZ* 69 (1975): 360–84.

Neville, L., *Authority in Byzantine provincial society, 950–1100* (Cambridge, 2004).

Osborne, J., 'Rome and Constantinople about the Year 700: The Significance of the Recently Uncovered Mural in the Narthex of Santa Sabina', in G. Bordi et al. (eds), *L'officina dello sguardo. Scritti in onore di Maria Andaloro 1, I luoghi dell'arte imagine, memoria, material* (Rome, 2014), 329–34.

Parani, M., '"The joy of the most holy Mother of God the Hodegetria the one in Constantinople": revisiting the famous representation at the Blacherna monastery, Arta', in S. Gerstel (ed.), *Viewing Greece: Cultural and Political Agency in the Medieval and Early Modern Mediterranean* (Turnhout, 2016), 113–45.

Pitarakis, B., 'Un groupe de croix-reliquaires pectorales en bronze à décor en relief attribuable à Constantinople avec le Crucifié et la Vierge Kyriotissa', *CahArch* 46 (1998): 81–102.

Reynolds, D., 'Monasticism and Christian Pilgrimage in Early Islamic Palestine c.614–c.950', PhD thesis, University of Birmingham, 2014.

Sanders, P., *Ritual, Politics and the City in Fatimid Cairo* (Albany, NY, 1994).

Ševčenko, N. P., 'Icons in the Liturgy', *DOP* 45 (1991): 45–57.

Tempesta, C., *L'icona murale di Santa Sabina all'Aventino* (Rome, 2010).

Van Dijk, A., 'Domus sanctae dei genetricis Mariae': Art and Liturgy in the Oratory of Pope John VII', in S. Kaspersen and E. Thunø (eds), *Decorating the Lord's Table: On the Dynamics Between Image and Altar in the Middle Ages* (Copenhagen, 2006), 13–42.

Vassilaki, M. (ed.), *Mother of God: Representations of the Virgin in Byzantine Art* (Aldershot, 2005).

Wickham, C. J., *Medieval Rome: Stability and crisis of a city, 900–1150* (Oxford, 2015).

6

'Middle-Class' Ideology of Education and Language, and the 'Bookish' Identity of John Tzetzes

Panagiotis A. Agapitos

In our postmodern world of deconstructed texts and textually absorbed contexts,[1] the search for 'text-based ideals and authorial identities' has led to essentially two types of approaches to medieval textual products. On the one hand, texts are scrutinised as to the ideologies expressing an overarching worldview of a ruling class,[2] while, on the other, texts are examined as to their intratextual strategies of authorial representation.[3] My aim here is to examine the class ideology and social-ethnic identity of John Tzetzes (c. 1110–70), a well-known teacher of the Komnenian era, who was also a prolific and versatile writer.[4] The case of Tzetzes is interesting for the purposes of the present volume, because he did not aestheticise himself as the object of his discourse in the manner that Michael Psellos did one century earlier, nor did he draw a clearly delineated high-style authorial portrait of himself,

---

[1] On this issue see the lucid analysis by Spiegel, 'History, Historicism', 59–72.

[2] Indicatively, see Agapitos, 'Εἰκόνα', on the image of the emperor in the ninth–tenth century; Loukaki, 'Ἰδανικός πατριάρχης', on the image of the patriarch in the twelfth century; Mullett, 'Literary Biography' on strategies of monastic vs imperial ideology in the twelfth-century *Life* of Cyril Philotheotes.

[3] For a first approach to authorial representations in the middle Byzantine period, see the various papers collected in Pizzone, *Author in Middle Byzantine Literature*. For Tzetzes in particular, see Agapitos, 'John Tzetzes'; Pizzone, '*Historiai* of John Tzetzes'; and Pizzone, 'Self-authorization'. All three studies have substantial bibliographies.

[4] Wendel, 'Tzetzes', still offers the best overview of Tzetzes' life and works; it can be profitably supplemented by Nesseris, *Παιδεία*, 1:158–97 and 2:515–40. For shorter presentations, see Hunger, *Hochsprachliche profane Literatur*, 2:59–63, and Gregoriades, *Ἰωάννης Τζέτζης*, 27–32. For various aspects of Tzetzes' social standing and views, see Grünbart, 'Tzurichos', and 'Byzantinisches Gelehrtenelend'; Rhoby, 'Ioannes Tzetzes'; Cullhed, 'Diving for Pearls'.

as his contemporary Eustathios of Thessaloniki had done.[5] On the contrary, Tzetzes virulently attacked the capital's 'ethereal rhetors' (ῥήτορες αἰθέριοι, *Hist.* 9.659)[6] for creating a false image of themselves by pretending to be learned and educated, while in reality they were 'thievish, temple-robbing clerics' (παπάδων ... κλεπτῶν ἱεροσύλων, *Hist.* 9.658). At the same time, Tzetzes presented himself as something else. But what was this 'something else' that he projected in many of his writings? It has often been described as his cantankerous and quarrelsome personality,[7] his pedantic approach to the classics,[8] or, more recently, his 'Roman' national identity.[9]

The chapter will take as its starting point Tzetzes' letter collection in order to examine three broader areas of ideology and identity: (1) the approach of Tzetzes to the middle and lower strata of society, partly in relation to his own education and linguistic skills;[10] (2) his understanding of social and ethnic identity in terms of his family lineage and professional lineage; (3) his use of vulgar humour and vituperation as a means of projecting a 'conservative' ideology.

Let us begin with Tzetzes' view of the middle and lower classes, and his own position in society. Tzetzes always perceives himself as acting in accordance with what is socially and professionally correct and explodes when he feels he has been treated improperly and unjustly. For example, he addresses a letter to the *kaisarissa* Anna in stringent tones of outrage (*ep.* 55).[11] Therein he asks of the noble lady to exact revenge from a certain person who has

---

[5] On Psellos see now Papaioannou, *Michael Psellos.* No proper study of Eustathios' authorial *persona* has been written; see Stone, 'The Panegyrical Personae', for some interesting observations.

[6] The *Histories* (or *Chiliades,* as they are conventionally referred to) are quoted from the edition by Leone: John Tzetzes, *Histories.*

[7] Wendel, 'Tzetzes', 1965–6.

[8] Hunger (ed.), 'Allegorien zur Odyssee', 7; Kaldellis, 'Classical Scholarship', 26.

[9] Kaldellis, *Hellenism,* 301–7.

[10] The letters of Tzetzes are quoted from the edition by Leone: John Tzetzes, *Letters.* See also Gregoriades, Ἰωάννης Τζέτζης, for a very useful Greek translation with notes. On letter-writing in Byzantium more generally, see the collected papers by Mullett, *Letters,* as well as the brief remarks by Grünbart, 'Byzantinische Briefkultur'. For a very recent and broad survey of letter-writing in Byzantium, see Riehle (ed.), *Byzantine Epistolography.* Tzetzes' letters go far beyond any 'conventional' generic norms of Byzantine epistolography, but they have remained unstudied in this respect, though they form a textual entity thoughtfully prepared by the author himself.

[11] John Tzetzes, *Letters,* ed. Leone, 75–7; tr. Gregoriades, 142–7. Most scholars agree that the addressee of Tzetzes' letter is Anna Komnene, daughter of John II Komnenos; see the prosopographical entry in Barzos, Ἡ γενεαλογία, 1:380–90 (no. 77). However, Barzos, Ἡ γενεαλογία, 1:194, suggested that the addressee is

threatened him with knives and blows (76.27–77.1). This person, who is employed in the lady's stables, happens to have married the daughter of a former priest of Adrianople. The letter discloses how this 'barbarian' and his priestly father-in-law have systematically caused problems to the metropolitan of Adrianople and to the abbots of the Pantokrator and Mosele monasteries. The 'barbarian' was discovered by the patriarch himself to hold heretical views (76.6–15). His father-in-law the priest, whom Tzetzes refuses to acknowledge as a holy man, is characterised as 'rogue priest' and 'rogue' (τζουριχοπρεσβύτερος and τζούριχος, 75.21–2, 76.11 and 24), while he is presented as a heretic and a deceiver who extracts money from innocent people by offering 'the false divine visions of a rogue' (τζουριχοψευδοθεοπτίας, 77.16). At the same time, the attacker of Tzetzes is characterised as 'the rascal son' (ὁ τζούριχος υἱός, 76.12 and 19–20) of a roguish father.[12]

Tzetzes points out to the *kaisarissa* that he would be absolutely capable of prevailing over this vile fellow with his own hands and the help of his servants, if she gave him the freedom and royal protection to do so. Thus, Tzetzes places himself in the middle of a social space with the *kaisarissa* on the one side and the priest's family on the other. The outraged teacher is certainly granting all respect to the princess while, at the same time, unleashing

---

the famous Anna Doukaina Komnene, daughter of Alexios I and author of the *Alexiad* (Anna no. 32); he has been followed in this by Grünbart, 'Tzurichos', 17, n. 14. Both women were born to the purple; however, given that Anna 77 was not a *kaisarissa* but a *panhypersebastē* on account of her husband Stephanos Kontostephanos, the probability that Anna 32 is the recipient of the letter is high.

[12] Grünbart, 'Tzurichos', examined the word *tzourichos* in this very letter, suggesting that it is actually the name of the heretic priest, a hypothesis that is not borne out by the text. The word also appears in John Tzetzes, *Letters*, no. 57, ed. Leone, 82.3: οἱ δὲ ῥηθέντες οὗτοι τζούριχοι καὶ τζουριχοχειροτόνητοι ἅγιοι; it is commented upon in John Tzetzes, *Histories*, 9.266–70: τὰς κεφαλὰς καὶ τοὺς ἡμῶν αὐθέντας καὶ δεσπότας | τηρεῖν, μὴ ὑποκλέπτεσθαι καὶ ἀπατᾶσθαι δόλοις | τοῖς τῶν κλεπτοαγίων τε καὶ τσουριχοαγίων, | τοὺς οὓς ἐχειροτόνησαν, ὠνόμασαν ἁγίους | ἄνθρωποι ἀλιτήριοι ὁμότροποι ἐκείνοις; and 361–5: εἰ λίτρας κλεπταββάσι τε καὶ τζουριχοαγίοις | ἐπὶ ἑνὶ τῷ μήλῳ τε δωρεῖσθε καὶ τῇ ῥόᾳ, | ἀνθρώποις συγγραφεῦσι δε μεταφρασταῖς βιβλίων | λέγετε μεταφράσαι μὲν μῆκος τοσαύτης βίβλου, | καὶ τότε δοίητε αὐτοῖς ὅπερ ἡμῖν δοκήσει. Grünbart did not take these passages into account. But the word is also found in Theodore Prodromos' *Ptōchoprodromika*, 2.13 (ms H) and 4.556–7 (mss SAC), ed. Eideneier, 163, 230. Eideneier, Ξοῦρες, following a suggestion of Phaidon Koukoules, sees the Ptochoprodromic τζούρουχος and τζουρουχία as related to ξυρίζω ('shave' or 'shear'), a rather improbable hypothesis. Though the etymology of the word remains unclear, the meaning approaches something like 'rogue, rascal' for τζούριχος and 'deceitful nonsense' for τζουριχία; see also my remarks in Agapitos, 'New Genres', 36, n. 161.

all his venom against the roguish priest and his villainous relatives. This self-positioning of Tzetzes in the middle of a social ladder is one of the more persistent themes in his works. Sometimes he presents himself as someone who takes the side of poor people. Thus, in *ep.* 57,[13] where he complains to a certain Megalonas, the middleman of Empress Irene (i.e. Bertha von Sulzbach, wife of Manuel I Komnenos) about the unfair payment for his work *Plot Summary of Homer*,[14] he comes to talk about some τρισάθλια ἀνθρωπάρια, 'wretched little people' (80.5). Tzetzes narrates in detail how he saved a poor would-be thief in his neighbourhood from certain death by a group of young bullies (80.9–81.13), while he expresses his pity towards a miserable woman with four small children selling apples which she carried on her back in an old basket, for having to pay duties to the various officials of the city prefect (81.27–82.2). He remarks that, contrastingly, many charlatan τζουριχοάγιοι or κρουστουλοάγιοι,[15] who are 'roguish saints or saints ordained by rogues' (τζούριχοι ἢ τζουριχοχειροτόνητοι ἅγιοι, 82.3), receive three or even four pounds of gold by sending through some ostensibly pious mediator of theirs[16] a pear or an apple or three figs in a small basket along with their blessings to the emperor or other aristocratic families, and no one ever accuses them of being thieves, while poor people are being harassed. Here the social space begins to take more nuanced contours, as Tzetzes introduces four types of persons on the social ladder. On the one side, the empress and below her the servant Megalonas; on the other, the false saints and below them the poor people of the capital like the desperate thief or the apple-selling woman. Tzetzes again places himself in the middle of this spectrum.

---

[13] John Tzetzes, *Letters*, ed. Leone, 79–84; tr. Gregoriades, 148–57.

[14] The Ὑπόθεσις τοῦ Ὁμήρου (see Wendel, 'Tzetzes', 1969) was originally dedicated to Irene-Bertha (Barzos, Ἡ γενεαλογία, 1:456–7). However, the writing was broken off when the empress refused through Megalonas to raise Tzetzes' wages. The work was finally completed after the empress's death (1160) with the financial support of Constantine Kotertzes, as a special preface to Book XVI (II) of the *Iliad Allegories* testifies (ed. Boissonade, 192). There exists no full critical edition of the text. For the *Iliad Allegories*, see the edition of Boissonade, for the *Odyssey Allegories* that of Hunger; for a complete translation with facing Greek text, see now *Iliad Allegories* and *Odyssey Allegories*, both tr. Goldwyn and Kokkini. On Tzetzes' relation with his patrons see Grünbart, 'Byzantinisches Gelehrtenelend', and Rhoby, 'Ioannes Tzetzes'.

[15] Could this appellation be a reference to the roguish monk Elias Kroustoulas, who figures in ten letters of Michael Psellos? See Dennis, 'Elias the Monk', for English translations of Psellos' letters, and Protogerou, Ρητορική θεατρικότητα, 144–74, for a detailed literary analysis.

[16] E.g. a 'miserable, pale (and old) nun' (John Tzetzes, *Letters*, ed. Leone, 79.21: δύστηνον καλογραΐδιον ὠχρόν) or a 'thievish little friar' (ibid. 80.1: κλεπταββαδίτζιον).

Indicative of Tzetzes' middle-class position is *ep.* 18,[17] addressed to Nike-phoros Serblias, secretary of the senate. Tzetzes asks Serblias to offer him the material to repair the lintel above his door and to clean the grass in the courtyard of his apartment building. Tzetzes explains that the edifice has three floors, and he lives on the second. Above him, on the third floor, lives a priest of the lower ranks (δευτερεῖα τῶν ἱεροπροσπόλων λαχών, 33.4) along with his many children and piglets (συντρέφεται δὲ τοῖς παισὶ καὶ συίδια, 33.7–8). All of them together urinate continuously just above Tzetzes' door, so that he is in danger of being washed away into the stormy sea by a flood of piss (33.8–16). The grotesque scene, very effective in its coarse humour, reveals, however, Tzetzes' deeper social and educational concerns. Though he is in the middle of the building, the boorish low-rank priest is above him, an inversion of proper order, especially when it comes to the abominable species of τζουριχοπρεσβύτεροι. Tzetzes does not tire in pointing out in his letters that he very consciously chose a 'free-spirited life needing few things, rather than using many things in an unfree life'[18] and a 'frugal life in a quiet corner.'[19] Such comments should not mislead us into reading them as indi-cations of Tzetzes' poverty or low station in Constantinopolitan society. Tzetzes does reveal in his letters (1) that he received all kinds of valuable gifts from various friends,[20] even though he objects to this custom of sending gifts along with letters;[21] (2) that he actually does have cash available when he needs it;[22] (3) that he even has slaves as his household servants.[23]

---

[17] John Tzetzes, *Letters*, ed. Leone, 31–4; tr. Gregoriades, 76–81.

[18] John Tzetzes, *Letters*, no. 19, ed. Leone, 36.6–7: ἀρκεῖ γὰρ ἐλευθερίως μικρά μοι καὶ πλειόνων ἀνελευθέρως οὐ κέχρημαι. On the role John's father Michael, also a teacher, played in his son's frugal upbringing and attitude to life, see a long passage in the *Exegesis to the Iliad* on Cato the Elder's father and Tzetzes' own scholia to the *Exegesis*, ed. Papathomopoulos, 15.3–28 and 128.10–23, along with *Hist.* 4.565–99. On the use of Cato by Tzetzes as a model, see Xenophontos, 'Living Portrait' (and further below in n. 35).

[19] John Tzetzes, *Letters*, no. 39, ed. Leone, 58.6–7: ἡρετισάμην βίον τὸν πενιχρὸν καὶ ἐγγώνιον.

[20] See e.g. *Letters*, nos 39 (cured fish from the Danube), 48 (partridges), 49 (a saddle with a bridle and a mule), 71 (silk garments), 80 (a Russian inkpot).

[21] See his very clear remarks in *Letters*, nos 48, 73 and 80.

[22] See John Tzetzes, *Letters*, no. 49, where he remarks that he has given a number of golden coins to doctors for his treatment, or no. 23, where he proposes to return the payment for his teaching to the father of a lazy pupil.

[23] See John Tzetzes, *Letters*, no. 49, where he reveals that he owns a σκλαβόπουλον who takes care of him when he is sick, or no. 104, on which see n. 47 below. In no. 80 he informs us that he has received a Bulgarian boy as servant, this being a gift from the metropolitan of Dristra.

Therefore, the inversion of proper order is something that Tzetzes is always ready to castigate – for example, by bluntly pointing out to persons of higher standing that they employ as their servants people who are immoral swindlers, uneducated boors or even heretics. Such persons include the already mentioned roguish priest from Adrianople and his villainous son-in-law (*ep.* 55), two appalling monks in the Holy Apostles (*ep.* 14), the disgusting secretary of the *sebastos* Isaac Komnenos (*ep.* 6) and the priestly sycophants denouncing to Emperor Manuel the newly elected patriarch Kosmas II (*ep.* 46). Generally speaking, priests and monks who make money out of people's credulity are a group for which Tzetzes reserves some of his most vitriolic attacks. Interestingly enough, in this group he places not only the τζουριχοάγιοι and τζουριχοπρεσβύτεροι, whom he perceives as belonging to a lower social level than himself, but he also places the teachers of higher standing close to the patriarch or the aristocracy. In an autograph iambic scholion of his in the late ninth-century codex Heidelbergensis Palatinus graecus 252 on Thucydides, Tzetzes attacks a 'wise band' of pig-like barbarians who, being ignorant, arbitrarily correct the old manuscripts of Herodotus and Homer, while they slander and ridicule him because he does not follow them but insists on keeping the old (and correct) rules of the art of discourse.[24] This group sits in the corners of the Portico and of the Dome, most probably a reference to teachers serving in imperial and patriarchal employment, some of whom were deacons or even priests, like Eustathios and Nikephoros Basilakes.[25] In his *Histories*, Tzetzes is far more explicit, when he refers to such teachers as βούβαλοι (*Hist.* 11.210–24) or

---

[24] Heid. Pal. gr. 252, fol. 45r (Luzzatto, *Tzetzes lettore*, 49–50): ἡ φύρσις ὅνπερ καὶ χυδαιότης βίου | ἐγγωνιῶντα τῇ Στοᾷ καὶ τῇ Θόλῳ | σύρει διαμπάξ, ἡ σοφὴ κουστωδία, | ἀνθ' οὗπερ αὐτοῖς οὐδαμῶς συνεισστρέχει | ὅτι τέ φησι τεχνικῶς δέον γράφειν | πεζοῖς ὁμοῦ λόγοις τε καὶ τοῖς ἐν μέτρῳ, | φύρειν δὲ μηδὲν μηδαμοῦ τὰ τῆς τέχνης ('Him [i.e. Tzetzes] whom the confusion and vulgarity of contemporary life squeezed in the corners of the Portico and of the Dome, continuously maligns – this wise band! – on account that he does not run along with them, since he says that one should methodically write discourses both in prose and in verse and not confuse the matters of art in any way and place').

[25] No study has been published on the image, either positive or negative, of teachers in the twelfth century. For such images in the early Byzantine period, see Loukaki, 'Le profil'. For a positive image of Tzetzes as teacher, see Mazzucchi, 'Ambrosianus C 222', 420, where two autograph scholia by a former pupil are edited from codex Ambr. C 222 inf. (late twelfth century), an important manuscript in the transmission of Tzetzian scholia to Aristophanes. For a positive, quasi-hagiographical, portrait of Eustathios written by his pupil Michael Choniates, see Michael Choniates, *Catechetical Sermon 19*, ed. Lambros, and the analysis by Agapitos, 'Literary *Haute Cuisine*', 238–41.

βουβαλοπαπάδες (*Hist.* 9.953–9), using 'buffalo' to signify a foolish and uneducated person. As becomes obvious from his letters and the *Histories*, Tzetzes resented the success of such hollow people because they destroyed the 'arts of discourse' by introducing novel and erroneous views on grammar and literature, and because they disfigured the minds of youths through their shallow teachings.[26] In contrast to these 'high-class' rhetors, 'middle-class' Tzetzes must earn his living from his teaching and his writings, a point he makes in no uncertain financial and social terms in his letters.[27]

All of the above makes it clear that Tzetzes viewed himself as standing in the middle of a social ladder. The question to be asked, of course, is if this 'middle' (Tzetzes never uses a specific term for it) represents some form of a structurally defined middle class or even an early form of bourgeoisie. A number of studies have pointed out the existence of a social group sometimes called *mesoi* ('those standing in the middle') in the first half of the fourteenth century,[28] while stratification and conscious social coherence or lack thereof have also been discussed for Byzantine society.[29] However, no attempt has been made to look at teachers and intellectuals of the eleventh and twelfth centuries as possibly forming a separate social group that could belong to a 'middle class', as has been done for the Palaiologan period.[30]

Now, Tzetzes might have placed himself in the middle of the capital's social space, but he also pointed with pride to the long lineages of his family

---

[26] See e.g. *Hist.* 12.223–46, where Tzetzes attacks the 'uneducated outcasts' (ἀμαθῆ καθάρματα) who compose foolish and barbaric grammatical exercises and simplify the complex treatises of ancient wise men.

[27] See e.g. *Letters*, no. 75, addressed to his former pupil John Triphyles about living from his 'craft', or nos 22 and 23, addressed to Theodoretos Kotertzes, father of Constantine, one of Tzetzes' laziest pupils, though he later paid his former teacher to finish the *Plot Summary of Homer* (see above n. 14).

[28] See, in particular, Oikonomidès, *Hommes d'affaires*, 114–23; Matschke and Tinnefeld, *Die Gesellschaft*, 99–157.

[29] For some important insights, see Beck, 'Senat und Volk'; Kazhdan, 'Small Social Groupings', and Kazhdan and Constable, *People and Power*, but also the various papers in Haldon (ed.), *A Social History of Byzantium*, though the volume does not include a separate treatment of the *mesoi*. The recent book by Kaldellis, *Byzantine Republic*, does not offer many new insights into social and political structures in Byzantium. For a detailed study of Thessaloniki and its social stratification in the 1340s, see Katsoni, 'Κοινωνική διαστρωμάτωση'.

[30] See Ševčenko, 'Society and Intellectual Life'; Matschke and Tinnefeld, *Die Gesellschaft*, 221–385. In contrast to these scholars, Gaul, 'Emperor's Men', 245 n. 1, uses the term 'middling stratum' to refer to a 'second-tier' aristocracy at the time of Andronikos II that could include learned men. But this is not my understanding of class as a social group.

and his profession. He referred to both these lineages in *ep.* 6, addressed to the *sebastos* Isaac Komnenos.[31] This particular letter, standing at the beginning of the collection, has caused some puzzlement to scholars because of its peculiar content, excessive form and irreverent way of addressing its high aristocratic recipient, to the point that it has been recently described as a fictive school exercise.[32] This puzzlement probably says more about the inadequacy of our methods in understanding Byzantine textual culture as a socio-historical and literary system than about any supposed intellectual failure on the part of Byzantine literati.[33] However, through a close reading of *ep.* 6, we discover that the central generic characteristic of the text (12.18–23) is its set-up as a public accusation of moral injury, a type of accusation that could not be made valid at a Byzantine court but which constitutes in Aristophanes' *Wasps* the main line of judicial parody in the grand *agōn* between Bdelykleon and his father Philokleon (526–723). In other words, Tzetzes plays with Isaac within a ludic and ludicrous frame in which the writer and the patron assume clearly defined comic roles dictated by a specific Aristophanic comedy.[34]

Within this frame, Tzetzes gives weight to his 'grave admonitions' by presenting himself, on the one hand, as of good social and ethnic lineage,

---

[31] John Tzetzes, *Letters*, ed. Leone, 9–15; tr. Gregoriades, 46–55. Tzetzes offers detailed exegetical comments on this letter in John Tzetzes, *Histories*, 5.550–6.669. The addressee is commonly identified with the purple-born *sebastokratōr* Isaac, younger brother of Emperor John II (on Isaac Komnenos, see now the relevant papers in Bucossi and Rodriguez Suarez, *John II Komnenos*). However, Tzetzes uses the title *sebastos* twice, which is exactly the title borne by Isaac Komnenos, governor of Berroia and first employer of Tzetzes, as pointed out by the anonymous reviewer of the present chapter, who argued for the identity of the two persons. One problem with this identification is that Tzetzes does not refer to his dismissal, nor does he make any suggestion that the addressee's secretary succeeded him (i.e. Tzetzes) in this job (on this dismissal see further below, p. 157). Therefore, I will tentatively retain the identification of the addressee with the *sebastokratōr* Isaac.

[32] Kaldellis, 'Classical Scholarship', 29.

[33] See the pertinent remarks of Katsoni, 'Ο Ιωάννης Τζέτζης', in her excellent analysis of a technical financial term in a series of Tzetzes' letters addressed to Alexios, a former pupil of his and later a tax officer.

[34] For a similar case between Tzetzes and the *sebastokratorissa* Irene, based on the *Knights*, see Agapitos, 'Vom Aktualisierungsversuch'. Though no Tzetzian commentary of the *Knights* survives, it is most probable that he had written one, as the detailed hypothesis preserved in codex Ambros. C 222 inf. attests; see John Tzetzes, *Commentarii in Aristophanem*, ed. Koster, 1121, where Tzetzes explicitly comments on the role-changing device in this particular Aristophanic play.

since he is of noble Iberian (qua Alanian) descent from his mother's side and of pure Hellenic descent from his father's side (10.2–6).[35] On the other hand, Tzetzes makes himself belong to an immense lineage of 'secretaries', beginning with the god Hermes and ending with the rhetor Philostratos, secretary of Empress Julia Domna in the early third century AD (10.20–12.7).[36] Obviously, the catalogue-like listing of all these names, spiced with some obscure information and snippets of anecdotal material, recalls in parodic form the Homeric catalogue of ships in *Iliad* II 484–762. The reason for conjuring up these genealogies is the secretary of Isaac, a person Tzetzes calls Lepreos (Λέπρεος, 'leprous').[37] This man is a scandal to the venerable lineage of secretaries, since he is ugly, ghost-like, sickly, vile, effeminate, completely illiterate, a true outcast.[38] Thus, Lepreos is given cumulatively all the characteristics of Aristophanic subaltern and liminal characters,[39] while Tzetzes (who had himself been a secretary at the beginning of his career) appears to belong to a heroic profession (οἱ γεγονότες τρισμάκαρες ἐκεῖνοι καὶ ἥρωές ποτε γραμματεῖς, 10.21–2). Tzetzes also appears to belong to a noble family. He presents this 'noble' family lineage with substantial details in a well-known passage of the *Histories*, where he attempts to demonstrate that his paternal family had been important in the capital since the times of Emperor Michael Doukas (1071–9).[40] There is no reason to doubt this detailed and exact information, especially since it offers a case parallel to the

---

[35] This good lineage is accentuated by his good looks, on which see John Tzetzes, *Iliad Allegories*, Proleg. 724–39 (like Palamedes and Cato the Elder, he was tall, strong of neck, symmetrically long-nosed and long-faced, quick-witted, modest, thin, blue-eyed, golden-skinned, light-brown-/reddish-haired and blond, but like Cato the Younger, he had a θερμή τε καὶ θυμώδης κρᾶσις, 'a hot and spirited temperament'), and John Tzetzes, *Histories*, 3.156–91 (many lines are identical with those of the *Iliad Allegories*); Tzetzes is Cato's ἔμψυχος ζωγραφία ('living portrait'), even to the point of having dirty hair from not washing them regularly out of a sense of austerity.

[36] Tzetzes offers detailed information on all of the persons catalogued in John Tzetzes, *Histories*, 5.783–6.324.

[37] On the pre-penultimate accent and meaning of λέπρεος (= λεπρός), see John Tzetzes, *Histories*, 5.682–98.

[38] John Tzetzes, *Letters*, no. 6, ed. Leone 10.17–18 and 12.9–11: πτῶμά τι καὶ μορμολύκιον ὄντα καὶ κάθαρμα καὶ τῆς σῆς εὐγενείας ἀλλότριον . . . λεμφώδη ὄντα καὶ εἰδεχθῆ, μυσαρόν τε καὶ κίναιδον, ἀφωνότερόν τε ἰχθύων καὶ ἀμαθέστερον. On the κάθαρμα as the φαρμακός, see John Tzetzes, *Histories*, 5.726–61.

[39] See e.g. the sycophant in the *Acharnians*, the seer Hierokles and the son of Kleonymos in *Peace* and the soothsayer and the dithyramb-composer in the *Birds*, Kinesias.

[40] John Tzetzes, *Histories*, 5.583–628. For a detailed historical analysis of the passage, see Gautier, 'La curieuse ascendance'.

family of Michael Psellos. The learned and ultimately successful Constantine/Michael enjoyed a middle-class family background that allowed him to become secretary of a provincial judge and from there to make the connections in order to enter imperial service at a basic level.[41] This is the crucial point at which John Tzetzes failed. But I will return to this matter further below. Let me just note here that I consider *ep.* 6 to Isaac to be a 'real' letter, but one which follows very clear and recognisable generic conventions by combining: (1) the Aristophanic staging and vocabulary; (2) the Homeric catalogues in parodic form; and (3) the middle-class narrator as the heroic defender of justice and propriety, another Aristophanic trait.[42] The letter is a joke between patron and writer, possibly in reaction to Theodore Prodromos' Ptochoprodromic poem II, also addressed to Isaac Komnenos sometime between 1145 and 1150.[43]

Finally, Tzetzes projects in his letters a 'conservative' ideology about society and education. This ideological position is primarily expressed through the use of Aristophanic 'vulgar' humour and crude vituperation. Thus, in *ep.* 14,[44] addressed to Constantine, *chartophylax* of Hagia Sophia, Tzetzes mercilessly satirises two recluse monks (ἔγκλειστοι), who have benefited in succession from staying in a cell (ἐγκλείστρα) at the Church of the Holy Apostles. The benefits are counted in revenues, food and sex.[45] The main point is that the innovations of the recent past as to keeping recluse cells in the grand churches of the capital should be cancelled, and the Church should return to its remoter and healthier past.[46] Similar, if on a smaller scale, is *ep.* 104, addressed by Tzetzes to his slave Demetrios Gobinas, who has escaped

---

[41] On Psellos' career, see Volk, *Der medizinische Inhalt*, 1–44.

[42] Like Dikaiopolis in the *Acharnians*, Bdelykleon in the *Wasps* and the farmer Trygaios in *Peace*.

[43] On this matter, see Agapitos, 'New Genres', 24 and n. 110.

[44] John Tzetzes, *Letters*, ed. Leone, 25–7; tr. Gregoriades, 68–73.

[45] John Tzetzes, *Letters*, no. 14, ed. Leone, 27.11–13: αἱ γὰρ ἐγκλεῖστραι τὰ νῦν, ἅγιε δέσποτα, γεγόνασιν ἀνθρωποχοιροτρόφια καὶ συμποσίων καὶ μοιχείας καταγωγαὶ ἤπερ ἐπαύλεις καὶ μάνδραι ψυχοσωτήριοι ('for the recluse cells have become these days, my holy lord, breeding farms for men and pigs, as well as base places for feasts and adultery, rather than dwellings and sheds for saving souls').

[46] The past as being stricter, more austere and thus politically and socially healthier is a central axiom of Aristophanes, at least in his earlier plays; see the debates between Just and Unjust Speech in the *Clouds* (889–1113) and between Aeschylus and Euripides in the *Frogs* (830–1098), respectively. At the same time, it is an important tenet of Byzantine culture to have to mask innovation in quite different areas from politics to literature; see, indicatively, my remarks in Agapitos, 'Teachers'; 'Mischung'.

from his service and now sells sausages in Philippoupolis.[47] We are immediately alerted to the fact that the escaped slave has become a vagabond and then a maker of sausages and sow's bellies, exactly the job of Agorakritos, the initially infamous and then reformed sausage-seller in Aristophanes' *Knights*. Tzetzes tries to convince Demetrios to return, not only because he (i.e. Tzetzes) is a far milder and more humane master than what is usually found in the capital, but also because in Constantinople Demetrios can truly become a highly successful ascetic saint and gain glory and money. Gobinas' hypothetical new profession brings us back to the image of the detested τζουριχοάγιοι. Tzetzes gives instructions to his slave on how to masquerade for a good show (151.15–17). We are right in the middle of the famous opening scene of the *Knights*, where the honest slaves of the Athenian Demos prepare the sausage-seller to fight the corrupt Paphlagonian slave (*Knights* 150–233). Gobinas should throw over his filthy body a monk's cloak, hang bells from his penis, tie wooden shackles around his feet or (and this is the greatest device!) bind iron fetters and chains around his body and neck, in order to be instantly proclaimed by the capital's noble gentry as the perfect ascetic saint. What I characterise as 'conservative' ideology, in this context, is illustrated by the image of the iron-bound ascetic. We find this type of 'saint' attacked by a number of high clergymen in the twelfth century,[48] particularly Eustathios of Thessaloniki, who in two of his sermons presents his audience with two vivid images of such fraudulent monks.[49] In another context, however, Eustathios inverts the negative image into a positive one and describes Emperor Manuel as a warrior ascetic who injures his body by the use of his own iron mail in battle.[50] That the emperor labours for his subjects is an important commonplace in panegyrical oratory,[51] but the identification of

[47] The letter is extensively commented upon in John Tzetzes, *Histories*, 13.218–380. See, specifically, ibid. 13.218–67 on ἀγυρτεύοντες or μηναγύρται (they are the καλανδισταί on Christmas Day, January First and Epiphany, jolly scoundrels of sorts) and 13.268–9 on ἀλλαντεύω (Χορδεύειν ἐστὶν ἔντερα προβάτων παραπλέκειν, | Ἀλλᾶς ἡ κωλοφάσσα δέ, τὸ ἀλλαντεύειν νόει).

[48] See Magdalino, 'The Byzantine Holy Man'.

[49] *Opuscula*, no. 13 (*On Hypocrisy*), § 36, ed. Tafel, 97.30–59, and no. 22 (*On the Stylite*), sections 33–8, ibid. 186.54–188.12, the latter being a very complex narrative sequence with an encased Thessalonian story on a false iron-fettered ascetic.

[50] This long and complex description is found in one of Eustathios' sermons for the opening of Lent; for the text, see Eustathios of Thessaloniki, *Lent Orations*, no. 1, ed. Schönauer, 38.776–42.902; Eustathios of Thessaloniki, *Opera minora*, no. 2, ed. Wirth, 41.72–45.18.

[51] Agapitos, 'Εἰκόνα', 315, with further bibliography and Karla, *Das literarische Porträt*, 677–8, on Manuel specifically.

battle labour with a special type of ascesis is not. Thus, in transgression of a convention, but in adherence with contemporary imperial propaganda,[52] Eustathios creates a novel image which would have been an outrage to Tzetzes and his sense of order.[53]

At the core of Tzetzes' world order lies his place as a professional. This place he began to carve out for himself when, at a young age, he was appointed secretary to the governor of Berroia, the *sebastos* Isaac Komnenos. In Berroia something went very wrong, and when John was twenty-one years old (that is, in c. 1131–2), the governor fired him, kept his horse and sent the young man back to the capital on foot. In a number of his teaching texts of the next decade (such as the hexametrical *Carmina Iliaca*, the unfinished *Exegesis to the Iliad* with its scholia and the unedited verse *Exegesis to Porphyry's Eisagōgē*), Tzetzes included various references to this disastrous episode in his life.[54] It is generally accepted that there had been a sexual affair between the young Tzetzes and the governor's licentious wife.[55] In carefully reading all relevant passages, I cannot accept this hypothesis. Tzetzes does describe the governor's wife as licentious, mischievous and cunning, and as engaging in sexual activities with other (in his view, disgusting) men. However, Tzetzes does not relate such activities to himself; she is only represented as plotting against him. Therefore, the reason for her hatred towards him must be sought elsewhere.

If we are to judge by the manner in which our hero communicates his very personal opinions to others (and he was forced at least once to apologise for his insulting behaviour),[56] it is probable that in some way Tzetzes

---

[52] See the relevant section in Magdalino, *Empire*, 454–70, on the image of Manuel in the last twenty years of his reign.

[53] E.g. in letter 66 (John Tzetzes, *Letters*, ed. Leone, 93–6; tr. Gregoriades, 172–7) Leo Charsianites, metropolitan of Dristra and friend of Tzetzes, when tormented by the Bulgarians who have arrested him, is represented as a martyr, not as a suffering ascetic.

[54] John Tzetzes, *Carmina Iliaca*, 2.137–62, 3.284–90 and 3.753–6, along with Tzetzes' own scholion to 3.284, ed. Leone, 34–5, 68–9 and 223–4; John Tzetzes, *Exegesis to the Iliad*, ed. Papathomopoulos, 21.12–23.7, 42.13–18; the relevant passage from the *Exegesis to Porphyry's Eisagōgē* has been edited by Cullhed, 'Diving for Pearls', 57–8, from codex Vindobonensis philologicus graecus 300, fol. 70r–v.

[55] Wendel, 'Tzetzes', 1961–2.

[56] See letter 16 (John Tzetzes, *Letters*, ed. Leone, 29–31; tr. Gregoriades, 74–7), wherein he suggests to his addressee (a bishop) that his insulting speech was, in fact, φιλικὴ παρρησία καὶ τὸ ἀστεῖον καὶ χάριεν ('friendly freedom of speech, urbane witticism and charm'). On urbanity and witticism, see Bernard, '*Asteiotes*'.

behaved inappropriately to the governor and his wife. Whatever the reason for his dismissal was, not only did Tzetzes sink into poverty, since he was left without revenues and was forced to gradually sell most of his books, but he also lost the kind of job that would afford him an entrance to imperial service, as it had done for Psellos. Despite the patrons of high standing that Tzetzes did have,[57] he never moved up the social ladder. He remained in the middle stratum, making a sort of virtue of this 'middle-class' position, since he chose to live 'a frugal life in his own quite corner.'[58] But that was not what he wished. And when in c. 1160 he failed to obtain an important educational position (probably a public professorship of rhetoric), his sense of outrage was directed against everybody and he unleashed a river of vitriolic abuse, excessively expressed in four iambic poems, a letter and a long comment in the *Histories*.[59]

To a substantial extent, Tzetzes did not differ in terms of social origins from other learned men of the eleventh and twelfth centuries such as John Mauropous, Michael Psellos, Nikephoros Basilakes or Michael Italikos. In fact, Tzetzes' life was off to a better start than that of Theodore Prodromos, who never entered civil service but always remained a teacher like his father. But Prodromos, despite his complaints about the level of education among his peers and the success of others, never failed in terms of social behaviour as Tzetzes did. And it was this failure that Tzetzes felt marked a disjunction in his life – that is, the gap between a good family lineage and his social status after 1131. This gap he tries to bridge with his 'pure Hellenic' identity,[60] an identity that is more based on his readings, especially of the homegrown

---

[57] He remembered the *sebastokratorissa* Irene with true warmth and admiration; see John Tzetzes, *Histories*, 11.42–6, the preface to John Tzetzes, *Theogony*, 31–45, ed. Bekker, 148, with a hidden reference to the Berroia episode, letter 56 (John Tzetzes, *Letters*, 77–9, ed. Leone; tr. Gregoriades, 146–9).

[58] See above nn. 18–19.

[59] The three poems attack the teachers Skylitzes and Gregory, who were both supported by the city prefect Andronikos Kamateros. See Leone's edition of two longer *Iambic Poems*, 135–44 (the poems are part of the peritextual material to the *Histories*). The third *Iambic Poem* has been edited by Pétridès, 'Vers inédits', from codex Parisinus graecus 2925 (fifteenth century), but it is also transmitted (with some variant readings and a different heading) by codex Vindobonensis philologicus graecus 321 (early fourteenth century), along with a fourth poem on the same topic, still unedited. On the role of Kamateros in this 'failure' of Tzetzes, see *Histories*, 11.210–24 and 353–8, along with John Tzetzes, *Letters*, no. 89, ed. Leone 129–30; tr. Gregoriades, 226–9; on the whole episode, see Wendel, 'Tzetzes', 1964–5.

[60] See John Tzetzes, *Letters*, no. 6, ed. Leone, 10.5–6: ἐκ δέ γε πατρὸς καθαρῶς τυγχάνοντα Ἕλληνα.

Athenian Aristophanes and his 'middle-class' heroes. One could even argue that his 'being a pure Hellene' is a form of critique against the 'Roman' identity of the Constantinopolitan elite.[61] It is through this 'middle-class' ideology and his 'bookish' identity as a Hellene that Tzetzes defined his place as a conscientious and traditionalist teacher of youths, a protector of poor individuals and a strict admonisher of intellectual swindlers and moral rogues.

Bibliography

Sources

Eustathios of Thessaloniki, *Lent Orations* . . . S. Schönauer (ed.), *Eustathios von Thessalonike: Reden auf die Große Quadragesima. Prolegomena, Text, Übersetzung, Kommentar, Indizes* (Frankfurt am Main, 2006).

Eustathios of Thessaloniki, *Opuscula* . . . T. L. F. Tafel (ed.), *Eustathii metropolitae Thessalonicensis Opuscula* (Frankfurt am Main, 1832; repr. Amsterdam, 1964).

Eustathios of Thessaloniki, *Opera minora* . . . P. Wirth (ed.), *Eustathii Thessalonicensis opera minora* (Berlin, 2000).

John Tzetzes, *Carmina Iliaca* . . . P. L. M. Leone (ed.), *Ioannis Tzetzae Carmina Iliaca* (Catania, 1995).

John Tzetzes, *Commentarii in Aristophanem* . . . W. J. W. Koster (ed.), *Johannis Tzetzae Commentarii in Aristophanem. Fasciculus III continens commentarium in Ranas et in Aves, argumentum Equitum* (Groningen, 1962).

John Tzetzes, *Exegesis to the Iliad* . . . M. Papathomopoulos (ed.), Ἐξήγησις Ἰωάννου γραμματικοῦ τοῦ Τζέτζου εἰς τὴν Ὁμήρου Ἰλιάδα (Athens, 2007).

John Tzetzes, *Iliad Allegories* . . . J. F. Boissonade (ed.), *Tzetzae Allegoriae Iliadis, accedunt Pselli Allegoriae quarum una inedita* (Paris, 1851; repr. Hildesheim, 1967); Engl. tr. A. J. Goldwyn and D. Kokkini, *John Tzetzes: Allegories of the Iliad* (Cambridge, MA, 2015).

John Tzetzes, *Histories* . . . P. L. M. Leone (ed.), *Ioannis Tzetzae Historiae* (Naples, 1968; 2nd ed. Galatina, 2017).

John Tzetzes, *Letters* . . . P. L. M. Leone (ed.), *Ioannis Tzetzae Epistulae* (Leipzig, 1972); Greek tr. I. Gregoriades, Ἰωάννης Τζέτζης: Ἐπιστολαί. Εἰσαγωγή, μετάφραση, σχόλια (Athens, 2001).

---

[61] On this issue on a broader scale see now Stouraitis, 'Roman Identity', 197–202, for the middle Byzantine period.

John Tzetzes, *Iambic Poems* ... P. L. M. Leone (ed.), 'Ioannis Tzetzae Iambi', *RSBV* 16–17 (1969–70): 127–56; S. Pétridès, 'Vers inédits de Jean Tzetzes', *BZ* 12 (1903) 568–70.

John Tzetzes, *Odyssey Allegories* ... H. Hunger (ed.), 'Johannes Tzetzes, Allegorien zur Odyssee, Buch 13–24', *BZ* 48 (1955): 4–48; H. Hunger (ed.), 'Johannes Tzetzes, Allegorien zur Odyssee, Buch 1–12', *BZ* 49 (1956): 249–310; Engl. tr. A. J. Goldwyn and D. Kokkini, *John Tzetzes: Allegories of the Odyssey* (Cambridge, MA, 2019).

John Tzetzes, *Theogony* ... I. Bekker (ed.), 'Die Theogonie des Johannes Tzetzes aus der bibliotheca Casanatensis', in *Abhandlungen der Königlichen Akademie der Wissenschaften zu Berlin aus dem Jahr 1840: Philosophische und Historische Klasse* (Berlin, 1840), 147–69 (repr. in I. Bekker, *Opuscula academica Berolinensia: Gesammelte Abhandlungen zur Klassischen Altertumswissenschaft, Byzantinistik und Romanischen Philologie, 1826–1871. Band 1: Aus den Abhandlungen der Preußischen Akademie der Wissenschaften, 1826–1847* [Leipzig, 1974], 443–65).

Michael Choniates, *Catechetical Sermon 19* ... S. P. Lambros (ed.), 'Χωρίον Μιχαὴλ Ἀκομινάτου περὶ Εὐσταθίου Θεσσαλονίκης', *Neos Hellenomnemon* 13 (1916): 359–61.

Theodore Prodromos, *Ptōchoprodromika* ... H. Eideneier (ed.), *Πτωχοπρόδρομος. Κριτικὴ ἔκδοση* (Heraklion, 2012).

Secondary Literature

Agapitos, P. A., 'Ἡ εἰκόνα τοῦ αὐτοκράτορα Βασιλείου Α΄ στὴ φιλομακεδονικὴ γραμματεία 867–959', *Hellenika* 40 (1989): 285–322.

Agapitos, P. A., 'Teachers, Pupils and Imperial Power in Eleventh-Century Byzantium', in N. Livingstone and Y. L. Too (eds), *Pedagogy and Power: Rhetorics of Classical Learning* (Cambridge, 1998), 170–91.

Agapitos, P. A., 'Mischung der Gattungen und Überschreitung der Gesetze: Die Grabrede des Eustathios von Thessalonike auf Nikolaos Hagiotheodorites', *JÖB* 48 (1998): 119–46.

Agapitos, P. A., 'New Genres in the Twelfth Century: The *schedourgia* of Theodore Prodromos', *Medioevo Greco* 15 (2015): 1–41.

Agapitos, P. A., 'Literary *Haute Cuisine* and Its Dangers: Eustathios of Thessalonike on Schedography and Everyday Language', *DOP* 69 (2015): 225–41.

Agapitos, P. A., 'John Tzetzes and the Blemish-Examiners: A Byzantine Teacher on Schedography, Everyday Language and Writerly Disposition', *Medioevo Greco* 17 (2017): 1–57.

Agapitos, P. A., 'Vom Aktualisierungsversuch zum kommunikativen Code: Johannes Tzetzes und der Epilog seiner Theogonie für die sebastokratorissa Eirene', in E. Kislinger and A. Külzer (eds), *Herbert Hunger und die Wiener Schule der Byzantinistik: Rückblick und Ausblick* (Vienna and Novisad, 2019), 271–90.

Barzos, K., *Ἡ γενεαλογία τῶν Κομνηνῶν* (Thessaloniki, 1984).

Beck, H. G., 'Senat und Volk in Konstantinopel: Probleme der byzantinischen Verfassungsgeschichte', *Sitzungsberichte der Bayerischen Akademie der Wissenschaften, Philosophisch-historische Klasse,* (München 1966), 1–75 (repr. in H. G. Beck, *Ideen und Realitäten in Byzanz*, London 1972, no. XII).

Bernard, F., '*Asteiotes* and the Ideal of the Urban Intellectual in the Byzantine Eleventh Century', *FS* 47 (2013): 129–42.

Bucossi, A., and A. Rodriguez Suarez (eds), *John II Komnenos, Emperor of Byzantium: In the Shadow of Father and Son* (Farnham, 2016).

Cullhed, E., 'Diving for Pearls and Tzetzes' Death', *BZ* 108 (2015): 53–62.

Dennis, G., 'Elias the Monk, Friend of Psellos', in John W. Nesbitt (ed.), *Byzantine Authors: Literary Activities and Preoccupations* (Leiden, 2003), 43–62.

Eideneier, H., 'Ξοῦρες', in *Φίλτρα. Τιμητικὸς τόμος Σ. Γ. Καψωμένου* (Thessaloniki, 1975), 32–7.

Gaul, N., 'All the Emperor's Men (and His Nephews): Paideia and Networking Strategies at the Court of Andronikos II Palaiologos, 1290–1320', *DOP* 70 (2016): 245–70.

Gautier, P., 'La curieuse ascendance de Jean Tzetzès', *RÉB* 28 (1970): 207–20.

Gregoriades, I., *Ἰωάννης Τζέτζης: Ἐπιστολαί. Εἰσαγωγή, μετάφραση, σχόλια* (Athens, 2001).

Grünbart, M., 'Tzurichos, ein Häretiker aus der ersten Hälfte des 12. Jhs. (Io. Tzetzes, ep. 55)', *BSl* 55 (1994): 15–18.

Grünbart, M., 'Byzantinisches Gelehrtenelend – oder wie meistert man seinen Alltag?', in L. M. Hoffmann and A. Monchizadeh (eds), *Zwischen Polis, Provinz und Peripherie* (Mainz, 2005), 413–26.

Grünbart, M., 'Byzantinische Briefkultur', *ActAntHung* 47 (2007): 117–38.

Haldon, J. (ed.), *A Social History of Byzantium* (Oxford, 2009).

Hunger, H., *Die hochsprachliche profane Literatur der Byzantiner*, 2 vols (Munich, 1978).

Kaldellis, A., *Hellenism in Byzantium: The Transformation of Greek Identity and the Reception of the Classical Tradition* (Cambridge, 2007).

Kaldellis, A., 'Classical Scholarship in Twelfth-Century Byzantium', in C. Barber and D. Jenkins (eds), *Medieval Greek Commentaries on the Nicomachean Ethics* (Leiden, 2009), 1–43.

Kaldellis, A., *The Byzantine Republic: People and Power in New Rome* (Cambridge, MA, 2015).

Karla, G., 'Das literarische Porträt Kaiser Manuels I. Komnenos in den Kaiserreden des 12. Jhs', *BZ* 58 (2008): 669–79.

Katsoni, P., 'Ο Ιωάννης Τζέτζης και ο κοκκιάριος: Πληροφορίες για το φορολογικό σύστημα και τη λειτουργία του στην επιστολογραφία της ύστερης βυζαντινής περιόδου', in T. G. Kolias and K. G. Pitsakis (eds), *Aureus: Τόμος αφιερωμένος στον καθηγητή Ευάγγελο Κ. Χρυσό* (Athens, 2014), 311–28.

Katsoni, P., 'Η κοινωνική διαστρωμάτωση της Θεσσαλονίκης στα χρόνια του κινήματος των ζηλωτών', *Makedonika* 43 (2020): 65–90.

Kazhdan, A. P., 'Small Social Groupings (Microstructures) in Byzantine Society', *JÖB* 32/2 (1982): 3–11.

Kazhdan, A. P., and G. Constable, *People and Power in Byzantium: An Introduction to Modern Byzantine Studies* (Washington, DC, 1982).

Loukaki, M., 'Ο ιδανικός πατριάρχης μέσα από τα ρητορικά κείμενα του 12ου αιώνα', in N. Oikonomidès (ed.), *Το βυζάντιο κατά τον 12o αιώνα. Κανονικό Δίκαιο, κράτος, κοινωνία* (Athens, 1991), 301–19.

Loukaki, M., 'Le profil des enseignants dans l'Empire Byzantin à la fin de l'Antiquité tardive et au début du Moyen Age (fin du VIe–fin du VIIe siècle)', in T. Antonopoulou, S. Kotzabassi and M. Loukaki (eds), *Myriobiblos: Essays on Byzantine Literature and Culture* (Munich, 2015), 217–43.

Luzzatto, M. J., *Tzetzes lettore di Tucidide: Note autografe sul Codice Heidelberg Palatino Greco 252* (Bari, 1999).

Magdalino, P., 'The Byzantine Holy Man in the Twelfth Century', in S. Hackel (ed.), *The Byzantine Saint. University of Birmingham, 14th Spring Symposium* (London, 1981), 51–66 (repr. P. Magdalino, *Tradition and Transformation in Medieval Byzantium* [Aldershot, 1991], no. VII).

Magdalino, P., *The Empire of Manuel I Komnenos, 1143–1180* (Cambridge, 1993).

Matschke, K. P., and F. Tinnefeld, *Die Gesellschaft im späten Byzanz: Gruppen, Strukturen und Lebensformen* (Köln, 2001).

Mazzucchi, C. M., 'Ambrosianus C 222 inf. (Graecus 886): Il codice e il suo autore. Parte seconda; L'autore', *Aevum* 78 (2004): 411–37.

Mullett, M., 'Literary Biography and Historical Genre in the Life of Cyril Philotheotes by Nicholas Kataskepenos', in P. Odorico and P. A. Agapitos (eds), *Les vies des saints à Byzance: Genre littéraire ou biographie historique?* (Paris, 2004), 387–409.

Mullett, M., *Letters, Literacy and Literature in Byzantium* (Aldershot, 2007).

Nesseris, I., 'Η παιδεία στην Κωνσταντινούπολη κατά τον 12ο αιώνα', PhD thesis, University of Ioannina, 2014 (2 vols).

Oikonomidès, N., *Hommes d'affaires grecs et latins à Constantinople (XIIIe–XVe siècles)* (Montreal and Paris, 1979).

Papaioannou, S., *Michael Psellos: Rhetoric and Authorship in Byzantium* (Cambridge, 2013).

Pizzone, A. (ed.), *The Author in Middle Byzantine Literature: Modes, Functions, and Identities* (Munich, 2014).

Pizzone, A., 'The *Historiai* of John Tzetzes: A Byzantine "Book of Memory"?', *BMGS* 41 (2017): 182–207.

Pizzone, A., 'Self-authorization and the Strategies of Autography in John Tzetzes: The *Logismoi* Rediscovered', *GRBS* 60 (2020): 652–90.

Protogerou, S. A., 'Ρητορική θεατρικότητα στο έργο του Μιχαήλ Ψελλού', PhD thesis, University of Cyprus, 2014.

Rhoby, A., 'Ioannes Tzetzes als Auftragsdichter', *Graeco-Latina Brunensia* 15 (2010): 155–70.

Riehle, A. (ed.), *A Companion to Byzantine Epistolography* (Leiden and Boston, 2020).

Ševčenko, I., 'Society and Intellectual Life in the Fourteenth Century', in *Actes du XIVe Congrès International des Études Byzantines (1971)* (Bucharest, 1974), 1: 69–92 (repr. I. Ševčenko, *Society and Intellectual Life in Late Byzantium: Collected Studies* [London, 1981], no. I).

Spiegel, G. M., 'History, Historicism, and the Social Logic of the Text', *Speculum* 65 (1990): 59–86.

Stone, A., 'The Panegyrical Personae of Eustathios of Thessaloniki', *Scholia* 18 (2007): 107–17.

Stouraitis, I., 'Roman Identity in Byzantium: A Critical Approach', *BZ* 107 (2014): 175–220.

Volk, R., *Der medizinische Inhalt der Schriften des Michael Psellos* (Munich, 1990).

Xenophontos, S., '"A Living Portrait of Cato": Self-fashioning and the Classical Past in John Tzetzes's *Chiliads*', *Estudios Bizantinos* 2 (2014): 187–204.

Wendel, C., 'Tzetzes Johannes', *RE* 7A (1948): 1959–2010.

7

Byzantium from Below: Rural Identity in Byzantine Arabia and Palaestina, 500–630

Daniel Reynolds

Rural identity in Arabia and Palaestina has received comparatively little attention from Byzantinists, despite the intensity of excavation at rural sites compared to other areas of the empire's former territories. This is a rather problematic omission in view of the region's later history as an area where we have explicit evidence of attempts by the Umayyads to formulate a public image distinct from that of their Roman predecessors and the region's diverse Christian population. As one of the earliest environments of Christian–Muslim interaction, this has placed Arabia-Palaestina centrally within debates about shifting identities in the wake of Islam. The recent popularity of studies devoted to assessing the impact of 'Arabisation' and 'Islamisation' as a component of a regional 'identity-shift' is a case in point.[1]

Such frameworks, focused on identity and transformation, have proven invaluable for understanding how individuals sought to express their own sense of identity in response to a new political order. But they have proved less successful for understanding the question of identity in relation to the plethora of social groups that confronted the Arab armies in c. 632. While studies have generally been content to discuss notions of 'Arabisation' and the social impact of conversion to Islam, attempts to define how far such developments represented sharp discontinuity with existing regional conventions remain in their infancy.[2]

The purpose of this chapter is to offer an examination of rural identity in Arabia-Palaestina prior to the Arab conquest. It will examine identities that were publicly conveyed by rural actors themselves in the contexts of

---

[1] Levy-Rubin, *Non-Muslims*; Griffith, *Church in the Shadow*.
[2] Di Segni and Tsafrir, 'Ethnic Composition'. One exception is the attention devoted to Jewish life in the region; see Fine, 'Between Liturgy and Social History'.

their communities, primarily through epigraphy and papyri, rather than attempting to theorise hidden or private identities. This scope reflects a basic limitation of the data. Although we may rightly hypothesise that reality was more complex than the homogenised identities familiar from epigraphy, we currently possess no counter-body of data through which to construct a coherent alternative. Moreover, to casually and entirely dismiss the epigraphic conventions employed by rural patrons is to reduce Arabian-Palestinian rural experience to a simplistic dichotomy of privately lived versus publicly constructed identities that denies the coexistence of both within an individual's perception of self. While epigraphy does not necessarily reflect the diversity within a historical community, the act of commissioning an inscription represented an important part of the construction of rural identities and was an act of identity formation that rural patrons themselves actively participated in. Although an imperfect source for understanding rural identities in Arabia-Palaestina, inscriptions offer direct access to conscious choices made by rural communities in the articulation of their own identity.

What Is 'Rural'?

What do we understand by the terms 'rural identity' and 'rural settlement'? What defines an individual, or social group, as 'rural' and thus categorically distinct from 'urban'? Whereas the material and social characteristics of the urban *polis* have been comparatively well explored in Arabia-Palaestina, our understanding of the material and social contexts that structured the lives of those in non-urban contexts is comparatively less refined.[3] Rural society has, in many cases, simply become a convenient epithet by which to classify an array of different settlements, landscapes and communities in opposition to the concept of 'the urban'.

An exploration of terminology is a useful introduction to the problem. By the sixth century, the commonly used terms *komē* (usually translated as 'village') and *chorion* (usually translated as 'land' or 'property') were habitually applied in Arabian-Palestinian sources to a range of settlements of varying scales, uses and plans. Of the hundreds of rural sites recovered through excavation, however, only a few can be identified by the names and terms employed by the communities that occupied them. In these cases, it

---

[3] Hirschfeld, 'Farms and Villages'; Stroumsa, 'People and Identities'; Ruffini, 'Village Life and Family Power'; Avni, *Byzantine-Islamic Transition*, 198–200.

is difficult to discern any consistent pattern. Throughout the documents recovered from Nessana, for example, the settlement is frequently referred to in various circumstances as a *kastron* ('fort'), a *komē* and a *chorion*, and occasionally by different terms within a single document.[4] The opening address of the contract preserved in P. Colt 26 (dated to 570) describes Nessana as a *komē* in the jurisdictional limits of Elousa (ἐν κώμῃ Νεσσ] άνοις ὁρίου πόλεως Ἐλούσης), but later refers to the same settlement as a *kastron*.[5] In a number of other documents, dated to between 548 and 682, a similarly fluid description of Nessana as both a *kastron* and a *chorion* may be observed.[6]

The implications of this ambiguity are simple: attempts to formulate theoretical criteria to distinguish between rural settlements under labels like *chorion, kastron* or *komē* risk categorising an array of sites and social groups in ways that their original occupants may not have, and, more importantly, that do not make sense of lived experiences. Archaeological research provides little additional consensus on this issue. Frequently, as in the case of settlements such as Horvat Hesheq or Rihab, the focus of excavators on the recovery of monumental buildings has meant that our understanding of the wider settlement context of these buildings remains limited.[7]

Approaches to rural landscapes in Byzantine Arabia-Palaestina based upon excavation are thus often forced to establish parallels between sites and communities that may have exhibited little economic or social uniformity with their contemporaries.[8] This situation is not unique to the region of Arabia-Palaestina, but it is a pertinent one. Although not the largest territory controlled by Byzantium at its sixth-century extent, the region is notable for both its environmental diversity and the complexity of its political and human geography over a small territorial area. Such a diverse natural patchwork, ranging from desert to Mediterranean ecosystems, had implications

---

[4] For a critique of the use of the term 'town', see Hirschfeld, 'Farms and Villages', 36–9.

[5] See also P. Colt 25, 5–7; P. Colt 18, 2, 7.

[6] P. Colt 19, 1; P. Colt 46, 5–6; P. Colt 55, 3; P. Colt 58, 5. These likely referred to defined areas of the settlement. See e,g, the important discussion of terminology employed in the Petra papyri in Kaimio, 'Terms in Connection with Houses', and Koenen, Kaimio and Daniel, 'Introduction: Terms Pertaining to Dwellings and Agriculture'. The interpretation of the *kastron* as part of the village of Nessana is supported by Wickham, *Framing the Early Middle Ages*, 452.

[7] Piccirillo, *Chiese e mosaici*, 69–80; Aviam, 'Horvath Hesheq – A Unique Church'.

[8] Decker, *Tilling*, 137–40, 204–27, and Kingsley, 'Economic Impact'.

for the economic and social organisation of rural communities across the region, even if we often lack the means to understand these in detail.[9]

Byzantium was also the inheritor of a complicated legacy of earlier traditions of urban and rural organisation which had shaped the landscape of Arabia-Palaestina long before the extension of Roman hegemony.[10] The larger fortified settlements of Nessana and Kastron Mefa'a, for example, still formed important components of the non-urban landscape of southern Palaestina and the southern Transjordan by AD 500, alongside smaller, more dispersed settlements.[11] In terms of scale and organisation, such *kastra* often housed large populations and were densely occupied within the area of their walled defences and could also be extremely complex in terms of their social and political organisation.

Yet, in spite of this complexity, such settlements were not formally defined as *poleis* ('cities'), and there are no indications that these communities and their governing 'elites' enjoyed more than local significance.[12] Certainly, such settlements were accorded no particular status that distinguished them from other, often substantially smaller, villages. But when compared to smaller settlements like Khirbet el-Mukhayyat or Khirbet es-Samra, two settlements described by their contemporaries as a *komē* and a *chorion*, respectively, the internal social and economic dynamics of a large rural *kastron* like Nessana become difficult to incorporate into a singular notion of an Arabian-Palestinian rural identity.[13]

What Is a Rural Community?

While buildings and structural environments direct our analysis of rural topography, such environments were equally defined by the people and communities that inhabited them. The factors that serve to define a site or community as 'urban' or 'rural' are socially constructed and reflective of human social practices and attitudes. In relation to Byzantine Palaestina

---

[9] Dauphin, *La Palestine Byzantine*, 85–119; Walmsley, 'Production, Exchange and Regional Trade', 265–343; Wickham, *Framing the Early Middle Ages*, 775; Kingsley, 'Economic Impact'; Bessard, 'Urban Economy', 377–421.

[10] Parker, *Romans and Saracens*; Bowersock, *Roman Arabia*; Lapin, *Economy, Geography, and Provincial History*; Fisher, 'New Perspective'; Esler, *Babatha's Orchard*.

[11] Hirschfeld, 'Farms and Villages'; Broshi, 'Population of Western Palestine', 2–3; Trombley, 'From Kastron to Qaṣr', 181.

[12] Wickham, *Framing the Early Middle Ages*, 240–1, 453; Kennedy, 'Syrian Elites', 186–7.

[13] Humbert, 'Khirbet es-Samra'; Di Segni, 'Greek Inscriptions', 439–40.

and Arabia, how, then, might we approach the question of what made an individual or community 'rural'?

One essential problem we face derives from our tendency to conceptualise Byzantine rural communities in Arabia-Palaestina as a coherent social group whose practices and activities can be straightforwardly distinguished from their urban counterparts. This segregation that we impose on our evidence invariably results in separate treatment of 'urban' and 'rural' communities in Palaestina-Arabia as coexistent but essentially distinct entities only superficially connected in economic and material terms. Such a model of compartmentalised urban and rural populations overlooks the substantial degree to which individuals or families operated in both spheres, connected by familial, economic or religious ties. Theodore, son of Obodianos, of Petra, for example, can be seen to have maintained links with smaller settlements like Kastron Zadakathon and Ogomon (κώμης Ογομων) while simultaneously cultivating connections with the cities of Augustopolis and Gaza.[14]

These connections often involved extended stays for such individuals and families at their rural properties. In the case of P. Petra 37, a tax receipt dated to 565/75, Theodore is described as temporarily residing in the *komē* of Kastron Zadakathon, where he appears to have retained some property.[15] A similar fluidity between urban and rural populations may be observed at Nessana.[16] Our sources offer no sense of how such individuals were perceived by the communities in which they temporarily resided. Nevertheless, they reveal clearly the overlapping nature of rural and urban existence for many individuals and family groups.

Although more ephemeral in the record, interactions between urban and rural communities by individuals of more modest social status also coincided with the connections cultivated by elites. Artisans and other skilled workers were one such group that evidently moved between the urban and rural landscapes of the region.[17] Slaves and servants (ambiguously referred

---

[14] P. Petra III, 25, 5, 9–10, 12–14, 17, 21; P. Petra I, 2, 20–3; P. Petra III, 29, 8. Evidence of letter exchange between urban bishops and the clergy of Nessana proffers a further example: P. Colt 50, 2; see also Koenen, 'Decipherment and Edition', 203–5, and P. Petra IV, 37, 103.

[15] P. Petra IV, 37, 2–3.

[16] Including Sergios, a former tax official of the city of Emesa; see Kirk and Welles, 'Inscriptions', 173, inscription 94. Individuals attested in the donation registers of the churches of Nessana who identify themselves as inhabitants of the city of Elousa; see P. Colt 79, 15, 41, 43 and 55.

[17] Di Segni, 'Varia Arabica', 587–8; Madden, *Corpus of Byzantine Church Mosaics*, 64–5.

to as δοῦλοι) are another. While sometimes attested in papyri in relation to agricultural property (but rarely in inscriptions), slaves represent one social group whose activities and identities are effectively irretrievable through modern lines of enquiry, though they evidently formed part of the wider social networks of the Arabian-Palestinian village.[18]

This is equally true for the presence of nomadic and semi-nomadic groups in the region, which are frequently invisible in epigraphy and overlooked by our tendency to conflate discussions of 'rural populations' with sedentary village communities.[19] Although a noted feature of the rural landscape by 500, nomadic communities are, invariably, defined in our sources by the perceptions of sedentary writers on the peripheries of these social networks. Nomadic groups are usually identified in our sources by the epithet *Sarakēnos* ('Saracen') – a phrase which is often implicitly assumed by modern commentators to correspond to modern conceptions of Arabs or Arabic speakers.[20] While it is evident that differences between nomadic groups like those identified as 'Saracens' and other residents of Nessana were acknowledged among contemporaries, the lived linguistic or social identities of those described as *Sarakēnoi* are unclear. Certainly, in the case of Nessana, there are no indications that the individuals labelled *Sarakēnoi* by the compilers of the papyri spoke Arabic or that they self-identified as belonging to a defined cultural or 'ethnic' group that linked them to the *Sarakēnoi* situated on the eastern peripheries of Arabia.[21]

Admittedly, this conclusion cannot be definitive, but certainly naming practices, particularly the use of Arabic cognates, have already been shown to be an inadequate signifier of an underlying 'Arabised' identity, and the material emanating from rural contexts in Palaestina and Arabia offers no exception. Within Nessana, individuals bearing names of Arabic, Greek and Nabataean origin coexisted in the settlement, often forming part of single- household units. In the family of Flavios Sergios, named in a property agreement dated to 562, names of varying linguistic origin may be observed among Sergios' extended kin. Sergios himself is identified by familiar patronymic convention as Sergios, son of Elias, son of Taim Obodas (Θεομοβοδος), but details in the document also reveal evidence of Sergios' two marriages: one to his aunt, Maria (who died prior

---

[18] P. Petra 15.65, 136–8; P. Petra 28.19; see Piccirillo, 'La Chiesa del Prete Wa'il', 322.

[19] The archaeological evidence is summarised in Avni, *Byzantine-Islamic Transition*, 281–3.

[20] Fisher, *Arabs and Empires*, 77–89.

[21] Fisher et al., 'Arabs and Christianity', 336–48, with further bibliography. Saracens are mentioned in the trading account preserved in P. Colt 51, 2, and P. Colt 89, 22.

to 562), which produced a son, Elias, and a later marriage to Mulaika, daughter of Abraham (Μολεχης Ἀβραάμιου), from which three sons, al-Alka (Αλολκαιος), Stephen and Zachary, emerge (P. Colt 21, 5–10). By the 560s, then, names which formally derived from Arabic (Mulaika, al-Alka), Greek (Elias, Stephen), Nabataean Aramaic (Taim Obodas) and Hebrew (Abraham), formed part of Sergios' immediate family network and were clearly not limited to particular factions within that family or, as is clear from other documents, within the context of the wider village.[22]

Evidently, the adoption of Greek names by individuals was also not necessarily a signifier of a shift towards a more Hellenised identity among Palestinian rural communities at the expense of other conventions. While the use of names of Greek, Latin or Christian origin (assuming, rather precariously, that such etymological distinctions were understood by contemporaries) were more frequently adopted by the most prominent power brokers in the settlements, this did not necessarily determine the conventions employed by their immediate kin or subsequent generations. Thus, Flavios Stephen's son and daughter, Flavios Anmos and Ania, described in P. Colt 22, both bore names of non-Greek origin.

Presenting Identity

Given the nature of our evidence, derived almost exclusively from legal documents and dedicatory inscriptions, discussions of rural identity in Byzantine Palaestina and Arabia are a discourse around performative identity: in essence, identities that were intended to be publicly staged for audiences already familiar with the conventions communicated by these media. The identities expressed through these materials were invariably intended to foreground two principal characteristics of an individual. The first was legal and established the status of a person in relation to the law, often as a freeborn inhabitant of a settlement or, in the case of slaves, as the property of another person or family. Papyri offer the most straightforward indication of these conventions, for what survives among the caches recovered from Nessana and Petra are almost exclusively legal in nature and comprised principally of land agreements and tax records, interspersed with a selection of private contracts. Dedicatory inscriptions often performed similar roles in legitimising the donor's status as a prominent member of the settlement and as a benefactor within the wider community. Such

[22] See also P. Colt 22 and P. Colt 24.

assertions of status were frequently reinforced by the visual and spatial context of the inscriptions within the physical space of rural church buildings. The use of particular visual devices to frame inscriptions, notably the *tabula ansata* rendered in mosaic, provide one such example.[23]

Often the positioning of dedicatory inscriptions in front of the main entrances to church buildings, or in front of areas used for the celebration of the eucharistic rite, ensured the visibility of such declarations to the attendant audience. In the *eukterion* of St George in Rihab, dated to 530, both conventions may be seen to work in tandem (Fig. 7.1).[24] The inscription, which attests to the donation of one Thomas, son of Gaianos, is clearly set within a *tabula ansata* and located directly before the main opening of the *bēma* (Fig. 7.2). The pattern was widely replicated across the region by the sixth century, including in Herodion, Kissufim and Khirbet el-Beiyudat.[25]

Figure 7.1 Rihab, Church of St George, eastern view of the nave and bema: Photo courtesy Daniel Reynolds, 2012.

[23] Meyer, *Legitimacy and Law*, 21–44. See also Leatherbury, *Inscribing Faith*, and Yasin, *Saints and Church Spaces*.

[24] Al-Hissan, 'New Archaeological Discoveries', and Blumell and Cianca, 'Oratory of St. George in Rihab'.

[25] Di Segni, 'Khirbet el-Beiyudat: The Inscriptions', 265–71; 'The Inscriptions at Khirbet el-Beiyudat', 164–9; Cohen, 'Kissufim'; Netzer, Birger-Calderon and Feller, 'The Churches of Herodium'.

Figure 7.2 Rihab, Church of St George, *tabula ansata*: Photo courtesy © Daniel Reynolds, 2012.

The second characteristic of note is linguistic: rural identity, for the most part, was conveyed in Greek. The extent to which the proliferation of Greek inscriptions in the region is an adequate reflection of the daily vernacular employed by the populations of Arabia-Palaestina is difficult to assess. While Greek continued to predominate in legal negotiations and inscriptions of rural communities even after the Arab conquest, a number of studies in recent years have drawn attention to the concurrent use of Christo-Palestinian Aramaic (CPA), and, more tentatively, a form of early Arabic among communities by the mid-sixth century.[26] Evidence for the use of these languages is generally better attested in monastic and rural contexts. Letters and fragmentary translations of biblical texts in CPA have been recovered from the excavations at Khirbet Mird and Deir 'Ain 'Abata, respectively, accompanied by a growing corpus of dedicatory inscriptions identified in the Transjordan.[27] The use of Arabic among the populations of

---

[26] Hoyland, 'Mount Nebo, Jabal Ramm', 29–46.
[27] Perrot, 'Un fragment Christo-Palestinien'; Verhelst, 'Les fragments du Castellion (Kh. Mird)'; Brock et al., 'The Semitic Inscriptions', 418.

the southern Transjordan and the Negev, for which very little epigraphic or written evidence survives, has also been proposed in recent debate.[28]

Complex linguistic environments were no less a feature of the daily activities of urban populations, including those of the Greek-speaking elite, even if they are sometimes less visible. One clear example of this survives from the Petra archive, in a property dispute dated to 591, which took place in Kastron Zadakathon between Theodore, son of Obodianos, and Stephen, son of Leontios, where the process of legal arbitration between the two parties, which was conducted and recorded in Greek, was accompanied by a presentation of evidence in Syriac(?) (τὰς μαρτυρ]ία[ς] τὰς αὐτὰς γράμμασιν Ἑλληνικοῖ καὶ Σ[υ]ρ[ια]κοῖς) in the presence of both parties (P. Petra IV 39, 364–7).[29] A roughly contemporary inscription from the Cathedral Church of Madaba, paraphrasing a biblical quotation in Aramaic but transcribed in Greek, provides an additional example of bilingualism among the urban communities of the region.[30]

Despite the gradual rise of CPA in documentary and epigraphic form by the sixth century, its use among rural communities appears seldom to have extended beyond the private sphere. As argued by Robert Hoyland, inscriptions in CPA were commonly relegated to a subsidiary position in comparison to their Greek counterparts and often located in more peripheral areas of church buildings.[31] In other contexts its use was limited to the more informal media of graffiti, ostraca and, in the case of Khirbet es-Samra, gravestones.[32]

The evidence from both Greek and CPA inscriptions is also centred on the individual. Rarely, rural donors affiliated themselves in these inscriptions with a defined community as residents of a particular *chorion* or *kastron*. Some occasional dedications on behalf of the community are known at Khirbet el-Mukhayyat and Kafr el-Makr – which petition God for the protection of the *komē* – paralleled by similar dedications at Madaba.[33] But examples of individuals seeking to present themselves in reference to their

---

[28] Al-Ghul, 'Early Arabic inscription from Petra'; Hoyland, 'Mount Nebo, Jabal Ramm', 34–5.

[29] This section of the text is filled with lacunae, and the identification of the language as Syriac is not certain. It is clear from the same passage, however, that evidence in another language was presented alongside evidence in Greek.

[30] Piccirillo, 'La Cattedrale di Madaba', 311.

[31] Hoyland, 'Mount Nebo, Jabal Ramm', 32.

[32] Kloner, 'The Cave Chapel of Horvat Qasra', 129–37, 29*-30*; Puech, 'Una iscrizione in cristo-palestinese', 289.

[33] Di Segni, 'Greek Inscriptions', 439–40; Piccirillo, 'La Cattedrale di Madaba', 311.

settlement of origin are scarce in dedications, and cases where individuals sought to situate themselves as part of a wider provincial or imperial superstructure are unknown. Where toponyms are attested, it is usually only to identify people who were in some sense 'out of place'. The donation registers for Nessana, for example, identify several individuals from Elousa and Sobata, who are listed as benefactors of the Church of Sts Sergios and Bakchos (P. Colt 79, 9–11, 14–16, 40–1). Pilgrim 'graffiti' from the Wadi Haggag also stress the identities of their inscribers as residents of Kastron Zadakathon.[34] Ideas of something that we would perceive as a 'civic identity' were generally expressed only in situations where an individual was removed from that community; in contrast, dedications sponsored individually by patrons who still resided in their place of commission never mention the locality. Rural identity, as expressed through papyri and epigraphy, was, it seems, intrinsically local – conveyed through an individual's association with their family and focused on promoting the status of a patron within a community that was likely already very aware of their broader social identity.

Public Identity in the Rural Sphere

The characteristics most frequently presented in constructing the public identity of rural communities were immediate to the individual and concerned with three principal qualities: an individual's gender – rarely stated but always implicit; a person's position within a wider family structure as a parent, spouse, sibling or child; and, finally, the person's vocation. The importance of the family as a social unit in Byzantium, as well as the ambiguity surrounding the definition of the commonly used term *oikos*, has been well acknowledged in previous studies.[35] The picture from Arabia-Palaestina mirrors this complexity and offers no certain indications that distinctions between an individual's immediate biological kin and other figures in a rural household or community were rigidly formalised. In epigraphic and papyrological convention, familial identity in the region was mediated in two principal ways by the sixth century: either collectively, whereby an individual stated their connection to an extended family network, or, more commonly, on more intimate terms, whereby connections to family were expressed through particular social relationships, whether consanguineal or marital.

[34] Negev, *The Greek Inscriptions from the Negev*, nos 72 and 104.
[35] Brubaker, 'Preface', with further references.

The Rural *Oikos*

By far the most ambiguous term in understanding the dynamics of the public identity of the rural family in Palaestina and Arabia is the concept of the *oikos*, which is invoked in church dedications of the sixth and seventh centuries across the region. A characteristic example appears in the western church of Horvat Mamshit, in the Negev, where a central mosaic medallion in the church entreats God for the salvation of the male donor Nilos, followed by further petitions to guard his household (K(YPI)E ΦΥΛΑΞΕ TON OIKON AYTOY).[36] Similar examples, which appeal directly for the protection or the salvation of the benefactor's *oikos*, appear in the dedications adorning the floors of the churches of Horvat Hesheq and Herodion.[37]

Rural dedications are never explicit in setting out and identifying the individual people that comprised an *oikos* – generally, I suspect, because the audiences for whom such dedications were intended were already well acquainted with the benefactor families. Certainly, the evidence alludes to the existence of prominent, and probably locally renowned, rural families exercising considerable control over the funding and management of church buildings at the level of individual villages after the year 500. The predominance of the George–Patrikios family at Nessana is a case in point, but more subtle allusions in the epigraphic corpus of other churches postdating 500 suggest a wider replication of these patterns across the region.[38] Within these communities, the identities of such prominent families and households may have been so familiar that dedications commissioned on behalf of their collective *oikos* required little further description of the individual actors to whom they referred.

While this often hinders more detailed understanding of the structure of individual households, one clear warning provided by the evidence is that the rather enclosed impression of the nuclear family proscribed by epigraphy seldom corresponded to the functioning of the rural *oikos* as a social and physical space. As is evident from the Nessana papyri, the inheritance laws that were commonly adhered to by rural communities in the region often involved the systematic division of an individual property between relatives and could result in cases of cohabitation and

---

[36] Madden, *Corpus of Byzantine Church Mosaics*, 170–1.
[37] Madden, *Corpus of Byzantine Church Mosaics*, 148–9, 170–1.
[38] Kraemer, *Excavations at Nessana*, 6–9; Ruffini, 'Village Life and Family Power'. Other examples of prominent village patrons or owners are discussion in Wickham, *Framing the Early Middle Ages*, 456.

shared ownership across several generations and kinship groups within the walls of a single building. An inheritance agreement dated to 566, brokered between Flavios Anmos and his sister Ania, provides one clear indication of this practice (P. Colt 22). The documents records how a house (οἰκοδομημάτων) located in Nessana, bequeathed to them by their grandfather, was evenly divided between the two siblings: Anmos received the two northern rooms of the building and Ania the two southern, with both consenting to mutual ownership and use of the vestibule and courtyard (P. Colt 22, 18–35).

That said, the immediacy of connections between spouses and children is so frequently foregrounded in the epigraphic convention that attempts to downplay the importance of the 'nuclear' family need to be handled cautiously. On some occasions, benefactors purposefully distinguished their immediate relatives from the wider framework of the *oikos* in the dedications that they commissioned in churches. While the central panel of the Church of Nilos in Horvat Mamshit, for example, commemorates the donation of Nilos and his extended *oikos*, an accompanying panel located in the eastern sector of the church eschews this convention in favour of a petition for Nilos' salvation and that of his own children (KAI TA TEKNA AYTOY).[39]

The most overt indication of the importance of the immediate family unit as a distinct component within the *oikos*, however, emerges from the sheer number of dedications in the region that identify the benefactor solely in the context of their agnatic family. Thus, in the current corpus, the most frequently attested figures alongside the main donor are generally parents, spouses and children, followed, to a lesser extent, by siblings.

This emphasis on the nuclear family was further expressed in chronological terms by limiting the portrayal of family identity to the generations that immediately preceded and followed a particular donor. While relationships to parents and children are habitually stressed in the epigraphic dedications of rural patrons, there are no known cases of donors situating themselves within a dynastic line that spanned several generations. Public identity in the village of sixth-century Arabia-Palaestina was, it seems, defined primarily in the context of living memory.

Rural Men

Following Roman convention, the idealised structure of the sixth-century Byzantine family habitually foregrounded its male members as the dominant

---

[39] Madden, *Corpus of Byzantine Church Mosaics*, 170–1.

figureheads of the public persona of the *oikos* and a person's connection to agnatic relatives. The conventions employed by rural patrons in Byzantine Palaestina and Arabia offer no exception to these general observations in terms of the broader gender bias in epigraphic material or how individual patrons sought to publicise their connections to wider familial or social networks. The dedicatory inscriptions of the Church of Horvat Hesheq name only three individuals – Demetrios, George and Somas – all of whom are men, and the prosopography of names that we may extract from the churches of Herodion, Khirbet el-Beiyudat and Rihab are also dominated by the presence of male figures.[40] Accordingly, the public identities of male donors in such contexts were generally negotiated with reference to male relations. Among the more familiar forms of this convention was the use of the patronymic, a device that served to stress the identity of an individual through the name and position of their father. The simplest expression of this connection followed the established epigraphic tradition of following the name of the subject (usually the patron) in the Greek nominative case with their father's name, inscribed in genitive form. A characteristic example of this convention emerges in the dedication of the church at Magen, where the principal donor, Aelianos, is described as 'Ailianos [son] of Zonainos the reader' (ΑΙΛΙΑΝΟΣ ΖΟΝΑΙΝΟΥ ΑΝΑΓΝΩΤΗΣ).[41]

In other cases, paternal relationships were promoted more explicitly through use of the title υἱός ('son') and, less frequently, the term τέκνον ('child'). At Horvat Hesheq, for example, the inscription, headed by the deacon Demetrios, introduces his son George as ΓΕΟΡΓΙΟΥ ΥΙΟΥ, and we may observe parallel adoption of these practices at the churches of St George at Khisfin and in the later phases of the church at Jabaliyah.[42]

Naming practices occasionally reinforced patrilineal associations through the naming of a child after a senior relative within the family, most commonly the father or a paternal grandparent. In the Church of St George at Horvat Hesheq, use of the name 'Demetrios' can be seen to have spanned two generations in the dedications commissioned in the church, as can the recurrence of the name Ouraos in Khisfin.[43] The situation finds a close parallel with the popularity of the names Sergios, George and Patrikios among

---

[40] Piccirillo, *Chiese e mosaici*, 63–90; Al-Hissan, 'New Archaeological Discoveries', 82; Madden, *Corpus of Byzantine Church Mosaics*, 18–19.
[41] Madden, *Corpus of Byzantine Church Mosaics*, 102.
[42] Madden, *Corpus of Byzantine Church Mosaics*, 64–5, 142–3.
[43] Madden, *Corpus of Byzantine Church Mosaics*, 142–3.

the prominent families of Nessana and the name Obodianos in the Petra papyri.[44]

Other forms of male connection could, however, be stressed in the absence of patronymic convention. Fraternal association was a common alternative, notably in cases where the foundation of a church or sponsorship of a programme of refurbishment was achieved through the collective efforts of an extended family. Thus, at Herodion, the dedicatory *tabula ansata* of the Church of St Michael commemorates the foundation by the two brothers Saphrika and Anael (ΣΑΦΡΙΚΑ ΚΑΙ ΑΝΑΗΛ ΑΔΕΛΦΩΝ) on behalf of their respective households.[45]

Rural Women

Women generally occupied a more peripheral role in the public image of the family in rural settlements of the sixth century, although the demands of daily life in agrarian communities evidently resulted in a more fluid negotiation of the formal ideals that were traditionally defined for elite, primarily urban, women. While this serves as a precaution in viewing epigraphic conventions as straightforward reflections of actual social practices and identities, attempts to understand the complexity and variation of women's experience in studies of rural life in the region, whether social, economic or legal, remain in their infancy.[46] While neither the Nessana nor Petra papyri are replete with women, they offer some examples in which women can be seen to act independently of male authority in ways that epigraphic formulas seldom convey. Such influence appears to have been partly predicated on a women's marital identity. Widows and divorced women appear to have been granted greater autonomy in exercising control over their property and custodianship of their children than their married counterparts, a scenario which echoes wider legal practices of the sixth century and earlier periods.[47] Thus in Nessana, Ania, widow of Phanes (γαμετὴ τοῦ μακαρ(ίου) Φ]ανῆτος), was able independently to negotiate her inheritance of familial property on an equal basis with her brother, Flavios Anmos (P. Colt 22, 7). This fluidity parallels the situations observed in urban contexts and, indeed, by contemporary rural communities in Egypt, notably Jeme.[48]

---

[44] Ruffini, 'Village Life and Family Power'; Koenen, 'Decipherment and Edition', 203–5.
[45] Madden, *Corpus of Byzantine Church Mosaics*, 65–6, 114–15.
[46] Sivan, *Palestine in Late Antiquity*, 275–301; Britt, 'Fama et memoria'.
[47] Arjava, *Women and Law*.
[48] Wilfong, *Women of Jeme*, 141–4.

Such extension of female authority in rural contexts was, nonetheless, often encased in a system of nomenclature that continued to situate a women's public identity in relation to her nearest male relative (whether living or deceased). Ania, for example, while freely engaged in her negotiations, was consistently defined through male association, as the daughter of Stephanos (Ανια Στεφάνου) (P. Colt 22).[49] While changes in marital status could, therefore, have tangible implications for the authority and identity exercised privately by women in rural society, the presentation of their formal public and legal identities still rendered masculine connections normative.

By far the most common way in which women are named as a component of rural communities is through church dedications that were issued on behalf of the corporate family, where they are acknowledged primarily for their roles as wives and mothers within extended households. This status was consistently subordinate to that of their husbands: whereas women could supplant their offspring in the order of the epigraphic register, there are no cases where a woman is named before her husband within the hierarchy of donors. A characteristic example of the familial tradition emerges from the Church of St George in Khirbet el-Mukhayyat, where a small dedicatory panel located between the columns in the nave of the church records the offering of Ammonios and Epiphania alongside their children John and Sergios.[50] Often, however, women are not explicitly named in inscriptions and are identified simply as anonymous appendages to their husbands, most commonly by the use of the term σύμβιος.[51]

While these two traditions represent the most common conventions in the representation of female status and familial identity, there are clear, albeit rare, examples where the authority exercised by individual women did subvert formalised epigraphic protocols. An interesting feature of both the churches of Khirbet el-Mukhayyat, for example, is that the familial identities of the two principle donors, Stephen and Elias, are not expressed in terms of their patrilineal line, but presented in reference to their mother, Komitissa, as ΤΗΚΝΑ ΚΟΜΙΤΙ(ΣΣΗΣ) (sic) ('children of Komitissa').[52] Another matronymic, this time identifying the donor Prokopios, son of Porphyria, also survives in the dedicatory panel of the Church of St George.[53]

---

[49] Cohen, 'Kissufim'; Britt, 'Fama et memoria', 125–7; Kennedy, 'Syrian Elites', 186.
[50] Di Segni, 'Greek Inscriptions', 442.
[51] Piccirillo, 'Province of Arabia', 107–9.
[52] Di Segni, 'Greek Inscriptions', 439–43.
[53] Ibid., 442–7. A similar representation of matrilineal heritage also emerges from the Church of the Bishop Sergios in Kastron Mefa'a; see Piccirillo, 'Le iscrizioni di Kastron Mefa'a', 262, inscription 19e.

What we cannot know, however, are the individual factors that facilitated the more overt declarations of matriarchal identity in these contexts. That such women were widows exercising control over their children's affairs is one potential explanation. Nevertheless, the inscriptions themselves are not explicit in asserting the marital status of such women, and we cannot assume that the loss of a husband represented the only means by which women could acquire their public identity. Certainly, in the case of the dedication by the donor Megale, in el-Rashidiyah, no indications are given as to her political or marital status, and similar examples of female donors acting independently of male relatives must caution against a straightforward understanding of female identity in Arabian-Palestinian villages as defined exclusively by patriarchal structures.[54]

One way in which some women appear to have been able to register a degree of autonomy in the expression of their identity is through their vocational role in the church, principally as nuns (μοναχή or ἀδελφή) or, occasionally, as deaconesses. These are better attested in urban assemblages than in rural churches, although rural counterparts are not unknown.[55] From the Church of St Basil in Rihab (594), we may identify the deaconess Zoe as one of the principal benefactors of the church, alongside a number of prominent male donors of the village.[56] Alongside these contributions to architectural programmes, more piecemeal evidence from liturgical furnishings also yields evidence for a wider system of independent female expression than mosaic epigraphy often permits us to observe, but, incidentally, in contexts that were separate from the public dedicatory inscription itself.[57]

Vocation

For women, vocation was an identity marker that could accompany, or sometimes replace, familial connections; the experience of rural men was often similar. Like women, vocational roles in the church provided one means by which male donors were permitted to appear publicly as lone individuals beyond the context of the family. One fairly typical example survives in the Church of St George of Khirbet el-Mukhayyat commemorating the priest

---

[54] Di Segni, 'Varia Arabica', 587–8.
[55] Meimaris, *Sacred Names*, 176–8; Madden, *Corpus of Byzantine Church Mosaics*, 150.
[56] Piccirillo, *Chiese e mosaici*, 70–2.
[57] Meimaris, *Sacred Names*, 232; Negev, *Wadi Haggag*, nos 72 and 104.

Barichas ΒΑΡΙΞΑΣ ΠΡΕΣΒΥΤΕΡΟΣ.[58] Similar cases of priests identifying themselves independently of family structures also emerge from the dedications commissioned in Jabaliyah (near Gaza), Hazor Ashdod and Horvat Bata, which clearly followed an earlier precedent exhibited in the fifth-century church at Evron.[59] Familial and clerical identities were not, however, mutually exclusive in a society where clerical marriages were a common feature of rural communities by the sixth century. Indeed, the combining of familial and clerical statuses was widespread. Such a synthesis can be clearly seen in the Patrikios–Sergios family of Nessana, but also in inscriptions across the region, at Beersheba, Jabaliyah and Magen.[60]

Clerical vocations (unsurprisingly) dominate in the largely ecclesiastical context of the epigraphic corpora of villages, and the majority of patrons who were identified by their vocation are those who were, in some manner, connected with the institutional church. 'Secular' roles are not unknown as an identity marker employed by patrons in the dedications that they commissioned, although women appear to have been excluded from emphasising any non-ecclesiastical vocation. The most prominent of such roles were those associated with village administration, such as *dioikētēs*, both of which are attested in papyrological and epigraphic formulas from the region in this period.[61] But other roles, including those of physicians and *scholastikoi*, accompanied by mentions of skilled craftsmen such as mosaicists and goldworkers, are also known (P. Colt 30; P. Colt 90) – the latter generally represent the lowest social group that can be identified by vocation in the corpus.

Visual Identities

While epigraphy and papyri substantially illuminate our understanding and awareness of rural literacy by the sixth century, such material often overshadows the individuals and communities for whom illiteracy and lack of, or partial, access to the written word were a daily feature of rural life.[62] Reading and writing are not absolute, or even necessarily mutually inclusive, skills, and individuals unable to engage with the more sophisticated written compositions of the rural elite of their settlement (let alone the

---

[58] Di Segni, 'Greek Inscriptions', 443.
[59] Madden, *Corpus of Byzantine Church Mosaics*, 73–4.
[60] Ibid. 64–8, 101–2.
[61] Meimaris and Kritikakou-Nikolaropoulou, 'Greek Inscriptions', 403–4; see also P. Colt 68.
[62] Stroumsa, 'People and Identities', 66–70.

larger corpus of late Roman literary production) were not necessarily also excluded from an understanding of information conveyed in epigraphic form. The formulaic protocols of the medium, which often saw remarkably similar inscriptions commissioned for the buildings of individual villages, would have facilitated legibility by creating an expected context and imposing a tight limit on the possible information to be deciphered.[63] Such figures were also able to participate in social situations where literacy was central to negotiation. As is evident from the occasional appearance in Nessana papyri of figures who signed formal agreements by proxy, individuals who were illiterate were often familiar with situations involving record-keeping and were often active participants within them (P. Colt 44; P. Colt 45). Thus, the formal identities that were commonly expressed by individuals in epigraphic or written form were often experienced as part of a wider social context where such identities could be expressed in person. Evidently, the predominance of the Sergios–Patrikios family in record-keeping in Nessana by the late sixth century resulted in the concentration of social networks around a single familial unit whose identity was known to those who engaged in the legal and economic affairs of the komē.[64]

Nonetheless, as noted by Leslie Brubaker, in an environment often characterised by considerable variation in literacy, images continued to play a central role in the communication of individual and familial identity.[65] Rural communities in Arabia-Palaestina provide no exception in this respect, and images and donor portraits were frequently employed at a village level to articulate the identity markers and family relationships otherwise expressed in written and epigraphic media.[66]

The portraits that survive are those rendered in floor mosaic, and all derive from schemes that formed part of the decorative programmes of churches. Whether or not comparable portraits of donors existed on the walls of such churches cannot be known, although examples rendered in wall mosaic and plaster in other provincial contexts, and fragments of figural subjects recovered from Kastron Mefa'a, Rehovot-in-the-Negev and Sobata, make this a possibility that cannot be lightly discredited.[67]

---

[63] Thus compare, e.g., the dedications of the churches of Rihab, which use very similar formulas in all of the dedications: Piccirillo, *Chiese e mosaici*, 63–88. See also Ruffini, 'Village Life and Family Power'.

[64] Ruffini, 'Village Life and Family Power'.

[65] Brubaker, 'Looking at the Byzantine Family'.

[66] Britt, 'Fama et memoria'; Habas, 'Donations and Donors'.

[67] Brubaker, 'Elites and Patronage'; Piccirillo, 'La Chiesa del Prete Wa'il'; Tsafrir, 'Northern Church', 65–7; Figueras, 'Mural Painting'.

The identities communicated in visual form by donors largely conformed to the established protocols of public identity more commonly expressed in epigraphic form, and the information conveyed by the two registers frequently intersected. The donor portraits that survive from the region are accordingly almost exclusively male and focused on patrilineal relationships, even in cases where women are otherwise named in the accompanying inscription. Thus, while women and matrilineal connections are a visible presence in St George in Khirbet el-Mukhayyat, only the portrait of a male donor, John, son of Ammonios, was ever explicitly identified by an accompanying inscription.[68] Even portraits of children, such as the figures named by *tituli* as 'the children of Sophia' and the 'children of John' in the Church of Bishop Sergios, Kastron Mefa'a, are identified more openly than images of women in the decorative programmes of rural churches.[69]

When they do appear in dedicatory images, portraits of women are often characterised by a higher degree of anonymity than those commemorating their male counterparts. The use of *tituli* to explicitly identify female subjects, for example, is almost unknown in rural contexts, with the exception of a single, and somewhat contentious, example from the Church of St Elias in Kissufim.[70] In contrast, male portraits are frequently adorned with them, even when they are placed in marginal locations.

The conventions employed in the visual depiction of women in dedications also reinforced their relative anonymity and separation from the public image of rural life. Images of prominent male donors in rural churches were seldom anonymous and commonly represented the subject accompanied by objects or attributes that communicated aspects of their status and social identity (whether actual or idealised). Frequently, this involved a depiction of the subject immersed in a particular activity. Although badly defaced by the later effects of iconoclasm, the nave mosaic of the Church of Bishop Sergios at Kastron Mefa'a preserves a portrait of Oudia, son of Esou, which shows the figure engaged in a liturgical procession, carrying a thurible and entering the open doors of a church.[71] Slightly lower in the same scheme, the figures of John, son of Porphyrios,

---

[68] Di Segni, 'Greek Inscriptions', 441; Piccirillo, 'The Churches on Mount Nebo', 222.

[69] Piccirillo, 'Le iscrizioni di Kastron Mefa'a', 262, inscriptions 19d and 19e; Piccirillo, 'I mosaici del complesso di Santo Stefano', 127–8.

[70] Cohen, 'Kissufim'; Britt, 'Fama et memoria', 125–7; Kennedy, 'Syrian Elites', 186.

[71] Piccirillo, 'I mosaici del complesso di Santo Stefano', 127; 'Le iscrizioni di Kastron Mefa'a', 262, inscription 19c. On iconoclasm, see Reynolds, 'Rethinking', with further references.

and Zognon, also censored by iconoclast intervention, are represented operating a mechanical device, presumably a plough or other agricultural machinery.[72] Whether or not these represent the activities that actually took place in a particular village cannot be known, and the careful qualifications offered by Henry Maguire's analysis of such schemes caution against straightforward interpretations of their designs as reflections of daily life within individual rural communities.[73] Nonetheless, such collective imagery indicates that even in symbolic terms, the public identity of the economically prosperous Christian *komē* was one largely communicated through the activities and efforts of its men.

Portraits of rural women in Arabia-Palaestina, however, are often static in form and more frequently represented in bust profile than fully standing portraits – even those surviving from urban contexts in Gerasa eschew depictions of women 'in action'.[74] The portrait in the Chapel of the Priest John in Khirbet el-Mukhayyat, for example, depicts a woman richly adorned with a diadem and earrings, but is restricted to a portrait of her face and shoulders. As Karen Britt has observed, the use of jewellery was a common signifier of female status in donor portraiture of the region, and one that had strong connections to the management of property and marital transaction.[75] Nonetheless, such emblems of authority could only be directly connected to an individual female patron by an audience to whom she was already known. In the context of the image itself, the portrait in the Chapel of Priest John contains no additional information (such as a *titulus*) that might allude to her wider social identity or link her to a known familial network. It is, in essence, a public image of an esoteric identity.

Representations of women in rural churches are, therefore, often more ahistorical than those of male donors: they are difficult to link to individuals that are named in the related epigraphic register and impossible to interpret in terms of their social roles in the village. This ambiguity is neatly reflected in the difficulty modern scholars often face when distinguishing portraits of actual human donors from feminised personifications of the seasons and other natural phenomena. One example from Kissufim (dated to 576), which features a portrait of Kalliora, continues to excite debate as to whether she is to be identified as the donor Kyria

---

[72] Piccirillo, 'L'identificazione', 37; 'Le iscrizioni di Kastron Mefa'a', 262, inscription 19c.
[73] Maguire, *Nectar and Illusion*, 12–26.
[74] Biebel, 'Mosaics', 302.
[75] Britt, 'Fama et memoria', 123–4.

Sylthous or a personification of good fortune.[76] Attempts to correlate the surviving portrait of Khirbet al-Mukhayyat's Chapel of Priest John with one of the two female donors mentioned in the dedication are similarly conjectural.

While it is difficult to contend that portraits of rural women were not intended to represent actual historical individuals who inhabited villages of the region in the sixth century, such correlations between portrait and subject were not communicated explicitly by the images themselves or their surrounding epigraphic devices. Visual recognition of female status and identity was, it seems, articulated primarily at a local level and communicated only to those already acquainted with the agent in question. In contrast, the correlation between *titulus* and male portraiture in rural contexts worked to ensure a wider recognition of the figure even to audiences not acquainted with the patron or his wider social network.

Image, Space and Word

Like the dedicatory *tabulae ansatae* that they frequently accompanied, the spatial context of images served to ensure the effectiveness of portraiture in communicating the key identity markers of gender, family and vocation in rural contexts. Where they exist, portraits are invariably located in prominent positions in the nave, usually set before the central *bēma* or directly in front of subsidiary altars in adjoining aisles and always orientated towards the gaze of the lay audience. Such calculated symbiosis between visual portraits and the written dedications, enshrined by the *tabula ansata*, was often reinforced by placing both formulas within a single decorative register. A clear example of this may be seen in the Church of St Paul at Kastron Mefa'a, where both the dedicatory inscription and a series of donor portraits are situated within a connected visual framework, bordered by a series of geometric patterns and set against a plain white field (Fig. 7.3).[77] Three portraits appear in the scheme, each accompanied by a *titulus* that identifies the portraits as belonging to the two brothers Sergis (sic) and Paul (the name of the father is not preserved) and another figure named Rabbous.[78] All three men are additionally named in the main inscription located above the image as the primary, and possibly only, donors of the

[76] Cohen, 'Kissufim'; Britt, 'Fama et memoria', 125–7; Kennedy, 'Syrian Elites', 186.
[77] Piccirillo, 'La Chiesa di San Paolo', 383–8.
[78] Ibid. 383–4.

Figure 7.3 Kastron Mefa'a, Church of St Paul, dedicatory panel. Photo courtesy M. Piccirillo 1997.

church building.[79] The portrait panel that flanks the main inscription consequently serves as an effective illustration of the same identities conveyed by the written dedication itself.

A later replication of this model emerges in the Church of St Stephen (dated to 718), also located in Kastron Mefa'a, where the central dedication is flanked by a series of (seven?) portraits incorporated within the same bordered panel.[80] Only one of these figures, a 'son of Samuel', is accompanied by a *titulus*, but this is sufficient to propose a possible familial link between this donor and one 'Elias son of Samuel', mentioned in the apse dedication dated to 756 (Fig. 7.4).[81] A fuller example, however, may be seen in the north aisle of the same church, where an inscription enveloping the two central portraits of the mosaic programme identifies the portraits as those of John and his father, John, son of Souades (Fig. 7.5).[82] An open-handed gesture

---

[79] Ibid.

[80] Piccirillo, 'L'identificazione', 39–41.

[81] Ibid.

[82] Piccirillo, 'Le iscrizioni di Kastron Mefa'a', 249, inscription 6d.

Figure 7.4 Kastron Mefa'a, Church of St Stephen, dedicatory panel. Photo courtesy S. Leatherbury/Manar al-Athar 2010.

Figure 7.5 Kastron Mefa'a, Church of St Stephen, north aisle. Photo courtesy © Daniel Reynolds, 2012.

by the figure on the left towards the neighbouring portrait intimates an association between the two: likely, given the nature of the accompanying inscriptions (all of which repeat similar formulas), a patrilineal connection. The subtle size disparity between the two figures also implies an attempt to establish the seniority of the figure to the viewer's left. Read in the context of the inscription, it appears that the gesture between father and child worked to legitimise the filial status of John in the context of the community of Kastron Mefa'a. The motif appears again in the main panel of the central nave, where a similar gesture by the scheme's central figure is directed to the viewer's right, towards another figure.[83]

Beyond familial associations, visual devices also appear to have been employed by rural patrons to convey information about their identities that written inscriptions occasionally omitted. This can be interpreted only partially, for the effects of later eighth-century iconoclasm have resulted in the defacement of most donor portraits in rural contexts.[84] However, the use of formal costume as a means of communicating the status and vocation of a patron is suggested by attributes that escaped iconoclast censure in some cases. Though iconoclastic activities have removed the main body of the original portraits within the Church of St Paul, what survives of the figure of Sergis is sufficient to identify the thurible that he once carried, which plausibly identifies him as a member of the diaconate – a status that is not otherwise attested in the main inscription.[85] Similarly, the portrait of Oudia, son of Esou, in the Church of the Bishop Sergios in Kastron Mefa'a, does not explicitly identify a clerical role for him, but the figure itself carries a thurible and enter an idealised representation of a church.[86]

Parallels in the churches of St Mary in Rihab and Bishop Leontios at Ya'amun also appear to have featured portraits of donors accompanied by weaponry.[87] In other examples, subjects of portraits can be seen engaging in agricultural pursuits, including harvesting and the tending of livestock.[88] In the portrait accompanying that of Sergis in the Church of St Paul at Kastron Mefa'a, presumably depicting either Constan-

---

[83] Piccirillo, 'I mosaici del complesso di Santo Stefano', 140, plate 30.

[84] Reynolds, 'Rethinking', with further references.

[85] Piccirillo, 'La Chiesa di San Paolo', 383–4.

[86] Piccirillo, 'I mosaici del complesso di Santo Stefano', 127; 'Le iscrizioni di Kastron Mefa'a', 262, inscription 19c.

[87] Turshan and Nassar, 'A Mosaic of the Book of Daniel'; Nassar and Turshan, 'Geometrical Mosaic Pavements'.

[88] Ibid.

tine or Rabbous, one of the figures can be seen carrying a basket filled with fruit corresponding to that flourishing on the trees within the scene (Fig. 7.3).[89]

More recent treatment of the subject has accordingly tended to organise conventions of donor portraiture in rural contexts into categories of formal and informal representation, the former including frontal images which appear in more static postures, such as that of John, son of John, son of Souades, accompanied by liturgical trappings or weaponry, and the latter representing figures engaged in agricultural and other rural activity. While this arrangement is broadly true in terms of the visual properties of the portraits, even those who made images that purportedly sought to represent donors engaged in the daily activities of the village were nonetheless conversant with the formal identities and roles associated with particular genders. The kinds of rural activity we observe in donor portraits, for example, are those that, normatively speaking, were a traditional male preserve. Hunting is a frequent theme of rural portraits in the region, and the decorative schemes adorning the churches of Bishop Sergios at Kastron Mefa'a, Khirbet el-Mukhayyat and Nitl are accordingly replete with images of men engaged in the pursuit of animals and wildfowl.[90]

Arguably, it is absence that most clearly expresses the restrictions of gender roles in relation to portraiture. Women, as we have seen, are generally invisible in the dedications, although in all probability they formed a substantial component of the economic and daily activities of the urban and rural *oikos*.[91] But depictions of children in rural churches also appear to have conformed to a formal ideal which minimised their association with the economic affairs and productive life of the rural community, despite the likelihood that children formed an active component of the labour force of agricultural property into the seventh century, as they had in earlier periods.[92] A surviving property dispute between Patrophilos, son of Bassos, and the widow Elaphia in Petra, for example, was essentially based around ownership of two slaves (who were brothers) aged around seven and four (P. Petra 28, 139–49).

The two sets of portraits of the 'children of Sophia' and 'children of John', in the nave of the Bishop Sergios Church at Kastron Mefa'a, are unique among the other portraits of the same scheme for their static depiction.

---

[89] Piccirillo, 'La Chiesa di San Paolo', 383–4.
[90] Piccirillo, 'Church of Saint Sergius at Nitl'.
[91] Schidel, 'The Most Silent Women'.
[92] Mirkovic, 'Child Labour and Taxes'.

Figure 7.6 Kastron Mefa'a, Church of Bishop Sergios, detail of the children of Sophia. Photo courtesy © Daniel Reynolds, 2012.

Whereas the images of adults in the scheme portray them engaged in a variety of agrarian pursuits, the representation of the two children is visibly static, presenting them standing in a front-facing position and not engaged in any particular activity. Similarly, whereas portraits of adult donors are furnished with weaponry or implements that associate them with particular vocations, those of children are instead depicted with flowers or small animals: the *tekna* of John hold a single flower and a basket, respectively, and those of Sophia are depicted in similar guise (Fig. 7.6). Children, like women, it seems, were excluded from the public image of the rural *komē* as a political and economic arena.

Conclusion

I have concentrated on the themes of family and gender in this chapter, primarily because it is these traits that are most frequently foregrounded in the dedications and papyri that were commissioned and produced directly by rural patrons. In this respect, they are the closest written source we have for understanding the nature of public identity in the rural sphere as it was presented by communities themselves, rather than how it was theorised by the clerical or urban elite from afar. Nevertheless, the public identities they suggest fit well with existing models of the Byzantine period and much later. Men retained their position as the dominant figures in the portrayal of the corporate family both in written and visual media, and their role as the individuals around whom others, including women and children, negotiated their own identities in the public space. Despite their demographic strength, women and children were frequently relegated to the peripheries of the public discourse.

These observations are hardly new in the context of established debate, but what is perhaps most surprising is the extent to which such formalised modes of public expression were able to permeate the practices of rural communities and patrons even in areas on the fringes of Byzantine imperial control and among groups, such as the Jafanids, whose patterns of social organisation may have borne little similarity to their contemporaries in other regions of the empire or, indeed, within the provinces of Arabia and Palaestina. Furthermore, these inscriptions are also testament to a particular type of rural 'class' in Arabia and Palaestina, the members of which were enfranchised by the economic developments of the late fifth century onwards to the extent that they possessed the means to sponsor such overt declarations of their public image. In this sense, the homogeneity in the conventions employed by rural patrons was likely an intentional act by benefactors as they sought confirmation and acceptance of their emerging social status – however modest, however local – through recourse to an established model of what it meant to be elite in the Byzantine world of the sixth century. This was, invariably, an identity grounded in Greek and expressed primarily through male connection.

Whether or not the formal conventions surveyed here adequately reflect how identity was exercised and understood on a daily basis in rural society is difficult to know. As addressed in this study, there are clear examples of individuals whose actions did subvert the roles that were formally prescribed in the public sphere, and allusions to many other individuals and groups whose lives were otherwise invisible to the epigraphic radar of the Byzantine village of Arabia-Palaestina. The appearance of local epigraphic traditions in CPA and the agency wielded by individual females are two clear examples of more complex ways of negotiating identity in the sixth and early seventh centuries that are now almost entirely lost to the modern gaze. While such examples, few as they are, allow us to penetrate the illusion of social homogeneity proposed by the epigraphic register, they offer us no complete alternative to nuance this picture, and any attempt to formulate a notion of 'private' or 'local' identities from such a limited corpus would result in a misrepresentation of such individuals and people.

Despite their homogeneity, we also cannot disregard the longevity of these conventions, which continued to be used in the public image of the rural family until well over a century after the collapse of Byzantine control in the region. In 718, with the foundation of the Church of St Stephen in Kastron Mefa'a, the use of Greek, patronymic convention and portrait still remained the dominant means by which public identity was expressed, and the Church as an institution and physical entity retained its role as the principal arena for such declarations of rural status.

By then, such conventions were being employed among communities with limited connections to Byzantium who may have had little memory of the origins of the formulas and practices they adopted in the articulation of their public presence. But these conventions are still to be seen in the church at Khirbet al-Shubaika, dated to 785/801, the last rural church in the region that we can date with precision to before the twelfth century.[93]

What is less clear is the extent to which these protocols continued beyond the late eighth century. One victim of the collapse of rural Christian patronage, which appears to have distinguished the ninth century, was precisely the epigraphic dedications in which rural patrons are most visible to modern commentators. Whether or not their disappearance marked an end to formal expressions of rural identity is impossible to know, though unlikely, but changes to the urban and fiscal organisation in the Abbasid Caliphate after the year 800 seem to have led to the evaporation of the enfranchised sedentary peasant class that had characterised the region in the fifth to eighth centuries. With this disappears our primary means of exploring the question of rural identity in the region prior to the Crusades.

The impression that emerges by the tenth century is that, overall, such ways of presenting identity survived. In a dedicatory votive inscription, dated to 985 and recovered from the excavations at the Tomb of the Theotokos, the identity of the primary donor Jābir, son of Musa, son of Mīkhā'īl, is referenced in relation to his paternal line, accompanied by his family alongside petitions for the salvation of all Christian monasteries.[94] His example bears comparison to a number of votive graffiti recovered from routes to Mount Sinai and dated to the same period, from male and female pilgrims, Christian and Muslim, all of whom stress connections to family and paternity.[95] The main shift we can see is linguistic: Arabic had,

---

[93] Madden, *Corpus of Byzantine Church Mosaics*, 186–7.
[94] Katsimbinis, 'New Findings at Gethsemani'.
[95] Kawatoko, Tokunaga and Iizuka, *Ancient and Islamic Rock*.

by then, replaced Greek as the dominant vernacular of public expression.[96] Nonetheless, familial and male connections had endured as one of the primary signifiers of public identity. Though armies waged war and dynasties rose and fell, 'the family' remained firm as the keystone of how individuals continued to situate themselves in relation to the wider world of the early medieval Levant.

Acknowledgements

I would like to thank Yannis Stouraitis and John Haldon for their generous invitation to submit a chapter to this volume. The research for this article was undertaken during my postdoctoral fellowship sponsored by the British Academy (2014–17). My thanks go to them for their generous support of my work. Lastly, I wish to thank my friend and colleague Rebecca Darley, who kindly offered her feedback and comments on a draft of this chapter.

In this chapter I have made several stylistic decisions that require note. For place names, I have used the versions which appear in recent publications to make them more accessible to the reader. The focus on the years 500 to 630 largely reflects the surviving evidence relating to rural communities. Nonetheless, there are clear indications of several of the characteristics outlined in this chapter prior to the year 500, and I do not intend to represent the sixth century as a period marking a drastic shift in how individual rural actors sought to convey their identity; Piccirillo, *Chiese e mosaici*, 52–3; Madden, *Corpus of Byzantine Church Mosaics*, 170–1.

Bibliography

Sources

P. Colt . . . C. J. Kraemer (ed.), *Excavations at Nessana: Non-Literary Papyri*, vol. 3 (Princeton, 1958).

P. Petra I . . . J. Frösén, A. Arjava and M. Lehtinen (eds), *The Petra Papyri I* (Amman, 2002).

P. Petra II . . . L. Koenen, J. Kaimio, M. Kaimio and R. W. Daniel (eds), *The Petra Papyri II* (Amman, 2013).

P. Petra III . . . A. Arjava, M. Buchholz and T. Gagos (eds), *The Petra Papyri III* (Amman, 2007).

---

[96] Griffith, *Church in the Shadow*.

P. Petra IV . . . A. Arjava, M. Buchholz, T. Gagos and M. Kaimio (eds), *The Petra Papyri IV* (Amman, 2011).

P. Petra V . . . A. Arjava, J. Frösén, J. Kaimio (eds), *The Petra Papyri V* (Amman, 2018).

Secondary Literature

Al-Ghul, O., 'An Early Arabic Inscription from Petra Carrying Diacritic Marks', *Syria* 8 (2004): 105–18.

Al-Hissan, A., 'The New Archaeological Discoveries of the al-Fudayn and Rahāb – al-Mafraq Excavation Projects, 1991–2001', *AAJord* 46 (2002): 71–94 (Arabic Section).

Arjava, A., *Women and Law in Late Antiquity* (Oxford, 1998).

Aviam, M., 'Horvath Hesheq – A Unique Church in Upper Galilee: Preliminary Report', in G. Claudio-Bottini, L. Di Segni and E. Alliata (eds), *Christian Archaeology in the Holy Land: New Discoveries. Essays in Honour of Virgilio C. Corbo* (Jerusalem, 1990), 351–78.

Avni, G., *The Byzantine-Islamic Transition in Palestine* (Oxford, 2014).

Bessard, F., 'The Urban Economy in Southern Inland Greater Syria from the Seventh Century to the End of the Umayyads', in L. Lavan (ed.), *Local Economies? Production and Exchange of Inland Regions in Late Antiquity* (Leiden, 2015), 377–421.

Biebel, F., 'Mosaics', in C. H. Kraeling (ed.), *Gerasa: City of the Decapolis* (New Haven, CT, 1938), 341–51.

Blumell, L., and J. Cianca, 'The Oratory of St. George in Rihab: The Oldest Extant Christian Building or Just Another Byzantine Church?' *Biblical Archaeology Review Online publications* (2008). <http://www.bib-arch.org/online-exclusives/oldest-church.pdf> (last accessed 15 January 2012).

Bowersock, G. W., *Roman Arabia* (Cambridge, MA, 1983).

Britt, K., 'Fama et memoria: Portraits of Female Patrons in Mosaic Pavements of Churches in Byzantine Palestine and Arabia', *Medieval Feminist Forum* 44/2 (2008): 119–43.

Brock, S., A. Canby, O. al-Ghul, R. G. Hoyland and M. C. A. Macdonald, 'The Semitic Inscriptions', in K. Politis (ed.), *The Sanctuary of Lot at Deir ʿAin ʿAbata in Jordan, Excavations 1988–2003* (Amman, 2012), 417–19.

Broshi, M., 'The Population of Western Palestine in the Roman-Byzantine Period', *BASOR* 236 (1979): 1–10.

Brubaker, L., 'Elites and Patronage in Early Byzantium: The Evidence from Hagios Demetrios at Thessalonike', in J. Haldon and L. Conrad (eds),

The Byzantine and Early Islamic Near East, VI: Elites Old and New (Princeton, NJ, 2004), 63–90.

Brubaker, L., 'Looking at the Byzantine Family', in L. Brubaker and S. Tougher (eds), *Approaches to the Byzantine Family* (Aldershot, 2013), 177–206.

Brubaker, L., 'Preface', in L. Brubaker and S. Tougher (eds), *Approaches to the Byzantine Family* (Aldershot, 2013), xix–xxv.

Cohen, R., 'A Byzantine Church and Its Mosaic Floors at Kissufim', in Y. Tsafrir (ed.), *Ancient Churches Revealed* (Jerusalem, 1993), 277–82.

Dauphin, C., *La Palestine Byzantine: Peuplement et Populations*, 3 vols (Oxford, 1998).

Decker, M., *Tilling the Hateful Earth: Agricultural Production and Trade in the Late Antique East* (Oxford, 2011).

Di Segni, D., 'Khirbet el-Beiyudat: The Inscriptions', in G. C. Bottini, L. Di Segni and E. Alliata (eds), *Christian Archaeology in the Holy Land: New Discoveries. Essays in Honour of Virgilio C. Corbo OFM* (Jerusalem, 1990), 265–73.

Di Segni, D., 'The Inscriptions at Khirbet el-Beiyudat', in Y. Tsafrir (ed.), *Ancient Churches Revealed* (Jerusalem, 1993), 164–9.

Di Segni, L., 'The Greek Inscriptions', in M. Piccirillo and E. Alliata (eds), *Mount Nebo: New Archaeological Excavations 1967–1997* (Jerusalem, 1998), 425–67.

Di Segni, L., 'Varia Arabica: Greek Inscriptions from Jordan', *Liber Annuus* 56 (2006): 578–92.

Di Segni, L., and Y. Tsafrir, 'The Ethnic Composition of Jerusalem's Population in the Byzantine Period (312–638 CE)', *Liber Annuus* 62 (2012): 405–54.

Esler, P. F., *Babatha's Orchard: The Yadin Papyri and an Ancient Jewish Family Tale Retold* (Oxford, 2017).

Figueras, P., 'Remains of a Mural Painting of the Transfiguration in the Southern Church of Sobata (Shivta)', *ARAM* 18–19 (2006–7): 127–51.

Fine, S., 'Between Liturgy and Social History: Priestly Power in Late Antique Palestinian Synagogues?' *JJS* 56 (2005): 1–9.

Fisher, G., 'A New Perspective on Rome's Desert Frontier', *BASOR* 336 (2004): 49–60.

Fisher, G., and P. Wood, with contributions from G. Bevan, G. Greatrex, B. Hamarneh, P. Schadler and W. Ward, 'Arabs and Christianity', in G. Fischer (ed.), *Arabs and Empires before Islam* (Oxford, 2015), 276–372.

Griffith, S. H., *The Church in the Shadow of the Mosque* (Princeton, 2008).

Habas, L., 'Donations and Donors as Reflected in the Mosaic Pavements of Transjordan's Churches in the Byzantine and Umayyad Period', in K. Kogman-Appel and M. Meyer (eds), *Between Judaism and Christianity: Art Historical Essays in Honor of Elisheva Elizabeth Revel-Neher* (Leiden and Boston, 2008), 73–90.

Hirschfeld, Y., 'Farms and Villages in Byzantine Palestine', *DOP* 51 (1997): 33–71.

Hoyland, R., 'Mount Nebo, Jabal Ramm, and the Status of Christian Palestinian Aramaic and Old Arabic in late Roman Palestine and Arabia', in M. C. A. Macdonald (ed.), *The Development of Arabic as a Written Language (Supplement to the Proceedings of the Seminar for Arabian Studies 40)* (Oxford, 2010), 29–46.

Humbert, J. B., 'Khirbet es-Samra du diocèse du Bostra', in Claudio-Bottini et al. (eds), *Christian Archaeology in the Holy Land: New Discoveries. Essays in Honour of Virgilio C. Corbo* (Jerusalem, 1990), 467–74.

Kaimio, J., 'Terms in Connection with Houses in 39 and Other Petra Papyri', in Arjava et al. (eds), *The Petra Papyri IV* (Amman, 2011), 9–22.

Katsimbinis, C., 'New Findings at Gethsemani', *Liber Annuus* 29 (1976): 277–80.

Kawatoko, M., R. Tokunaga and M. Rizuka, *Ancient and Islamic Rock Inscriptions of South Sinai* (Tokyo, 2006).

Kennedy, H., 'Syrian Elites from Byzantium to Islam: Survival or Extinction?' in J. Haldon (ed.), *Money, Power and Politics in Early Islamic Syria: A Review of Current Debates* (Farnham and Burlington, VT, 2010), 181–200.

Kingsley, S., 'The Economic Impact of the Palestinian Wine Trade in Late Antiquity', in S. Kingsley and M. Decker (eds), *Economy and Exchange in the East Mediterranean During Late Antiquity* (Oxford, 2001), 45–67.

Kirk, G., and C. B. Welles, 'The Inscriptions', in H. D. Colt (ed.), *Excavations at Nessana (Auja Hafir Palestine)*, vol. 1 (London, 1962).

Kloner, A., 'The Cave Chapel of Horvat Qasra', *'Atiqot* 19 (1990): 129–37 (Hebrew), 29*–30* (English summary).

Koenen, L., 'The Decipherment and Edition of the Petra Papyri: Preliminary Observations', in L. Schiffman (ed.), *Semitic Papyrology in Context: A Climate of Creativity. Papers from a New York University Conference Marking the Retirement of Baruch A. Levine* (Leiden, 2003), 201–26.

Koenen, L., J. Kaimio and R. W. Daniel, 'Introduction: Terms Pertaining to Dwellings and Agriculture in 17', in A. Arjava et al. (eds), *The Petra Papyri IV* (Amman, 2011), 1–22.

Lapin, H., *Economy, Geography, and Provincial History in Later Roman Palestine* (Tübingen, 2001).

Leatherbury, S., *Inscribing Faith in Late Antiquity: Between Reading and Seeing. Image, Text, and Culture in Classical Antiquity* (London and New York, 2020).

Levy-Rubin, M., *Non-Muslims in the Early Islamic Empire: From Surrender to Coexistence* (Cambridge, 2011).

Madden, M., *Corpus of Byzantine Church Mosaics from Israel and the Palestinian Territories* (Leuven, Paris, Walpole, MA, 2014).

Maguire, H., *Nectar and Illusion: Nature in Byzantine Art and Literature* (Oxford, 2012).

Meimaris, Y. E., *Sacred Names, Saints, Martyrs and Church Officials in the Greek Inscriptions and Papyri Pertaining to the Christian Church of Palestine* (Athens, 1986).

Meimaris, Y. E., and K. I. Kritikakou-Nikolaropoulou, 'The Greek Inscriptions', in K. Politis (ed.), *Sanctuary of Lot at Deir 'Ain 'Abata in Jordan Excavations 1988–2003* (Amman, 2012), 393–416.

Meyer, E. A., *Legitimacy and Law in the Roman World: Tabulae in Roman Belief and Practice* (Cambridge, 2004).

Mirkovic, M., 'Child Labour and Taxes in the Agriculture of Roman Egypt: Pais and Aphelix', *Scripta Israelica Classica* 24 (2005): 139–49.

Nassar, M., and N. Turshan, 'Geometrical Mosaic Pavements of the Church of Bishop Leontios at Ya'amun (Northern Jordan)', *PEQ* 143 (2011): 41–62.

Negev, A., *Inscriptions of Wadi Haggag, Sinai* (Jerusalem, 1977).

Negev, A., *The Greek Inscriptions from the Negev* (Jerusalem, 1981).

Netzer, E., R. Birger-Calderon and A. Feller, 'The Churches of Herodium', in Y. Tsafrir (ed.), *Ancient Churches Revealed* (Jerusalem, 1993), 219–32.

Parker, S. T., *Romans and Saracens: A History of the Arabian Frontier* (Winona Lake, IN, 1986).

Perrot, C., 'Un fragment Christo-Palestinien découvert à Khirbet Mird', *Revue Biblique* 70 (1963): 506–55.

Piccirillo, M., *Chiese e mosaici della Giordania Settentrionale* (Jerusalem, 1981).

Piccirillo, M., 'La Cattedrale di Madaba', *Liber Annuus* 31 (1981): 299–332.

Piccirillo, M., 'La Chiesa del Prete Wa'il a Umm al-Rasas – Kastron Mefaa in Giordania', in F. Manns and E. Alliata (eds), *Early Christianity in Context: Monuments and Documents* (Jerusalem, 1993), 313–34.

Piccirillo, M., 'L'identificazione storica di Umm al-Rasas con Mefaa', in M. Piccirillo and E. Alliata (eds), *Umm al-Rasas, Mayfa'ah I: Gli Scavi del Complesso di Santo Stefano* (Jerusalem, 1994), 37–46.

Piccirillo, M., 'I mosaici del complesso di Santo Stefano', in M. Piccirillo and E. Alliata (eds), *Umm al-Rasas, Mayfa'ah I: Gli Scavi del Complesso di Santo Stefano* (Jerusalem, 1994), 121–64.

Piccirillo, M., 'Le iscrizioni di Kastron Mefa'a', in M. Piccirillo and E. Alliata (eds), *Umm al-Rasas, Mayfa'ah I: Gli Scavi del Complesso di Santo Stefano* (Jerusalem, 1994), 241–69.

Piccirillo, M., 'La Chiesa di San Paolo à Umm al-Rasas – Kastron Mefaa', *Liber Annuus* 47 (1997): 375–94.

Piccirillo, M., 'The Churches on Mount Nebo: New Discoveries', in M. Piccirillo and E. Alliata (eds), *Mount Nebo: New Archaeological Excavations 1967–1997* (Jerusalem, 1998), 221–44.

Piccirillo, M., 'The Church of Saint Sergius at Nitl: A Centre of the Christian Arabs in the Steppe at the Fates of Madaba', *Liber Annuus* 51 (2001): 267–84.

Puech, E., 'Una iscrizione in cristo-palestinese', in M. Piccirillo and E. Alliata (eds), *Umm al-Rasas, Mayfa'ah I: Gli Scavi del Complesso di Santo Stefano* (Jerusalem, 1994), 289–90.

Reynolds, D., 'Rethinking Palestinian Iconoclasm', *DOP* 71 (2017): 1–64.

Ruffini, G., 'Village Life and Family Power in Late Antique Nessana', *TAPA* 141 (2011): 201–25.

Schidel, W., 'The Most Silent Women of Greece and Rome: Rural Labour and Women's Life in the Ancient World', *Greece & Rome* 42/2 (1995): 202–17.

Sivan, H., *Palestine in Late Antiquity* (Oxford, 2008).

Stroumsa, R., 'People and Identities in Nessana', PhD thesis, Duke University, 2009.

Trombley, F., 'From Kastron to Qaṣr: Nessana between Byzantium and the Umayyad Caliphate ca.602–689. Demographic and Microeconomic Aspects of Palaestina III in Interregional Perspective', in E. Bradshaw Aitken and J. M. Fossey (eds), *The Levant: Crossroads of Late Antiquity* (Leiden, 2014).

Tsafrir, Y., 'The Northern Church', in Y. Tsafrir (ed.), *Excavations at Rehovot-in-the-Negev*, vol. 1 (Jerusalem, 1988), 22–77.

Turshan, N., and M. Nassar, 'A Mosaic of the Book of Daniel in the Ya'amun Church', *GRBS* 5 (2011): 340–9.

Verhelst, S., 'Les fragments du Castellion (Kh. Mird) des évangiles de Marc et de Jean (P84)', *Le Muséon* 116 (2003), 15–44.

Walmsley, A., 'Production, Exchange and Regional Trade in the Islamic East Mediterranean: Old Structures, New Systems?', in I. L. Hansen and C. Wickham (eds), *The Long Eighth Century* (Leiden, Boston and Cologne, 2000), 265–344.

Wickham, C., *Framing the Early Middle Ages* (Oxford, 2005).

Wilfong, T. G., *Women of Jeme: Lives in a Coptic Town in Late Antique Egypt* (Ann Arbor, MI, 2002).

Yasin, A-M., *Saints and Church Spaces in the Late Antique Mediterranean: Architecture, Cult, and Community* (New York, 2009).

8

Community-Building and Collective Identity in Middle Byzantine Athens

Fotini Kondyli

Communities are dynamic and socially constituted institutions that rely on day-to-day interaction, shared experiences and shared qualities that allow their members to define and distinguish themselves from others.[1] Community building often involves physical spaces that function as focal points of placemaking activities that include social encounters, daily rituals and practices that endow places with meaning and value.[2] Cities are the physical manifestation of such interactions among different social and economic groups, both elite and non-elite.[3]

Byzantine cities often do not correspond to modern urban aesthetics, nor do they easily conform to their Greco-Roman predecessors, making it easy for scholars to misunderstand or disapprove of them. Furthermore, despite the numerous publications on Byzantine cities that explore how local and regional conditions shape and manifest in the urban fabric, comparisons with Constantinople continue to inform our expectations of urban realities in the provinces.[4] Provincial cities could be small, messy,

---

[1] For a definition of community and the role of archaeology in understanding ancient communities, see Yaeger and Canuto, 'Archaeology of Communities'.

[2] Low and Lawrence-Zúñiga, 'Locating Culture'; Friedmann, 'Place and Place-Making', 152–5; Cresswell, *Place*; Ashmore, 'Ancient Placemaking'.

[3] Smith, 'Social Construction', esp. 73, 78; Cowgill, 'Origins and Development'; Fisher and Creekmore, 'Making Ancient Cities'.

[4] A renewed interest in Byzantine urbanism has produced numerous publications on the archaeology of Byzantine cities and on the nature of Byzantine urbanism. I mention here a small number of very recent edited volumes and monographs that exemplify that interest: for edited volumes, see Daim and Drauschke, *Byzanz*; Kiousopoulou (ed.), *Βυζαντινές πόλεις*; Albani and Chalkia (eds), *Heaven and Earth*; for late antique cities, see Saradi, *Byzantine City in the Sixth Century*; Jacobs, *Aesthetic Maintenance*; Dey, *Afterlife*; Lenski, *Constantine and the Cities*; for middle and late Byzantine cities, see Kalligas, *Monemvasia*; Bouras, *Byzantine Athens*; Daim and Ladstätter (eds), *Ephesos*.

'organically' developed and haphazardly built, characterised at times by a distinct lack of civic buildings and monumentality. This 'organic' scenario often becomes synonymous with unplanned, crowded, chaotic, unsophisticated and *ad hoc* urban developments.[5] However, such labels mask the intentionality and the decision-making processes included in organic development and undermine the study of the social and spatial practices involved in city-making.[6] Spaces are socially produced and are shaped and conceptualised through social interaction.[7] Such encounters are not always harmonious and peaceful; they can equally involve conflict, disagreement, indifference and/or collaboration. But the engagement in such processes is what ultimately creates shared spaces and experiences, and enhances a sense of belonging – that is, emotional and socio-economic ties among community members and with specific localities.

In this chapter I discuss city-making processes in middle Byzantine Athens as mechanisms of collectiveness and belonging. I seek the spatial and material imprint of community-building in an urban setting, focusing on evidence of placemaking activities such as architectural transformations, repurposing of buildings and spaces and new constructions that became key loci of interaction among city-dwellers. Emphasis is placed on the micro-scale, on the study of changes in Athens' streets and neighbourhoods that involved the participation of the local inhabitants but rarely required that of the provincial or imperial authorities.[8] I thus examine several spaces and structures that were modified and repurposed, such as chapels, burial sites, streets and wells, and seek to understand how such minor

---

[5] On the lack of planning and the organic development of Byzantine cities, see Angold, 'Medieval Byzantine City', 14; Bouras, 'Byzantine Cities in Greece', 48, 62; 'Μεσοβυζαντινές καί ύστεροβυζαντινές πόλεις'. For Athens specifically, see Bouras, 'Byzantine Athens', 174; Kazanaki-Lappa, 'Medieval Athens', 643.

[6] For a discussion of Byzantine urban planning beyond the organic development, see Buchwald, 'Byzantine Town Planning'. On 'organic' patterns and the variety of choices and decisions inherited in such urban designs, see Kostof, *City Shaped*, 43–69; Smith, 'Form and Meaning'. For urban social and spatial practices, see Lavan, 'Late Antique Urban Topography'.

[7] The scholarship on socially produced and constructed spaces is vast. I reference here as indicative of such discussions Tilley, *Phenomenology of Landscape*; Low, *Theorizing the City*, 111–201; Lefebvre, *Rhythmanalysis*; 'Production of Space'; and Cresswell, *Place*.

[8] For the study of interaction on the micro-scale, see Yaeger and Canuto, 'Archaeology of Communities', and Smith, 'Neighborhoods and Districts'; see also Knappett's criticism on archaeologists' lack of ability to consider and interlink the different scales of interaction (micro-/meso-/macro-): Knappett, *Archaeology of Interaction*, 25–33.

changes speak to collectiveness and identity negotiation within a Byzantine city. I particularly consider the role of non-elites in these urban transformations and argue that their time, labour and even financial investment, on the one hand, and their ability to make decisions and implement them, on the other, informed their identities and strengthened their sense of belonging within their community and city.

City Administration

Based on its hands-off policies, the imperial government has been characterised as indifferent towards the provinces in the middle Byzantine period (i.e. the ninth to twelfth centuries). The central administration's main interests included collecting tax revenues and defending imperial sovereignty; the day-to-day management of the provinces and their cities was outside the scope of such objectives and was thus left in the hands of the provincial governors.[9] The powers of provincial governors were extensive and enabled them to impact and even improve life in their provinces, but governors were rarely stationed at Athens. They preferred to reside at Thebes or to remain at Constantinople and leave lower-ranking officials in charge.[10] The governors' brief time in office and frequent absences from the provinces translated to a lack of interest in the well-being of the cities and their infrastructure and protection.[11] Furthermore, both high- and lower-ranking officials used their appointments to increase their personal wealth, by abusing their power, raising taxes, demanding gifts and so forth.[12] The unchecked power of provincial officials and their abuses seems

---

[9] As Neville has pointed out, this kind of apathy does not necessarily indicate a weak state but rather a specific style of government focused on a narrow set of objectives. Neville's chronological scope ends at the beginning of the twelfth century, and thus she does not take into consideration the changes in the administration in the twelfth century and its complete breakdown at the end of that century; Neville, *Authority*, 39–65.

[10] For the civilian administration, see Herrin, 'Byzantine Provincial Government', 275–82.

[11] For the brief duration of civilian and administrative appointments in comparison to ecclesiastical ones, see Herrin, 'Byzantine Provincial Government', 67, Table 3.1.

[12] E.g. governors' official visits to the cities were resented by the inhabitants because they were accompanied by demands in gifts, payments in gold and other concessions; Michael Choniates' efforts to ban such visits at Athens are indicative of the provincial governors' greed and ramifications that threatened the revenues and the well-being of provincial cities: Herrin, 'Byzantine Provincial Government', 76–7; Shawcross, 'Golden Athens', 82.

to have escalated in the twelfth century, particularly in the reign of the late Komnenoi and the Angeloi, when the imperial administration started deteriorating. The provinces felt the state's neglect and weakness, which manifested in heavy taxation and the draining of provincial resources as well as the lack of defence, all of which caused great resentment and alienation in the provinces and gave rise to subaltern powers.[13]

In contrast to military and civic officials, bishops and metropolitans held long-tenured offices that allowed them to invest in the well-being of their cities and to build strong and long-lasting networks of cooperation, thus providing a degree of continuity and stability in the administration of their dioceses.[14] In the case of Athens, a series of energetic and ambitious bishops in the eleventh and twelfth centuries – most notably Michael Choniates – were able to mobilise their network of family and friends involved in the imperial administration in order to protect Athens' revenues, reduce the power of provincial governors and obtain significant tax exemptions for their sees and for the city overall.[15] An imperial chrysobull pertaining to Athens' tax exemptions and privileges in the late twelfth century highlights the metropolitans' strategies to protect the city from external pressures and speaks to the kind of autonomy they were trying to achieve for their city.[16] Due to such efforts, Athens enjoyed some degree of legal and fiscal autonomy, and the Athenian metropolitans became the primary source of stability and authority in the province and the city.[17]

[13] Herrin, 'Byzantine Provincial Government', 60, 82, 86–90; Neville, *Authority*, 119–35. For provincial separatist movements in that period, see Angold, *Byzantine Empire*, 307–10, and more recently Anagnostakis, 'From Tempe to Sparta'.

[14] Shawcross sees the metropolitans' efforts to increase the city's autonomy and obtain tax exemptions as evidence of shifting allegiances that serve local rather than imperial interests: Shawcross, 'Golden Athens', 91; Herrin maintains that metropolitans remained loyal to imperial authority and sees Choniates' stand against Sgouros under that prism: Herrin, 'Byzantine Provincial Government', 74.

[15] For the role of bishops in middle Byzantine Athens, see Herrin, 'Byzantine Provincial Government', 67–9, 76; Angold, *Church and Society*, 203–12; Kaldellis, *Christian Parthenon*, 121–9; Shawcross, 'Golden Athens', 78–85. See also Angold, 'Medieval Byzantine City', 9–10, and Neville, *Authority*, 122–3, for a general discussion on the bishops' role in the middle Byzantine period.

[16] Shawcross presents this chrysobull as apt proof of Choniates' power and the city's autonomy: Shawcross, 'Golden Athens', 82. Angold and Herrin are more sceptical about the reinforcement of the chrysobull's terms on the ground: Herrin, 'Byzantine Provincial Government', 68–9, 76–7; Angold, *Church and Society*, 205.

[17] Herrin, 'Byzantine Provincial Government', 60; Angold, 'Medieval Byzantine City', 10–11.

The tensions between oppressive and unchecked governors, energetic and well-connected bishops and the imperial court – tensions well illustrated in Choniates' correspondence – highlight the dynamic between different groups and their claims to the city, and exemplify the role of regional and local actors.[18] Within such a political framework, interesting questions arise about the day-to-day administration of the city and the planning and management of the city's built environment. It invites an opportunity to consider the presence of other economic and political institutions and the role of the Athenian people, both elite and non-elite, in the running of their city. For example, city councils played a key role in the life of the city, deciding on issues of infrastructure and rights of property. They even represented the city as a legal and political entity, making decisions about its political course of action, including resisting or surrendering when under attack. These city councils were comprised by local elites and non-elites including representatives of specific professions, guilds and other collectives who brought their own experiences, interests and perceptions of Byzantine Athens and its needs.[19]

The political tensions in the city, coupled with the metropolitans' complaints about the poor living conditions and heavy taxation, led earlier scholars to conclude that by the end of the twelfth century, Byzantine Athens was nothing more than a small and insignificant town.[20] More recent studies, however, view Athens in a positive light and point to a vibrant, densely populated and prosperous city.[21] More specifically, nine decades of excavation by the American School of Classical Studies at the Athenian Agora and the recent metro excavations around Athens have revealed numerous Byzantine residential and industrial quarters and provided substantial archaeological evidence for a prosperous and densely populated city.[22] Similarly, Kaldellis's discussion of the Christian Parthenon, and specifically the development of the cult of the Virgin Mary Atheniotissa and the 'branding' of

---

[18] For Choniates' correspondence, see Michael Choniates, *Letters*, ed. Kolovou.
[19] On Byzantine city councils' role and composition, see Kontogiannopoulou, Τοπικά συμβούλια.
[20] Setton, 'Athens in the Later Twelfth Century'; Herrin, 'Collapse'.
[21] Herrin was able to point early on to a growing population in Athens: Herrin, 'Ecclesiastical Organization'. For the prosperity of the city, see Kazanaki-Lappa, 'Medieval Athens', 639; Camp, 'Athenian Agora: 1998–2001', 246; Bouras, 'Byzantine Athens', 173–7.
[22] Camp, 'Athenian Agora: 1998–2001', 246. See also, Bouras, *Byzantine Athens*, 66–83; Parlama and Stampolidis, *City Beneath the City*.

this cult, has provided a new appreciation of Athens as a key locus of pil-grimage and as a source of financial gains and civic pride for the city.[23] My discussion of middle Byzantine Athens focuses on the area of the Athenian Agora, based on the results of the Athenian Agora excavations, and brings together evidence from the Agora's legacy data and from more recent and published excavation results (Fig. 8.1).[24] For the purposes of this chapter, I limit my discussion to two different types of built environment: streets and burial sites within residential areas. Despite their different functions and architectural vocabulary, they speak to placemaking activities that offered opportunities for interaction, collective action and shared experiences.

Figure 8.1 Aerial view of the Athenian Agora. Photo courtesy American School of Classical Studies at Athens, Agora Excavations.

---

[23] Kaldellis, *Christian Parthenon*, 129–44.
[24] For a discussion on archaeological legacy data, see Allison, 'Dealing with Legacy Data', and Faniel et al., 'Challenges of Digging Data'. For the Athenian Agora, see Hartzler, 'Applying New Technologies'.

The Making of Sacred Places in Byzantine Athens

During the 1990s and early 2000s, the Athenian Agora excavations brought to light a Byzantine neighbourhood on the northern outskirts of the Agora (sections BE, BZ and BH), with numerous Byzantine houses organised east and west of a north–south-running road and two small chapels which each contained the remains of numerous burials (Fig. 8.2).[25] The first chapel was found in the southeast area of section BE and was in use in the middle and perhaps also in the late Byzantine period, coinciding with the main phases of habitation in the area (Fig. 8.3).[26] The chapel was of small dimensions, located in a residential area between middle Byzantine houses. A crudely built rubble wall divided the chapel's interior into two spaces, a narthex and

Figure 8.2 Medieval 'superimposed' state plan of post-Roman, Byzantine and premodern structures in sections BE, BH, and BZ. Shear 1997, 522, Fig. 7.

---

[25] Shear and Camp, 'Αρχαία Αγορά (1990)'; Shear, 'Athenian Agora', 521–46; Camp, 'Αμερικάνικη Σχολή'; 'Athenian Agora: 1998–2001', 242–6; 'Athenian Agora: 2002–2007', 629–33.

[26] For the chapel, see Shear and Camp, 'Αρχαία Αγορά (1992)', 18; Shear, 'Athenian Agora', 535–7.

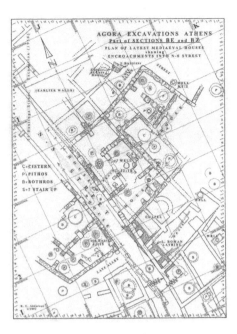

Figure 8.3 Plan of Byzantine structures in sections BE and BZ, Camp 2003, 242, Fig. 1.

a main *naos* with the *bēma* (Fig. 8.4).[27] Despite the destruction and intrusions from later activity that seriously damaged the east side of the chapel, the archaeologists were able to distinguish two phases of construction. In the first phase, two late Roman walls that were still standing became the north and south walls of the chapel, and a small dividing rubble wall created a narthex to the west and a tiny main *naos* and *bēma* to the east. A clearer architectural plan emerged in the second phase of construction, when a tile floor was laid down in the narthex, a new dividing wall between the narthex and the main *naos* replaced the previous one, a new rubble apse was constructed and three buttresses abutting the exterior walls were added to support the chapel's roof. This phase should be dated to the middle Byzantine period, most likely the tenth to early eleventh centuries, based on the pottery found associated with these levels and with the walls and buttresses.[28]

---

[27] Shear, 'Athenian Agora', 536.

[28] Shear gives no conclusive date for the construction of the chapel and focuses on its later phases that correspond to the late Byzantine period, based on thirteenth- to fourteenth-century pottery sherds found in the burial vault chamber of the chapel. The late Byzantine pottery should be associated with the latest use of the area that

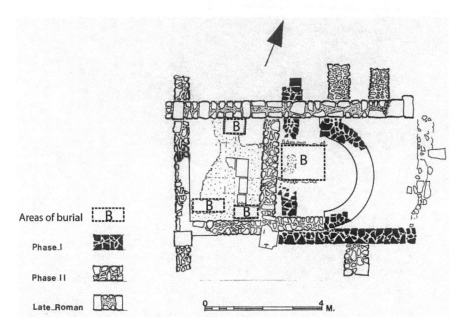

Figure 8.4 Plan of Byzantine chapel with the location of burials based on Shear 1997, 536, Fig. 10.

Besides the chapel's location between houses in a densely populated area, its function as a burial site is equally interesting. In the southwest corner of the narthex, the burial of a single individual in an extended position with the head towards the west was discovered; this seems to be the earliest burial on the site.[29] Two tile-lined cists were also discovered in the north wall and the southeast corner of the narthex, respectively, which contained

also destroyed the east part of the chapel, including the vaulted burials. In the excavation reports of 1992 and 1993, the excavators make it very clear that the first period of the chapel's use should be dated to the tenth century, perhaps even the early eleventh. While Shear also mentions that the deposits under the narthex tile floor are of the tenth century, he concludes that it is not possible that the church could be dated so early, without giving any explanation for this claim: Shear, 'Athenian Agora', 537.

[29] This burial was found at a lower level compared to the other burials in the narthex, one metre under the tile floor. The fact that this burial did not pierce through the tile floor in the narthex makes it earlier than the other burials and the floor itself: Shear, 'Athenian Agora', 536.

numerous individuals, both adults and children (Fig. 8.5).[30] In the chapel's main area, a stone-built burial vault dominated the entire space under the *naos*'s floor. Although the area was disturbed by later activities, the traces of plaster in the walls and floor, the traces of vaulting on the side walls and the large number of disarticulated human bones clearly suggest that this was an ossuary, most likely filled up to the roof with human bones. While the discussion of Byzantine mortuary practices is beyond the scope of this article, it is interesting to note that we have the remains of different types of burials (from single individual to multiple burials, from a vaulted room to tile-lined cists) in different locations (narthex and main *naos*) and in different periods (earlier burials in the narthex and later burials in the main *naos*); the motivations and symbolic meaning of such choices relate to religious and social attitudes towards life and death.

Figure 8.5 Tile burial by the north wall of the chapel's narthex. Photo courtesy American School of Classical Studies at Athens, Agora Excavations.

[30] These burials have pierced the tile floor for the deposition of the deceased and postdate the floor, although their exact date remains unknown: Shear, 'Athenian Agora', 536. For the burials of adults and children in the narthex during the middle Byzantine period, see Teteriatnikov, 'Burial Places', 143–8; Marinis, *Architecture and Ritual*, 73–6.

Southeast of this chapel, another one, identified as Aghios Nikolaos, was discovered in the extreme southeast corner of section BH.[31] The excavators identified four main building phases in the structure based on a series of architectural alterations and additions, such as a better demarcated narthex and possibly the addition of side aisles (Fig. 8.6).[32] The earliest burial lies underneath the narthex's west wall, clearly suggesting that the burial preceded the narthex's construction. The burial is of a male individual in extended position, his head to the west, and is fully covered with large terracotta tiles (Fig. 8.7).[33] What is interesting to note here is that the practice of burials in this area coincided with the earliest phases of the church and probably took place outside the church, if we accept the archaeologists'

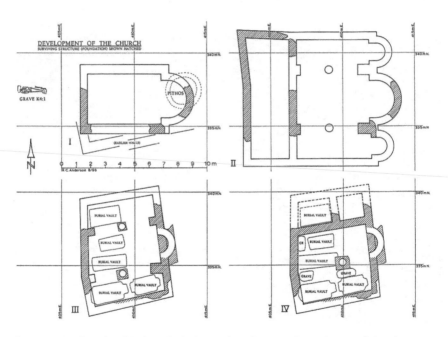

Figure 8.6 Church of Aghios Nikolaos: plan showing four phases of development, Shear 1997, 540, Fig. 12.

[31] For the identification of the church, see Shear, 'Athenian Agora', 544–6.
[32] For the main phases and architecture of the church, see Shear and Camp, 'Αρχαία Αγορά (1992)', 18; Shear, 'Athenian Agora', 538–43, Figs 11–12. For a different interpretation of the church's architecture, see Bouras, *Byzantine Athens*, 136.
[33] Shear, 'Athenian Agora', 541.

Figure 8.7 Tile burial outside Aghios Nikolaos (phase I). Photo courtesy American School of Classical Studies at Athens, Agora Excavations.

Figure 8.8 Vaulted burial chamber in the *naos*, Aghios Nikolaos. Photo courtesy American School of Classical Studies at Athens, Agora Excavations.

architectural reconstruction of the chapel in phase I without the narthex.[34] After the construction of the narthex, a second individual was buried in a similar extended position just west of the wall (thus adjacent but outside the narthex) and laid out parallel to it in a north–south orientation. Although no evidence exists for the date of the first burial, pottery sherds associated with the second one date to the twelfth century.[35] The majority of burials found within the church belong to its third main phase, when the church was rebuilt after destruction, and five vaulted ossuaries were added in the main *naos* and the south aisle (Fig. 8.8). In one of the cists, glazed bowls of the late thirteenth to fourteenth centuries suggest that this church continued to function as a funerary chapel well into the Frankish period and provide a *terminus ante quem* for the construction of the third phase of the church.[36]

The biography of the church of Aghios Nikolaos provides some parallels with the small chapel at section BE. They are both located in a densely populated residential area, they both coincide with a time of intense building activity in the area of the Agora (eleventh century) and they both emerge as focal points of religious and ritual activity in the same part of Athens.[37] Their size, simplicity in architectural design and location suggest that these were not elite private foundations but burial chapels used by the people

---

[34] There were no finds directly associated with the burial, but the layers around the burials produced some pottery fragments of the eleventh century [BH Lot 89]. The narthex wall postdates the burials, since it sits on top of them; the wall has been dated between the second half of the twelfth and the early thirteenth century based on the pottery found within the wall fabric, including a champlevé bowl [P31971]. Thus, that first burial took place somewhere between the eleventh century and the first half of the twelfth century; this date is also supported by two late eleventh-century coins [N10551, N10552] found immediately in the northwest corner of the narthex wall, under a Doric column in secondary use: Shear, 'Athenian Agora', 540–2, Fig. 12.

[35] Pottery associated with the burial points to a mid twelfth- to early thirteenth-century date [BH Lot 14]. The fact that the burial respects the line of the west wall of the narthex also suggests that it postdates the construction of the narthex and cannot be dated to before the mid-twelfth century: Shear, 'Athenian Agora', 541.

[36] The two glazed bowls [P32067, P32068], dated to the late thirteenth to fourteenth century, had traces of burning in them and could have been used for incense burning during or after the burial: Shear and Camp, 'Αρχαία Αγορά (1992)', 18; Shear, 'Athenian Agora', 543–4.

[37] Recent excavations at Chersonesos revealed a Byzantine funerary chapel with multiple burials within a residential area that provides a good comparison for the situation at Athens: Rabinowitz, Sedikova and Henneberg, 'Daily Life', 460–9.

living around them.[38] Their biography as funerary chapels begins with one
initial interment of a single individual in the narthex or outside it, and continues with their gradual transformation to chapels with multiple burials
and ossuaries found both in the narthex and the nave. Note that both chapels display the same relationship between type and location of burials:
both have tile-covered burials only in the narthex and burial vaults for a
larger number of individuals in the remainder of the space. These common burial practices speak to people's shared beliefs about life, death and
the treatment of the dead, and point to rituals that confirm and reaffirm
peoples' membership to a religious community. It is these shared ideas and
practices that create and maintain communities even if each funerary chapel served the needs of individual families. Considering the different types
of burials, the number of the deceased and the long use of each chapel, it
is possible to imagine that these small funerary chapels were used by more
than a single household, perhaps serving the needs of a number of houses
around the church. Regardless of ownership, the existence and function of
the funerary chapels required the participation of the neighbourhood in
two ways. First, some kind of agreement among neighbours was required
to be able to locate burials so close to their residences. Second, through
prayer, rituals of commemoration and liturgy, the entire neighbourhood
could participate in the commemoration of the dead buried in these chapels and in the salvation of their souls.[39] This kind of interaction transformed empty plots in residential areas into places of religion and ritual,
instigated new functions and meaning in existing spaces and stimulated
encounters among people beyond the family realm, allowing a sense of
belonging anchored in social ties and shared beliefs as well as in specific
localities.

---

[38] Bouras also reaches the same conclusion for Aghios Nikolaos and suggests that this
was a small neighbourhood church, pointing to the lack of monumentality and small
size: Bouras, *Byzantine Athens*, 136. Compare, e.g., the two funerary chapels' size,
building material and close proximity to other buildings with the magnificent church
of the Holy Apostles, which is also located in the area of the Agora, and contained
burials. For the Holy Apostles, see Frantz, *Church of the Holy Apostles* and Bouras,
Byzantine Athens, 131–4.

[39] For the role of communities in burial and post-mortem rituals and especially the
commemoration of the dead, see Abrahamse, 'Rituals of Death' and Velkovska,
'Funeral Rites', 39–42; for the importance of prayer, see Wortley, 'Death, Judgment,
Heaven', and Marinis, 'He Who Is at the Point of Death', esp. 73, 78; for different
mechanisms and strategies of commemoration and their architectural manifestations, see Ousterhout, 'Remembering the Dead'.

Southwest of the two chapels, archaeologists have also discovered
another area of Byzantine burials in section MM, excavated during the 1930s
(Fig. 8.9). In section MM, three ossuaries with numerous burials were discovered adjacent to a middle Byzantine house, named the Middle House
Block by the excavators.[40] The first ossuary was built of rubble stone and very
soft lime mortar and had visible stairs on its east side, so people could visit
and reuse it on multiple occasions (Fig. 8.10).[41] Inside, there were at least sixteen skeletons; on the uppermost layers, there was a single individual buried
in the southeast corner with no burial goods except from a twelfth-century
coin found in the general layer of the burial.[42] Below it, another level was
discovered containing at least eight disarticulated skeletons with bones disturbed and scattered. Further down, another layer of burials was found with
at least seven skeletons almost intact and in order, all positioned with their
heads to the west.[43] The absence of finds makes the dating of this ossuary
extremely difficult; based on the level of its cut and its general stratigraphic
position, it was probably in use at least in the eleventh to twelfth centuries,
if not earlier, coinciding with the principle period of habitation in the adjacent house.[44] Immediately west of this ossuary, another was found, built with
fieldstones and broken tile, and with a vaulted top built with lime mortar.[45]

---

[40] A more detailed publication on the archaeology and architecture of the Byzantine
layers in section MM is currently under preparation.

[41] This was a rectangular chamber, 1.05 m x 2.28 m, with the long axis east–west:
Excavation notebook MM-1, 39.

[42] This is a coin of Manuel I Komnenos (1143–80), [N33229]: Excavation notebook
MM-1, 38.

[43] For the number of skeletons and the sequence of burials, see Excavation notebook
MM-I, 39–40. Without more detailed notes on the ossuaries, it is difficult to assess
the nature and sequence of events, but I am more inclined to think that we are
dealing with the coexistence of primary and secondary burials based on both well-
articulated and completely disturbed and incomplete burials.

[44] The top part of the ossuary's wall and the upper part of the steps leading to the ossuary
correspond to a general floor level (52.50 m to 52.40 m) in the Middle Block, present
in the room at 38/Θ (Excavation notebook MM-I, 146), in Area 36–41/IB-KA (Excavation notebook MM-II, 293; note that four coins found in that area between 53 m
and 52.50 m date to the eleventh century [N33466, N33467, N33468, N33469]) and
Area 37–40/IB-IE (Excavation notebook MM-II, 294). This general level corresponds
to the so-called brown-glaze period of the settlement, dated to the tenth and, in some
areas, up to the early eleventh centuries (Excavation notebook MM-IV, 695–7).

[45] The ossuary's south and east walls were disturbed by later structures, but based on
the surviving features, this was a rectangular 0.60 m x 1.90 m structure, with the long
axis running east–west, and a height of 1.45 m based on the surviving part of the
vault: Excavation notebook MM-II, 168–9.

This second ossuary seems to have disturbed an earlier burial group, remains of which were found in the northeastern corner, suggesting that this area was already used for burials before the construction of the three ossuaries. The ossuary contained six skulls but a larger number of long bones, attesting to the presence of more individuals. Again, there were no finds or burial goods, but the construction of the ossuary corresponds to the previous ossuary's stratigraphic level and should be considered contemporary.[46] Finally, further east along the south face of the south wall of the house, a third ossuary was discovered with at least ten skulls at the west end of the floor, the other bones lying in confusion in the east part.[47]

Figure 8.9 The Byzantine remains at section MM with the Hephaisteion in the background. Photo courtesy American School of Classical Studies at Athens, Agora Excavations.

[46] Excavation notebook MM-II, 169.
[47] The ossuary was bound to the north and west by foundations associated with the Middle House Block. The construction resembled the other two ossuaries with unplastered walls built with fieldstones. Its size was 0.85 m along the north–south axis and at least 1 m along the east–west: Excavation notebook MM-VII, 1219.

Figure 8.10 Byzantine Osteotheke at the south edge of section MM, with steps visible. Photo courtesy American School of Classical Studies at Athens, Agora Excavations.

As mentioned above, the dating of these burials is very difficult, but based on the general stratigraphic levels of all three ossuaries, they must have been in use in the eleventh and twelfth centuries, if not earlier. The fact that the area around the ossuaries was densely populated during their use raises questions about the identity of the deceased and their relations with those living in that neighbourhood. The location of the ossuaries is important: they were situated on an empty space between houses that could have functioned also as a small alley, providing easy access to the burials. The fact that the easternmost ossuary disturbed an older burial points to a long tradition of burials in that area and its recognition as a sacred space and as a resting place for the dead throughout the middle Byzantine period. Whether the deceased all belonged to a single extended family or to different social groupings such as neighbours, friends or even different family groups occupying the adjacent house at different times, the multiple burials in the ossuaries still speak to shared experiences, rituals and spaces that could reaffirm and strengthen familial and community ties and become their physical manifestations. I consider the ossuaries' proximity to the house – as in the case of the funerary chapels – also to be meaningful. Such spatial arrangements speak to overlapping geographies shared by the dead and the living that enabled social interaction and mapped out people's social ties and group memberships marked by a physical location.[48] The burials around and adjacent to houses can also be seen as an effort to embed individuals' and groups' life histories in that of the settlement and the community, thus transforming personal experience and loss into collective social memory.

Shared Spaces – Shared Experiences

Placemaking activities are not limited to religious and ritual spaces but extend to neighbourhoods, streets, open spaces and areas outside and around houses. I now turn my discussion to streets as focal points of encounter, social interaction and community-building. In section MM, immediately north of the three ossuaries discussed above, the archaeologists also excavated three Byzantine house blocks, the West, Middle and East (following the names mentioned in the excavation notebooks), divided by two streets running north–south (Fig. 8.11a–b).[49] The entire section MM must have been severely damaged by a widespread fire that affected three house blocks and the streets in between them, based on the layers of destruction, ash and debris identified in different parts of the section.[50] The fire took place sometime in the first half of the twelfth century based on relevant finds and the stratigraphic sequence of occupation.[51] Of note in the

---

[48] For the interaction of the dead and living and the role of the living in the salvation of the deceased's soul, see Wortley, 'Death, Judgment, Heaven'; on burials as manifestations of identity and focal points of social memory, see Cannon, 'Spatial Narratives', 194–5; for cross-cultural perspectives of burials in and around houses and their participation in the construction of family and community narratives, see Adams and King, 'Residential Burial'.

[49] For a general discussion of the chronology and architecture of these houses, see Excavation notebook MM-IV, 698–714; for an earlier discussion of section MM and its archaeology, see Setton, 'Archaeology of Medieval Athens', 248–53.

[50] For the fire, see Excavation notebook MM-IV, 701–2; for ash and charcoal layers pointing to a widespread fire, see Excavation notebook MM-II, 259, 262. For the East House Block, see Excavation notebook MM-III, 470; for the West House Block, see Excavation notebook MM-III 513.

[51] This date is based mainly on the coins and pottery found in the layers of ash and charcoal between the pre-fire floor (Floor III) and the post-fire floor (Floor II) in the East House Block, where the evidence of fire is better preserved. The majority of coins below the pre-fire floor date from the second half of the eleventh century to the

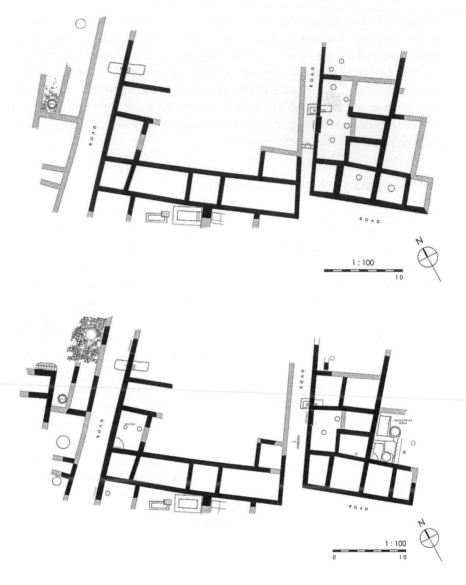

Figure 8.11 Plan of section MM in the middle Byzantine period (a) pre-fire; (b) post-fire. Drawings by F. Kondyli and L. Leddy.

pre- and post-fire houses are the architectural alternations in the exterior walls of the Middle and East House Blocks and the street between them. In the pre-fire phase, the entire exterior east wall of the Middle House Block was built at a wide angle, approaching towards the exterior wall of the

East House Block and allowing space for a very small and irregular street between the two houses. Within the street, the excavators discovered the foundations of a wall running east–west, abutting the exterior west wall of the East House Block and probably the external east wall of the Middle House Block. That wall foundation carried a threshold for a gate or a door that would have closed off the street or at least controlled access to this part of the street (Fig. 8.12).[52]

Figure 8.12 Foundation walls of street gate and exterior walls of Middle and East House Blocks, section MM. Original photo courtesy American School of Classical Studies at Athens, Agora Excavations.

first decades of the twelfth [N 33443, N33596, N33597]. On the destruction layers, coins of Alexios I [N 33442, N33552, N35948], John II [N33591] and Manuel I Komnenos are present [N33648]. The majority of coins and pottery associated with the time of the repairs found around the mouth of pithoi that were filled with destruction debris [N33595, N33664, N33665, N33666] and rebuilt walls [Excavation notebook MM-III, 498, Coin no. v.4.36 #7] date to the twelfth century, and to the time of Manuel Komnenos in particular. In one of the rooms in the East House Block a coin of Alexios I [N33443] and a sgraffito plate [P7382] dated to the mid-twelfth century were found together in the fire layer between the pre- and post-fire floors and further support the idea that the fire occurred in the first half of the twelfth century.

[52] Excavation notebook MM-IV, 748–51.

The fire significantly damaged the external walls of both houses, which were almost immediately rebuilt. In the post-fire phase, the exterior east wall of the Middle House Block retreated to the west by as much as 1.50 m in the southeast corner and slightly changed orientation to become parallel with the west wall of the East House Block.[53] Because of that move, a more spacious and wider street now measuring 3.40 m across was formed, but the wall with the gate was destroyed (compare the street in Fig. 8.11a–b).[54] Reasons for the abandonment of the gate in the post-fire phase could be many, including, among others, pressure from neighbours who wanted easier access in crossing the street, a lack of funds or interest in the gate's rebuilding or even a change in the house's residents. These alterations in the post-fire phase that resulted in a wider and more easily accessible street offer an example of how local inhabitants regulated traffic, debated and decided upon what was public and private and contributed to the amelioration of living conditions for themselves and their neighbours.

A similar example is provided by the discovery of a well in section BE in the northwest part of the Agora that provided water for the neighbourhood. This well was located at the edge of an alley next to a house in use during the middle Byzantine period.[55] There is no doubt that the well was intended for public use: the hard-packed gravel surface around it is typical of the roads' stratigraphy, while the large amount of intact pots found in it, i.e. water jugs, amphorae, pitchers, points to its use by more than one household (Fig. 8.13).[56] This well shares similar characteristics with numerous other wells excavated in middle Byzantine Athens: they are small and not extremely well built, lack monumentality, and many of them are in fact earlier, ancient Greek or Roman structures that had been rediscovered, cleaned, had their shafts raised, and were then reused in the Byzantine period.[57] The well in section BE was originally of a Roman date that was cleaned and reused in the tenth and eleventh centuries.[58] The reuse of an

---

[53] Excavation notebook MM-IV, 701, 761.

[54] Excavation notebook MM-II, 219.

[55] The well is Deposit K 1:2. For a detailed discussion of the well and that neighbourhood, see Shear and Camp, 'Αρχαία Αγορά (1992)'; Shear, 'Athenian Agora'; Camp, 'Athenian Agora: 1998–2001' and Bouras, *Byzantine Athens*.

[56] Shear, 'Athenian Agora', 533–4, n. 81.

[57] Two similar wells, originally of Roman date, that were reused in the middle Byzantine period can be found inside two houses in the area: Shear, 'Athenian Agora', 523, 528.

[58] For the date and time span of the well's use, see Shear and Camp, 'Αρχαία Αγορά (1992)', 17–18, and Shear, 'Athenian Agora', 534. The twenty coins, all anonymous folles from the late tenth to the end of the eleventh century [BE 861, BE 863,

earlier well and its simple construction point to a local, *ad hoc* solution to supplying water. The well's location in a small alley rather than a major road further supports the idea that it was built by the residents on that street to serve localised needs. Its position next to the entrance of a Byzantine house in the west might suggest that the residents of this house were somehow involved in its construction (whether by building it or by allowing it to be built and used publicly). They were certainly affected by it, since the well's presence would have transformed the area outside the house into a focal point of neighbourhood interaction. The entrance to the house leads to a large rectangular room used as a storeroom, based on the three large pithoi sunk in its floor.[59] One can easily imagine the residents of this house taking advantage of the well's proximity to their storeroom for household activities, such as cleaning and food preparation, and for watering the animals that transported produce from the fields or the market to the house. The well thus became an extension of the house, with household activities spilling outside its walls and expanding to the street and to the area around the well. At the same time, the public use of the well created a focal point of communal interaction, transforming the alley into a social space where people gathered, benefited from public amenities and created common experiences.[60]

The street in section MM and the well in BE exemplify architectural alterations undertaken by the local inhabitants, who provided amenities for themselves, their neighbourhoods and communities. In the micro-scale of the street and the neighbourhood, the architectural framework of the city is the result of interaction, negotiation and collaboration among the local inhabitants, who emerge as important agents in the making of their city. While the widening of the street and the use of a well are easily understood as responses to practical needs involving daily mundane actions, they are also associated with placemaking processes, creating shared spaces that become spatial opportunities for people to

---

BE 864, BE 866–9, BE 871, BE 873–5, BE 877–84, BE 887–8] and the lead seal [IL1802] typical of the period of the Macedonian dynasty found together with the pottery inside the well suggest the primary time of the well's use and abandonment. After the end of the eleventh century, debris and rubble from destroyed buildings in the vicinity were thrown into the well, putting an end to its function as a water source in the first half of the twelfth century.

[59] Shear, 'Athenian Agora', 531–3.

[60] For a discussion of public wells/fountains as spaces of social interaction in ancient cities, especially for women, see Cohen, 'Seclusion, Separation'.

Figure 8.13 Public well at section BE. Photo courtesy American School of Classical Studies at Athens, Agora Excavations.

interact, connect and negotiate their role in their community. In that light, Byzantine Athens can be understood as a collective endeavour that involved shared actions, rights and responsibilities that brought people together and ultimately enhanced their sense of belonging.

Conclusion

The examples discussed in this chapter speak to the vast amount of information brought to light by the Athenian Agora excavations and the potential that such material holds for a better understanding of Byzantine urbanism and collective identity. In discussing them here, I do not wish to generalise about the living conditions and social practices in middle Byzantine Athens by extrapolating from a few chapels and spaces between houses located at the Agora. My intention has been two-fold: to show how the study of archaeological and architectural data can contribute to questions of societal structures and to draw attention to the daily, even mundane, actions of non-elites that nevertheless had the power to transform urban spaces and bring people together. As such, I have approached the building of chapels and burial sites in residential areas as important placemaking activities that produced spaces shared among the dead and the living and created new sacred geographies that involved collective participation beyond the family realm. In the examples of the street and the well, I highlighted shared responsibilities and rights pertaining to the transformation of the built environment and argued for the role of ordinary people in the negotiation of public and private spheres, in providing amenities, in instigating architectural changes and in impacting the living conditions of their city. I hope to have shown that city-making involved the interaction of different groups and that non-elites had an important role to play in the development of their cities. In the absence of a strong state in the provinces and with absentee local authorities, the inhabitants of the city, elite and non-elite, became architects and urban planners.[61] This kind of participation in city-making is fundamental in building communities and reinforcing collective identities. Such processes of identity building at the local and regional scale are, furthermore, a window to the formation and transformation of Byzantine societal structures and provide a foundation for the study of people's membership in a pan-Byzantine identity.

Acknowledgements

I am grateful to Yannis Stouraitis for the invitation to present some of my preliminary results from my project, *Inhabiting Byzantine Athens*, first at the workshop in Vienna and now in this edited volume. I am also deeply indebted to Professor John McK. Camp II, Director of the Athenian Agora excavations, and to all the Agora staff members for their continuous support, guidance and generosity. This research was supported by the Archaeological Institute of America (AIA) with the Anna C. and Oliver C. Colburn Fellowship (2014–15). The University of Virginia also supported me and my students in the field/study season of 2015, for which I am grateful. Finally, I owe great thanks to Laura Leddy for her architectural drawings and for being willing to chase walls in the old excavation notebooks with me and help me reimagine Byzantine Athens.

---

[61] For the political significance of such activities, see Kondyli, 'View from Archaeology'.

Bibliography

Sources

Michael Choniates, *Letters* ... F. Kolovou (ed.), *Michaelis Choniatae Epistulae* (Berlin, 2001).

Secondary Literature

Abrahamse, D., 'Rituals of Death in the Middle Byzantine Period', *GOTR* 29/2 (1984): 125–34.

Adams, R. L., and S. M. King, 'Residential Burial in Global Perspective', *Archeol. Pap. Am. Anthropol. Assoc.* 20/1 (2010): 1–16.

Albani, J., and E. Chalkia (eds), *Heaven and Earth. Cities and Countryside in Byzantine Greece* (Athens, 2013).

Allison, P., 'Dealing with Legacy Data – An Introduction', *Internet Archaeology* 24 (2008). https://doi.org/10.11141/ia.24.8.

Anagnostakis, I., '"From Tempe to Sparta": Power and Contestation Prior to the Latin Conquest of 1204', in A. Simpson (ed.), *Byzantium, 1180–1204: 'The Sad Quarter of a Century'?* (Athens, 2015), 135–57.

Angold, M., 'The Shaping of the Medieval Byzantine City', *BF* 10 (1985): 1–37.

Angold, M., *The Byzantine Empire, 1025–1204: A Political History* (London and New York, 1997).

Angold, M., *Church and Society in Byzantium under the Comneni, 1081–1261* (Cambridge, 2000).

Ashmore, W., 'On Ancient Placemaking', in Ö. Harmanşah (ed.), *Of Rocks and Water: Towards an Archaeology of Place* (Oxford, 2014), 40–7.

Bouras, C., *Byzantine Athens, 10th–12th Centuries* (Athens, 2010).

Bouras, C., 'Μεσοβυζαντινές καί ὑστεροβυζαντινές πόλεις ἀπό τήν σκοπιά τῆς πολεοδομίας καί τῆς ἀρχιτεκτονικῆς', in Kiousopoulou (ed.), *Βυζαντινές πόλεις* (Rethymno, 2012), 1–14.

Bouras, C., 'Byzantine Athens, 330–1453', in J. Albani and E. Chalkia (eds), *Heaven and Earth: Cities and Countryside in Byzantine Greece* (Athens, 2013), 168–79.

Bouras, C., 'Byzantine Cities in Greece', in J. Albani and E. Chalkia (eds), *Heaven and Earth: Cities and Countryside in Byzantine Greece* (Athens, 2013), 45–73.

Buchwald, H., 'Byzantine Town Planning – Does it Exist?', in M. Grünbart, E. Kislinger, A. Muthesius and D. Stathakopoulos (eds), *Material Culture and Well-being in Byzantium (400–1453): Proceedings of the International Conference (Cambridge, 8–10 September 2001)* (Vienna, 2007), 57–74.

Camp, J. McK. II, Ἀμερικάνικη Σχολή Κλασικών Σπουδών, *Ἀρχ.Δελτ.* 54/ B1 (1999): 69–70.

Camp, J. McK. II, 'Excavations in the Athenian Agora: 1998–2001', *Hesperia* 72/3 (2003): 241–80.

Camp, J. McK. II, 'Excavations in the Athenian Agora: 2002–2007', *Hesperia* 76/4 (2007): 627–63.

Cannon, A., 'Spatial Narratives of Death, Memory, and Transcendence', *Archeol. Pap. Am. Anthropol. Assoc.* 11/1 (2002): 191–9.

Cohen, D., 'Seclusion, Separation, and the Status of Women in Classical Athens', *Greece and Rome* (2nd series) 36/1 (1989): 3–15.

Cowgill, G. L., 'Origins and Development of Urbanism: Archaeological Perspectives', *Annual Review of Anthropology* 33 (2004): 525–49.

Cresswell, T., *Place: A Short Introduction* (Malden, MA, 2013).

Daim, F., and J. Drauschke, *Byzanz – das Römerreich im Mittelalter*, 4 vols (Mainz, 2010).

Daim, F., and S. Ladstätter (eds), *Ephesos in byzantinischer Zeit* (Mainz, 2011).

Dey, H. W., *The Afterlife of the Roman City* (Cambridge, 2014).

Faniel, I., E. Kansa, S. W. Kansa, J. Barrera-Gomez and E. Yakel, 'The Challenges of Digging Data: A Study of Context in Archaeological Data Reuse', in *JCDL 2013 Proceedings of the 13th ACM/IEEE-CS Joint Conference on Digital Libraries* (New York, 2013), 295–304. http://dx.doi. org/10.1145/2467696.2467712.

Fisher, K. D., and A. T. Creekmore III, 'Making Ancient Cities: New Perspectives on the Production of Urban Places', in A. T. Creekmore III and K. D. Fisher (eds), *Making Ancient Cities: Space and Place in Early Urban Societies* (Cambridge, 2014), 1–31.

Frantz, A., *The Church of the Holy Apostles (The Athenian Agora, XX)* (Princeton, NJ, 1971).

Friedmann, J., 'Place and Place-Making in Cities: A Global Perspective', *Planning Theory & Practice* 11/2 (2010): 149–65.

Hartzler, B., 'Applying New Technologies', in J. McK. Camp II and C. Mauzy (eds), *The Athenian Agora. New Perspectives on an Ancient Site* (Mainz, 2009), 128–37.

Herrin, J., 'The Collapse of the Byzantine Empire in the Twelfth Century: A Study of a Medieval Economy', *University of Birmingham Historical Journal* 12/2 (1970): 186–203.

Herrin, J., 'Realities of Byzantine Provincial Government: Hellas and Peloponnesos, 1180–1205', *DOP* 29 (1975): 253–84.

Herrin, J., 'The Ecclesiastical Organization of Central Greece at the Time of Michael Choniates: New Evidence from the Codex Atheniensis 1371', in *Actes du XVe Congrès international d'études byzantines*, 4 vols (Athens, 1980), 4:131–7.

Jacobs, I., *Aesthetic Maintenance of Civic Space: The 'Classical' City from the 4th to the 7th c. AD* (Leuven and Walpole, MA, 2013).

Kaldellis, A., *The Christian Parthenon: Classicism and Pilgrimage in Byzantine Athens* (Cambridge, 2009).

Kalligas, H. A., *Monemvasia: A Byzantine City State* (London and New York, 2010).

Kazanaki-Lappa, M., 'Medieval Athens', in A. E. Laiou, C. Bouras, C. Morrison, N. Oikonomides and C. Pitsakis (eds), *The Economic History of Byzantium: From the Seventh through the Fifteenth Century*, 3 vols (Washington, DC, 2002), 3:639–46.

Kiousopoulou, T. (ed.), *Οι βυζαντινές πόλεις. 8ος–15ος αιώνας. Προοπτικές της έρευνας και νέες ερμηνευτικές προσεγγίσεις* (Rethymno, 2012).

Kondyli, F., 'The View from Archaeology', in F. Kondyli and B. Anderson (eds), *The Byzantine Neighborhood: Urban Space and Political Action* (Abingdon, Oxon; New York, NY, 2022), 44–68.

Kontogiannopoulou, A., *Τοπικά Συμβούλια στις Βυζαντινές Πόλεις. Παράδοση και Εξέλιξη (13ος–15ος αι.)* (Athens, 2015).

Knappett, C., *An Archaeology of Interaction: Network Perspectives on Material Culture and Society* (Oxford, 2011).

Kostof, S., *The City Shaped: Urban Patterns and Meanings through History* (London, 1991).

Lavan, L., 'Late Antique Urban Topography: From Architecture to Human Space', in L. Lavan and W. Bowden (eds), *Theory and Practice in Late Antique Archaeology* (Leiden and Boston, 2003), 169–95.

Lefebvre, H., *Rhythmanalysis: Space, Time and Everyday Life* (London and New York, 2004).

Lefebvre, H., 'The Production of Space', in J. J. Gieseking, W. Mangold, C. Katz, S. Low and S. Saegert (eds), *The People, Place, and Space Reader* (London, 2014), 289–94.

Lenski, N. E., *Constantine and the Cities: Imperial Authority and Civic Politics* (Philadelphia, 2016).

Low, S. M., *Theorizing the City: The New Urban Anthropology Reader* (New Brunswick, NJ, 1999).

Low, S. M., and D. Lawrence-Zúñiga, 'Locating Culture', in S. M. Low and D. Lawrence-Zúñiga (eds), *The Anthropology of Space and Place: Locating Culture* (Malden, MA, 2003), 1–47.

Marinis, V., *Architecture and Ritual in the Churches of Constantinople: Ninth to Fifteenth Centuries* (Cambridge, 2014).

Marinis, V., "'He Who Is at the Point of Death'': The Fate of the Soul in Byzantine Art and Liturgy', *Gesta* 54/1 (2015): 59–84.

Neville, L., *Authority in Byzantine Provincial Society, 950–1100* (Cambridge, 2004).

Ousterhout, R., 'Remembering the Dead in Byzantine Cappadocia: The Architectural Settings for Commemoration', in *Architecture of Byzantium and Kievan Rus from the 9th to the 12th Centuries, Materials of the International Seminar, November 17–21* (St Petersburg, 2010), 89–100.

Parlama, L., and N. Stampolidis, *Athens: The City Beneath the City. Antiquities from the Metropolitan Railway Excavations* (Athens, 2000).

Rabinowitz, A., L. Sedikova, and R. Henneberg, 'Daily Life in a Provincial Late Byzantine City: Recent Multidisciplinary Research in the South Region of Chersonesos', in F. Daim and J. Drauschke (eds), *Byzanz – das Römerreich im Mittelalter*, 4 vols (Mainz, 2010): 2 ('Schauplätze'), 425–77.

Saradi, H. G., *The Byzantine City in the Sixth Century: Literary Images and Historical Reality* (Athens, 2006).

Setton, K. M., 'Athens in the Later Twelfth Century', *Speculum* 19/2 (1944): 179–207.

Setton, K. M., 'The Archaeology of Medieval Athens', in J. Mundy, R. W. Emery and B. N. Nelson (ed.), *Essays in Medieval Life and Thought, Presented in Honor of Austin Patterson Evans* (New York, 1955), 227–58.

Shawcross, T., 'Golden Athens: Episcopal Wealth and Power in Greece at the Time of the Crusades', in N. G. Chrissis and M. Carr (eds), *Contact and Conflict in Frankish Greece and the Aegean, 1204–1453: Crusade, Religion and Trade between Latins, Greeks and Turks* (Farnham, 2014), 65–96.

Shear, T. L., 'The Athenian Agora: Excavations of 1989–1993', *Hesperia* 66/4 (1997): 495–548.

Shear, T. L., and J. McK. Camp II, 'Αμερικάνικη Σχολή Κλασικών Σπουδών, Αρχαία Αγορά', *Αρχ.Δελτ.* 45/Β1 (1990): 28.

Shear, T. L., and J. McK. Camp. II, 'Αμερικάνικη Σχολή Κλασικών Σπουδών, Αρχαία Αγορά', *Αρχ.Δελτ.* 47/Β1 (1992): 17–20.

Smith, M. E., 'Form and Meaning in the Earliest Cities: A New Approach to Ancient Urban Planning', *Journal of Planning History* 6/1 (2007): 3–47.

Smith, M. E., 'The Archaeological Study of Neighborhoods and Districts in Ancient Cities', *Journal of Anthropological Archaeology* 29/2 (2010): 137–54.

Smith, M. L., 'Introduction: The Social Construction of Ancient Cities', in M. L. Smith (ed.), *The Social Construction of Ancient Cities* (Washington, DC, 2003), 1–36.

Teteriatnikov, N. B., 'Burial Places in Cappadocian Churches', *GOTR* 29 (1984): 141–57.

Tilley, C., *A Phenomenology of Landscape: Places, Paths, and Monuments* (Oxford, 1994).

Velkovska, E., 'Funeral Rites according to the Byzantine Liturgical Sources', *DOP* 55 (2001): 21–51.

Wortley, J., 'Death, Judgment, Heaven, and Hell in Byzantine "Beneficial Tales"', *DOP* 55 (2001): 53–69.

Yaeger, J., and M. A. Canuto, 'Introducing an Archaeology of Communities', in J. Yaeger and M. A. Canuto (eds), *The Archaeology of Communities: A New World Perspective* (London and New York, 2000), 1–15.

Part II

Centre and Periphery

9

Provincial Rebellions as an Indicator of Byzantine 'Identity' (Tenth–Twelfth Centuries)

Jean-Claude Cheynet

Anthony Kaldellis has vigorously revived the debate about Byzantine identity and reproached historians for overusing the term 'Byzantines' instead of 'Romans'. There is no doubt that the Byzantines considered themselves Romans and the heirs to Rome, since, despite all the changes endured by the empire during its thousand-year existence, the devolution of imperial power was never interrupted in the New Rome, with 1204 constituting a particular case. The population of the empire could have formed a community united by a feeling of affiliation to *Rhōmania*. The author insists on the traits of a premodern nation state, having at its disposal an administration that was effective and covered the whole empire, using the same money, weights and measures and so forth. It is a surprisingly Jacobin conception of the empire, and a very cosmopolitan point of view.[1] Without question, imperial administration made available to the *basileis* certain means of doing things that we do not find in other Christian states before the last centuries of the Middle Ages. Yet, if we consider the measures, they sometimes differed, often under the same name, in the different provinces of the empire,[2] and if we consider the law, the importance of local customs is well attested. But one cannot deny the existence of unifying factors, since, from the perspective of their neighbours, in particular the Islamic powers, the group of *Rums* is well distinguished from the *Ifranj* (the Latins), who, nevertheless, are also Christians.[3]

---

[1] Kaldellis, *Hellenism in Byzantium*; see now the elaboration of this thesis in Kaldellis, *Romanland*.

[2] See Schilbach, *Byzantinische Metrologie*. It is true that it is also necessary to be aware of chronological evolution.

[3] On the Rums in Egypt, see in particular Jacoby, 'Byzantine Trade', esp. 43–5.

In this short chapter, I will not seek to participate in the debate about what Byzantine identity might be – a very fashionable but quite ambitious subject – because the answer to the question of what it was to be Roman was surely not unanimous among the emperor's subjects. This would have depended on whether one was Greek or not, or from Constantinople or the provinces and, in the latter case, on whether one lived in a city or in the countryside.[4] It is certain that the power of the 'Romans' extended over a specific territory, Asia Minor and Europe, since the Turks, who occupied Anatolia and settled there, founded the so-called Sultanate of Rum. This quickly turned into 'Turchia'.[5] Three centuries later, the Ottomans, who had established themselves in the west, named the entirety of the conquered lands 'Rumelia'. The name of the territory was not, therefore, linked to a specific political power, but kept the name of the people who had long lived there.

The study of provincial revolts, especially in the eleventh century, allows us to better understand what constituted – if not Byzantine identity, at least – the glue that maintained the empire for so many centuries, or the disaffection of the peoples who, on the contrary, contributed to its crumbling. The empire was actually not linked to a particular territory, even if the memory of the old borders had always remained alive for the ruling elites of the capital. For that reason, it was able to lose its eastern provinces in the seventh century and central and eastern Anatolia in the eleventh century without the sense of 'Romanness' being lost among the elites. From this point of view, it does not compare to modern states with stable boundaries that enclose an area called the 'mother country'. The notion of *patris*, used by the chroniclers, referred to the city in which a subject of the empire was born, or even to Constantinople; but the 'queen of cities' was not a 'homeland' common to all the emperor's subjects. Some weeks or months after April 1204, residents of Thrace felt no solidarity with the Constantinopolitans who had been ruined and driven out by the Latin conquerors.[6]

Two types of provincial rebellions are to be distinguished: those which were led by great generals, most often coming from the upper aristocracy, and whose objective it was to seize the throne; and those that were purely local and the leaders of which were not always famous figures. In the first case, the promoter of the revolt claimed himself to be the reformer of the empire and used the same ideals, at least in his propaganda, as those that

[4] See most recently Stouraitis, 'Roman Identity in Byzantium'.
[5] Cahen, *Turquie pré-ottomane*, 102–3.
[6] Niketas Choniates, *Historia*, ed. van Dieten, 593–4.

were valued by the elites of the capital. The second kind of rebellion, the objectives of which were more modest and often linked to the burden of taxation, but which could also be the consequence of ethnic dissent, allows us to determine, at least partially, by which links the rebels felt themselves to belong to the empire or not. They were much more common than the first kind, but they are less often described by the chroniclers, because they often took place rather far from the capital and did not put at stake the survival of the empire.

The feeling of solidarity among the empire's population was not based on a common Greek culture, at least not before the Palaiologan period, when the empire became almost exclusively populated by Greek-speaking people. Religion formed a common bond, but the non-Chalcedonians had long inhabited important regions both in the east and in the west, without it having much influenced their loyalty to the empire, except during some notable crises. The attitude of the Syrian population in the reconquered provinces of Syria and Mesopotamia was unambiguous. The Syriac patriarch, John, defended his dogmatic position before the metropolitan of Melitene, who reproached him for not accepting the confession of the emperor, to which he responded: 'We are under the orders of the holy emperor in everything, as we must, but we will not change to your confession.'[7]

If we want to distance ourselves from the point of view of the capital's elites – towards whom all the imperial pomp and all propaganda centred on the sovereign, his virtues and his concern for the common good were directed – we have to look at the rare documents that give voice to the provincials. One of the most famous of these, the *Consilia et narrationes*, was written by Kekaumenos, a figure whose exact social profile is unknown, but who belonged to the aristocracy.[8] This is, indeed, an officer who seems familiar with both Constantinople, where he sometimes stayed, and the provinces of the empire, where he most likely engaged in his work, and he

---

[7] Michael the Syrian, *Chronicle*, ed. and tr. Chabot, 3:142. According to the same author, the judge in Melitene – a certain Chrysoberges, who came from a large family of ecclesiastical figures which produced several patriarchs and metropolitans – wished that John had avoided his summons to Constantinople, because he appreciated the prelate so much (ibid. 140).

[8] We have two relatively recent editions available: the first is *Consilia et narrationes*, ed. and transl. G. G. Litavrin, *Sovety i rasskazy Kekavmena* (Moscou, 1972). Charlotte Roueché has also produced an annotated English translation with an introduction accompanied by a very rich bibliography. Available at <http://www.ancientwisdoms.ac.uk/library/kekaumenos-consilia-et-narrationes> (last accessed 24 March 2022).

shows himself to be particularly sensitive to the fate of their inhabitants, all while proclaiming his attachment to the *basileus*. The whole work counsels the reader to always respect the authority of the emperor, without discussing the merits of his actions. There is not much about his career, but in the episodes he relates, he shares the activities of his famous, near-contemporary relative Katakalon Kekaumenos, to whose entourage he undoubtedly belonged. Katakalon became a monk under Constantine X Doukas;[9] the author of the *Consilia et narrationes* likewise retired at an early date, at the latest under Michael VII Doukas. He may have, like Katakalon, retired in the *thema* of Koloneia.

According to the information given by the author himself, the Kekaumenos family is representative of all those coming from the Caucasus to engage in the service of the empire, especially under Basil II, who needed men for his war against the Bulgarians.[10] Among his ancestors there was a *stratēgos* of Hellas, but also a *toparchēs*, an enemy of the empire. Moreover, there was Demetrios Polemiarchos, who fought the Byzantines on behalf of the Bulgarians, and another relative by marriage, Nikoulitzas, who offered the latter his services.[11] Anthroponymy suggests that the Kekaumenoi had probably forged ties with some large Anatolian families, as evidenced by the names of the Adralestos[12] and Delphinas[13] families, whose misadventures Kekaumenos recounts.

A certain Nikoulitzas Delphinas resided in his fortified *oikos* in Larissa, Hellas. Although the author does not specify – as he does in the case of another relative, Maios – that the story is based on the first-hand account of the protagonist, the text seems to be inspired by Nikoulitzas' own report and

---

[9] Michael Psellos, *Letters*, no. 59, ed. Papaioannou, I, 219–20.

[10] Savvidis, 'Byzantine Family of Kekaumenos', to be supplemented by Savvidis, 'Armeno-Byzantine Family of Cecaumenus', and Roueché, 'Introduction to Kekaumenos', IV ('The author and his family'), where we must correct a point of detail: the Katakalon who participated in the conspiracy of Diogenes in 1094 is certainly the grandson of the famous general, not his son.

[11] Lemerle, *Prolégomènes*, 46–50.

[12] A relative of Romanos Lekapenos by that name was a *domestikos tōn scholōn* at the beginning of the tenth century; see *Theophanes Continuatus (liber VI)*, ed. Bekker, 400; John Skylitzes, *Synopsis*, ed. Thurn, 214. One of his descendants contracted a union with the Diogenes family, since the sources mention a Diogenes Adralestos, *stratēgos* of the Anatolians, as well as with John Tzimiskes (John Skylitzes, *Synopsis*, ed. Thurn, 292). Thus Nikoulitzas and Romanos IV Diogenes may have been distantly related.

[13] A Delphinas who commanded troops of Bardas Phokas, a rebel against Basil II, in 989 found a disgraceful death in Abydos; see John Skylitzes, *Synopsis*, ed. Thurn, 336.

seeks to justify his behaviour, which Constantine X Doukas and his entourage deemed suspicious. Nikoulitzas was accused of plotting a rebellion
against this emperor with a troop of Vlachs. It is impossible to determine to
what extent Nikoulitzas' story is true or not; we should rather try to understand the dynamics at work among the Vlachs of the region in order to grasp
the degree to which they considered themselves Romans or not.

Nikoulitzas was a provincial notable well rooted in his city, since his
grandparents had settled in the time of Tsar Samuel, who kept them there
when he took possession of this still well-fortified city.[14] He must have
belonged to high society, since he had the ability to communicate with the
emperor. Thus, he would have warned that the Vlachs of the region of Larissa were about to rebel, not because of ethnic dissent, but because of the
new conditions of the tax levy.[15] One can wonder about the causes of this
tax increase, which went against the fundamental principle of the stability
of tax levies. Sedentary farmers and pastoralists did not accept what seemed
to them a fiscal *kainotomia*. They were willing to pay the amounts they had
always paid, but no more. Why had the emperor taken this risk? First, at
that time the ruler was forced, in an emergency, to recruit soldiers to face
any external threats. Secondly, this measure was a result of the devaluation
of the currency, which had been noticeable since the time of Constantine
Monomachos but was accentuated during his reign. To compensate for the
devaluation of the *nomisma*, it was necessary to increase the number of
raised levies to keep the former level of tax, expressed in weight of gold.
The levy of taxes was accepted by the population on the condition that they
be protected against approaching enemies and could quietly go about their
business. This principle explains why additional requisitions for the army
were raised in the provinces that were threatened or likely targets of enemy
attacks. Under Constantine X, Asia Minor was already subjected to Turkish
raids and the Danube frontier was no longer able to stop the peoples of the
steppes, but Hellas and the region of Larissa were still untouched by the war.
The justification for the tax increase was not tangible at this time and could
appear to taxpayers as an exaction. There existed no real solidarity between
the provinces.

Having come to Constantinople on business, Nikoulitzas met the
prōtosynkellos George the Corinthian, whose name attests that he also
came from the *thema* of Hellas. George advised him to talk directly to

---

[14] Kekaumenos, *Consilia et narrationes*, ed. Litavrin, 252.
[15] Ibid. 254.

Constantine Doukas about the planned rebellion of the Vlachs. But the latter refused to receive Nikoulitzas, deferring every personal interview. This episode reminds us that being known to the emperor did not give immediate access to his person. From then on, the Kekaumenos relative found himself caught in the crossfire: should he stay loyal to the sovereign and risk him and his family being killed by the leaders of the plot, or submit to their demands and in turn be considered a rebel? For the Vlachs, the participation of Nikoulitzas in their revolt seemed indispensable for the success of their enterprise, on account of his social influence, being in charge of a large household; his support for the movement would boost it by providing it with new adherents who had wavered up to this point. However, his position did not allow him to oppose the insurgents and be certain that he would emerge victorious from a possible conflict.

Kekaumenos certainly defended his relative, but he exposed a real dilemma, one with which any provincial notable who did not reside in a garrison town was eventually confronted. Kekaumenos' presentation of the rebel leaders is also illuminating. They belonged to the aristocracy, as evidenced by the use of a transferable name, well attested elsewhere – that of the Vlach Beriboes. Some of them had received imperial honours: John Greminiates, for example, was made *prōtospatharios*, but it seems he lost this dignity, which in principle was for life.[16] Nikoulitzas himself had also received this title and his son Gregoras was granted the title of *spatharokandidatos*. This son was later promoted to a higher rank by Romanos IV Diogenes. Greminiates perhaps owed his title to the intercession of the most powerful notable of the region, Nikoulitzas himself, in the same way that Eustathios Boïlas owed his titles of *prōtospatharios* and *hypatos* to his masters, the Apokapai.[17] As for Nikoulitzas himself, he could have been directly rewarded by an emperor, like his son, who obtained a promotion when he went to Constantinople.

When Nikoulitzas was not received by the emperor, he had to make a decision. Kekaumenos reports discussions between his relative and the leaders of the rebellion. He began with a moral argument, saying that breaking the peace by opposing the emperor with arms would provoke divine wrath; on a more prosaic level, however, he reminded the rebels that the sovereign had the means to gather many troops against whom they would have no chance of winning, and that they could lose their crops

---

[16] The title *apoprōtospatharios* seems to be a *hapax*; see Kekaumenos, *Consilia et narrationes*, ed. Litavrin, 256.

[17] Lemerle, *Le testament de Boïlas*, 55–6.

and herds. Curiously enough, he did not justify the imperial decision by reminding the rebels that obedience was due to the sovereign, but instead weighed the pros and cons of this insurrection, with the latter clearly prevailing over the former. Meanwhile, Nikoulitzas, who exercised no official function and therefore had no delegated authority from the emperor, did not dare take the initiative to punish the leaders of the rebellion with blinding or death, a right which remained the prerogative of the emperor. As a result, without slaying the leaders, Nikoulitzas could no longer prevent the insurgency. Unable to persuade the rebels, he chose to go along with them. However, he did not lose contact with the imperial court, leading negotiations behind the scenes.

Nikoulitzas indeed found himself simultaneously the bearer of the demands of the Larisseans and their allies and, in the words of Kekaumenos, submissive to the emperor, because it was never about rejecting imperial power but only about putting himself in a position to obtain concessions. And he was not disappointed, since Constantine X renounced tax increases and promised a full amnesty, despite skirmishes already underway that had caused some damage. But these proposals met with scepticism, because the rebels, having prepared for war, no longer wanted to give it up; they also feared a trap – and not without reason. This allowed the negotiation to advance, something which happened in two stages: first an imperial chrysobull was sent, guaranteeing with an oath the emperor's pardon, then icons arrived that forbade the emperor from committing perjury. Added to that was the promise of honours or chrysobulls with the beneficiary name left blank.[18] This move obviously presupposed that the guarantee given by the icons and the shared interest in imperial honours were equally appreciated. This assurance, given by the church and confirmed by the patriarch John Xiphilinos himself, was not enough for Nikoulitzas, who did not escape the imperial anger and exile.

This revolt of the Vlachs highlights the mechanisms that attached provincial populations to the empire. The lack of solidarity could have been ethnic, but during the revolt that criterion is never mentioned by the Vlachs. This was not always the case, since, at the end of the twelfth century, they joined the Bulgarians, who then proclaimed their independence. The difference between the Vlachs and Bulgarians lay in the fact that the latter had, upon arrival in the Balkan Peninsula, forged a state separate from Constantinople, and therefore they had at their disposal a model of

[18] Laiou, 'Emperor's Word'.

dissent. The discrepancy could have been religious, but, in fact, the pro-
tective value of icons was shared by both sides. Moreover, the Vlachs are
highlighted because, without question, they provided the largest number
of mobilised men with some expertise in the use of arms, but they were not
the only participants in the uprising. The Larisseans, who themselves were
not mere nomads, had sided with them.

It should be noted that these groups were never considered 'Romans'.
According to the chroniclers of the eleventh and twelfth centuries, ethnic groups – Vlachs, Bulgarians, Armenians of Philippoupolis or Troas –
remained separate from the rest of the population. The army included
Bulgarian *tagmata*, and the former Bulgarian state had disappeared in
favour of Byzantine themes. Until the reign of Isaac II Angelos, these
Bulgarians recognised the imperial authority. They paid taxes, and
they were within the Patriarchate of Constantinople, yet without being
seen by these Constantinopolitan chroniclers as Romans. Similarly, the
Armenika themata were distinct from the *Rhomaïka themata* due to the
composition of their population, the majority of whom were probably
Armenians, whose loyalty was always suspect. This contrast proves that
those administrative districts established more recently were not seen to
be fully Roman.

The rebels felt connected not to the basileus of Constantinople himself,
but rather to the person most capable of representing them before him.
Apparently, no civil servant of the empire was residing in Larissa, although
in principle this was the capital of the *thema* of Hellas, and its metropolitan could, if need be, recall the central authority; however, no metropolitan
appears to interfere in the Nikoulitzas story at any point. Like Kitros, which
was destroyed by the rebels without there being any reference to a prior
battle, Larissa did not house any garrison at that time.[19] It was at Servia that
the rebels met with resistance for the first time; mediation could therefore
be carried out only through local notables.

As with all provincial populations, the link was first fiscal, but the matter was also decided based on common religious values that allowed negotiations, and on the recognition, both by local people and by the emperor,
of the role the family naturally played, especially for provincial towns. Yet
the religious community and the idea of an imperial state emanating from

---

[19] This is again surprising, since the *stratēgos* resided there. It will be assumed that the
latter and his troops had been sent to another more threatened province, e.g. in the
Paradounavon, attacked by the Ouzes under Constantine X Doukas. From the year
1018, peace reigned in Hellas.

the common good for which the sovereign has taken responsibility are not mentioned in the words towards the Thessalians which Kekaumenos attributes to his relative. This mindset explains why, a century earlier, the inhabitants of this region had defected to Samuel without much resistance, seeking only to safeguard their interests. These interests were determined by who was victorious: the Bulgarian tsar or emperor Basil II.[20] Under Constantine X, such a seesaw game was unthinkable, since the empire's frontier had been taken to the Danube, barring the Vlachs from any hope of relying on an outside force. It is true that Kekaumenos accuses the Vlachs of perfidy and duplicity, of not respecting their oaths, and that he does not hesitate to take his demonstration back to the time of Emperor Trajan, who conquered the Dacians, their ancestors. In the eyes of our author, the Vlachs are not considered Romans; in essence, they cannot be, because of their lack of loyalty to God and the emperors.[21]

Kekaumenos' personal position is not devoid of ambiguity. If he never misses the opportunity to bring to mind that one must be perfectly loyal to the emperor of Constantinople, who always ends up winning,[22] and to fight for him until death if necessary, his advice regarding the *toparchēs* of the border, which are extensively developed, are disconcerting, even if they are imbued with realism. He praises the *toparchēs* that does not yield to the lure of submission to the emperor.[23] Better to be a friend (*philos*) of the emperor than his subject (*doulos*). This is certainly not an incitement to disobey imperial orders, but a counsel of distrust, not so much with regard to the *basileus*, who is to be respected and loved, but vis-à-vis his entourage, supposed to be looking systematically to harm the *toparchēs*, who has become a subject to the empire. This mistrust is also recommended to him with regard to the *stratēgoi* of the border, who will necessarily want to take possession of his territory. Apparently, Kekaumenos does not share the idea of a Christian Romanness which would have a vocation to dominate the *oikoumenē*.

It is also in this light that we can measure the reaction of the inhabitants of the islands of Lake Pousgouse, which has the name Lake Skleros

---

[20] Larissa was taken by Samuel while the Byzantine armies were busy fighting the rebellion of Bardas Skleros until 979 (John Skylitzes, *Synopsis*, ed. Thurn, 330), but it was back under imperial rule in 997 when Nikephoros Ouranos left his baggage there before defeating Samuel on the edges of Spercheios (ibid. 341).

[21] Kekaumenos, *Consilia et narrationes*, ed. Litavrin, 268–70.

[22] This is the conclusion of the Nikoulitzas episode: Kekaumenos, *Consilia et narrationes*, ed. Litavrin, 268.

[23] Ibid. 298–306.

in some sources.[24] They faced emperor John II Komnenos, to whom they refused any allegiance. We have the surprised, even outraged, comments of the Constantinopolitan historians John Kinnamos and Niketas Choniates, and we may even surmise the point of view of the inhabitants, at least as reported by these two authors.[25] The islanders had lost, it seems, every local intermediary that was personally linked to the emperor and allowed to conduct real negotiations. For two generations they were subject to Seljuk authority, which, no doubt, levied taxes on them and protected them from exactions. To call this balance into question was to break off fruitful business transactions and, above all, to expose themselves to the reprisals of the Sultan of Ikonion, a town a short distance from the lake. Moreover, given their isolation and the separation of the territory, if they remained under the firm control of imperial power thanks to the no man's land forged by the father of John II, Alexios I Komnenos, the *basileus* would not be able to defend them effectively. Thus, they refused to follow him, resisting by force, unlike the Christians of the region near Philomelion, which the Emperor Alexios had brought under guard to imperial territory a generation earlier. In their decision, neither common language (Greek), nor common religion (Christianity) – indeed hardly threatened by the Seljuk sultans, who did not have an active policy of proselytisation – nor the memory of their grandparents being 'Romans' weighed heavily on their vital interests of the moment. This attitude contrasts with that of the Christians, or at least the Chalcedonians, who a generation or two after the Arab conquest were still waiting on the return of the *basileus*, the owner of recently lost provinces which he had possessed from time immemorial.

The role of the state apparatus was crucial. The administration, by its presence, constantly brought to mind the existence of a central power, even if some parts of the provinces, for example the *Sklabēniai* on one occasion, escaped his direct control.[26] Among these structures, the army held first place, yet not so much as an instrument of coercion but as one to ensure local peace, something it could not promise the residents of Lake Pousgouse.

The same observations could be recorded for another part of the empire, situated in its western margins: Italy. Italian possessions, directly administered by the empire, were lost during the eleventh century, to the benefit of the Normans. They were composed roughly of Lombard Puglia, with its Latin language and local law, turned towards the Church of Rome, and

---

[24] Note mention of the lake in Belke and Restle, *Galatien und Lykaonien*, 218.
[25] John Kinnamos, *Epitome*, ed. Meineke, 22; Choniates, *Historia*, ed. van Dieten, 37–8.
[26] *ODB*, s.v. Sklavinia, Ezeritai and Melingoi.

Greek-speaking Calabria, attached to the Patriarchate of Constantinople. The titles conferred by the Byzantines integrated those who benefited from them into the aristocracy and were deemed highly desirable by those who received them.[27] They forged a common language of honours, appreciated beyond the political boundaries of the empire. Many rebellions broke out again, most often linked to fiscal innovations which were felt, not without reason, to be abuses. These rebellions rarely required the reinforcement of the local Byzantine troops because their scale was limited; an exception was the one headed by the Lombard – possibly of Armenian descent, given his name – Meles, who was able to find an outside ally, the German emperor Henry II.[28] Weak links between the empire and the Italian provinces resulted in the almost complete absence of local representation of the Italian aristocracy in Constantinople, with the exception of the Lombard Argyros, the son of Meles, and his family. They recognised themselves as subjects of the *basileus*, but did they consider themselves Romans? Ultimately, the Lombards of Puglia, governed by few officials from Constantinople, submitted themselves to Norman rule by coercion.

In comparison, the behaviour of the Venetians was very different, because from the early ninth century onwards, they had became independent of Constantinople, without ever being in open revolt, while remaining close allies. The doges regularly received higher imperial dignities. The Byzantines regarded them as *isopolitai*, indeed servants of the emperor, but they did not go so far as to call them Romans. The Duchy of Naples presents the same situation in the ninth century. The Neapolitans were independent in fact and belonged to the category of *philoi*, but their dukes were also receiving regular imperial dignities and dated their official acts by the year of the reign of the emperor of Constantinople.

From the time that the emperor was no longer able to ensure security against invasions, the loyalty of the people, who felt abandoned, wavered. The indigenous population rallied behind those whose military value gave them hope for the safeguarding of their lives and property. The rapid advance of the Turks in Asia Minor provides some well-known examples of this behaviour. At Amaseia, in Paphlagonia, the residents wanted to keep the Frankish troops of Roussel de Bailleul and obey their leader, who then rebelled against the *basileus* Michael VII but effectively defended the region

---

[27] Martin, 'Usage des dignités impériales'; Peters-Custot, 'Titulatures byzantines'.

[28] The most complete account remains that of Gay, *Italie méridionale*, 410–15. On society and administration, see now S. Consentino (ed.), *Companion to Byzantine Italy*, in particular the chapters by S. Cosentino, V. Prigent and V. Falkenhausen.

against the Turks. Similarly, provinces southeast of the empire – Antioch, Edessa, Cilicia and Melitene – let themselves be ruled by Philaretos Brachamios, a Chalcedonian Armenian who somehow resisted the Turks and, with his subordinates, subsequently negotiated agreements with Malik Shah to reduce the Turkish attacks and their devastating impact on the regional economy. Philaretos, faithful to Romanos IV Diogenes, refused to recognise the authority of Michael VII and rebelled, before turning to Nikephoros Botaneiates in 1078. Then he acted as he liked, but continued to recognise the at least nominal authority of emperor Alexios I Komnenos, from whom he received very high honours. Philaretos was not loyal to 'Romanness', but rather to a political faction. It is difficult to know how he was perceived by the local population. Was he seen as the master, more or less independent, of a vast territory, or as the legitimate representative of the emperor, which he wanted to be, if we judge by the titles of his many seals? The two local chroniclers, Matthew of Edessa, an Armenian, and Michael the Syrian, a Syriac, who lived considerably later than the fall of Philaretos, present him in a very negative light, but only because he was Chalcedonian.[29]

When the situation worsened and Philaretos was brushed away by the Turks, his lieutenants held on for a long time by turning to Malik Shah, renowned for his tolerance and simultaneously carrying Byzantine and Persian titles, such as Gabriel of Melitene, formally *doux* and emir, and Thoros of Edessa.[30] The people of Melitene and Edessa certainly did not really feel Roman, let alone Seljuk; first and foremost they were inhabitants of their city and Christians that were attached to the Armenian, Greek or Syriac Churches. The walls of their city confined their horizon. However, they let the leaders of their city maintain an allegiance to the emperor of Constantinople. It took at least two generations of abandonment by the imperial administration for that state of mind to change, sometimes radically. What differentiates the opinions of Aristakes of Lastivert and Matthew of Edessa on the actions of *basileis* in the east in the last third of the eleventh century is the half-century of neglect by the imperial administration of the provinces populated by Armenians, including Cilicia.

[29] The literature on Philaretos is rich. We may cite, among others, Yarnley, 'Philaretos: Armenian Bandit'; Dédéyan, *Arméniens entre Grecs*, 5–357; Cheynet, *Société byzantine*, 390–410; Seibt, 'Philaretos Brachamios'.

[30] Gabriel of Melitene and Het'um of Edessa inscribed on their seals written in Greek, where they boasted of their Byzantine honours, the title of emir conferred by the Seljuks: Zacos, *Byzantine Lead Seals*, no. 464, and Cheynet, *Sceaux de la collection Zacos*, no. 34.

More innovative in its motivations was the movement of Theodore Mangaphas under the reign of Isaac II Angelos. The context was similar to the previous examples. After the death of Manuel I Komnenos in 1180, the Seljuk Turks had taken the military initiative in Anatolia and were conducting raids in the rich valley of the Meander. Philadelphia was the military capital of the *thema* of the Thrakesians. In 1189/90 while Isaac II was blocked in Constantinople due to difficult negotiations for the passage through the empire of the German crusade of Frederick Barbarossa and was not able to protect the provinces of Asia Minor, Theodore Mangaphas took possession of Philadelphia with the complicity of local officials.[31] The story of Niketas Choniates is not developed enough for the author to have reported the reasons put forward by Mangaphas, but it corresponds well to a time of Seljuk advancement. The city protected the route which prohibited the Turks from marching to Smyrna. Mangaphas obtained the support of the Lydians, whose loyalty was affirmed with oaths, had himself proclaimed *basileus* and struck currency. This whole process is consistent with the proclamation of all rebellions. What is less known is that this emperor did not then take the road to Constantinople but was content to build a state limited to the province where he lived. In the past, there was no lack of dissent from peripheral regions, but that was due either to claims of ethnic independence, as in the case of the Serbs and Bulgarians, or to an expression of discontent on a specific point of imperial policy, almost always about fiscal affairs. With Mangaphas, we have the example of a Greek population that turned to a *basileus* who had no intention of competing for the supreme power in Constantinople. The arrival of the emperor in person did not discourage the support of Mangaphas. After a long siege without results, Isaac II negotiated, but the agreement was not respected, because the *doux* set up by the emperor forced Mangaphas to seek refuge from the sultan of Ikonion, who granted him the right to raise the support of Turkmens, with whose backing he came to ravage Lydia. This episode, still exceptional before 1204, reflects the fragility of this city's membership in the empire, although it constituted the heart of the Byzantine military system. Can these provincial dissidents, who did not recognise the authority of the ruler of Constantinople, be considered Romans? Niketas Choniates, who reports the facts and who was from the region affected by the rebellion of Mangaphas, does not pose the question, so for him it was not conceivable.

[31] Cheynet, 'Philadelphie'. On the striking of coins by Mangaphas, see recently Papadopoulou, 'Coinage and Economy', 184–6.

Conclusion

The influence coming from Constantinople was not non-existent. The empire indeed used a common currency, the *nomisma*, which conveyed the traditional idea of imperial power. Undoubtedly, the local population, who saw the coins circulating for tax payments, could not read the inscriptions on them, but they recognised a portrait of an emperor, without perhaps identifying him, and the representation of Christ on the obverse, who brought his protection to the emperor, all while being the guarantor of the good government of the latter.

What defined a provincial Byzantine? Recognition of the power of the one who sat in Constantinople, whoever it was. When usurpers attempted to take over, they led supporters, as with Bardas Phokas, who was followed by the major part of Asia Minor when he opposed Basil II. It is likely that the provincials, who were not directly involved in the army on one side or the other, waited for the outcome of the conflict to know whom to submit to.[32] But once one of the two protagonists was a winner, he was recognised as the master to obey – except perhaps by the recalcitrant core of those loyal to the vanquished one – in exchange for his protection.

Time was a fundamental factor. When a population was led for generations by the imperial administration, it could not conceive of obeying another master. To take a much earlier example, the residents of the eastern provinces conquered by the Muslims waited for one or two generations for the return of the imperial administration under whose authority they had lived for centuries. The Vlachs of Hellas, for generations the subjects of the *basileus*, never imagined negotiating without having him as interlocutor. This impression of the endurance of the Roman Empire was shared not only by the indigenous population, but also by their opponents. Sultan Alp Arslan, who defeated Romanos Diogenes, could not conceive of conquering Anatolia, as it seemed to him that the empire had had it from all eternity.[33]

The link between the capital and the provinces was broken after 1204. Until then, the sovereign, heir of Constantine, was a Greek, loyal to the Patriarchate of Constantinople, even if he sometimes came from a lineage that had emigrated one or two generations earlier. For over three

---

[32] Abū Shujāʿ al-Rūḏrawārī, *Ḏayl kitāb tajārib al-umam*, ed. and tr. Amedroz and Margoliouth, 30–1.

[33] Aristakes Lastivertsi, *History*, tr. Canard and Berbérian, 128.

centuries, in fact, only Greeks had reigned in Constantinople. In April 1204, the population of the empire was faced with a unique choice. If it was the possession of Constantinople that primarily defined attachment to the empire, it was necessary in this case to turn to the emperor who held the city, even if he was Latin, and this is probably what happened in the first instance for part of the population, especially in the capital, where part of the administration was maintained, but also in the provinces, as in Adrianople, where Theodore Branas integrated himself in the settings of the empire.[34] But, this identification of the Latin emperor with the legitimate power clashed with the idea that the emperor was Greek-speaking and, perhaps more importantly, someone loyal to the Patriarchate of Constantinople. If this was not the case, then there existed no determining element for knowing which was the good pretender, since he could not occupy the city that legitimised imperial authority. It is, therefore, around the imperial title that this was reconstituted, which explains the eagerness of the pretender Theodore Laskaris to take up the title, but also the relative slowness of the proclamation of Theodore Angelos, who did not conceive of taking that title without having at his disposal a substitute capital, Thessaloniki.

This dichotomy between town and emperor left traces after 1261. However, the imperial title retained its value until the end of the empire by giving the *basileus* of the Romans an influence far superior to that which its political means could allow him to hope. The repercussions throughout Europe of the fall of Constantinople shows that it was not only the loss of a declined city, still of strategic interest, which was at issue.

The dissident movements highlight the difficulty of emphasising the traits that would allow us to declare firmly the elements of identity common to all the emperor's subjects. Outside of Constantinople, loyalty to the *basileus* depended on the length of presence of the imperial administration there, the inhabitants of the old Roman *themata* being considered by the Byzantines themselves more loyal than those of the provinces reconquered starting from the tenth century. Although the *themata Armenika* were part of the empire, they were perceived by the heads of the army as different from the traditional *themata*, according to, among others, the testimony of Michael Attaleiates when he describes the expeditions of Romanos Diogenes

---

[34] His union with Agnes of France, daughter of Louis VII, without doubt facilitated the agreement. See recently, van Tricht, 'Byzantino-Latin Principality'.

against the Turks.[35] The Roman generals were willing to abandon those *themata* populated by foreigners. However, even in this favourable context, the awareness of belonging to the eternal Roman Empire faded rather quickly after one or two generations of having been taken away from imperial power, as the behaviour of the inhabitants of Lake Pousgouse showed.

This solidarity with Constantinople staggered when the populations of outlying provinces had the feeling of being fiscally abused or poorly defended, and they rebelled because a chance to appeal to an opponent of the Byzantines then presented itself. The latter were well aware of this when they accused those populations, like the Armenians, of double dealing. Only Christian solidarity limited the appeal to Muslim powers, though betrayals were not rare. To counteract this centrifugal tendency, the emperors had to create direct personal links with the influential families among these populations. The eyes of the provincials and peripheral princes remained, with a few exceptions, turned towards Constantinople as a potential giver of wealth and military protection. The civil, military and ecclesiastical authorities contributed to the cohesion of the whole, limiting dissent in time and space, and this is why 1204 marked an irreversible break.[36]

Acknowledgements

The text was translated from French into English by Dr Adam Carter McCollum.

Bibliography

Sources

Abū Shujāʿ al-Rūḏrawārī, *Ḏayl kitāb tajārib al-umam* ... H. F. Amedroz and D. S. Margoliouth (ed. and tr.), *The Eclipse of the ʿAbbasid Caliphate: Original Chronicles of the Fourth Islamic Century*, vol. 3 (Oxford, 1921).

---

[35] At a council of war, Attaleiates advised that the *themata* ravaged by the Turks, that is, the *Armenika themata* which were the first to be affected, should be abandoned to their fate, and that intact *themata*, that is, the big traditional *themata*, should be defended, and he took the decision to the generals: Michael Attaleiates, *History*, ed. Tsolakis, 106. The *Armenika themata* implicitly oppose the *Rhomaïka themata* that Michael VII tries to defend when they, in turn, are undermined by the Turks: ibid. 141.

[36] Angold, *Fourth Crusade*, 125–6.

Aristakes Lastivertsi, *History* . . . M. Canard and H. Berbérian (tr.), *Aristakès de Lastivert, Récit des malheurs de la nation arménienne* (Brussels, 1973).

Niketas Choniates, *Historia* . . . I. A. van Dieten (ed.), *Nicetae Choniatae Historia* (Berlin and New York, 1975).

John Kinnamos, *Epitome* . . . E. Meineke (ed.), *Ioannis Cinnami Epitome rerum ab Ioanne et Alexio Comnenis gestarum* (Bonn, 1836).

John Skylitzes, *Synopsis* . . . J. Thurn (ed.), *Ioannis Scylitzae Synopsis historiarum* (Berlin and New York, 1973).

Kekaumenos, *Consilia et narrationes* . . . G. G. Litavrin (ed. and tr.), *Sovety i rasskazy Kekavmena* (Moscow, 1972); C. Roueché (ed. and Engl. tr.), *Kekaumenos, Consilia et Narrationes* (SAWS edition, 2013). Available at <https://ancientwisdoms.ac.uk/library/kekaumenos-consilia-et-narrationes/> (last accessed 17 June 2021).

Michael Attaleiates, *History* . . . E. Tsolakis (ed.), *Michaelis Attaleiatae Historia* (Athens, 2011).

Michael Psellos, *Letters* . . . S. Papaioannou (ed.), *Michael Psellus. Epistulae*, 2 vols (Berlin and Boston, 2019).

Michael the Syrian, *Chronicle* . . . Jean-Baptiste Chabot (ed. and tr.), *Chronique de Michel le Syrien, patriarche jacobite d'Antioche (1166–1199)*, 4 vols (Paris, 1905–10; repr. Brussels, 1963).

Theophanes Continuatus (liber VI) . . . I. Bekker (ed.), *Theophanes Continuatus, Ioannes Cameniata, Symeon Magister, Georgius Monachus* (Bonn, 1838).

Secondary Literature

Angold, M., *The Fourth Crusade: Event and Context* (Harlowe, 2003).

Belke, K., and M. Restle, *Tabula Imperii Byzantini 4: Galatien und Lykaonien* (Vienna, 1984).

Cahen, C., *La Turquie pré-ottomane* (Istanbul and Paris, 1988).

Cheynet, J.-C., 'Philadelphie, un quart de siècle de dissidence, 1182–1206', in H. Ahrweiler (ed.), *Philadelphie et autres études* (Paris, 1984), 39–54.

Cheynet, J.-C., *La société byzantine. L'apport des sceaux* (Paris, 2008).

Cheynet, J.-C., *Sceaux de la collection Zacos (Bibliothèque nationale de France) se rapportant aux provinces orientales de l'Empire byzantin* (Paris, 2001).

Cosentino, S. (ed.), *A Companion to Byzantine Italy* (Leiden and Boston, 2021).

Dédéyan, G., *Les Arméniens entre Grecs, Musulmans et Croisés: étude sur les pouvoirs Arméniens dans le Proche-Orient méditerranéen (1068–1150)* (Lisbon, 2003).

Gay, J., *L'Italie méridionale et l'Empire byzantin depuis l'avènement de Basile 1er jusqu'à la prise de Bari par les Normands (867–1071)* (Paris, 1904).

Jacoby, D., 'Byzantine Trade with Egypt from the Mid-Tenth Century to the Fourth Crusade', *Θησαυρίσματα* 30 (2000): 25–77.

Kaldellis, A., *Hellenism in Byzantium: The Transformation of Greek Identity and the Reception of the Classical Tradition* (Cambridge, 2007).

Kaldellis, A., *Romanland: Ethnicity and Empire in Byzantium* (Cambridge, 2019).

Laiou, A., 'The Emperor's Word: Chrysobulls, Oaths and Synallagmatic Relations in Byzantium (11th–12th c.)', *TM* 14 (2002): 347–62.

Lemerle, P., *Prolégomènes à une édition critique et commentée des Conseils et Récits de Kékauménos* (Brussels, 1960).

Lemerle P., 'Le testament de Boïlas', in P. Lemerle, *Cinq études sur le XIe siècle byzantin* (Paris, 1977), 15–63.

Martin, J.-M., 'De l'usage des dignités impériales en Italie (fin du viiie–début du xiie siècle)', *TM* 16 (2010) = *Mélanges Cécile Morrisson*: 533–48.

ODB: The Oxford Dictionary of Byzantium, A. P. Kazhdan editor-in-chief, A.-M. Talbot executive editor, 3 vols (New York and Oxford, 1991).

Papadopoulou, P., 'Coinage and the Economy at the End of the Twelfth Century: An Assessment', in A. Simpson (ed.), *Byzantium, 1180–1204: 'The Sad Quarter of a Century'* (Athens, 2015), 184–96.

Peters-Custot, A., 'Titulatures byzantines en Pouille et Calabre', in J.-M. Martin, A. Peters-Custot and V. Prigent (eds), *L'héritage byzantin en Italie. Les cadres juridiques et sociaux et les institutions publiques* (Rome, 2012), 643–58.

Roueché, C., 'Introduction to Kekaumenos', in *Kekaumenos, Consilia et Narrationes* (SAWS edition, 2013). Available at <https://ancientwisdoms. ac.uk/library/kekaumenos-consilia-et-narrationes/intro-kekaumenos/ index.html> (last accessed 16 June 2021).

Savvidis, A. G. C., 'The Armeno-Byzantine Family of Cecaumenus: Addenda et Corrigenda', *Journal of Oriental and African Studies* 2 (1990): 224–6.

Savvidis, A. G. C., 'The Byzantine Family of Kekaumenos (Late 10th–Early 12th Century)', *Δίπτυχα* 4 (1986–87): 12–27.

Schilbach, E., *Byzantinische Metrologie* (Munich, 1970).

Seibt, W., 'Philaretos Brachamios – General, Rebell, Vasall', in E. Chrysos and E. Zachariadou (eds), *Καπετάνιος και Λόγιος/Captain and Scholar: Papers in Memory of Demetrios I Polemis* (Andros, 2009), 281–95.

Stouraitis, Y., 'Roman Identity in Byzantium: A Critical Approach', *BZ* 107 (2014): 175–220.

Van Tricht, P., 'The Byzantino-Latin Principality of Adrianople and the Challenge of Feudalism (1204/06–ca 1227–28): Empire, Venice and Local Autonomy', *DOP* 60 (2007): 1–18.

Yarnley, C. J., 'Philaretos: Armenian Bandit or Byzantine General', *REArm*, nouvelle série 9 (1972): 331–53.

Zacos, G., *Byzantine Lead Seals*, vol. 2, compiled and ed. by John W. Nesbitt (Bern, 1985).

10

Provincial Separatism in the Late Twelfth Century: A Case of Power Relations or Disparate Identities?

Alicia Simpson

At the time when the German crusading army under Frederick I Barbarossa was traversing Byzantine lands, that is, in 1189–90, the anonymous author of the *Historia de expeditione Friderici Imperatoris* recorded that

> the kingdom was split into four . . .; in Cyprus a certain man of royal blood named Isaac had usurped the royal dignity for himself; beyond the Hellespont . . . a certain Theodore was in rebellion in the region of Philadelphia, while Kalopeter the Vlach and his brother Asan with the Vlachs subject to them were exercising tyrannical rule over much of Bulgaria.[1]

The author was referring to the regions of the Lower Danube controlled by the Vlach chieftains Peter and Asen, the important city of Philadelphia and its neighbouring lands in southwestern Anatolia ruled by the local magnate Theodore Mangaphas and the wealthy island of Cyprus that had been seized by the imperial relative Isaac Komnenos. What is remarkable in his description is not the knowledge of Byzantine internal affairs, but rather the observation that the Byzantine Empire was already in the process of dissolution.

The individuals in question had rebelled against imperial authority and were self-proclaimed rulers. Theodore Mangaphas and Isaac Komnenos had even usurped the imperial title and minted their own coinage. The territories under their control were located in frontier regions of the empire, and they all received, at one point or another, some form of outside assistance: from the Cumans in the case of Peter and Asen, the Normans of Sicily in the case

---

[1] *Crusade of Frederick Barbarossa*, ed. Chroust, 32–3, tr. Loud, 63–4.

of Isaac Komnenos and the Turks in the case of Theodore Mangaphas. The rebels themselves do not appear to have had much in common: the Vlachs Peter and Asen were foreign subjects of the empire; Theodore Mangaphas was a local magnate with no known connections to the imperial family or court; and Isaac Komnenos was a grand-nephew of the late emperor Manuel I Komnenos (1143–80) and a former governor of Cilicia. Nevertheless, their rebellions converged into the 'perfect storm', since they represented the major problems confronting the imperial government in the late twelfth century: ethnic separatism in the periphery; the rise of a locally powerful aristocracy in the provinces; and the imperial ambitions of members of the extended Komnenian family.

The phenomenon of rebellions and usurpations in Byzantium has received considerable attention in the scholarly literature of the past decades, from Jean-Claude Cheynet's fundamental study of internal strife in the eleventh and twelfth centuries, to more recent treatments examining the manifold manifestations of political subversion in Byzantium.[2] In this context, the alleged omnipotence of the imperial office has now been replaced by a model of inherent vulnerability that is especially noticeable in the middle Byzantine period, while the hitherto neglected role of the populace in the Byzantine political process, most notably in times of regime change, has been high-lighted.[3] At the same time there has been growing interest in elucidating the political, economic, religious and cultural links between Constantinople and its provinces, and also in detecting distinct ethnic and regional identities.[4] Here the focus has been rightly placed on the eleventh and twelfth centuries, when the letter collections of provincial bishops allow us to explore such issues in greater depth, and when the centrifugal movements in the empire's periphery give rise to new political entities.[5]

Several rebellions of the late twelfth century – rebellions such as those noted by the author of the *Historia de expeditione Friderici Imperatoris* – led to the creation of independent polities in the empire's outlying terri-tories and the establishment of autonomous provincial centres in its core

---

[2] Cheynet, *Pouvoir et contestations*; Angelov and Saxby (eds), *Power and Subversion*. See also Chapter 9 in this volume.

[3] Lilie, 'Zentralbürokratie und Provinzen'; Kaldellis, *Byzantine Republic*.

[4] Lilie, 'Zentralbürokratie und Provinzen'; Cheynet, 'Efficacité administrative'; Neville, *Authority in Byzantine Provincial Society*; Holmes, 'Provinces and Capital'; Herrin, *Margins and Metropolis*.

[5] See e.g. Mullett, 'Byzantium and the Slavs'; Stephenson, 'Byzantine Conceptions of Otherness'; Nerantzi-Varmazi, 'Identity of the Byzantine Province'.

regions. For this reason, they have been categorised as separatist movements and generally understood in terms of a crisis or breakdown in the
relations between the centre and the periphery.[6] Admittedly, there is strong
evidence to support this view. Paul Magdalino observed that 'at no previous time in the empire's history had its ruling class and the ownership of
its resources been so disproportionally concentrated in the capital.'[7] He was
referring not only to the pattern of landholding in the empire – according to
the documentation of the late twelfth century, the major landholders were
all based in Constantinople and were either imperial relatives or important
individuals and families associated with the regime – but also to the literary evidence regarding Constantinopolitan 'exclusivity' vis-à-vis ethnic foreigners and provincials, which seems to have reached a climax in the years
immediately before and after the Latin conquest of Constantinople in 1204.[8]

Scholars have noted that the 'exclusivity' of Constantinople bred detachment in the provinces, where local interests tended to prevail, often in
opposition to the interests of the imperial government. This is not surprising considering the nature of imperial authority in the provinces, which,
according to the current consensus, was largely restricted to the collection
of revenue, the provision of security from foreign invasion and the sup-
pression of rebellion.[9] In such conditions, locally prominent figures with
or without official capacity assumed an important role in provincial affairs.
It was precisely such figures, including men like Theodore Mangaphas
in Philadelphia or Leo Sgouros in the Argolid, who established independent rule over a particular region in the period under discussion.[10] What
is more, revisionist work has shown that the hold of the central government in the empire's outlying territories was intermittent and loose.[11] Here
Constantinople ruled through local potentates, often only nominally. It is
therefore no coincidence that potentates such as Roupen III of Cilicia or
Stephen Nemanja of Serbia were the first to secede from imperial rule in
the late twelfth century. The fact that these separatist movements begin to
appear only after the death of Manuel Komnenos in 1180 seems to confirm

---

[6] The prevailing views concerning the problem of provincial separatism are discussed
by Simpson, 'Perceptions and Interpretations', 22–8.

[7] Magdalino, 'Constantinople and the Outside World', 160.

[8] Ibid. 153, 160.

[9] Neville, *Authority in Byzantine Provincial Society*.

[10] Angold, 'Archons and Dynasts'.

[11] Stephenson, *Byzantium's Balkan Frontier*; Holmes, *Basil II and the Governance of
Empire*.

the degeneration of the imperial government in the final decades of the twelfth century. Under such circumstances, foreign potentates, provincial magnates and discontented imperial relatives discovered that there were more advantages in autonomy than in subjection to Constantinople.

This explanation, though perfectly valid when it comes to understanding power relations between the capital and its provincial regions, leaves little room for anything else. But there were certainly more reasons for the rise of provincial separatism in the twelfth century. This was, after all, a period in which ethnic and military boundaries were increasingly blurred: a time when both 'internal' and 'external' barbarians threatened the integrity of the empire; when deviant religious practices were condemned and persecuted; and when the identity of the Romans was redefined in juxtaposition to foreigners.[12] In what follows, I would like to revisit the rebellions mentioned above with the aim of discerning their individual characteristics and questioning their aims. Specifically, I will be asking whether the rebellions belong to the category of provincial separatism and whether they can be regarded as the outcome of a 'problematic' relationship between the centre and its provinces. I will begin with the Vlach-Bulgarian revolt, since the current interest in *ethnogenesis* and state formation in southeastern Europe during the Middle Ages has yet to modify our understanding of this major event, which led to the establishment of the Second Bulgarian Empire. The dominant – but by no means universally accepted – view holds that the Vlach-Bulgarian rebellion was a case of regional disaffection which turned into ethnic separatism. More specifically, the rebellion was caused by the rapacity of the imperial government, i.e. the extraordinary tax levied by Isaac II Angelos (1185–95) in the region of the Haimos Mountains, and gradually evolved into a struggle for independence because of the continued success enjoyed by the rebels. In other words, a revolt against the excessive demands of the capital was transformed into a movement for political independence due to the weakness of the capital.

Recent studies, however, have brought back the ethnic dimension of the revolt. This ethnic dimension proved instrumental in the creation of the Second Bulgarian Empire and was recognised by the contemporary historian Niketas Choniates, who stated unequivocally that from the outset, the intention of the rebels was 'to unite the rule of Mysia and Bulgaria into one

---

[12] See discussion in Laiou, 'Foreigner and Stranger', and, more generally, Innes, 'Historical Writing'; Kaldellis, *Ethnography after Antiquity*; Stouraitis, 'Roman Identity', 185–206.

empire as in olden times'.[13] Significantly, it is also borne out by the initial actions of the rebels: (1) the appropriation of the cult of St Demetrios, who abandoned the Romans to assist the Vlachs and the Bulgarians in their struggle for freedom; (2) the coronation of the rebel leader Theodore as Peter, in reminiscence of the Bulgarian tzar Peter I; and (3) the assault on Preslav, capital of the old Bulgarian Empire. These actions confirm that the desire for political autonomy was not an afterthought and that from the beginning, the expressed goal of the rebellion was the restoration of the Bulgarian Empire.[14] This does not mean that the rebellion should be seen as a Bulgarian 'national' revival, for the Second Bulgarian Empire, like most medieval empires, was multiethnic in character, but rather that the leaders of the revolt used the idea of the restoration of the Bulgarian Empire to gain popular support and justify their bid for independence from Byzantine domination.[15]

But if the leaders of the rebellion, the Asenids, employed such ideas, then we must assume that they had found willing listeners. Although there is no evidence of pre-existing discontent with Byzantine authority or autonomous tendencies among the Vlach and Bulgarian populations involved in the rebellion, there is much to confirm that the Vlachs and the Bulgarians, like other populations inhabiting the empire's periphery, had maintained their distinct identities, however imprecise or ambiguous these may have been.[16] It is well known that Byzantine authors employed the toponym 'Bulgaria' to refer to the territories belonging to the administrative theme of Bulgaria and also to the lands of the Lower Danube, both of which had been part of the old Bulgarian Empire. Less attention has been paid to their use of the ethnonym 'Bulgarians' to refer to these same territories (e.g.: γῆ τῶν Βουλγάρων, ἡ τῶν Βουλγάρων χώρα, τὰ Βουλγάρων ὅρια).[17] This means that the 'Bulgarian lands', though subject to the empire, were considered separate entities, inhabited by different peoples, and therefore clearly distinguishable from Byzantine lands proper. For the historian of the Latin East, William the Tyre, this arrangement was shocking, and when describing the region of the northern Balkans, he writes that the Greeks ignore that the name Bulgaria is actually a symbol of their shame.[18]

---

[13] Niketas Choniates, *Historia*, ed. van Dieten, 374: τὴν τῶν Μυσῶν καὶ τῶν Βουλγάρων δυναστείαν εἰς ἓν συνάψουσιν, ὡς πάλαι ποτὲ ἦν.

[14] Ibid. 371–2.

[15] See Dall'Aglio, 'Qualche considerazione'; 'Shifting Capitals'.

[16] Angelov, 'Die bulgarischen Länder'; Scholz, 'Erforschung der Integration Bulgariens'.

[17] See Kolia-Dermitzaki, 'Εἰκόνα τῶν Βουλγάρων', with the sources.

[18] William of Tyre, *Chronicle*, ed. Huygens, 1:166; tr. Babcock and Krey, I, 121.

But they did not ignore it. In the often-cited phrase of Theophylact, archbishop of Ohrid, Bulgaria was a βάρβαρος οἰκουμένη, the barbarian part of the civilised world.[19] Yet the archbishop's condescending attitude towards the Bulgarians was accompanied by a respect for the traditions of the old Bulgarian Empire, which was rooted in his attempts to reconcile the natives to Byzantine rule. In fact, Theophylact did not hesitate to recognise the Bulgarians as a distinct people possessing their own language, culture and institutions, and even as a 'holy nation' on a par with the Romans.[20] Historical and apocalyptic literature of the late eleventh century, mostly of west Bulgarian origin and written in Church Slavonic, promoted a historical consciousness that was evident in the links between the past, present and future of the Bulgarian peoples, their origins and role in history.[21] It is therefore not surprising that whenever the Bulgarians rebelled, Byzantine authors, including Niketas Choniates, invoked their inherent desire for freedom and emancipation from Byzantine rule.[22] Modern scholars, on the other hand, have been reluctant to see such rebellions in the same light, since they involved peoples of various ethnic origins and were either provoked by changes in Byzantine policy or coincided with more general unrest. These observations, though true enough, do not invalidate the desire for autonomy. A case in point is the uprising of Peter Deljan (1040–1), which aimed at a restoration of the old Bulgarian Empire and swiftly became part of the Bulgarian historical-apocryphal tradition.[23] Yet the revolt also involved factors such as the withdrawal of the Byzantine armies from the region of the uprising some years before, the replacement of the Bulgarian archbishop of Ohrid with a Greek one, and, not least, the arbitrary decision of the imperial government to change the collection of taxes in the Bulgarian lands from kind to cash, all of which encouraged separatism.[24]

The Vlach-Bulgarian rebellion of the late twelfth century involved similar factors. It has been established that for much of the twelfth century, the lands of the Lower Danube were stripped of imperial armies and characterised by

---

[19] Theophylact of Ohrid, *Letters*, no. 13, ed. Gautier, 171.2.
[20] On Theophylact's views, see Mullett, 'Byzantium and the Slavs'; *Theophylact of Ochrid*, 266–74; Stephenson, 'Byzantine Conceptions of Otherness', 249–51; *Byzantium's Balkan Frontier*, 152–4.
[21] See Tăpkova-Zaimova and Miltenova, *Historical and Apocalyptic Literature*, and the discussion in Kaimakamova, 'Culture historique des Bulgares'.
[22] Kolia-Dermitzaki, 'Εικόνα των Βουλγάρων'.
[23] Kaimakamova, 'Uprising of Peter Delian'.
[24] Stephenson, *Byzantium's Balkan Frontier*, 135–8; Curta, *Southeastern Europe*, 282–4.

impoverished or semi-destroyed settlements. The general disregard for the region, coupled with the imperial policy of recruiting the local populations into the armed forces, gave rise to a local military elite that was based on the forts along the Haimos Mountains.[25] It was probably from this elite that the Asenids and other prominent Vlach commanders like Ivanko-Alexios and Dobromir Chrysos sprang. The latter, according to Choniates, had not initially joined the rebellion and was therefore expected to fight alongside the imperial armies with the 500 countrymen under his command as an ally (ἔνσπονδος) of the Romans.[26] If the case of Dobromir Chrysos is indicative, and there is no reason to think otherwise, then it is obvious that such arrangements fostered political separatism. For Choniates, the area controlled by the rebels was known as Mysia or Zagora and lay beyond Roman borders. For the Byzantine troops called upon to fight against the rebels, it was a foreign land.[27] That is precisely the reason why, when attempting to galvanise support for their rebellion, the Asenids had only to overcome the fears of the compatriots and not any sentiments of loyalty to Constantinople.[28] In the end, the *de facto* separate existence of the region and the distinct identity of its inhabitants are what allowed a trivial cause – that is, the extraordinary tax levied by Isaac II Angelos – to lead to a rebellion of such massive proportions.

Very different was the case of the self-proclaimed emperor Isaac Komnenos in Cyprus. A grand-nephew of Manuel I Komnenos and former governor of Cilicia, Isaac rebelled against imperial authority and used the money and provisions sent to him from Constantinople to sail to Cyprus with a large force. Carrying forged letters of appointment, he presented himself as the new governor of the island, but within a short time, probably by 1184, he had established his own independent rule. His rebellion has been viewed as a case of provincial separatism *par excellence* despite Cheynet's insistence that Isaac's ultimate ambition was the throne.[29] This ambition is evident in the contemporary sources of the period and confirmed by Isaac's coinage, where he is represented in imperial attire, holding a sceptre and an orb and identified in the accompanying inscription

[25] Madgearu, *Byzantine Military Organization*, 144–66.
[26] Niketas Choniates, *Historia*, ed. van Dieten, 487.
[27] Ibid. 430, 398; see Curta, *Southeastern Europe*, 362.
[28] Niketas Choniates, *Historia*, ed. van Dieten, 371–2.
[29] Cheynet, *Pouvoir et contestations*, 116–17, 130–1, 454. See Grünbart, 'Ascension of Isaakios Komnenos', who argues that Isaac seized Cyprus and established his own dominion on the island as an anti-emperor only because he thought it too dangerous to head to Constantinople.

as ICAAKIOC ΔΕCΠΟΤΙC – that is, bearing the title commonly used by Byzantine emperors in the twelfth century.[30] For Choniates, Isaac desired but never attained the throne. Having fled to Cyprus, he was immediately suspected of planning usurpation. The emperor at the time, Andronikos I Komnenos (1183–5), feared that Isaac would sail from Cyprus and put an end to his tyrannical rule. He had Isaac's prominent supporters in the capital charged with treason and publicly executed, but made no moves against the usurper himself.[31]

Thus, for a time Isaac remained the unlawful ruler of Cyprus (τυραννεύων τῆς Κύπρου), refusing to subject himself to the emperor and withholding the revenues due to Constantinople. With the assistance of the Norman Sicilian fleet, he defeated the Byzantine forces sent by the new emperor Isaac II Angelos to recover the island in 1186. However, following the conquest of the island by Richard I of England in 1191 and Isaac's release from Frankish captivity in Palestine some years later, the tyrant rekindled his love for the throne and conspired to attain the imperial title. This time around, Isaac sought refuge with the sultan of Konya, Kaykhusraw I, but was unable to induce him or the other Turkish lords of Anatolia to support his cause. Though recalled to Constantinople by Alexios III Angelos (1195–1203), he refused to return, saying that he knew how to rule and not how to be ruled, and in the end died of poison, probably administered by an imperial agent.[32]

Significantly, the Latin chroniclers consistently brand Isaac a false emperor, a cruel and perfidious tyrant who had usurped the imperial title.[33] Likewise, Michael the Syrian portrays Isaac as a rebel who revolted against the emperor of Constantinople. He relates that Isaac even forced the bishops of the island to ordain a patriarch who then crowned him emperor, and thus in Cyprus a new emperor and a new patriarch were proclaimed in opposition to the emperor and patriarch in Constantinople.[34] All this means that Isaac's imperial claims were not limited to Cyprus, though his rebellion resulted in the *de facto* secession of the island from Constantinople. But this should not be regarded as provincial separatism; rather, it was the incidental outcome of the foiled ambitions of a member of the Komnenian family. In this context, it is significant to note that Isaac's rebellion did not

---

[30] For Isaac's coinage, see Hendy, *Catalogue of Byzantine Coins*, 354–64.
[31] Niketas Choniates, *Historia*, ed. van Dieten, 291–4.
[32] Ibid. 369–70, 463–5. On Isaac as a defector, see Beihammer, 'Defection', 625.
[33] Neocleous, 'Imaging Isaak Komnenos'.
[34] Michael the Syrian, *Chronicle*, tr. Chabot, 3:402.

enjoy the support of the local population. Let us recall that Isaac assumed control of the island with forged letters of appointment. A contemporary western source says that Isaac was accepted by the Cypriots because he was a relative of the late emperor Manuel,[35] but all the sources agree that his regime was brutal and oppressive.[36] St Neophytos the Recluse, a precious local voice with nothing but scorn for the tyrant, relates how Isaac 'utterly despoiled the land, and perpetually harassed the lives of its rich men.'[37] The same author tells us that when Cyprus was captured by Richard I of England, 'all [the Cypriots] ran unto him [Richard] and Isaac was abandoned by the people.'[38] Richard then confirmed to the *archontes* of the land the laws and institutions by which they were governed at the time of Manuel.[39]

It has been noted that St Neophytos refers to the emperor and the empire during Isaac's independent rule (and even after the English conquest in 1191) as if Cyprus were still under Byzantine authority.[40] The monk Neilos, who drew up the *typikon* of the Monastery of the Theotokos of Machairas in 1210, had secured from the legitimate emperors, Isaac II and his successor Alexios III, various concessions and donations for the monastery, and it is clear that he anticipated the restoration of Byzantine rule on the island.[41] It is difficult to tell whether Neophytos' and Neilos' sentiments of loyalty to Constantinople were shared by most Cypriots. Nevertheless, there are very clear indications that the Cypriots identified closely with the empire and that they perceived their culture to be inextricably linked to the Byzantine world.[42] On the other hand, Constantinopolitan attitudes towards the island and its residents are said to have been mixed, while sentiments of metropolitan superiority are evident, as they are for most provinces.[43] Cyril Mango's contention that 'Cyprus was governed on a colonial basis' has since been qualified,[44] but there is evidence to suggest

---

[35] Roger of Howden, *Gesta*, ed. Stubbs, 2:168. See Galatariotou, *Making of a Saint*, 216.
[36] Cf. Neocleous, 'Imaging Isaak Komnenos'.
[37] Neophytos the Recluse, *Concerning the Misfortunes of the Land of Cyprus*, tr. Cobham, 12.
[38] Ibid. For the attitude of the Cypriots, see Nicolaou-Konnari, 'Conquest of Cyprus', 53–9.
[39] Roger of Howden, *Gesta*, ed. Stubbs, 2:168. See Nicolaou-Konnari, 'Conquest of Cyprus', 61.
[40] Galatariotou, *Making of a Saint*, 216.
[41] *Byzantine Monastic Foundation Documents*, no. 34, 3:1107–75.
[42] Galatariotou, *Making of a Saint*, 216–21.
[43] Ibid. 221–4.
[44] Mango, 'Chypre Carrefour', 8.

that the Cypriots were viewed as 'foreigners', notably the ἔθνος Κυπρίων of John Skylitzes and the γένος Κύπριος of Niketas Choniates.[45] There is, however, no evidence whatsoever that a 'problematic' relationship between Constantinople and Cyprus or a 'distinct' Cypriot identity played a role in the events of the late twelfth century. The secession of Cyprus occurred because of the geographical isolation and distance of the island from the capital, and also because Isaac Komnenos allied himself with the Sicilian Normans, whose armies had recently been defeated by the imperial forces in the Balkans. The Sicilian fleet sailed to the rescue of the usurper and prevented the almost certain Byzantine recovery of the island in 1186.[46]

This brings us to the final case under discussion: the rebellion of Theodore Mangaphas, which, like that of Isaac Komnenos in Cyprus, has been traditionally viewed as a case of provincial separatism.[47] Mangaphas, a native magnate of Turkish origin in Philadelphia,[48] rebelled in 1188–9, and having secured the allegiance of the inhabitants of Philadelphia and its environs, he proclaimed himself emperor and proceeded to mint his own coinage. Isaac II campaigned against Mangaphas and besieged him in Philadelphia. Forced to retreat due to the advance of the Third Crusade, the emperor negotiated a settlement whereby Mangaphas renounced the imperial title, returning to his previous (unknown) post, while the citizens of Philadelphia also returned to their previous allegiance to the emperor.[49] But the settlement was short-lived, and by 1191 Basil Batatzes, the *doux* of Thrakesion, had forced Mangaphas into exile. The latter sought refuge at the court of Kaykhusraw I of Konya and requested auxiliary forces.[50]

---

[45] John Skylitzes, *Synopsis*, ed. Thurn, 429; Niketas Choniates, *Historia*, ed. van Dieten, 534.

[46] As is clear from the account of Theodosios (*Encomium*, ed. Sakellion and Vionis, 177), which should be read as a corrective to that of Niketas Choniates, *Historia*, ed. van Dieten, 369–70. For the Byzantine notion of islands as distinct from the mainland and isolated by the sea, see Malamut, *Îles de l'Empire byzantin*, 1:26–31.

[47] See Cheynet, 'Philadelphie'; *Pouvoir et contestations*, 123, 134–5, 454–5. See also Chapter 9 in this volume.

[48] For Mangaphas' Turkish origins and position in Philadelphia, see Korobeinikov, *Byzantium and the Turks*, 52, with the accompanying notes; 'Byzantine-Seljuk Border', 64–6.

[49] In 1190 Mangaphas may have been the anonymous *doux* of Philadelphia mentioned by the crusader sources. If so, he was hostile to the crusaders despite the treaty that had been signed between Isaac II and Frederick Barbarossa. See Korobeinikov, 'Byzantine-Seljuk Border', 68–71.

[50] Niketas Choniates, *Historia*, ed. van Dieten, 399–400.

Michael the Syrian quotes a letter of the sultan mentioning the arrival of a 'nephew' of the king of the Romans who had come from Philadelphia and had declared his submission before the sultan's throne.[51] Mangaphas, with the Turkish mercenaries under his command, invaded Byzantine territory and plundered the regions of Laodikeia, Phrygia and Caria. Having returned to the Seljuk court, he was eventually handed over to Byzantium at the request of Isaac II, though Kaykhusraw is said to have insisted that the rebel should suffer no harm.[52]

Choniates sees Mangaphas as a pretender to the throne and a defector to the enemy.[53] After all, many of the rebels who aimed for the throne had begun their rebellions in the provinces and proceeded to march towards Constantinople, rallying supporters to their cause along the way. More importantly, Mangaphas had issued his own coinage, where he was represented in imperial attire, holding a sceptre, with the inscription Θεόδωρος Βασιλεὺς ὁ Μαγκαφᾶς.[54] In an Epiphany oration (1190) Choniates makes reference to the rebellion of the 'faithless' Philadelphians, who had substituted the true emperor (Isaac) with an idol (Mangaphas) and fought against the imperial armies with the assistance of their Turkish neighbours.[55] The rebellion, which evidently enjoyed the support of the local population as well as that of the neighbouring Turks, was a serious challenge to Isaac's authority. This explains why the emperor himself campaigned against the rebel and why he felt compelled to extract oaths of allegiance to his person from the citizens of Philadelphia and also to take hostages for their good behaviour.

But should Mangaphas' rebellion be taken as a case of provincial separatism? In answering this question, it is important to consider that this was not the first time the Philadelphians had rebelled. As recently as 1182 – that is, six years earlier – they had followed the *doux* of Thrakesion, John Komnenos Batatzes, who was resident in Philadelphia, in his rebellion against the usurper Andronikos I Komnenos. But once Batatzes had been defeated, they submitted to Andronikos, and quite slavishly, if we believe Choniates.[56] Likewise, once Mangaphas' rebellion had been defeated, they again submitted to the emperor. In both cases the Philadelphians supported their local

---

[51] Michael the Syrian, *Chronicle*, tr. Chabot, 3:394–5.
[52] Niketas Choniates, *Historia*, ed. van Dieten, 400–1.
[53] Ibid. 420. For Mangaphas as a defector, see Beihammer, 'Defection', 605–6, 631–2.
[54] Hendy, *Catalogue of Byzantine Coins*, 392–6; Penna and Morrisson, 'Usurpers and Rebels', 40–1.
[55] Niketas Choniates, *Orations*, no. 9, ed. van Dieten, 92–3.
[56] Niketas Choniates, *Historia*, ed. van Dieten, 262–4.

leaders until forced into submission by the imperial armies. What is more, it apparently made no difference to them that Isaac's own family hailed from Philadelphia – they still preferred Mangaphas. Indeed, Choniates rebukes the Philadelphians for their disloyalty when he says that they had forgotten all the benefices they had previously received from the emperor's father (i.e. Andronikos Angelos).[57] But the Angeloi were no longer resident in Philadelphia and therefore could no longer represent the interests of the local population. The Mangaphades, on the other hand, were, and it is significant that they remained prominent in the region even in later times.[58] The entire episode illustrates that in the case of Philadelphia, local loyalties – no doubt encouraged by the city's frontier status – were more important than state loyalties, but also that the central government, relying largely on its armies, still managed to control provincial revolts.[59]

In this context, it is important to note that recent studies have challenged the very notion of provincial independence in the late twelfth century, making the crucial distinction between separatism and loss of control of the provinces.[60] Indeed, it is difficult to imagine that Mangaphas would have succeeded – or that he indeed intended – to carve out an independent state in Anatolia. Instead, his actions over time betray a certain opportunism. Initially taking control of Philadelphia and then over the whole of Lydia, he styled himself emperor. He then struck his own coins and attempted to win over the neighbouring provinces. These seem like the actions of a usurper, and this is precisely how they were interpreted by contemporaries.[61] Subsequently, Mangaphas was forced to relinquish the imperial title and seek refuge in Konya, only to re-emerge soon afterwards with his

---

[57] Niketas Choniates, *Orations*, no. 9, ed. van Dieten, 92.

[58] See *Byzantine Monastic Foundation Documents*, no. 35, 3:1176–95.

[59] The frontier status of Philadelphia and its consequent defensive needs are well illustrated by a passage in the *Historia de expeditione Friderici Imperatoris*, where the governor of the city brags to the German crusaders that Philadelphia 'had for a long time and single-handedly defended the cult and honour of the Christian faith by resisting the neighbouring Turks and other peoples': *Crusade of Frederick Barbarossa*, ed. Chroust, 74, tr. Loud, 98. See also the similar sentiments voiced by George Akropolites, *History*, ed. Heisenberg and Wirth, 105, tr. Macrides, 277.

[60] Smyrlis, 'Sybaris on the Bosporos', 174–5, who argues that the 'locally powerful were not that powerful and that their allegiance was incomparably less important to the emperors than that of the high aristocracy in the capital'.

[61] See Papadopoulou, 'Coinage and Economy', 185–6, who stresses that the issuing of coinage by Mangaphas should be taken into consideration when assessing his aspirations and goals.

Turkish mercenaries. This time around, Mangaphas did not attempt to restore his power in the region but rather engaged in widespread plunder, before returning to his Turkish overlord. These seem like the actions of a defector. It was probably not until late 1203 that Mangaphas, like many others, took advantage of the political chaos in Constantinople to establish independent rule in Philadelphia. George Akropolites observed that

> in the confusion of the conquest of the city of Constantine commanders appeared, one from one place, another from another; those who were prominent over the others made the land they had under their control their personal realm, having set out to do this either by their own initiative or because they were summoned to the defence of the land by its inhabitants.[62]

From his base in Philadelphia, Mangaphas emerged as one of the rulers who disputed power in Anatolia until he was defeated by Theodore Laskaris, most probably in 1205.[63] These, then, were the actions of a political opportunist who sought whatever he could gain; as his circumstances changed, so did his ambitions.

In conclusion, it seems that the description of the crusader chronicler in 1189–90 turns out to be substantially correct. Let us recall that in noting the disturbances in the empire at that time, he recorded that: (1) the Vlachs were exercising tyrannical rule over much of Bulgaria; (2) Isaac Komnenos had usurped the royal dignity in Cyprus; and (3) Mangaphas was in rebellion in Philadelphia. Thus what we are confronted with here are three distinct cases, where the Vlach-Bulgarians represent political separatism, Isaac Komnenos attempted usurpation and Theodore Mangaphas – though he aimed for the throne – provincial revolt. The nature and limitations of imperial authority in these frontier provinces certainly played a part in these movements. We need only consider the loose control of the imperial government over the lands of the Lower Danube, the geographic isolation of the island of Cyprus and the proximity of Philadelphia to the Turkish border. Issues of identity, on the other hand, come into play only in the case

---

[62] George Akropolites, *History*, 7.25–35, ed. Heisenberg and Wirth, 12: tr. Macrides, 120. For the revolts in Greece at the onset of the thirteenth century – most notably that of Leon Sgouros in the Argolid – see, most recently Anagnostakis, 'From Tempe to Sparta', 145–57, with the bibliography.

[63] For Mangaphas' position at this time, see Cheynet, 'Philadelphie', 48–50; Korobeinikov, *Byzantium and the Turks*, 137–8.

of the Vlach-Bulgarians, who sought and gained independence from Constantinople. For their part, the Cypriots retained their loyalty to Byzantium but rebelled against Latin rule in 1192. Thereafter, the Lusignans were able to establish themselves as rulers only because 'the land had no master, for the duke [Isaac Komnenos] was dead and the emperor far away'.[64] The Philadelphians repeatedly followed their local leaders in rebellion against the central government, but once their city had been integrated into the territories controlled by Theodore I Laskaris, it assumed an important role as part of the region of Philadelphia–Nymphaion–Magnesia, which formed the heartland of the Empire of Nicaea.[65]

Having said that, it is clear that the convergence of such distinct movements (political separatism, usurpation and provincial revolt) in the final decades of the twelfth century was due to the political instability at the centre, and here I mean the questionable legitimacy of Manuel's successors and their failure to firmly establish their rule in a time of increasing external and internal pressures.[66] In the end, whatever the form of challenge to imperial authority, the end result was one and the same, and as our crusader chronicler rightly observed, 'every kingdom divided against itself is brought to desolation'.[67]

Bibliography

Sources

Byzantine Monastic Foundation Documents, ed. J. Thomas and A. C. Hero, *Byzantine Monastic Foundation Documents. A Complete Translation of the Surviving Founders' Typika and Testaments*, 5 vols (Washington, DC, 2000).

Crusade of Frederick Barbarossa . . . A. Chroust (ed.), *Quellen zur Geschichte des Kreuzzuges Kaiser Friedrichs I.* (Berlin, 1928); Engl. tr. G. A. Loud, *The Crusade of Frederick Barbarossa: The History of the Expedition of the Emperor Frederick and Related Texts* (Farnham, 2013).

---

[64] Leontios Machairas, *Recital*, 19–20. See Kyrris, 'Cypriot Identity', 563.
[65] George Akropolites, *History*, ed. Heisenberg and Wirth, 105, tr. Macrides, 277; and the comments of Macrides, 279, n. 3.
[66] Smyrlis, 'Sybaris on the Bosporos', 160–73, who upholds the damning testimony of Niketas Choniates.
[67] *Crusade of Frederick Barbarossa*, ed. Chroust, 33, tr. Loud, 62 (quoting Luke 11:17).

George Akropolites, *History* ... A. Heisenberg (ed.), *Opera*, 2 vols (Leipzig, 1903); repr. with corrections P. Wirth (Stuttgart, 1978); Engl. tr. R. Macrides, *George Akropolites: The History* (Oxford, 2007).

John Skylitzes, *Synopsis* ... J. Thurn (ed.), *Ioannes Scylitzae, Synopsis historiarum* (Berlin and New York, 1973).

Leontios Machairas, *Recital Concerning the Sweet Land of Cyprus, Entitled "Chronicle"*, R. Dawkins (ed. and tr.) (Oxford, 1932).

Michael the Syrian, *Chronicle* ... J. B. Chabot (ed. and Fr. tr.), *Chronique de Michel le Syrien, Patriarche Jacobite d'Antioche (1166–1199)*, 4 vols (Paris, 1899–1924 repr. Brussels, 1960)

Neophytos the Recluse, *De calamitatibus Cypri, Concerning the Misfortunes of the Land of Cyprus*, Engl. tr. C. D. Cobham, *Excerpta Cypria: Materials for a History of Cyprus* (Cambridge, 1908; repr. Nicosia, 1969), 10–13.

Niketas Choniates, *Historia* ... J. L. van Dieten (ed.), *Nicetae Choniatae Historiae*, 2 vols (Berlin and New York, 1975).

Niketas Choniates, *Orations* ... J. L. van Dieten (ed.), *Orationes et epistulae* (Berlin and New York, 1973).

Roger of Howden, *Gesta* ... W. Stubbs (ed.), *Gesta Regis Henrici Secundi et Ricardi Primi*, 2 vols (London, 1867).

Theodosios, *Encomium* ... I. Sakellion and C. Vionis (eds), Ἀκολουθία ἱερά τοῦ ὁσίου καὶ θεοφόρου πατρός ἡμῶν Χριστοδούλου τοῦ θαυματουργοῦ (Athens, 1884).

Theophylact of Ohrid, *Letters* ... P. Gautier (ed. and tr.), *Theophylacti Achridensis Epistulae* (Thessaloniki, 1986).

William of Tyre, *Chronicle* ... R. B. C. Huygens (ed.), *Willemi Tyrensis Archiepiscopi Chronicon*, 2 vols (Turnhout, 1986); Engl. tr. E. A. Babcock and A. C. Krey, *William, Archbishop of Tyre: A History of Deeds done Beyond the Sea*, 2 vols (New York, 1941).

Secondary Literature

Anagnostakis, I., '"From Tempe to Sparta": Power and Contestation prior to 1204', in A. Simpson (ed.), *Byzantium, 1180–1204: 'The Sad Quarter of a Century'?* (Athens, 2015), 135–57.

Angelov, D., and M. Saxby (eds), *Power and Subversion in Byzantium* (Farnham, 2013).

Angelov, D., 'Die bulgarischen Länder und das bulgarische Volk in den Grenzen des Byzantinischen Reiches im XI.–XII. Jahrhundert (1018–1185)', in *Proceedings of the XIIIth International Congress of Byzantine Studies* (London, 1967), 149–66.

Angold, M., 'Archons and Dynasts: Local Aristocracies and Cities of the Later Empire', in M. Angold (ed.), *The Byzantine Aristocracy, IX to XIII Centuries* (Oxford, 1984), 236–49.

Beihammer, A., 'Defection across the Border of Islam and Christianity: Apostasy and Cross-Cultural Interaction in Byzantine-Seljuk Relations', *Speculum* 86/3 (2011): 597–651.

Cheynet, J.-C., 'Philadelphie, un quart de siècle de dissidence, 1182–1206', in H. Ahrweiler (ed.), *Philadelphie et autres etudes* (Paris, 1984), 45–54 (= *The Byzantine Aristocracy and its Military Function* [Aldershot, 2006], no. IX).

Cheynet, J.-C., 'Point de vue sur l'efficacité administrative entre les Xe et XIe siècles', *BF* 19 (1993): 7–16.

Cheynet, J.-C., *Pouvoir et contestations à Byzance (963–1210)* (Paris, 1991).

Curta, F., *Southeastern Europe in the Middle Ages, 500–1250* (Cambridge, 2006).

Dall'Aglio, F., 'Qualche consideratione sulla fondazione del "Secondo Regno Bulgaro"', *RicSlav* 9 (2011): 55–64.

Dall'Aglio, F., 'Shifting Capitals and Shifting Identities: Pliska, Preslav, Tărnovo and the Self- Perception of a Medieval Nation', *Bulgaria Mediaevalis* 2 (2011): 587–601.

Galatariotou, C., *The Making of a Saint: The Life, Times and Sanctification of Neophytos the Recluse* (Cambridge, 1993).

Grünbart, M., 'How to Become an Emperor: The Ascension of Isaakios Komnenos (of Cyprus)', in S. Roggi and M. Grünbart (eds), *Medieval Cyprus: A Place of Cultural Encounters* (Münster, 2015), 11–27.

Hendy, M., *Catalogue of the Byzantine Coins in the Dumbarton Oaks Collection and in the Whittemore Collection*, vol. 4, Part 1 (Washington, DC, 1999).

Herrin, J., *Margins and Metropolis: Authority across the Byzantine Empire* (Princeton, 2013).

Holmes, C., 'Provinces and Capital', in L. James (ed.), *A Companion to Byzantium* (Sussex, 2010), 55–66.

Holmes, C., *Basil II and the Governance of Empire (976–1205)* (Oxford, 2005).

Innes, M., 'Historical Writing, Ethnicity and National Identity: Medieval Europe and Byzantium in Comparison', in S. Foot and C. F. Robinson (eds), *The Oxford History of Historical Writing*, vol. 2: *400–1400* (Oxford, 2012), 539–74.

Kaimakamova, M., 'Byzance et la culture historique des Bulgares aux XIe–XIIe siécles', in K. Nikolaou and K. Tsiknakes (eds), *Βυζάντιο και Βούλγαροι (1018–1185)* (Athens, 2008), 123–40.

Kaimakamova, M., 'The Uprising of Peter Delian (1040–1041) in a New Old Bulgarian Source', *Paleobulgarica* 8 (1986): 227–40.

Kaldellis, A., *Ethnography after Antiquity: Foreign Lands and Peoples in Byzantine Literature* (Philadelphia, 2013).

Kaldellis, A., *The Byzantine Republic: People and Power at New Rome* (Cambridge, MA, 2015).

Kolia-Dermitzaki, A., 'Η εικόνα των Βουλγάρων και της χώρας τους στις Βυζαντινές πηγές του 11ου και 12ου αιώνα', in K. Nikolaou and K. Tsiknakes (eds), *Βυζάντιο και Βούλγαροι (1018–1185)* (Athens, 2008), 59–89.

Korobeinikov, D., 'The Byzantine-Seljuk Border in Times of Trouble: Laodikeia in 1174–1204', in A. Simpson (ed.), *Byzantium, 1180–1204: 'The Sad Quarter of a Century'?* (Athens, 2015), 49–81.

Korobeinikov, D., *Byzantium and the Turks in the Thirteenth Century* (Oxford, 2014).

Kyrris, C., 'Cypriot Identity, Byzantium and the Latins, 1192–1489', *History of European Ideas* 19, nos 4–6 (1994): 563–73.

Laiou, A., 'The Foreigner and the Stranger in 12th Century Byzantium: Means of Propitiation and Acculturation', in M.-T. Fögen (ed.), *Fremde der Gesellschaft: historische und sozialwissenschaftliche Untersuchungen zur Differenzierung von Normalität und Fremdheit* (Frankfurt am Main, 1991), 71–98.

Lilie, R.-J., 'Die Zentralbürokratie und die Provinzen zwischen dem 10. und dem 12. Jahrhundert. Anspruch und Realität', *BF* 19 (1993): 65–75.

Madgearu, A., *Byzantine Military Organization on the Danube, 10–12th Centuries* (Leiden, 2013).

Magdalino, P., 'Constantinople and the Outside World', in D. Smythe (ed.), *Strangers to Themselves: The Byzantine Outsider* (Aldershot, 2000), 149–62.

Malamut, E., *Les îles de l'Empire byzantin: VIIIe–XIIe siècles*, 2 vols (Paris, 1998).

Mango, C., 'Chypre Carrefour du monde Byzantin', in *XVe Congrès International d'Etudes Byzantines. Rapports et co-rapports*, vol. 5/5 (Athens, 1976), 1–13 (= *Byzantium and Its Image* [London, 1984], no. XVII).

Mullett, M., 'Byzantium and the Slavs: The Views of Theophylact of Ochrid', *Annuaire de l'Université de Sofia 'St. Kliment Ohridski' de recherché slavo-byzantines 'Ivan Dujčev'* 87/6 (1994): 55–70.

Mullett, M., *Theophylact of Ochrid. Reading the Letters of a Byzantine Archbishop* (Birmingham, 1997).

Neocleous, S., 'Imaging Isaak Komnenos of Cyprus (1184–1190) and the Cypriots: Evidence from the Latin Historiography of the Third Crusade', *Byz* 83 (2013): 297–338.

Nerantzi-Varmazi, V., 'The Identity of the Byzantine Province in the 12th Century', *EKEE* 23 (1997): 9–14.

Neville, L., *Authority in Byzantine Provincial Society, 950–1100* (Cambridge, 2004).

Nicolaou-Konnari, A., 'The Conquest of Cyprus by Richard the Lionheart and Its Aftermath: A Study of the Sources and Legend, Politics and Attitudes in the Year 1191–1192', *EKEE* 26 (2000): 25–123.

Papadopoulou, P., 'Coinage and the Economy at the End of the Twelfth Century: An Assessment', in A. Simpson (ed.), *Byzantium, 1180–1204: 'The Sad Quarter of a Century'?* (Athens, 2015), 179–94.

Penna, V., and C. Morrisson, 'Usurpers and Rebels in Byzantium: Image and Message through Coins', in D. Angelov and M. Saxby (eds), *Power and Subversion in Byzantium* (Farnham, 2013), 21–42.

Scholz, C., 'Probleme bei der Erforschung der Integration Bulgariens in das Byzantinische Reich, 1018–1186', in L. M. Hoffmann and A. Monchizadeh (eds), *Zwischen Polis, Provinz und Periphere. Beiträge zur byzantinischen Geschichte und Kultur* (Wiesbaden, 2005), 337–47.

Simpson, A., 'Perceptions and Interpretations of the Late Twelfth Century', in A. Simpson (ed.), *Byzantium, 1180–1204: 'The Sad Quarter of a Century'?* (Athens, 2015), 13–34.

Smyrlis, K., 'Sybaris on the Bosporos: Luxury, Corruption and the Byzantine State under the Angeloi', in A. Simpson (ed.), *Byzantium, 1180–1204: 'The Sad Quarter of a Century'?* (Athens, 2015), 159–78.

Stephenson, P., 'Byzantine Conceptions of Otherness after the Annexation of Bulgaria (1018)', in D. Smythe (ed.), *Strangers to Themselves: The Byzantine Outsider* (Aldershot, 2000), 245–57.

Stephenson, P., *Byzantium's Balkan Frontier. A Political Study of the Northern Balkans, 900–1200* (Cambridge, 2000).

Stouraitis, Y., 'Roman Identity in Byzantium: A Critical Approach', *BZ* 107 (2014): 175–220.

Tăpkova-Zaimova, V., and A. Miltenova, *Historical and Apocalyptic Literature in Byzantium and Medieval Bulgaria* (Sofia, 2011).

11

Irrevocable Blood: Violence and Collective Identity Formation in the Late Twelfth Century

Dionysios Stathakopoulos

War is a violent teacher,[1] and it seems that violence does most of the teaching. In this chapter I would like to explore the relationship between violence and collective identity formation: just as the latter requires interaction with, and more often opposition to, the Other,[2] so does violence; to erupt, its object must first be othered. War is, of course, primarily a repertoire of violence: people are killed and abused, things are destroyed; but there are differences in *how* people are killed and abused, *what* things are destroyed and *how* these things are depicted – and that difference is meaningful.

Violence is a useful analytical concept. By its sheer force it demands to be taken seriously. It imposes and codifies difference: victims of violence are different from its perpetrators. In the cases I will discuss below, it is the latter who impose the distinction by tailoring the violence towards specific attributes of their victims, thus making sure that the difference is clearly understood. The ritualised aspects of the violent acts I will explore in this chapter constitute a distorting mirror that is held to the Other, a mirror of misrecognition, showing them to be heretic, impure, effeminate and animal-like, and the violence meted out to them attempts to fix this distorted image, to impose the perpetrator's discourse (strong, masculine, hegemonic). The resistance to accept it is what triggers the strengthening of identity and, of course, the mirroring of violence. A victim is made to understand that the specific violence meted out to them is a result of a difference and that this difference makes the violence possible and justifiable in the eyes of its perpetrator. Moreover, physical group violence additionally functions as a catalyst for existing differences and tensions. Once it

---

[1] Thucidides, *History*, 3.82.2.
[2] Jenkins, *Social Identity*, 102–13.

erupts, it makes the return to a period where difference was debated principally through discourse much more difficult and stimulates a more acute expression of difference, facilitating in this way the formation of distinct identities.

In the case of collective identity formation in the Byzantine Empire, a privileged role has been assigned to the contact and conflict with westerners, especially Normans and crusaders, from the twelfth century onwards.[3] Despite (or perhaps as a result of) close proximity, the self-perception of each side crystallised into a form that was unlike, or even the polar opposite of, that Other.[4] The fact that prejudice against the Other was rife on both sides is well attested: numerous studies have collected and analysed evidence that shows the disdain and even hatred that (some) Byzantines exhibited towards the Latins (as they are often collectively called, increasingly after the eleventh century) and vice versa.[5] For the following discussion it is not central to assume that each side's identity was internally coherent and/or fixed, but rather that it was increasingly secure in terms of being different to that specific Other. This relational and dynamic aspect in identity construction is crucial.[6]

The Byzantines clearly knew that not all Latins were the same (geographically, politically or linguistically) but their increasing use of a few terms to denote all westerners suggest that for the particular purposes of a number of late twelfth-century authors (to stay in the period I will be exploring), they could be treated as a 'unified entity,'[7] as a block of people who were *unlike* them. The use of the term 'Greeks' to denote the Byzantines in western sources suggests a similar attitude. These two groups differed in a number of constituent traits: they owed loyalty and allegiance to different polities, spoke different languages, practised their faith differently and had different customs. While it may be difficult to isolate the exact external components of this identity as reflected in our sources, certainly the difference in

---

[3] Page, *Being Byzantine*; Kaldellis, *Hellenism in Byzantium*, 334–68; Stouraitis, 'Roman Identity in Byzantium', esp. 199, 214; 'Reinventing Roman Ethnicity', 82–3.

[4] Messis, 'Lectures sexuées', with previous bibliography; Hunger, *Graeculus perfidus*, 36–46.

[5] Kazhdan, 'Latins and Franks'; Koder, 'Image of the Other'; Hunger, *Graeculus perfidus*; Gounarides, 'Εικόνα των Λατίνων'; Mitsiou, 'Byzantines and "Others"'; and the studies of Kolbaba, *Byzantine Lists*; 'Byzantine Perceptions'.

[6] Sociolinguists have been recently operating with the term 'identity in interaction': see Bucholtz and Hall, 'Identity and Interaction'.

[7] Kazhdan, 'Latins and Franks', 86.

religious faith and custom was particularly marked and easily identifiable, but there was also a set of political and cultural markers at play which, for the lack of a more plausible alternative term, I would refer to as ethnic.[8] The combination of ethnoreligious differences, therefore, added an additional level to how the Byzantine or Latin Other would be perceived, conceptualised and, more importantly for this study, handled. In order to critically reflect on the instances of violence that I will discuss below, it is important to make use of the heuristic tools and terminology of recent studies on violence, especially ethnic and religious violence by historians, sociologists and political scientists. This will have a twofold effect: to introduce these case studies from Byzantine history into the larger debate on the causation and function of violence and its effect on identity formation and therefore to test their interpretative value, as well as to provide a degree of abstraction that can make certain parameters more clear, even though these might not have been necessarily evident to the contemporary authors who recorded them. As Brubaker and Laitin correctly acknowledge, we 'are no longer blind to ethnicity, but we may be blinded by it'.[9]

The sack of Constantinople by the Fourth Crusade in 1204 and the establishment of Latin states in the territories once controlled by the empire undoubtedly represent a watershed regarding the relationship between Byzantines and Latins. However, I will focus on two events that preceded it and which for a long time were seen as the stepping stones that led to it:[10] the massacre of the Latins in Constantinople in 1182[11] and the sack

---

[8] In a number of publications Anthony Kaldellis has argued in favour of regarding this identity as national (Kaldellis, *Hellenism in Byzantium*, 42–119; 'Review of G. Page, *Being Byzantine*'; 'From Rome to New Rome'). I am, on the one hand, convinced by the critique of Stouraitis ('Roman Identity in Byzantium' and 'Byzantine Romanness') against this use and, on the other, unconvinced that adopting the term 'national' offers an interpretative advantage. I find the term 'ethnic' less partisan and thus preferable. Stouraitis, 'Roman Identity in Byzantium', 204–6, *pace* Susan Reynolds, opts for the alternative term 'regnal Romanness' to denote the collective identity of Byzantines as subjects of the empire. In any case, the current heated debate on identity is a very welcome phenomenon in the usually rather theoretophobic field of Byzantine Studies, but in this text I see myself as a spectator rather than a participant in it.

[9] Brubaker and Laitin, 'Ethnic and Nationalist Violence', 428.

[10] Brand, *Byzantium Confronts the West*, 43, writes of the events of 1182: 'One of the causes of the Fourth Crusade had been set in motion.' See also Madden, 'Outside and Inside'.

[11] Shawcross, 'Ethnic and Religious Violence', esp. 287–8, 306–7, touches on the events of 1182 but sets them in a very different framework.

and occupation of Thessaloniki by the Normans in 1185. I will offer a close reading of these two pivotal events with the aim of exploring how they contributed to the process of collective identity formation. It is also important to declare what this chapter does not aim to do. As already indicated, I will not be commenting on the current heated debate on Byzantine identity. For my purpose it is not important to proclaim whether the Byzantines had a predominantly political, religious, cultural or national identity; my aim is to shed light on the process, and not the outcome, on change and not on fixity.

To begin with, it will be useful to offer a brief outline of the events in question.[12] After the death of Manuel I in September 1180, the government of his heir, the young Alexios II, was in the hands of a regency headed by his mother, Manuel's second wife, Maria of Antioch. The *prōtosebastos* Alexios Komnenos, a nephew of Manuel, emerged as the grey eminence at the court, while rumours abounded that he had become the empress's lover. The regency was opposed by the *pophyrogennētē* Maria, Manuel's daughter from his first marriage to Bertha of Sulzbach, and her husband, the *kaisar* Renier of Montferrat. Things came to a head between the two parties in early 1181, when Maria, Renier and some followers barricaded themselves inside the Hagia Sophia while street battles broke out, and there was looting and destruction of aristocratic homes in the vicinity of the building. Both sides made use of Latin forces, although contemporary sources suggest that Maria of Antioch and the *prōtosebastos* relied heavily on the Latins in Constantinople and showed a marked preference for them.[13] Andronikos Komnenos, Manuel's cousin and a constant antagonist to his power, was summoned to intervene; he arrived across the water from Constantinople in May 1181 and gradually won over a number of important civil and military officers as well as public opinion. After he had had Alexios arrested

---

[12] The key sources are: Eustathios of Thessaloniki, *Capture of Thessaloniki*, tr. Melville Jones (which also reprints the text of the critical edition by Kyriakides); William of Tyre, *Chronicle*, 22.5, 22.11(10)–14(13), ed. Huygens, 2:1012–13, 1020–5. I have decided against using the account of Niketas Choniates (but for occasional cross-references); Choniates devotes little space to the massacre of 1182 (of which he was probably an eyewitness), while his description of the capture of Thessaloniki in 1185 is clearly based on Eustathios; see Simpson, *Niketas Choniates*, 224–9. The major studies are: Brand, *Byzantium Confronts the West*, 31–43, 160–75; Holmes, 'Shared Worlds?'; Neocleous, 'Tyrannus Grecorum'; 'Greeks and Italians'; Harris, *Byzantium and Crusades*, 121–30.

[13] William of Tyre, *Chronicle*, 22.5.11–12(10–1), ed. Huygens, 2:1013, 1020–1; Eustathios, *Capture*, 28, tr. Melville Jones), 34–5); Niketas Choniates, *Historia*, ed. van Dieten, 246–7; see Lilie, *Handel und Politik*, 527, 535.

and blinded, he instigated an attack against the resident Latins in Constantinople in April 1182: a large number of people were killed, the Latin
Quarters were burned down and survivors were sold into slavery.[14] Those
who fled by ship plundered a number of sites and monasteries in the sea of
Marmara and killed some of the population they encountered.[15]

Once Andronikos secured the capital, he gradually removed all those
who had claims to the throne (Maria and Renier, Maria of Antioch and ultimately Alexios II) and reigned as sole emperor. Another Alexios Komnenos,
a nephew of the *prōtosebastos*, arrived at the court of William II of Sicily and
incited the Norman ruler to attack Byzantium. A boy alleged to be Alexios
II arrived in Sicily as well, and William decided to launch a major campaign
against the empire in 1185.[16] After landing at Dyrrachium and easily taking
the city in June, the Normans moved against Thessaloniki by land and sea
in August 1185. They captured the city within less than a month and held it
until November of the same year, subjecting its population to violence and
looting.

The two events are often presented together in a linear genealogy of
violence between Byzantines and Latins,[17] although they are actually
quite different. The massacre of 1182 is a case of violence meted out to a
minority group with a distinct ethnic and religious background (the Latins
of our sources were actually mostly Pisan and Genoese merchants)[18] by
a mercenary force and an urban mob representing the dominant ethnic
group of the empire, incited by a usurper, albeit one with blood ties to
the regime and in control of substantial authority. In current scholarship,
such an event is termed a deadly ethnic riot, 'an intense, sudden, though
not necessarily wholly unplanned, lethal attack by civilian members of one
ethnic group on civilian members of another ethnic group, the victims
chosen because of their group membership.'[19] The Latin merchants that
were attacked in Constantinople had most probably been residents of the
city for a long time. William confirms this when he writes that the 'guests'

---

[14] The enslavement is recorded only by William of Tyre, *Chronicle*, 22.13(12), ed.
Huygens, 2:1024.

[15] William of Tyre, *Chronicle*, 22.14(13), ed. Huygens, 2:1024–5, tr. Atwater and Krey,
2:466–7.

[16] Eustathios, *Capture*, 51–2, tr. Melville Jones, 60–5.

[17] See the discussion in Madden, 'Outside and Inside', 727–30.

[18] This is because Venetians had been expelled by Manuel I in 1171; see Lilie, *Handel
und Politik*, 526–39.

[19] Horowitz, *Deadly Ethnic Riot*.

(of the Greeks) 'had not deserved such treatment and were far from anticipating anything of the kind; those to whom they had given their daughters, nieces, and sisters as wives and who, by long living together, had become their friends.'[20] Some of these Latins would have been Byzantine subjects – they certainly were to be tried in Byzantine courts (this did not change until 1198)[21] – and therefore in terms of political loyalty and identity they were, at least in theory, not different from those who attacked them. What made them different was their ethnoreligious identity, or at least the one projected onto them.[22]

On the other hand, the Norman sack of Thessaloniki was primarily an act of war between two states, the ethnoreligious component of the violence not being its primary or defining characteristic a priori – the city was attacked as a strategic target and a lucrative place for looting, but not primarily because it was inhabited by people of a different ethnic and/or religious label.[23] One might reasonably argue that it is methodically unsound to compare the two events, given their difference. My aim, however, is to focus on one common aspect between them, the violence inflicted from one ethnoreligious group upon another, and to suggest a trajectory of its impact. This is possible because even a casual glance at the sources recording these events will not fail to spot that their descriptions match. This is understandably the case in Eustathios of Thessaloniki, one of the main sources for the massacre of 1182 and the principal one for the siege and capture of his see in 1185.[24] His narrative links the two events, causally suggesting that 'it is from this action [the events of 1182] that our present woes [the sack of Thessaloniki] came upon us.'[25] As recent scholarship has emphasised, the narrative strategies of Eustathios are complex and should not be reduced to a 'rhetoric of polarized religious identity', which is his constant point of

---

[20] William of Tyre, *Chronicle*, 22.13(12), ed. Huygens, 2:1025, tr. Atwater and Krey, 2:465.

[21] Jacoby, 'Byzantine Outsider', esp. 136–7; 'Imperial Court'; Lilie, *Handel und Politik*, 299.

[22] I would like to thank Yannis Stouraitis for drawing my attention to this point.

[23] Eustathios, *Capture*, 117, tr. Melville Jones, 130–1, suggests so when he records that the Latins justified their acts of violence in Thessaloniki as a result of their having taken the city by force.

[24] Niketas Choniates also records the Norman capture of Thessaloniki, but his account is clearly based on Eustathios. As far as I know, there are no other detailed accounts on what happened in Thessaloniki. The only western source that records the sack of Thessaloniki merely mentions it in passing: *Annales Ceccanenses*, ed. Pertz, 287.

[25] Eustathios, *Capture*, 28, tr. Melville Jones, 34–5.

reference when describing these two events.[26] This is undoubtedly correct, but is not central to my discussion. Despite rhetorical flourishes, Eustathios' reference to violence should be seen as depicting actual occurrences. There are two facts that corroborate this. On the one hand, we have the testimony of William of Tyre, who wrote down his account of the massacre of 1182 shortly thereafter, based on survivors' accounts related to him in Syria, to which they fled.[27] William could not have known Eustathios' text – leaving aside whether William knew Greek, he had died in either 1184 or 1185, before Eustathios' text had been written[28] – and therefore the similarities in both accounts corroborate each other. On the events of 1185, on the other hand, Eustathios is the sole source. This discrepancy is probably due to the fact that, as a rule, it is the victims of atrocities that report them and very rarely their perpetrators. Furthermore, we are informed that Eustathios preached and circulated his text to an audience which included survivors of the Norman sack and occupation shortly after the liberation of the city;[29] for these reasons it would seem improbable that his account on the very specific instances of violence would have been invented. As far as the scope of this chapter is concerned, therefore, I will operate on the assumption that the violence described in these texts did occur and did have consequences.

First, I would like to present a close reading of these two events, placing emphasis on the ethnoreligious aspects of the violence they record. As is to be expected, certain events are common in both descriptions: killing, burning of parts of the city, looting. They are both part of the stock and trade of the way the capture of cities is described in the Greek and Latin literary tradition,[30] as well as reflecting what actually took place. There are differences as well: while both Eustathios and William record the killing of non-combatants, especially women and children – William as a result of them being trapped within their burning houses, Eustathios much more

---

[26] Holmes, 'Shared Worlds?' 40, 48, quote on 49. Neocleous, 'Greeks and Italians', 233, 250, is right to question hatred between Byzantines and Latins as the reason for the massacre (as scholars of previous generations had done), but, in my mind, he downplays its significance in order to support his theory of *convivencia* between the two groups.

[27] William of Tyre, *Chronicle*, 22.14(13), ed. Huygens, 2:1025.

[28] On William's death, see Edbury and Rowe, *William of Tyre*, 20–2; on the fact that he was probably not familiar with Greek, see Huygens, *Willelmi Tyrensis Chronicon*, 1:2–3.

[29] See also Magdalino, 'Eustathios and Thessalonica', 231.

[30] On this motif see Paul, 'Urbs Capta'; Fan Chiang, 'Urban Civilians' Experience', 62–8.

brutally and directly – Eustathios makes a point of additionally recording that pregnant women were killed both in 1182 and 1185, while also recording the raping of women (nuns in one instance) in Thessaloniki.[31] Furthermore, William writes that survivors of the massacre were sold into slavery, a fact unrecorded by Eustathios.

Violence directed towards religious buildings and members of the clergy is a motif equally shared by both texts. In the case of 1182, William records the burning of churches and the killing of clergy and monks.[32] The murder of a high-ranking Roman clergyman, the subdeacon John, is attested by both authors; William, however, includes additional information that emphasises the ritual aspect of the killing, as he relates that John's severed head was tied to the tail of a dog and trailed through the streets, which was clearly meant to humiliate the clergyman's religion.[33] Eustathios, on the other hand, includes much more information on the defiling, rather than the destruction, of churches in Thessaloniki: he records people being killed in them and Latins stripping or riding horses inside the buildings, as well as a wide range of actions that were meant to defile liturgical objects, such as urinating on sacred objects, attacking the shrine of St Demetrios with axes or giving church vestments to prostitutes to wear.[34]

Both authors record the defiling of dead bodies: William mentions exhumed corpses being dragged out in the streets in 1182,[35] while Eustathios relates that in Thessaloniki dead bodies were staged in unseemly poses with dead animals, making it appear as if they were kissing or having intercourse (symplokē); dead humans and animal carcasses resulting from the Norman onslaught were not allowed to be buried, but were burned together; and dead bodies were stripped and looted.[36] Finally, both sources record that an ecclesiastical charitable institution was attacked (the hospital of St John in Constantinople, the xenōn of the Church of Thessaloniki) and its sick and infirm inmates killed – Eustathios adds that the attackers

---

[31] On pregnant women being killed, see Eustathios, *Capture*, 29 (in 1182) and 105 (in 1185), tr. Melville Jones, 35, 118–19; rape: 99, 125, tr. Melville Jones, 114–15, 138–9; William of Tyre, *Chronicle*, 22.13(12), ed. Huygens, 2:1023.

[32] William of Tyre, *Chronicle*, 22.13(12), ed. Huygens, 2:1023–4.

[33] Ibid. 22.13(12), ed. Huygens, 2:1023; Eustathios, *Capture*, 29, tr. Melville Jones, 34–5.

[34] Eustathios, *Capture*, 99 (killing of priests in churches), 101–3 (looting and defiling church vessels, riding inside churches, stripping in churches, attacking the shrine of St Demetrios), 109 (vestments given to prostitutes), tr. Melville Jones, 114–15, 114–17, 122–3.

[35] William of Tyre, *Chronicle*, 22.13(12), ed. Huygens, 2:1023.

[36] Eustathios, *Capture*, 98, 107, tr. Melville Jones, 112–15, 120–1.

destroyed all medical drugs they found.[37] This is where the common motifs between William and Eustathios and the events of 1182 and 1185 end.

For some events in 1185 which do not correspond to those in 1182, Eustathios clearly suggests that the violence meted out to the population of Thessaloniki was fuelled by religious prejudice. I have already mentioned the defiling of churches and sacred objects; to these one can add the mocking and disrupting of church services, prohibiting the use of *sēmantra* or – allegedly – contaminating bread sold to the Byzantine population with lard to make it ritually impure and make them unknowingly break their religious fasting.[38] Furthermore, Eustathios informs us that the Latins in Thessaloniki first prohibited all Greeks from wearing any headgear and then proceeded to cut the long hair and beards of the Greeks in order to make them like themselves: clean-shaven and sporting bowl cuts.[39]

Despite the differences already discussed above and given that I take these accounts as historically reliable, we are confronted with a wide range of violent acts that transcend the usual repertoire of violence in warfare. They are instances of ritualised violence that include the violation or desecration of sacred spaces, times or objects[40] and the display of power through disrespect and humiliation, including on the bodies of the ethnoreligious Other. The following definition is, in my mind, very helpful in describing the events outlined above as instances of ethnic (or ethnoreligious) violence:

> [V]iolence perpetrated across ethnic lines . . . and in which the putative ethnic difference is coded – by perpetrators, targets, influential third parties, or analysts – as having been integral rather than incidental to the violence, that is, in which the violence is coded as having been meaningfully oriented in some way to the different ethnicity of the target.[41]

I have suggested above that violence leaves a mark (or maybe a stain) in history. But by the same token it is a sensational event that may obscure its causes and effects, both to its contemporaries and to us, the later exegetes. Scholars of the period have been only too eager to situate these instances

---

[37] William of Tyre, *Chronicle*, 22.13(12), ed. Huygens, 2:1023–4; Eustathios, *Capture*, 134–5, tr. Melville Jones, 144–9.

[38] Eustathios, *Capture*, 99, 114–15, 122, tr. Melville Jones, 114–15, 124–7, 134–5.

[39] Ibid. 109, 119, tr. Melville Jones, 122–3, 130–3.

[40] Brubaker and Laitin, 'Ethnic and Nationalist Violence', 445.

[41] Ibid. 428.

of violence in a recognisable context: they were precursors to the sack of Constantinople in 1204 and helped to explain it.[42]

While acknowledging that cultural difference may often be the bedrock within which the roots of ethnoreligious violence can be found, scholars working on ethnic and religious violence have introduced a number of qualifications: violence is a process, not an outcome,[43] a form of conflict, not a degree. Indeed, '[e]ven where violence is clearly rooted in pre-existing conflict, it should not be treated as a natural, self-explanatory outgrowth of such conflict, something that occurs automatically when the conflict reaches a certain intensity, a certain "temperature".'[44] In other words, we should not treat the outbreaks of violence in 1182 and 1185 as a natural culmination of the discourse of difference that had been brewing for some time but regard them as a new stage or form of this conflict.

The initial causes of the two events that led to violence may well have been opportunistic. I use this term in the sense employed by Laiou to characterise the conflicts between Latins and Byzantines in the twelfth century.[45] She suggests that although there had been plans to attack Byzantium, or even actual attacks against it, by crusaders before 1204, these were never at the core of crusader ideology, but had developed in response to what was seen by the Latins as Byzantine intransigence, hostility or even treacherous alliances with Muslims. Likewise, when Andronikos I chose to target the Latins in Constantinople, he did so to punish those who had supported the *prōtosebastos*, to secure Constantinople and preemptively counteract any resistance. In my mind, the fact that those targeted were Latins was not intrinsic to their being targeted. One could easily assume that any group that antagonised Andronikos would have been attacked, whether they belonged to his own ethnoreligious group or not, as the key reason was political dominance.[46]

As I have stated above, I think that the ethnoreligious element was equally opportunistic in the case of the Norman attack against Thessaloniki in 1185: the city and its population were not targeted for any other reason

---

[42] See above n. 10.
[43] Kalyvas, *Logic of Violence*, 21.
[44] Brubaker and Laitin, 'Ethnic and Nationalist Violence', 425–6, quote on 426.
[45] Laiou, 'Byzantium and the Crusades', esp. 17, 38–40.
[46] See Harris, *Byzantium and the Crusades*, 121–30. A further motivation for the attack of the mob would have been looting, no doubt also fuelled by the increasing economic privileges granted to the Italian merchants in the empire and especially Constantinople; see Jacoby, 'Byzantine Outsider', 142; Lilie, *Handel und Politik*, 535–7.

than being a strategically accessible and manageable target – as opposed
to Constantinople, the assumed target of the Normans, which was neither
of the two. The above suggestions may explain *why* the violence broke out,
but they do not explain the forms it took. This was a result of interpretation
by the authors of our sources, a fact commonly accepted in current scholarship that sees 'the "ethnic" quality of ethnic violence [as] not intrinsic to the
act itself; it emerges through after-the-fact interpretive claims'.[47] Eustathios
can be seen as utilising the bouts of violence against his flock to construct
and elaborate a vision of belonging together, of shared collective identity as
victims, that may not be systematic or always coherent but is nevertheless
powerful and suggests the readiness of his audience to accept it.

As we might expect, there were other forces at play. In the case of 1182,
competition for power and resources and the fear that one (ethnoreligious)
community (the Latins in Constantinople) would overwhelm and dispos-
sess the other (the Byzantine population in the city)[48] played a crucial role
as rumours and fears were instrumentalised by both sides in the conflict
(the regency of Alexios II versus Andronikos and his allies) for their own
goals.[49] Given that such outbursts of violence had not occurred before, one
can ask why the Constantinopolitans would fear that the Latins would wish
to exterminate them or vice versa. Again, recent approaches make clear
that when told by leaders that they are targets for violence, people often
react in this way, despite the fact that the outbreak of such violence may
seem logically implausible, as it is felt that even the slight chance of such
danger must be preemptively avoided.[50]

Once unleashed – even if its consequences were not fully thought out –
the violent conflict developed its own dynamic and could not be controlled.
The difficulty lies in the fact that we now have no way of knowing whether the
ritual aspects of the violence, those that clearly position them as instances of
ethnoreligious violence, were actually preconceived, planned and/or ordered
by the leaders of the conflicts, or whether we must accept that they were
quasi-spontaneous, a gruesome improvisation by its perpetrators.

Violence may have the discourse of difference as one of its causes, but its
outbreak fosters and amplifies this difference and makes boundaries more

---

[47] Brubaker and Laitin, 'Ethnic and Nationalist Violence', 444.
[48] See Williams, 'Sociology of Ethnic Conflicts', 62–3.
[49] Eustathios, *Capture*, 28, tr. Melville Jones, 34–5: 'Latins might plunder the city and
place the Greeks in servitude under them'; William of Tyre, *Chronicle*, 22.13(12), ed.
Huygens, 2:1023.
[50] Brubaker and Laitin, 'Ethnic and Nationalist Violence', 439.

pronounced.[51] It is as if the discourse leapt off the page and into the streets. A few examples can illustrate this. Some of the incidents of ethnoreligious violence described above clearly echo items found in the popular literature of prejudice, for example the lists of errors of the Latins circulated in Byzantium. The fact that Latins – especially members of the clergy – were clean-shaven was regarded by the Byzantines as a Judaising trait by Michael Keroularios; Theophylaktos of Ohrid also mentions it, while later sources, such as Constantine Stilbes shortly after 1204, added effeminacy to the insult (the shaven Latins look like women), a claim shared with Michael Choniates, who suggested that shaving one's beard instantly transformed one from a man to a woman, like the hermaphrodites of ancient Greece.[52] William of Tyre had made the following observation in his text (unconnected to the events above): 'For Orientals, both Greeks and other nationalities cherish the beard with most earnest care, and if perchance even one hair be pulled from it, this insult is regarded as the highest dishonor and ignominy.'[53]

Similarly, the cases of contaminating food with the aim of ritual damage (mixing lard into bread) equally echo Byzantine accusations of Latin dietary transgressions, especially regarding Lenten fasting.[54] There may well even have been other such instances – although, admittedly, the links are less straightforward. Latins making the Byzantines remove their headgear may be a jumbled reaction to Byzantine objections to Latin headgear (laity and clergy not distinct by the hats they wore, clergy approaching the altar with a covered head).[55] The desecration of tombs may also point to the mutual suspicion and objections towards the way each community regarded burials, as attested in Byzantine lists of the errors of the Latins.[56] The disruption and mocking of liturgical services by the Latins could also be connected to Byzantine disapproval of Latin customs, especially during Lent.[57]

These Byzantine accusations must have been known to some extent in the west – for example, as a result of public debates with members of the Orthodox Church that took place under John II and Manuel I or through the translation of Greek lists of the errors of Latins, such as the one by Hugo

[51] Yosmaoğlu, *Blood Ties*, 217; Brubaker and Laitin, 'Ethnic and Nationalist Violence', 439.
[52] Kolbaba, *Byzantine Lists*, 56–7; see also Messis, 'Lectures sexuées', 164–70, with literature on hair and beards.
[53] William of Tyre, *Chronicle*, 11.11, ed. Huygens, 1:511, tr. Atwater and Krey, 1:480.
[54] Kolbaba, *Byzantine Lists*, 34–5, 41–3, 46–7.
[55] Ibid. 62, 199.
[56] Ibid. 58, 195.
[57] Ibid. 55–6, 58–61, 63–4, 65, 67–9, 193.

Eteriano in the 1160s or 1170s.[58] Even though only a small group of people would have had access to the actual texts themselves, it seems safe to assume that some pedestrianised version could have reached larger groups. We can also assume that, as is often the case, the leaders in the attacks against the ethnoreligious Other (who would have been better educated and belonged to higher social strata) would have used such information to bestow meaning on the violence perpetrated under their command.[59] Despite the fact that the close mirroring of the acts of violence and the motifs in the literature of prejudice can be seen as a narrative strategy to reinforce the discourse of difference, there is nothing to suggest that some of these violent acts should not be seen as being tailored to reverse the accusations of heterodoxy or heresy flung upon the Latins by the Byzantines.

The nature of the connection between the theological and pastoral literature of prejudice and these acts of ethnoreligious violence may not be as straightforward as my account possibly suggests, but only more research on the question will be able to provide more specific answers.

Recently, Yannis Stouraitis argued that warfare was conducive to the process of reconstruction and reformulation of the community's (that is, the Byzantines') collective identity towards the consolidation of a vision of the Romans as an ethnic group circumscribed by cultural boundaries rather than as a geopolitical community demarcated by the boundaries of imperial authority, as had been the case in the previous period.[60] My suggestion is that these outbreaks of violence were the outliers of the warfare that Stouraitis has pointed to. These may not have been the first instances in which Byzantines inflicted violence on Latins and vice versa,[61] but it is telling that they are the first ones in which these acts of violence, especially the ritualised ones, are recorded in detail. In my mind, this suggests a certain shift. While Byzantine authors writing under Manuel I's reign suggested a reluctance – even if we assume it was only a rhetorical one – to shed the blood of fellow Christians,[62] the hardening of attitudes that

---

[58] Bucossi, 'Filioque Controversy'; 'Dibattiti teologici'.
[59] Brubaker and Laitin, 'Ethnic and Nationalist Violence', 426–7.
[60] Stouraitis, 'Reinventing Roman Ethnicity', 82–5.
[61] See e.g. the attacks against various Byzantine cities in the Norman campaigns against the empire in the early 1080s, the Venetian raid of Corfu in 1123, the Norman raids against Greece in 1147 or the Venetian campaign of reprisals against Manuel I after 1171.
[62] Anna Komnene, *Alexias*, 10.9, ed. Reinsch and Kambylis, 308–9; Manganeios Prodromos, *Poem* 20, v. 96 in E. and M. Jeffreys, 'Wild Beast from the West', 109; see also Stouraitis, 'Byzantine War against Christians', 96–7, 100–1, 107.

followed the events of 1182 and 1185 promote the detailed recording of acts of violence that target the ethnoreligious other. It is as if a line had been crossed and both sides could not go back to the previous state of precarious balance.

Instances of ethnoreligious violence proliferate thereafter, as do anti-Latin treatises, both seemingly feeding off each other.[63] The attacks of the Constantinopolitan mob against the Latins in the city in 1187 and again in 1203 included killings, looting and arson, but were fended off quite quickly, and thus a more pronounced use of violence could be prevented.[64] The violence to which the inhabitants of Constantinople were subjected by the conquering armies of the Fourth Crusade, on the other hand, resembles in many ways the incidents recorded in 1182 and 1185. Apart from the wide-spread murder of civilians (recorded by both Latin and Byzantine sources), the latter refer to rape, the defiling of churches and holy objects and the desecration of tombs and looting.[65] Obviously, as these events occurred during a state of war, violence across ethnoreligious lines became the norm, rather than the horrible exception.

Violence teaches both sides the importance of otherness. To paraphrase Rousseau's 'master and slave corrupt each other',[66] perpetrator and victim corrupt each other into being, into defining the image of each other through misrecognition, dominance and submission.[67] By demonstrating power on the bodies of those attacked and conquered, both directly and ritually, difference is permanently defined and coded. The identity of each side is strengthened by the fact that they belong to one of the two catego-ries of victim or perpetrator, and it remains firm even as the roles occasion-ally reverse.

---

[63] Kolbaba, 'Byzantine Perceptions', 117.

[64] Neocleous, 'Greeks and Italians', 240–9; Jacoby, 'Greeks of Constantinople', 54; Brand, *Byzantium Confronts the West*, 81–4, 247–8.

[65] Two key Byzantine accounts on the violence employed in 1204 are Constantine Stilbes, *Errors of the Latin Church*, 340–426, ed. and tr. Darrouzès, 81–6, and Niketas Choniates, *Historia*, ed. van Dieten, 572–9; for a number of studies that discuss the events of 1204 with reference to the violence, see Brand, *Byzantium Confronts the West*, 258–69; Angold, *Fourth Crusade*, 75–108; Phillips, *Fourth Crusade*, 253–80; and Papadopoulou, 'Niketas Choniates'.

[66] Rousseau, *Emile*, Book 2; translation from Taylor, 'Politics of Recognition', 45.

[67] Taylor, 'Politics of Recognition' is a seminal study on how a demeaning image of the Other can be imposed through conquest and on the implications of such actions on the formation of identities.

In her thought-provoking study on violence in late Ottoman Macedonia, İpek Yosmaoğlu referred to Hannah Arendt's maxim (violence can destroy power; it is utterly incapable of creating it) in order to suggest that violence can, in fact, help create something with actual power – a nation.[68] Perhaps we can push for another, intermediary stage and see violence helping a collective Byzantine ethnocultural identity to push through.

Acknowledgements

I would like to thank Myriam Fotou and Yannis Stouraitis for their astute comments and suggestions on previous drafts of the text. The text has also profited from being discussed with Aslihan Akışik Karakullukcu, Koray Durak, Nevra Necipoğlu, Youval Rotman and Kostis Smyrlis – I thank them all for their valuable suggestions.

Bibliography

Sources

Annales Ceccanenses ... G. H. Pertz (ed.), 'Annales Ceccanenses', in Monumenta Germaniae Historica. Scriptores, vol. 19 (Hanover, 1866), 275–302.

Anna Komnene, Alexias ... D. R. Reinsch and A. Kambylis (eds), Annae Comnenae Alexias, 2 vols (Berlin, 2001).

Constantine Stilbes, Errors of the Latin Church ... J. Darrouzès (ed. and tr.), 'Le mémoire de Constantin Stilbès contre les Latins', REB 21 (1963): 50–100.

Eustathios of Thessaloniki, Capture of Thessaloniki ... J. R. Melville Jones (tr.), The Capture of Thessaloniki (Canberra, 1988).

Niketas Choniates, Historia ... J. A. van Dieten (ed.), Niketae Choniatae Historia (Berlin, 1975).

Thucidides, History ... H. S. Jones and J. E. Powell (eds), Thucydidis historiae, 2 vols (Oxford, 1942) (repr. 1:1970, 2:1967).

William of Tyre, Chronicle ... R. B. C. Huygens (ed.), Willelmi Tyrensis Archiepiscopi Chronicon, 2 vols (Turnhout, 1986); Engl. tr. E. Atwater and A. C. Krey, William, Archbishop of Tyre: A History of Deeds Done Beyond the Sea, 2 vols (New York, 1943).

---

[68] Yosmaoğlu, Blood Ties, 287.

Secondary Literature

Angold, M., *The Fourth Crusade: Event and Context* (Harlow and New York, 2003).

Brand, C. M., *Byzantium Confronts the West 1180–1204* (Cambridge, MA, 1968).

Brubaker, R., and D. D. Laitin, 'Ethnic and Nationalist Violence', *Annual Review of Sociology* 24 (1998): 423–52.

Bucholtz, M., and K. Hall, 'Identity and Interaction: A Sociocultural Linguistic Approach', *Discourse Studies* 7 (2005): 585–614.

Bucossi, A., 'Dibattiti teologici alla corte di Manuele Comneno', in A. Rigo, A. Babuin and M. Trizio (eds), *Vie per Bisanzio. VIII Congresso dell'Associazione Italiana di Studi Bizantini*, vol. 1 (Bari, 2012), 311–21.

Bucossi, A., 'Seeking a Way out of the Impasse: The Filioque Controversy during John's Reign', in A. Bucossi and A. Rodriguez (eds), *John II Komnenos, Emperor of Byzantium: In the Shadow of Father and Son* (Farnham, 2016), 121–34.

Edbury, P., and J. G. Rowe, *William of Tyre: Historian of the Latin East* (Cambridge, 1988).

Fan Chiang, S.-C., 'Urban Civilians' Experience in the Romano-Persian Wars, 502–591 CE', PhD thesis, King's College London, 2015.

Gounarides, P., 'Η εικόνα των Λατίνων την εποχή των Κομνηνών', *Symmeikta* 9 (1994): 157–71.

Harris, J., *Byzantium and the Crusades*, 2nd ed. (London, 2014).

Holmes, C., 'Shared Worlds? A Question of Evidence', in C. Holmes, J. Harris and E. Russell (eds), *Byzantines, Latins and Turks in the Eastern Mediterranean World after 1150* (Oxford, 2012), 31–58.

Horowitz, D. L., *The Deadly Ethnic Riot* (Berkeley, Los Angeles and London, 2001).

Hunger, H., *Graeculus perfidus – Italos itamos: il senso dell'alterita'nei rapporti greco-romani ed italo-bizantini* (Rome, 1987).

Huygens, R. B. C., *Willelmi Tyrensis Archiepiscopi Chronicon*, 2 vols (Turnhout, 1986).

Jacoby, D., 'Between the Imperial Court and the Western Maritime Powers: The Impact of Naturalizations on the Economy of Late Byzantine Constantinople', in A. Ödekan, N. Necipoğlu and E. Akyürek (eds), *The Byzantine Court: Source of Power and Culture* (Istanbul, 2013), 95–101.

Jacoby, D., 'The Byzantine Outsider in Trade (c. 900–c. 1350)', in D. Smythe (ed.), *Strangers to Themselves: The Byzantine Outsider* (Aldershot, 2000), 129–47.

Jacoby, D., 'The Greeks of Constantinople under Latin Rule, 1204–1261', in T. F. Madden (ed.), *The Fourth Crusade: Event, Aftermath, and Perceptions* (Aldershot, 2008), 53–73.

Jeffreys, E., and M. Jeffreys, 'The "Wild Beast from the West": Immediate Literary Reactions in Byzantium to the Second Crusade', in A. E. Laiou and R. Parviz Mottahedeh (eds), *The Crusades from the Perspective of Byzantium and the Muslim World* (Washington, DC, 2001), 101–16.

Jenkins, R., *Social Identity*, 3rd ed. (London and New York, 2008).

Kaldellis, A., *Hellenism in Byzantium. The Transformation of Greek Identity and the Reception of the Classical Tradition* (Cambridge, 2007).

Kaldellis, A., 'Review of G. Page, *Being Byzantine*', *The Medieval Review* (2009). Available at <https://scholarworks.iu.edu/journals/index.php/tmr/article/view/16788/22906> (last accessed 28 September 2021).

Kaldellis, A., 'From Rome to New Rome, from Empire to Nation-State. Reopening the Question of Byzantium's Roman Identity', in L. Grig and G. Kelly (eds), *Two Romes. Rome and Constantinople in Late Antiquity* (Oxford, 2012), 387–404.

Kalyvas, S. N., *The Logic of Violence in Civil War* (Cambridge, 2006).

Kazhdan, A., 'Latins and Franks in Byzantium: Perception and Reality from the Eleventh to the Twelfth Century', in A. E. Laiou and R. Parviz Mottahedeh (eds), *The Crusades from the Perspective of Byzantium and the Muslim World* (Washington, DC, 2001), 83–100.

Koder, J., 'Latinoi – The Image of the Other according to Greek Sources', in C. Maltezou and P. Schreiner (eds), *Bisanzio, Venezia e il mondo francogreco (XIII–XV secolo)* (Venice, 2002), 25–39.

Kolbaba, T. M., *The Byzantine Lists. Errors of the Latins* (Urbana and Chicago, 2000).

Kolbaba, T. M., 'Byzantine Perceptions of Latin Religious "Errors": Themes and Changes from 850 to 1350', in A. E. Laiou and R. Parviz Mottahedeh (eds), *The Crusades from the Perspective of Byzantium and the Muslim World* (Washington, DC, 2001), 117–43.

Laiou, A. E., 'Byzantium and the Crusades in the Twelfth Century: Why Was the Fourth Crusade Late in Coming?', in A. E. Laoiu (ed.), *Urbs capta: The Fourth Crusade and Its Consequences* (Paris, 2005), 17–40.

Lilie, R.-J., *Handel und Politik zwischen dem byzantinischen Reich und den italienischen Kommunen Venedig, Pisa und Genua in der Epoche der Komnenen und der Angeloi (1081–1204)* (Amsterdam, 1984).

Madden, T. F., 'Outside and Inside the Fourth Crusade', *The International History Review* 17 (1995): 726–43.

Magdalino, P., 'Eustathios and Thessalonica', in C. N. Constantinides, N. M. Panagiotakes, E. Jeffreys and A. D. Angelou (eds), *ΦΙΛΕΛΛΗΝ. Studies in Honour of Robert Browning* (Venice, 1996), 225–38.

Messis, C., 'Lectures sexuées de l'altérité. Les Latins et identité romaine menacée pendant les derniers siècles de Byzance', *JÖB* (2011): 151–70.

Mitsiou, E., 'The Byzantines and the "Others". Between "Transculturality" and Discrimination', in C. Gastgeber and F. Daim (eds), *Byzantium as Bridge between West and East* (Vienna, 2015), 65–74.

Neocleous, S., 'Tyrannus Grecorum: The Image and Legend of Andronikos I Komnenos in Latin Historiography', *Medioevo greco* 12 (2012): 195–284.

Neocleous, S., 'Greeks and Italians in Twelfth-Century Constantinople: *Convivencia* or Conflict?', in B. Crostini and S. La Porta (eds), *Negotiating Co-Existence: Communities, Cultures and Convivencia in Byzantine Society* (Trier, 2013), 221–50.

Page, G., *Being Byzantine. Greek Identity Before the Ottomans, 1200–1420* (Cambridge, 2008).

Papadopoulou, T., 'Niketas Choniates and the Image of the Enemy after the Latin Capture of Constantinople', in J. Koder and I. Stouraitis (eds), *Byzantine War Ideology between Roman Imperial Concept and Christian Religion. Akten des Internationalen Symposiums (Wien, 19.–21. Mai 2011)* (Vienna, 2012), 87–98.

Paul, G. M., '"Urbs Capta": Sketch of an Ancient Literary Motif', *Phoenix* 36 (1982): 144–55.

Phillips, J., *The Fourth Crusade and the Sack of Constantinople* (New York, 2004).

Shawcross, T., 'Ethnic and Religious Violence in Byzantium', in M. S. Gordon, R. W. Kaeuper and H. Zurndorfer (eds), *The Cambridge World History of Violence*, vol. 2: AD 500–AD 1500 (Cambridge, 2020), 287–312.

Simpson, A., *Niketas Choniates. A Historiographical Study* (Oxford, 2013).

Stouraitis, Y., 'Byzantine War Against Christians – An *Emphylios Polemos*?', *Symmeikta* 20 (2010): 85–110.

Stouraitis, Y., 'Roman Identity in Byzantium: A Critical Approach', *BZ* 107 (2014): 175–220.

Stouraitis, Y., 'Byzantine Romanness: From Geopolitical to Ethnic Conceptions', in W. Pohl, C. Gantner, C. Grifoni and M. Pollheimer (eds), *Transformations of Romanness in the Early Middle Ages: Early Medieval Regions and Identities* (Berlin, 2018), 123–39.

Stouraitis, Y., 'Reinventing Roman Ethnicity in High and Late Medieval Byzantium', *Medieval Worlds* 5 (2017): 70–94.

Taylor, C., 'The Politics of Recognition', in A. Gutmann (ed.), *Multicultur-alism: Examining the Politics of Recognition* (Princeton, 1994), 25–73.

Williams, R. M., 'The Sociology of Ethnic Conflicts: Comparative International Perspectives', *Annual Review of Sociology* 20 (1994): 49–79.

Yosmaoğlu, I., *Blood Ties: Religion, Violence and the Politics of Nationhood in Ottoman Macedonia, 1878–1908* (Ithaca and London, 2014).

12

Adjustable Imperial Image-Projection and the Greco-Roman Repertoire: Their Reception among Outsiders and Longer-Stay Visitors

Jonathan Shepard

Byzantium's leadership was keenly aware of the impression its activities and the sheer longevity of its empire made on outsiders, and this was one reason for its encouragement of external potentates to send envoys or to pay a visit to Constantinople themselves.[1] Yet in the early Middle Ages only a few persons made the round trip to Constantinople, whether as traders, envoys or potentates. Even Arab observers seem to have been less than well informed, and fresh, accurate data about material resources and current goings-on in the empire were correspondingly hard to come by.[2] Rumours throve, many being propagated deliberately by the imperial authorities. So long as means of verification were few, such disinformation was often effective, especially as few 'barbarian' regimes were capable of crosschecking the latest intelligence with written reports of even a few years earlier.[3] Such conditions gave the imperial government scope to 'change its story' – literally so, in the refashioning of narratives of quite recent episodes and bilateral agreements,[4] but also figuratively, accentuating different facets of the empire according to circumstances.

---

[1] Shepard, 'Byzantine Diplomacy', 51–2.

[2] Winkelmann, 'Probleme', 19–20, 26–9; Treadgold, 'Remarks', 211–12; Haldon, *Warfare*, 102–3, 314 n. 6, 106; El Cheikh, *Byzantium Viewed by the Arabs*, 5–9.

[3] On Charlemagne's record-keeping, which seems to have been meticulous, see e.g. McCormick, *Charlemagne's Survey*, 153–8, 163–5, 177–81; Davis, *Charlemagne's Practice*, 294–311, 317–22.

[4] This is exemplified by the specious reinterpretation of Patriarch Nicholas Mystikos' coronation of Symeon of Bulgaria, concocted shortly after the event in 913: Symeon Logothetes, *Chronicon*, 135.11, ed. Wahlgren, 301.80–3; Shepard, 'Symeon of Bulgaria', 21–4; idem, 'Introduction', xxi–xxii; Mladjov, 'Crown and Veil'.

Our aim here is to consider the workings of imperial image-projection towards foreign courts in the early Middle Ages and to compare them with the ways in which the empire's condition was presented subsequently, in the era of Alexios I Komnenos. The underlying question is what adjustments occurred at a time when Constantinople was attracting outsiders in sizeable numbers. Most obviously, it is a matter of communications, the fact that travel grew more frequent and outsiders were better-informed about the empire. But this is not the full story. One seems to observe in Alexios Komnenos' era something deeper-seated than tactical shifts in image-projection to cater for the many foreigners – especially westerners – with whom he had to do business. Prolonged quasi-social interaction with the 'Latins', especially Normans, observing their manners, appreciating their values and partaking of a kindred soldierly outlook, may have helped to foster a rather different self-image on the part of Alexios and some other members of the ruling elite.

How far the change was, in Alexios' case, calibrated is virtually impossible to adjudge. It begs the question of where the border between contrived image and a sense of personal identity lies. At his deathbed, Alexios' wife deplored his penchant for, and mastery of, 'all sorts of deceits, decking out your language with contradictory meanings'.[5] Eschewing any attempt at systematic answering, we shall sketch the fluctuations in Byzantium's geopolitical circumstances over the tenth and eleventh centuries, along with concomitant shifts in image-projection. Two themes loom in the background: the fact that the armed forces seem to have been at their peak in the mid-eleventh century, in terms of both size and the articulacy of the senior officers;[6] and the fact that the abrupt downturn from what still appeared to visitors a stance of 'imperial arrogance' in the mid-1060s[7] was witnessed by many outsiders, notably westerners. The empire's infirmities were laid bare. Alexios Komnenos grew up in these circumstances and had, essentially, to live by his wits in the course of his first command, quashing the insurrection of Roussel through a deal with a Turkish war-band.[8]

---

[5] Niketas Choniates, *Historia*, ed. van Dieten, 7.

[6] On the armed forces' overall numbers in the eleventh century, see Cheynet, 'Effectifs de l'armée byzantine', with the reservations expressed by Haldon, *Warfare*, 315, n. 71. For the elaboration of the military ethos and sense of support from warrior saints, see Kazhdan and Epstein, *Change in Byzantine Culture*, 104–19; Cheynet, *Société byzantine*, 2:413–14, 473–97, 563–81; Holmes, *Basil II*, 176–7, 278–94; White, *Military Saints*, 61–3.

[7] *Annales Altahenses maiores*, ed. von Giesebrecht and von Oefele, 67.

[8] Cheynet, *Pouvoir et contestations*, 78–9; Shepard, 'Man-to-Man', 756–8.

Our prime aim is to consider Alexios' response to circumstances in which improvisation was quintessential to statecraft and strategy alike. The emperor's changes of tack were open to scrutiny to an unprecedented extent. In particular, one may note the criticism of Alexios voiced by some Norman participants in the First Crusade and most stridently by Bohemond. In the early 1100s the emperor was having to cope with a propaganda campaign. Bohemond instigated hagiographical texts, recounting his miraculous escape from Turkish captivity and the clutches of the 'most cruel' emperor, 'a fanatical heretic'. His prisoner's silver chains were exhibited and dedicated to the monastery of Saint-Léonard-de-Noblat in Haute Vienne during his recruiting tour.[9] Bohemond also disseminated letters, reinforcing charges of the Greek church's heresy with vilification of Alexios Komnenos for alleged breaches of the undertakings he had made to the crusaders in 1096/7. Bohemond was behind the revision of the text of an early narrative of the crusade which, in the form of the *Gesta Francorum*, soon spawned further versions of events casting Alexios as the villain of the piece.[10] Imperial image-projection was now having to respond to a well-informed adversary's agenda. Alexios' was not an identity of convenience forced upon him by outsiders. But he needed to counter propaganda capable of mustering against him an army in the name of Christ. This was a far cry from the ambassadorial exchanges recorded in chronicles three centuries earlier, when data on Byzantine affairs was hard for outsiders to come by.

Regulated Image-Projection

Firstly, one may glance at a few episodes from the era of Charlemagne, who was perhaps the hungriest of all early medieval rulers for news about his borderlands and beyond. In 813 Pope Leo III wrote to him, relaying what 'some Greek men', newly arrived from the east, had said about an attempted palace coup. The pope added that another informant had supplied divergent details; he forwarded both versions on the assumption that the Frankish ruler wanted to know it all.[11] The episode was almost wholly fictitious.

---

[9] *Miracula Beati Leonardi Confessoris*, ch. 7, 164. See Flori, *Bohémond d'Antioche*, 253–64, 275–7.

[10] Holtzmann, 'Geschichte des Investiturstreites', 282; Flori, *Bohémond d'Antioche*, 275–6; Flori, 'Anonyme Normand', 735–44; Malamut, *Alexis Ier Comnène*, 412–13; von Falkenhausen, 'Boemondo e Bisanzio', 117–18.

[11] Leo III, *Letters*, ed. Hampe, 99–100; Wickham, 'Ninth-Century Byzantium', 246; Sansterre, 'Informations parvenues en Occident', 373–8.

Stuart Airlie has drawn attention to two letters addressed to Charlemagne by, respectively, Abbot Maginarius of St Denis and Pope Hadrian I, recounting Maginarius' misadventures while trying to glean information south of Benevento in 788. Airlie concludes: 'The letter shows how difficult it was to obtain reliable information from the more distant regions of the empire, from the borderlands and from beyond the borders.'[12] He further notes the dilemma of 'Louis the Pious' in 826, who was 'uncertain how to deal with a Bulgarian delegation, as rumours had reached him that the Bulgarian ruler had already been killed.'[13]

Frankish rulers might be expected to have been even less sure about reports from the eastern empire itself. The *Annales Regni Francorum* recount 'the many and illustrious victories' won by Emperor Nikephoros I over the Bulgars before perishing in battle and being succeeded by Michael I.[14] This representation of Nikephoros' incursion into Bulgaria in 811 as successful and stymied only by death in action may well reflect a Byzantine embassy's report to Charlemagne soon afterwards. And, as Daniel Ziemann observes, the misleadingly positive account of Byzantium's situation probably led Charlemagne to agree to peace, accepting acclamation as *basileus* by the envoys and confirming the Treaty of Aachen.[15] Yet only two years later, Byzantine envoys were singing a rather different tune. Still accentuating the positive, and claiming that Khan Krum had been gravely wounded by Leo V, they acknowledged his encampment just outside Constantinople's walls and, according to one chronicle, now 'sought help against the Bulgars and other barbarous peoples.'[16] The Frankish sources show no sign of scepticism. Apparently their authors did not see the claims of Roman-style victories

---

[12] Airlie, 'Partes, termini', 220: 'Der Brief führt vor Augen, wie schwierig es war, verlässliche Informationen aus den entfernteren Regionen des Reichs, den Grenzgebieten und von jenseits der Grenzen zu erhalten.' See *Codex Carolinus*, ed. Gundlach, 655–7.

[13] Airlie, 'Partes, termini', 220: 'verunsichert, wie er mit einer bulgarischen Gesandtschaft umgehen sollte, da ihm das Gerücht zu Ohren gekommen war, der bulgarische Herrscher sei bereits getötet worden'; Borgolte, 'Experten der Fremde', 960–1.

[14] *Annales Regni Francorum*, ed. Kurze, 136; Ziemann, 'Dangerous Neighbours', 93. On the theme of 'victory' in imperial messages to external potentates, and on its connection with the triumphs periodically staged in Constantinople, see McCormick, *Eternal Victory*.

[15] *Annales Regni Francorum*, ed. Kurze, 136; Ziemann, 'Dangerous Neighbours', 102. See also Hartmann, *Karl der Große*, 227–8; Davis, *Charlemagne's Practice*, 364–77.

[16] *Chronicon Laurissense breve*, ed. Schnorr von Carolsfeld, 38; *Annales Regni Francorum*, ed. Kurze, 139; Ziemann, 'Dangerous Neighbours', 101.

in Moesia provincia being followed by a request for military aid soon afterwards as inconsistent.

One could cite other examples of ninth-century imperial image-projection combining reports of victories with requests for help, notably Theophilos' demarches to the west after the fall of Amorion in 838. The following year, a Byzantine embassy arrived at the court of Louis the Pious in Ingelheim, reporting the victories their own emperor had won and urging Louis and his subjects to render thanks to 'the Giver of all victories'.[17] This was followed up by the mission of Theodosios Baboutzikos, which in the spring or early summer of 842 reached the court of Louis' son and successor, Lothar I. Baboutzikos' aim was to induce the Franks to undertake operations against the Muslims who were overrunning Byzantine Sicily, and to send an army to serve with Theophilos in the east.[18] This demarche was probably the occasion for the delivery of the Papyrus of St Denis to the western emperor.[19] There is not, to my knowledge, any hint in western sources of awareness of the parlousness of Theophilos' position in the aftermath of Amorion's fall.

This serves merely to confirm that data on Byzantine affairs was hard to come by, and image-projection through embassies and lavish gifts was correspondingly straightforward. One might expect things to change when communications between the Bosporus and the outside world burgeoned, and more travellers visited Constantinople, passed by the capital en route to the Holy Land or made short-range trips across the border. A marked increase in written communications, in the journeying of individuals, and in commercial exchanges between Byzantium and distant peoples is discernible from around the mid-tenth century. That was when the sea link to the land of Rus and points north came into intensive use.[20] Nikephoros Phokas' reconquest of Crete rendered sea voyages to the west less perilous, albeit never secure.[21] There followed an upsurge in land travel following

---

[17] *Annales Bertiniani*, s.a. 839, ed. Grat et al., 30; Shepard, 'Rhos Guests', 41–6; Borgolte, 'Experten der Fremde', 962–3.

[18] See the slightly divergent versions in Joseph Genesios, *On the Reigns*, ed. Lesmüller-Werner and Thurn, 50; *Theophanes Continuatus*, 3.37, ed. Signes Codoñer and Featherstone, 194–5; and John Skylitzes, *Synopsis*, ed. Thurn, 79.

[19] Dölger, 'Pariser Papyrus', 206–8; Shepard, 'Rhos Guests', 45–7; idem, 'Theodosios' Voyages', 70–3; Signes Codoñer, *Emperor Theophilos*, 324–7.

[20] Gnezdovo serves as a 'litmus test': Shepard, 'Constantinople', 257–9; Pushkina, Murasheva and Eniosova, 'Gnezdovskii arkheologicheskii kompleks', 262–73; Eniosova and Pushkina, 'Finds of Byzantine Origin'.

[21] Malamut, *Îles de l'empire Byzantin*, 1:88–90, 2:546–51, 559; Kislinger, 'Reisen und Verkehrswege', 369–71.

the subjugation of Bulgaria in 1018.[22] That significant change was already occurring in the mid-tenth century seems clear enough from a number of suggestive items of evidence. For example, in 960 the Venetian political leadership expressed concern about an apparently burgeoning slave trade, as well as about 'this wicked and extraordinary offence'. The 'offence' was on the part of unauthorised individuals who were intruding on the Venetian leaders' role as supervisors of message-bearing between Byzantium and the west. A decade later, John Tzimiskes put pressure on the Venetians to halt their trafficking of strategic materials with the Muslims, a measure signalling how buoyant this trade actually was.[23] More to the point of our underlying question (above, p. 288) are the implications of this easing of communications: the likelihood that rapid adjustments to the empire's image would become harder to perform once journeys to and from the Byzantine dominions multiplied and information about events there was diffused more widely.

So long as the economy was prospering, and ample resources were at the authorities' disposal, this scarcely mattered: after all, glamorous image-projection was more often than not in line with reality. One might consider the various ways in which the government spread the word about spectacular victories and the acquisition of holy relics from beyond the border.[24] There are grounds for supposing a more emphatic display of 'Roman' characteristics on the part of the authorities than had been feasible in preceding eras. For example, the triumph John Tzimiskes celebrated after his Danubian campaign seems to have been modelled on descriptions of triumphs in Republican Rome, judging from a contemporary tract purporting to describe it.[25] Resuscitation of ancient monuments as well as military considerations and the need for ready-made building materials probably

---

[22] Shepard, 'Communications', 219, 220, 228–9. Specifically on Macedonian roads, see Popović and Breier, 'Tracing Byzantine Routes'. For roads more generally, see Laiou, 'Regional Networks', 127–8, 130.

[23] *Urkunden zur älteren Handels- und Staatsgeschichte*, nos 13, 14, ed. Tafel and Thomas, 1:21, 26–8. On the 971 ban, see Lopez and Raymond, *Medieval Trade*, 333–5; Jacoby, 'Venetian Commercial Expansion', 374, 380, 382.

[24] John I Tzimiskes' letter to the Armenian king of kings Ashot III combines both these qualities: Matthew of Edessa, *Chronicle*, 1:19–21, tr. Dostourian, 29–33; Walker, '"Crusade" of John Tzimisces', 320–1, 325–7. For the amassment of relics by victorious armies in this era, see also Kalavrezou, 'Helping Hands', 67–79; Engberg, 'Romanos Lekapenos'.

[25] The tract, although hypothetical rather than still extant, has been identified and partially reconstructed by Kaldellis, 'Original Source', 37–8, 47–8, 52.

played a part in the refortification of the Danube border in the 970s and 980s.[26] And the outer gate added to Constantinople's Golden Gate may date from Nikephoros II's reign. In Cyril Mango's words, 'it would have looked from a distance not unlike the face of a Roman triumphal arch'.[27] Triumphs continued to be celebrated until the mid-eleventh century, with military success and classicising lore being purveyed to eminent outsiders.[28] The silk depicting an imperial *adventus* found in the tomb of Bishop Gunther of Bamberg suggests as much. He probably received it as a gift from the emperor while passing through Constantinople in the mid-1060s.[29]

Byzantine Military Culture's Diffusion among Northern Warriors

Image-projection at an elite level is less of a concern to me, however, than the diffusion of lore and culture to outsiders through somewhat different streams, the most important of which were the armed forces. Liudprand might mock the Byzantines' recourse to foreigners to swell the ranks of expeditionary forces, but that large numbers of them were now serving for varying lengths of time seems clear; and some units had their own officers.[30] For example, the units of Rus, Khazars, Bulgarians, 'Turks' (probably Hungarians) and others serving with the Byzantines in Syria in the 950s were very large, and interpreters were needed to make liaison possible.[31] Although many will have kept apart, there are hints of communication and even socialising to the point of friendship, at least among the higher ranks. The question of what kind of 'culture' this entailed is impossible to answer confidently, raising as it does such questions as what went on in Byzantine officers' messes, the officers' openness to foreign-born commanders and what marks their word-of-mouth exchanges could have left in Byzantine

---

[26] Shepard, 'Imperial Outliers', 379–80; Madgearu, *Byzantine Military Organization*, 102–8, 112–14.

[27] Mango, 'Triumphal Way', 186.

[28] McCormick, *Eternal Victory*, 178–84, 187–8, 198–205.

[29] Prinzing, 'Bamberger Gunthertuch', 219–20, 230 and n. 52; Jacoby, 'Bishop Gunther', 276–8 and n. 59; Prinzing, 'Nochmals zur historischen Deutung'.

[30] Liudprand of Cremona, *Relatio*, chs 30, 44, 45, ed. Chiesa, 200, 206, 207. See also Haldon, *Warfare*, 116–17; Shepard, 'Uses of the Franks', 288, 290–1, 294.

[31] For the employment of interpreters who 'alone . . . could understand their languages', see Mutanabbi, tr. in Vasiliev, *Byzance et les Arabes*, II.2, 333, and the almost contemporaneous historical commentary on the poem of Mutanabbi, ibid. 331; see Vasiliev, *Byzance et les Arabes*, II.1, 353 and n. 1.

or external sources. And, of course, the barbarians' own languages and cultures varied greatly.

Speculative as any treatment of these issues must be, four considerations give reason to suppose that Byzantine middlebrow military culture is not utterly irrecoverable, and that outsiders could have partaken of it. Firstly, one gains an inkling of officers' cultural horizons from the digests of ancient materials and the revisions and the new writings on military matters that proliferated in the tenth and eleventh centuries. Debate was underway between writers and their readers over the relative merits of ancient tactics and present-day practice, comparisons being drawn between the enemies of Greco-Roman armies, such as Alexander the Great's, and current foes.[32] Secondly, Charlotte Roueché has reconstructed the thought-world of the higher-ranking officers. They had received elementary training in rhetoric through *progymnasmata*. Accordingly, they had a taste for maxims, manifest fables and tales of Greco-Roman campaigns and heroes, linking these with factual details of ancient tactics along with practical recommendations on contemporary warfare, and they were apt to consult works of 'compilation literature' that mixed these genres. This conclusion rests heavily but not exclusively on Roueché's study of the *Counsels and Tales* of Kekaumenos, a veteran of mid-eleventh-century campaigning.[33] Thirdly, *Counsels and Tales* implies a fair degree of communication between its author and foreign-born commanders, including Harald Hardrada, with whom he seems to have struck up an acquaintance.[34] Dealings with such commanders are still more prominent in a work written by his namesake, Katakalon Kekaumenos. Parts of this work were, in my opinion, incorporated by John Skylitzes into his chronicle. Conversations with Georgians, Pechenegs and Varangians are implied. They evince the same taste for stratagems as can be found in *Counsels and Tales* and other works emanating from military circles.[35]

Fourthly and finally, there are hints in *non*-Byzantine sources of motifs and tales of stratagems circulating among some of the peoples who provided military manpower for the empire in the tenth and eleventh centuries. I have

---

[32] Sullivan, 'Byzantine Instructional Manual', 228–9, 256–7; Shepard, 'Middle Byzantine Military Culture', 477.

[33] Roueché, 'Literary Background', 114–17; eadem, 'Rhetoric', 30–7; Holmes, 'Compilation Literature', 76–8.

[34] Kekaumenos, *Consilia et Narrationes*, ed. Roueché, 97.20–1; Shepard, 'Middle Byzantine Military Culture', 481–2.

[35] Shepard, 'Middle Byzantine Military Culture', 480, 482.

in mind the stories woven into the *Rus Primary Chronicle* and Scandinavian sagas. Of particular note is the stratagem of tying firebrands to homing pigeons or other birds, thereby setting fire to the roofs where the birds had their nests and forcing the inhabitants of a town to surrender.[36] Adolf Stender-Petersen drew attention to similar ploys in Greco-Roman literature and highlighted a parallel in an Armenian writer's reference to a ruse devised by Alexander the Great. Writing in the heyday of northerners' service with the Byzantine armed forces, Stephen of Taron states that Alexander had set fire to a palace by means of flaming birds. Stephen likens to Alexander's feat the ruse of a near-contemporary ruler, Ibn Khosrow ('Adud al-Dawla): he required the inhabitants of a town to give up their household dogs as a symbol of submission and then set fire to the dogs, who duly ran home and set the town ablaze.[37] Stender-Petersen suggested returnees from Byzantium and the stories they heard during military service were the likeliest sources for this and other tales in the *Rus Primary Chronicle* and the sagas.[38] He may well have cast his net too wide in ascribing to such veterans many of the classicising stories in Saxo Grammaticus and the sagas, as Roland Scheel points out.[39] However, the importance of oral traditions relayed from the distant past as a source for the *Rus Primary Chronicle* has been reaffirmed by Timofei Gimon,[40] while Stender-Petersen's thesis of a cultural dialogue between northern mercenary commanders and imperial army officers looks more plausible in light of Roueché's studies.

If socio-cultural exchanges between outsiders and Byzantine officers were quite lively below the level of imperial image-projection, one would expect disinformation of the sort practised on Charlemagne to become harder to pull off. Such expectations are vindicated by, for example, a detailed account of Romanos IV's mishaps at Manzikert, that symbol of imperial humiliation.[41] The account comes in William of Apulia's *Deeds of Robert Guiscard*, and his information is probably derived from western

---

[36] *Povest' Vremennykh Let*, ed. Adrianova-Peretts, Likhachev and Sverdlov, 28–9; *Russian Primary Chronicle*, tr. Cross and Sherbowitz-Wetzor, 81; Snorri Sturluson, *Haralds Saga*, 6, ed. Bjarni Aðalbjarnarson, 76–7; Shepard, 'Middle Byzantine Military Culture', 473.

[37] Stephen of Taron, *Universal History*, tr. Greenwood, 246; Stender-Petersen, *Varäger-sage*, 147–8, 151–3.

[38] Stender-Petersen, *Varägersage*, 85–101, 127–9, 141–54, 248–53.

[39] Scheel, *Skandinavien und Byzanz*, 1:302–3 n. 38, 416–22.

[40] Gimon, 'Ian' Vyshatich', 103–10.

[41] See the reassessment by Cheynet, 'Mantzikert'. That Manzikert still appeared a debacle in the eyes of military men is suggested by the attitude of Anna Komnene, presumably reflecting her father's outlook. See Buckley, *Alexiad*, 46, 142, 265–6.

warriors on the scene.[42] Soon a Norman commander, Roussel, was setting up a lordship in Asia Minor.[43] Image-projection conveyed by embassies proclaiming victories will have lost its edge once events in the empire could be divulged by such foreign-born warriors. They themselves constituted part of its military resources and, if Stender-Petersen's thesis holds true, their own commanders might have learned Greek and at least a smattering of the Greco-Roman culture in vogue among Byzantine-born officers. This would not have prevented them from partaking of a certain 'Roman-ness', in the broadest sense of a glorious military tradition, but the cult of heroes in this culture did not necessarily pivot on the emperor of the day.[44]

Heroes in Anglo-Norman and Italo-Norman Literary Culture

If Byzantine military culture's motifs and tales of classical stratagems found favour among the Rus and Scandinavians, it might be expected to have resonated even more loudly among the Normans, who harboured clerical students of the classical world. Stender-Petersen himself drew attention to stratagems and narrative structures in Anglo-Norman and slightly later works, which, he argued, could have reached the British Isles via Scandinavia.[45] But he did not allow for the vibrancy of the Channel-coast Normans' contacts with their kinsmen in southern Italy and Sicily or directly with the Byzantine lands.[46] And he wrote before the huge numbers of the 'Franks' – especially Normans – entering imperial service gained recognition. One might surmise a priori that the examples of Greco-Roman lore identified by Stender-Petersen in the *Rus Primary Chronicle* and the sagas had counterparts in the materials that

---

[42] William of Apulia, *Gesta Roberti Wiscardi*, 3.1–92, ed. Mathieu, 164–8. For the numbers of westerners in imperial service around the time of Manzikert, see Shepard, 'Uses of the Franks', 303–4. See also Mathieu, 'Source négligée', 96–8, 103.

[43] Michael Attaleiates, *History*, tr. Kaldellis and Krallis, ed. Pérez Martín, 350–1, 360–5; Nikephoros Bryennios, *History*, 2.19, ed. and tr. Gautier, 182–9; *Skylitzes Continuatus*, ed. Tsolakes, 161; Shepard, 'Uses of the Franks', 300–1.

[44] The criteria for determining endowment with 'Roman' qualities were labile. See Page, *Being Byzantine*, 46–51, 67–71; Stouraitis, 'Roman Identity'; idem, 'Being "Roman" in Byzantium'.

[45] Stender-Petersen, *Varägersage*, 131–9, 189–93, 209. The 'commonplace' nature of some motifs, including the stratagems, is emphasised by Scheel, who also underlines the late date of our extant written Scandinavian narratives, in comparison with Anglo-Norman and other Latin texts: Scheel, *Skandinavien und Byzanz*: e.g. 1:417–28, 2:723–6.

[46] Ciggaar, *Western Travellers*, 178–83. See also Ciggaar, 'Bilingual Word Lists', 172–5.

French-speaking, especially Norman, warriors brought back from Byzantine service from the mid-eleventh century onwards.

To substantiate this surmise would require expertise in Anglo-Norman, French and also southern Italian literary cultures. And the hazards of trying to distinguish between indigenous Italo-Latin and Greco-Italian literary themes and those flourishing under the patronage of the Normans are obvious. So I shall merely highlight a couple of features of eleventh-century Norman historical writing and political culture before turning back to Byzantium. First, the earliest accounts of Duke William's conquest of England show classicising tendencies and invoke eastern imperium in their attempts to legitimise his rule there. According to the *Song of the Battle of Hastings*, almost certainly composed soon afterwards, William even had a 'Greek' craftsman manufacture his golden crown (*stemma*), while one of the slayers of Harold is likened to a son of Hector (*Hectorides*).[47] William of Poitiers, another contemporary, compares William's organisation of the Channel crossing with Julius Caesar's, finding William braver and a better strategist. He also remarks on the 'Greeks'' request for warriors from the Duke to fight 'Babylon.'[48] He recounts the *adventus* ceremonies that greeted William back in Normandy in 1067, likening Rouen's welcome to that of Rome for Pompey.[49] To read more into this than the tropes of classically educated French churchmen may seem rash. But one should recall that two sons of William's steward had recently served at the imperial court. One was a *prōtospatharios*,[50] a dignity just above that of the *spatharokandidatos* Harald Hardrada,[51] William's rival for the throne of England in 1066. Earlier that year, the incumbent of the throne, Edward the Confessor, had himself been buried with an *enkolpion* and a silk of, most probably, Byzantine manufacture.[52] So William of Poitiers and others could presuppose acquaintance with Byzantine court manners on the part of

---

[47] Guy, Bishop of Amiens, *Carmen de proelio Hastingae*, 757–62, 794 (on the crown); 537–8, 563 (on *Hectorides*), ed. and tr. Barlow, 44–5, 46–7, 32–3, 34–5.

[48] William of Poitiers, *Gesta Guillelmi ducis*, 2.39–40, 1.59, ed. Davis and Chibnall, 168–75, 96–7.

[49] Ibid. 2.41 (176–7).

[50] *Chronicle of Sainte-Barbe-en-Auge*, ed. Sauvage, 56–7; Ciggaar, 'Byzantine Marginalia', 49–52.

[51] Kekaumenos, *Consilia et Narrationes*, ed. Roueché, 97.20–1. On the titles, see Oikonomides, *Listes de préséance*, 297.

[52] Ciggaar, 'England and Byzantium', 89–95. Granger-Taylor, 'Silk from the Tomb', inferred from the silk's lower quality that it was not a diplomatic gift from Byzantium. See, however, for evidence of such contacts, Cheynet, 'London Byzantine Seals'.

leading families of northern France and the Anglo-Scandinavian world, alongside whatever individual returnees picked up in Byzantine officers' messes.

In northern Europe, literary conceits were just one of many cards to play in dynastic ambitions, as, for instance, the name 'Philip' being given by Henry of France to his eldest son in 1052. The name seemingly recalls that of the father of Alexander the Great, while also averring the 'Macedonian' ancestry of the child, through his mother, Princess Anne of Rus, and her putative grandmother, the sister of Basil II.[53] The choice of name could have been in response to the pretensions of William of Normandy, whose ambitions were alarming the French king. Here, invocation of Alexander the Great alongside the eastern imperial dynasty served to bolster Philip's rights to succeed Henry. But for the Normans in the south, possessing both *force majeure* and knowledge of Byzantium's predicament, such invocations had connotations of entitlement to the eastern throne. This may be the significance of the name given to Guiscard's daughter, 'Olympias', which was the name of the mother of Alexander the Great. Vera von Falkenhausen has suggested that Guiscard's choice signalled a *Herrschermutter*: her son would be a mighty conqueror. She further noted that the personal names 'Olympias' and 'Alexander' appear to come into use in southern Italy *only* in the Norman period, although the *Alexander Romance* had been known there since its translation into Latin in Naples in the tenth century.[54] Could not talk of Alexander and other Greco-Roman heroes have been brought home to Guiscard by returnees from Byzantium, the portentousness of Olympias' name being understood? Guiscard's own brother, Hubert, may have served in Byzantium and given his son the name of Constantine. Early imperial history and literary lore about heroes such as Alexander was, in other words, readily accessible to Norman leaders by the third quarter of the eleventh century.[55]

---

[53] Other candidates, such as the emperor Philip the Arabian (AD 244–9), seem far less plausible (*pace* Dunbabin, 'What's in a Name?', 959–68). See also Bogomoletz, 'Anna of Kiev', 307.

[54] See von Falkenhausen, 'Olympias', 57–9, 68–72, n. 76; Ciggaar, *Western Travellers*, 277; Skinner, 'And Her Name Was . . . ?', 36–7, n. 44. On a more general – perhaps subversive – tendency to signal political and ethnic allegiance by the choice of Greek names in Apulia and Lombard ones at Amalfi from the later eleventh century onwards, see ibid. 38.

[55] There are grounds for supposing that Guiscard's brother Hubert ('Humbertus'), whose death is recorded in the *Breve Chronicon Northmannicum* s.a. 1071, was the father of Constantine Humbertopoulos, a senior commander at the time of Alexios Komnenos' coup d'état in 1081: *Breve Chronicon Northmannicum*, ed. Cuozzo, 171; Seibt, 'Europäische Aristokraten', 84–6; Shepard, 'Man-to-Man', 761.

Such questions are speculative. What is certain is that soon Norman leaders were commissioning historical works which represented their own enterprises in epic terms. These invoked warfare for the faith on 'infidel Sicily'.[56] But their primary aim was to portray the leaders as Greco-Roman heroes, whose success shows that they are legitimate. Thus, according to Geoffrey Malaterra, Count Roger of Sicily, 'familiar with many authors, having had the histories of the ancients recited to him, decided, on the advice of his men, to have his hard-won triumphs committed . . . [to writing] . . . for the sake of posterity'.[57] Geoffrey, while implicitly criticising Norman *aviditas dominationis*,[58] presents Count Roger as heroic; his fleet is comparable to Alexander's.[59] He seems to have been writing in 1098, around the same time as William of Apulia. The latter compares his epic of Guiscard's *Deeds* to Vergil's *Aeneid*, and hints that his patron, Roger Borsa, should be as generous as Octavian was to Vergil.[60] It is probably no coincidence that Geoffrey and William seem to have begun writing their works while the First Crusade was underway. Their patrons were rivals, partly of one another but primarily of Bohemond, who was then distinguishing himself on the *iter sacrum*.[61] Unable to pose as warriors for Christ like Bohemond, the two Rogers were vying as to which of the three of them was the worthiest inheritor of the Greco-Roman past. Roger Borsa was, in effect, doing so vicariously through an epic, commemorating his father who had bequeathed him southern Italy but who had perished in his bid to acquire the Roman Empire, too. A key theme of William of Apulia is that the Greeks, under weak leadership such as Michael VII's, had

---

[56] Geoffrey Malaterra, *De rebus gestis*, 1.40, ed. Pontieri, 25.

[57] Ibid. preface (4).

[58] Wolf, *Making History*, 155, 164, 168.

[59] Geoffrey Malaterra, *De rebus gestis*, 3.40, ed. Pontieri, 62; Wolf, *Making History*, 175.

[60] William of Apulia, *Gesta Roberti Wiscardi*, 5.413–14, ed. Mathieu, 258; Wolf, *Making History*, 123–4, 128–9, 146–7. This statement leaves little room for doubt as to whom William was primarily addressing, even if he wrote at the request of Pope Urban II, as his prologue avers: William of Apulia, *Gesta Roberti Wiscardi*, prologus, line xi, ed. Mathieu, 98.

[61] On the date of the composition of these works, see William of Apulia, *Gesta Roberti Wiscardi*, ed. Mathieu, 12–13; Wolf, *Making History*, 123–4, 146–7; Brown, 'Gesta Roberti Wiscardi', 162, 164; Frankopan, *Call from the East*, 82. On Bohemond's feats in the east, see Flori, *Bohémond d'Antioche*, 165–75. For Count Roger's coolness towards Bohemond, see Becker, *Graf Roger I. von Sizilien*, 68–70. Duke Roger's attitude can scarcely have been more fulsome, given Bohemond's alacrity in exploiting a rumour of his death in 1093. *Pace* Brown, 'Gesta Roberti Wiscardi', 165, the 'Bohemond problem' was amplified for his fellow de Hautevilles, and not resolved, by his departure for the east in 1096.

lost their ancestors' courage;[62] the Normans, whom he often terms *Galli*,[63] are now rightful leaders, while contending with Fate in the manner of Homeric heroes. Guiscard had fought like Achilles but was 'no less clever than Ulysses', hence his nickname: 'Guiscard' meant 'wily'.[64] Guiscard is also likened to Cicero. Thus, Byzantium's uniquely privileged access to Greco-Roman culture and to Romanness in conjunction with superior military capability was under challenge from well-informed outsiders, whose writers could parade classical history and lore to legitimise new regimes at the empire's expense.

Such works need not herald further aggression. Indeed, they are part of broader cultural developments in southern Italy from the later eleventh century onwards, involving the composition of the *laudes* of a city in classical literary terms as well as hagiographical ones.[65] Geoffrey's patron, Count Roger, was on amicable terms with Alexios I Komnenos, and Geoffrey goes so far as to state that Bohemond, in taking up the Cross, was merely resuming the aggressiveness of his father, Guiscard.[66] William of Apulia, for his part, repeatedly expressed admiration for Alexios' 'manly' generalship, even styling him *imperii rector Romani maximus*.[67] Such terminology denoted acceptance of Alexios' legitimacy and, by implication, the vanity and unlawfulness of any future assault on the empire, a possible sideswipe at Bohemond's ambitions. However, in the wake of easier communications, it raised the question of what image an eastern emperor should now project towards western or, indeed, other outsiders: scarcely one of uncontestable Romanness and blithe obfuscation of disasters. Adjustability of the old school, switching from triumphalism to requests for aid, was no longer an option.

---

[62] William of Apulia compares Michael unfavourably with Romanos IV Diogenes and, indeed, Alexios: *Gesta Roberti Wiscardi*, 3.1–6, 5.31–2, ed. Mathieu, 164, 236–8; Brown, '*Gesta Roberti Wiscardi*', 172–3.

[63] E.g. William of Apulia, *Gesta Roberti Wiscardi*, 1.21, 1.44, 1.55, 1.61, 1.160, 1.162, 1.169, 1.189, 1.195, ed. Mathieu, 100, 102, 106, 108. See e.g. Wolf, *Making History*, 130.

[64] William of Apulia, *Gesta Roberti Wiscardi*, 2.129–30, ed. Mathieu, 138.

[65] Oldfield, *Urban Panegyric*.

[66] Geoffrey Malaterra, *De rebus gestis*, 4.24, ed. Pontieri, 102.

[67] William of Apulia, *Gesta Roberti Wiscardi*, 5.31–2, 4.568, ed. Mathieu, 236–8, 243. See Brown, '*Gesta Roberti Wiscardi*', 173, 175. On Count Roger's amicability towards Alexios, see Orderic Vitalis, *Historia Ecclesiastica*, 7.5, ed. and tr. Chibnall, 4:14–15; Shepard, 'Man-to-Man', 760–2.

Alexios I Komnenos' Adjustable Image and Sense of Identity

Perhaps unsurprisingly, Alexios presented himself to outsiders as a supplicant, eschewing festivities even when things were going well. Reportedly,
he forbade an extravagant *adventus* in Constantinople to celebrate his campaign against the Seljuk sultan in 1116.[68] According to Anna Komnene, he
was no more enthusiastic about the idea of a historical record of his labours,
despite his wife's urgings.[69] Alexios was mainly on the defensive, coping with
shortages of resources and fiscal problems until at least the early 1100s.[70] In
that sense, adopting the stance of supplicant, highlighting the faith held in
common with western sources of military manpower, and resorting to gifts
of relics rather than of gold, represents pragmatic adaptation to reduced circumstances: reliance on an image long available in the diplomatic repertoire.
Indeed, a reactive stance could not fail to colour imperial image-projection.
As already noted (p. 289), in the early 1100s Alexios had to respond to the
propaganda emanating from Bohemond. From this perspective, one might
view in negative terms the cumulative effect of thousands of outsiders serving in the imperial forces, some commanders' absorption of Greco-Roman
lore, the transmission home of news of defeats, and the fillip such familiarity
may have given to presenting upstart regimes on the empire's periphery in
classicising terms designed to legitimise them.

However, it is clear that Alexios felt at home in the role of military
champion, seeking outsiders' help while himself patrolling what amounted
to a perpetual borderland. This was not an image of convenience. From
the outset Alexios had to deal with a medley of strangers, striking up face-
to-face relationships with, for example, several leading Turks.[71] Trying to
fathom feelings (as against poses assumed for *raisons d'état*) is risky. Nonetheless, an interrelationship is discernible between the images he projected
towards the west, towards his subjects and towards himself (his sense of
identity and values). I shall outline four considerations that are consistent
with this impression.

Firstly, Alexios' military ethos is patent in his readiness to lead from
the front, concern for practical issues like weaponry and logistics and

---

[68] Anna Komnene, *Alexiad*, 15.7.2, ed. Reinsch and Kambylis, 1:482.20–1; Malamut,
Alexis Ier Comnène, 436; Buckley, *Alexiad*, 268.
[69] Anna Komnene, *Alexiad*, 15.11.1, ed. Reinsch and Kambylis, 1:494.
[70] On Alexios' fiscal problems and the protracted nature of his monetary and tax
reforms, see Harvey, 'Financial Crisis', 179–82.
[71] Brand, 'Turkish Element', 12–13, 16–17.

penchant for stratagems, ancient or modern. His tastes, owing much to family background and early military experiences of improvisation, reflect the 'middlebrow military culture' of Kekaumenos' *Counsels and Tales*, in which he was most probably raised.[72]

Secondly, this culture comprised a kind of stockpot of stories and lore of which foreign-born commanders partook – easterners of Armenian and Georgian heritage, most probably northerners, and certainly westerners. Alexios was able to converse with many, presumably thanks to their learning some Greek rather than his knowing simple phrases of a Romance language.[73] One of the advantages of westerners of the sort whom he paraded before Bohemond at Deabolis in 1108 was that the churchmen and notables from southern Italy, at least, were likely to have some grasp of Greco-Roman lore and literature.[74] Rather than eroding his imperial dignity, such knowledge gave an adept leader like Alexios the opportunity to play the part of classical hero: on occasion Alexander or other grandees, but more often the wily navigator Odysseus.[75] He was thereby able to place himself in a robust military cultural tradition, which did not pivot on the figure of the emperor of the day, and which was in vogue among Byzantines and westerners alike.

Thirdly, by way of supporting this last proposition, one may glance back at William of Apulia's *Deeds of Robert Guiscard*. William praises Alexios' leadership and courage, even while portraying Guiscard and his warriors in Homeric guise and assuming his readers' familiarity with Greco-Roman lore. If these literary traits call to mind the *Alexiad*'s portrayal of Alexios, this is probably no coincidence. Scholars have long noted similarities

---

[72] Alexios' childhood and education can be inferred only from much later, partisan texts such as the *Alexiad*. But that his mother's family was, like his father's, of an essentially military cast is clear: Barzos, Γενεαλογία τῶν Κομνηνῶν, no. 6, 49–52; Cheynet, 'Les Dalassènoi'.

[73] The half-brother of Bohemond, Guy de Hauteville, is represented as conversing freely with Alexios, a probable reflection of the Greek spoken by members of the Norman elite now in southern Italy: *Gesta Francorum*, 9.27, ed. and tr. R. Hill, 63–4; Malamut, *Alexis Ier Comnène*, 402, 421. Alexios' reliance on intermediaries is shown by the episode when he had to ask 'one of the Latin interpreters' what had been said by a crusader, whose lips he had seen moving: Anna Komnene, *Alexiad*, 10.10.6–7, ed. Reinsch and Kambylis, 1:316.

[74] Anna Komnene, *Alexiad*, 13.12.28, ed. Reinsch and Kambylis, 1:423; Marquis de la Force, 'Conseillers latins', 154, 163–4.

[75] The depiction in the *Alexiad* of Alexios as the Odysseus-like helmsman coping with waves of troubles, and its likely emanation from Alexios himself, is mooted in Shepard, 'Anna Komnena and the Past'. A similar line was independently taken by Dyck, 'Iliad and Alexiad'. See also below, p. 304.

between the texts, and Ferdinand Chalandon suggested a common source for their account of Guiscard's campaign in the Balkans.[76] Peter Frankopan has argued for the availability of William's entire text to Anna. Showing how similar in all but chronology are many passages and (not always accurate) details about the Norman campaign of 1081–5, he points to what could perhaps be a misunderstanding on the translator's part of the word *honor* in William's Latin text.[77] If Frankopan's thesis holds good, it offers further evidence for a certain cultural commonality between members of the Komnenian milieu and the ruling elite in southern Italy. The heroic virtues being pooled were not of a particularly Christian cast; neither was that sense of inexorable Fate and waves of misfortunes which are discernible in William of Apulia and the *Alexiad* alike.[78]

This leads to a fourth consideration, or rather a series of questions. If Alexios adjusted his image's format, perhaps detaching it from the city of Constantinople to foreground the borderlands and a wider range of Greco-Roman heroes, values, and perhaps even notions of Fate, what fixed points of identity remained, and what made his imperial entitlement credible? One must take into account the diverse tendencies Alexios seems to have nurtured: his stance as a kind of *akritēs* and the apparent patronage at the Komnenian court for epic Digenes themes[79] and, in contrast, the enthusiasm Alexios' envoys reportedly expressed for restoring imperial authority

---

[76] Chalandon, *Domination normande*, 1:xxxix–xl. See also other views on the interrelationship, e.g. William of Apulia, *Gesta Roberti Wiscardi*, ed. Mathieu, 38–46; Loud, 'Anna Komnena and Her Sources', 50, 52.

[77] William of Apulia, *Gesta Roberti Wiscardi*, 4.260–1, ed. Mathieu, 218; Anna Komnene, *Alexiad*, 4.1.3, ed. Reinsch and Kambylis, 1:121.36; Frankopan, 'Turning Latin into Greek', 88–9 n. 57, 90–1.

[78] For intimations of the reluctance of Guiscard's men to participate in his Balkan expedition, followed by shipwreck, heavy loss of life and Guiscard 'not know[ing] how to turn back from what he had begun', see William of Apulia, *Gesta Roberti Wiscardi*, 4.128–31, 4.215–25, 4.230–1, ed. Mathieu, 210, 216.

[79] Alexios' self-image is, most probably, transmitted by Anna's blow-by-blow account of such episodes as his parrying of three Norman assailants in a cavalry engagement: *Alexiad*, 4.6.8, ed. Reinsch and Kambylis, 1:135. For the circulation of tales of Digenes Akrites and the borders in various circles, including Komnenian households, from the end of the eleventh century on, see Magdalino, 'Byzantine Snobbery', 68–9; Beaton, *Medieval Greek Romance*, 49; Jeffreys (ed. and tr.), *Digenis Akritis*, lvi–lvii; Pryor and Jeffreys, 'Alexios, Bohemond', 66–7; de Medeiros, 'Construcción de los dos palacios', 59–66, 70–2; Mamangakes, 'Αυτοκράτορας, λαός και Ορθοδοξία', 404–24. I am very grateful to João Vicente de Medeiros for making the latter work known to me. See also below, p. 307.

over the city of Rome in 1112.[80] But may not Alexios' pose as champion of the faith and correct doctrine have constituted the key fixed point, while his 'leading of the charge' against the dualist heresy of the Bogomils gave proof of his unique credentials for rulership to Christians in both the east *and* the west? And was not this perhaps the prime reason for his commission to Euthymios Zigabenos to compile the *Armoury of Doctrine*?

It is, I suggest, significant that the imagery of the hero battling against monsters and the helmsman steering his ship to port features in the *Armoury of Doctrine*, too. Zigabenos depicts himself as navigating through 'a vast sea of impiety' on behalf of the emperor, while Alexios features as the 'faithful lord for battling the unfaithful', marshalling the works of 'champions of the true faith' for Zigabenos to set in order, and destroying the 'dragon' of Bogomilism, thereby 'raising a trophy . . . loftier and more wondrous than all his other many and splendid trophies'.[81] In this way, that sense of fortune's fickleness over the outcomes of battles which Anna imputes to Alexios' generalship, and which probably reflects his outlook, gains Christian anchorage and a sense of direction: tossed by waves like Odysseus and suffering spectacular defeats, Alexios could still provide comprehensive protection – a *Panoplia* – for the souls of his subjects and himself. One may recall the miniature that shows him presenting the first part of this book to Christ.[82] Through this array of religious correctness, Alexios offered a counterbalance to the blind chance that appeared to bedevil his earthly affairs. Besides offering reassurance to his subjects (if not himself), he was refuting the accusations of Bohemond and other western enemies that he harboured false teachings and heretics. This exemplifies the coherent interrelationship between outward-facing image and image-projection towards his subjects mentioned earlier.

A distinctive feature of all this was its celebration of imperial cunning as a virtue. Euthymios Zigabenos praises Alexios' 'dexterous grasp and handling of public affairs', his stratagems and his 'responses at once circumspect and full of shrewdness to the ambassadors of the great nations'.[83] And he highlights Alexios' feat of outwitting the Bogomil leader, Basil. By

---

[80] Johannes Turmair (Aventinus), *Annales ducum Boiariae*, 6.2, ed. Riezler et al., 2:187; Kahl, 'Römische Krönungspläne', 265–9; Koder, 'Letzte Gesandtschaft', 134–5.

[81] Euthymios Zigabenos, *Panoplia dogmatikē*, *PG* 130:19, 24, 1332. See also the original pamphlet written by Euthymios Zigabenos, upon which his *Armoury of Doctrine* drew: Euthymios Zigabenos, *On the Heresy of the Bogomils*, ed. Ficker, 90.27–9, 110.14–20, 111.7–14.

[82] Spatharakis, *Portrait in Byzantine Illuminated Manuscripts*, Fig. 80 and 122–8.

[83] Euthymios Zigabenos, *Panoplia dogmatikē*, *PG* 130:20, 21.

offering him a seat in his own quarters and conversing with him genially, 'intelligently taking on the role of the pupil, Alexios easily deceived him who had misled many into perdition.'[84] Alexios' ability when 'attacked from all sides . . . to find a way through impasses . . . adapting to new situations to good effect' was, according to Zigabenos, well known.[85] Indeed, twenty or so years earlier, on 6 January 1088, Alexios, 'fertile in invention', was lauded for his ability to bemuse barbarians with speeches: Theophylact of Ohrid compares him with the speechmakers in Homer's epic, following up the attack of an Odysseus with the milder approach of a Menelaos. In this way he had won over the Pechenegs.[86] To Alexios' more sympathetic subjects, his practice of statecraft was at one with the defence of true religion. Outsiders were, however, on the receiving end of this statecraft and, as noted above, ever more were frequenting Constantinople. Alexios' reputation for 'trickiness' shows in William of Tyre's description of his scorpion-like behaviour: 'while you have nothing to fear from its face, you will do well to avoid the sting in its tail.'[87] Alexios' penchant for encounters of the kind that disarmed Basil the Bogomil, Pechenegs and individual Latins alike carried with it the potential to engender charges of deceit and betrayal.

One should not rule out the possibility that Alexios tried to forestall such criticism by supplementing his role of supplicant with that of penitent sinner. This theme seems common to the projection of his image for both external and domestic consumption. He confessed to 'sin above all men' to the abbot of Montecassino in a letter sent, significantly, in June 1098, thus soon after his turnaround at Philomelion which had effectively left the besiegers of Antioch to their fate.[88] Moreover, a large-scale painting of the Last Judgement on a wall of the Blachernai Palace showed Alexios penitent among the sinners, awaiting Christ's verdict and possible hellfire.[89] This

---

[84] Euthymios Zigabenos, *On the Heresy of the Bogomils*, ed. Ficker, 90.10–12; Euthymios Zigabenos, *Panoplia dogmatikē*, PG 130:1290, 1292.

[85] Ibid. 130:21.

[86] Theophylact of Ohrid, *Orations*, no. 4, ed. and tr. Gautier, 222–5.

[87] William of Tyre, *Chronicle*, 10, 12, ed. Huygens, 1:467. On the 'two voices' in William's account of crusader relations with the Byzantines, see Edbury and Rowe, *William of Tyre*, 136. The authors allow for the availability to William of oral traditions 'which consistently vilified Alexius': ibid. 134.

[88] *Letters on the History of the First Crusade*, ed. Hagenmeyer, 11.152–3.

[89] For the text of the poem that describes the depiction of Alexios as on the left side of Christ's throne: Nikolaos Kallikles, *Poems*, no. 24, ed. and tr. Romano, 101–2, esp. lines 14–15; Magdalino and Nelson, 'Emperor in Byzantine Art', 125–6; Kepetzi, 'Empereur', 235–44; Parani, *Reality of Images*, 39, n. 121.

would have been visible to members of the ruling elite and western visitors and was at least consistent with Alexios' regard for monks and the efficacy of their prayers.[90] The painting's themes of judgement and penance are also in key with John Zonaras' report that 'certain monks' had prophesied that Alexios would not die before he had made, in effect, a pilgrimage to Jerusalem and laid down his crown at the Holy Sepulchre.[91]

There was, then, a certain coherence to Alexios Komnenos' image-projection, as also in his sense of what was good for his soul. How many of Alexios Komnenos' subjects or foreign contemporaries found it convincing is hard to adjudge. One cannot ignore the chorus of execration from chroniclers of the crusades or assume that all the hostility emanates from Bohemond's propaganda campaign. Nonetheless, one suspects that the very vehemence owes something to the effectiveness of Alexios in winning over individual outsiders to his cause and, often, his service. And if the criticism also reflects great sophistication and familiarity with Greco-Roman culture on the part of elites on Byzantium's western periphery and beyond, this may owe something to a newish 'open-door' policy towards employment of foreign military manpower. What is certain is that image-projection of the sort practised in the earlier Middle Ages, masking abrupt adjustments according to circumstances behind thin veneers of 'Roman-ness', was no longer viable.

Manuel Komnenos as Aftermath

This did not prevent emperors from essaying what might be termed 'high-style Romanising' image-projection when resources allowed. But even when they did so, the spotlight now was more on their personal qualities and epic accomplishments, as in the case of Manuel I Komnenos. He revived with relish ceremonies such as *adventus* and triumphs in Constantinople. According to Kinnamos, Manuel even staged his solemn entry into Antioch in 1159 along the lines of triumphs in the capital. This display of what he envisaged as reabsorption of Antioch within 'Roman' dominions was accompanied by ritual self-abasement on the part of the city's Frankish prince, Reynald de Châtillon.[92] Manuel was also inclined to send upbeat

[90] Malamut, *Alexis Ier Comnène*, 246–9, 258–66.
[91] John Zonaras, *Epitome*, 18.28.10–12, ed. Büttner-Wobst, 3:760; Magdalino, *Manuel I Komnenos*, 34.
[92] John Kinnamos, *History*, ed. Meineke, 187; Magdalino, *Manuel I Komnenos*, 69. For other instances of Manuel's triumphs and grand receptions in Constantinople, see ibid. 75–7, 241–3.

messages to foreign potentates, in a style reminiscent of those sent out in the eighth and ninth centuries. One letter, addressed to the Plantagenet king Henry II of England, represents even the battle of Myriokephalon in fairly positive terms.[93] These somewhat brazen projections of success and a positive image were, however, complementary – and perhaps secondary – to the incessant campaigning and other ventures Manuel undertook in deliberately swashbuckling style. Comparisons between his activities and garb and those of Digenes Akrites were expressly drawn in works such as the fourth poem of the *Ptōchoprodromika*. This was, most probably, composed by Theodore Prodromos around 1150. At that time Manuel was closely concerned with the region of the Middle Euphrates, Digenes' old stomping ground; Manuel was attempting to reimpose direct rule through buying key strongholds from the widowed countess of Edessa.[94] It seems to have been around this time, too, that tales from the frontier were strung together into some sort of life story of Digenes Akrites, constituting the rough-hewn prototype of what are known as the Escorial and the Grottaferrata versions of the epic.[95]

The image of Manuel on the Tigris and the Euphrates, a fearless warrior who had charged into the fray, rallied imperial troops and saved the day, was already being propagated just after his accession: a court oration describes Manuel's heroism during his father's campaigns of 1137 and 1138.[96] The orator Michael Italikos mentions in passing that Manuel had western cavalrymen under his command, and that they 'were all astonished (τεθήπασι)' at his feats.[97] Manuel's temperament and personal inclinations seem to have been perfectly attuned to western martial tastes, as witnessed in his no less public participation in jousting.[98] Such pursuits amounted to deliberate projection of an image, and one may gauge its effectiveness

---

[93] Significantly, Manuel did not attempt to disguise the scale or the seriousness of his losses, but he made clear his own valorous role in the combat and stressed that the sultan found it prudent to request peace terms. See Roger of Howden, *Chronica*, ed. Stubbs, 2:102–4; Vasiliev, 'Manuel Comnenus', 236–41; Magdalino, *Manuel I Komnenos*, 96, 98.

[94] Theodore Prodromos, *Ptōchoprodromika*, 4.116, 189–92, ed. Eideneier, 204, 207; William of Tyre, *Chronicle*, 17.16–17, ed. Huygens, 2:781–5; Magdalino, *Manuel I Komnenos*, 66; Kaldellis, *Hellenism*, 248–9; Pryor and Jeffreys, 'Alexios, Bohemond', 66–7.

[95] Jeffreys, *Digenis Akritis*, lvi–lvii (intro.).

[96] Michael Italikos, *Letters and Orations*, no. 44, ed. Gautier, 286–7.

[97] Ibid. 286.7–8.

[98] Jones and Maguire, 'Jousts'.

from the famous eulogy of William of Tyre. He describes Manuel as well-disposed towards westerners and 'a great-souled man of incomparable energy'. According to William, Latins 'from all over the world, nobles and also men of lesser rank, regarded him as their great benefactor and eagerly thronged to his court'.[99]

Manuel seems to have been rather more adept than his grandfather, Alexios, in aligning the image he projected to outsiders with his style of military leadership and his recreational activities. Whether by accident or design, he avoided episodes like the mismatch between exacting oaths of *fides* and of *hominium* and taking personal command of operations that so exposed Alexios to charges of treachery by Bohemond at Antioch in 1098. What is certain is that the doings of emperors and other events in Byzantium were now open to the scrutiny of articulate outsiders in a quite different manner from those of the ninth century. The emperor could still prevaricate, dissimulate and lay claim to greater material resources or more splendid victories than realities warranted. But much now depended on his personal example and the figure he cut, especially in war. Alexios I Komnenos was, I suggest, all too well aware of the new challenge to adjustable image-projection. His self-presentation as the worst of sinners may be a reflection of this.

Bibliography

Sources

Anna Komnene, *Alexiad* . . . D. R. Reinsch and A. Kambylis (eds), *Annae Comnenae Alexias*, 2 vols (Berlin and New York, 2001).

Annales Altahenses maiores . . . W. von Giesebrecht and E. L. B. von Oefele (eds), *Annales Altahenses maiores* (Hanover, 1891).

Annales Bertiniani . . . F. Grat et al. (eds), *Annales de Saint-Bertin* (Paris, 1964).

Annales Regni Francorum . . . F. Kurze (ed.), *Annales Regni Francorum inde ab a. 741 usque ad a. 829*, MGH ScriptRerGerm 6 (Hanover, 1895).

Breve Chronicon Northmannicum . . . E. Cuozzo (ed.), 'Il Breve Chronicon Northmannicum', *Bulletino dell'Istituto storico italiano per storico italiano per il Medio Evo e Archivio Muratoriano* 83 (1971): 131–232.

Chronicle of Sainte-Barbe-en-Auge . . . R. N. Sauvage (ed.), *La chronique de Sainte-Barbe-en-Auge* (Caen, 1907).

---

[99] William of Tyre, *Chronicle*, 22.11(10), ed. Huygens, 2:1020.

Chronicon Laurissense ... H. Schnorr von Carolsfeld (ed.), 'Das Chronicon Laurissense breve', *Neues Archiv der Gesellschaft für ältere deutsche Geschichtskunde* 36 (1911): 13–39.

Codex Carolinus ... W. Gundlach (ed.), 'Codex Carolinus', in *MGH, Epistolae* 3, *Merowingici et Karolini Aevi* 1 (Berlin, 1892), 468–657.

Digenis Akritis ... *Digenis Akritis: The Grottaferrata and Escorial versions*, ed. and tr. E. Jeffreys (Cambridge 1998).

Euthymios Zigabenos, *On the Heresy of the Bogomils* ... G. Ficker (ed.), in *Die Phundagiagiten: ein Beitrag zur Ketzergeschichte des byzantinischen Mittelalters* (Leipzig, 1908), 89–111.

Euthymios Zigabenos, *Panoplia dogmatikē* ... *PG* 128–30.

Geoffrey Malaterra, *De rebus gestis* ... E. Pontieri (ed.), *De rebus gestis Rogerii Calabriae et Siciliae comitis et Roberti Guiscardi ducis fratris eius*, 3 fasc. (Bologna, 1927–8).

Gesta Francorum ... R. Hill (ed. and tr.), *Gesta Francorum et aliorum Hierosolimitanorum: The Deeds of the Franks and the Other Pilgrims to Jerusalem* (London and Edinburgh, 1962).

Guy, Bishop of Amiens, *Carmen de proelio Hastingae* ... F. Barlow (ed. and tr.), *The Carmen de Hastingae Proelio of Guy Bishop of Amiens* (Oxford, 1999).

Johannes Turmair (Aventinus), *Annales ducum Boiariae* ... S. Riezler et al. (eds), *Johannes Turmair's genannt Aventinus sämmtliche werke: Auf veranlassung Sr. Majestät des königs von Bayern*, 6 vols (Munich, 1880–1908).

John Kinnamos, *History* ... A. Meineke (ed.), *Epitome rerum ab Ioanne et Alexio Comnenis gestarum*, *CSHB* (Bonn, 1836).

John Skylitzes, *Synopsis* ... H. Thurn (ed.), *Synopsis historiarum*, *CFHB* 5 (Berlin and New York, 1973).

John Zonaras, *Epitome* ... T. Büttner-Wobst (ed.), *Ioannes Zonarae Epitome Historiarum*, 3 vols, *CSHB* (Bonn, 1841–97).

Joseph Genesios, *On the Reigns* ... A. Lesmüller-Werner and H. Thurn (eds), *Regum libri quattuor*, *CFHB* 14 (Berlin, 1978).

Kekaumenos, *Consilia et Narrationes* ... C. Roueché (ed. and tr.), *Consilia et Narrationes* (SAWS edition, 2013). Available at <http://www.ancientwisdoms.ac.uk/library/kekaumenos-consilia-et-narrationes/> (last accessed 24 March 2016).

Leo III, *Letters* ... K. Hampe (ed.), 'Leonis III. papae epistolae X', in *MGH, Epistolae* 5, *Karolini Aevi* 3 (Berlin, 1899), 85–104.

Letters on the History of the First Crusade ... Hagenmeyer, H. (ed.), *Die Kreuzzugsbriefe aus den Jahren 1088–1100* (Innsbruck, 1901).

Liudprand of Cremona, *Relatio de legatione Constantinopolitana* ..., in P. Chiesa (ed.), *Liudprandi Cremonensis opera omnia*, *CCCM* 156 (Turnhout, 1998), 185–218.

Matthew of Edessa, *Chronicle* ... A. E. Dostourian (tr.), *Armenia and the Crusades: Tenth to Twelfth Centuries. The Chronicle of Matthew of Edessa* (Lanham, MD, 1993).

Michael Attaleiates, *History* ... A. Kaldellis and D. Krallis (tr.), I. Pérez Martín (ed.), *Michael Attaleiates: The History* (Cambridge, MA, 2012).

Michael Italikos, *Letters and Orations* ... P. Gautier (ed.), *Lettres et discours de Michel Italikos* (Paris, 1972).

Miracula Beati Leonardi Confessoris ... , in *Acta sanctorum Novembris* 6, 160–8.

Nikephoros Bryennios, *History* ... P. Gautier (ed. and tr.), *Nicephori Bryennii Historiarum libri quattuor, CFHB* 9 (Brussels, 1975).

Niketas Choniates, *Historia* ... J. L. van Dieten (ed.), *Nicetae Choniatae Historia*, 2 vols, *CFHB* 11 (Berlin and New York, 1975).

Nikolaos Kallikles, *Poems* ... R. Romano (ed. and tr.), *Nicola Callice, Carmi* (Naples, 1980).

Orderic Vitalis, *Historia Ecclesiastica* ... M. Chibnall (ed. and tr.), *The Ecclesiastical History of Orderic Vitalis*, 6 vols (Oxford, 1969–80).

Povest' Vremennykh Let ... V. P. Adrianova-Peretts, D. S. Likhachev and M. B. Sverdlov (eds), *Povest' Vremennykh Let*, 2nd ed. (St Petersburg, 1996).

Roger of Howden, *Chronica* ... W. Stubbs (ed.), *Chronica magistri Rogeri de Houedene*, 4 vols (London, 1868–71).

Russian Primary Chronicle ... S. H. Cross and O. P. Sherbowitz-Wetzor (tr.), *The Russian Primary Chronicle: Laurentian Text* (Cambridge, MA, 1953).

Skylitzes Continuatus ... E. T. Tsolakes (ed.), *Η συνέχεια της χρονογραφίας του Ιωάννη Σκυλίτζη* (Thessaloniki, 1968).

Snorri Sturluson, *Haralds Saga* ... , in Bjarni Aðalbjarnarson (ed.), *Heimskringla*, 3 vols, *Íslenzk Fornrit* 26–8 (Reykjavik, 1941–51). (Reykjavik, 1951).

Stephen of Taron, *Universal History* ... T. Greenwood (tr.), *The Universal History of Step῾anos Tarōnec῾i* (Oxford, 2016).

Symeon Logothetes, *Chronicon* ... S. Wahlgren (ed.), *Symeonis magistri et logothetae Chronicon, CFHB* 44.1 (Berlin and New York, 2006).

Theodore Prodromos, *Ptōchoprodromika* ... H. Eideneier (ed.), *Πτωχοπρόδρομος* (Herakleion, 2012).

Theophanes Continuatus, ed. J. Signes Codoñer and J. Featherstone, *Chronographiae quae Theophanis Continuati nomine fertur Libri I–IV, CFHB* 53 (Berlin and Boston, 2015).

Theophylact of Ohrid, *Orations* ... P. Gautier (ed. and tr.), *Théophylacte d'Achrida: Discours, traités, poésies, CFHB* 16.1 (Thessaloniki, 1980).

Urkunden zur älteren Handels -und Staatsgeschichte ... G. L. F. Tafel and G. M. Thomas (eds), *Urkunden zur älteren Handels-und Staatsgeschichte der Republik Venedig*, 3 vols (Vienna, 1856–7).

William of Apulia, *Gesta Roberti Wiscardi* ... M. Mathieu (ed. and tr.), *La geste de Robert Guiscard* (Palermo, 1961).

William of Poitiers, *Gesta Guillelmi ducis* ... R. H. C. Davis and M. Chibnall (eds and tr.), *The Gesta Guillelmi of William of Poitiers* (Oxford, 1998).

William of Tyre, *Chronicle* ... R. B. C. Huygens (ed.), *Guillaume de Tyr Chronique*, 2 vols, CCCM 63/63A (Turnhout, 1986).

Secondary Literature

Airlie, S., 'Partes, termini, confinia regnorum. Innere und äußere Grenzen', in *Kaiser und Kalifen. Karl der Große und die Mächte am Mittelmeer um 800* (Darmstadt, 2014), 214–29.

Barzos, K., *Η γενεαλογία τῶν Κομνηνῶν*, 2 vols (Thessaloniki, 1984).

Beaton, R., *The Medieval Greek Romance*, 2nd ed. (London, 1996).

Becker, J., *Graf Roger I. von Sizilien: Wegbereiter des normannischen Königreichs* (Tübingen, 2008).

Bogomoletz, W. V., 'Anna of Kiev, an Enigmatic Capetian Queen of the Eleventh Century', *French History* 19 (2005): 299–323.

Borgolte, M., 'Experten der Fremde. Gesandte in interkulturellen Beziehungen des frühen und hohen Mittelalters', in *Le relazioni internazionali nell'alto medioevo* (Spoleto, 2011), 945–92.

Brand, C. M., 'The Turkish Element in Byzantium, Eleventh–Twelfth Centuries', *DOP* 43 (1989): 1–25.

Brown, P., 'The *Gesta Roberti Wiscardi*: A "Byzantine" History?', *JMH* 37 (2011): 162–79.

Buckley, P., *The Alexiad of Anna Komnena: Artistic Strategy in the Making of a Myth* (Cambridge, 2013).

Chalandon, F., *Histoire de la domination normande en Italie et Sicile*, 2 vols (Paris, 1907).

Cheynet, J.-C., 'Mantzikert: un désastre militaire?', *Byz* 50 (1980): 410–38.

Cheynet, J.-C., *Pouvoir et contestations à Byzance (963–1210)* (Paris, 1990).

Cheynet, J.-C., 'Les effectifs de l'armée byzantine aux Xe–XIIe s.', *CahCM* 38 (1995): 319–35.

Cheynet, J.-C., *La société byzantine. L'apport des sceaux*, 2 vols (Paris, 2008).

Cheynet, J.-C., 'The London Byzantine Seals', in J.-C. Cheynet, *Société byzantine*, 2 vols (Paris, 2008), 1:145–59.

Cheynet, J.-C., 'Les Dalassènoi', in J.-C. Cheynet, *Société byzantine*, 2 vols (Paris, 2008), 2:413–71.

Ciggaar, K. N., 'England and Byzantium on the Eve of the Norman Conquest', *Anglo-Norman Studies* 5 (1982): 78–96.

Ciggaar, K. N., 'Byzantine Marginalia to the Norman Conquest', *Anglo-Norman Studies* 9 (1987), 43–69.

Ciggaar, K. N., *Western Travellers to Constantinople: The West and Byzantium, 962–1204* (Leiden, 1996).

Ciggaar, K. N., 'Bilingual Word Lists and Phrase Lists: For Teaching or For Travel?', in R. Macrides (ed.), *Travel in the Byzantine World* (Aldershot, 2002), 165–78.

Davis, J., *Charlemagne's Practice of Empire* (Cambridge, 2015).

Dölger, F.. 'Der Pariser Papyrus von St. Denis als ältestes Kreuzzugsdokument', in F. Dölger, *Byzantinische Diplomatik* (Ettal, 1956): 204–14.

Dunbabin, J., 'What's in a Name? Philip, King of France', *Speculum* 68 (1993): 949–68.

Dyck, A., 'Iliad and Alexiad: Anna Comnena's Homeric Reminiscences', *GRBS* 27 (1986): 113–20.

Edbury, P. W., and J. G. Rowe, *William of Tyre, Historian of the Latin East* (Cambridge, 1988).

El Cheikh, N., *Byzantium Viewed by the Arabs* (Cambridge, MA, 2004).

Engberg, S. G., 'Romanos Lekapenos and the Mandilion of Edessa', in J. Durand and B. Flusin (eds), *Byzance et les reliques du Christ* (Paris, 2004), 123–42.

Eniosova, N., and T. Pushkina, 'Finds of Byzantine Origin From the Early Urban Centre Gnezdovo in the Light of the Contacts Between Rus' and Constantinople (10th–early 11th Centuries AD)', in L. Bjerg, J. H. Lind and S. M. Sindbæk (eds), *From Goths to Varangians. Communication and Cultural Exchange between the Baltic and the Black Sea* (Aarhus, 2013), 213–55.

Flori, J., *Bohémond d'Antioche: chevalier d'aventure* (Paris, 2007).

Flori, J., 'De l'Anonyme Normand à Tudebode et au *Gesta Francorum*. L'impact de la propagande de Bohémond sur la critique textuelle des sources de la première croisade', *RHE* 102 (2007): 717–46.

Frankopan, P., *The First Crusade: The Call from the East* (Cambridge, MA, 2012).

Frankopan, P., 'Turning Latin into Greek. Anna Komnene and the *Gesta Roberti Wiscardi*', *JMH* 39 (2013): 80–99.

Gimon, T. V., 'Ian' Vyshatich i ustnye istochniki drevnerusskoi nachal'noi letopisi', in G. V. Glazyrina (ed.), *Drevneishie gosudarstva Vostochnoi*

Evropy. 2011 god. Ustnaia traditisiia v pis'mennom tekste (Moscow, 2013), 65–117.

Granger-Taylor, H., 'Silk from the Tomb of Edward the Confessor', in D. Buckton (ed.), *Byzantium: Treasures of Byzantine Art and Culture* (London, 1994), no. 166, 151–3.

Haldon, J., *Warfare, State and Society in the Byzantine World 565–1204* (London, 1999).

Hartmann, W., *Karl der Große* (Stuttgart, 2010).

Harvey, A., 'Financial Crisis and the Rural Economy', in M. Mullett and D. Smythe (eds), *Alexios I Komnenos: Papers of the Second Belfast Byzantine International Colloquium, 14–16 April 1989* (Belfast, 1996), 167–84.

Holmes, C., *Basil II and the Governance of Empire (976–1025)* (Oxford, 2005).

Holmes, C., 'Compilation Literature and Byzantine Political Culture in the Tenth and Eleventh Centuries', *DOP* 64 (2010): 55–80.

Holtzmann, W., 'Zur Geschichte des Investiturstreites 2. Bohemund von Antiochien und Alexios I', *NA* 50 (1935): 270–82.

Jacoby, D., 'Bishop Gunther of Bamberg, Byzantium and Christian Pilgrimage to the Holy Land in the Eleventh Century', in L. Hoffmann and A. Monchizadeh (eds), *Zwischen Polis, Provinz und Peripherie. Beiträge zur byzantinischen Geschichte und Kultur* (Wiesbaden, 2005), 267–85.

Jacoby, D., 'Venetian Commercial Expansion in the Eastern Mediterranean, 8th–11th centuries', in M. Mundell Mango, *Byzantine Trade (4th–12th Century): The Archaeology of Local, Regional and International Exchange* (Aldershot, 2009), 371–91.

Jones, L., and H. Maguire, 'A Description of the Jousts of Manuel I Komnenos', *BMGS* 26 (2002): 104–48.

Kahl, H.-D., 'Römische Krönungspläne im Komnenenhause? Ein Beitrag zur Entwicklung des Zweikaiserproblems im 12. Jahrhundert', *Archiv für Kulturgeschichte* 59 (1977): 259–320.

Kalavrezou, I., 'Helping Hands for the Empire: Imperial Ceremonies and the Cult of Relics at the Byzantine Court', in H. Maguire (ed.), *Byzantine Court Culture from 829 to 1204* (Cambridge, MA, 1997), 53–79.

Kaldellis, A., *Hellenism in Byzantium: The Transformations of Greek Identity and the Reception of the Classical Tradition* (Cambridge, 2007).

Kaldellis, A, 'The Original Source for Tzimiskes' Balkan Campaign (971) and the Emperor's Classicizing Propaganda', *BMGS* 37 (2013): 35–52.

Kazhdan, A. P., and A. W. Epstein, *Change in Byzantine Culture in the Eleventh and Twelfth Centuries* (Berkeley, Los Angeles and London, 1985).

Kepetzi, V., 'Empereur, piété et remission des péchés dans deux *ekphraseis* byzantines: image et rhétorique', *Deltion tēs Christianikēs archaiologikēs etaireias* 20 (1999): 231–44.

Kislinger, E., 'Reisen und Verkehrswege in Byzanz. Realität und Mentalität, Möglichkeiten und Grenzen', in I. Iliev and A. Nikolov (eds), *Proceedings of the 22nd International Congress of Byzantine Studies, Sofia 2011. Plenary Papers* (Sofia, 2011), 341–87.

Koder, J., 'Die letzte Gesandtschaft Alexios' I. Komnenos bei Paschalis II', in E.-D. Hehl, I. H. Ringel and H. Seibert (eds), *Das Papsttum in der Welt des 12. Jahrhunderts* (Stuttgart, 2002), 127–36.

Laiou, A. E, 'Regional Networks in the Balkans in the Middle and Late Byzantine Periods', in C. Morrisson (ed.), *Trade and Markets in Byzantium* (Washington, DC, 2012), 125–46.

Lopez, R. S., and I. W. Raymond (eds), *Medieval Trade in the Mediterranean World: Illustrative Documents*, repr. with a foreword by O. R. Constable (New York, 2001).

Loud, G., 'Anna Komnena and Her Sources for the Normans of Southern Italy', in I. Wood and G. Loud (eds), *Church and Chronicle in the Middle Ages: Essays Presented to John Taylor* (London, 1991), 41–57.

McCormick, M., *Eternal Victory: Triumphal Rulership in Late Antiquity, Byzantium and the Early Medieval West*, 2nd ed. (Cambridge, 1990).

McCormick, M., *Charlemagne's Survey of the Holy Land: Wealth, Personnel, and Buildings of a Mediterranean Church between Antiquity and the Middle Ages* (Cambridge, MA, 2010).

Madgearu, A., *Byzantine Military Organization on the Danube, 10th–12th Centuries* (Leiden, 2013).

Magdalino, P., 'Byzantine Snobbery', in M. Angold (ed.), *The Byzantine Aristocracy IX to XIII Centuries* (Oxford, 1984), 58–78.

Magdalino, P., *The Empire of Manuel I Komnenos 1143–1180* (Cambridge, 1993).

Magdalino, P., and R. Nelson, 'The Emperor in Byzantine Art of the Twelfth Century', *BF* 8 (1982): 123–83.

Malamut, E., *Les îles de l'empire Byzantin*, 2 vols (Paris, 1988).

Malamut, E., *Alexis Ier Comnène* (Paris, 2007).

Mamangakes, D. A., 'Ο αυτοκράτορας, ο λαός και η Ορθοδοξία: Αλέξιος Α΄ Κομνηνός (1081–1118). Κατασκευάζοντας την δημόσια αυτοκρατορική εικόνα', PhD thesis, University of Athens, 2014.

Mango, C., 'The Triumphal Way of Constantinople and the Golden Gate', *DOP* 54 (2000): 173–88.

Marquis de la Force, 'Les conseillers latins du Basileus Alexis Comnène', *Byz* 11 (1936): 153–65.

Mathieu, M., 'Les *"Gesta Roberti Wiscardi"* de Guillaume d'Apulie: une source negligée de la Bataille de Mantzikert', *Byz* 20 (1950): 89–103.

de Medeiros Publio Dias, J. V., 'La construcción de los dos palacios: la composición del Poema de Diyenís Acrita y la reivindicación de la hegemonía anatólica de Alejo Comneno', *Erytheia* 31 (2010): 55–73.

Mladjov, I., 'The Crown and the Veil: Titles, Spiritual Kinship, and Diplomacy in Tenth-Century Bulgaro-Byzantine Relations', *History Compass* 13 (2015): 171–83.

Oikonomides, N., *Les listes de préséance byzantines des IXe et Xe siècles* (Paris, 1972).

Oldfield, P., *Urban Panegyric and the Transformation of the Medieval City, 1100–1300* (Oxford, 2019).

Page, G., *Being Byzantine: Greek Identity Before the Ottomans, 1200–1420* (Cambridge, 2008).

Parani, M. G., *Reconstructing the Reality of Images: Byzantine Material Culture and Religious Iconography (11th–15th Centuries)* (Leiden, 2003).

Popović, M., and M. Breier, 'Tracing Byzantine Routes – Medieval Road Networks in the Historical Region of Macedonia and Their Reconstruction by Least-Cost Paths', in *Proceedings of the 16th International Conference on Cultural Heritage and New Technologies* (Vienna, 2011), 464–75.

Prinzing, G., 'Das Bamberger Gunthertuch in neuer Sicht', *BSl* 54 (1993): 218–31.

Prinzing, G., 'Nochmals zur historischen Deutung des Bamberger Gunthertuch auf Johannes Tzimiskes', in M. Kaimakamova, M. Salamon and M. Smorąg-Różycka (eds), *Byzantium. New Peoples, New Powers. The Byzantino-Slav Contact Zone, from the Ninth to the Fifteenth Century* (Kraków, 2007), 123–32.

Pryor, J. H., and M. H. Jeffreys, 'Alexios, Bohemond, and Byzantium's Euphrates Frontier: A Tale of Two Cretans', *Crusades* 11 (2012): 31–86.

Pushkina, T., V. Murasheva and N. Eniosova, 'Gnezdovskii arkheologicheskii kompleks', in N. Makarov (ed.), *Rus' v IX–X vekakh. Arkheologicheskaia Panorama* (Moscow, 2012), 242–73.

Roueché, C., 'The Literary Background of Kekaumenos', in C. Holmes and J. Waring (eds), *Literacy, Education and Manuscript Transmission in Byzantium and Beyond* (Leiden, 2002), 111–38.

Roueché, C., 'The Rhetoric of Kekaumenos', in E. Jeffreys (ed.), *Rhetoric in Byzantium* (Aldershot, 2003), 23–37.

Sansterre, J.-M., 'Les informations parvenues en Occident sur l'avènement de l'empereur Léon V et le siège de Constantinople par les Bulgares en 813', *Byz* 66 (1996): 373–80.

Scheel, R., *Skandinavien und Byzanz: Bedingungen und Konsequenzen mittelalterlicher Kulturbeziehungen*, 2 vols (Göttingen, 2015).

Seibt, W., 'Europäische Aristokraten auf byzantinscher Karriereleiter: ein sigillographischer Beitrag zur Prosopographie des 11. Jahrhunderts', in M. Altripp (ed.), *Byzanz in Europa. Europas östliches Erbe. Akten des Kolloquiums 'Byzanz in Europa' vom 11. bis 15. Dezember 2007 in Greifswald* (Turnhout, 2011), 82–96.

Shepard, J., 'Anna Komnena and the Past', paper, Courtauld Institute for Art, May 1987 (unpublished).

Shepard, J., 'Symeon of Bulgaria – Peacemaker', *Annuaire de l'Université de Sofia 'St. Kliment Ohridski', Centre de Recherches Slavo-Byzantines 'Ivan Dujčev'* 83/3 (1989): 9–48.

Shepard, J., 'Byzantine Diplomacy, AD 800–1204: Means and Ends', in J. Shepard and S. Franklin (eds), *Byzantine Diplomacy* (Aldershot, 1992), 41–71.

Shepard, J., 'The Uses of the Franks in Eleventh-Century Byzantium', *Anglo-Norman Studies* 15 (1993): 275–305.

Shepard, J., 'The Rhos Guests of Louis the Pious: Whence and Wherefore', *EME* 4 (1995): 41–60.

Shepard, J., 'Constantinople – Gateway to the North: the Russians', in C. Mango and G. Dagron (eds), *Constantinople and its Hinterland* (Aldershot, 1995), 243–60.

Shepard, J., 'Imperial Outliers: Building and Decorative Works in the Borderlands and Beyond', in P. Stephenson (ed.), *The Byzantine World* (London, 2010), 372–85.

Shepard, J., 'Introduction', in J. Shepard, *Emergent Elites and Byzantium in the Balkans and East-Central Europe* (Farnham, 2011), xix–xxxv.

Shepard, J., 'Middle Byzantine Military Culture, Harald Hardrada and Tall Stories', in N. Y. Gvozdetskaja, I. G. Konovalova, E. A. Melnikova and A. V. Podossinov (eds), *Stanzas of Friendship. Studies in Honour of Tatjana N. Jackson* (Moscow, 2011), 473–82.

Shepard, J., 'Theodosios' Voyages', in S. M. Sindbæk and A. Trakadas (eds), *The World in the Viking Age* (Roskilde, 2014), 68–73, 88–99.

Shepard, J., 'Communications across the Bulgarian Lands – Samuel's Poisoned Chalice for Basil II and His Successors', in V. Gjuzelev and G. Nikolov (eds),

South-Eastern Europe in the Second Half of 10th–the Beginning of the 11th Centuries: History and Culture (Sofia, 2015), 217–35.

Shepard, J., 'Man-to-Man, Dog-Eat-Dog, Cults-in-Common: The Tangled Threads of Alexios' Dealings with the Franks', *TM* 21/2 (2017): 749–88.

Signes Codoñer, J., *The Emperor Theophilos and the East, 829–842: Court and Frontier in Byzantium During the Last Phase of Iconoclasm* (Farnham, 2014).

Skinner, P., 'And Her Name Was … ? Gender and Naming in Medieval Southern Italy', *Medieval Prosopography* 20 (1999): 23–49.

Spatharakis, I., *The Portrait in Byzantine Illuminated Manuscripts* (Leiden, 1976).

Stender-Petersen, A., *Die Varägersage als Quelle der Altrussischen Chronik* (Aarhus, 1934).

Stouraitis, I., 'Roman Identity in Byzantium: A Critical Approach', *BZ* 107 (2014): 175–220.

Stouraitis, Y., 'What Did It Mean to be 'Roman' in Byzantium?', in J. Shepard et al. (eds), *Byzantine Spheres: The Byzantine Commonwealth Re-evaluated* (Oxford, forthcoming).

Sullivan, D., 'A Byzantine Instructional Manual on Siege Defense: The *De obsidione toleranda*', in J. W. Nesbitt (ed.), *Byzantine Authors: Literary Activities and Preoccupations* (Leiden, 2003), 139–266.

Treadgold, W., 'Remarks on the Work of Al-Jarmî on Byzantium', *BSl* 44 (1983): 205–12.

Vasiliev, A. A., 'Manuel Comnenus and Henry Plantagenet', *BZ* 29 (1929–30): 233–44.

Vasiliev, A. A., *Byzance et les Arabes*, II.2: *Extraits des sources Arabes*, tr. M. Canard (Brussels, 1950).

Vasiliev, A. A., *Byzance et les Arabes*, II.1: *La dynastie macédonienne (867–959)*, ed. and tr. H. Grégoire and M. Canard (Brussels, 1968).

von Falkenhausen, V., 'Olympias, eine normannische Prinzessin in Konstantinopel', in *Bisanzio e l'Italia. Raccolta di studi in memoria di Agostino Pertusi* (Milan, 1982), 56–72.

von Falkenhausen, V., 'Boemondo e Bisanzio', in C. D. Fonseca and P. Ieva (eds), *'Unde boat mundus quanti fuerit Boamundus'. Boemondo I di Altavilla, un normanno tra Occidente e Oriente* (Bari, 2015), 105–23.

Walker, P. E., 'The "Crusade" of John Tzimisces in the Light of New Arabic Evidence', *Byz* 47 (1977): 301–27.

White, M., *Military Saints in Byzantium and Rus, 900–1200* (Cambridge, 2013).

Wickham, C., 'Ninth-Century Byzantium Through Western Eyes', in L. Brubaker (ed.), *Byzantium in the Ninth Century: Dead or Alive?* (Aldershot, 1998), 245–56.

Winkelmann, F., 'Probleme der Informationen des al-Garmi über die byzantinischen Provinzen', *BSl* 43 (1982): 18–29.

Wolf, K. B., *Making History: The Normans and their Historians in Eleventh-Century Italy* (Philadelphia, 1995).

Ziemann, D., 'Dangerous Neighbours: The Treaty of Aachen and the Defeat of Nikephoros I', in M. Ančić, J. Shepard and T. Vedriš (eds), *Imperial Spheres and the Adriatic: Byzantium, the Carolingians and the Treaty of Aachen (812)* (Abingdon, 2018), 93–107.

13

Two Paradoxes of Border Identity: Michael VIII Palaiologos and Constantine Doukas Nestongos in the Sultanate of Rūm

Dimitri Korobeinikov

After the battle at Mantzikert in 1071, a considerable number of Byzantine aristocratic families continued to hold their ancestral possessions despite now being under sway of the victorious Seljuks. There was a phenomenon of divided families, with members of the same clan continuing to enjoy political careers on both sides of the Byzantine-Seljuk border. The number of families with 'double' Byzantine-Seljuk affiliation was enormous: the Komnenoi, Gabrades, Maurozomoi, Tornikioi, Bardachlades, Pakourianoi (a branch of the 'Greek' Hethoumides), to list but a few. Little is known about the identity of those who remained Byzantine in the Seljuk territory. However, one can assume that the semi-independent position of some Byzantine lords now outside the borders of the empire did not disappear after the Seljuk conquest.

The self-portraits of the Byzantine courtiers who became Seljuk can also be found in sources from a later period, the thirteenth century. Close relations, and sometimes alliances, between the two states, Byzantium (and the Nicaean Empire) and the Seljuk Sultanate of Rūm,[1] allowed those many members of the Byzantine aristocracy who were at odds with the emperor to seek asylum at the Seljuk court. They sometimes had relatives in Rūm, and in most cases their new fortune was built up with grants and gifts from the sultan. The traditional political and social influence of the Greek aristocracy continued in the Sultanate. Two cases, that of Michael Palaiologos, the future emperor Michael VIII (1259–82), and that of his mysterious *parakoimōmenos tēs megalēs sphendonēs*, give insights into the minds of the noble refugees.

---

[1] Korobeinikov, *Byzantium and the Turks*, 289–97. I wish to express my heartfelt thanks to Dr M. E. Martin (Oxford), who read a draft of this chapter and offered various suggestions. All possible mistakes are, however, mine.

Michael Palaiologos, the son of Andronikos Palaiologos (d. between 1248 and 1252), the *megas domestikos*[2] (highest-ranking military official of Byzantium), and Theodora (the daughter of Alexios Palaiologos and Irene Angelina, elder daughter of Emperor Alexios III Angelos [r. 1195–1203]),[3] was the head of the aristocratic *fronde* in the Empire of Nicaea. He was arrested twice on suspicion of disloyalty.[4] Nonetheless, sometime between the end of 1253 and November 1254, the emperor John III Batatzes (1221–54) appointed him *megas konostablos*.[5] When governing the provinces of Mesothynia and Optimates, the Nicaean frontier territory on the Sangarios River, Michael Palaiologos received the news in 1256 that the emperor was going to arrest him.[6] Michael crossed the Sangarios River and arrived at the Seljukid border zone, and there his large caravan was robbed by the frontier Turkmens who took into slavery his servants and retainers, so he arrived at Konya 'denuded of everything'.[7]

The sultan 'Izz al-Dīn Kay-Kāwūs II (1246–56; 1257–61) appointed Michael the commander of the Christian part of the Seljukid army. He fought on the Seljukid side against the Mongols in the battle at Sultanhanı before 23 Ramaḍān AH 654 (14 October 1256). When Baiju, the famous Mongol commander-in-chief, finally defeated the sultan, Michael Palaiologos escaped. He rushed northwards from the battlefield to Kastamonu and then to Nicaea.[8] According to George Pachymeres,

---

[2] Macrides, *George Akropolites*, 243–4, n. 6. Cheynet and Vannier, *Études prosopographiques*, 177, n. 32. Cheynet and Vannier suggested another date for Andronikos Palaiologos' death (1247).

[3] Geanakoplos, *Emperor Michael Palaeologus*, 17–18; Papadopulos, *Versuch*, 1–2; Cheynet and Vannier, *Études prosopographiques*, 176–9, 185–6, nn. 32, 33.

[4] Failler, 'Chronologie et composition', 9–20; Geanakoplos, *Emperor Michael Palaeologus*, 21–4.

[5] George Akropolites, *History*, 64, ed. Heisenberg, 1:134.10–12; George Pachymeres, *History*, 1.7, ed. Failler, 1:37.1–11; Geanakoplos, *Emperor Michael Palaeologus*, 26; Angold, *Byzantine Government in Exile*, 187–8.

[6] George Akropolites, *History*, 64, ed. Heisenberg, 1:134.7–136.7; George Pachymeres, *History*, 1.9, ed. Failler, 1:43.6–20; *PLP*, no. 21528; Talbot, 'Michael VIII Palaiologos', in *ODB*, ii.1367.

[7] George Pachymeres, *History*, 1.9, 6.24, ed. Failler, 1:43.21–45.1, 613.17–20; George Akropolites, *History*, 22–3, ed. Heisenberg, 1:36.8–25.

[8] George Akropolites, *History*, 65, ed. Heisenberg, 1:137.9–138.18. On sections 64–5 and 69 in Akropolites (which narrate the story of Michael's sojourn in Rūm), see the excellent commentaries in Macrides, *George Akropolites*, 312–19, 325–8, and Zhavoronkov (tr.), *George Akropolites*, 112–15, 117–18, 268–70, 275.

While in the foreign land, he [Michael Palaiologos], standing side by side in battle together with his men under the imperial banners (σημαίαις βασιλικαῖς), was the best at [fighting] against the enemies of the sultan, in order to please the emperor, if somehow the latter could have heard [about that]. He then felt sorry so much that [finally] he deliberately chose to go back [to his homeland]. He came forward to speak to the then [metropolitan] of Ikonion and used him as a mediator to the emperor so that, if possible, [the latter], having verily suppressed his anger now, would give him the warrant letters (τὰ πιστὰ γράμμασι); and this would be [the chance] for him, [Michael], to return. The hierarch supplied the embassy with the letters (γράμμασι σχεδιάσαντος τὴν πρεσβείαν);[9] the sovereign granted his pardon (κατένευσε τὴν συμπάθειαν); and [Michael] returned back with the imperial charters (βασιλικαῖς συλλαβαῖς) of safety [guaranteeing] that he would suffer nothing fatal from the [emperor's] anger. And the emperor kindly accepted the humble one: he embraced him as he arrived, and gave his pardon (συμπαθεῖ)[10] to him, as [Michael]

---

[9] The term ἡ πρεσβεία meant, strictly speaking, 'embassy', and for σχεδιάζω the dictionaries suggest the basic meaning of a swift and careless action: 'to do a thing offhand or on the spur of the moment; to play off-hand': LSJ, 1744 (and Supplement, p. 288); Sophocles, *Greek Lexicon*, 1062; Chantraine, *Dictionnaire étymologique*, 4:1080; Lampe (ed.), *A Patristic Greek Lexicon*, 1357. The Byzantine dictionaries listed four meanings of σχεδιάζειν: (1) ἐγγίζειν and πλησιάζειν ('to bring near, approach'); (2) ἐκ τοῦ παρατυχόντος λέγειν ('to speak offhand') and τὸ εἰκῇ ἀποφαίνεσθαι ('to give an opinion without plan or purpose, at a venture'); (3) λέγεται δὲ καὶ ἐπὶ τοῦ ταχέως ποιεῖν ('to speak and do at once', cf. Stephanus, *Thesaurus Graecae Linguae*, 8:1646–7: 'ex tempore aliquid facio, et tumultuario opere'); (4) ἑτοιμάζειν ('to get ready, prepare, furnish'): Photios, *Φωτίου τοῦ πατριάρχου λέξεων συναγωγή*, 2:561.21–2; *Lexica Segueriana*, 378.13; *Suidae Lexicon*, 4:489.29–30; Hesychius of Alexandria, *Lexicon*, ed. Schmidt, 1426; Pseudo-Zonaras, *Lexicon*, 1:887.7. It is Pseudo-Zonaras' translation, ἑτοιμάζειν, which I accept.

[10] Pachymeres uses the noun ἡ συμπάθεια ('sympathy') and the verb συμπαθέω ('to sympathise') in the sense of 'pardon, immunity' and 'to pardon': George Pachymeres, *History*, 1.9, ed. Failler, 1:45.8–12. However, Akropolites also employs the same term in his own direct speech addressed to Theodore II, in which he, Akropolites, predicted to the emperor that Michael Palaiologos would soon ask for 'immunity' (συμπαθείας), a permission for safe return: George Akropolites, *History*, 64, ed. Heisenberg, 1:135.15; Macrides, *George Akropolites*, 314–15, n. 6. This meaning is derived from the fiscal term for 'tax immunity'; see Kekaumenos, *Strategicon*, ed. and tr. Litavrin, 276.21, 507–8. The dictionary of Pseudo-Zonaras, whose wording is close to that of Pachymeres', uses συμπάθεια in order to explain the term ἐπιχώρησις ('concession, permission'): *Lexicon*, 807.1.

confessed that he acknowledged his unpardonable crimes. [Theodore II] then restored him to his previous dignity [of *megas konostablos*].[11]

This is the information about Michael's sojourn in Rūm from September 1256 until the beginning of 1257 provided by the Byzantine sources, Akropolites and Pachymeres. An additional source – an amalgamation of Pachymeres and George Akropolites with an unidentified account – is that of Nikephoros Gregoras. The general outline of his story is close to that of Pachymeres and Akropolites: Gregoras lists Michael's flight to the Seljuks, his battle with the 'Scythians', i.e. the Mongols,[12] and, finally, the pardon granted by Theodore II and Michael's consequent return to Nicaea.[13] However, other details in Gregoras, mostly those concerning the battle with the Mongols and the return of Michael Palaiologos to Theodore II, cannot be found elsewhere. They were obviously taken from an additional source.

According to Gregoras, when Michael Palaiologos arrived in Konya, the sultan 'with all speed' (πάσῃ σπουδῇ) was gathering his forces against the Mongols and:

As there were many Romans under his power, who in olden time became his subjects (lit. 'were enslaved'), he enrolled them into a division, formed the army and assigned [them to the command] of the general Palaiologos (ὑπὸ στρατηγῷ τῷ Παλαιολόγῳ). They were invested with the foreign Roman, rather than the native [Seljuk], dress and weapons, in order to bemuse the Scythians (i.e. the Mongols) when the latter realised that the Roman allied force had just arrived.[14]

Thus, it is Gregoras who suggests that the 'Byzantine' detachment in Seljuk service was indeed composed of the Greeks of Rūm. He likewise relates some details of the oaths given by Michael Palaiologos to Theodore II. That Theodore II sent the oaths guaranteeing Michael's personal safety is mentioned by Akropolites, Pachymeres and Gregoras;[15] but that Michael

---

[11] George Pachymeres, *History*, 1.9., ed. Failler, 1:45.1–12.
[12] On the designation of the Mongols as 'Scythians', see Moravcsik, *Byzantinoturcica*, 2:282.
[13] Nikephorus Gregoras, *History*, 3.2, ed. Schopen, 1:57.19–60.3.
[14] Ibid. 3.2, ed. Schopen, 1:58.19–59.1.
[15] George Akropolites, *History*, 69, ed. Heisenberg, 1:144.20–3; George Pachymeres, *History*, 1.9, ed. Failler, 1:45.4–12; Nikephorus Gregoras, *History*, 3.2, ed. Schopen, 1:59.10–14; Dölger and Wirth, *Regesten*, no. 1842. On the nature of this oath on the part of the emperor to his subject, exceptional in Byzantine history, see Macrides, *George Akropolites*, 327–8, n. 9.

in his turn 'confessed that he acknowledged his unpardonable crimes', is noted only by Pachymeres. The text of Gregoras is more explicit:

> And thus the Roman land received back Palaiologos, but not before he himself gave assurances, through the most solemn oaths, of guarantees of his good faith in regard to the emperor: to always remain within the limits of submission, to never seek the empire for himself, to forget (lit. 'to leave to the past') [everything] that had been said against him, and henceforth with his future deeds to clean himself from the now faint (lit. 'dead') suspicion, and moreover to always keep and maintain the same goodwill and love to the same emperor Theodore and his son John, and the successors-to-be in their dynasty and the empire.[16]

What was Michael Palaiologos' ultimate goal when he decided to seek asylum in Rūm? Was he really guilty of preparing a revolt against the emperor? Did he move to Rūm asking for military help from the Seljuks in the seizure of the Nicaean throne (hence his riches which were most unfortunately taken by the frontier Turkmens)?[17] Or did he intend, albeit unwillingly, to settle permanently in the Sultanate, thus becoming a member of the Byzantine aristocracy abroad? However, the political context casts doubt on the suggestion concerning the revolt. There existed a Nicaean-Seljuk treaty against the Mongols, concluded in 1243 during the reign of John III Batatzes.[18] Emperor Theodore Laskaris confirmed this agreement three times: twice in 1254–5,[19] and the last time in the spring of 1256, just before Michael Palaiologos' flight.[20] It is unlikely that the Seljuks, who were under constant threat from the Mongols, had wanted to establish a new emperor in Nicaea; on the contrary: it was the Greeks of Nicaea who for a while helped to crush the Seljuk Sultanate after the latter was defeated by the Mongols.[21] Moreover, it is the text of Gregoras that clarifies the meaning of '[Michael's] unpardonable crimes' in Pachymeres. These do not refer to Michael's 'plots' just before his flight to Rūm (that suspicion is called 'dead' in Gregoras), but rather to his desertion from

---

[16] Nikephorus Gregoras, *Historia Byzantina*, 3.2, ed. Schopen, 1:59.14–24.

[17] Prinzing, 'Ein Mann τυραννίδος ἄξιος'. See also Macrides, *George Akropolites*, 317, n. 5.

[18] George Akropolites, *History*, 41, ed. Heisenberg, 1:69.17–70.9; Dölger and Wirth, *Regesten*, no. 1776.

[19] Dölger and Wirth, *Regesten*, nos 1824, 1825.

[20] George Akropolites, *History*, 61, ed. Heisenberg, 1:125.9–13; Ibn Bībī, *Histoire des Seldjoucides d'Asie Mineure*, 284, tr. Duda, 270; Dölger and Wirth, *Regesten*, no. 1830.

[21] Angelov, *Byzantine Hellene*, 161–74.

the important post in Mesothynia and, according to Theodore II (whose words were preserved by Akropolites), to the fact that 'he did not stay in Roman lands even if he were to suffer these terrible things (i.e. blinding), preferring to fare ill among his own people than to fare well in a foreign land.'[22] That is why Michael was asked 'to forget [everything] that had been said against him', as the emperor's threats to blind him and the arrest of his uncle, the *megas chartoularios*, also called Michael,[23] were the chief reasons for Michael Palaiologos' decision to seek asylum in Rūm.[24] Pachymeres and Akropolites attributed the suspicions to only the emperor Theodore II Laskaris,[25] but it is Gregoras who states that Michael fled because of the envy (ὁ φθόνος) of Theodore II's retainers;[26] the same 'envy' is mentioned in Michael's two *typika* and the laudatory orations of George of Cyprus and Manuel Holobolos.[27]

I suggest that the prospect of becoming a Seljuk courtier for the rest of his life was real for Michael Palaiologos in 1256. There are two extant *typika* of Michael's, written towards the end of his life, sometime in 1280–1, where he describes his *curriculum vitae*, including, of course, his stay in the Rūm. The *typika* are highly trustworthy in the sense that they are concerned with the events of 1256–7, since part of the story was provided later by Michael Palaiologos himself. (The main core of the text was written in 1261, when Michael managed to re-conquer Constantinople from the Latins.) The *typikon*, which features strong elements of autobiography and which Michael VIII had commissioned for the monastery of his patron saint, the Archangel Michael, on Mount Auxentios near Chalcedon, contains the most detailed explanation of Michael's motives during his sojourn in Rūm. The text reads:

> I had therefore to leave my native land, that of the Romans, I mean, and I fled to a foreign country. I entered Persian [Seljuk] territory, facing many

22 George Akropolites, *History*, 64, ed. Heisenberg, 1:135.1–4; tr. Macrides, *George Akropolites*, 312.
23 On him, see Cheynet and Vannier, *Études prosopographiques*, 174–6, n. 31.
24 George Akropolites, *History*, 64, ed. Heisenberg, 1:134.25–135.1; George Pachymeres, *History*, 1.9, ed. Failler, 1:43.6–20.
25 George Akropolites, *History*, 64, ed. Heisenberg, 1:134.18–135.1; George Pachymeres, *History*, 1.9, ed. Failler, 1:43.14: τῆς ἀρχῆς ὑποψίαν.
26 Nikephorus Gregoras, *History*, 3.2, ed. Schopen, 1:58.1–13.
27 Τυπικὸν τῆς ἐν τῷ περιωνύμῳ βουνῷ τοῦ Αὐξεντίου κατὰ τὴν ἐπαρχίαν Χαλκηδόνος βασιλικῆς μονῆς, 790, tr. Dennis 1, 1231; Michael VII Palaiologos, 'De vita sua', 453, tr. Dennis 2, 1243; George (Gregory) of Cyprus, 'Oratio laudatoria', *PG* 142:364; Siderides, 'Μανουὴλ Ὁλοβώλου ἐγκώμιον', 177; Manuel Holobolos, *Orationes*, ed. Treu, 1:34.23–9.

dangers along the way, it should be noted, from all of which I was rescued by God. I remained for quite a while with the ruler of the Persians.
There I often led a contingent of our Persian enemies nobly into battle
against the Atarioi [Mongols]. This people migrated from lands to the
East not a long time ago. They have been raised to war, gladly shed blood,
and are spirited like a herd of cattle. Borne along by the situation and
yielding to necessity, I endured. What was accomplished there let others
say. I feel no obligation to speak about such things myself. But I shall sum
up everything by saying just one thing, and let the all watching eye [of
God] be witness to my words. During the time I spent in Persia I engaged
in absolutely nothing, in word, in deed, in plot, or in attempt against the
ruler of the Romans at that time, the blessed late emperor, my cousin
[Theodore II Laskaris] or against the realm of the Romans. Rather, with
God's help, I intended and carried out in practice only what would benefit them. The spirit of envy soon dissipated and in a short time I left
Persia and again returned to the land of the Romans, subjected myself to
the ruler and again loyally performed the services he commanded. These
things then happened before I became emperor.[28]

Here Emperor Michael VIII Palaiologos shows that his self-consciousness
comprised elements of a border identity. The idea of being Byzantine while
actually being Seljuk was a logical outcome of the maxims of Kekaumenos,
who had advised to seek the favours of the emperor but at the same time keep
the ancestral possessions outside the control of the empire.[29] Kekaumenos,
however, wrote at a time when no Seljuk polity was yet present in Asia Minor.
Michael's duplicity was no secret for his subjects. When Pachymeres wrote
that, in 1256, Michael 'was the best at [fighting] against the enemies of the sultan, in order to please the emperor', he alluded to the same idea that Michael
expressed in his *typikon*. Of course, the political *amicitia* between the Seljuk
Sultanate of Rūm and the Byzantine (Nicaean) Empire[30] allowed the notion
of being simultaneously Byzantine and Seljuk, but Michael's text avoided
stressing that. On the contrary, he described the 'Persian territory', i.e. the
Sultanate of Rūm, as a hostile and dangerous land and even called his fellow
Rūmī Greeks, who spoke the same language as he did, 'our Persian enemies'.

---

[28] Τυπικὸν τῆς ἐν τῷ περιωνύμῳ βουνῷ τοῦ Αὐξεντίου κατὰ τὴν ἐπαρχίαν Χαλκηδόνος
βασιλικῆς μονῆς, 791; tr. Dennis 1, 1231.

[29] Kekaumenos, *Strategicon*, ed. and tr. Litavrin, 314–15; Kekaumenos, *Consilia et
Narrationes*, English tr. C. Roueché, ch. 5: 'Advice to a toparch'.

[30] Korobeinikov, *Byzantium and the Turks*, 289–94.

If Michael did indeed try to present himself as a Byzantine patriot, his text nonetheless contained some logical discrepancies, appropriately noted later by Pachymeres. Pachymeres seemed to have been aware of Michael's *typikon*, as only he, Theodore Skoutariotes and Michael VIII use the extremely rare form *Atarioi* for the Mongols (Tatars).[31]

Can Michael VIII's behaviour in Rūm be seen as a case of so-called 'situational identity'? If so, it was remembered for a long time: until the end of the thirteenth century, when the final versions of his *typika* were composed and Pachymeres began writing his *History*. But the picture of the forced adaptation to harsh circumstances of the future Byzantine emperor, who arrived 'denuded of everything' at the gates of Konya, so carefully painted by Akropolites and Michael himself in his *typika*, is not in accordance with the data of other sources. He arrived at a friendly country, was met by his relatives (including the sultan himself)[32] and on the whole managed to use his 'Persian adventure' to his own profit. The Byzantine source that explicitly suggests a direct connection between Michael's flight to Rūm (and his subsequent return to Nicaea) in 1256–7 and his step-by-step usurpation of the Byzantine throne in the years between 1258 and 1261 is a poem of Manuel Philes, written sometime at the beginning of the fourteenth century.[33] The poem is dedicated to St Stephen the First Martyr (Acts 6:5,8–7:60), whose monastery in Constantinople was established, or restored, by a certain *parakoimōmenos tēs megalēs sphendonēs* ('chamberlain of the great seal') who was later buried there. However, the most intriguing aspect of the poem is its description of the circumstances of the first meeting between the *parakoimōmenos* and Michael Palaiologos:

> When the hero Michael Palaiologos Doukas
> fled the envy which is hostile to man[34]
> and went to the land of the Persians from that of the Ausonians[35]

---

[31] Korobeinikov, 'Ilkhans', 398–401.

[32] On the dynastic relations between the Seljuks of Rūm and the Palaiologoi, see Korobeinikov, 'Byzantine Emperors'.

[33] Manuelis Philes, *Carmina*, ed. Miller, 2:260–3 (poem 242).

[34] I translate the expression τὸν μισάνθρωπον φθόνον, which literally means 'envy that abhors mankind'.

[35] Originally, the 'Ausonian land' and the 'Ausonians' meant Italy and Italians (including the Romans). As such, it also meant 'Byzantium' and the 'Byzantines', who considered themselves as 'Romans'. Interestingly, 'Ausonia' could also have meant 'Ionia', i.e. the western shore of Asia Minor: Herodianus Grammaticus, 'De prosodia catholica', 3 (1): 296.7–10; Herodianus Grammaticus, Περὶ παρωνύμων, 3 (2): 877.40–878.2.

before [obtaining] the crown of his royal accession and power,
he met with him [i.e. the future *parakoimōmenos*] before [meeting] any
  nobleman
and deemed worthy his words of advice about himself,
for he considered him the wisest of all men,
very [strong] and capable of enduring in battle.
Then, having him as his great helper,
he [i.e. Michael] from there [Persia] came here [to Nicaea], desiring
  [to return],
and at once took hold of the realm of the Ausonians.
In exchange, he honoured him,
who had earlier appeared [to have been] of good repute among the satraps
because of the dignities [he had received] in reward,
with the honour of the Chamberlain of the Greatest Seal.[36]

That man, now the *parakoimōmenos tēs megalēs sphendonēs*, was so grateful to St Stephen, who helped him to endure in 'Persia' and then to return to
Byzantium, that he established in St Stephen's name the monastery in Constantinople in which he eventually passed away as a monk; he was buried by
his former servant, now also a monk by the name of Dionysios, probably the
hēgoumenos of the same monastery. He earlier served his master in 'Persia'.[37]

The wording in Philes is not exceptional: like other later authors, he mentions the 'envy which is hostile to man' which forced Michael to flee from the
Nicaean empire. However, it is only Philes who connects Michael's sojourn
in Rūm in 1256 with his enthronement that took place on 1 January 1259.[38]

Philes gives no clue as to the name of Michael's 'great helper' (συνεργός)
in Rūm, save his later title. Originally, the term *parakoimōmenos* ('chamberlain') designated the eunuch who slept in the emperor's chamber and
thus had direct access to the sovereign. Under Michael VIII Palaiologos,

---

[36] Manuelis Philes, *Carmina*, ed. Miller, 2:261.21–35: Ἐπεὶ δὲ φυγὼν τὸν μισάνθρωπον
φθόνον / Ἐξ Αὐσόνων γῆς ἦλθεν εἰς γῆν Περσίδος / Ὁ βασιλειῶν καὶ κρατῶν πρὸ
τοῦ στέφους / Ἥρως Μιχαὴλ Παλαιολόγος Δούκας, / Τούτῳ πρὸ παντὸς εὐγενοῦς
ἐντυγχάνει, / Καὶ τῶν κατ' αὐτὸν ἀξιοῖ βουλευμάτων, / Ὁρῶν σοφὸν τὸν ἄνδρα τῶν
ἄλλων πλέον / Καὶ καρτερικὸν ἀκριβῶς πρὸς τὰς μάχας. / Εἶτα συνεργὸν εὐτυχῶν
τοῦτον μέγαν / Ἐκεῖθεν ἥκει δεῦρο τοῦ σκοποῦ χάριν, / Καὶ γίνεται μὲν Αὐσονάρχης
αὐτίκα, / Τιμᾷ δὲ τιμῇ τοῦ παρακοιμωμένου / Τῆς σφενδόνης τὸν ἄνδρα τῆς ὑπερτάτης,
/ Φανέντα καὶ πρὶν εὐκλεῆ τοῖς σατράπαις / Ἐκ τῶν πρὸς ἀντάμειψιν ἀξιωμάτων.

[37] Manuelis Philes, *Carmina*, ed. Miller, 2:262.36–60; on Dionysios, see *PLP*, no. 5435.

[38] George Pachymeres, *History*, 1.29, 2.4, 6.36, ed. Failler, 1:115.5–6, 137.7, 667.7–10;
Kleinchroniken, ed. Schreiner, 1:75 (6).

the office, no longer restricted to the eunuchs, was divided between the 'chamberlain of the great seal' (*parakoimōmenos tēs megalēs sphendonēs*) and the 'proper' chamberlain (*parakoimōmenos tou koitōnos*).[39] While the latter served as head of the pages and the *valets-de-chambre*,[40] the former was keeper of the emperor's private seal for the letters addressed to the emperor's family: his mother, wife and his co-emperor son. He also held the emperor's sword if its bearer, the *prōtostratōr*, was absent.[41] The 'great seal' was a signet ring: the first known *parakoimōmenos tēs megalēs sphendonēs*, Isaac Doukas, brother of the emperor John III Batatzes, was referred to in the Byzantine-Genoese treaty documents of March–July 1261 as *parachimemoni magni anuli imperii sui Isachii Ducis* and *parachimomenos magni anuli imperii nostri Ysachius Duca* ('chamberlain of the great signet of our imperial majesty Isaac Doukas').[42] According to Pseudo-Kodinos, the 'great seal' was used for the wax sealing of the private letters of the emperor:[43] if so, a signet ring was a more appropriate tool than a seal, which actually was a misnomer for σφενδόνη.[44]

The reform of the chamberlain's offices took place as early as 1260:[45] Pachymeres wrote that by the beginning of 1261, Michael VIII had received two refugees from the Sultanate of Rūm, the Basilikos, natives of Rhodes and the Sultan's retainers, whom he knew from his sojourn in the Sultanate in 1256; he then granted them Byzantine court titles. One of the brothers, Basil, became the 'proper' chamberlain (*parakoimōmenos tou koitōnos*);[46] he thus cannot be identified with our *parakoimōmenos tēs megalēs sphendonēs*.[47]

However, the title of *parakoimōmenos* (without the addition *tēs megalēs sphendonēs* or *tou koitōnos*) continued being employed in the sources,

---

[39] Guilland, 'Le parakimomène', 198–200 (repr. in id., *Recherches*, 1:208–9).

[40] Pseudo-Kodinos, *Traité des offices*, 176.6–14; Guilland, 'Le parakimomène', 198 (repr. in id., *Recherches*, 1:208).

[41] Pseudo-Kodinos *Traité des offices*, 175.23–176.5. The *parakoimōmenos tēs megalēs sphendonēs* held the sixteenth position in the list of the court dignitaries: ibid. 137.12, 156.4–12, 300.11–2, 305.9–10, 307.10–2, 320.31–321.38, 334.43–335.44, 344.18–9, 347.15–6.

[42] Pieralli, *Corrispondenza diplomatica*, 142.298–300, 50.6–7; Dölger and Wirth, *Regesten*, nos. 1890, 1892.

[43] Pseudo-Kodinos, *Traité des offices*, 175.23–32.

[44] Kazhdan, 'Sphendone', in *ODB*, iii.1936–7.

[45] See Guilland, 'Le parakimomène', 198–9 (repr. in id., *Recherches*, 1:208–9).

[46] George Pachymeres, *History*, 2.24, ed. Failler, 1:183.1–19, *PLP*, nos 2452, 2458.

[47] It seems that the last *parakoimōmenos* before the division of the office was George Zagarommates (d. 1261), the 'chamberlain' under Theodore II between 1254 and 1258 and uncle (θεῖος) of Michael VIII: *PLP*, no. 6417; George Akropolites, *History*, 75, ed. Heisenberg, 1:154.20–155.10; Zhavoronkov (tr.), *George Akropolites*, 123–4, 281–4

including the fourteenth-century lists of the court dignitaries:[48] in Byzantium until 1367[49] and in the Empire of Trebizond until 1432.[50]

The list of *parakoimōmenoi tēs megalēs sphendonēs* under Michael VIII, including those mentioned as 'chamberlains' only,[51] comprises five names:[52]

and n. 935; Macrides, *George Akropolites*, 339–42 and n. 11; Βυζαντινὰ ἔγγραφα τῆς Μονῆς Πάτμου, ed. Branouse and Nystazopoulou-Pelekidou, 1:128; 2:156–63; *Acta et diplomata graeca*, ed. Miklosich and Müller, 4:11, 31 and 232–6; 5:259; 6:191, 199 and 231; Ahrweiler, 'Smyrne', 177–8.

[48] Pseudo-Kodinos, *Traité des offices*, 309.8. Pachymeres himself is a good example: though he had mentioned Basil Basilikos as the *parakoimōmenos tou koitōnos* by 1261, he afterwards made reference to the *parakoimōmenos* John Makrenos in 1262–3 without any clarification of his court functions: was he the holder of the 'great seal' or the head of the chamber offices? George Pachymeres, *History*, 3.16–17, ed. Failler, 1:11.16, 273.5–10, 275.16–277.16. According to Failler, John Makrenos was the *parakoimōmenos tēs megalēs sphendonēs*: George Pachymeres, *History*, 2, part 5: Index, 34, 49. But this is merely a suggestion; cf. *PLP*, no. 92605 (*parakoimōmenos*) and Guilland, 'Le parakimomène', 199 (repr. in id., *Recherches*, 1:209) (*parakoimōmenos tou koitōnos*). Likewise, in documentary sources one can find the titles *parakoimōmenos tēs megalēs sphendonēs* and *parakoimōmenos* in reference to one and the same person: *Acta et diplomata graeca*, ed. Miklosich and Müller, 4:257–8.

[49] *PLP*, no. 91760: Theophylaktos Dermokaites, the *oikeios* of Emperor John V Palaiologos (1341–7; 1354–91).

[50] *PLP*, no. 24789: Michael Sampson, the half-brother of the *amērtzantarios* Theodore Sampson (*PLP*, no. 24788). On this famous family in the Empire of Trebizond, see *PLP*, nos 24785–90; its last representative, Manuel Sampson, had been settled in Rumeli on the orders of the Ottoman authorities by 1484–7: Karpov, *Istoriia Trapezundskoi imperii*, 440–1.

[51] When only the title of the *parakoimōmenos* is mentioned under the Palaiologoi, there is a strong suspicion that this means the holder of the 'great seal', who ranked higher than the *parakoimōmenos tou koitōnos*. The traditional Byzantine antiquarian way of naming suggests the continuing usage of the older forms, in this case the shortened form of the 'chamberlain'.

[52] According to the *PLP*, there were no fewer than twenty *parakoimōmenoi* in Byzantium (including the Empire of Trebizond) between 1258 and 1461: *PLP*, nos 209, 1180, 2458, 5298, 5691, 5829, 6417, 8665, 10955, 92605 (16358), 20201, 24106, 24789, 25210, 27276, 27305, 29122, 29580, 30954, 91760. Of these, ten (nos. 2458, 5691, 5829, 6417, 8665, 92605 [16358], 20201, 24106, 27276, 30954) were *parakoimōmenoi* between 1258 and 1307: George Zagarommates under Theodore II (no. 6417), six under Michael VIII and three under Andronikos II until c. 1307: Dionysios Drimys c. 1300 (no. 5829); a certain Rhaoul, also c. 1300 (no. 24106); and John Komnenos Choumnos, the *parakoimōmenos tēs megalēs sphendonēs* after 1307 (no. 30954). It should be noted that Constantine Doukas Nestongos (no. 20201) was the last *parakoimōmenos* under Michael VIII and the first one under Andronikos II. As to the six *parakoimōmenoi* under Michael VIII, I exclude Basil Basilikos (no. 2458) from the list, as he was the *parakoimōmenos tou koitōnos*.

1. John, whose seal as *parakoimōmenos* and *pansebastos*, dated to the middle of the thirteenth century, is extant; this John might have been identical to John Makrenos (3) below.[53] However, according to N. P. Likhachev, John could be identified with John Phagomodes, *sebastos* and *parakoimōmenos*, whose seal also survives; its *terminus a quo* is the end of the twelfth century.[54]

2. Isaac Doukas, *sebastokratōr, pansebastos sebastos* and *parakoimōmenos tēs megalēs sphendonēs*, brother of the emperor John III Batatzes and uncle (*avunculus*) of Michael VIII, who died in Genoa in 1261.[55]

3. John Makrenos, *parakoimōmenos* (probably *tēs megalēs sphendonēs*) in 1262–3.[56] He was among the generals sent by John III Batatzes to fight against Michael II Angelos Doukas, despot in Epiros (1230–67), during the campaign in the winter of 1252–3.[57] As *parakoimōmenos*, he was sent together with *megas domestikos* Alexios Philes[58] under the command of Michael VIII's half-brother, the *sebastokratōr* Constantine,[59] to

---

[53] *PLP*, no. 8665; Laurent, *Bulles métriques*, no. 484; George Pachymeres, *History*, 3.16, ed. Failler, 1:273, n. 4.

[54] Likhachev, *Molivdovuly grecheskogo Vostoka*, 296–7 (LXXXI.8). On the Phagomodes, the local family from Smyrna of which Constantine Phagomodes, *pansebastos* and close retainer of the emperor in 1225, was a representative, see *Acta et diplomata graeca*, ed. Miklosich and Müller, 4:190, 252; Ahrweiler, 'Smyrne', 160; *PLP*, nos 29548, 29549. However, no representative of the Phagomodes family is listed in the *PBW*.

[55] George Akropolites, *History*, 51, ed. Heisenberg, 1:101, lines 6–18; George Pachymeres, *History*, 1.8, 1.21, 8.19, ed. Failler, 1:41.15–19, 93.1–8; 2:173.2–7 (Pachymeres never mentions Isaac Doukas Batatzes by name, only through various marriage connections); *Annali genovesi*, 4:42–3; Pieralli, *Corrispondenza diplomatica*, 142.298–300, 150.5–7; *PLP*, no. 5691; Dölger and Wirth, *Regesten*, no. 1892; Polemis, *The Doukai*, 109, n. 73; Macrides, *George Akropolites*, 269–70, n. 5.

[56] *PLP*, nos 92605, 16358; Ahrweiler, 'Smyrne', 146; Guilland, 'Le parakimomène', 199 (repr. in id., *Recherches*, 1:209); Failler, 'Chronologie et composition', 85–103. His name is known only from the headline of ch. 17 in George Pachymeres, *History*, 1.17, ed. Failler, 1:275.21. Failler (George Pachymeres, *History*, 2, part 5: Index, 34 and 49) suggested that John Makrenos was the chamberlain of the Great Seal (μεγάλης σφενδόνης).

[57] George Akropolites, *History*, 49, ed. Heisenberg, 1:89.20–90.31, Zhavoronkov (tr.), *George Akropolites*, 89–90, 240–1 and n. 657; Macrides, *George Akropolites*, 249–59 and n. 14.

[58] George Pachymeres, *History*, 2.13 and 3.16, ed. Failler, 1:155.1, 273.9, 275.19; *PLP*, no. 29809.

[59] George Akropolites, *History*, 77, 82, ed. Heisenberg, 1:160.16–161.8, 173.10–11; Zhavoronkov (tr.), *George Akropolites*, 126, 132, 288–9 and n. 975; Macrides, *George Akropolites*, 347, 350–1 n. 15, 366; Nikephorus Gregoras, *History*, 3.5, 4.1, ed. Schopen, 1:72.16–18 and 79.11–80.11; *PLP*, no. 21498; Cheynet and Vannier, *Études prosopographiques*, 178, n. 16; Papadopulos, *Versuch*, 6; Polemis, *The Doukai*, 161, n. 149.

Monemvasia to fight against William II Villehardouin, Prince of Achaia (1246–78). Initially successful, both John Makrenos and Alexios Philes were then taken captive in the battle at Makry Plagi in the Peloponnese in 1263;[60] Philes soon died in captivity, but John Makrenos, while in Achaia, was reported to have married Theodora, daughter of Theodore II Laskaris, widow of Matthew de Valaincourt, Baron of Damala and Veligosti.[61] Michael VIII Palaiologos appeared to have convinced himself that John Makrenos wanted to become emperor through this marriage connection; he then exchanged John for the Latin prisoners of war, brought him back to Byzantium and 'at once deprived him of his eyes' (παρασχεδὸν τῶν ὀφθαλμῶν ἀφαιρεῖται).[62]

4. Gabriel Sphrantzes, cousin (αὐτανέψιος) of John Doukas Angelos,[63] son of Michael II of Epiros.[64] Once the *parakoimōmenos tēs megalēs sphendonēs*, he had been deprived of his office and blinded on the orders of the emperor before August 1280.[65] He thus must have held the office sometime between 1263 and 1280.

5. Constantine Doukas Nestongos, who was already the *parakoimōmenos tēs megalēs sphendonēs* when he followed Andronikos II, a co-emperor at that time, to the military expedition along the Meander valleys which ended in the restoration of Tralles (Aydın) in 1280. Between 1280 and 1283/4 Nyssa (Sultanhisar) was taken by the frontier Turks; its governor, the '*parakoimōmenos* Nostongos', i.e. Constantine Doukas Nestongos, was taken captive.[66] He was soon released, probably ransomed, and then witnessed the Byzantine-Venetian treaty of 15 June 1285 as *avunculo imperii nostri parachimumeno magnesfendonis domino Constantino Duca Nestingo* ('the maternal uncle, the Chamberlain of the Great Seal of our empire, lord Constantine Doukas Nestongos').[67] Further information

---

[60] *Chronicle of Morea*, ed. Kalonaros, 190–227.4546–5465, ed. Schmitt, 301–56.4546–5465; *Kleinchroniken*, ed. Schreiner, 1:599 (5); Geanakoplos, *Emperor Michael Palaeologus*, 158–9, 173–4.

[61] According to Zhavoronkov (tr.), John Makrenos indeed married Theodora: Zhavoronkov (tr.), *George Akropolites*, 280, n. 922; 345, Table 2. On Matthew de Valaincourt and his family, see *PLP*, no. 2555, and Lock, *Franks*, 76, 83, 89.

[62] Pachymeres, *Relations historiques*, 1:275.16–277.16.

[63] *PLP*, no. 205; Polemis, *The Doukai*, 95, n. 50.

[64] *PLP*, no. 220; Polemis, *The Doukai*, 93–4, n. 48.

[65] George Pachymeres, *History*, 6.25, ed. Failler, 1:621.24–623.2; *PLP*, no. 27276.

[66] George Pachymeres, *History*, 6.20–1, ed. Failler, 1:593.6–11 and 599.10–4.

[67] *Urkunden zur Handels- und Staatsgeschichte*, ed. Tafel and Thomas, 3:339; Polemis, *The Doukai*, 151–2, n. 132.

about him can be found in Greek charters, in which he appeared as a powerful landowner in Prinobaris near Smyrna; it seems that he reduced his
political activity after 1285. The first document, issued in February, in the
fourth indiction (i.e. in 1276, 1291 or 1306), was signed by 'the slave of the
emperor', *parakoimōmenos tēs megalēs sphendonēs* Constantine Doukas
Nestongos.[68] Two other documents, of March and April 1307, concern his
paroikoi ('peasant tenants') who tried to occupy the lands of the Lembi-
otissa monastery near Smyrna.[69] In both charters Constantine Nestongos
is labelled the 'uncle' (θεῖος) of Emperor Andronikos II, 'the most noble
Doukas' and, again, *parakoimōmenos tēs megalēs sphendonēs*.[70]

One should exclude the 'chamberlains' John (1) and Isaac Doukas (2)
as possible candidates for our *parakoimōmenos tēs megalēs sphendonēs*: if
John's seal is attributed to Phagomodes, it belongs to the first half of the thirteenth century, before 1256. As to Isaac Doukas, it seems improbable that
emperor John III Batatzes' brother was an émigré in Rūm in 1256; besides,
he died in Genoa and was buried in the city's cathedral of St Laurence. His
grave could not have been in the monastery of St Stephen in Constantinople.

If Philes wrote his poem in strict chronological sequence, the best possible candidate for our *parakoimōmenos tēs megalēs sphendonēs* would have
been John Makrenos (3), because his appointment to this office took place
in 1261–2, soon after Michael Palaiologos' enthronement. However, some
details in Philes' verses exclude him: our hero, Michael's chief supporter
while in Rūm in 1256, began the construction of St Stephen's monastery
when, 'still alive and seeing the sun, he laboured with his body',[71] while John

---

[68] *Acta et diplomata graeca*, ed. Miklosich and Müller, 4:103–4.
[69] Ibid. 4:257–60; Ahrweiler, 'Smyrne', 153–4, 165 and 173. However, Ahrweiler thought
that our 'chamberlain' Constantine Doukas Nestongos (*PLP*, no. 20201) was identical
with the *megas hetaireiarchēs* Nestongos Doukas, the *kephalē* ('governor') of Magnesia
and *doux* of the *thema* of Neokastra, mentioned by Pachymeres for 1304–6: George
Pachymeres, *History*, 11.16, 11.24, 12.14, 12.23, 12.30, 13.27, ed. Failler, 2:441.28–443.33,
471.24–475.28, 549.25–551.4, 573.4–16, 593.1–24, 687.1–15). This identification has
been rejected by scholars; see *PLP*, no. 20725 (Nestongos Doukas); George Pachymeres,
History, 2, part 5: Index, 37; Polemis, *The Doukai*, 152, n. 133.
[70] *Acta et diplomata graeca*, ed. Miklosich and Müller, 4:257: τοῦ θείου τῆς βασιλείας μου
τοῦ παρακοιμωμένου τῆς μεγάλης σφενδόνης, κυροῦ Ἰωάννου Δούκα τοῦ Νεοστόγγου
(read Κωνσταντίνου, 'Constantine', instead of Ἰωάννου, 'John': Ahrweiler, 'Smyrne',
173); *Acta et diplomata graeca*, ed. Miklosich and Müller, 4:258: τοῦ πανευγενεστάτου
Δούκα καὶ παρακοιμωμένου τῆς μεγάλης σφενδόνης τοῦ Νεοστόγγου.
[71] Manuelis Philes, *Carmina*, ed. Miller, 2:262.43: Ἔτι μὲν οὖν ζῶν καὶ βλέπων τὸν
ἥλιον ἔκαμνε τῷ σώματι.

Makrenos and Gabriel Sphrantzes (4) (whose family was connected almost entirely to the Balkans[72]) were most likely blinded when middle-aged on the orders of Michael VIII. The strong pro-Michael Palaiologos sentiments in the poem of Philes were at variance with the real circumstances of Makrenos' and Sphrantzes' lives. Besides, a closer look at the poem's structure reveals that though Philes followed the chronological sequence, he described the events, which were separated by years, as if these were almost simultaneous. That leaves no option but to accept the opinion of R. Janin, who suggested that Constantine Doukas Nestongos was indeed the benefactor of St Stephen's monastery in Constantinople.[73] Of all of Michael VIII's *parakoimōmenoi tēs megalēs sphendonēs*, only Constantine Doukas Nestongos had a long and prominent career.

How did Constantine end up in Rūm? One can only guess. As Constantine was still alive in 1307, and as his political career began only in the 1280s, it seems that in 1256 he was of a relatively young age, being of the same generation as, or even a later than, Michael Palaiologos. But he was already in Rūm and enjoyed 'good reputation' among the 'satraps' at the moment of Michael's arrival.

It seems that Constantine Doukas Nestongos was Michael Palaiologos' first cousin. According to Polemis, Constantine might have been the brother of Alexios Doukas Nestongos (Nostongos), the governor (*kephalē*) of Thessalonike and *pinkernēs* ('cupbearer of the emperor') who is mentioned as a 'first cousin' (ἐξάδελφος) of Michael VIII in 1267.[74]

Who might Constantine Doukas Nestongos' father have been? The imperial branch of the Doukas family that was related to the Palaiologoi in the thirteenth century was that of Emperor John III Doukas Batatzes and his brother Isaac Doukas (2), the *parakoimōmenos tēs megalēs sphendonēs*.[75] Theodora, wife of Michael VIII, whom he married in 1253/4, shortly before his flight, was a granddaughter of Isaac Doukas,[76] and Michael VIII himself called John III his great-uncle (θεῖος).[77] Indeed, Michael VIII's maternal grandmother,

---

[72] George Pachymeres, *History*, 6.32, ed. Failler, 1:641.1–19.

[73] Janin, *Géographie ecclésiastique*, 477; cf. *PLP*, no. 5435; Kidonopoulos, *Bauten*, 62–5.

[74] *Actes de Zographou*, nos 7:22.125, 24.178; Polemis, *The Doukai*, 151–2, n. 131–2; *PLP*, no. 20727.

[75] Polemis, *The Doukai*, 106–11, n. 72–6.

[76] George Akropolites, *History*, 51, ed. Heisenberg, 1:101.6–18, Zhavoronkov (tr.), *George Akropolites*, 251–2, n. 703–8; Macrides, *George Akropolites*, 269–70, n. 6; *PLP*, nos 21380, 21528; Talbot, 'Theodora Palaiologina', 295.

[77] George Akropolites, *History*, 78, ed. Heisenberg, 1:162.19–22; Michael VII Palaiologos, 'De vita sua', 451, tr. Dennis 2, 1243; cf. Zhavoronkov (tr.), *George Akropolites*, 289, n. 980.

Irene Komnene, daughter of Alexios III, was the second cousin of John III Batatzes, whose mother[78] was the daughter of Isaac Doukas Angelos.[79] The latter was the brother of Andronikos Angelos,[80] who was the father of the emperors Isaac II and Alexios III.

The Nestongoi were also connected with John III Batatzes and the Angeloi. According to Akropolites, in 1224/5 Andronikos Nestongos, the first cousin (πρωτεξάδελφος) of John III, plotted against the emperor. Andronikos' brother Isaac Nestongos, a certain Makrenos (probably the father of John Makrenos [3]) and many other notables were among the conspirators. The plot was unsuccessful; Isaac Nestongos and Makrenos were sentenced to blinding and having their hands amputated, but Andronikos Nestongos was only imprisoned in the fortress of Magnesia. Shortly afterwards, he escaped (by the wish of the emperor as Akropolites suggests) and would have run away to the land of the Muslims, i.e. to the Sultanate of Rūm, where he then lived and died.[81] According to Barzos, Andronikos and Isaac Nestongoi were the sons of a certain Nestongos and the daughter of Isaac Doukas Angelos, the latter being the uncle of Emperor Isaac II (1185–95, 1203–4).[82]

Was this Andronikos Nestongos the father of Constantine Doukas Nestongos? The wording in Philes seems to suggest that Constantine's sojourn in the Sultanate of Rūm lasted for several years before 1256: the patron saint of Constantine Doukas Nestongos, St Stephen, did not just help Constantine return to Byzantium, but 'indeed miraculously drew out that man from Persia by putting [him] on the hook of the fishing-line.'[83] The statement alludes to the apostles, 'the fishers of men' (Matthew 4:18–19);

---

[78] On her, see Barzos, Γενεαλογία τῶν Κομνηνῶν, 2:851–7, n. 190.

[79] On Isaac Doukas Angelos, see ibid. 1:673–4, n. 96.

[80] Isaac Doukas Angelos and Andronikos Angelos were sons of Constantine Angelos, husband of Theodora Komnene, daughter of Emperor Alexios I (1081–1118). On Andronikos Angelos, see Barzos, Γενεαλογία τῶν Κομνηνῶν, 1:656–62, n. 93; Polemis, The Doukai, 86, n. 39.

[81] George Akropolites, History, 23, ed. Heisenberg, 1:36.18–37.25; Angold, Byzantine Government in Exile, 40–1.

[82] Barzos, Γενεαλογία τῶν Κομνηνῶν, 2:857–8, n. 190a; Zhavoronkov (tr.), George Akropolites, 200–1, n. 362. On the relation between John III Batatzes and Michael VIII and his wife Theodora Doukaina Palaiologina, see the tables in Zhavoronkov (tr.), George Akropolites, 349 (Table 5); Cheynet and Vannier, Études prosopographiques, 185–6. On the earlier Nestongoi, see Cheynet, 'Les Nestongoi', 599–607. See also Table 13.1 in this chapter.

[83] Manuelis Philes, Carmina, ed. Miller, 2:262.41–2: Σὺ γὰρ ἐκεῖνον εἷλες ἐκ τῆς Περσίδος, / Ἄγκιστρον ἐνθεὶς ὁρμιᾶς τεραστίων.

and the word ἄγκιστρον ('hook') in Philes, used by Christ himself in Matthew 17:27, was often interpreted in the apostolic teachings as a spiritual tool with which a human being was drawn out for a higher purpose, ultimately for their salvation.[84] In other words, when he was back in Byzantium after 1256, Constantine Doukas Nestongos did not return to his previous state of being 'Roman' (as indeed Michael Palaiologos did) – he emerged into a new life in Christ. Moreover, Constantine's servant, who later became the monk Dionysios, was not a Byzantine who followed Nestongos into exile – on the contrary, Constantine Doukas Nestongos 'was his master while in the Persian land,'[85] as if they met in Rūm for the first time. If Constantine Doukas Nestongos was a son of Andronikos Nestongos, he must have been born in, or brought at a young age to, Rūm, since he was younger than Michael Palaiologos. That is why Michael met him only when he himself was in Rūm in 1256.

There were other Nestongoi at the court of Theodore II; they are thought to have been descendants of either of the rebel brothers, Andronikos or Isaac Nestongos.[86] I do not think that Constantine Doukas Nestongos was a son of the blinded Isaac Nestongos, brother of Andronikos. If such were the case, Constantine Doukas Nestongos should have been born in Nicaea and later, like Michael Palaiologos, have run away from the ever suspicious Theodore II Laskaris just before 1256. However, the Nestongos family is reported to have been in favour of Theodore II during his short reign; a representative of the family, George Nestongos (Nostongos), who was in charge of the emperor's table (*epi tou kerasmatos*, i.e. *epi tēs trapezēs*), 'boasted about himself' in front of other members of the aristocracy, and especially against his cousin (αὐτανέψιος) Michael Palaiologos, the future emperor. George was so dear to Theodore II that despite his illustrious pedigree, which was potentially dangerous to the Laskarid dynasty, the emperor wanted to make him his son-in-law.[87] Other Nestongoi were George's brother Michael, whom Michael VIII made *protosebastos* in 1259;[88] Theodore Nestongos, the

---

[84] *Matthäeus-Kommentare*, ed. Reuss, 222–3, n. 212; Lampe (ed.), *Patristic Greek Lexicon*, 20 (s.v. ἄγκιστρον).

[85] Manuelis Philes, *Carmina*, ed. Miller, 2:262.54: ἐκεῖνον ἐν γῇ Περσικῇ σχὼν δεσπότην.

[86] See Zhavoronkov (tr.), *George Akropolites*, 259 and n. 760, 273 and n. 866.

[87] George Pachymeres, *History*, 1.21, 1.27, ed. Failler, 1:95.1–12, 107.10–22. Cf. Theodore Skoutariotes, *Additamenta*, ed. Heisenberg, 1:42, 293.10–17; Theodore Skoutariotes, *Chronicle*, ed. Sathas, 524.5–11; Macrides, *George Akropolites*, 303, n. 12, 325, n. 6; *PLP*, no. 20724.

[88] George Pachymeres, *History*, 2.13, 12.2, ed. Failler, 1:155.18–21 and 2:515.1–6; *PLP*, no. 20726.

defender of Melenikon (Melnik) in 1255;[89] and, finally, the *epi tēs trapezes* Isaac Nestongos, who surrendered Ohrid to Michael II of Epiros in 1257; only then did Theodore II suspect Isaac to have been a traitor.[90] But no Nestongos was sentenced to blinding or amputation under Theodore II; even Isaac might have survived and was later able to sign a document as a landowner near Smyrna in 1281.[91]

Andronikos Nestongos, who died in Rūm, was the first cousin of John III; he was therefore the great-uncle of Theodora (the wife of Michael VIII and granddaughter of John III's brother Isaac Doukas [see Table 13.1]). If Constantine Doukas Nestongos was Andronikos Nestongos' son,[92] this fact alone implies that he was also the uncle (θεῖος) of Empress Theodora and the great-uncle (also θεῖος in its broader sense)[93] of Andronikos II, son of Michael VIII and Theodora. However, this interpretation needs additional support, as the term θεῖος is not very precise: its chief meaning was, and still is, 'brother of the father or mother,'[94] but in Byzantine and modern Greek it can also refer to the cousin of the father or mother.[95] The Byzantine-Venetian treaty of 15 June 1285, which mentions the *parachimumeno magnesfendonis domino Constantino Duca Nestingo*, translates the θεῖος of the Greek original as *avunculus*. The term *avunculus* generally means 'uncle,' but while in classical Latin it referred to the mother's brother, in medieval Latin it could also mean 'father's brother' and, rarely, 'cousin.'[96] The 'great-uncle'

---

[89] George Akropolites, *History*, 9, ed. Heisenberg, 1:115.5–15; on the date, see ibid. 59, ed. Heisenberg, 1:119.24–5, Zhavoronkov (tr.), *George Akropolites*, 261, n. 776, Macrides, *George Akropolites*, 281–2, 294.

[90] George Akropolites, *History*, 68 and 72, ed. Heisenberg, 1:142.9–12, 151.1–15, Macrides, *George Akropolites*, 325, n. 6; *PLP*, no. 20200.

[91] *Acta et diplomata graeca*, ed. Miklosich and Müller, 4:123; *PLP*, no. 20199; Zhavoronkov (tr.), *George Akropolites*, 273, n. 866.

[92] So Kidonopoulos, *Bauten*, 64; Savvides, Βυζαντινά στασιαστικά καί αὐτονομιστικά κινήματα, 214–16.

[93] For θεῖος meaning 'great-uncle', see Blum's translation of Akropolites, *History*, 78, ed. Heisenberg, 1:162.19–22: Blum (tr.), *George Akropolites*, 177. See also Gómez, 'Théodôra Palaiologina Philanthrôpènè', 131; Chantraine, *Dictionnaire étymologique*, 2:426.

[94] Stephanus, *Thesaurus Graecae Linguae*, 5:276–7; LSJ, 788; Anthimos of Ghaza, Λεξικὸν τῆς ἑλληνικῆς γλώσσης, 2:43; Kriaras, Λεξικό, 7:94; Frisk, *Griechisches etymologisches Wörterbuch*, 1:658.

[95] Demetrakos, Μέγα λεξικόν, 7:3312.

[96] Glare, *Oxford Latin Dictionary*, 221; Niermeyer, *Mediae Latinitatis Lexicon Minus*, 75; Blaise, *Dictionnaire latin-français*, 87; Forcellini et al., *Lexicon totius latinitatis*, 1:418; Stephanus, *Dictionarium*, 1:81; Du Cange et al., *Glossarium*, 1:496; Diefenbach, *Supplementum*, 63; Latham, *Revised Medieval Latin Word-List*, 40; Ernout and Meillet, *Dictionnaire étymologique*, 109–10.

Table 13.1 The Nestongoi, Angeloi and Palaiologoi: Constantine Doukas Nestongos as 'uncle' (θεῖος) of Andronikos II.

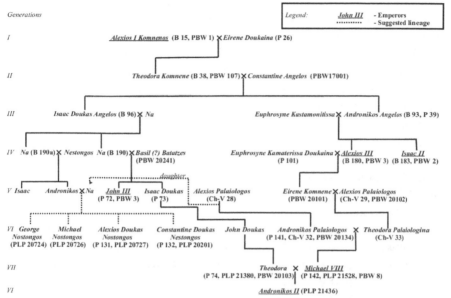

Abbreviations (other than those already mentioned): B (K. Barzos, Ἡ Γενεαλογία τῶν Κομνηνῶν, 2 vols (Thessaloniki, 1984)); Ch-V (J.-C. Cheynet, J.-V. Vannier, Études prosopographiques (Paris, 1986), chapter: "Les premiers Paléologues", pp. 168-187); P (D.I. Polemis, The Doukai. A Contribution to the Byzantine Prosopography (London, 1968))

was called *avunculus magnus* (or simply *avunculus*), the 'great-great-uncle' was *avunculus maior*; and the 'great-great-great-uncle' was *avunculus maximus*.[97] The Greek term for 'great-uncle' was usually πρόθειος.[98] The intersection between the meanings of θεῖος and *avunculus* reduces the list of possible connotations to either 'uncle' (brother of the father or mother) or 'great-uncle' (brother of the grandfather or grandmother). This thus suggests a close relation between Constantine Doukas Nestongos and the Palaiologos dynasty, though in the documents Constantine is never named Palaiologos, Komnenos or Angelos.

Indeed, the links between the Nestongoi and the Palaiologoi were very close. Of all the Nestongoi mentioned above, there were at least four who were relatives of Michael VIII Palaiologos. They were our Constantine Doukas Nestongos, θεῖος (*avunculus*) of Andronikos II; Alexios Doukas Nestongos (Nostongos), governor (*kephalē*) of Thessalonike in 1267 and ἐξάδελφος (first

[97] Glare, *Oxford Latin Dictionary*, 221.
[98] Chantraine, *Dictionnaire étymologique*, 2:426.

cousin) of Michael VIII; and, finally, George and Michael Nestongos (Nostongos), who, according to Pachymeres, were the αὐτανέψιοι of Michael VIII Palaiologos. Despite Pachymeres' tendency towards archaisation, his wording is precise: the term αὐτανέψιος means only 'first cousin' in his *History* as far as the Byzantine aristocracy is concerned.[99] It should be noted that Michael VIII's mother Theodora had no sister or brother;[100] this means that Michael VIII's aunt must have been an otherwise unknown sister of his father, the *megas domestikos* Andronikos Palaiologos (d. 1247), and that this aunt was the mother of George and Michael Nestongos. Given the fact that the chief meaning of θεῖος was 'uncle', and that Constantine Doukas Nestongos' father was most likely Andronikos Nestongos, one may suggest that all four Nestongoi (George, Michael, Alexios and Constantine) were brothers, the sons of the rebel Andronikos Nestongos. If Constantine was born in Rūm, then the aunt of Michael Palaiologos, the wife of Andronikos Nestongos, must have joined her husband in exile.

My chief concern has been to demonstrate the closest possible relationship between Constantine Doukas Nestongos and Michael VIII Palaiologos, but one can advance another interpretation: Constantine might have been Michael VIII's first cousin, and he was almost certainly a distant uncle of Theodora, Michael VIII's wife.

Thus, when he came to Rūm in 1256, Michael Palaiologos did not encounter a 'blind marsh, or Scythian cold, or waterless sands, full of wild beasts', as Theodore Metochites would later describe the Sultanate.[101] Indeed, he found himself in a Byzantine environment. The first noble person he met in the most difficult circumstances, after he was deprived of everything by the Turkmen nomads, was Constantine Doukas Nestongos, his first cousin (if one accepts Polemis' view) or the uncle of his wife Theodora (if one accepts Andronikos Nestongos as Constantine's father).

In Philes' poem, the difference between the images of Michael Palaiologos and Constantine Doukas Nestongos is profound. While Michael returned safely to Nicaea, his helper in Rūm, Constantine, after his own return to the Byzantine Empire, was described as if he was a convert, despite the fact

---

[99] George Pachymeres, *History*, 1.7, 1.21, 1.22, 2.13, 6.16, 6.25, 7.12, ed. Failler, 1:37.4, 95.7, 95.25, 155.20, 581.16, 621.27; 2:49.16; Failler, 'Pachymeriana quaedam', 187–91.

[100] Cheynet and Vannier, *Études prosopographiques*, 178–9, n. 33.

[101] Theodore Metochites, Βασιλικὸς δεύτερος, in MS Cod. Vindobon. Philol. Gr. 95, f. 154r; Theodore Metochites, Οἱ Δύο Βασιλικοὶ Λόγοι, ed. Polemis, 376.9–10. This is a citation from Plutarch, *Vitae parallelae*, i (Thes.1.1), 1.4–5; Metochites, Οἱ Δύο Βασιλικοὶ Λόγοι, ed. Polemis, 377, n. 259. See also Ševčenko, 'Decline of Byzantium', 178, n. 46.

that he represented just the first generation of his family in the Sultanate. Accordingly, Pachymeres, when mentioning the Basilikos brothers, the natives of Rhodes, friends of Michael VIII Palaiologos and the favourites of Kay-Kāwūs II,[102] refused to call them 'Romans', Byzantines. Besides Greek, they knew Arabic and Turkish. Only when they moved to Nicaea in 1260–1 and received the titles of *parakoimōmenos tou koitōnos* and *megas hetaireiarchēs*, respectively, did they get the chance to 'become Roman' (κατὰ ῾Ρωμαίους μετασχηματισθέντες).[103] Likewise, Michael VIII called his fellow Rūmī Greeks 'Persian enemies', thus denying their Byzantine identity, though the Cappadocian inscriptions show that these Greeks continued to commemorate the Byzantine emperors as their sovereigns.[104] Only Gregoras, himself a native of Heracleia Pontike, a remote Byzantine outpost surrounded by the Turks from the 1300s, noticed that the Rūmī Greeks were once 'Romans', thus implying that they were no longer Romans and that Byzantine manners and usages were alien to them. The Byzantine attitude had changed. What seemed to have been acceptable during the times of John Kinnamos and Niketas Choniates was no longer deemed suitable in the middle of the thirteenth century.

We are facing two paradoxes. The catastrophe of 1204, when the crusaders took Constantinople, had almost no repercussions in Asia Minor, save for the foundations of the empires of Trebizond and Nicaea. However, Nicaea, in her relations with the Sultanate of Rūm, inherited all the connections and diplomatic traditions that Byzantium had enjoyed before 1204. One can notice the same changes of loyalty between Nicaea and Rūm on the part of the members of the aristocratic elites after 1204.

The difference between Nicaea and Byzantium before 1204 was evident – while the empire of the Komnenoi and the Angeloi was multiethnic, Nicaea emerged as an almost entirely Greek state.[105] From the sixties of the thirteenth century, the border identity seems to have been no longer tolerated by the 'real' Byzantines who lived within the empire. This coincided with the reforms of Michael VIII Palaiologos that aimed at unification of the Byzantine eastern border.

---

[102] On them, see Shukurov, *Byzantine Turks*, 121–2, 242, 363.
[103] George Pachymeres, *History*, 2.24, 6.12, 6.24, ed. Failler, 1:183.1–19, 575.14–20, 615.11–21.
[104] Jolivet-Lévi, *Études Cappadociennes*, 289; Thierry and Thierry, *Nouvelles églises rupestres*, 202; Laurent, 'Note additionnelle', 367–71; Bees, *Inschriftaufzeichnung*, 7; Korobeinikov, 'Byzantine Emperors'.
[105] Ahrweiler, 'Expérience nicéenne', 21–40.

The second paradox was rooted in Michael VIII himself, as his self-consciousness bore evident traces of the border identity, which is why he felt so guilty for his flight to Rūm. It was he, then, who conducted the reforms that greatly reduced the independence of the people on the Byzantine side of the empire's eastern frontier in Asia Minor. The border identity as a historical phenomenon never ceased to exist, but the Byzantine aristocracy outside Byzantium in Asia Minor had almost disappeared as a powerful political stratum by the end of the thirteenth century.

Bibliography

Sources

Acta et diplomata ... F. Miklosich and I. Müller (eds), *Acta et diplomata graeca medii aevi*, 6 vols (Vienna, 1860–90).

Actes de Zographou, ed. W. Regel, E. Kurtz and B. Korablev, *Vizantiiskii Vremennik* 13 (1906): prilozheniie (repr. Amsterdam, 1969).

Aelius Herodianus Grammaticus, 'De prosodia catholica', in *Grammatici Graeci*, ed. A. Lentz, 3 vols (Leipzig, 1867–70; repr. Hildesheim, 1965), 3(1):3–547.

Aelius Herodianus Grammaticus, Περὶ παρωνύμων, in *Grammatici Graeci*, ed. A. Lentz, 3(2):849–97.

Annali genovesi di Caffaro e de' suoi continuatori dal MXCIX al MCCX-CIII, ed. C. Imperiale di S. Angelo, 5 vols (Rome, 1890–1929).

Βυζαντινὰ ἔγγραφα τῆς Μονῆς Πάτμου, ed. E. L. Branouse and M. Nystazo-poulou-Pelekidou, 2 vols (Athens 1980).

Chronicle of Morea ... P. P. Kalonaros (ed.), Τὸ Χρονικὸν τοῦ Μορέως (Athens, 1940).

Chronicle of Morea ... J. Schmitt (ed.), τὸ Χρονικὸν τοῦ Μορέως (London, 1904).

George (Gregory) of Cyprus, 'Oratio laudatoria in Imperatorem Dominum Michaelem Palaeologum', in J.-P. Migne (ed.), *Patrologiae cursus completus, series graeco-latina*, 161 vols (Paris, 1857–66), 142:col. 364.

George Akropolites, *History* ... A. Heisenberg (ed.), Georgii Acropolitae, *Opera*, 2 vols (Leipzig, 1903; repr. with corrections by P. Wirth, Stuttgart, 1978), vol. 1: R. Macrides (tr.), *George Akropolites, The History* (Oxford, 2007). Engl. tr. R. Macrides, *George Akropolites, The History* (Oxford, 2007).

George Pachymeres, *History* ... Albert Failler (ed.), *Georgius Pachymeres, Relations historiques*, 5 vols (Paris, 1984–2000).

Hesychius of Alexandria, *Lexicon* ... M. Schmidt (ed.), *Hesychii Alexandrini lexicon (P–W)*, (Halle, 1861–2; repr. Amsterdam, 1965).

Ibn Bībī, *Histoire des Seldjoucides d'Asie Mineure, d'après l'abrégé du Seldjouknämeh d'Ibn-Bībī: texte persan*, ed. M. T. Houtsma (*Recueil de textes relatifs à l'histoire des Seldjoucides* 4) (Leiden, 1902); tr. H. W. Duda, *Die Seltschukengeschichte des Ibn Bībī* (Copenhagen, 1959).

Kekaumenos, *Strategikon* ... G. G. Litavrin (ed. and tr.), *Kekavmen, Sovety i rasskazy* (St Petersburg, 2003). Engl. tr. C. Roueché, *Consilia et Narrationes* (SAWS, 2013). Available at <https://ancientwisdoms.ac.uk/library/kekaumenos-consilia-et-narrationes/> (last accessed 17 December 2021).

Kleinchroniken ... P. Schreiner (ed.), *Chonica minora*, CFHB 13, 3 vols (Vienna, 1975–9).

Lexica Segueriana: Collectio verborum utilium e differentibus rhetoribus et sapientibus multis (Συναγωγὴ λέξεων χρησίμων ἐκ διαφόρων σοφῶν τε καὶ ῥητόρων πολλῶν) (recensio aucta e cod. Coislin. 345), in *Anecdota Graeca*, ed. L. Bachmann, 2 vols (Leipzig, 1828).

Manuel Holobolos, *Orationes* ... M. Treu (ed.), *Programm des königlichen Viktoria-Gymnasiums zu Potsdam, 1906–1907*, 2 vols (Potsdam, 1906–7).

Manuelis Philae, *Carmina, ex codicibus Escurialensibus, Florentinis, Parisinis et Vaticanis*, ed. E. Miller, 2 vols (Paris, 1855–7).

Matthäeus-Kommentare aus der griechischen Kirche, ed. J. Reuss (Berlin, 1957).

Michael VIII Palaiologos, *Typikon* ... A. Dmitrievskii (ed.), *Τυπικὸν τῆς ἐν τῷ περιωνύμῳ βουνῷ τοῦ Αὐξεντίου κατὰ τὴν ἐπαρχίαν Χαλκηδόνος βασιλικῆς μονῆς τοῦ Ἀρχιστρατήγου Μιχαήλ, ἧς κτήτωρ ὁ βασιλεὺς Μιχαὴλ πρῶτος τῶν Παλαιολόγων*, in *Opisanie liturgicheskikh rukopisei, khraniaschikhsia v bibliotekakh pravoslavnogo Vostoka*, 2 vols (Kiev, 1895), 1: *Τυπικά*, Part 1: *Pamiatniki patriarshikh ustavov i ktitorskie monastyrskie tipikony*, pp. 769–94.

Michael VII Palaiologos, 'Imperatoris Michaelis Palaeologi de vita sua', ed. H. Grégoire, *Byz* 29–30 (1959–60): 447–76.

Nikephoros Gregoras, *History* ... L. Schopen and I. Bekker (eds.), *Nicephori Gregorae Byzantina Historia*, 3 vols (Bonn, 1829–55).

Photios, *Φωτίου τοῦ πατριάρχου λέξεων συναγωγή*, ed. R. Porson, 2 vols (Cambridge, 1822).

Plutarch, *Vitae Parallelae* ... K. Ziegler (ed.), *Plutarchi vitae parallelae*, vol. 1.1, 4th edn. (Leipzig, 1969).

Pseudo-Kodinos, *Traité des offices*, ed. J. Verpeaux (Paris, 1976).

Pseudo-Zonaras ... J. A. H. Tittmann (ed.), *Iohannis Zonarae lexicon ex tribus codicibus manuscriptis*, 2 vols (Leipzig, 1808; repr. Amsterdam, 1967).

Suidae Lexicon, ed. A. Adler, 5 vols (Leipzig, 1928–38).

Theodore Metochites, Οἱ Δύο Βασιλικοὶ Λόγοι, ed. I. Polemis (Athens, 2007).

Theodore Skoutariotes, *Additamenta ad Georgii Acropolitae Historiam*, in Georgii Acropolitae, *Opera*, ed. Heisenberg (rev. Wirth, 1978): 1:42, 277–302.

Theodore Skoutariotes, *Chronicle* ... K. N. Sathas (ed.), Μεσαιωνικὴ Βιβλιοθήκη, 7 vols (Venice, 1872–94), 7:1–556.

Urkunden zur Handels- und Staatsgeschichte ... G. L. F. Tafel and G. M. Thomas (eds), *Urkunden zur älteren Handels- und Staatsgeschichte der Republik Venedig*, 3 vols (Vienna, 1856–7).

Secondary Literature

Ahrweiler, H., 'L'expérience nicéenne', *DOP* 29 (1975): 21–40.

Ahrweiler, H., 'L'histoire et la géographie de la région de Smyrne entre les deux occupations turques (1081–1317), particulièrement au XIII siècle', *TM* 1 (1965): 1–204.

Angelov, D., *The Byzantine Hellene. The Life of Emperor Theodore Laskaris and Byzantium in the Thirteenth Century* (Cambridge, 2019).

Angold, M., *A Byzantine Government in Exile. Government and Society under the Laskarids of Nicaea* (Oxford, 1975).

Anthimos of Ghaza, Λεξικὸν τῆς ἑλληνικῆς γλώσσης, 3 vols (Vienna, 1835–7).

Barzos, K., Ἡ γενεαλογία τῶν Κομνηνῶν, 2 vols (Thessaloniki, 1984).

Bees, N., *Die Inschriftaufzeichnung des Kodex Sinaiticus graecus 508 (976) und die Marie Spiläotissa Klosterkirche bei Sille (Lykaonien) mit Exkursen zur Geschichte des Seldshukidentürken* (Berlin, 1922).

Blaise, A., *Dictionnaire latin-français des auteurs du Moyen-Age. Lexicon Latinitatis Medii Aevi: praesertim ad res ecclesiasticas investigandas pertinens* (Turnhout, 1975).

Blum, W. (tr.), *George Akropolites, Die Chronik* (Stuttgart, 1989).

Chantraine, P., *Dictionnaire étymologique de la langue grecque: histoire des mots*, 4 vols (Paris, 1968–77).

Cheynet, J.-C., 'Les Nestongoi, un exemple d'assimilation réussie', in J. C. Cheynet, *La société byzantine: L'apport des sceaux*, 2 vols (Paris, 2008), 2:599–607.

Cheynet, J.-C., and J.-V. Vannier, *Études prosopographiques* (Paris, 1986).

Demetrakos, D., Μέγα λεξικόν ὅλης τῆς ἑλληνικῆς γλώσσης, 15 vols (Athens, 1953).

Dennis, G. (tr.), '*Typikon* of Michael VIII Palaiologos for the Monastery of the Archangel Michael on Mount Auxentios near Chalcedon', in J. Thomas and A. C. Hero (eds) with assistance of G. Constable, *Byzantine Monastic Foundation Documents: A Complete Translation of the Surviving Founders' Typika and Testaments*, 5 vols (Washington, DC, 2000), 3:1207–36 (cited as Dennis 1).

Dennis, G. (tr.), '*Typikon* of Michael VIII Palaiologos for the Monastery of St. Demetrios of the Palaiologoi-Kellibara in Constantinople', in Thomas, Hero and Constable (eds), *Byzantine Monastic Foundation Documents*, 1237–53 (cited as Dennis 2).

Diefenbach, G. L. A., *Supplementum lexici mediae et infimae latinitatis* (Frankfurt am Main, 1857).

Dölger, F., *Regesten der Kaiserurkunden des oströmischen Reiches, 565–1453, 3. Teil* (with the assistance of P. Wirth): *Regesten von 1204–1282* (Munich, 1977).

Du Cange, C. D. F., et al., *Glossarium mediae et infimae latinitatis*, 10 vols (Niort, 1883–7).

Ernout, A., and A. Meillet, *Dictionnaire étymologique de la langue latine: histoire des mots* (Paris, 1951).

Failler, A., 'Chronologie et composition dans l'Histoire de Georges Pachymère' [part 1], *REB* 38 (1980): 5–103.

Failler, A., 'Pachymeriana quaedam', *REB* 40 (1982): 187–99.

Forcellini, E., et al., *Lexicon totius latinitatis*, 6 vols (Padua, 1864–1920; repr. Bonn, 1965).

Frisk, H., *Griechisches etymologisches Wörterbuch*, 3 vols (Heidelberg, 1960–72).

Geanakoplos, D. J., *Emperor Michael Palaeologus and the West, 1258–1282. A Study in Byzantine–Latin Relations* (Cambridge, MA, 1959).

Glare, P. G. W. (ed.), *Oxford Latin Dictionary* (Oxford, 1968).

Gómez, R. E., 'Théodôra Palaiologina Philanthrôpènè et son lignage du 13ᵉ au 15ᵉ siècle', *REB* 66 (2008): 125–72.

Guilland, R., 'Études sur l'histoire administrative de l'Empire byzantin: le parakimomène', *Études Byzantines* 2 (1944): 191–201; repr. in R. Guilland, *Recherches sur les institutions byzantines*, 2 vols (Berlin, 1967), 1:202–15.

Janin, R., *La géographie ecclésiastique de l'Empire byzantine, première partie: Le siège de Constantinople et le patriarchat oecuménique. Tome III: Les églises et les monastères* (Paris, 1969).

Jolivet-Lévi, C., *Études Cappadociennes* (London, 2002).

Karpov, S. P., *Istoriia Trapezundskoi imperii* (St Petersburg, 2007).

Kidonopoulos, V., *Bauten in Konstantinopel 1204–1328. Verfall und Zerstörung, Restaurierung, Umbau und Neubau von Profan- und Sakralbauten* (Wiesbaden, 1994).

Korobeinikov, D., *Byzantium and the Turks in the Thirteenth Century* (Oxford, 2014).

Korobeinikov, D., 'The Ilkhans in the Byzantine Sources' in T. May, B. Dashdondog and C. P. Atwood (eds), *New Approaches to Ilkhanid History* (Leiden, 2020), 385–424.

Korobeinikov, D., 'Byzantine Emperors and Sultans of Rūm: Sharing Power?' in S. Tougher (ed.), *The Emperor in the Byzantine World. Papers from the Forty-Seventh Spring Symposium of Byzantine Studies* (London and New York, 2019), 83–111.

Kriaras, E., et al., *Λεξικό τῆς μεσαιωνικῆς ἑλληνικῆς δημώδους γραμματείας, 1100–1669*, 21 vols (Thessaloniki, 1969–2019).

Lampe, G. W. H. (ed.), *A Patristic Greek Lexicon* (Oxford, 1961).

Latham, R. E., *Revised Medieval Latin Word-List from British and Irish Sources* (Oxford, 1965).

Laurent, V., *Les bulles métriques dans la Sigillographie byzantine* (Athens, 1932).

Laurent, V., 'Note additionnelle. L'inscription de l'église Saint-Georges de Bélisérama', *RÉB* 26 (1968): 367–71.

Likhachev, N. P., *Molivdovuly grecheskogo Vostoka* (Moscow, 1991).

Lock, P., *The Franks in the Aegean, 1204–1500* (London and New York, 1995).

Moravcsik, G., *Byzantinoturcica*, 2 vols (Berlin, 1958).

Niermeyer, J. F., *Mediae Latinitatis Lexicon Minus* (Leiden, 1976).

Papadopulos, A. T., *Versuch einer Genealogie der Palaiologen, 1259–1453* (Munich, 1938; repr. Amsterdam, 1962).

Pieralli, L., *La corrispondenza diplomatica dell'imperatore bizantino con le potenze estere nel tredicesimo secolo (1204–1282). Studio storicodiplomatistico ed edizione critica* (Vatican City, 2006).

Polemis, D. I., *The Doukai. A Contribution to Byzantine Prosopography* (London, 1968).

Prinzing, G., 'Ein Mann τυραννίδος ἄξιος. Zur Darstellung der rebellischen Vergangenheit Michels VIII. Palaiologos', in I. Vassis, G. S. Henrich and D. R. Reinsch (eds), *Lesarten. Festschrift für Athanasios Kambylis zum 70. Geburtstag* (Berlin and New York, 1998), 188–97.

Savvides, A. G. C., *Βυζαντινά στασιαστικά καί αὐτονομιστικά κινήματα στά Δωδεκάνησα καί στή Μικρά Ἀσία, 1189–c. 1240* (Athens, 1987).

Ševčenko, I., 'The Decline of Byzantium Seen through the Eyes of Its Intellectuals', *DOP* 15 (1961): 167–86.

Shukurov, R., *The Byzantine Turks, 1204–1461* (Leiden, 2016).

Siderides, X., ʿΜανουὴλ Ὀλοβώλου ἐγκώμιον εἰς τὸν αὐτοκράτορα Μιχαὴλ Η΄ τὸν Παλαιολόγον, *EEBS* 3 (1926): 168–91.

Sophocles, E. A., *Greek Lexicon of the Roman and Byzantine Periods (from b.c. 146 to a.d. 1100)* (Cambridge, 1914; repr. Hildesheim, Zürich and New York, 1992).

Stephanus (Estienne), H., *Thesaurus Graecae Linguae*, ed. C. B. Hase, G. Dindorf and L. Dindorf, 9 vols (Paris, 1831–65; repr. Graz, 1954).

Stephanus (Estienne), R., *Dictionarium, seu Latinae linguae thesaurusinterpretation*, 2 vols (Paris, 1536).

Talbot, A.-M., ʿEmpress Theodora Palaiologina, wife of Michael VIIIʾ, *DOP* 46 (1992): 295–303.

Thierry, N., and M. Thierry, *Nouvelles églises rupestres de Cappadoce. Région du Hasan Dağı* (Paris, 1963).

Zhavoronkov, P. I. (tr.), *George Akropolites, Istoriia* (St Petersburg, 2005).

14

The Coriander Field: Ideologies and Identities in Post-Roman Ravenna

Francesco Borri

In the middle of the ninth century, Adreas Agnellus wrote the history of Ravenna's bishops. This is a collection of biographies starting from the mythical Apolinaris and including George, who occupied Ravenna's see in Agnellus' days. The book is a kaleidoscope of marvellous stories which are, however, often difficult to interpret. Among them, we find the narrative of Ravenna's darkest hour – the Adriatic town's humiliation at the hands of a wicked emperor – and of the final victory of the Ravennates against their tormentors on the Coriander Field. This narrative has gone somewhat unnoticed and, being a story of battle and lay heroism, unlocks a suggestive hidden textual layer which partially escapes the master narrative of Agnellus' book. The account enables us to grasp a number of aspects regarding the troubled identity of the Ravennates in the decades preceding and following the fall of the exarchate in 751, along with the ideology that supported this identity. These are the years of Constantinople's loss of hegemony in the northern Adriatic and the transformation of Italian Romanness which triggered a profound identity crisis in Ravenna.[1] The narrative is staged in the first years of Emperor Justinian II's second bloody reign (705–11), when the conflict with the emperor escalated, something which made it into one of the most dramatic accounts of the entire *Book of Pontiffs of the Church of Ravenna*.[2]

An Odd Story for a Start

The whole incident has a loose chronology and is contextualised in the biographies of Felix, who was archbishop between 709 and 725, and his

---

[1] On Romanness, see Pohl et al. (eds), *Transformations of Romanness*.
[2] On the sequence, see Brown, 'Justinian II'; Haldon, *Byzantium in the Seventh Century*, 76–8.

successor John, who ruled until 744.[3] In the narrative, a number of citizens of Ravenna joined the imperial soldiers in the dethronement – by the mutilation of ears and nose and in aiding the exile – of an otherwise unknown emperor named Constantine. The incident closely resembles the dethronement of Emperor Justinian II, which occurred in 695 and was known to both the Patriarch Nikephoros and Theophanes the Confessor who wrote at the end of the eighth and the beginning of the ninth century, respectively.[4] Constantine, like Justinian II, was eventually able to regain the empire by viciously retaliating against his persecutors.[5] As the story goes, having punished the inhabitants of Constantinople, the wicked emperor turned his dark thoughts to Ravenna.[6] Writing at the end of the eighth century, Paul the Deacon reports that Justinian II, the model for Agnellus' Constantine, had a nose made of gold and that for every drop of nasal mucus, he had somebody killed.[7]

In Agnellus' book, Emperor Constantine ordered the kidnapping of Ravenna's high-ranking citizens. An officer called Monstraticus led the expedition, sailing to the northern Adriatic on a peculiar route through Sicily. Landing close to Ravenna, he set up his encampment on the banks of the River Po and sent envoys to the town, while spreading the news that the citizens were invited to visit his tent. Many queued in front of Monstraticus' pavilion, but once inside, the unlucky persons were subdued, tied up in pairs and thrown into the ship's hold. Once this was full, armed soldiers entered the town, harassing, killing and burning. After causing much grief, they sailed back to Constantinople, and night fell on Ravenna. In the tense hours that followed, the Ravennates realised the tragedy that had just occurred. Bishop Felix and Agnellus' ancestor Little John (*Iohanicis*), two of Ravenna's best, were among the captives sailing towards Constantinople.[8]

The author continues his narrative, drawing a skilful parallel between the two cities. On the one hand, we have the gory description of the torments endured by the men of Ravenna at the hands of the emperor and the terrible death of Little John, but not before he predicted the end of Justinian. On the other, we see the desperation of the Ravennates back home, stripped of their leader and spiritual guidance. Days after the abduction,

---

[3] Agnellus, *Liber pontificalis*, 136–53, ed. Deliyannis, 312–31.
[4] Theophanes, *Chronographia*, ed. de Boor, 566; Nikephoros, *Short History*, 40, ed. and tr. Mango, 96.
[5] Agnellus, *Liber pontificalis*, 137, ed. Deliyannis, 312.
[6] Ibid. 137, ed. Deliyannis, 312–13.
[7] Paul the Deacon, *Historia Langobardorum*, VI, 32, ed. Bethmann and Waitz, 175.
[8] Agnellus, *Liber pontificalis*, ed. Deliyannis, 137, ed. Deliyannis, 314–15.

having received the news of the deaths of many townsmen, the Ravennates gathered on the sandy beaches not far from town, in the wake of the
newly elected warlike and pious Duke George, son of Little John. Once
in Ravenna, the duke delivered a vibrant speech to the gathered crowd,
comparing the empire to a poisonous snake sinisterly rising from the Black
Sea. Afterwards, he foretold Ravenna's revival and enlisted the various
military forces of the town, splitting them into the late antique divisions
of the Roman army: *bandi*, with the flags preceding the marching troops,
and *numeri*.

George's speech is among the liveliest passages of the episode and,
together with bishop Gratiosus' prophecy, one of the most exciting sections
of the whole book.[9] The duke's words emphasise the importance of Roman
traditions for the self-representation of the Ravennates. At the same time,
they also depict the eastern Romans in utterly negative tones through the
use of eschatological metaphors. This tense dialectic between the imperial
heritage of Ravenna and hostility towards the empire dominates the entire
narrative.

The narrative continues to tell that the emperor was killed and bishop
Felix was permitted to return to Ravenna with honours and gifts meant to
compensate for the torments he had endured.[10] Here the story could have
found its fitting conclusion, but, instead, it escalates to a more climactic,
albeit somewhat unexpected, ending. In fact, we are informed that, at a later
point, Monstraticus returned with his troops to the mouth of the River Po to
meet the enemy in the *Campus Coriandri* – the Coriander Field – an open
space northeast of Ravenna where the 'Greek' army had taken position.[11]

After the beginning of the hostilities, the Italian soldiers deployed what
seemed to be a feigned flight by retreating to the *stadium tabulae* with the
intention of relining, counterattacking and routing the 'Greek' army.[12] As
soon as the soldiers of Ravenna charged their enemy, a giant bull appeared
on the field, raising dust with his hooves and blinding the enemies accompanied by a loud voice crying from the sky: 'Quick, men of Ravenna, victory will be yours today!'[13] The 'Greek' line broke and the defeated army

---

[9] On Gratiosus, see Agnellus, *Liber pontificalis*, ed. Deliyannis, 166, 343–8.

[10] Ibid. 142, ed. Deliyannis, 320–2.

[11] Ibid. 153, ed. Deliyannis, 330–1.

[12] The *stadium Tabulae* is mentioned also ibid. 22, ed. Deliyannis, 168–9.

[13] Ibid. 153, ed. Deliyannis, 331: 'Eia Rauennani, fortier pugnate! Victoria vestra erit
heude'. The mystical bull in ibid: 'apparuit inter utrosque exercitus quasi effigies
magni tauri et coepit cuntra Graecorum exercitum pedibus puluerum exspargere'.

ran to the ships for salvation, but were reached by the Ravennates in boats and other vessels. The local army won the day, slaughtering the 'Greeks' and throwing their corpses into the waters. The melee was so deadly that nobody dared to fish for one year in the stream where the massacre took place.[14] This battle was fought on 26 June, the day of Sts John and Paul, and the date became a local festivity that was celebrated on Agnellus' days.

This is an odd, puzzling story. As is often the case in Agnellus' book, the narrative structure and style seem incoherent to our taste, presenting the reader with some peculiarities. To begin with, the very topic of the story – a battle – is atypical. It is one of the very few descriptions of a melee in the Latin literature of the early Middle Ages, when readers and authors were apparently uninterested in military matters.[15] The narrative is even more anomalous in Agnellus' context, where warriors and military feats are generally condemned, as is the case with many early medieval histories.[16] Second, extensive sections of his account are epic in character, a further element that is uncommon in the rest of the *Book of Pontiffs of the Church of Ravenna*. And, finally, a secondary authorial will acting on an older story can be identified. This becomes especially manifest in some sections of the narrative such as in Little John's trial, where the emperor of Constantinople was, in fact, restored to his alleged identity of Justinian II.

Significantly, the whole account is so poorly attested that we may doubt its historicity. The first part seems to be a creative enrichment of the laconic witness of the *Liber pontificalis*, in which we read that the patrician Theodore, the leader of the army of Sicily ('primi exercitus Siciliae'), reached Ravenna with the fleet around the year 700, because of the town's hostilities against Rome.[17] There, Theodore seized the revenues of the church and

---

[14] Ibid. 153, ed. Deliyannis, 331: 'ut per annos .vi. ex Patereno nullus inde umquam piscem comederet'.

[15] Halsall, *Warfare and Society*, 1–6.

[16] Goffart, 'Conspicuously Absent'.

[17] *Liber pontificalis*, 90, ii, ed. Duchesne, I, 389: 'Mittens quippe Iustinianus imperator Theodorum patricium et primi exercitus Siciliae, cum classe Ravennam civitatem coepit, praefatum archiepiscopum arrogantem in navi vinctum tenuit, et omnes rebelles quos ibi repperit conpendibus strinxit, divitias eorum abstulit et Constantinopolim misit'. The odd journey of Monstraticus, who rounded Trapani, Sicily, before entering the Adriatic, echoes the Vergilian tradition on Aeneas' journey to Italy (*Aeneid* III, 707). This too seems to be a misplacement of the Sicilian origin of the commander. Could the 'primi ... Siciliae' have been misinterpreted, mistaking Theodore's dignity for a stopover in the journey? It is more certain that the colourful detail of the men being tied up two-by-two originated with the *Liber pontificalis*.

arrested and secured the arrogant bishop together with the other rebels, all of whom he chained with shackles before sailing back to Constantinople, where Felix was blinded and exiled to the Pontic regions ('exul in Pontica transmissus est regione'), as was customary. Towards the end of the biography, we read of the fall of Justinian and the bishop's return.[18] Yet, the *Liber pontificalis* does not hint at the battle that followed. Paul the Deacon, writing a generation before Agnellus and concluding his *History of the Lombards* with the death of King Liutprand in 744, did not record the clash, although he did narrate the misadventures of Justinian II and the first Lombard occupation of Ravenna of c. 740.[19] Similarly, Theophanes and Nikephoros, the above-mentioned chroniclers who also recorded Justinian's reign, are silent on this episode too. Because of this silence, the account of the battle seems to have relied on a local and, perhaps, fictional tradition. It was, nevertheless, an important account, useful in reconstructing the tormented identity of the Ravennates in the aftermath of the empire's withdrawal.

Epic Fragments

Almost a century ago, Nino Tamassia and Vincenzo Ussani proposed that the narrative concerning the conflict between the emperor and Ravenna was drawn from an epic poem centred on the years-long war between Ravenna and Constantinople which ended with the death of Justinian II.[20] The limits of this interpretation have been noted for many years.[21] Yet, almost three decades ago, Joaquín Martínez Pizarro validated the idea of these two scholars to some extent. He proposed that many of the narrative elements present in Agnellus' story were indeed fragments of an older story, epic in character.[22] He added that the nature of this epic had been partially misjudged by Tamassia and Ussani, proposing, instead, that the lost tale began with the expedition of Monstraticus, in chapter 137 of Deliyannis' (and, previously, Holder-Egger's) edition, and ended with the battle of the Coriander Field in chapter 153. Martínez Pizarro recognised elements that were consistent within these chapters and pointed out a difference with the

---

[18] *Liber pontificalis*, 90, ix, ed. Duchesne, I, 391.
[19] Paul the Deacon, *Historia Langobardorum*, VI, 31 and 54, ed. Bethmann and Waitz, 175, 183–4.
[20] Tamassia and Ussani, 'Epica e storia'.
[21] Fasoli, 'Rileggendo', 716.
[22] Martínez Pizarro, *Writing Ravenna*, 183–8.

rest of the book, such as the above-mentioned epic-style long sections of the narrative. Other stylistic differences were the flowery Vergilian language used to describe the waterscapes and landscapes, such as the 'glassy fields' ('uitrea rura') portraying the sea, and the usage of antiquated names for the men of Ravenna, who were called Melisenses, and the 'Greeks', who were instead named Pelasgians ('Pelasgi').[23] Above all, Martínez Pizarro highlighted Agnellus' major reworking of this narrative. Here, the author's principal concern was, in fact, to tell the story of his ancestor Little John – as mentioned earlier, it is while narrating his dramatic trial in Constantinople that the emperor's name is restored to Justinian – as well as to offer a biography of Archbishop Felix – whose role in the epic tale must remain a matter of opinion – rather than the epic itself. While doing this, he must have handled a tale whose chronology was perhaps loose enough to be framed in a chain of biographies, incorporating it with further stories and details such as the actions of Little John or the catalogue of the gifts granted by Emperor Philippikos to Felix.[24]

I also believe that the narrative section of Agnellus' book, which tells the whole story culminating at the Coriander Field, stems from a lost narrative, epic in character, which remains unknown to us. In order to access the hidden narrative that emerges at a textual level in the *Book of Pontiffs of the Church of Ravenna*, it is necessary to focus on the anomalies in Agnellus' story, which may well be clues to a lost context.

To begin with, the figure of George constitutes the most evident anomaly. He is handsome and skilled, showing the makings of a leader, and was the first local ruler raised by the Ravennates themselves. Coming to town at its most tragic moment, he electrified his audience with his powerful words and majestic gestures. In a long speech, Homeric in style, he enlisted the armed forces from both Ravenna and its surroundings, inciting his companions to a just fight against the evil empire.[25] It is a very successful literary piece that leads us to picture the men gathering from the flat shores and swampy plains as well as the pre-Apennine hills and see them converge at the waterways in order to patrol them for the danger approaching from the sea. Yet, George's role appears to be somehow mutilated. After this highly promising entrance, he disappears completely from the book, and the reader is left to wonder about his destiny and role in the events that followed.

---

[23] Martínez Pizarro, *Writing Ravenna*, 184–5, lists these elements.
[24] Agnellus, *Liber pontificalis*, 143, ed. Deliyannis, 322.
[25] Tamassia and Ussani, 'Epica e storia', 13.

George's perfect antagonist would have been Monstraticus. This peculiar name is used in chapters 137 and 153 and is the most evident clue for the unity of the textual section singled out by Martínez Pizarro. That chapter 153 was originally the climactic ending of Agnellus' source becomes manifest in the opening line, where we read that Monstraticus returned ('uenit iterum') to Ravenna, believing himself to be as successful as he had been before ('putante, se ut antea euaderet').[26] For decades it has been clear that Monstraticus is not a name, but a dignity, and most probably a corrupted form of *monostratēgos*.[27] It remains an open question whether, in the Latin version of the narrative, the name could have been a reference to *monstrum*, meaning an unnatural thing or portent, or *monstrare*, pointing out the striking gathering of numerous soldiers.

This epic and eschatological language and the use of these archaic names to describe the two armies was perhaps intended to extol their attributes. We know that antiquated, sometimes barely understandable, ethnonyms were a characteristic of panegyrics, texts read in public to praise powerful rulers and aristocrats. A famous example are the Franks, associated with the Sicambrians of the past.[28] Of the two names we find in Agnellus' book, 'Pelasgians' is the less problematic. According to ancient Greek authors, Pelasgians were their forerunners in the Aegean, and they have been associated with the Etruscans and other non-Hellenic populations in Italy. The Pelasgian tradition was alive in ancient Ravenna, so the inhabitants of the early medieval town may have been acquainted with the label.[29] In the given context, the name seems to have been an archaic and possibly derogatory synonym for eastern Romans.

The name 'Melisenses', on the other hand, is a riddle. With the partial exception of the *Melisenses Urbis* in Martin's biography, the name is found only in this account of the confrontation with the 'Greeks'.[30] It is not attested elsewhere, and it may have been antiquated already in Agnellus' day. On one occasion, the author commented on 'Melisenses id est Ravenniani cives', offering a possible explanation of the obscure name to his audience.[31] If the

---

[26] Agnellus, *Liber pontificalis*, 153, ed. Deliyannis, 331.
[27] Holder-Egger, 'Glossarium', 635; Tamassia and Ussani, 'Epica e storia', 26; Lazard, 'Origine des hellénismes', 286.
[28] Reimitz, *History*, 90; Gerbending, *Rise of the Carolingians*, 20–2.
[29] Briquel, *Les Pélasges*, 31–53.
[30] Agnellus, *Liber pontificalis*, 167, ed. Deliyannis, 348.
[31] Ibid. 153, ed. Deliyannis, 331; 139, ed. Deliyannis, 316: *Rauennenses qui est Melisenses*. See Tamassia and Ussani, 'Epica e storia', 17. In the Catalogo Santi Muratori of Classe archive (http://www.classense.ra.it/, accessed 18 October 2016), two archivists have

name was hardly intelligible in the ninth century, it is even more trouble-
some for us to find its meaning today. Any tentative answer to this question
is lost in the meanders of historiography, and the suggestions listed here by
no means claim comprehensiveness. Tamassia and Ussani have proposed an
association with bees, stemming from the Greek noun μέλισσα, translating
Melisenses as 'those from bees' ('quelli delle api').[32] The two authors record
a lyric passage of the book *Della geografia trasportata al morale*, written
by the seventeenth-century Jesuit historian Daniello Bartoli (1608–85). In a
wonderfully evocative passage, the author records the habits of the inhabitants of Ostiglia, who travelled up the River Po in flat boats loaded with hives.
During their long breaks they let the bees graze the flower fields on the
banks of the river in order to return home with a load of honey and wax.[33]
This narrative was written with some chronological distance from Agnellus'
times. However, bees could have been a symbol of kingship and authority,
such as the description of a bee flying to the heavens from the head of King
Wamba (672–80) recorded by Julian of Toledo at the end of the seventh century.[34] This may have been because the bellicose nature of the flying insect
was already chronicled by Vergil, whose *Georgics* (IV 67–87) feature a long
description of the bees and record their warlike attitude. Paul the Deacon
also knew the passage.[35] It must have been due to Vergil's authority that, in
the seventh century, Isidore of Seville narrated a story about the armies and
king of these peculiar creatures.[36]

---

left information on index cards. The oldest reported interpretation of Montanari,
'Sunto', 118, which read *Melisenses* as a corrupted form of *Aemilianeses*, is descriptive
of Ravenna's inland allies from Emilia. The second, much more charming but even
less convincing, reports the idea of A. Zaccarini, published in *Il Nuovo Ravennate*
28 (1989): 25 (which I could not access), according to whom Melisenses was a name
describing the *glauco-melati* eyes of the Ravennates, a colour that is also difficult to
for Italian native speakers, perhaps something like 'shining honey'.

[32] Tamassia and Ussani, 'Epica e storia', 27–8, n. 1.

[33] Bartoli, *Geografia trasportata*, 1–2.

[34] Julian of Toledo, *Historia Wambae regis*, 4, ed. Levison, 504: 'Nam mox e vertice
ipso, ubi oleum ipsum perfusum fuerat, evaporatio quaedam fumo similis in modum
columnae sese erexit in capite, et e loco ipso capitis apis visa est prosilisse, quod
utique signum cuiusdam felicitatis sequuturae speciem portenderet'. On this passage, see Martínez Pizarro, *Writing Ravenna*, 184; Collins, 'Julian of Toledo', 46–8.

[35] Paul the Deacon, *Historia Langobardorum* IV, 37, ed. Bethmann and Waitz, 130:
'ingentes animos angusto in pectore versans' (quoting *Georgica* IV, 83).

[36] Isidore of Seville, *Etymologies*, XII, 8, ed. Lindsay, II, n.p.: 'exercitum et reges habent,
proelia movent'. See Goulon, 'Quelques aspects'; Gillet, 'Goths and Bees', 159–62.

Évelyne Patlagean, instead, noted a similarity between the Melisenses of Agnellus and the Μίληντος quarter of Augustopolis mentioned in the Greek *Life of St Gregentios*, the archbishop of Taphar.[37] Albrecht Berger, the latest editor of the *bios*, suggested that the name Melisenses is connected to another place name among the many listed in the *Life of St Gregentios*. According to Berger, the Μελικὴ πόλις, in which Gregentios' friend Leon eventually became ruler, should be identified with Ravenna.[38] And, indeed, it seems that the name Melisenses may have been meant to recall the city's deeper past. Many decades ago, in an almost forgotten book, G. P. Berti thought that the name Melite or Melitea was the original, and eventually lost, name of Ravenna.[39] Similar names are actually attested around Ravenna in modern cartography; these may have been, however, dependent on Agnellus' witness.[40] We know that in the aforementioned life of Gregentios, the city of Padua is called Ἀντηνόρα, because of the mythical Trojan hero Antenor, the legendary founder of the city. It could be possible that, as in the case of Padua, the name Melisenses similarly echoes a mythical founder. We know of a certain Melissos, the legendary king of Crete, but any relationship between Crete and Ravenna is missing here.[41] More suggestive is that in the *Patria of Constantinople*, a narrative possibly dating to the tenth century, we read of the mythical Μελίας, king of Thrace in the days of Byzas, the first founder of Byzantium.[42]

Therefore, the odd name may have echoed one of an ancient and forgotten hero, the richness of Italy or the bright or warlike nature of the Ravennates, or even something irreparably lost to us due to our limited knowledge of the oldest history of Ravenna.[43] With more certainty, it can be stated that the peculiar naming aimed at recalling the ancient, pre-Roman past of the city, as did the name 'Pelasgian'.

These two obscure names fitted the epic narrative of the clash at the *Campus Coriandri*. The Coriander Field was an open area close to a fluvial

---

[37] *Life and Works of St Gregentios*, 7, ed. Berger, 132. See Patlagean, 'Moines grecs', 586. A centre called Augustopolis between Aquileia and Istria can be found in George of Cyprus, *Descriptio orbis Romanis*, ed. Gelzer, 31.617.

[38] *Life and Works of St Gregentios*, 3, ed. Berger, 264.

[39] Berti, *Ravenna*, 88–113.

[40] Fabbi, 'Ravenna romana', 129. Filippo Borgatti records the *Portus Leonis seu Pyrotolo*, in the region of the Gauls, *Aegones seu Melisenses*: Borgatti, *Agro ferrarese*.

[41] See also Orioli, 'Passio sancti Apolinaris', 19.

[42] *Patria of Constantinople*, ed. and tr. Berger, 6–7.

[43] Deliyannis, *Ravenna*, 21–4; Magnani, 'Percorsi mitici'; Morpurgo, 'Ravenna'.

harbour granting access to the River Po and the Adriatic.[44] It was an arena well suited for a great battle against the 'Greeks', who would have approached by sea. Agnellus' audience was apparently well acquainted with the place, since we read in the book that the Church of St Eusebius was built not far from the field, so that the place was a part of the everyday landscape.[45] Also, locations like the *stadium tabulae*, which was the stage of a given episode of the battle, may have been extant physical places. It is possible, therefore, that by the time Agnellus wrote his work, the battle had entered the Ravennates' social memory.

Although the narrative culminates with the combat, the military details provided by its source seem to have been rather poor.[46] The conflict is mostly depicted as a just war, and with the loud cry announcing the victory of the Ravennates we begin to uncover the deeper meaning of the short narrative. The battle cry from the sky was an omen of victory according to an old and trusted epic trope.[47] In the story, moreover, we read that all the Ravennates fought with the typical weapons appropriate for each age: the young used actual tools of war, while the old fought with prayers instead. The idea of a battle fought on two levels, terrestrial and celestial, was at the very core of Christian ideology and gained additional strength in the age of Charlemagne.[48]

In the following lines we reach the climactic end of the battle, with the Ravennates pursuing the routed Byzantines in the waters. At first glance, the tragic detail could seem just like a straightforward account of a battle close to a waterway in which the losing side, the enemy, tragically looks to

---

[44] Agnellus, *Liber pontificalis*, 153, ed. Deliyannis, 331. See Calzolari, 'Delta padano', 164; Novara, 'Edifici teoderciani', 47.

[45] Agnellus, *Liber pontificalis*, 86, ed. Deliyannis, 253. On the church, see Deliyannis, *Ravenna*, 144.

[46] The Ravennates won the battle thanks to a feigned flight, which consisted of a faked rout performed by cavalry forces aiming to lure the enemy into pursuit (Halsall, *War-fare and Society*, 189–90). The flying forces lined up again in another place in order to charge the now open lines of the enemies and rout them. Like the encirclement of Hannibal and Aetius, it was one of the basic principles of military culture and an old and trusted *topos* of ancient literature. Readers acquainted with ancient literature may have encountered this old tactic.

[47] The closest association I found is *Chronicle of Fredegar*, III, 65, ed. Krusch, 110. The God of Hosts normally spoke through his prophets, avoiding such bombastic perfor-mances. Yet, Old Testament associations may have been there, and a passage from the book of Isaiah describes the Lord as a warrior ('sicut vir proeliator') shouting above his enemies ('vociferabitur et conclamabit'): Is. 42, 13; see also Mt. 3, 17.

[48] Alberi, 'Army of God's Camp'.

the ships for salvation. Moreover, we know that the fiercest moment of an ancient or medieval battle was the pursuit, where men desperately resisted their enemies with weapons and hoped to find salvation in a hasty retreat.[49] Agnellus' account seems coherent with both these assumptions.

Yet, behind this apparent simplicity lies a much more complex narrative. To begin with, the image of 'Greeks' running to their ships was a recognisable episode of the Trojan War, magnificently told in book XII of the *Iliad*. In the story, Hector, favoured by the god Apollo, led the outnumbered Trojans through the enemy lines, storming their camp and forcing them to their vessels. It was only the determination of Ajax that prevented the Achaeans from sailing back to Greece.[50] However, the 'Greeks' in Agnellus' narrative had no Ajax among them, and, unable to put up a fight on the shores of the River Po, ended up dying tragically in the waters. The narrative reflects, again, the difficult position of the Ravennates, caught between their imperial heritage and their antagonism towards Constantinople. The inability of the 'Greeks' to fight was indeed a classic Roman trope and a crucial element in the construction of their stereotypes.[51]

Also, a drowned army was a strong trigger for the narrative's audience. It had powerful associations with the Christian discourse of the early Middle Ages. At around the time of Agnellus, Paul the Deacon recounted how the army of the tyrant Alahis ended their lives at the bottom of the Adda River.[52] Almost three centuries earlier, the army of Eugenius drowned in the Frigidus River in the battle that was fought in the area in 394, and the troops of Maxentius submitted to the River Tiber at the mournful end of the battle at the Milvian Bridge.[53] All these succumbing armies were perceived as the legions of Satan, menacing the Christian Empire of Constantine and Theodosios (or the pious kingdom of Cunicpert). The matrix for all the stories can be found much deeper in history, in the most influential narrative of the Middle Ages, the biblical Book of Exodus, where the Pharaoh's army drowned in the waves of the Red Sea while pursuing the people of Israel (Ex. 14:28). The episode of

---

[49] Halsall, *Warfare and Society*, 111.

[50] On the early medieval reception of the narrative centred on Troy, see Wolff, *Troja*, 63–5.

[51] Sidebottom, *Ancient Warfare*, 12. See also, Baldeson, *Romans*, 30–58.

[52] Paul the Deacon, *Historia Langobardorum*, V, 41, ed. Bethmann and Waitz, 160.

[53] On the Battle of the Frigidus see Springer, 'Schlacht am Frigidus'; on that of the Milvian Bridge, see Kuhoff, 'Schlacht an der Milvischen Brücke', as well as the monograph by Van Dam, *Remembering Constantine*.

the 'Greeks' feeding the fish of the Po River could hardly have been based on a witness's account of the battle, but rather described the soldiers of Constantinople, that is, of the legitimate Roman Empire, as a heathen army attacking Christian Ravenna, a point of no return in the relationships between Ravenna and Constantinople.

The dramatic clash may have concluded the epic tale, and after this we meet no further clues to this story in Agnellus' book. Surmising a little, we could reconstruct the story as follows. First, Monstraticus is sent by the emperor to punish Ravenna, and then, in the aftermath, the surviving Ravennates make Duke George their leader, announcing the war against Constantinople and the recovery of the Adriatic city. Following this, for reasons unknown to us – perhaps, George's election was a provocation or an act of defiance? – Monstraticus returned with the army to be soundly crushed at the Coriander Field. And, finally, the battle ends with a victory representing the empire's final defeat and is celebrated until Agnellus' days.

Being a Ravennate after Rome

This fragmentary narrative, with its local perception of imperial authority and the conflict of the Ravennates against it, is revealing of a transient political situation. The story may have been composed between the reign of Justinian II and Agnellus' days. These were, in fact, tense and dramatic years, which saw the withdrawal of the empire from northern Italy and the Carolingian takeover of the Lombard kingdom together with Romania. It was also a time that saw the disbandment of the imperial army in Italy and the final demise of the Roman identity in vast regions of the peninsula, which, up to the eighth century, was still embraced by the officers and gentlemen of imperial Italy.[54] Having captured Ravenna, King Aistulf prided himself on having divinely obtained the rule over the Roman people.[55] Still, Paul the Deacon described the *Romani*, the subjects of the empire mostly linked to service in the army, as the antagonists of the Lombards and their kings up to the eighth century. In a curious passage he similarly referred to the 'Romans of Ravenna'.[56]

With the disappearance of the empire from northern Italy, any form of Roman identity became difficult outside Rome. This was destined to become

---

[54] Brown, *Gentlemen and Officers*. See also Halsall, *Warfare and Society*, 44–5.
[55] *Leges Ahistulfi*, ed. Beyerle, 194: *traditum nobis a Domino populm Romanorum*.
[56] Paul the Deacon, *Historia Langobardorum*, IV, 35, ed. Bethmann and Waitz, 135: *cum Ravennatibus Romanis*.

a major issue in Italy in the centuries to come.[57] In a city like Ravenna, an imperial capital with obscure roots beyond its Roman past, these transformations may have triggered a profound identity crisis. In this specific context, the lost epic could be understood as a search for new sources of legitimisation outside the Roman Empire which could reinvent the town's roots.[58] As I have suggested above, the name Melisenses could be read in these terms. And, as we have seen, this peculiar name opposed the Pelasgian one, which is a highly characteristic definition for the eastern Romans, and occurred elsewhere only in the so-called seventeenth book of Paul's *Roman History*. The *Roman History* is a series of sixteen books which Paul completed before writing the *History of the Lombards*. It runs from the foundations of the city up to the reign of Justinian.[59] The seventeenth book is instead an anonymous and later collection of accounts stemming from the *History of the Lombards* which deals with the history of the empire and continues the *Roman History* up to the eighth century. Introducing his work, the compiler interpolated Paul's fragments with the only original section of the whole book: 'thus as it has been described, when the empire of the Romans had already ceased among the Italians (*Itali*) and many people were raging against them, the empire passed into Pelasgian rule (*ius*)'.[60] In the days of the compiler, the Roman Empire had abandoned Italy, becoming Pelasgian.

The seventeenth book was probably composed in northern Italy at the beginning of the ninth century. Maya Maskarinec has suggestively argued that the text delegitimised Romanness as a source of political authority.[61] In fact, while recording the history of the Romans in the seventh and eighth centuries, the anonymous compiler depicted a gloomy spiral of failure to narrate the long agony which, from his historical perspective, represented the history of the empire in the first centuries of the Middle Ages. The compiler had an eastern conception of empire and carefully avoided reporting Paul's passages dealing with the Romans of imperial Italy scattered in the *History of the Lombards*. Even more revealing is that, once faced with the necessity of including passages mentioning these Romans,

---

[57] Giardina, *Italia Romana*, 3–116.
[58] Paul the Deacon, *Historia Romana*, XVII, 1–53, ed. Crivellucci, 239–68. On the narrative, see Maskarinec, 'Who Were the Romans?' 336–54.
[59] Cornford, 'Paul the Deacon's Understanding'.
[60] Paul the Deacon, *Historia Romana*, XVII, 1, ed. Crivellucci, 239: 'Quum iam, ut premissum est, Romanorum desineret apud Italos imperium plurimeque gentes irruerent contra ipsos ad iusque pertransierat Pelasgum'.
[61] Maskarinec, 'Who Were the Romans?' 350.

he used pronouns in order to avoid mentioning them in reference to the inhabitants of the peninsula. Thanks to a highly selective approach to history, the compiler aimed to deprive the Italian subjects of Constantinople, and the Ravennates among them, of their Romanness. In the introduction, which I have just quoted in full, the inhabitants of Roman Italy were called 'Italians' (*Itali*), a rather unusual label poorly evidenced among ancient authors.[62] However, this odd label could help make sense of Agnellus' reference and description of the raging bull among the armies.

The narrative element of the bull appearing on the battlefield is peculiar. In the *Book of Pontiffs of the Church of Ravenna* it is an isolated narrative element, and by the time Agnellus was writing, it had apparently lost its meaning. That supernatural entities could lead armies to victory was an old and beloved trope in the Mediterranean world. In antiquity there are abundant examples of the Dioscuri, who often granted triumphs to the Greek and Roman armies.[63] This idea survived in the Christian Empire, as the already mentioned Battle of the Frigidus may show, as well as in post-Roman Europe.[64] Around the time of Agnellus, this idea was still vividly present in Italy. Paul the Deacon, at the end of the eighth century, narrates that in the Battle of Camerino the blessed Sabinus was seen leading the Lombard army against the Romans.[65] Yet Sabinus, the other military saints and the Dioscuri were all young and handsome men riding white horses: figures syncretising Christian and military values and identity.

The image of the bull, notwithstanding the possible associations with strength and masculinity, goes further back in history than this particular interpretative matrix. Writing in the first century BC, Varro reported that the name of Italy grew alongside and in association with the image of a bull (*taurus*) or calf (*vitulus*). According to one story, the incoming Greeks, impressed by the majesty of local cattle, named the peninsula *Italia*, which meant 'land of the bulls'.[66] Columella recalled Varro's etymology.[67] More revealing is that Festus, writing in the second century AD, also quotes Varro, and the entry survives in Paul the Deacon's summary of the original, compiled at the end

---

[62] Giardina, *Italia Romana*, 117–38.
[63] Cracco Ruggini, 'Simboli di battaglia', 265–72; Pritchett, *Greek State at War*, 11–46.
[64] Cameron, *Last Pagans*, 103–4.
[65] Paul the Deacon, *Historia Langobardorum*, IV, 16, ed. Bethmann and Waitz, 121–2.
[66] Varro, *Res rusticae*, II, 5, iii: 'tauros uocabat italos'; Varro, *De lingua latina*, V, 19, xcvi: 'uitulus, quod graece antiquitus ἰταλός, aut quod plerique uegeti, uegitulus'.
[67] Columella, *Res rusticae*, VI, praef.: 'quod olim Graeci tauros italos vocabant'. See Josephson, *Columella-Handschriften*.

of the eighth century.[68] He also records the story in his *History of the Lombards*.[69] Therefore, it seems that an association between Italy and the bull was well known when Agnellus' source was writing. Moreover, the mentions of the *Itali*, the Pelasgians and the *taurus* leading an army to victory in contiguous contexts suggest that, between the eighth and the ninth centuries, the bull could have become a symbol of identity not only for the Italians who had been left without their Romanness but, above all, for the Ravennates.

A further association bears mentioning. We know that on at least one occasion the bull became the antagonist of Rome. On a silver coin minted during the closing months of the Social War in the first century BC, a wolf was pictured being trampled by a massive bull standing above him. The inscription, in the Oscan language, is *VITELIU*, meaning 'the bull', and recalls the ancient name of Italy.[70] No author narrating the tense years of the Social War describes the issue and, apart from the coin, there appears to be no other link between the Italian League and the bull. Emma Dench has proposed that the bull was meant as a symbol for the Italian people fighting Rome, but her idea has not been universally accepted.[71]

We do not know if Agnellus' source had seen the coin, but we know that ancient coinage was widely circulated for a long time. Ermanno Arslan has shown how, during the reign of Theodoric, the old iconographies of the she-wolf and the eagle, for centuries dismissed from imperial coinage, were minted again.[72] This means that some coins were kept for centuries, and men living many generations later were still acquainted with old iconographic models. Moreover, some Carolingian productions from the second decade of the ninth century also imitated Roman analogues in order to depict Charlemagne as a Roman emperor, with models possibly based on Gordianus III, Diocletian or Constantine, rulers whose coins had been minted many centuries before. This suggests that a rich variety of ancient

---

[68] Festus, *De verborum significatu*, ed. Lindsay, 94: 'Italia dicta, quod magnos italos, hoc est boves, habeat. Vituli etenim ab Italis sunt dicti'.

[69] Paul the Deacon, *Historia Langobardorum*, II, 24, ed. Bethmann and Waitz, 86: 'Sive ob hoc Italia dicitur, quia magni in ea boves, hoc est itali, habentur'.

[70] The coin was mentioned in Campana, *Monetazione degli insorti*, 50–1. Moreover, Burnett, 'Coinage of the Social War'. On the political background, see Dart, *Social War*, 130–1. On the iconography of the wolf, see Mazzoni, *She-Wolf*.

[71] Dench, *From Barbarians*, 212–17; 'Sacred Springs', 48–9. See also Pobjoy, 'First Italia', 201–2. Different views, together with a discussion of the literature just cited, can be found in Tataranni, 'Toro, lupa e guerriero', where the bull is instead interpreted as a symbol of the Samnites only.

[72] Arslan, 'Struttura delle emissioni monetarie'.

iconographic models was available to the post-Roman die cutters.[73] Finally, we know that many early medieval women and men considered ancient Roman coins as sources of prestigious iconographies, sometimes bearing the power of charms and talismans, with their age being proportional to their power.[74] That, in the epic author's mind, the raging bull at the Coriander Field was an antagonist to the wolf of Rome or New Rome must remain suggestive speculation, but it seems very probable that, stripped of their Romanness, the Ravennates had to find their identity from a deeper place in history in which an Italian identity may have acquired significance.

Conclusion: Fighting the Crisis

In chapters 137 to 153 of Agnellus' *Book of Pontiffs of the Church of Ravenna*, we find a story which, in the context of the book, makes sense only to some extent. Here, Agnellus actually attributed to the battle and its preambles some importance, making it a sort of narrative watershed.[75]

The story is what survives of an older narrative, epic in character and focused on a showdown between Ravenna and Constantinople, the meaning of which may have been mostly lost by the middle of the ninth century. This forgotten epic was told against the backdrop of the waning of the empire, the crumbling of Italian Romanness and the increasing tension with Constantinople. This lost tale was thrilling and full of biblical and classical images, and was viciously abusive against the eastern Romans. Its protagonists were given archaic names meant to recall a forgotten past. I have suggested that it was a story narrated to avenge the town's frustrated honour during the reign of Justinian II and that it explains the subsequent decline of the empire which, from contemporary sources, seems to have been an obscure and surely not ostentatious event. In my opinion, it is very significant in order to comprehend the troubled identity of its inhabitants during these difficult years.

From the fragments we get a glimpse of the anxious relationship with the empire in the decades around Constantinople's withdrawal in 751. On the one hand, the idea of empire was paramount in the town, as we have

---

[73] Garipzanov, *Symbolic Language*, 211–13, with references.

[74] Maguire, 'Magic and Money'.

[75] After the narrative on the battle, the empire moved from Constantinople to Aachen. We find no comment on the Byzantine withdrawal, the Lombard conquest of Ravenna or the following Frankish takeover of the city. In the pages of Agnellus' book, the Frankish emperors silently substitute the 'Greek' ones.

seen from George's catalogue of the armed forces of Ravenna and its surroundings. On the other, however, this imperial idea needed to be delivered from the lumbering presence of Constantinople and the burden of ancient Rome. In post-Roman Ravenna, complex intellectual acrobatics were developed in order to overcome this identity crisis. We can see how boundaries were skilfully shifted in order to represent the Ravennates, who had to turn to the Italian bull, an old myth on the peninsula, as a symbol of identity.

The story was apparently repeated in order to avenge the humiliation that Ravenna had endured at the hands of Emperor Justinian II, by describing a triumphant city rising proudly defiant and able to mercilessly crush its former masters. Nonetheless, dark clouds gathered over the Coriander Field, and the account, far from recording a triumph, actually highlights how frail Ravenna's position was when facing the loss of empire and reflects the awe that Constantinople still inspired at the time.

Acknowledgements

Research for the current article was made possible thanks to the funding of the FWF Project 24823: The Transformation of Roman Dalmatia. I would like to thank Richard Corradini, Andreas Fischer, Stefano Gasparri, Cinzia Grifoni, Walter Pohl, Helmut Reimitz, Alessia Rovelli, Francesca Tataranni, Katharina Winckler and Veronika Wieser for their help and valuable suggestions.

Bibliography

Sources

Patria of Constantinople ... A Berger (ed. and tr.), *Accounts of Medieval Constantinople: The Patria* (Cambridge, MA and London, 2013).

Agnellus, *Liber pontificalis* ... D. Deliyannis (ed.), *Agnellus Ravennas: Liber pontificalis Ecclesiae Ravennatis* (Turnhout, 2006).

Chronicle of Fredegari ... B. Krusch (ed.), *Fredegarii et aliorum Chronica. Vitae sanctorum* (Hanover, 1888), 1–193.

Festus, *De verborum significatu* ... W. M. Lindsay (ed.), *Sexti Pompei Festi De verborum significatu quae supersunt cum Pauli epitome* (Leipzig, 1913).

George of Cyprus, *Descriptio orbis Romanis* ... H. Gelzer (ed.), *Georgii Cypri descriptio orbis Romanis* (Leipzig, 1890).

Isidore of Seville, *Etymologies* ... W. M. Lindsay (ed.), *Isidori Hispalensis episcopi Etymologiarum sive Originum libri XX*, 2 vols (Oxford, 1911).

Julian of Toledo, *Historia Wambae regis* ... W. Levison (ed.), in B. Krusch and W. Levison (eds), *Passiones vitaeque sanctorum aevi Merovingici* (Hanover and Leipzig, 1910), 486–535.

Liber Pontificalis ... L. Duchesne (ed.), *Le Liber Pontificalis: Texte, introduction et commentaire*, 3 vols (Paris, 1886–92).

Leges Ahistulfi ... F. Beyerle (ed.), *Leges Langobardorum, 643–866: Die Gesetze der Langobarden* (Witzenhausen, 1962), 194–204.

Life and Works of St Gregentios ... A. Berger (ed.), *Archbishop of Taphar: Introduction, Critical Edition and Translation*, with a contribution by G. Fiaccadori (Berlin, 2006).

Nikephoros, *Short History* ... C. Mango (ed. and tr.), *Nikephoros Patriarch of Constantinople: Short History* (Washington, DC, 1990).

Paul the Deacon, *Historia Langobardorum* ... L. Bethmann and G. Waitz (eds), *Historia Langobardorum*, in *Scriptores rerum Langobardicarum et Italicarum saec. VI–IX* (Hanover, 1878), 12–187.

Paul the Deacon, *Historia Romana* ... A. Crivellucci (ed.), *Pauli Diaconi Historia Romana* (Rome, 1914).

Theophanes, *Chronographia* ... C. de Boor (ed.), *Theophanis chronographia* (Leipzig, 1883).

Secondary Literature

Alberi, M., '"Like the Army of God's Camp": Political Theology and Apocalyptic Warfare at Charlemagne's Court', *Viator* 41 (2010): 1–20.

Arslan, E., 'La struttura delle emissioni monetarie dei Goti in Italia', in *Teodorico il grande e i goti d'Italia: Atti del XIII Congresso internazionale di studi sull'alto Medioevo* (Spoleto, 1993), 517–54.

Baldeson, J. P. V. D., *Romans and Aliens* (London, 1979).

Bartoli, D., *Della geografia trasportata al morale* (Milan, 1664).

Berti, G. P., *Ravenna nei primi tre secoli dalla sua fondazione con un'appendice sui rapporti delle origini di Roma con Ravenna* (Ravenna, 1877).

Borgatti, F., *L'agro ferrarese in età romana* (Ferrara, 1906).

Briquel, D., *Les Pélasges en Italie: Recherches sur l'histoire de la légende* (Rome, 1984).

Brown, T. S., *Gentlemen and Officers: Imperial Administration and Aristocratic Power in Byzantine Italy, A.D. 554–800* (Rome, 1984).

Brown, T. S., 'Justinian II and Ravenna', *BSl* 56 (1995): 29–36.

Burnett, A., 'The Coinage of the Social War', in U. Wartenberg, R. Witschonke and A. Burnett (eds), *Coins of Macedonia and Rome: Essays in Honour of Charles Hersh Hardcover* (London, 1998), 65–72.

Calzolari, M., 'Il delta padano in età romana: idrografia, viabilità, insediamento', in F. Berti, M. Bollini, S. Gelichi and J. Ortalli (eds), *Genti del delta da Spina a Comacchio: Uomini, territorio e culto dall'antichità all'alto Medioevo* (Ferrara, 2007), 153–72.

Cameron, A., *The Last Pagans of Rome* (Oxford, 2011).

Campana, A., *La monetazione degli insorti durante la Guerra sociale (91–87 a.C.)* (Modena, 1987).

Collins, R., 'Julian of Toledo and the Royal Succession in late Seventh Century Spain', in P. H. Sawyer and I. Wood (eds), *Early Medieval Kingship* (Leeds, 1977), 30–49.

Cornford, B., 'Paul the Deacon's Understanding of Identity, His Attitude to Barbarians, and His "Strategies of Distinction" in the *Historia Romana*', in R. Corradini, C. Pössel and P. Shaw (eds), *Texts and Identities in the Early Middle Ages* (Vienna, 2006): 47–60.

Cracco Ruggini, L., 'Simboli di battaglia ideologica nel tardo ellenismo', *Studi storici in onore di Ottorino Bertolini*, 2 vols (Pisa, 1972), 1:170–300.

Dart, C. J., *The Social War, 91 to 88 BCE: A History of the Italian Insurgency against the Roman Republic* (Aldershot, 2015).

Dench, E., *From Barbarians to New Men: Greeks, Romans and the Perceptions of People from Central Apennine* (Oxford, 1995).

Dench, E., 'Sacred Springs to Social War: Myths of Origins and the Question of Identity in Central Apennines', in T. J. Cornell and K. Lomas (eds), *Gender and Ethnicity in Ancient Italy* (London, 1997), 43–51.

Fabbi, F., 'Ravenna romana nelle ricostruzioni storiche grafiche e cartografiche', in M. Mauro (ed.), *Ravenna romana I* (Ravenna, 2001), 107–32.

Fasoli, G., 'Rileggendo il Liber Pontificalis di Agnello Ravennate', *Settimane* 17 (1970): 457–95.

Garipzanov, I., *The Symbolic Language of Authority in the Carolingian World (c. 751–877)* (Leiden, 2008).

Gerbending, R. A., *The Rise of the Carolingians and the Liber Historiae Francorum* (Oxford, 1987).

Giardina, A., *L'Italia romana: Storie di un'identità incompiuta* (Rome and Bari, 2004).

Gillet, A., 'The Goths and the Bees in Jordanes: A Narrative of No Return', in U. Betka and J. Burke (eds), *Byzantine Narrative: Papers in Honour of Roger Scott* (Melbourne, 2006), 149–63.

Goffart, W., 'Conspicuously Absent: Martial Heroism in the Histories of Gregory of Tours and Its Likes', in K. Mitchell and I. Wood (eds), *The World of Gregory of Tours* (Leiden, 2002), 365–93.

Goulon, A., 'Quelques aspects du symbolisme de l'abeille et du miel à l'époque patristique : héritage antique et interprétations nouvelles', in L. Holtz, J.-C. Fredouille and M.-H. Jullien (eds), *De Tertullien aux Mozarabes I: Antiquité tardive et christianisme ancien (III⁻–VI⁻ siècles). Mélanges offerts à Jacques Fontaine à l'occasion de son 70e anniversaire* (Paris, 1992), 525–35.

Haldon, J., *Byzantium in the Seventh Century: The Transformation of a Culture* (Cambridge, 1990).

Halsall, G., *Warfare and Society in the Barbarian West, 450–900* (London, 2003).

Holder-Egger, O., 'Glossarium', in *Monumenta Germaniae Historica: Scriptores rerum Langobardicarum et Italicarum saec. VI–IX* (Hanover, 1878), 633–6.

Josephson, Å., *Die Columella-Handschriften* (Uppsala, 1955).

Kuhoff, W., 'Die Schlacht an der Milvischen Brücke: Ein Ereignis von weltgeschichtlicher Tragweite', in G. Weber and K. Ehling (eds), *Konstantin der Große: Zwischen Sol und Christus* (Mainz, 2011), 10–20.

Lazard, S., 'De l'origine des hellénismes d'Agnello', *Revue de linguistique romane* 40 (1976): 255–98.

Magnani, S., 'I percorsi mitici nell'Adriatico e il problema delle origini di Ravenna', *Ravenna Studi e Ricerche* 5 (1998): 173–96.

Maguire, H., 'Magic and Money in the Early Middle Ages', *Speculum* 72 (1997): 1037–54.

Martínez Pizarro, J., *Writing Ravenna: the* Liber pontificalis *of Andreas Agnellus* (Ann Arbor, MI, 1995).

Maskarinec, M., 'Who Were the Romans? Shifting Scripts of Romanness in Early Medieval Italy', in W. Pohl and G. Heydemann (eds), *Post-Roman Transitions: Christian and Barbarian Identities in the Early Medieval West* (Turnhout, 2013): 297–363.

Mazzoni, C., *She-Wolf: The Story of a Roman Icon* (Cambridge, 2010).

Montanari, T., 'Sunto della storia del Po', *Il Politecnico* 18 (1926): 33–55, 65–79, 104–18.

Morpurgo, G., 'Ravenna, Spina e la tradizione pelasgica', in F. Boschi (ed.), *Ravenna e l'Adriatico dalle origini all'età romana* (Bologna, 2013), 9–20.

Novara, P., 'Gli edifici teoridiciani', in E. Marraffa and V. Moronia (eds), *Ravenna la città che sale: Da Teodorico al XX secolo, città, cultura, spazio urbano* (Ravenna, 1993), 33–55.

Orioli, G., 'La Passio sancti Apolinaris secondo il codice petropolitano', *Ravenna: Studi e ricerche* 8 (2001): 13–62.

Patlagean, E., 'Les moines grecs d'Italie e l'apologie des thèses pontificales (VIIIe–IXe siècles)', *StMed* 5 (1964): 579–602.

Pobjoy, M., 'The First Italia', in E. Herring and K. Lomas (eds), *The Emergence of State Identities in Italy in the First Millennium BC* (London, 2000), 187–211.

Pohl, W., C. Gantner, C. Grifoni and M. Pollheimer (eds), *Transformations of Romanness in the Early Middle Ages: Regions and Identities* (Berlin, 2017).

Pritchett, W. K., *The Greek State at War, Part III* (Berkeley and Los Angeles, 1979).

Reimitz, H., *History, Frankish Identity and the Framing of Western Ethnicity, 550–850* (Cambridge, 2015).

Sidebottom, H., *Ancient Warfare: A Very Short Introduction* (Oxford, 2004).

Springer, M., 'Die Schlacht am Frigidus als quellenkundliches und literaturgeschichtliches Problem', in R. Bratož (ed.), *Westillyricum und Nordostitalien in der spätrömischen Zeit* (Ljubljana, 1996), 45–94.

Tamassia, N., and V. Ussani, 'Epica e storia in alcuni capituli di Agnello Ravennate', *Nuovi studi medievali* 1 (1923): 9–40.

Tataranni, F., 'Il toro, la lupa e il guerriero: l'immagine marziale dei Sanniti nella monetazione degli insorti italici durante la guerra sociale (90–88 a.C.)', *Athenaeum* 93 (2005): 291–304.

Van Dam, N., *Remembering Constantine at the Milvian Bridge* (Cambridge, 2011).

Wolff, K., *Troja: Metamorphose eines Mythos* (Berlin, 2009).

15

Cultural Policy and Political Ideology: How Imperial was the Norman Realm of Sicily?

Annick Peters-Custot

In recent years the medieval Mediterranean has been the focus of research concerning cultural contacts, *convivencia* and multiculturalism. Often evoked, these concepts have become almost banalities. However, they speak volumes about the way in which historians interact with contemporary issues such as religious coexistence and pluralistic societies in the Mediterranean. The current pervasive discourse of tolerance, cultural exchange, minorities and contacts does not necessarily influence the historical approach, but promotes the focus on these arguments.[1]

Most often, the cultural groups of the Mediterranean world have been studied from a religious viewpoint, inserted into the political framework: that is to say that each religious sphere (Christianity, Islam, Judaism) is the object of a state-focused study divided into subgroups (the Arab world, the Ottoman world, the Persian world, the Byzantine world, the Latin world, and so forth). Then the focus becomes more finely differentiated (Mozarabic Christians in Al-Andalus, Christian minorities in Islamic Sicily, Jewish communities in Islamic Persia, etc.) in order to conduct comparative analyses: what it meant to be Jewish in Capetian France, in the Byzantine Empire or in

---

[1] See e.g. the call for papers for the Seventh International Conference on the Mediterranean World and the quote of Edgar Morin: 'At a conference hosted in 2013 by the Arab World Institute (Paris) with the support of the Cultural Council of the Mediterranean Union, sociologist Edgar Morin sounded the alarm, warning against rising nationalist identity politics in Mediterranean countries: "The Mediterranean is fading as a common point of cultural identity. Can we save the Mediterranean? Can we restore and, even better, develop its sense of community? Can we reenergize this sea of exchanges and encounters, this melting pot of cultures, this engine of culture and civilization?"' Available at <http://medworlds7.univ-tln.fr/appel-a-contribution> (last accessed 9 May 2018).

Islamic Syria. Dynamics of coexistence and cohabitation in daily life, peaceful or not, harmonious or not, are also compared (the famous *convivencia* theme[2]), and even if the word 'tolerance' has now become almost taboo and is rarely used in academic discourse, the story of 'living together' is, in fact, seen through this logic: tolerance or no tolerance, that is the question. To address this issue, two main directions have recently been taken: juridical studies and anthropological input in the field of cultural contacts.

Since the frontiers and the content of minorities and communities are fortunately less and less described in terms of ethnicity, historians increasingly privilege medieval criteria such as law. Indeed, in the Middle Ages, *lex* was used for both 'law' and 'religion' (*lex Iudeorum, lex Christi, lex Mahometi*, etc.).[3] Whatever the debate on personal or territorial law could be, the medieval documentation often defines the people by their law.[4] Consequently, numerous scholarly works and research programmes have focused on the legal regimes of minorities, in particular in the medieval Mediterranean.[5] Such studies often end up confronting the problematic and frequent opposition between human rights and the law, on the one hand, and the application of rights, on the other. Such frequent distortions reflect the flexibility in the application of the law, submitted to individual interpretations, local situations and one-off issues.[6] This flexibility may finally weaken the comparative method based on legal regimes.

On the other hand, historical analysis has finally come to focus, and quite often, too, on the dynamics of minorities, particularly on cultural dynamics: cultural transfers, acculturation, Romanisation, barbarisation, Hellenisation, Latinisation, Islamisation and so forth. These words are not similar to each other but all have in common the notion of cultural policy towards communities. Some of these notions, in particular that

---

[2] Although this term has been primarily used to describe the situation in the medieval Al-Andalus, its potential usefulness for other political contexts has been explored; see e.g. Crostini and La Porta (eds), *Negotiating Co-Existence*.

[3] I am grateful to John Tolan for bringing that to my attention.

[4] Peters-Custot, *Grecs de l'Italie*, 33–9.

[5] See e.g. the RELMIN (Legal Status of the Religious Minorities in the Euro-Mediterranean World) research programme, directed by John Tolan (University of Nantes) and which benefited from the financial support of the European Research Programme (ERC). Available at <http://telma.irht.cnrs.fr/outils/relmin/index/> (last accessed 9 May 2018).

[6] E.g. Tolan et al. (eds), *Jews in Early Christian Law*.

of acculturation, are imported from anthropology.[7] It should be noted that sources never provide information concerning cultures meeting one another, but rather men, objects, human groups.[8] Furthermore, anthropological and sociological definitions of culture are not compatible, and historians often need to choose between them. Equally problematic to the notion of 'culture' is the notion of 'identity'. Many works have demonstrated the analytical weakness of the criteria of identity and self-determination for the members of social elites who rarely seem to identify with or even be bound to only one community through shared cultural practices.[9] On the contrary, it is commonplace to notice that social dividing lines between the members of what is considered to have been a single cultural community are often stronger than shared unifying elements. How could it be possible, in this context, to speak of community or identity?[10]

It also seems quite difficult to describe systematically the situation and evolution of communities from only a juridical or an anthropological point of view. Social determination supersedes the anthropological vision of culture and its communal expressions; the documentation rarely provides access to the feeling of being – or not – a member of the community. And what seems evident is that the juridical and anthropological foci, respectively, weakened our attention to political determination, as if the political framework were an old-fashioned and outdated interpretative system. Is it a specific feature of our post-twentieth-century period to relegate political ideologies because of an obsessional fear of those which, until recently, influenced, most often negatively, world history?

In my opinion, all these questions should be reviewed regarding the political aspect of the cultural issues. I will take the example of the realm of Sicily under Hauteville domination. In fact, the Italian 'Mezzogiorno' is considered to be a laboratory for the analysis of medieval Mediterranean

---

[7] About the notion of acculturation, see Peters-Custot, 'Usage de l'acculturation'.

[8] The motto of the great Parisian museum of primary arts, named 'Musée du quai Branly – Jacques Chirac', is, on the contrary, to be 'the place where the cultures are conversing' ('Le lieu où dialoguent les cultures'). But this is cultural marketing, not scientific reflection.

[9] Very illuminating is Nef, *Conquérir et gouverner*, 11–13.

[10] On identity, see Tony Judt, a historian of nineteenth- and twentieth-century Europe: 'Identity is a dangerous word. It has no respectable contemporary uses', in 'The Edge People', *The New York Review of Books*, 23 February 2010; quoted by Tolan, 'Constructing Christendom', 278.

communities, and for notions of identity and community.[11] The questions I will be investigating are: how did the ideology of royal power manifest itself during the so-called Norman period? How did the king deal with the particularities of the multicultural landscape of his realm? Was there a specific policy towards minorities and, if so, how could we define its contents and origins?

Even though my approach here cannot be exhaustive, I would like to present some aspects of Norman policy towards its various subject groups, seeking to deduce its ideological connotations.

The Norman Realm of Sicily: A Territorial and Cultural Mosaic

Norman Italy was far from being a unified territory, even politically. Its regional diversity resulted from the situation prior to the Norman conquest. The terms and stages of this conquest did not weaken that diversity; on the contrary, they reinforced it.[12]

This plurality is indeed inscribed in the landscape, since the geographical distribution of the different groups can be easily mapped. Naturally, I have no intention of denying the reality of individual and collective mobility, as we shall see. Still, at a macro-geographical scale, communities were spread throughout quite homogeneous areas that did not correspond exactly to the political entities.[13] At the very moment when the conquest started, there was a so-called Longobardian southern Italy – the word 'Longobardian' having

---

[11] The bibliography of the Norman kingdom of Sicily, with all its political, socio-economical, religious, linguistic and cultural aspects, has no end, and it seems it would not be useful to present an extensive inventory of all the scientific production on these themes. On questions regarding Norman ethnogenesis, Greek identity and communities, Sicilian 'Mozarabs' and Sicilian Arab-speaking Jews, see e.g. Canosa, *Etnogenesi normanne*. See Peters-Custot, *Grecs de l'Italie*, for the Greeks of Southern Italy; Colafemmina, *Storia degli ebrei*, for the Apulian Jews; Colafemmina, *Jews in Calabria*, for the Calabrian Jews; Bresc and Nef, 'Mozarabes de Sicile', and Nef, 'Histoire des "mozarabes"', for the Sicilian 'Mozarabian'; and Bresc, *Arabes de langue*, for the Sicilian Jews. See also di Carpegna Falconieri, '*Militia* a Roma', and Nef, 'Groupes religieux', for reflections on medieval collective identities, minorities and communities.

[12] On this story, see Martin, *Italies normandes*; Bouet and Neveux (eds), *Normands en Méditerranée*; Taviani-Carozzi, *Terreur du monde*; *Cavalieri alla conquista del Sud*; Peters-Custot, *Grecs de l'Italie*, 225–33; on the Hauteville conquest of the island of Sicily, see Nef, *Conquérir et gouverner*, 21–63.

[13] See Peters-Custot, 'Convivencia between Christians'.

no ethnical connotation[14] – which included the Longobardian principalities (Salerno, Capua-Benevento) as well as most of Byzantine Apulia, which had become a *thema*, and the Catepanate of Italy. In this area the population lived mainly under Longobardian law, wrote documents in Latin and were of Christian confession, mostly of the Latin rite, even if, between the papacy and the Byzantine emperors, the ecclesiastical policy was quite complex.

Next to that there was the 'Byzantine', or at least the Italo-Greek, southern Italy, which included southern and central Calabria, the southern part of Apulia (Salento) and a residual Christian population in the northeast of Sicily, in the region called Val Demone. Whether under Byzantine authority or not, these zones had Greek-speaking populations living under Byzantine law and confessing Christianity according to the eastern tradition. Another small part was the 'Roman' southern Italy, exclusively based upon the Tyrrhenian dukedoms (Naples, Amalfi, Gaeta), where the population were most conscious of their own specific characteristics, for example the practice of Roman-Justinianic law, and some cultural pretensions bound to original social selection criteria, such as the one called the 'Neapolitan pseudo-Hellenism'.[15] Finally, there was the island of Sicily, which at the time of the Norman conquest was split between rival emirs in what has been called a *taifa* system (in parallel with the *taifas* of the same period in Spain), and which was inhabited by an Arabic-speaking and mostly Muslim population living under Islamic law.

The mobility of the population may have, indeed, slightly changed this general landscape. Merchants coming from the Tyrrhenian dukedoms are known in Byzantine Calabria and in the Longobardian principality of Salerno, and above all, in the 970s, quite massive Italo-Greek movements are discernible in the documents, going north and creating sorts of Greek-speaking 'enclaves' in southern Basilicata,[16] Taranto[17] and, less extensively, in Rome and Naples.[18] For administrative and political reasons, the Byzantine population of Longobardian Bari in Apulia was important in the first half of the eleventh century. However, generally speaking, the mosaic of populations also had a territorial character. The imperial logic preserved this pluralism in the two broader zones: the *dhimmi* status shaped the juridical position of

---

[14] See Martin, 'Romani e Longobardi'.
[15] Martin, 'Hellénisme'.
[16] Peters-Custot, 'Monastère de Carbone'.
[17] Martin, 'Κίνναμος Ἐπίσκοπος'.
[18] Peters-Custot, 'Construction de la norme monastique'.

the Jewish and Christian populations of Islamic Sicily, while the Byzantine administration accepted the practice of Longobardian law.[19]

The conquest of Greek-speaking southern Calabria and the southern part of Apulia was quite efficient and rapid, under the supervision of two of the most important members of the Hauteville family, Duke Robert Guiscard and his young brother Count Roger I. The latter also led the conquest of Sicily, which lasted many years. Sicily was penetrated rather than conquered by the Normans.[20] In any case, the outcome of the conquest of these two parts of the future 'Norman' realm[21] was a centralised rule which certainly aimed at preserving a strong public authority similar to that which had existed under Islamic or Byzantine rule. By contrast, authority in the northern territories underwent fragmentation due to longer military expeditions led by different lords in Aversa, Capua, Byzantine Apulia and Salerno. This process induced a landlord system quite similar to the recently imported western feudal system. Even after the royal unification of the Norman territories in 1130, the sovereign did not manage to subjugate these regions and their feudal *milieu*. However, the principality of Taranto in Norman Apulia probably maintained some administrative and ideological legacy of Byzantine origins, led by the Hauteville Prince of Taranto, Bohemond, a son of Robert Guiscard. Naples was the last territory to surrender, long after the emergence of the kingdom, in 1137. Even after the Hauteville period, this original zone maintained its politically distinctive character against the papacy and the Anjou dynasty in the second half of the thirteenth century. Naples is only one example that illustrates a reality common to all the territories under Hauteville power: the initial mosaic did not dissolve under the Norman monarchy. Shall we interpret this phenomenon as a lack of ability, a lack of will for integration, or a combination of both? We have to keep in mind that the subjected populations of Norman Italy were not minorities, at least from a demographical point of view: in Sicily or Calabria, for example, the conquerors always remained a numerical minority.

The Political Administration of Cultural Issues

Having no expertise beyond the study of the Greek communities of Norman Italy, I will mainly address the question of the administering of

---

[19] Lefort and Martin, 'Sigillion du catépan'.
[20] For Roger I, the most recent biography is Becker, *Graf Roger I*. See also *Documenti greci e latini*, ed. Becker.
[21] Many of the invaders were not 'Norman' at all: see Ménager, 'Pesanteur et étiologie'.

this population. Nevertheless, I will attempt to put into perspective the studies of Annliese Nef on Norman Sicily in order to attempt a broader approach that is often missing from historical studies, including mine, which artificially disconnect Sicily and Calabria, even though these were unified under the Hauteville administration and, to a large extent, through the population itself. [22]

The question is: were there different Norman political practices for each category of population (Greek, Sicilian, Jewish and 'Latin' people) or was there a single policy towards the different groups, which may have known variations (Muslims should not be treated like Christians, for instance) but was nonetheless informed by the same ideological background?

Regarding the political attitude towards the Italo-Greek populations in the County of Calabria, the County of Sicily and the Kingdom of Sicily, it is now largely accepted that, particularly in the religious field, they did not undergo a 'Latinisation' process.[23] Christians who lived according to the eastern rite were not forced to 'convert' or become Latinised. The peculiarities of eastern ecclesiology – such as the ordination of married men – were duly maintained and respected, and even included in the king's law; in fact, the sons of the Greek priests were included by the king in the ecclesiastical jurisdiction.[24]

Yet we cannot deny the existence of an ecclesiastical and monastic policy of the Hauteville sovereigns, sanctioned by the Apostolica Legazia privilege which had been given by the pope to Count Roger I at the end of the eleventh century. This explicitly identified the count – and later the king – as the

---

[22] Nef, *Conquérir et gouverner la Sicile islamique*; Peters-Custot, 'Construction royale'; see also Nef, 'Imaginaire impérial'.

[23] Peters-Custot, *Grecs de l'Italie*, 289–306 ; *Bruno en Calabre*, 44–54.

[24] A few Hauteville deeds regarding the foundation or refoundation of episcopal sees in Calabria express the fact that the bishop's jurisdiction includes the Greek priests' sons. See e.g. the refoundation deed of Squillace's see, dated 1096, by Roger I: *Documenti greci e latini*, no. 54, ed. Becker, 212–17, at 215. Another example can be found in the redefinition of Calabria, the jurisdiction of the bishop of Cosenza, by William, the duke of Apulia, dated 1113 and mentioning the Latin and Greek priests of the episcopal see. The deed has been lost, but is known through Frederick II's confirmation, dated 1223: *Historia diplomatica Friderici secundi*, t. II, vol. 1, ed. Huillard-Bréholles, 390. See also the deed of Empress Constance, Henry VI's widow, for the archbishop of Taranto, dated December 1197: *Urkunden der Kaiserin Konstanze*, no. 44, ed. Kölzer, 136–44, at 142.9–10. All these documents are the product of the sovereign's decision in his or her capacity as the head of the given realm's church.

pope's permanent legate in Sicily and in Calabria.[25] The Hauteville sovereign thus earned complete autonomy and authority over the ecclesiastical matters of those two areas, such as defining the episcopal sees and the jurisdictional territories of the bishops, and appointing the bishops and the most important abbots.[26] At the same time, he avoided introducing tithes on private incomes, a practice which was absent from Islamic Sicily as well as from Byzantine Calabria, and found other ways of financing the churches, keeping them under his control.[27] So there was an ecclesiastical and monastic policy, but no religious policy: the sovereign never did interfere in dogmatic debates, the question of married priests or any such affairs. On the contrary, he got involved in the management of bishoprics and monasteries, and managed the Greek institutions just as he did with the Latin ones without distinguishing between them. In the Middle Ages, these actions always formed part of the typical policy of sovereigns, who claimed to be the heads of their respective Churches, not in a feudal manner, but as an expression of public authority.

The result was clear: Christianity throughout Norman Italy was diversified and remained so. Was this the result of a conscious policy of flexibility? Eastern Christianity was preserved and even sustained – I mention here only the foundation of the great Archimandritate of SS. Salvatore di Messina[28] – not as part of an Italo-Greek Church but as a part of the prince's Church. The counts and kings made poor use of diversity, not due to lack of political awareness but due to lack of utility. I am more and more convinced that we should not speak of an 'Italo-Greek Church' under the Hauteville. The Italo-Greek ecclesiastical structures, and the Christians themselves, were a simple part of a whole – the king's Church. Therefore, 'king's Church' seems to me a more meaningful label.

Some other aspects of the Norman government indicate that there were no policies specifically targeting the Greek populations of the kingdom: Byzantine law was kept in use, the Italo-Greek notarial milieu maintained the writing of Greek deeds and even the Norman lords looked to their

---

[25] The most important study on this subject remains Fodale, *Comes et Legatus Siciliae*.

[26] For the Sicilian sees, see Nef, 'Géographie religieuse'; Nef, *Conquérir et gouverner*, 448–55; and for the Calabrian sees, cf. Peters-Custot, 'Les remaniements'.

[27] See Toomaspoeg, *Decimae*, with Peters-Custot, 'Review of Toomaspoeg, *Decimae*'.

[28] See Scaduto, *Il monachesimo basiliano*; von Falkenhausen, 'L'archimandritato'; Peters-Custot, *Grecs de l'Italie*, 296–306.

help and abilities to produce valid deeds.[29] The Italo-Greek subjects of the Hauteville were not subject to any particular political treatment if we leave aside their confessional peculiarities. So, in regard to this population, the Hautevilles' slogan could be said to have been: 'an indifferent difference'. This paradoxical expression may reflect the awareness of the Christian unity within the kingdom. On the other hand, that same expression could not be used to appropriately describe the situation of the Muslims in the realm, despite the many elements the two subgroups had in common.

The Court Milieu

Were the Greek members of the Hauteville court conceived as the representatives of a community (that of the Greeks of Norman Italy)? Were they part of a lobby inside the court? Was there a link between their presence – or their absence – at the court, and the king's general policy towards their community?[30]

The Palermitan court was home to various types of Greek-speaking individuals: a first, well-educated group, consisted of members of a high-level cultural milieu whose job was to support the actions of the sovereign and his ideological and political image. A second group, less prestigious, wrote the Greek deeds of the count and later of the king,[31] and led the king's current administrative action.

Beside this group of the sovereign's servants, the Norman court actually contained a smaller circle of high-level Greek-speaking intellectuals. There was certainly little sense of identification between those intellectuals and the Italo-Greek population, since they were only rarely of Italo-Greek origin. Neilos Doxopater and George of Antioch,[32] the most important

---

[29] Peters-Custot, *Grecs de l'Italie*, 375–99. Greek-speaking writers continued to monopolise the notarial milieu of some Calabrian towns at the beginning of the thirteenth century, forcing local lords to seek the services of some Latin monks to get Latin deeds written down. For example, in 1217, Andrea di Pagliara, lord of Mesoraca, Calabria, had a deed written by William, monk of the Cistercian abbey of Sant'Angelo di Frigillo, having the approval of the town's Greek notary Peregrinus, who could not write in Latin: *Carte latine*, no. 110, ed. Pratesi. From then on, Guillaume wrote all the Latin deeds of Mesoraca until 1219, always with the Greek notary's approval: ibid. nos 112, 113, 119.

[30] See von Falkenhausen, 'I gruppi etnici'.

[31] See Brühl, *Diplomi e cancelleria*.

[32] On George of Antioch, see De Simone, 'Il mezzogiorno', 261–93 and Nef, *Conquérir et gouverner*, 311–14.

representatives of this milieu, belonged to this category of refugees. Their presence at Palermo alongside the presence of many intellectuals coming from the Islamic world demonstrates above all how attractive the Hauteville court was for Greek-speaking and other individuals around the Mediterranean. Their activity at Palermo was thus a key element of a Norman political ideology aiming to configure an international profile.

Under this upper-class group, there was a second group that brought together notaries and administrative agents. Their appointment was linked to their linguistic and diplomatic skills – they were bilingual and, in some cases, trilingual. To the extent that the chancery was actually trilingual – I will not address the term's relevance, which has been criticised – Italo-Greek notaries had their part in it due to their technical skills and the technical service they provided to the sovereign. After king Roger II's death in 1154, his successors took into account the considerable weakening of the Greek-speaking element in the kingdom, which followed the unification of 1127, when Roger II brought Apulia under his jurisdiction. According to Annliese Nef, William II even favoured an Islamisation of the court and the administration.[33] Therefore, knowledge of Greek, which previously was an advantage for pursuing a career in the central administration, became useless and even disadvantageous. The regression of the Italo-Greek element in the circles of power reflected the fact that this group never exerted political pressure and was never a power lobby. Moreover, based on the absence of any documentation, it seems doubtful that these notaries and administrative agents had any awareness of a common identity binding them with the other Italo-Greeks of the kingdom. Given that the social barriers were stronger than their cultural consciousness and even though their social status depended on this very same cultural background, their loyalty and identification lay rather with the court culture and environment than with the Italo-Greek community.

Nevertheless, from the time of Count Roger I, even before a real chancery was established, and until the end of the Hauteville dynasty, that multilingual court was able to produce royal deeds in the three main languages considered as the languages of the king: Latin, Greek and Arabic. This multilingual culture of writing, quite original for the areas of the west, is well known and has been thoroughly studied. Modern works that focused on this notarial and diplomatic production shed light on many salient features.[34]

---

[33] Nef, *Conquérir et gouverner*, 328–51.

[34] For the most recent approach to this topic, see Peters-Custot, 'Documentary Multilingualism'. Some important elements are to be found in Nef, *Conquérir et gouverner*, 73–116, focused on the chancery's production for Sicily.

First, at the beginning of the Norman conquest, the written language was decided by the use of notaries found *in situ*: indeed, at this time the conquerors did not have a rich notarial tradition, and the language used for written matters was less chosen by than imposed on them through the demographical context: Latin in Apulia, Greek in Calabria, Arabic in Sicily, and so forth. Moreover, for some kinds of documentation (such as lists of peasants or land inventories), the count or duke had to rely on the local communities' cooperation. In that case, the practical provisions were directly registered in the language of the partners of the sovereign's agents.[35]

Subsequently, when a linguistic choice emerged thanks to the appointment of notaries by the public authority, this choice derived less from the beneficiary's language than from the category of the respective deeds. For example, the public deeds concerning ecclesiastical policy were mostly written in Greek for Calabria and Sicily, even if the beneficiary was not Greek-speaking (such as a Latin monastery or bishop). This thematic specialisation of the Greek language in public deeds found an echo in high-register Greek literature, which was more or less dedicated to ecclesiastical and not theological matters, as is sometimes alleged.[36] On the other hand, the Arabic language was used in Sicily mostly for tax matters. The linguistic monopoly in both fields could be associated with specific legacies that the Norman conquerors inherited from the previous administration of the respective areas: the Islamic and the Byzantine.

There was thus a functional use of written languages bound to ideology, since the written language of public authority cannot be distinguished from the political forms it conveys. By using the Greek language, the Norman counts and kings also adopted the archetypical form of the Byzantine public deed, the *sigillion*. This was not a naïve selection. The linguistic choice was not, at this time, linked to practical constraints anymore, but proceeded from political choice, since language went beyond words to express a political ideology.[37]

On the other hand, the multilingualism of the chancery did not imply that the same was true of the deeds themselves. Studies recently made on the written production of the count and later king of Sicily have revealed a sort of fragmented use of languages on functional bases, as mentioned.[38] But the small number of genuinely multilingual documents – which present the same

---

[35] Nef, 'Conquêtes'; Peters-Custot, 'Comportement'; 'Les *plateae* calabraises'.

[36] Nef, *Conquérir et gouverner*, 202.

[37] The best study on this theme remains that of Breccia, 'Il *sigillion*'.

[38] Peters-Custot as cited above n. 34, and Nef, *Conquérir et gouverner*, 73–116.

text in two different languages – reflects a clear choice: not to have the sovereign's word translated. The Latin monasteries or bishops, for example, could not get a direct understanding of the Greek deeds produced for them without enlisting the help of this exclusive environment of bilingual individuals – the bilingual public agents. Besides, writing in Greek or Arabic could make it difficult to produce forgeries. In a nutshell, for all these reasons we can assume that there was a real policy of public deeds which was based on ideology, and which was not a linguistic policy, since the counts and kings never promoted multilingualism in their territories, but on the contrary, created a sort of state monopoly on multilingualism in order to maintain a public monopoly on common authority.[39]

The King's Multifaceted Representation

My final point will be on the multiple practices of representation of the Hauteville king, not only through iconography, but in all media. Many works have studied the representation of the Norman king through the image of a Byzantine emperor or, on the contrary, his manifestation according to the Islamic ruling image.[40]

Obviously, Arab authors, and particularly the Arab geographers visiting the Palermitan court, included Roger II in their world. For them, the Hauteville king was a part of the Islamic world.[41] There is also no doubt that in other contexts or communication media the king wanted to present himself in a Latin or Byzantine manner. Did the king seek to address differently his subjects who had various linguistic, cultural and iconographic standards? Did he want to correspond with their own different cultural references? It is difficult to say with certainty, because the lack of Byzantine imperial testimonies regarding southern Italy before the conquest makes it difficult to know whether the Italo-Greeks previously had access to iconographic representations of the *basileus*. Monetary circulation could be a medium providing such an access, but in Calabria in particular, the real currency was not purely Byzantine before the Normans, but Islamic, as demonstrated by many studies.

The king's multifaceted image causes problems of interpretation and makes it difficult to provide a synthetic approach to the king's representation.

---

[39] On the subject, see Nef, 'Peut-on parler de "politique linguistique"'.
[40] See e.g. Nef, *Conquérir et gouverner*, esp. 119–45; Vagnoni, *La sacralità regia*.
[41] See De Simone, 'Il mezzogiorno'; Nef, 'Dire la conquête'.

For example, in her masterful study on Norman Sicily and the king's images, Annliese Nef, by restricting her research to the 'elements commonly considered "Islamic"', excludes many of the sovereign's representational forms that were not Islamic.[42] However, the Norman kings' issue was to rule over not only Islamic Sicily, but also Latin Apulia and Byzantine Calabria.[43] We know, for example, of an *Ordo* for the royal coronation, probably dating from Roger II's reign, that has been studied by Reinhard Elze and is attested in four manuscripts written in the Sicilian kingdom.[44] This *Ordo* took its inspiration from the Romano-Germanic Pontifical, dated to the tenth century. From this point of view, the Sicilian king was a western sovereign. Besides, the Hauteville matrimonial policy systematically preferred Latin princesses. But, on the other hand, in the Sicilian churches, built by the king or by one of his relatives (Martorana, Monreale), the king is represented as a *basileus*. These images did not act as representations of contemporary reality, since the royal clothes matched neither those of the Norman king nor those of the twelfth-century *basileus*. This iconographic distortion is particularly striking regarding the Martorana mosaics. The representation had been copied from a tenth-century Byzantine iconographic model that was two centuries old at the time of the mosaic's creation.[45] However, the choice of a Byzantine model for the public image of the Sicilian king could not have been accidental. It was made on purpose and had a meaning. The problem is how to provide an interpretative synthesis of this three-faced representation from an ideological viewpoint. Isolating the Islamic or the Byzantine elements of this multifaceted image would not allow us to attempt a holistic approach, which still needs to be done.

Another example comes from epigraphy: the very famous trilingual inscription of the hydraulic clock at Palermo was a glorification of the Norman king.[46] Yet it presented a very brief, plain and little-inspired Latin text.[47] The Arabic and the Greek texts, on the contrary, both had quite dignified

---

[42] Nef, *Conquérir et gouverner.*
[43] Peters-Custot, 'Construction royale'.
[44] Elze, 'Zum Königtum'.
[45] See Cutler, *The Hand of the Master*, esp. 203–35; Kitzinger, *Mosaics of St Mary's of the Admiral.*
[46] This inscription can be found in *Recueil des inscriptions grecques*, no. 198, ed. Guillou, 216–18.
[47] Ibid. 217: *Hoc opus horologii precepit fieri dominus et magnificus rex Rogerius anno incarnationis Dominice MCXLII mense Martio indictione V, anno vero regni ejus XIII. Feliciter.*

royal titles. For Nef, who considered only the Arabic part, such a titulature indicates the 'figure of a learned sovereign, devoted to the kingdom's protection, who rules the hours as well as his administration.'[48] But she neglects to study the Greek part of this inscription.[49] The Greek text was as complex and broad, with a spectacular title – ὁ κραταιὸς δεσπότης Ῥογέριος ῥὴξ ἐκ Θεοῦ σκηπτροκράτωρ: 'the powerful lord Roger, king by the grace of God and holder of the sceptre' – attributing to the king the function of the wise sovereign who rules the water's stream and produces an infallible knowledge of the hours: this is regarded as an unprecedented miracle (Ὦ θαῦμα καινόν).[50] The Greek and the Arabic versions are the same, and both glorify the king, unlike the Latin version. The Greek and Arabic languages can both be considered as the languages of power, solemnity and greatness of the king's authority: they convey the royal ideology. This is no coincidence, considering that they are the languages of the two great Mediterranean imperial worlds: the Islamic and the Byzantine.

This imperial dimension is reinforced through royal ecclesiastical authority which, from Constantine the Great and Theodosios onwards, resulted from the integration of divine election into Roman imperial ideology. In fact, the papal bull of 1098 allowed the sovereign to rule over religious diversity in an independent and original manner.[51] For corresponding images, the best model was Byzantine. As a *basileus*, King Roger was directly crowned by Christ, thus taking his power from a non-earthly authority. These adapted Byzantine ideological models contributed alongside other inherited models – like the Islamic image – to the Norman king's sacral dimension. Yet, never did the Norman kings take the title of *basileus*, which was monopolised by the Byzantine emperors. They adopted the classical title of *rex* written in Greek letters (ῥὴξ), which was the Byzantine title given to western sovereigns. Moreover, they never took the title of *emir*; instead, with the same wisdom, they preferred that of *malik*.[52]

---

[48] The Arabic text can be translated as follows: 'The royal, revered, supreme majesty of Roger – may God perpetuate his days and help his banners! – has ordered the construction of this machine in order to mark the hours in the capital of Sicily, protected by God, in the year 536'. I have adapted this text from the French translation in *Recueil des inscriptions grecques*, ed. Guillou, 217.

[49] Peters-Custot, 'Construction royale'.

[50] Ὦ θαῦμα καινόν· ὁ κραταιὸς δεσπότης | Ῥογέριος ῥὴξ ἐκ Θ(εο)ῦ σκηπτροκράτωρ | Τὸν ῥ(οῦ)ν χαλινοῖ τῆς ῥε(ού)σης (οὐ)σίας | Γνῶσιν νέμων ἄπταιστον ὡρῶν τ(οῦ) χρόν(ου) | τῷ ιβ΄ τῆς βασιλείας χρόνῳ μηνὶ Μαρτίῳ | ἰνδ(ικτιῶνος) ε΄ ἔτ(ους) ϛχν΄.

[51] Fodale, *Comes et Legatus Siciliae*.

[52] Nef, *Conquérir et gouverner*, 186.

Conclusion

In terms of handling the kingdom's various communities and cultural diversity, the Hauteville monarchy expressed an ideology that could be qualified as 'ecumenical', the aim of which was not to merge the different elements, but on the contrary to maintain diversity and make well-directed use of it, since the royal power was the only one able to exercise power over all these communities as a whole. The king spoke to each one of them in their own language; he was a Pentecost-king. His rule exceeded the frontiers of Christianity.[53] The diversity of his subjects – even the Muslims or the Jews – reasserted the king's ecumenicity.

Concerning the Greek people, the Hauteville king never had a cultural policy. Greek people were welcome at the Palermitan court, their skills in Greek and notarial writing being in high demand, in particular until the middle of the twelfth century. Moreover, they were the only repositories of a Byzantine inheritance still prestigious in the western world and keepers of a model of the sovereign as leader of his Church; a model that disappeared in the west after the Concordat of Worms in 1122. The court was indeed quite a cosmopolitan melting pot, but the members of the Greek-speaking elite did not come from southern Italy or Sicily; instead, they were foreign refugees. In this sense, the appeal of the Palermitan court was also a sign of the kingdom's imperial character.

The Hauteville regime, then, adopted an imperial ideology regarding the people's identity which was also applied to non-Christians. The comparison most frequently made by historians between the juridical status and situation of religious minorities in the Islamic and the Christian world, respectively, does not make much sense for the Norman kingdom of Sicily. Even though this was undoubtedly a Christian kingdom, it took up many juridical elements of *dhimmi* status and applied them to its Muslim communities. Its ideology was therefore both Byzantine and Islamic, since it was an imperial one.

These results regarding the links between imperial ideologies and how these were adapted to kingdoms and cultural communities could be compared, first, with the political strategies of other conquering kingdoms, including the management of people of different languages, cultures and religions (in particular in the Iberian Peninsula); and second, with what has recently been shown regarding the medieval Norman world – that is, the

---

[53] See Nef, 'Imaginaire impérial'.

imperial vision of the Anglo-Norman monarchy after 1066.[54] Surely this comparative approach would provide us with a broader overview of the links between minorities and ideologies in some medieval pseudo-imperial constructions.[55]

Bibliography

Sources

Carte latine di abbazie calabresi . . . A. Pratesi (ed.), *Carte latine di abbazie calabresi provenienti dall'Archivio Aldobrandini* (Vatican City, 1958).

Urkunden der Kaiserin Konstanze . . . T. Kölzer (ed.), *Die Urkunden der Kaiserin Konstanze* (Hanover, 1990).

Documenti greci e latini di Ruggero I . . . J. Becker (ed.), *Edizione critica dei documenti greci e latini di Ruggero I, conte della Calabria e della Sicilia (1080–1101)* (Rome, 2013).

Historia diplomatica Friderici secondi . . . ed. J.-L.-A. Huillard-Bréholles (ed.), *Historia diplomatica Friderici secundi* (Paris, 1852–61; repr. Turin, 1963).

Recueil des inscriptions grecques d'Italie médiévale, ed. A. Guillou (Rome, 1996).

Secondary Literature

Bates, D., *The Normans and Empire* (Oxford, 2013).

Becker, J., *Graf Roger I. von Sizilien. Wegbereiter des normannischen Königreichs* (Tübingen, 2008).

Bouet, P., and F. Neveux (eds), *Les Normands en Méditerranée dans le sillage des Tancrède, Colloque de Cerisy-la-Salle (24–27 septembre 1992)* (Caen, 1994).

---

[54] See Bates, *Normans and Empire*, who uses the concept of empire as a framework for new analysis on the story of the Anglo-Norman states, emphasising the cross-Channel and continental dimensions of the subject, to present a new interpretation of a broader history of England, the British Isles and northern France in the eleventh and twelfth centuries.

[55] See, for a first approach, a comparative study between the coronation processes of William the Conqueror and Roger I of Sicily in Madeline and Peters-Custot, 'De Guillaume Ier'.

Breccia, G., 'Il *sigillion* nella prima età normanna. Documento pubblico e semipubblico nel Mezzogiorno ellenofono (1070–1127)', *Quellen und Forschungen aus Italienischen Archiven und Bibliotheken* 79 (1997): 1–27.

Bresc, H., *Arabes de langue, juifs de religion: l'évolution du judaïsme sicilien dans l'environnement latin, XIIᵉ–XIVᵉ siècles* (Paris, 2001).

Bresc, H., and A. Nef, 'Les Mozarabes de Sicile (1100–1300)', in E. Cuozzo and J.-M. Martin (eds), *Cavalieri alla conquista del Sud. Studi sull'Italia normanna in onore di Léon-Robert Ménager* (Rome and Bari, 1998), 134–56.

Brühl, C., *Diplomi e cancelleria di Ruggero II* (Palermo, 1983).

Canosa, R., *Etnogenesi normanne e identità variabili. Il retroterra culturale dei Normanni d'Italia fra Scandinavia e Normandia* (Turin, 2009).

Colafemmina, C., *Documenti per la storia degli ebrei in Puglia nell'Archivio di Stato di Napoli* (Bari, 1990).

Colafemmina, C., *The Jews in Calabria* (Leiden, 2012).

Crostini, B., and S. La Porta (eds), *Negotiating Co-Existence: Communities, Cultures and 'Convivencia' in Byzantine Society* (Trier, 2013).

Cutler, A., *The Hand of the Master. Craftmanship, Ivory, and Society in Byzantium (9th–11th Centuries)* (Princeton, NJ, 1994).

De Simone, A., 'Il mezzogiorno normanno-svevo visto dall'Islam africano', in *Il mezzogiorno normanno-svevo visto dall'Europa e dal mondo mediterraneo. Atti delle tredicesime giornate normanno-sveve, Bari, 21–24 ottobre 1997* (Bari, 1999), 261–93.

di Carpegna Falconieri, T., 'La *militia* a Roma: il formarsi di una nuova aristocrazia (secoli VII–VIII)', in J.-M. Martin, A. Peters-Custot and V. Prigent (eds), *L'héritage byzantin en Italie. II. Les cadres juridiques et sociaux et les institutions publiques* (Rome, 2012), 559–83.

Elze, R., 'Zum Königtum Rogers II. von Sizilien', *Festschrift Percy Ernst Schramm zu seinem siebzigsten Geburtstag*, 2 vols (Wiesbaden, 1964), 1:102–16.

Fodale, S., *Comes et Legatus Siciliae. Sul privilegio di Urbano II e la pretesa Apostolica Legazia dei Normanni di Sicilia* (Palermo, 1970); repr. in S. Fodale, *L'Apostolica Legazia e altri studi su Stato e Chiesa* (Messina, 1991), 9–157.

Kitzinger, E., *The Mosaics of St Mary's of the Admiral in Palermo* (Washington, DC, 1990).

Lefort, J., and J.-M. Martin, 'Le sigillion du catépan d'Italie Eustathe Palatinos pour le juge Byzantios (décembre 1045)', *Mélanges de l'Ecole française de Rome. Moyen Âge* 98 (1986): 525–42.

Madeline, F., and A. Peters-Custot, 'De Guillaume Ier à Roger II de Sicile: Autour de l'impérialité des premiers couronnements royaux normands (1066–1130); *Annales de Normandie*, 69.1 (2019): 165–98.

Martin, J.-M., 'Κίνναμος Ἐπίσκοπος – Cennamus episcopus. Aux avant-postes de l'hellénisme sud-italien vers l'an Mil', *RSBN* 27 (1991): 89–99.

Martin, J.-M., *Italies normandes (X^e–XIIe siècles)* (Paris, 1994).

Martin, J.-M., 'Hellénisme politique, hellénisme religieux et pseudo-hellénisme à Naples (VIIe–XIIe siècle); *Νέα Ῥώμη* 2 = Ἀμπελοκήπιον. *Miscellanea Vera von Falkenhausen* (2005): 59–77.

Martin, J.-M., 'Romani e Longobardi' in M. Boccuzzi and P. Cordasco (eds), *Civiltà a contatto nel Mezzogiorno normanno-svevo. Economia Società Istituzioni* (Bari, 2018), 79–102.

Martin, J.-M., and E. Cuozzo (eds), *Cavalieri alla conquista del Sud. Studi sull'Italia normanna in memoria di Léon-Robert Ménager* (Bari, 1997).

Ménager, L.-R., 'Pesanteur et étiologie de la colonisation normande d'Italie et Appendice. Inventaire des familles normandes et franques émigrées en Italie méridionale et en Sicile (XIe–XIIe siècle); in *Roberto Il Guiscardo e il suo tempo. Atti delle prime giornate normanno-sveve (Bari, 1973)* (Bari, 1975), 203–29, 279–410; repr. in R. Ménager, *Hommes et Institutions de l'Italie normande* (London, 1981), no. IV.

Nef, A., 'Conquêtes et reconquêtes médiévales: une réduction en servitude généralisée? (Al-Andalus, Sicile et Orient latin); in *Les formes de la servitude: esclavages et servages de la fin de l'Antiquité au monde moderne. Actes de la table ronde de Nanterre (12–13 décembre 1997)* = *Mélanges de l'Ecole française de Rome. Moyen Âge* 112/2 (Rome, 2000), 579–607.

Nef, A., 'Géographie religieuse et continuité temporelle dans la Sicile normande (XIe–XIIe siècles): le cas des évêchés; in P. Henriet (ed.), *À la recherche de légitimités chrétiennes. Représentations de l'espace et du temps dans l'Espagne médiévale (IXe–XIIIe siècle)* (Lyon and Madrid, 2003), 177–94.

Nef, A., 'Peut-on parler de «politique linguistique» dans la Sicile du XIIe siècle? Quelques réflexions préliminaires; in J. Dakhlia (ed.), *Trames de langues. Usages et métissages linguistiques dans l'histoire du Maghreb* (Paris, 2004), 41–57.

Nef, A., 'L'histoire des "mozarabes" de Sicile. Bilan provisoire et nouveaux matériaux; in C. Aillet, M. Penelas and P. Roisse (eds), *¿Existe una identidad mozárabe? Historia, lengua y cultura de los cristianos de al-Andalus (siglos IX–XII)* (Madrid, 2008), 255–86.

Nef, A., *Conquérir et gouverner la Sicile islamique* (Rome, 2011).

Nef, A., 'Imaginaire impérial, empire et oecuménisme religieux: quelques réflexions depuis la Sicile des Hauteville', *Cahiers de Recherches Médiévales et Humanistes* 24 (2012): 227–49.

Nef, A., 'Les groupes religieux minoritaires et la question de leur structuration en communautés dans les sociétés médiévales chrétiennes et islamiques', in J. Dakhlia and W. Kaiser (eds), *Les musulmans dans l'histoire de l'Europe*, vol. 2: *Passages et contacts en Méditerranée* (Paris, 2013), 413–40.

Nef, A., 'Dire la conquête et la souveraineté des Hauteville en arabe (jusqu'au milieu du XIIIᵉ siècle)', *Tabularia* (2015). Available at <http://www.unicaen.fr/mrsh/craham/revue/tabularia/print.php?dossier=doss ier13&file=01nef.xml> (last accessed 9 May 2018).

Peters-Custot, A., 'Le Monastère de Carbone au début du XIVᵉ siècle', *Mélanges de l'Ecole française de Rome. Moyen Âge* 114/2 (2002): 1045–66.

Peters-Custot, A., 'Les remaniements de la carte diocésaine de l'Italie grecque lors de la conquête normande: une politique de latinisation forcée de l'espace? (1059–1130)', in P. Rodriguez (ed.), *Pouvoir et territoire. Colloque du CERHI, Saint-Etienne, 7–8 novembre 2005* (Saint-Etienne, 2007), 57–77.

Peters-Custot, A., *Les Grecs de l'Italie méridionale post-byzantine. Une acculturation en douceur (IXᵉ–XIVᵉ siècles)* (Rome, 2009).

Peters-Custot, A., 'Review of Toomaspoeg, *Decimae, Francia-Recensio* 2011/1'. Available at <http://www.perspectivia.net/content/publikationen/francia/ francia-recensio/2011-1/MA/toomaspoeg_peters-custot> (last accessed 29 June 2021).

Peters-Custot, A., 'Construction royale et groupes culturels dans la Méditerranée médiévale: le cas de la Sicile à l'époque des souverains normands', *Le Moyen Âge* 118/3–4 (2012): 679–86.

Peters-Custot, A., 'Comportement social et comportement culturel des élites rurales calabro-grecques d'après les actes de la pratique (XIᵉ–XIIIᵉ siècles)', in L. Feller, M. Kaplan and C. Picard (eds), *Élites rurales méditerranéennes, Vᵉ–XVᵉ siècles = Mélanges de l'Ecole française de Rome. Moyen Âge*, 124/2 (Rome, 2012), 359–74.

Peters-Custot, A., 'Convivencia between Christians: The Greek and Latin Communities of Byzantine South Italy (IXth–XIth centuries)', in B. Crostini and S. La Porta (eds), *Negotiating Co-Existence: Communities, Cultures and 'Convivencia' in Byzantine Society* (Trier, 2013), 203–20.

Peters-Custot, A., 'De l'usage de l'acculturation' Ménestrel (2013). Available at <http://www.menestrel.fr/?-acculturation-&lang+fr> (last accessed 28 June 2021).

Peters-Custot, A., *Bruno en Calabre. Histoire d'une fondation monastique dans l'Italie normande: S. Maria* de Turri *et S. Stefano del Bosco* (Rome, 2014).

Peters-Custot, A., 'Les *plateae* calabraises d'époque normande. Une source pour l'histoire économique et sociale de la Calabre byzantine?' *Cahiers de Recherches Médiévales et Humanistes* 28/2 (2014): 389–408.

Peters-Custot, A., 'The Documentary Multilingualism and the Social Status of Effective Multilingualism in the Norman Southern Italy, 11th–12th Centuries', in G. Mandalà and I. Pérez Martín (eds), *Multilingual and Multigraphic Documents and Manuscripts of East and West* (Piscataway, NJ, 2018), 293–314.

Peters-Custot, A., 'Construction de la norme monastique dans l'Italie méridionale, entre moines italo-grecs et moines latins aux IXe–XIe siècles', in O. Delouis and M. Mossakowska-Gaubert (eds), *La vie quotidienne des moines en Orient et en Occident, IVe-Xe siècles. II. Questions transversales* (Cairo, 2019), 445–67.

Scaduto, M., *Il monachesimo basiliano nella Sicilia medievale. Rinascita e decadenza, sec. XI–XIV* (Rome, 1982).

Taviani-Carozzi, H., *La terreur du monde. Robert Guiscard et la conquête normande en Italie* (Paris, 1996).

Tolan, J., N. de Lange, L. Foschia and C. Nemo-Pekelman (eds), *Jews in Early Christian Law. Byzantium and the Latin West, 6th–11th Centuries* (Turnhout, 2014).

Tolan, J., 'Constructing Christendom', in J. Hudson (ed.), *'The Making of Europe': Essays in Honour of Robert Bartlett* (Leiden, 2016), 277–98.

Toomaspoeg, K., *Decimae. Il sostegno economico dei sovrani alla Chiesa del Mezzogiorno nel XIII secolo. Dai lasciti di Eduard Sthamer e Norbert Kamp* (Rome, 2009).

Vagnoni, M., *La sacralità regia dei Normanni di Sicilia: un mito?* (Bari, 2012).

von Falkenhausen, V., 'L'archimandritato del S. Salvatore in lingua Phari di Messina e il monachesimo italo-greco nel regno normanno-svevo (secoli XI–XIII)', in G. Fallico, A. Sparti and U. Balistreri (eds), *Messina. Il ritorno della memoria. Mostra sotto l'Alto Patronato del Presidente della Repubblica Italiana On. Oscar Luigi Scalfaro e di S.M. il Re di Spagna Don Juan Carlos I. Messina, Palazzo Zanca – 1 marzo/28 aprile 1994* (Palermo, 1994), 65–79.

von Falkenhausen, V., 'I gruppi etnici nel Regno di Ruggero II e la loro partecipazione al potere', in *Società, potere e popolo nell'età di Ruggero II. Atti delle 3° giornate normanno-sveve (Bari, 23–25 mai 1977)* (Bari, 1979), 133–56.

16

Changes in Identity and Ideology in the Byzantine World in the Second Half of the Twelfth Century: The Case of Serbia

Vlada Stanković

The twelfth century brought a paradigm-shifting change to the region of southeast Europe, exemplified by the case of the creation of medieval Serbia in the form and with the features that would characterise this polity until the end of the Middle Ages. The Serbia of the 1160s onwards and the Serbia of the eleventh and first half of the twelfth centuries were two clearly and conspicuously different political formations. This is particularly true regarding identity, ideology and religion, three basic features and markers of political self-perception and self-representation in the Middle Ages, which became unified in a coherent political platform that would serve to create the basis of the more than two-century-long rule of the Nemanjić dynasty in Serbia.

In the early twelfth century, Serbia was still an insufficiently defined polity that was situated in the deep Balkan hinterland of the Byzantine Empire under the formal but distant and somewhat lax control of Constantinople. Constantinopolitan influence and even control was exercised indirectly, mainly through Hungary from the north or Diokleia from the southwest. By the second half of the twelfth century, however, the Serbian kingdom had emerged as a clearly profiled, recognisable and politically and ideologically defined entity that was now subordinate to the empire of Constantinople through a personal bond of its ruler to the Byzantine emperor. Mirroring the new epoch that had commenced through a changed relationship with the emperor, Serbia's new ruler Stephen Nemanja, chosen personally and installed as the great zhupan by Emperor Manuel I Komnenos in the mid-1160s, closely and adeptly followed the main features of the political and ideological culture of the Byzantine capital at the time of Manuel Komnenos. From this point on, there would be no doubt which political centre medieval Serbia was orientated towards, and to whose political and cultural sphere it belonged.

The questions of identity, its understanding, characteristics and trans-formations in medieval Serbia have never been addressed in scholarship. It was always tacitly assumed, and from the time of the influential and voluminous early twentieth-century *Geschichte der Serben* by Constantine Jireček practically codified, that the identity of the Serbs was an unchange-able constant, from the early Middle Ages (the time of the Serbs' settle-ment into the Balkans and their first mentions in the Byzantine sources) until the end of the Middle Ages and beyond, all the way to the modern era. The overwhelming influence of modern national attitudes, which coloured the narrative of 'national' history, was never seriously re-examined and only gained strength, scholarly legitimacy and popularity with the rise of nationalist policies and ideologies in the twentieth century.[1] Those poli-cies led scholars to continually read modern national aspirations into past contexts to seek to group different territories under a single 'nation'. This resulted in deep, essential misrepresentations of medieval developments in the highly diverse, volatile and extremely complex region of southeastern Europe.[2] It also led to different entities – with quite distinctive political tra-ditions – being indiscriminately placed under the umbrella of one single, currently dominant 'nation' and viewed as just geographically divided ema-nations of the same and unalterable, strongly fixed national identity, as it was formulated in the nineteenth and twentieth centuries.

---

[1] The new nation state provided an ideal frame for the development of that simplis-tic 'national' historiography in the nineteenth and early twentieth centuries, which acquired additional prominence in the 1970s and the decades that followed. The question of identity in the early and central Middle Ages in Dalmatia and Croatia has been receiving increasing scholarly attention in recent times; see Dzino, *Becom-ing Slav*, with Curta, *Making of the Slavs*, both challenging the predominant view based on uncritical acceptance of the scarce information from the written sources. See Geary, *Myth of Nations*.

[2] In the case of Serbia, notions such as a 'Serbian Nation' or 'Serbian Lands' offered opportunities to divide the nation-hued narratives and ideas into periods, geograph-ical regions and polities that bore no relation to the modern-day nation states or national borders. In this respect, the most indicative example is the collective work under the title *History of the Serbian Nation* (*Istorija srpskog naroda*), the first two volumes of which, published in 1981 and 1984, respectively, are dedicated to the Middle Ages. This mishmash of somewhat hurriedly composed, superficial over-views, which was conceptualised in the 1970s, starts with prehistory (!), combining both the territorial and the national principle to further the idea of the unchanging national being, while discarding this obvious absurdity as a mere technicality that stands in the way of a correct grasping of national history.

There is hardly a better example of this historiographical paradox, which led to the establishment of a false perspective based on the projection of modern ideas into the past, than the still predominant view of Diokleia and Serbia, and their historical developments, in the eleventh and twelfth centuries.[3] In the second half of the eleventh century, two polities similar in size but with very different political traditions coexisted and overlapped in the heart of the Balkan Peninsula: Diokleia on the Adriatic coast and in the Adriatic hinterland (roughly today's Montenegro) and Serbia, a mountainous region in the central and southwestern part of present-day Serbia, with the town-fortress of Ras as its focal point. Added to the importance of Ras as a central point of the region – both for the Serbian polity which grew around it and as an outpost of Constantinople's direct influence deep into the Balkan hinterland – was the fact that it was also the main religious centre and a bishopric of the Archbishopric of Ohrid (founded in 1019–20 by Emperor Basil II) that ruled over the vast territories in the Balkans, including the Serbian polity in its entirety. It was the dual, and to a degree schizophrenic, natures of the political traditions of these two closely connected yet quite distinctive polities that gave birth to a new regional political elite in the late eleventh and twelfth centuries through processes whose basic features, dynamics and even prosopography are covered by almost complete silence in the historical sources and therefore remain essentially unknown.

What is known, however, is that from the late eleventh century onwards, Diokleia and Serbia formed a specific political unity representing – at least nominally – the far outposts of Byzantine power in the Balkans, with the prevalence of the former until the last years of the eleventh century and the subsequent dominance of the latter starting at the beginning of the twelfth century. This process is clearly observable in the Byzantine diplomatic formulas, which were stable and remained almost unchanged from the late eleventh century until as late as 1217. The Byzantine imperial chancery in this period consistently regarded Diokleia and Serbia as two distinctive political units under the dominance of whichever ruler – from either polity – was currently stronger; the close ties of that ruler with Constantinople

---

[3] The name Serbia is often replaced in scholarship by that of 'Rascia', drawing on the naming of the fluctuating Serbian polity in the Latin sources from Dalmatia westwards. In those sources, Rascia represents a common denomination for Serbia centred around the town of Ras and based on the geographical rather than the 'national' principle. That should not, however, prevent us from using the term Serbia for the polity in question, which is attested both in Byzantine – starting from the earliest mentions in the *De administrando imperio* – and Serbian sources throughout the Middle Ages.

and the Byzantine imperial family were the key elements for regarding him as a personal political client of the emperor.

Such was the case with Constantine Bodin, who in the early years of Alexios I Komnenos' reign received from the emperor the exalted title of *prōtosebastos* and was awarded the dignity of the *ruler: exousiastēs of Diokleia and Serbia*. Little changed in the Byzantines' attitudes until 1217, when the Serbian Great Zhupan Stephen the First-Crowned received a royal crown from Rome and Pope Honorius III. Even after the papal legates crowned him as king, Stephen, who was a former son-in-law of the Byzantine emperor, remained strongly bonded to the old political traditions and administrative divisions.[4] Both Diokleia and Serbia were well-formed political entities, regardless of the question of the ethnicity of the ruling families and ethnic structure of the population, and despite the fact that two brothers, Vukan, the older, and Stephen, the younger, ruled Diokleia and Serbia, respectively. They were understood as such both in Constantinople and in Rome, from the political as well as the religious standpoint. Constantinople played a major role in shaping those polities as local political units included in the administrative system of the empire, while the papacy clearly distinguished between Diokleia, on the one hand, and Serbia, settled in the deeper Adriatic hinterland, on the other, and accordingly had a different approach and policy towards each.[5]

When we discard the obsolete, chiefly nineteenth-century misconceptions about continuous and unchangeable ethnic identity in these regions, and especially the notion that both Diokleia and Serbia were in essence just two Serbian principalities with different names, we can begin to assess more adequately and correctly the process of change in political balance between the two polities from the end of the eleventh until the middle of the twelfth century. This, then, was the period in which Serbia emerged not only as a dominant force in the region – territorially demarcated by the traditional Bulgarian lands in the east, Hungary in the north and the Byzantine Empire in the south and southeast – but also as a completely new political phenomenon.

---

[4] Cheynet, 'Place de la Serbie'; Demetrios Chomatenos, *Ponēmata*, no. 10, ed. Prinzing, 55–6; Stanković, 'Character and Nature'. Stephen, who received the exalted title of *sebastokratōr* after his marriage to Eudokia, the daughter of Alexios III Angelos, was treated as a peer and close relative both in Nicaea and in Epirus, despite his divorce from Eudokia and subsequent marriage to Anna Dandolo, the granddaughter of the Doge of Venice, Enrico Dandolo; Stanković, 'Stronger than it Appears'; 'Rethinking'.

[5] *Register Innocenz' III*, 167 (176) (Vukan's letter to the pope, July–August 1199); 168 (177) (Stephen's letter to the pope, July–August 1199); Moore, *Pope Innocent III*, 73–5; Cheynet, 'Place de la Serbie'; Stanković, 'Stronger than It Appears', 45–7.

In the latter part of the twelfth century, Serbia was a thoroughly reshaped and remodelled polity, both in comparison to Diokleia in the eleventh century – the time of its dominance over Serbia – and Serbia proper from the first half of the twelfth century. Serbia in the late eleventh and the first half of the twelfth century was a loosely defined polity with murky features, whose great zhupans (and their relatives) bore strange names of Hungarian origin (Uroš, Beloš) – being political clients of both Byzantine emperors and Hungarian kings – and about whose religious orientation and relations with the bishops of Ras nothing is known. The political turnaround that occurred in the second half of the twelfth century with the activities and policies of Stephen Nemanja was based on his conscious efforts to change the ideological basis of his polity by strongly embracing not only the political primacy of the Byzantine emperor, but Constantinopolitan Orthodoxy – and its representatives in Serbia as his spiritual counterparts, allies and helpers, as well. For the first time in the history of medieval Serbia, Stephen Nemanja's Serbia had a clearly defined religious policy, with bishops of Ras becoming accomplices in the creation of an emerging novel political formation.[6]

Realising the distinction between Diokleia and Serbia, as well as the fact that there was no direct, unbroken continuity in policy between Diokleia and Serbia, enables us to better understand many of the otherwise incomprehensible and problematic questions regarding the rise of Stephen Nemanja in the late 1150s and 1160s: his political manoeuvres, the high-profile political and ritual moves, their consequences and the reactions they provoked from his sidelined siblings, who all found their place in the still remarkably understudied Serbian medieval historiographical texts. In the case of Stephen Nemanja, his story was told in the *Lives* written by his two sons, St Sava and Stephen the First-Crowned.

When put into this perspective, the change that occurred in the 1150s and 1160s in the relationship between Constantinople and Serbia can be understood better when placed in the correct historical context of the time of the emperor Manuel Komnenos. Although Stephen Nemanja was the protagonist of change in Serbia, it was made possible by Manuel Komnenos' diplomatic *modus operandi*. This change complied perfectly with the ways the emperor devised and conducted his ambitious policies, chose allies and clients and insisted on creating personal dominance over his

---

[6] St Sava, *Life of St Simeon*, 173 (unnamed bishop of Ras who baptised Stephen Nemanja); Stephen the First-Crowned, *Life of St Simeon*, 55–6 (unnamed bishop of Ras who baptised Stephen Nemanja); 63 (Bishop Euthimios); 74 (Bishop Kallinikos).

political protégées by demanding absolute and unequivocal fealty from them through a ceremonial recognition of his overlordship.

Stephen Nemanja was in this respect a perfect choice. Stemming from one of the mightier families that had battled for political prevalence in Serbia and Diokleia, Nemanja was the youngest of four brothers – just like Manuel himself. For some reason, he was chosen by the emperor over his older brothers, at least one of whom had previously held the position of great zhupan of Serbia with the blessing of the same emperor. Manuel's intention to break the cycle of constant internal struggles that led to frequent changes of Serbian great zhupans and thus undermined his authority by causing political instability in the region, forced him to look for a loyal, preferably young, local noble who could become his faithful client and to seek a solution to the annoying disturbances in the empire's Balkan hinterland, which were supposed to have been put to rest with the emperor's personal victory in 1150 in the region of today's northwest Serbia. The emperor's choice of Stephen Nemanja would turn out to be the crucial move in obtaining stable dominance over the region that connected Byzantium with the lands of Manuel's mother, over which he also established an indisputable prevalence with the installation of Bela III as King of Hungary in 1172.

Emperor Manuel's emphasis on tying his chosen client personally to himself underscored the importance he ascribed to having a reliable person in charge of the region that acquired special importance in the empire's policies of his time. Before becoming the new Serbian great zhupan, Manuel's new protégé had to undergo a series of ritual transformations that would ensure his loyalty to the emperor – and Byzantine Orthodoxy – in exchange for a special status not only within his and other Serbian rival families, but also within the Byzantine elite. Those ritual transformations included the second baptism in the episcopal Church of St Peter and Paul in the town of Ras and an equally ritual 'renaming' through receiving the two highly distinctive names of Stephen and Nemanja. In exchange, and as a sign of his new position, Nemanja received from the emperor the vast territory in 'the border region' between Byzantium and Serbia as his personal, permanent possession (*patrimonium*) together with the right to rebuild the dilapidated Byzantine churches and monasteries on his land. Additionally, Stephen Nemanja received an undisclosed imperial title ('carski san'), as unequivocally stated by his son and successor Stephen the First-Crowned, the *sebastokratōr*.[7] Stephen Nemanja's renovation of

---

[7] Stephen the First-Crowned, *Life of St Simeon*, 56–62.

Byzantine churches and erection of new foundations in the territories received by emperor Manuel were the first such activities in medieval Serbia – not taking into account, as argued above, Diokleia and its separate development and distinct political traditions. With that in mind, the strong reaction of Nemanja's older brothers against his activities becomes understandable, as does their correct recognition of the youngest brother's aspirations for predominance over them, of which his *ktetorship* was an unequivocal political statement.

In choosing and personally rewarding Stephen Nemanja, the emperor Manuel Komnenos revealed in no uncertain terms his designs for Nemanja to become the great zhupan of Serbia, and the first local Serbian ruler with a direct personal bond with the Byzantine emperor. Sources reveal nothing about the identity of Stephen Nemanja's wife and the mother of his sons, Anna. However, when the historical context of the time is fully taken into account, marrying his new client to a member of the numerous Komnenian family would perfectly fit Emperor Manuel Komnenos' usual policy of marital diplomacy.[8] The little information about her life seems to give strength to this argument. At the time of Stephen Nemanja's abdication in 1196, when he took a monastic vow and became the monk Simeon, his wife Anna followed suit, becoming a nun and assuming the name Anastasia. She retreated to a nunnery dedicated to the Virgin Mary in Ras, while Stephen Nemanja-Simeon retreated to his Studenica monastery, before going to Mount Athos, where he joined their son Sava. Retreating to one's monastery, designed as the founder's mausoleum, was a well-established and highly symbolical practice of the Komnenoi from the time of Alexios I Komnenos' ascension to the throne onwards. This had changed the topography of Constantinople in a strongly ideological manner, and Stephen Nemanja's and Anna's simultaneous taking of the monastic vow, followed by their retreat to their respective monasteries, was a perfect *imitatio* of the Komnenian imperial practice.[9]

Two of the above-mentioned important and highly symbolic ritual transformations that the founder of the Serbian medieval dynasty underwent in the process of becoming emperor Manuel Komnenos' favourite client and the great zhupan of Serbia deserve particular attention: Stephen Nemanja's second baptism and the question of his names and their meaning and significance.

---

[8] Magdalino, *Manuel*, 209–17.
[9] Stanković and Berger, *Komnenoi and Constantinople*; St Sava, *Life of St Simeon*, 161; Stephen the First-Crowned, *Life of St Simeon*, 75.

Second Baptism

The ritual second baptism of Stephen Nemanja is explicitly mentioned by both of Nemanja's sons, St Sava and Stephen the First-Crowned, in their respective *Lives* of their father.[10] It was a highly ritualised gesture of the future founder of the dynasty, who had originally been baptised according to the Latin rite in his birthplace, the town of Ribnica (modern-day Podgorica, the capital of Montenegro). The significance and the ritual character of this gesture is additionally highlighted by the fact that the second baptism was performed in the episcopal Church of St Peter and Paul in Ras by the hand of the Byzantine bishop of Ras. It represented a conscious political as well as religious move that sanctified Nemanja's bond with Byzantine Orthodoxy, the Bishopric of Ras, the Archbishopric of Ohrid and through these with the emperor himself, who had had sole authority over the Archbishopric of Ohrid since its foundation in 1019–20 by Emperor Basil II.

Doubts expressed in relatively recent Serbian historiography about the truthfulness of the accounts of Nemanja's sons regarding the second baptism, and the attempts to explain away their specific mentioning of *baptism* as inexact comprehension of the simple ritual of anointment, rest on a complete misunderstanding of the historical context of the time and are deeply coloured by contemporary attitudes towards the question of re-baptism among Orthodox and Catholic Christians.[11] Even worse, such superficial and actually ahistorical musings misread the sources themselves and underestimate the power of ritual in the Middle Ages. In his account, St Sava insists on the symbolical meaning of the number two throughout his father's entire life, emphasising Stephen Nemanja's 'two baptisms, two monastic vows and two burials'.[12] It should be underlined that Sava was writing around the year 1208, at a time when there was as yet no Serbian church but only the Archbishopric of Ohrid, which was dominant throughout the Balkans. Stephen Nemanja's second baptism in Ras was politically and ideologically loaded, and represented the beginning of a new phase in Byzantine–Serbian relations and a new phase in the history of medieval Serbia that was strongly characterised by the ruling elite's adherence to Byzantine Orthodoxy and by the rulers' clear goal to become, and remain, an integral part of the Byzantine imperial family.

[10] St Sava, *Life of St Simeon*, 173; Stephen the First-Crowned, *Life of St Simeon*, 55–6.
[11] Maksimović, 'Άγιοι Σέρβοι βασιλείς'.
[12] St Sava, *Life of St Simeon*, 173–4. Sava also placed a strong emphasis on the significance of his father's ritual acceptance of Constantinopolitan Orthodoxy.

Stephen Nemanja's Names

The question of the names of Stephen Nemanja has never been seriously analysed in scholarship. The fact that he bore the 'typical' ruler's name Stephen, as did the first Christian ruler of medieval Hungary and some rulers of Diokleia – the name that in its basic meaning (*stephanos*: 'wreath') signified power – overshadowed at least three important facts: first, that Stephen Nemanja was the first ruler to bear the name Stephen in medieval Serbia (again, not in Diokleia: in the ninth century, according to the *De administrando imperio*, when the first Christian names appear among the Serbian 'nobility', there was one Stephen, along with Peter and then Paul and Zachary);[13] second, that we still do not know the origin and the etymology of the name Nemanja, leaving aside highly tentative etymological assertions that it was of Slavic origin;[14] and third, that all three of Stephen Nemanja's older brothers bore typically Slavic names, in complete contrast to the youngest brother. Only the last four letters of the oldest brother's name survived (... omir), suggesting a very common Slavic name, while two other brothers were named Stratzimir or Strashimir, and Miroslav.[15]

I would, therefore, like to suggest that the name *Nemanja* also had a ritual meaning, as Stephen obviously had its own. While Stephen Nemanja's successors all bore the name Stephen as a distinctive sign of rulership, not a single member of his ramified lineage, which ruled over Serbia, Diokleia and neighbouring lands until 1371, bore the name Nemanja.[16] And while one can be tempted to find a Slavic origin for this name, its first occurrences in relation to the Serbian great zhupan are found in a Byzantine text: in an oration by Eustathios of Thessalonike from the year 1172 for the

---

[13] Constantine Porphyrogennetos, *De administrando imperio*, 32, ed. Moravcsik, tr. Jenkins, 154–9.

[14] Loma, 'Personenname *Nemanja*'.

[15] *Old Serbian epigrams and inscriptions*, no. 2, 3; no. 3, 3; no. 6, 3; no. 10, 5–6.

[16] In his *Life* of their father, St Sava calls his older brother and great zhupan, Stephen the First-Crowned, 'Stephen Nemanja': St Sava, *Life of St Simeon*, 160, 172; cf. similarly Demetrios Chomatenos, *Ponēmata*, no. 10, ed. Prinzing, 55–6 (dating from 1217). It seems, nevertheless, that they were both using Nemanja as a patronymic, since Stephen the First-Crowned never used Nemanja as his second name in his edicts or writings: in his version of his father's *Life*, written in the 1210s, he introduces himself simply as Stephen: Stephen the First-Crowned, *Life of St Simeon*, 55. This is also how Stephen Nemanja calls his son, *Zbornik*, no. 9, 69. It is also indicative that among the three sons of Stephen Nemanja, only his second son and eventual heir, Stephen, bore a Christian name, while the oldest Vukan ('wolf') and youngest Rastko (apotropaic, meaning 'to grow'), the future St Sava, bore Slavic names, which is hardly accidental.

occasion of Emperor Manuel's triumphal entrance in Constantinople with Stephen Nemanja as one of his 'captives'.[17] In its Greek form Νεεμάν, the name is identical with the name Νεεμάν in the Old Testament (2 Kings 5), the commander of the Syrian armies who suffered from a kind of leprosy or skin disease and was cured by the prophet Elisha through ritual cleansing in the river Jordan, emerging from the ritual seven dips in the Jordan as a 'new man', accepting the God of Israel and renouncing his former beliefs.

The similarities of the two rituals are too obvious not to be taken into account in a serious analysis of the radical change that Stephen Nemanja brought to medieval Serbia and the entire region of southeastern Europe, pointing at the same time to the highly developed understanding of the political culture and its symbolic manifestations in the peripheral Byzantine regions of the Balkans. With a bishop performing the ritual of 'coming to the other side', Nemanja's plausible change of name or acquisition of the Christian, mystic power-wielding name Stephen, which characterised many a ruler in the previous generations in Diokleia and elsewhere in the region, testifies also to the intensity of the rivalry between the Papacy and the west, on the one hand, and Constantinople, on the other, in the highly contested territory from the Adriatic hinterland to the heart of the Balkans and beyond.

Stephen Nemanja's transformation brought a completely novel element to the policy of medieval Serbia: a strong and unyielding Orthodox–Constantinopolitan orientation. Once Diokleia is liberated from the false assumption of being just 'one of the states of the Serbs', and the incorrect understanding of an unchanging ethnic identity is replaced with a much more adequate situational, political-regional-social-religious identity, it becomes clear that by turning towards Constantinople, Stephen Nemanja made a complete change that proved to be a decisive step in the history of medieval – and not only medieval – Serbia. The case of the twelfth-century revolutionary change of Serbia represents the most successful example of Byzantine policy towards southeastern Europe resulting in Serbia's unwavering, long-term political and spiritual orientation towards the Byzantine world.[18]

---

[17] Eustathios of Thessalonike, *Opera minora*, no. 13 ('M'), ed. Wirth, 217. See also *Actes de Chilandar*, no. 4, 107: κῦρ Στέφανος ὁ Νεεμάν, διὰ δὲ τοῦ μοναχικοῦ σχήματος Συμεὼν μετονομασθείς.

[18] Stanković, 'Rethinking'. Stephen Nemanja's actions, his relations with the empire and his time, in general, are still profoundly misunderstood in scholarship, even when his changing the course of Serbian polity in the Middle Ages is recognised, as e.g. in Ćirković, *The Serbs*, 34: 'The reign of Stefan Nemanja represented an essential turning point in the development of the Serbian state, although this became apparent

Serbia after Stephen Nemanja was a defined, yet incomplete, polity that cannot be considered independent, since it adhered to the Byzantine ideological tenet of God-given authority and, in a practical sense, to the Byzantine model of governance of kinsmen with Constantinopolitan Orthodoxy, providing religious sanction for such a loyalty through recognising the Serbs as one of its legitimate constituent 'nations'.[19] By creating a new identity for himself, however, Stephen Nemanja radically changed the identity of Serbia in the Middle Ages. Stephen Nemanja provided an ideological basis to his new polity that his offspring would keep throughout the late Middle Ages and that would outlive the physical disappearance of his line, which comprised three main principles: Byzantine political ideology; inclusion into the Byzantine political system based on kinship ties; and Constantinopolitan Orthodoxy.[20] With the help of the second factor – close kinship relations with Byzantine ruling families both in the east (Nicaea) and in the west (Epirus) – the sons of Stephen Nemanja, Stephen the First-Crowned and Sava, managed to create an autonomous Orthodox Church, first by creating the cult of their father as a holy protector of his lineage (and, sequentially, of his *patria*, Serbia) and then by obtaining imperial permission from their cousin Emperor Theodore I Laskaris in Nicaea to establish an autocephalous Archbishopric of Serbia in 1218/9. Together with the royal crown, received a year before that from Pope Honorius III, the brothers thus rounded off – politically, religiously and ideologically – Stephen Nemanja's new political formation: medieval Serbia.

Acknowledgements

This chapter was conceived while I was a Willis F. Doney member at the Institute for Advanced Study in Princeton, NJ, in 2014/15. I am particularly grateful to Patrick Geary for his vision and for insightful and thought-provoking comments on my ongoing research projects *Creating the Rule of Kinsmen in Southeast Europe in the Twelfth and Thirteenth Centuries* and *A History of Medieval Serbia*, partial results of which are presented here. The Ohio State University's Hilandar Research Library provided me with an opportunity to examine the Hilandar edicts, especially the *chrysoboulos*

only after his death. His era had much more in common with the period of his predecessors than with that of his successors, particularly with regard to relations with the Byzantine Empire.' Similarly, Maksimović, 'Byzantinische Herrscherideologie'.

[19] *Actes de Chilandar*, no. 4, 108: 'μοναστήριον ἀποκαταστῆναι εἰς ὑποδοχὴν χρηματίζον τοῖς ἀπὸ τοῦ σερβικοῦ γένους'.

[20] *Zbornik*, no. 9, 68–9.

logos of Emperor Alexios III Angelos from 1198, and my thanks go to the monks of the Hilandar monastery and the library's then curator, Predrag Matejić. I owe special gratitude to Yannis Stouraitis, who kindly invited me to participate in the discussion on identity in the Byzantine world and showed infinite patience while this contribution was completed somewhere between the US, Belgrade and Cyprus.

Bibliography

Sources

Actes de Chilandar . . . M. Živojinović, V. Kravari and C. Giros (eds), *Actes de Chilandar I. Des origins à 1319* (Paris, 1998).

Constantine Porphyrogennetos, *De administrando imperio* . . . ed. G. Moravcsik (ed.) and R. J. H. Jenkins (tr.), *Constantinus Porphyrogenitus: De administrando imperio*, 2nd ed. (Washington, DC, 1967).

Demetrios Chomatenos, *Ponēmata* . . . G. Prinzing (ed.), *Demetrii Chomateni Ponemata diaphora* (Berlin and New York, 2002).

Eustathios of Thessalonike, *Opera minora* . . . P. Wirth (ed.), *Eustathii Thessalonicensis Opera minora magnam partem inedita* (Berlin and New York, 2000).

Magdalino, *Manuel* . . . P. Magdalino, *The Empire of Manuel I Komnenos, 1143–1180* (Cambridge, 1993).

Old Serbian epigrams and inscriptions . . . Stojanović, L., *Stari srpski zapisi i natpisi* (Belgrade, 1902).

Register Innocenz' III . . . O. Hageneder and A. Haidache (eds), *Die Register Innocenz' III*, vol. 1 (Graz and Cologne, 1964).

St Sava, *Life of St Simeon* . . . V. Ćorović (ed.), *Spisi svetog Save* (Belgrade and Sremski

Karlovci, 1928), 151–75.

Stephen the First-Crowned, *Life of St Simeon* . . . Jovanović, T. (ed.), *Žitije svetog Simeona* (Despotovac, 2019), 53–109.

Zbornik . . . Mošin, V., S. Ćirković and D. Sindik (eds), *Zbornik srednjove-kovnih ćiriličnih povelja i pisama Srbije, Bosne i Dubrovnika I, 1186–1321* (Belgrade, 2011).

Secondary Literature

Cheynet, J.-C., 'La place de la Serbie dans la diplomatie Byzantine à la fin du XIe siècle', *ZRVI* 45 (2007): 89–97.

Ćirković, S., *The Serbs* (Malden, Oxford and Carlton, 2004).

Curta, F., *The Making of the Slavs. History and Archaeology of the Lower Danube Region, c. 500–700* (Cambridge and New York, 2001).

Dzino, D., *Becoming Slav, Becoming Croat. Identity Transformation in Post-Roman and Early Medieval Dalmatia* (Leiden and Boston, 2010).

Geary, P. J., *The Myth of Nations* (Princeton, 2002).

Istorija srpskog naroda, ed. Sima Ćirković, vols 1–2 (Belgrade, 1981–4).

Jireček, K., *Geschichte der Serben*, vols 1–2 (Gotha, 1911).

Loma, A., 'Der Personenname *Nemanja*: Ein neuer Ausblick', *ZRVI* 45 (2008): 109–16.

Maksimović, L., 'Byzantinische Herrscherideologie und Regierungsmethoden im Falle Serbien. Ein Beitrag zum Verständnis des byzantinischen Commonwealth', in C. Scholz and G. Makris (eds), *Πολύπλευρος νοῦς. Miscellanea für Peter Schreiner zu seinem 60. Geburtstag* (Munich and Leipzig, 2000), 174–92.

Maksimović, L., 'Οι Ἅγιοι Σέρβοι βασιλείς', in E. Kountoura-Galake (ed.), *Οι ήρωες της Ορθόδοξης εκκλησίας: οι νέοι άγοι, 8ος–16ος αιώνας* (Athens, 2004), 107–22.

Moore, J. C., *Pope Innocent III (1160/1–1216): To Root Up and To Plant* (Leiden and Boston, 2003).

Stanković, V., 'The Character and Nature of Byzantine Influence in Serbia: Policy–Reality–Ideology (11th–end of the 13th century)', in M. Angar and C. Sode (eds), *Serbia and Byzantium: Proceedings of the International Conference Held on 15 December 2008 at the University of Cologne* (Frankfurt am Main, 2013), 75–93.

Stanković, V., 'Stronger than It Appears? Byzantium and Its European Hinterland after the Death of Manuel Komnenos', in A. Simpson (ed.), *Byzantium, 1180–1204: 'The Sad Quarter of a Century'?* (Athens, 2015), 35–48.

Stanković, V., 'Rethinking the Position of Serbia within the Byzantine *Oikoumene* in the Thirteenth Century', in V. Stanković (ed.), *The Balkans and the Byzantine World before and after the Captures of Constantinople, 1204 and 1453* (Lanham, 2016), 89–100.

Stanković, V., and A. Berger, 'The Komnenoi and Constantinople before the Building of the Pantokrator Complex', in S. Kotzabassi (ed.), *The Pantokrator Monastery in Constantinople* (Berlin and Boston, 2013), 3–32.

Index